T0185822

Pivotal Certified Spring Enterprise Integration Specialist Exam

A Study Guide

Lubos Krnac

Apress®

Pivotal Certified Spring Enterprise Integration Specialist Exam

ISBN-13 (pbk): 978-1-4842-0794-9

ISBN-13 (electronic): 978-1-4842-0793-2

Managing Director: Welmoed Spahr
Lead Editor: Steve Anglin
Technical Reviewer: Manuel Jordan Elera
Editorial Board: Steve Anglin, Louise Corrigan, Jonathan Gennick, Robert Hutchinson,
    Michelle Lowman, James Markham, Susan McDermott, Matthew Moodie, Jeffrey Pepper,
    Douglas Pundick, Ben Renow-Clarke, Gwenan Spearing
Coordinating Editor: Mark Powers
Copy Editor: Sharon Wilkey
Compositor: SPi Global
Indexer: SPi Global
Artist: SPi Global
Cover Designer: Anna Ishchenko

Distributed to the book trade worldwide by Springer Science+Business Media New York, 233 Spring Street, 6th Floor, New York, NY 10013. Phone 1-800-SPRINGER, fax (201) 348-4505, e-mail orders-ny@springer-sbm.com, or visit www.springeronline.com. Apress Media LLC is a California LLC and the sole member (owner) is Springer Science+Business Media Finance Inc. (SSBM Finance Inc.). SSBM Finance Inc. is a Delaware corporation.

For information on translations, please e-mail rights@apress.com, or visit www.apress.com.

Apress and friends of ED books may be purchased in bulk for academic, corporate, or promotional use. eBook versions and licenses are also available for most titles. For more information, reference our Special Bulk Sales–eBook Licensing web page at www.apress.com/bulk-sales.

Any source code or other supplementary materials referenced by the author in this text is available to readers at www.apress.com/9781484207949. For detailed information about how to locate your book's source code, go to www.apress.com/source-code/. Readers can also access source code at SpringerLink in the Supplementary Material section for each chapter.

Contents at a Glance

iii

Contents

About the Author

I started my career as an embedded software developer, and these capabilities were also the focus of my studies. But soon I changed to Java and Spring development. I worked hard for nearly seven years on web and enterprise projects of various sizes and domains. I gained Spring Enterprise Integration Specialist certification in 2014.

I am naturally amazed by the Spring ecosystem; reinventing the wheel is not an option for me. A huge passion of mine is automation and testing. I am lazy and strongly believe that developers shouldn't be doing repetitive tasks. That is why the examples for this book (https://github.com/lkrnac/book-eiws-code-samples) are all covered by tests. One of the reasons that Spring is my framework of choice is its testability.

I write blog posts on my site, www.lkrnac.net, that are often republished on DZone, Java Code Geeks, and Web Code Geeks. I am also interested in modern JavaScript development: ES6, Node.js, Grunt, Gulp, LoopBack, and AngularJS. My Twitter handle is @luboskrnac and my e-mail address is lubos.krnac@gmail.com.

About the Technical Reviewer

Manuel Jordan Elera is an autodidactic developer and researcher who enjoys learning new technologies for his own experiments and creating new integrations.

Manuel won the 2010 Springy Award—Community Champion and Spring Champion 2013. In his little free time, he reads the Bible and composes music on his guitar. Manuel is known as dr_pompeii. He has tech reviewed numerous books for Apress, including *Pro Spring, Fourth Edition* (2014); *Practical Spring LDAP* (2013); *Pro JPA 2, Second Edition* (2013); and *Pro Spring Security* (2013).

Read his 13 detailed tutorials about many Spring technologies and contact him through his blog at www.manueljordanelera.blogspot.com. You can also follow him on his Twitter account, @dr_pompeii.

Acknowledgments

My biggest acknowledgement goes to my wife, Eva, and daughter, Mia, for the endless support, patience, and love they have provided me, and not only during my work on this book. Thanks very much!

My mom, dad, and family played a huge part by supporting me from childhood and helping me to get to this point. Thank you very much!

I greatly appreciate all the friends and colleagues I have had the privilege to work and live with during my career in Slovakia and Ireland. I learned a lot from you, either when I was mentored by you or when I was mentoring you. Thank you very much!

I can't forget all my nontechnical friends. You'll probably never read this, but you played, and hopefully will continue to play, an important part in my life. Thank you very much!

Another big part of the acknowledgements for this book belongs to the Apress team. You were extremely helpful in introducing me to the publishing world. Steve Anglin dragged me into this book's authorship; Mark Powers managed my progress; Matthew Moodie provided editing and suggestions; and Sharon Wilkey, Chris Nelson, and Dhaneesh Kumar enhanced the final form of the content. Thanks very much!

A special acknowledgement goes to Manuel Jordan for his valuable guidance, insight, and technical expertise while creating this content. Thanks very much!

Introduction

Java, with its rock-solid JVM, dominates the enterprise world. Spring is a major Java platform used within distributed systems. Understanding the Spring portfolio is essential for enterprise Java developers. The demand for Spring skills is skyrocketing.

This books covers all the major features that the Spring portfolio provides for enterprise development and prepares you for the Pivotal Certified Enterprise Integration Specialist with Spring exam. When you become Pivotal certified, you will have one of the most valuable credentials in Java.

The exam topics covered include tasks and scheduling, remoting, Spring Web Services framework, RESTful services with Spring MVC, Spring JMS module, JMS and JTA transactions with Spring, and batch processing with the Spring Batch and Spring Integration frameworks. This book covers them by explaining examples and focusing on major architectural considerations and concepts. The examples are the biggest contributor to the page count and are open sourced on GitHub (`https://github.com/lkrnac/book-eiws-code-samples`).

One of the important aspects of this book is its focus on new and modern abstractions provided by the Spring frameworks. Therefore, most of the features are shown with Java annotations (if they exist) alongside established XML configurations. Most of the examples are also based on the Spring Boot framework. Spring Boot adoption has been exponential because of its capability to significantly simplify Spring configuration according to sensible opinionated defaults. But Spring Boot is not the target of the exam, so all the features are also covered with plain Spring configuration examples.

What You'll Learn

This book covers the following topics:

- How to use Spring to create concurrent applications and schedule tasks

- How to do remoting to implement client/server applications

- How to work with Spring Web Services to create loosely coupled web services and clients

- How to use Spring MVC to create RESTful web services and clients

- How to integrate JMS for asynchronous messaging-based communication

- How to use local JMS transactions with Spring

- How to configure global JTA transactions with Spring

- How to use Spring Integration to create event-driven pipes-and-filters architectures and integrate with external applications

- How to use Spring Batch for managed, scalable batch processing that is based on both custom and built-in processing components

Who This Book Is For

This book is for developers and architects who have experience programming and developing with the Spring Framework. An understanding of Java is essential for this book, as well as knowledge of the dependency injection pattern and Spring features for the Inversion of Control container. All other features needed for the exam are covered from scratch, with a focus on providing an understanding to beginners as well as valuable material for intermediates and experts.

How This Book Is Structured

- Chapter 1 explores Spring abstractions for asynchronous processing and compares them to plain Java support. It also covers Spring scheduling support.

- Chapter 2 compares Spring RMI support with Java RMI APIs and explains the Spring HttpInvoker abstraction, as well as Hessian and Burlap protocol support provided by Spring.

- Chapter 3 dives into the Spring Web Services framework and its features. It shows how Spring facilitates the Contract First style of SOAP web service development as well as client-side support.

- Chapter 4 presents REST principles and the main HTTP features. It then highlights Spring MVC usage for REST services and compares it to JAX-RS APIs. This chapter also covers client-side support and Spring test support that's useful for REST APIs.

- Chapter 5 shows Java abstractions for the Java Message Service (JMS) and compares them to Spring abstractions. It covers both messaging paradigms (peer-to-peer and publish/subscribe) and explains how to read and send messages synchronously and how to listen asynchronously.

- Chapter 6 covers JMS acknowledgment modes and transaction support. It subsequently dives into how to use them with the Spring JMS module.

- Chapter 7 introduces JTA transactions and shows how to use them with Spring.

- Chapter 8 takes a look at the Spring Integration framework and its message, message endpoint, and message channel types. It also focuses on topics such as interceptions, synchronous vs. asynchronous message passing, and error handling.

- Chapter 9 discusses features of the Spring Batch framework, including its domain model, executing batch processing, passing parameters into Job, transitioning state, providing interception, and controlling batch flow. It also dives into the advanced topics of providing scaling and parallel processing.

Conventions

All the examples are written so that no artificial wrapping is needed. Italics is used for emphasis of particular aspects of the content. I believe that bullets make the options in the content much more readable and memorable, so they are often used to list the features discussed.

Prerequisites

Because we use Java, the operating system is not important. The examples in this book sometimes use Java 8 features, so you need to have Java 8 installed.

It is also important to have the Spring Tools Suite (STS) IDE (Spring's flavor of Eclipse) available because Spring Integration and Spring Batch use its visualizations. It can be downloaded from the Spring site, `http://spring.io/tools/sts/all`. At the time of writing this book, the latest version was 3.7.1.RELEASE. You can use plain Eclipse with the Spring Tools Suite plug-in installed, but using the STS product is recommended.

All examples use the most common Java build tool, Maven, so you will need an Internet connection to build the examples. A separate Maven installation is not needed, as STS contains an embedded Maven installation out of the box.

You can use other popular Java IDEs such as IntelliJ IDEA or NetBeans, but you will lose the visualization features of STS for the Spring Integration and Spring Batch examples.

Throughout the content, we introduce various tools such as Lombok, PlantUML, ObjectAid, and the DHC REST/API client plug-in for Chrome. The use as well as the installation of these tools is explained as we use them. Because we use a Chrome plug-in, you need to have a Chrome browser available. But feel free to use any HTTP querying tool of choice instead of the DHC REST/API client plug-in; in that case, Chrome is not needed at all.

Downloading the Code

Code examples are hosted on GitHub: `https://github.com/lkrnac/book-eiws-code-samples`. Execute the command `git clone https://github.com/lkrnac/book-eiws-code-samples` from your command line.

Contacting the Author

I am eager to hear your feedback on this book. If you find any problems in the content or examples, please submit the issue on the GitHub repository for this book's examples: `https://github.com/lkrnac/book-eiws-code-samples`. My personal web site, `www.lkrnac.net/about`, contains all the possible links for reaching me. The most effective way to contact me is to send e-mail to `lubos.krnac@gmail.com` or tweet to `@luboskrnac`.

CHAPTER 1

■ ■ ■

Tasks and Scheduling

With rising numbers of cores and increasing processor speed in computers nowadays, it is crucial for applications to be able to use this computational power. Let's compare a processor to yourself at work. Imagine you get stuck with a task, and only your experienced teammate can help you with it. But he's at lunch. You could switch to a different task or wait for him. But when you decide to wait for your teammate's help and study your social account for a moment, your progress at work is blocked. You are not productive at all until your mentor comes back. What if he doesn't return? Your employer wouldn't be happy.

Now imagine an application that needs to access the file system, a database, or a third-party system via Hypertext Transfer Protocol (HTTP). The application's action is a blocking operation: the CPU is doing nothing while waiting for an input/output (I/O) response. At the same time, new requests are coming in and waiting to be processed. Such a scenario is a textbook example of a performance bottleneck.

This situation can be solved by diverting the CPU's attention to a separate thread of execution. The stack and context of the current thread are parked (so the processor can continue computation later, as if the thread was never terminated), and the CPU starts computing a different thread for a short amount of time. This context switching between threads allows the CPU to prioritize the processing pipeline and focus on tasks that need to be processed instead of tasks that are waiting for I/O responses. This concept is commonly called *multitasking*, *multithreading*, or *concurrent processing*.

Threads are valuable for applications that

- Are I/O intensive (for example, applications storing and reading data from a database)

- Are serving requests from multiple clients (for example, web applications)

- Want to use full power of all CPU cores

Multithreading covers immediate parallel execution. It is commonly triggered by user action—for example, sending a request from a web browser or via actions executed in the application's graphical user interface (GUI). But some processing can't rely on external triggering. This is where another important concept of concurrent programming comes into play: *task scheduling*. Execution can be planned at a certain time to start once or even repeatedly. Examples include background batch processing and housekeeping quiet hours.

The ability to create maintainable, concurrent code has become an important part of a developer's knowledge base. However, this is hard. The evolution of languages has led to various abstractions that can help with this implementation. It is crucial to understand how these abstractions can be applied, to achieve the best performance.

All of the projects from Spring's enterprise portfolio rely on multithreading. That is why you need to understand Spring constructs for threading and scheduling. This chapter also highlights their benefits against standard Java APIs. But it does not cover complicated parts such as synchronization, locking, deadlocks, or sharing resources.

Multithreading in Java

Developing asynchronous concurrent applications isn't trivial. Early Java versions provided threading abstractions that were hard to maintain. Let's quickly gather the basic concepts and skip the less important parts.

Java SE

In the Java world, the primary element of multithreading is the java.lang.Runnable interface (shown in Listing 1-1).

Listing 1-1. Runnable Interface

```java
package java.lang;

public interface Runnable {
    public abstract void run();
}
```

A Java developer implements this interface and places the concurrent logic into the Runnable.run() method. *It doesn't take nor return any parameters.*

For controlling concurrent execution, the java.lang.Thread class can be used. When the method Thread.start() is executed, the Java virtual machine (JVM) kicks off a new thread, while the current thread also continues processing—kind of. The CPU switches its attention between these two tasks, and the developer can't predict at which point the attention of the processor will be given to a particular piece of code. If the CPU has multiple cores, both threads can be running simultaneously, leveraging the best allocation of computational power.

Thread creation is a CPU- and memory-expensive operation. Also, direct java.lang.Thread usage turned out to be too low level and often led to unmaintainable code. Therefore, Java SE 5 introduced the new java.util.concurrent package, which utilizes reuse of threads in so-called *thread pools*. The main interface java.util.concurrent.Executor is shown in Listing 1-2.

Listing 1-2. Executor Interface

```java
package java.util.concurrent;

public interface Executor {
    void execute(Runnable command);
}
```

The basic concept is to wrap the concurrent behavior into a class implementing the java.lang.Runnable interface and pass it to a thread pool for execution. The thread pool (an implementation of java.util.concurrent.Executor) takes care of executing the concurrent code in a parallel thread of execution.

A crucial subinterface of java.util.concurrent.Executor introduced with Java SE 5 concurrency utilities is java.util.concurrent.ExecutorService, shown in Listing 1-3.

Listing 1-3. Partial ExecutorService Interface Signature

```
package java.util.concurrent;

public interface ExecutorService extends Executor {
    void shutdown();
    boolean isShutdown();
    boolean isTerminated();
    boolean awaitTermination(long timeout, TimeUnit unit)
        throws InterruptedException;
    <T> Future<T> submit(Callable<T> task);
    <T> Future<T> submit(Runnable task, T result);
    Future<?> submit(Runnable task);
    ...
}
```

ExecutorService provides two groups of operations on top of the thread pool. One group is used to terminate thread execution. Here are the main players from this category:

shutdown: The thread pool doesn't accept new tasks for execution.

isShutdown: Indicates whether the thread pool is scheduled for shutdown (some threads can still be running).

isTerminated: Indicates whether the thread was terminated (all threads are finished).

awaitTermination: Blocks current threads until all tasks are finished.

The second group of ExecutorService methods is designed for submitting tasks for execution. As you can see from the declaration, they have complicated-looking signatures. Newcomers are java.util.concurrent.Future<V> and java.util.concurrent.Callable<V>. They are designed for use cases that java.util.Runnable can't handle, such as returning a value from a thread and populating exceptions into the caller thread.

As its name suggests, Future wraps a value returned later by the concurrent logic. The value type is specified by generic type V. It will be filled in the future by a forked thread. The caller thread can grab it by calling Future.get(). But the caller thread will be blocked until the value is filled by the forked thread. Optionally, we can pass a time-out to Future.get(long timeout, TimeUnit unit) when it's not suitable to block the caller for a long time.

java.util.concurrent.Callable is the interface designed for task declaration, similar to java.lang.Runnable. But it provides more possibilities than java.lang.Runnable, because its method can return a value and throw an exception. See Listing 1-4.

Listing 1-4. Callable Interface

```
package java.util.concurrent;

public interface Callable<V> {
    V call() throws Exception;
}
```

The thread-pool abstraction java.util.concurrent.ExecutorService has various implementations. Most notable is the class java.util.concurrent.ThreadPoolExecutor, which has various constructors to configure its properties. Thread-pool properties can be used for fine-grained tuning of thread pools. The most important properties of java.util.concurrent.ThreadPoolExecutor are as follows:

> corePoolSize: The number of threads to keep in the pool

> maximumPoolSize: The maximum number of threads to allow to run concurrently

> keepAliveTime with unit: The keep-alive time-out for threads that exceed corePoolSize

> workQueue: The queue for waiting threads that are submitted for execution when there aren't enough worker threads in the pool

We can create thread pools directly via java.util.concurrent.ThreadPoolExecutor constructors, but a more convenient way is to create them via the factory class java.util.concurrent.Executors, as shown in Listing 1-5.

Listing 1-5. Partial Executors Class Signature—Factory Methods for Basic Thread Pools

```
package java.util.concurrent;

public class Executors {
    public static ExecutorService newFixedThreadPool(int nThreads);
    public static ExecutorService newSingleThreadExecutor();
    public static ExecutorService newCachedThreadPool();

    //introduced in Java SE 8:
    public static ExecutorService newWorkStealingPool();
    public static ExecutorService newWorkStealingPool(int parallelism)

    ...
}
```

Executors contain many more factory methods that enable powerful control over your thread pools, but in most cases the preceding methods should be enough. The first three factory methods use java.util. concurrent.ThreadPoolExecutor as a thread-pool implementation. Each factory creates it with different constructor parameters.

newFixedThreadPool(int nThreads) creates a thread pool of a fixed size. The desired size of the pool is passed into this factory method as a parameter. This pool will start execution of a new thread immediately if the nThreads limit is not reached. When the pool contains nThreads running threads, any subsequent tasks submitted for execution will be waiting in the queue until one of the running threads finishes its work or is interrupted. So when an unexpected peak event occurs, threads are blocked, but this situation doesn't overload the whole application.

newSingleThreadExecutor() creates a thread pool with only one thread. If this single worker thread is currently running, subsequent submitted tasks will be queued.

newCachedThreadPool() creates a thread pool that reuses finished threads. It creates new ones only when there isn't an idle one in the pool. This pool is handy if we need to serve a lot of short tasks. Because creation of a thread is a CPU- and memory-intensive operation, we may benefit from reusing the same thread instances.

The last two factory methods shown in Listing 1-3 were introduced in Java SE 8. They use `java.util.concurrent.ForkJoinPool` as their underlying thread-pool implementation. Introduced in Java SE 7, this implementation uses a unique algorithm of CPU load distribution between threads called *work-stealing*. Idle threads can "steal" work from busy threads rather than waiting silently.

`Executors.newWorkStealingPool()` creates a thread pool with a size equal to the number of cores on the machine it's currently running on. Thus it tries to use CPU power most effectively, because having more running threads than cores leads to frequent context switching, which isn't a resource-free operation. But this type of thread pool isn't suitable for I/O-bound processing. The reason is related to the number of threads again. If threads are mostly waiting on I/O operations and there aren't other threads in the pool able to keep CPU cores busy, a lot of CPU cycles are wasted on waiting. A much better fit for such I/O-bound operations is a fixed thread pool with a number of cores bigger than the available cores. A better fit is a cached thread pool.

`Executors.newWorkStealingPool(int parallelism)` creates a pool that doesn't take into account the number of cores on the current machine, but rather optimizes the pool to the given parallelism level. So the pool size is optimized toward the number of threads specified by `parallelism`. Unless you are a skilled user of `ForkJoinPool`, use the default parallelism, equal to the number of available cores (`Executors.newWorkStealingPool()` without the `parallelism` parameter).

■ **Note**   The fork/join algorithm is beyond the scope of this book. To become familiar with this algorithm's special features, the Oracle tutorial for fork/join pools provides a good explanation: `http://docs.oracle.com/javase/tutorial/essential/concurrency/forkjoin.html`. Javadoc documentation for `java.util.concurrent.ForkJoinPool` and `java.util.concurrent.ForkJoinTask` provides a detailed explanation of why this type of pool isn't suitable for I/O-bound operations.

The parameters of a thread pool (especially its size) can significantly improve or diminish performance of parallel processing. It is important to understand the nature of concurrent tasks processed by a thread pool. Various considerations affect thread-pool configuration. For example, a developer needs to understand whether parallel tasks are CPU bound, I/O bound, or mixed.

If we are dealing with CPU-bound operations, we want to keep the number of threads as close to the number of cores on the machine as possible. This avoids frequent switching between threads causing unnecessary overhead when there is enough processing to keep the CPU busy.

If we are processing I/O-intensive operations, we generally want to have a larger number of threads available, because we don't want the CPU to waste cycles on blocking I/O operations. But the number of threads can't be too large, because the overhead of switching threads can decrease performance. Balance needs to be found.

Balance needs to be found also for mixed types of processing. There isn't any guidance for tuning configuration when I/O- and CPU-intensive operations are mixed within one thread pool. A developer may consider splitting the tasks into various threads if it helps. But such splitting doesn't make sense for `ForkJoinPool`, because is it optimized toward the number of cores on the current machine. Therefore, we likely want to have only one instance of it reserved for processing CPU-intensive operations.

Trying to guess the thread-pool configuration is impossible. It needs to be backed up by performance testing, or at least by benchmarking or micro-benchmarking of certain modules. Performance testing with the environment as close as possible to that experienced in production, and with a similar load as expected in production, will lead to more accurate results than benchmarking modules in isolation.

■ **Note** If you want to dive deeper into thread-pool sizing alongside other crucial aspects of thread pools, this article by Brian Goetz provides a short, decent introduction to this complicated topic: `www.ibm.com/developerworks/library/j-jtp0730/index.html`.

Implementations of the `java.util.concurrent.Executor` interface effectively made the `java.lang.Thread` class obsolete, because they abstract out the need for low-level thread handling and provide the same flexibility.

After all this theory, it's time to show an example. See Listing 1-6.

Listing 1-6. Simple Asynchronous Task (0101-java-concurrency)

```java
package net.lkrnac.book.eiws.chapter01.javaconcurrency;

import java.util.Random;
import java.util.concurrent.Callable;
public class SimpleTask implements Callable<String> {
  private static final int SIMULATE_IO = 1000;
  private final Random random = new Random();

  @Override
  public String call() throws Exception {
    Integer value = random.nextInt();
    String threadName = Thread.currentThread().getName();

    Thread.sleep(SIMULATE_IO);
    if (value % 2 == 0) {
      throw new UnsupportedOperationException(threadName + " threw exception");
    }
    return threadName + " generated number " + value;
  }
}
```

The class `SimpleTask` is our logic that should be executed concurrently. It implements the `java.util.concurrent.Callable` interface with the generic type `String` to specify a return value type passed from the concurrent logic to the caller thread. It also contains various statements that highlight these features of the `java.util.concurrent` package:

- Generates a random `value` to simulate an error in the form of `UnsupportedOperationException` thrown from the concurrent logic.

- Simulates a blocking I/O operation with `Thread.sleep(SIMULATE_IO)` call. It blocks concurrent logic for 1 second.

- Returns a `String` value in the case of success.

But notice that this mechanism doesn't allow asynchronous code to accept parameters. `SimpleTask` is called from the class shown in Listing 1-7.

Listing 1-7. Caller of Asynchronous Tasks (0101-java-concurrency)

```java
package net.lkrnac.book.eiws.chapter01.javaconcurrency;

import java.util.ArrayList;
import java.util.Collection;
import java.util.concurrent.ExecutionException;
import java.util.concurrent.ExecutorService;
import java.util.concurrent.Future;
import java.util.concurrent.TimeUnit;

public class SimpleTaskExecutor {
  private final ExecutorService executorService;
  private final int execCount;

  public SimpleTaskExecutor(ExecutorService executorService, int execCount) {
    super();
    this.executorService = executorService;
    this.execCount = execCount;
  }

  public void executeTasks() throws InterruptedException {
    Collection<Future<String>> results = new ArrayList<>(execCount);
    long start = System.currentTimeMillis();
    SimpleTask task = new SimpleTask();
    for (int idx = 0; idx < execCount; idx++) {
      results.add(executorService.submit(task));
    }

    executorService.shutdown();
    executorService.awaitTermination(Integer.MAX_VALUE, TimeUnit.DAYS);

    results.forEach(result -> {
      try {
          System.out.println(result.get());
      } catch (InterruptedException | ExecutionException exception) {
          System.out.println(exception.getLocalizedMessage());
      }
    });
    System.out.println("Elapsed time: " + (System.currentTimeMillis() - start));
  }
}
```

This class takes two properties via the constructor. First, executorService represents the thread pool used for managing concurrent execution. We are using an instance of java.util.concurrent. ExecutorService, so we can execute this concurrent processing against different thread pools. The second constructor parameter specifies the number of tasks to execute on the thread pool.

The concurrent execution itself happens in the executeTasks() method. At the beginning, it creates a collection of Future instances to gather results from concurrent tasks. After that, it saves the execution start time into the variable start. Subsequently, in the for loop, it submits one SimpleTask after another to the thread pool for execution. Future results are gathered in the results collection. At this stage, the thread pool starts executing tasks in parallel.

When all the tasks are submitted for execution and our work is being processed in the background, two commands are included that can be used to shut down the thread pool politely(without interrupting all the currently running threads). After calling executorService.shutdown(), the thread pool rejects further task submissions. After the awaitTermination call, the current thread would be blocked until the last thread from the thread pool finishes its execution.

Finally, we loop through results of concurrent task executions and log them to the console. Each result is of type java.util.concurrent.Future; therefore, the call result.get() waits for the thread to finish, if it's still running. This is not our case because we already did that to all threads by calling awaitTermination. You might notice that the behavior would be practically the same without the awaitTermination call, because the reading of results would wait for threads also.

Calling result.get() can carry exceptions from parallel logic; therefore, we catch them and log the error message to the console. The ability to return values and bubble up exceptions from concurrent logic is a big advantage introduced in Java SE 5 with the java.util.concurrent package.

Last, we write to the console the elapsed time of parallel processing. This allows us to compare various thread-pool implementations. The remaining class is the main Java concurrency example highlighted in Listing 1-8.

Listing 1-8. Main Class of Concurrency Example (0101-java-concurrency)

```
package net.lkrnac.book.eiws.chapter01.javaconcurrency;

import java.util.concurrent.ExecutorService;
import java.util.concurrent.Executors;

public final class Application {
  private static final int EXEC_COUNT = 10;

  public static void main(String... args) throws InterruptedException {
    ExecutorService fixedThreadPool = Executors.newFixedThreadPool(EXEC_COUNT);
    SimpleTaskExecutor executorFast = new SimpleTaskExecutor(fixedThreadPool, EXEC_COUNT);
    executorFast.executeTasks();

    ExecutorService workStealingPool = Executors.newWorkStealingPool();
    SimpleTaskExecutor executorSlow = new SimpleTaskExecutor(workStealingPool, EXEC_COUNT);
    executorSlow.executeTasks();
  }
}
```

The main class specifies the number of tasks to execute as 10. The main method first creates a fixed thread pool with 10 fixed threads. Then we create SimpleTaskExecutor to execute 10 tasks on this thread pool. Finally, we again execute 10 tasks, but this time on ForkJoinPool. When we run this small application, the console output may look like Listing 1-9.

Listing 1-9. Console Output of Java Concurrency Example

```
pool-1-thread-1 generated number -1212896919
java.lang.UnsupportedOperationException: pool-1-thread-2 threw exception
java.lang.UnsupportedOperationException: pool-1-thread-3 threw exception
pool-1-thread-4 generated number -776274655
java.lang.UnsupportedOperationException: pool-1-thread-5 threw exception
pool-1-thread-6 generated number 233198511
pool-1-thread-7 generated number -1552830437
```

```
pool-1-thread-8 generated number -819640425
pool-1-thread-9 generated number -144950271
pool-1-thread-10 generated number 2002956537
Elapsed time: 1091
ForkJoinPool-1-worker-1 generated number 1209832625
java.lang.UnsupportedOperationException: java.lang.UnsupportedOperationException:
ForkJoinPool-1-worker-2 threw exception
ForkJoinPool-1-worker-3 generated number 2024148305
ForkJoinPool-1-worker-0 generated number 39272021
java.lang.UnsupportedOperationException: java.lang.UnsupportedOperationException:
ForkJoinPool-1-worker-1 threw exception
ForkJoinPool-1-worker-2 generated number -281172827
java.lang.UnsupportedOperationException: java.lang.UnsupportedOperationException:
ForkJoinPool-1-worker-3 threw exception
ForkJoinPool-1-worker-0 generated number 36551191
java.lang.UnsupportedOperationException: java.lang.UnsupportedOperationException:
ForkJoinPool-1-worker-1 threw exception
java.lang.UnsupportedOperationException: java.lang.UnsupportedOperationException:
ForkJoinPool-1-worker-2 threw exception
Elapsed time: 3005
```

Notice the big difference in the elapsed times of the same concurrent processing on different thread pools. As you may remember, our concurrent task (Listing 1-6) contains a delay, simulating a blocking I/O operation 1,000 milliseconds long. The fixed thread pool (with pool size 10) is able to execute 10 given tasks in parallel and straight away after submission. So after the blocking I/O delay of 1 second, all threads finish, and the whole parallel execution takes only a little bit more than 1 second. In fact, the CPU was waiting mostly for the blocking I/O operation to finish.

The second ForkJoinPool uses only four threads for execution, because the machine it was executed on has four CPU cores. So after four threads are already running, further submitted tasks are waiting in the queue to get a free thread-pool worker. At the time, only four tasks can be served. So simple math explains why the second parallel execution on ForkJoinPool took 3 seconds.

Such a scenario is an example of how important it is to understand the nature of tasks being executed by our thread pool. Generally, we want to increase thread-pool size if I/O-bound operations are being processed (but not too much). Or we can align the thread-pool size as close as possible to the available core count in the case of CPU-bound operations. But this isn't a general rule for every case. Performance testing or benchmarking should apply. Bear in mind that you can have various thread pools for various purposes in your application, so it's crucial to understand the behavior of your whole application under load.

Java EE

In the Java Platform, Enterprise Edition (Java EE), use of Java SE concurrency APIs is considered bad practice. Until Java EE 7, enterprise developers couldn't use any specific concurrent API that would be managed by the container (concurrency should be handled exclusively by the application container). Because Java EE standards didn't provide any concurrency support, various mechanisms specific to application containers were created:

- CommonJ
  - WebSphere
  - WebLogic

- Java EE Connector Architecture (JCA) work managers
  - JBoss (now WildFly)
  - GlassFish

Java EE 7 finally introduced Concurrency Utilities that allowed application developers to use managed concurrency APIs.

■ **Note** Java EE 7 Concurrency Utilities are beyond the scope of this book. Please refer to the Java EE 7 tutorial for more information: `http://docs.oracle.com/javaee/7/tutorial/concurrency-utilities.htm#GKJIQ8`.

Task Scheduling

Some use cases require scheduling of tasks for later execution. For this purpose, Java has the interface `java.util.concurrent.ScheduledExecutorService`, shown in Listing 1-10.

Listing 1-10. ScheduledExecutorService Interface Signature

```
public interface ScheduledExecutorService extends ExecutorService {
    public ScheduledFuture<?> schedule(Runnable command,
                                    long delay, TimeUnit unit);

    public <V> ScheduledFuture<V> schedule(Callable<V> callable,
                                    long delay, TimeUnit unit);
    public ScheduledFuture<?> scheduleAtFixedRate(Runnable command,
                                    long initialDelay,
                                    long period,
                                    TimeUnit unit);
    public ScheduledFuture<?> scheduleWithFixedDelay(Runnable command,
                                    long initialDelay,
                                    long delay,
                                    TimeUnit unit);
}
```

The important mechanisms are the last two methods. They facilitate recurring scheduling, whereby a task is triggered at certain time intervals. This is most commonly used for batch processing of jobs that doesn't involve user interaction. Two important scheduling configurations are available:

> *Fixed Delay*: The time between the end time of the previous thread and the start of subsequent execution is specified (think of it as a constant gap between scheduled threads). The next start time is hard to predict because it depends on the end time of the previous execution.

> *Fixed Rate*: The start time of each scheduled thread is specified. So the gap between threads varies. If thread execution time is longer than the scheduled rate, the start time of the next task execution is delayed until the previous one finishes. So scheduled tasks wouldn't be executed concurrently.

With this support, we can schedule implementations of the `java.lang.Runnable` and `java.util.concurrent.Callable<V>` interfaces. But notice that we are not able to schedule `java.util.concurrent.Callable<V>` for recurring scheduling.

Implementation of a scheduled thread pool is `java.util.concurrent.ScheduledThreadPoolExecutor`. It can be created via its constructor or via a factory method provided by the class `java.util.concurrent.Executors`. The signature of this factory method is shown in Listing 1-11.

Listing 1-11. Partial Executors Class Signature—Scheduling Factory Method

```java
package java.util.concurrent;

public class Executors {
    ...
    public static ScheduledExecutorService newScheduledThreadPool(int corePoolSize);
    ...
}
```

Let's explore how we would use this mechanism. Listing 1-12 highlights a simple task as an implementation of the `java.lang.Runnable` interface.

Listing 1-12. Simple Task (0104-java-scheduling)

```java
package net.lkrnac.book.eiws.chapter01.javascheduling;

import java.text.DateFormat;
import java.text.SimpleDateFormat;
import java.util.Date;
import java.util.Locale;

public class ScheduledTask implements Runnable {
  private final DateFormat dateFormat = new SimpleDateFormat("HH:mm:ss:SSS",
      Locale.getDefault());

  public void run() {
    System.out.println(dateFormat.format(new Date()) + " - job kicked off");
  }
}
```

This task simply outputs the time when it was started to the console. Listing 1-13 shows how we schedule this task.

Listing 1-13. Simple Task Scheduling (0104-java-scheduling)

```java
package net.lkrnac.book.eiws.chapter01.javascheduling;

import java.util.concurrent.Executors;
import java.util.concurrent.ScheduledExecutorService;
import java.util.concurrent.TimeUnit;
```

```java
public class SimpleScheduler {
  public void scheduleTask() {
    ScheduledExecutorService executor = Executors.newScheduledThreadPool(1);
    ScheduledTask task = new ScheduledTask();
    executor.scheduleAtFixedRate(task, OL, 1, TimeUnit.SECONDS);
  }
}
```

ScheduledThreadPoolExecutor with only one worker thread is created via the Executors.
newScheduledThreadPool(1) factory method call. Subsequently, a SimpleTask instance is scheduled at
a fixed rate of 1 second with no initial delay. If we run the schduleTask() method of SimpleScheduler,
console output would look like Listing 1-14.

Listing 1-14. Console Output of Java Scheduling Example

```
10:20:25:469 - job kicked off
10:20:26:469 - job kicked off
10:20:27:468 - job kicked off
10:20:28:468 - job kicked off
10:20:29:468 - job kicked off
...
```

SimpleTask outputs the current time to the console every second. Because we are using recurring
scheduling in this example, this execution would continue further—potentially until the JVM of our
application would be stopped forcibly.

But such limited scheduling often isn't suitable for enterprise applications. Fortunately, a popular
library called Quartz Scheduler is commonly used for complex scheduling. It also provides enterprise
features such as distributed transaction propagation, job persistence, and clustering features. But most
notable are these scheduling features:

- Indicate a certain time of the day (with millisecond precision)

- Indicate certain days of the week/month/year

- Exclude days specified by a given calendar (useful for excluding public holidays)

- Specify an explicit number of executions

- Repeat until date/time

Multithreading with Spring

You might be wondering where Spring comes into this game. Spring is a well-known provider of fine-grained
abstractions on top of common Java technologies. It removes a lot of boilerplate code by providing three
main abstractions used for executing and scheduling tasks:

- TaskExecutor

- Trigger

- TaskScheduler

org.springframework.core.task.TaskExecutor

The purpose of this interface is to provide an abstraction for executing asynchronous tasks. It extends the `java.util.concurrent.Executor` interface, but doesn't introduce a changed API contract in comparison to pure Java SE abstractions. See Listing 1-15.

Listing 1-15. TaskExecutor Interface Signature

```
public interface TaskExecutor extends Executor {
        @Override
        void execute(Runnable task);
}
```

TaskExecutor abstracts away the Java SE 5 Executor interface so it can be used as a superinterface for non-Java SE 5 thread pools. `TaskExecutor` is an umbrella for these thread executors:

> `SimpleAsyncTaskExecutor`: Creates a new thread for each task. Supports a limited number of threads (unlimited by default). When this limit is reached, execution of subsequent tasks is blocked until some of the threads finish execution.

> `SyncTaskExecutor`: Task execution is performed synchronously in the calling thread. Mainly intended for testing purposes.

> `ConcurrentTaskExecutor`: Wraps the provided `java.util.concurrent.Executor` and exposes it as `TaskExecutor`. It is useful when the developer wants to create a custom Java SE 5 thread pool and use it in a Spring environment. Not very common. In most cases, you would probably want to use `ThreadPoolTaskExecutor`.

> `SimpleThreadPoolTaskExecutor`: Subclass of `org.quartz.simpl.SimpleThreadPool` (Quartz Scheduler's implementation of a thread pool). It is useful because it can understand Spring's life-cycle callbacks.

> `ThreadPoolTaskExecutor`: Wrapper for `java.util.concurrent.ThreadPoolExecutor`. Enables you to create configurable thread pools with parameters such as `corePoolSize`, `maxPoolSize`, `keepAliveSeconds`, and `queueCapacity`.

There are also some Java EE implementations of `TaskExecutor`. These implementations act as a bridge between the Spring environment and multithreading support of the enterprise application container where the configuration of thread pools is located:

> `org.springframework.jca.work.WorkManagerTaskExecutor`: Adapter for the JCA 1.5 `javax.resource.spi.work.WorkManager` interface.

> `org.springframework.scheduling.commonj.WorkManagerTaskExecutor`: Adapter for the CommonJ `commonj.work.WorkManager` interface.

> `org.springframework.jca.work.glassfish.GlassFishWorkManagerTaskExecutor`: Adapter for the GlassFish JCA WorkManager.

> `org.springframework.jca.work.jboss.JbossWorkManagerTaskExecutor`: Adapter for the JBoss JCA WorkManager.

All these task executors can be declared as standard Spring beans via the `@Bean` annotation or the `<bean/>` tag. An example is shown later in this chapter, in the "Configuring Asynchronous Tasks" section.

org.springframework.scheduling.Trigger

The Trigger interface, shown in Listing 1-16, is designed for determining the next execution time based on a previous execution. It is used by Spring for scheduling.

Listing 1-16. Trigger Interface

```
public interface Trigger {
        Date nextExecutionTime(TriggerContext triggerContext);
}
```

It has two implementations:

CronTrigger: Allows triggering based on Cron expressions.

PeriodicTrigger: Allows you to specify Fixed Rate or Fixed Delay triggers. For switching between them, it exposes a flag via PeriodicTrigger. setFixedRate(boolean fixedRate). The default triggering is Fixed Delay.

■ **Note**   Cron is used within Unix systems for job scheduling. A Cron expression has six parts separated by spaces. Each part specifies the minute, hour, day of month, month, day of week, and year. The year is not mandatory, so commonly only five parts are used. But the original Cron expression allows triggering with the shortest intervals 1 minute long. Therefore, Spring uses a Quartz Scheduler style of Cron syntax. It uses seven parts instead of six, and the first one is in seconds. The year is not mandatory, as with Unix Cron. With powerful placeholders for each part, it is possible to specify complicated patterns for scheduling (for example, * */10 9-17 * * MON-FRI represents triggering every 10 minutes during work hours). Understanding Cron expressions isn't in the scope of this book, but it's important to know that Spring integrates this powerful triggering mechanism. For more information about the Quartz flavor of Cron expressions, go to www.quartz-scheduler.org/ documentation/quartz-2.1.x/tutorials/crontrigger.

Task Scheduler

org.springframework.scheduling.TaskScheduler, shown in Listing 1-17, is Spring's abstraction for scheduling tasks.

Listing 1-17. TaskScheduler Interface Signature

```
public interface TaskScheduler {
        ScheduledFuture<?> schedule(Runnable task, Trigger trigger);
        ScheduledFuture<?> schedule(Runnable task, Date startTime);
        ScheduledFuture<?> scheduleAtFixedRate(Runnable task, Date startTime, long period);
        ScheduledFuture<?> scheduleAtFixedRate(Runnable task, long period);
        ScheduledFuture<?> scheduleWithFixedDelay(Runnable task, Date startTime, long delay);
        ScheduledFuture<?> scheduleWithFixedDelay(Runnable task, long delay);
}
```

As you can see from the interface declaration, Spring can schedule one-time or recurring jobs based on a fixed rate and fixed delay approach. It can also use the Trigger interface for complex Cron-based scheduling.

Although it's important to remember how TaskExecutor and Trigger interfaces work, we don't need to use them directly. Spring provides powerful annotations and XML tags for configuring multithreading and scheduling behavior. So TaskExecutor and Trigger are used under the hood.

Configuring Asynchronous Tasks

For enabling multithreading support, Spring provides the class-level annotation @EnableAsync. A class annotated with @EnableAsync should be used in conjunction with the @Configuration annotation. So the @EnableAsync annotation basically switches on Spring asynchronous support.

The @Async method-level annotation is designed to define asynchronous logic. Such tasks will be executed in a separate thread. This annotation provides much wider possibilities when the developer designs asynchronous APIs. Earlier sections about the Callable<T> interface explained that Java SE APIs can return value and bubble up exceptions from asynchronous code. Passing parameters into asynchronous logic is a unique feature of @Async annotation that Spring provides. But methods annotated by @Async have two important limitations:

- The method must return void or Future<T> (similar to Callable<T>).

- The method can't be used with life-cycle callbacks (for example, @PostConstruct).

@Async annotation has one optional parameter, which specifies the name of the task executor bean used for executing asynchronous logic. Let's explore use of these annotations in an example. Listing 1-18 shows logic that will be executed in a separate thread.

Listing 1-18. Asynchronous Task (0102-async-job example project)

```
package net.lkrnac.book.eiws.chapter01.async.task;

import java.util.concurrent.Future;
import org.springframework.scheduling.annotation.Async;
import org.springframework.scheduling.annotation.AsyncResult;
import org.springframework.stereotype.Component;

@Component
class AsyncTask {
  private static final int SIMULATE_IO = 1000;

  @Async("customTaskExecutor")
  public Future<String> call(int parameter) throws InterruptedException {
    String threadName = Thread.currentThread().getName();

    Thread.sleep(SIMULATE_IO);
    if (parameter % 2 == 0) {
      throw new UnsupportedOperationException(threadName + " threw exception");
    }
    return new AsyncResult<String>(threadName + " have parameter " + parameter);
  }
}
```

The class AsyncTask is annotated with the @Component annotation, which specifies that the AsyncTask class is a candidate for component scanning by Spring. This class has only one method, call. First it reads the name of the current thread. Then it simulates a blocking I/O operation, which is 1 second long. Finally, it simulates an error if the given parameter is odd, or the return name of the thread if the given parameter is even. This behavior is in place to highlight possibilities of this API.

But this method is special, which is declared by the @Async annotation. It will be executed in a separate thread. Notice that it can take any number of parameters, as opposed to the Callable<T> interface. To be able to return a value into the caller thread, it wraps the result into AsyncResult<String>. AsyncResult<T> is Spring's implementation of the Future interface.

Listing 1-19 shows how we can call asynchronous logic.

Listing 1-19. Caller of Asynchronous Logic (0102-async-job)

```
package net.lkrnac.book.eiws.chapter01.async.task;

import java.util.ArrayList;
import java.util.Collection;
import java.util.concurrent.ExecutionException;
import java.util.concurrent.Future;
import org.springframework.beans.factory.annotation.Autowired;
import org.springframework.stereotype.Component;

@Component
public class Caller {
  private final AsyncTask asyncTask;
  @Autowired
  public Caller(AsyncTask asyncTask) {
    this.asyncTask = asyncTask;
  }

  public void kickOffAsyncTasks(int execCount) throws InterruptedException {
    Collection<Future<String>> results = new ArrayList<>(execCount);

    long start = System.currentTimeMillis();
    for (int idx = 0; idx < execCount; idx++) {
      results.add(asyncTask.call(idx));
    }

    results.forEach(result -> {
      try {
        System.out.println(result.get());
      } catch (InterruptedException | ExecutionException e) {
        System.out.println(e.getLocalizedMessage());
      }
    });
    System.out.println("Elapsed time: " + (System.currentTimeMillis() - start) + " ms");
  }
}
```

The AsyncTask bean is injected into the Caller class via constructor injection. The method kickOffAsyncTasks executes this asynchronous logic. It first takes the number of tasks to execute as a parameter and allocates the collection for gathering Future<String> results. We track the start and end time of execution and write it to the console. The execution of each thread is started by calling results. add(asyncTask.call(idx)), which calls the asynchronous method, passes a parameter to it, and stores the Future<String> object for retrieving return values later. An interesting aspect is the ability to pass parameters to asynchronous logic. It is possible because Spring's proxy mechanism for AsyncTask handles multithreading behavior with propagating parameters. Notice that the multithreading example in Listing 1-6 is based on java.util.concurrent.Callable<T> not being able to pass parameters to the thread directly. This is a big advantage of Spring's multithreading support.

After the first for loop, all threads are submitted for execution. Finally, we loop through the results collection and output return values to the console. Calling result.get() would wait for the thread to finish its job. In addition, a try-catch block handles errors penetrated from asynchronous logic.

You might ask where and how the thread pool is involved in this setup. Let's explore it in Listing 1-20.

Listing 1-20. Main Configuration of Spring Async Example with Fork/Join Pool (0102-async-job)

```
package net.lkrnac.book.eiws.chapter01.async;

import java.util.concurrent.Executor;
import java.util.concurrent.Executors;
import net.lkrnac.book.eiws.chapter01.async.task.Caller;
import org.springframework.boot.SpringApplication;
import org.springframework.context.ApplicationContext;
import org.springframework.context.annotation.Bean;
import org.springframework.context.annotation.ComponentScan;
import org.springframework.context.annotation.Configuration;
import org.springframework.scheduling.annotation.EnableAsync;

@Configuration
@ComponentScan(basePackageClasses = Caller.class)
@EnableAsync
public class AsyncConfigurationSmallerPool {
  @Bean
  public Executor customTaskExecutor() {
    return Executors.newWorkStealingPool();
  }

  public static void main(String... args) throws InterruptedException {
    ApplicationContext context = SpringApplication.run(AsyncConfigurationSmallerPool.class,
    args);
    Caller caller = context.getBean(Caller.class);
    caller.kickOffAsyncTasks(10);
  }
}
```

This Spring configuration scans the package for Spring beans where the Caller class is located. So with Caller, the AsyncTask bean is registered into the Spring IoC container. The first method, customTaskExecutor, registers the thread-pool bean into the context. java.util.concurrent.Executor is used as a bean type to allow for variability of thread-pool implementation. So it's obvious that we can use any of the executors that Spring provides as well as the standard Java SE java.util.concurrent thread-pool implementations. In this case, java.util.concurrent.ForkJoinPool is created with the help of the java.util.concurrent.Executors factory class. This pool creates a number of worker threads equal to the number of cores of the machine it's running on (which is four in this example).

This bean is registered with the name customTaskExecutor; Spring uses the name of the bean registration method as the bean name when it isn't configured explicitly. Notice that this name is the same as the parameter of the @Async annotation in the class AsyncTask in Listing 1-18. So this bean will be used for executing the AsyncTask.call method.

The second method in this class is main. The signature of this method should be familiar to every Java developer. Yes, it's the famous main method that turns this class into a command-line utility. The array args can take arguments from the command line, but we don't use this feature in this case. What happens in the body of this method is interesting. It uses a feature of a relatively new project from the Spring portfolio called *Spring Boot*. We can think of the Spring Boot project as a convention over the configuration wrapper for the Spring Framework. It can significantly simplify and reduce the Spring configuration needed for building modern Java applications, but at the same time it doesn't reduce the variability of Spring configuration features. Starting a new Spring project without it wouldn't make sense nowadays.

■ **Note**   The Spring Boot project is beyond the scope of this book, because it's not part of Enterprise Integration with Spring certification. If you want to learn more about this useful project, take a look at the "Getting Started" section of the Spring Boot reference documentation: http://docs.spring.io/spring-boot/docs/current/reference/htmlsingle/#getting-started.

SpringApplication.run will kick off the application with the given Spring configuration and command-line arguments. It is used to simply bootstrap our asynchronous application. This method returns the created Spring context instance, which is used to find the Caller bean and explicitly execute asynchronous code. The possible console output after running this application is shown in Listing 1-21.

Listing 1-21. Possible Console Output for Fork/Join Pool

```
java.lang.UnsupportedOperationException: java.lang.UnsupportedOperationException:
ForkJoinPool-1-worker-1 threw exception
ForkJoinPool-1-worker-2 have parameter 1
java.lang.UnsupportedOperationException: java.lang.UnsupportedOperationException:
ForkJoinPool-1-worker-3 threw exception
ForkJoinPool-1-worker-0 have parameter 3
java.lang.UnsupportedOperationException: java.lang.UnsupportedOperationException:
ForkJoinPool-1-worker-1 threw exception
ForkJoinPool-1-worker-3 have parameter 5
java.lang.UnsupportedOperationException: java.lang.UnsupportedOperationException:
ForkJoinPool-1-worker-0 threw exception
ForkJoinPool-1-worker-2 have parameter 7
java.lang.UnsupportedOperationException: java.lang.UnsupportedOperationException:
ForkJoinPool-1-worker-3 threw exception
ForkJoinPool-1-worker-1 have parameter 9
Elapsed time: 3039 ms
```

Notice we used java.util.concurrent.ForkJoinPool as a thread-pool implementation. It uses parallelism equal to the number of CPU cores provided. We can think about parallelism as the core size of the pool. So this thread pool will have four worker threads, because four cores are available on the machine.

We can find this fact in Listing 1-21. Fork/join pool worker threads are named with the suffix -worker-X, where X specifies the ID of the thread.

An interesting statistic is the elapsed time of the whole execution. It took more than 3 seconds. Notice that simulating the blocking I/O operation in AsyncTask from Listing 1-18 took only 1 second. But then why does the overall execution take 3 seconds? The reason is again in the incorrect thread-pool type used to handle this type of asynchronous logic. When we are dealing with blocking I/O operations, it is a good idea to make sure the size of the pool is bigger than the number of CPU cores, so the CPU doesn't have to wait for a slow blocking I/O operation. Let's show what would happen if we use the thread pool from Listing 1-22.

Listing 1-22. Main Configuration of Spring Async Example with ThreadPoolExecutor (0102-async-job)

```
package net.lkrnac.book.eiws.chapter01.async;

import java.util.concurrent.Executor;
import net.lkrnac.book.eiws.chapter01.async.task.Caller;
import org.springframework.boot.SpringApplication;
import org.springframework.context.ApplicationContext;
import org.springframework.context.annotation.Bean;
import org.springframework.context.annotation.ComponentScan;
import org.springframework.context.annotation.Configuration;
import org.springframework.scheduling.annotation.EnableAsync;
import org.springframework.scheduling.concurrent.ThreadPoolTaskExecutor;

@Configuration
@ComponentScan(basePackageClasses = Caller.class)
@EnableAsync
public class AsyncConfigurationBiggerPool {
  private static final int EXEC_COUNT = 10;

  @Bean
  public Executor customTaskExecutor() {
    ThreadPoolTaskExecutor threadPool = new ThreadPoolTaskExecutor();
    threadPool.setCorePoolSize(EXEC_COUNT);
    return threadPool;
  }

  public static void main(String... args) throws InterruptedException {
    ApplicationContext context = SpringApplication.run(AsyncConfigurationBiggerPool.class,
    args);
    Caller caller = context.getBean(Caller.class);
    caller.kickOffAsyncTasks(EXEC_COUNT);
  }
}
```

This code uses Spring's org.springframework.scheduling.concurrent.ThreadPoolTaskExecutor implementation of the thread pool. We configured the core pool size of 10 to be the same as the number of tasks being executed asynchronously. Listing 1-23 shows possible output for this thread-pool configuration.

Listing 1-23. Console Output for ThreadPoolExecutor

```
java.lang.UnsupportedOperationException: customTaskExecutor-1 threw exception
customTaskExecutor-2 have parameter 1
java.lang.UnsupportedOperationException: customTaskExecutor-3 threw exception
customTaskExecutor-4 have parameter 3
java.lang.UnsupportedOperationException: customTaskExecutor-5 threw exception
customTaskExecutor-6 have parameter 5
java.lang.UnsupportedOperationException: customTaskExecutor-7 threw exception
customTaskExecutor-8 have parameter 7
java.lang.UnsupportedOperationException: customTaskExecutor-9 threw exception
customTaskExecutor-10 have parameter 9
Elapsed time: 1024 ms
```

Now the overall execution took much less time than with the fork/join pool. This clearly shows how crucial it is for the developer to understand asynchronous behavior and tune the thread-pool parameters accordingly.

XML Configuration for Task Execution

Spring's Java-based configuration is a modern younger brother of XML configuration. If you need to use XML configuration for legacy reasons, Spring allows you to define asynchronous behavior with the task namespace. To replicate Listing 1-23 with XML configuration, use the XML in Listing 1-24.

Listing 1-24. XML Configuration for Asynchronous Job (0102-async-job)

```
<?xml version="1.0" encoding="UTF-8"?>
<beans xmlns="http://www.springframework.org/schema/beans"
  xmlns:xsi="http://www.w3.org/2001/XMLSchema-instance"
  xmlns:task="http://www.springframework.org/schema/task"
  xmlns:context="http://www.springframework.org/schema/context"
  xsi:schemaLocation="http://www.springframework.org/schema/task
  http://www.springframework.org/schema/task/spring-task-4.0.xsd
               http://www.springframework.org/schema/beans http://www.springframework.org/
               schema/beans/spring-beans.xsd
               http://www.springframework.org/schema/context http://www.springframework.org/
               schema/context/spring-context-4.0.xsd">

  <context:component-scan base-package="net.lkrnac.book.eiws.chapter01.async.task" />
  <task:executor id="customTaskExecutor" pool-size="10" queue-capacity="20" />
  <task:annotation-driven executor="customTaskExecutor" />
</beans>
```

Our AsyncTask and Caller beans are located in the package net.lkrnac.book.eiws.chapter01. async.task, where they are component scanned. So their @Component annotations are still needed, for registration into the Spring IoC container. The <task:executor/> tag creates a ThreadPoolTaskExecutor instance as a thread-pool implementation. If we need to use a different implementation, it needs to be specified with a standard bean definition. The AsyncTask annotation doesn't need the custom task executor name parameter anymore, because the thread-pool reference is configured by the executor parameter in the <task:annotation-driven/> tag. We use the customTaskExecutor instance defined by the <task:executor/> tag.

The `<task:executor/>` tag has various parameters:

pool-size: This optional parameter can have two forms:

- A single value specifies the number of threads to keep in the pool, even if they are idle (the core pool size).

- A range of values, separated by a dash (for example, 5-25). The first value specifies the core pool size (the default value is 1). The second value specifies the maximum pool size (the default value is Integer.MAX_INT). If the range isn't specified, the default core size is 1 and the maximum pool size is Integer.MAX_INT.

queue-capacity: Specifies the capacity for ThreadPoolTaskExecutor's BlockingQueue. Queue is used for storing scheduled tasks when there aren't free threads in pool. When the capacity of the queue is reached, the task executor rejects further thread submissions. The default queue capacity is Integer.MAX_INT. This value is often not desirable, because OutOfMemory problems can occur if a lot of threads are queued. So it's always a good idea to limit queue-capacity.

rejection-policy: Specifies the rejection behavior when the queue capacity is reached. Options are as follows.

- ABORT: The thread pool throws TaskRejectedException when an additional task is submitted. This is the default behavior.

- CALLER_RUNS: Logic is executed synchronously in the caller thread. It allows you to keep the caller thread busy until subsequent tasks are submitted for execution. In the meantime, some threads from the thread pool may finish and free some capacity.

- DISCARD: The submitted task is silently discarded.

- DISCARD_OLDEST: The task at the head of the queue is discarded.

Configuring Scheduled Tasks

Scheduling configuration is enabled by the @EnableScheduling class-level annotation. It should be used with the @Configuration annotation. A class annotated with @EnableScheduling and @Configuration can be imported by the @Import annotation into another Spring configuration class. The second option is to component scan such an annotated class.

The @Scheduled method-level annotation defines logic that should be scheduled for recurring execution. It can't take any parameters nor return any value. An annotation can have these parameters:

fixedDelay: Numeric value in milliseconds

fixedRate: Numeric value in milliseconds

cron: String Cron expression

initialDelay: Delay first start in milliseconds

Exactly one of the parameters fixedDelay, fixedRate, or cron must be specified. Otherwise, registering such a bean into the Spring context would fail. The last parameter, initialDelay, is optional. It would be useful when we don't want to schedule a first iteration immediately but rather want to defer this execution to a later time. Listing 1-25 shows an example of this annotation.

Listing 1-25. Scheduled Task Example (0103-scheduled-job)

```
package net.lkrnac.book.eiws.chapter01.scheduling.task;

import java.text.DateFormat;
import java.text.SimpleDateFormat;
import java.util.Date;
import java.util.Locale;
import org.springframework.beans.factory.annotation.Autowired;
import org.springframework.scheduling.annotation.Scheduled;
import org.springframework.stereotype.Component;

@Component
public class ScheduledTask {
  private static final int SCHEDULING_DELAY = 1000;

  private final DateFormat dateFormat = new SimpleDateFormat("HH:mm:ss:SSS",
      Locale.getDefault());

  @Scheduled(fixedRate = SCHEDULING_DELAY)
  public void call() {
    System.out.println(dateFormat.format(new Date()) + " - job kicked off");
  }
}
```

ScheduledTask is a Spring bean with one method annotated by the @Scheduled annotation. In this case, we use the fixed-rate scheduling method with 1-second intervals. This method simply prints the current time to the console. The Spring configuration looks like Listing 1-26.

Listing 1-26. Scheduled Task Configuration (0103-scheduled-job)

```
package net.lkrnac.book.eiws.chapter01.scheduling;

import org.springframework.boot.SpringApplication;
import org.springframework.context.annotation.ComponentScan;
import org.springframework.context.annotation.Configuration;
import org.springframework.scheduling.annotation.EnableScheduling;

@Configuration
@ComponentScan
@EnableScheduling
public class ScheduledConfiguration {
  public static void main(String... args) {
    SpringApplication.run(ScheduledConfiguration.class, args);
  }
}
```

This example uses the @EnableScheduling annotation to enable the scheduling feature. It also uses a component scan to register Spring beans from the current package and its subpackages. The last notable aspect of this class is usage of Spring Boot to simply execute this configuration as an executable JAR application. When we run this Java application, we should see output similar to Listing 1-27.

Listing 1-27. Scheduled Task Console Output

```
19:36:34:454 - job kicked off
19:36:35:454 - job kicked off
19:36:36:454 - job kicked off
19:36:37:454 - job kicked off
...
```

Our job is scheduled for execution each second. This application would have this behavior until we terminate it forcibly.

XML Configuration for Scheduling

It is also possible to configure scheduling with XML by using the task namespace, which has various tags for scheduling support. The first one is <task:scheduler>, used to configure the ThreadPoolTaskScheduler thread pool that will be driving scheduling. <task:scheduler> has one mandatory parameter, id, which specifies the name of the scheduler bean and the prefix for worker thread names. The second parameter, pool-size, is optional and specifies the core size of the thread-pool implementation used for scheduling. When it's not explicitly specified, the default value is 1, indicating that a single thread will be used to execute scheduled logic.

The second top-level element for scheduling support is <task:scheduled-tasks>. It can have various <task:scheduled> subelements, where each subelement specifies one scheduled task. <task:scheduled> can have one of these parameters:

> fixed-delay: Numeric value in milliseconds

> fixed-rate: Numeric value in milliseconds

> cron: String Cron expression

One of them has to be specified. The next parameter is the optional initial-delay. It may be used to delay initial iteration by a given number of milliseconds. The last two parameters, ref and method, are mandatory. They specify a reference to a Spring bean and the name of the method that will be scheduled. *This method has to be void and can't accept parameters.*

Also, the top-level element, <task:scheduled-tasks>, has one optional parameter, scheduler, used to define the scheduler bean reference. If it isn't specified, a single-threaded executor is used for scheduling tasks defined as subelements. Listing 1-28 shows the configuration.

Listing 1-28. Examples of XML Configuration Support for Scheduling

```xml
<task:scheduler id="customScheduler" pool-size="10"/>
<task:scheduled-tasks scheduler="customScheduler">
        <task:scheduled ref="bean1" method="method1" cron="*/10 9-17 * * * MON-FRI"/>
        <task:scheduled ref="bean2" method="method2" fixed-delay="1000"/>
        <task:scheduled ref="bean3" method="method3" fixed-rate="1000"/>
</task:scheduled-tasks>
```

Summary

This chapter described Spring's APIs for multithreading and scheduling and compared them with pure Java SE multithreading support. It is important to bear in mind that multithreading is a double-edged sword. Throwing a pool of threads on the problem can slow computation, because switching context between threads can become more expensive than the computation itself. This can happen especially when there are many more running threads than CPU cores in the system. In addition, multithreaded logic could be too simple and not worth the cost of context switching. So figuring out the correct level of parallelism isn't a trivial job and requires a good understanding of the problem and the surrounding environment. Benchmarking and accurate performance testing are always a good idea when problems are being solved by multithreading.

■ **Note** In addition to multithreading, you can use other approaches to solve problems of blocking I/O operations. But these are beyond the scope of this book. For more information, you can research Java Futures and Reactive Extensions (for example, see the RxJava library at `https://github.com/ReactiveX/RxJava`) and Actor systems (for example, Spring Reactor at `https://github.com/reactor/reactor` or Akka at `http://akka.io/`). A good example of an aggressive nonblocking I/O approach is the event loop in Node.js (`https://nodejs.org/`) that naturally evolved from the web browser's event loop.

CHAPTER 2

■ ■ ■

Remoting

Let's compare the Ultrabook (Dell's super thin laptop) to a desktop PC. Most people would probably go for an Ultrabook these days, because it's lighter, silent, and can be carried nearly everywhere. So does a desktop PC have any advantage at all, apart from its lower price? Yes—it is modular. What would you do with an Ultrabook when its processor breaks or its power connector burns out? These kinds of problems would likely make the Ultrabook unrepairable. But if this happened to a desktop PC's monitor or power supply, those can be replaced easily. The capability to replace PC components is supported by standardized connectors. They allow us to build a whole PC by using components from different vendors.

Now imagine a big cloud service provider. The infrastructure of this system is closer to PC architecture in terms of our PC vs. Ultrabook metaphor. Enterprise systems are composed of applications that are often implemented in different programming languages and are running on machines located in various parts of the world. It is obvious that these applications need to communicate with each other via common protocols, so that a broken application eventually can be replaced without affecting the whole enterprise.

Spring remoting support is an abstraction umbrella for interapplication communication mechanisms used in the enterprise world. These technologies can be categorized into two basic groups based on their nature: synchronous and asynchronous.

Let's start with method invocation technologies (synchronous communication):

- Remote Method Invocation (RMI)

- HTTPInvoker: Java serialization over HTTP

- Hessian: Lightweight binary HTTP-based protocol designed by Caucho Technology

- Burlap: XML-based version of Hessian

- Java API for XML Web Services (JAX-WS): Replaced JAX-RPC with the introduction of Java EE 5, covered in Chapter 3

And now consider technologies for message passing (asynchronous communication):

- Java Message Service (JMS): Covered in Chapter 5

- Advanced Message Queuing Protocol (AMQP): Covered by the Spring AMQP project and out of the scope of this book

As you can see, the Spring umbrella is rich. But each of these technologies also can be used without Spring. So the question is, what benefits do the Spring abstractions provide? For remoting technologies, the benefits are as follows:

- Decouples remoting logic from application code

- Propagates a declarative paradigm to configure and expose services

- Supports various protocols with consistent APIs

- Translates checked exceptions into runtime exceptions

Let's explore each of these technologies and Spring's abstractions in more detail.

■ **Note**   Hessian and Burlap were included in previous versions of the Enterprise Integration with Spring certification, but were removed from the latest version, which covers Spring 4.0 features. Therefore, they are beyond the scope of this book.

Remote Method Invocation

As its name suggests, *Remote Method Invocation* (RMI) is used for executing methods located on a remote JVM or system. RMI provides a convenient way to integrate distributed systems. Developers don't need to convert data models into another format in order to communicate with the remote system. To transfer data between JVMs, serialization is used. Serialization is a standard Java mechanism to convert data and code into binary form, so they can be stored or sent through the wire.

Initial implementations of RMI worked only for inter-JVM communication. They were based on the Java Remote Method Protocol (JRMP). To make RMI more flexible, the RMI over Internet Inter-Orb Protocol (RMI-IIOP) was developed. This version is based on the Common Object Request Broker Architecture (CORBA) standard and can be used for intercommunication of diverse systems. The important take-away of this is that RMI-IIOP makes method invocation possible with non-JVM runtime environments.

As mentioned, RMI is used for communication between remote environments potentially located on different hosts. So two sides are involved. One side exposes logic. The second side consumes the exposed RMI method. Both sides are able to communicate via the network, because the JRMP provides an RMI registry. Each side of the communication registers a proxy object into the RMI registry, and these objects then communicate with each other with the help of a standard Java serialization mechanism.

In order to understand each other, the client and server need to have a common contract available on both sides. This contract in the RMI world isn't anything other than a standard Java interface. The method provider needs to implement this interface, and the RMI client needs it during the remote method call. There are two ways to ensure that this contract is available on both sides:

- The interface is located in a shared JAR library that would be used by both sides as a dependency.

- The interface is duplicated with the same signature on both sides.

Each approach has its pros and cons. Extracting into a shared library creates complexity around handling and maintaining that shared library. Duplicating an interface on both sides obviously creates the risk of making the interface incompatible on one of the sides.

It may seem like developers can take any call and easily expose it via RMI without any changes. But this isn't exactly the case. Certain RMI contract specifics need to be fulfilled:

- The contract interface needs to extend the `java.rmi.Remote` interface.

- The exposing method must throw a `java.rmi.RemoteException`.

- The class implementing the RMI method (logic that will be shared) needs to extend `java.rmi.server.UnicastRemoteObject`.

- The class implementing the RMI method needs to have an explicit constructor, which must throw java.rmi.RemoteException.

- The client consuming the RMI method needs to handle the checked exception java.rmi.RemoteException.

Another important part of the contract is serialization. Each parameter, return type, and implementing class itself needs to be serializable. For the service implementation class, this is ensured via extending java.rmi.server.UnicastRemoteObject.

Let's explore RMI contract specifics in examples. Our shared interface is highlighted in Listing 2-1.

Listing 2-1. Shared Interface Between Client and Server

```
package net.lkrnac.book.eiws.chapter02.rmi.java;

import java.rmi.Remote;
import java.rmi.RemoteException;

public interface BarService extends Remote {
  String serveBar(String param) throws RemoteException;
}
```

This interface with identical signatures is located in two example projects, 0201-java-rmi-service and 0201-java-rmi-client. Of course, you can use any type as a parameter, as long as it is shared on both sides of the communication and fulfills the serialization requirements. Listing 2-2 shows the service logic that is located in the class implementing the shared interface on the server.

Listing 2-2. Example of RMI Service Implementation (0201-java-rmi-service)

```
package net.lkrnac.book.eiws.chapter02.rmi.java;

import java.rmi.RemoteException;
import java.rmi.server.UnicastRemoteObject;

public class BarServiceImpl extends UnicastRemoteObject implements BarService {
  private static final long serialVersionUID = 1L;

  protected BarServiceImpl() throws RemoteException {
  }

  @Override
  public String serveBar(String param) throws RemoteException {
    return "Bar service response to parameter: " + param;
  }
}
```

As you can see, all these java.rmi API details are invasive to the application code. It is obvious that exposing a method via RMI wouldn't always be a refactoring-free operation. You can see that the implementation class itself needs to be serializable (as do the parameters and return value as well). Listing 2-3 shows RMI code that creates the RMI registry and starts the server. It is the last piece of our server example.

Listing 2-3. Example of Exposing the RMI Service (0201-java-rmi-service)

```
package net.lkrnac.book.eiws.chapter02.rmi.java;

import java.rmi.AlreadyBoundException;
import java.rmi.RemoteException;
import java.rmi.registry.LocateRegistry;
import java.rmi.registry.Registry;

public class RmiServer {
  private static final int RMI_PORT = 10201;

  public static void main(String... args) throws RemoteException,
      AlreadyBoundException {
    BarServiceImpl engine = new BarServiceImpl();
    Registry registry = LocateRegistry.createRegistry(RMI_PORT);
    registry.bind("BarService", engine);
  }
}
```

In this case, we are creating an RMI registry and thus exposing the RMI method on port 10201. BarService is the RMI name that identifies our method. So it is possible to expose various methods that will be bound to different RMI names. This concept is similar to Spring MVC request mappings.

The next piece of our RMI puzzle is the client side. The name of this example project is 0201-java-rmi-client. Listing 2-4 shows the main client class.

Listing 2-4. RMI Client Example (0201-java-rmi-client)

```
package net.lkrnac.book.eiws.chapter02.rmi.java;

import java.rmi.NotBoundException;
import java.rmi.RemoteException;
import java.rmi.registry.LocateRegistry;
import java.rmi.registry.Registry;

public class FooClient {
  private static final int RMI_PORT = 10201;

  public static void main(String... args) throws RemoteException,
      NotBoundException {
    System.out.println(new FooClient().callService("Main method"));
  }

  public String callService(String parameter) {
    Registry registry;
    try {
      registry = LocateRegistry.getRegistry(RMI_PORT);
      BarService barService = (BarService) registry.lookup("BarService");
      return barService.serveBar(parameter);
    } catch (RemoteException | NotBoundException e) {
      throw new RuntimeException(e);
    }
  }
}
```

The method callService tries to find the RMI registry on port 10201. If callService can't find the registry, NotBoundException is thrown. This is another invasive aspect of the pure Java RMI API. The registry is then searched for the RMI object based on the name. Finally, the actual RMI call is performed.

When we run server example 0201-java-rmi-service, it creates an RMI registry and remains running, exposing the service. After running client example 0201-java-rmi-client, it will try to establish a connection to the remote RMI registry and call the remote method. Listing 2-5 shows the console output after running the client example.

Listing 2-5. Console Output of the RMI Example

```
Bar service (Java RMI) response to parameter: Main method
```

You might be wondering where Spring enters the equation and how it helps with the RMI. Let's focus on that now.

Spring RMI Support

Spring always tries to iron out the API flaws of existing technologies. Java RMI is no exception. Spring allows for noninvasive RMI exposure. This means we can forget about RemoteException, UnicastRemoteObject, and the Remote interface altogether. We can expose existing code without changes. The only contract requirement needed with Spring is serialization. But Spring can't avoid it. Serialization is in the nature of this distributed technology.

RMI registry handling is also much easier with Spring. Spring tries to see whether there is an RMI registry on given port. If not, an RMI registry is created on demand. Let's explore Spring's RMI constructs in an example. Listing 2-6 shows the service interface.

Listing 2-6. Shared Interface (0202-spring-rmi-java-config-service and 0202-spring-rmi-java-config-client)

```
package net.lkrnac.book.eiws.chapter02.rmi.spring.javaconfig;

public interface BarService {
  public String serveBar(String param);
}
```

Listing 2-7 shows the implementation.

Listing 2-7. Shared Interface and Service Implementation (0202-spring-rmi-java-config-service)

```
package net.lkrnac.book.eiws.chapter02.rmi.spring.javaconfig.service;

import net.lkrnac.book.eiws.chapter02.rmi.spring.javaconfig.BarService;
import org.springframework.stereotype.Service;

@Service
public class BarServiceImpl implements BarService {
  @Override
  public String serveBar(String param) {
    return "Bar service 0202 response to parameter: " + param;
  }
}
```

As you can see, no RMI-specific code is needed. This is a huge advantage over the pure Java RMI API, because we can expose any method via RMI without refactoring. The only requirement is serialization of all types in the method signature. The RmiServiceExporter bean is needed in the Spring context for RMI registry binding and registering, as shown in Listing 2-8.

Listing 2-8. Spring RMI Service Configuration (0202-spring-rmi-java-config-service)

```
package net.lkrnac.book.eiws.chapter02.rmi.spring.javaconfig.service;

import net.lkrnac.book.eiws.chapter02.rmi.spring.javaconfig.BarService;
import org.springframework.context.annotation.Bean;
import org.springframework.context.annotation.ComponentScan;
import org.springframework.context.annotation.Configuration;
import org.springframework.remoting.rmi.RmiServiceExporter;

@Configuration
@ComponentScan
public class ServiceConfiguration {
  private static final int RMI_PORT = 10202;

  @Bean
  public RmiServiceExporter registerService(BarService barService) {
    RmiServiceExporter rmiServiceExporter = new RmiServiceExporter();
    rmiServiceExporter.setServiceName("BarService");
    rmiServiceExporter.setService(barService);
    rmiServiceExporter.setServiceInterface(BarService.class);
    rmiServiceExporter.setRegistryPort(RMI_PORT);

    return rmiServiceExporter;
  }
}
```

barService bean is injected by Spring, so that it can be used for registering a service to the RMI register. Otherwise, the RMI server code is pretty straightforward.

Let's take a look at the client side in Listing 2-9.

Listing 2-9. Spring RMI Client Configuration (0202-spring-rmi-java-config-client)

```
package net.lkrnac.book.eiws.chapter02.rmi.spring.javaconfig.client;

import net.lkrnac.book.eiws.chapter02.rmi.spring.javaconfig.BarService;
import org.springframework.context.annotation.Bean;
import org.springframework.context.annotation.Configuration;
import org.springframework.remoting.rmi.RmiProxyFactoryBean;

@Configuration
public class ClientConfiguration {
  @Bean
  public BarService createBarServiceLink() {
    RmiProxyFactoryBean rmiProxyFactoryBean = new RmiProxyFactoryBean();
    rmiProxyFactoryBean.setServiceUrl("rmi://localhost:10202/BarService");
    rmiProxyFactoryBean.setServiceInterface(BarService.class);
    rmiProxyFactoryBean.afterPropertiesSet();
    return (BarService) rmiProxyFactoryBean.getObject();
  }
}
```

First we create `org.springframework.remoting.rmi.RmiProxyFactoryBean`. This factory class is used to create RMI proxy objects. It has a few mandatory properties:

- The remote location of the RMI registry. Spring uses the URL notation of the RMI endpoint definition.

- The service interface class definition.

Calling `rmiProxyFactoryBean.afterPropertiesSet()` applies the configured RMI settings and binds the factory to the remote RMI register. The last call is `rmiProxyFactoryBean.getObject()`, where we create a proxy object that will simulate the service bean. And that's it. `BarService` is now a bean in our client Spring IoC container. Listing 2-10 shows how this bean can be used in client business logic.

Listing 2-10. Use of RMI Client Proxy Bean (0202-spring-rmi-java-config-client)

```
package net.lkrnac.book.eiws.chapter02.rmi.spring.javaconfig.client;

import javax.annotation.PostConstruct;
import net.lkrnac.book.eiws.chapter02.rmi.spring.javaconfig.BarService;
import org.springframework.beans.factory.annotation.Autowired;
import org.springframework.stereotype.Component;

@Component
public class FooClient {
  private final BarService barService;

  @Autowired
  public FooClient(BarService barService) {
    this.barService = barService;
  }

  @PostConstruct
  public void callBarService() {
    System.out.println(barService.serveBar("FooClient"));
  }
}
```

In any Spring bean, we can inject an RMI proxy bean and use it with exactly the same API as we would call the server implementation directly. This is because Spring translates checked `java.rmi.RemoteException` into unchecked `org.springframework.remoting.RemoteAccessException`. So we can completely hide the fact that we are calling a remote method from the business logic.

When we run server example `0202-spring-rmi-java-config-service` and subsequently client example `0202-spring-rmi-java-config-client`, we can see the console output shown in Listing 2-11.

Listing 2-11. Console Output of Spring RMI Example

```
Bar service 0202 response to parameter: FooClient
```

If you are using XML context for legacy reasons, Spring provides support for it also. In fact, it is similar to the Java configuration, without any special XML namespaces. Therefore, we skip the definition of the service interface and its implementation for XML examples. They are the same as in Listing 2-6 and Listing 2-7, only the packages are slightly different.

The server XML RMI configuration looks like Listing 2-12.

Listing 2-12. Spring RMI XML Server Configuration (file bar-service-context.xml in example project
0203-spring-rmi-xml-config-service)

```
<beans xmlns="http://www.springframework.org/schema/beans"
  xmlns:xsi="http://www.w3.org/2001/XMLSchema-instance"
  xmlns:context="http://www.springframework.org/schema/context"
  xsi:schemaLocation="http://www.springframework.org/schema/beans
    http://www.springframework.org/schema/beans/spring-beans.xsd
    http://www.springframework.org/schema/context
    http://www.springframework.org/schema/context/spring-context-4.0.xsd">

  <context:component-scan base-package=
     "net.lkrnac.book.eiws.chapter02.rmi.spring.xmlconfig.service" />

  <bean class="org.springframework.remoting.rmi.RmiServiceExporter">
    <property name="serviceName" value="BarService" />
    <property name="service" ref="barServiceImpl" />
    <property name="serviceInterface"
      value="net.lkrnac.book.eiws.chapter02.rmi.spring.xmlconfig.BarService" />
    <property name="registryPort" value="10203" />
  </bean>
</beans>
```

The beginning of the file contains a definition of the standard Spring XML namespace context and bean. First we perform a component scan of the package where the service implementation is located. Then we register the RMI service exporter bean. The XML configuration is using standard Spring bean registration syntax.

Notice the different port number than in Listing 2-8. This difference indicates that this configuration is located in a different project, but the service interface and its implementation are exactly the same. It is easier to handle integration tests when different projects within an integration test suite are using different ports.

As Listing 2-13 shows, the client XML configuration is interestingly less verbose than the Java configuration.

Listing 2-13. Spring RMI XML Client Configuration (file foo-client-context.xml in example project
0203-spring-rmi-xml-config-client)

```
<?xml version="1.0" encoding="UTF-8"?>
<beans xmlns="http://www.springframework.org/schema/beans"
  xmlns:xsi="http://www.w3.org/2001/XMLSchema-instance"
  xmlns:context="http://www.springframework.org/schema/context"
  xsi:schemaLocation="http://www.springframework.org/schema/beans
    http://www.springframework.org/schema/beans/spring-beans.xsd
    http://www.springframework.org/schema/context
    http://www.springframework.org/schema/context/spring-context-4.0.xsd">

  <bean id="barService"
    class="org.springframework.remoting.rmi.RmiProxyFactoryBean">
    <property name="serviceUrl" value="rmi://localhost:10203/BarService" />
    <property name="serviceInterface"
      value="net.lkrnac.book.eiws.chapter02.rmi.spring.xmlconfig.BarService" />
  </bean>
</beans>
```

This example is the client counterpart for the XML server configuration in Listing 2-14. Therefore, port 10203 is used. You may notice that it is similar to the Java configuration. Notice that in the Java client configuration example in Listing 2-9, we had to create the proxy bean explicitly. In this case, Spring will create it automatically, so it's enough to register only the factory bean.

As you can see, these examples document the API enhancements Spring provides for RMI. Although it's easy to expose services via RMI and much easier with Spring, there are a few architectural risks when using RMI. First of all, every type that is part of the contract has to be serializable. This is restrictive, because both sides need to have the same version of each return type or parameter. So changes to the contract need to be aligned on both sides. This creates a tight coupling between the RMI exporter and consumer.

Another problem is the inability to use various versions of the same API contract. Of course, the contract should be as stable as possible. But sometimes changes are required. Other approaches, such as SOAP or REST, allow extending the API without needing to change the client. RMI serialization is not suitable for such changes. Each change to types used in the RMI method signature needs to be reflected on the client.

Another significant downside of RMI is that it can communicate with only the JVM runtime. This is solved by the RMI over CORBA implementation (RMI-IIOP). CORBA is a standard defined by Object Management Group (OMG) and designed for communication between different platforms. RMI-IIOP with Spring is similar to pure RMI. The only difference is to add a JNDI prefix to Spring RMI classes. So, for example, instead of `RmiServiceExporter`, we would use `JndiRmiServiceExporter` for RMI-IIOP. But even when CORBA seemed a promising technology for implementing distributed systems, it didn't gain widespread adoption because of various problems with the protocol or its implementations.

■ **Note** Diving into CORBA and its problems is beyond the scope of this book. Wikipedia is good place to start investigation: `https://en.wikipedia.org/wiki/Common_Object_Request_Broker_Architecture#Problems_and_criticism`

All these weak points of RMI can lead to questions, including why to use RMI at all. But it does have one more advantage (alongside simplicity and better performance than SOAP and REST): it doesn't require a web server to communicate. Pure RMI can perform communication between JVMs without using additional abstractions or libraries. This can be handy in Java-based embedded systems that need to communicate remotely.

Spring RMI Summary

It is important to remember that Spring provides many benefits compared to the pure Java RMI API. First, on the server side:

- Decouples server business logic from the remoting protocol because we can expose business services without changes.

- Service method doesn't need to throw `java.rmi.RemoteException`.

- Service interface doesn't extend `java.rmi.Remote`.

- Service implementation doesn't extend `java.rmi.server.UnicastRemoteObject`.

- Service constructor doesn't need to throw `java.rmi.RemoteException`.

- Binding to the RMI registry can be done automatically by Spring.

Second, on the client side:

- Existing code doesn't have to be changed when invoking a remote method, because the client doesn't need to handle checked java.rmi.RemoteException when the service method is used. Spring translates it into unchecked RemoteAccessException.

- Decouples client business logic from remoting mechanism, so remoting protocols can be easily replaced.

Spring HttpInvoker

HttpInvoker is a technology similar to RMI. It also uses standard Java serialization and deserialization. But it uses a different protocol to transfer serialized data. RMI uses JRMP, and PMI-IIOP uses CORBA. In contrast, as its name suggests, HttpInvoker uses HTTP. This is probably the most widely used protocol nowadays, because it fuels the whole Web. HTTP provides a significant advantage over other protocols, because it is most likely to be widely supported by network infrastructures. For example, RMI or CORBA can be blocked by firewall rules, but HTTP is enabled in most firewalls.

When a remote call is performed, it uses an HTTP POST request and serializes parameters and response values via standard Java serialization. So it has similar performance to RMI. But HttpInvoker is officially supported by the Spring team as the preferred remoting approach, because it doesn't need to use any special remoting contracts (remote interfaces, remote exceptions, proxies). It also doesn't rely on the mechanism of an RMI registry. That is why Spring documentation considers HttpInvoker lightweight compared to other remoting mechanisms.

HttpInvoker can be served in several ways:

- From the servlet container (Java EE)

- Via HttpRequestHandlerServlet (without Spring MVC support)

- Via DispatcherServlet (with Spring MVC support)

- Via simple Java HTTP server implementation (Java SE)

No special runtime is needed for the latter implementation. The standard Java runtime is enough. For the first two, on the other hand, a Java EE servlet container is needed.

Each HttpInvoker solution uses a similar approach for bean exposure. It wraps the target service bean and the service interface into an HttpInvokerServiceExporter/SimpleHttpInvokerServiceExporter. This bean is registered in the Spring container and exposed via the previously mentioned HTTP communication mechanisms. Let's explore each approach with examples. Listing 2-14 contains an example service interface and implementation that will be exposed.

Listing 2-14. Shared Interface and Service Implementation

```
public interface BarService {
  String serveBar(String param);
}

import org.springframework.stereotype.Service;

@Service
public class BarServiceImpl implements BarService {
  @Override
  public String serveBar(String param) {
    return "Bar service response to parameter: " + param;
  }
}
```

This service interface contract and service implementation are used across all HttpInvoker examples in this chapter.

HttpInvoker Served via HttpRequestHandlerServlet

Examples of HttpInvoker served via `HttpRequestHandlerServlet` can be found in code examples under projects 0204-http-invoker-handler-servlet-java-config and 0205-http-invoker-handler-servlet-xml-config. First we need to wrap our service interface into `HttpInvokerServiceExporter` and register it as a Spring bean, as shown in Listing 2-15.

Listing 2-15. HttpInvoker Server Configuration Example

```
package net.lkrnac.book.eiws.chapter02.httpinvoker.handlerservlet.javaconfig.server;

import net.lkrnac.book.eiws.chapter02.httpinvoker.
        handlerservlet.javaconfig.shared.BarService;
import org.springframework.context.annotation.Bean;
import org.springframework.context.annotation.ComponentScan;
import org.springframework.context.annotation.Configuration;
import org.springframework.remoting.httpinvoker.HttpInvokerServiceExporter;

@Configuration
@ComponentScan
public class ServerConfiguration {
  @Bean
  public HttpInvokerServiceExporter barExporter(BarService barService) {
    HttpInvokerServiceExporter httpInvokerServiceExporter =
        new HttpInvokerServiceExporter();
    httpInvokerServiceExporter.setService(barService);
    httpInvokerServiceExporter.setServiceInterface(BarService.class);
    return httpInvokerServiceExporter;
  }
}
```

This is a pretty straightforward Spring Java configuration that scans for Spring components in the current package (also in subpackages) and registers a service exporter bean. Notice that this bean has the name barExporter (which is the name of the bean method by default). The bean name is important, because it needs to match the servlet name configured in the servlet descriptor configuration. The target service barService instance is injected and configured via the `HttpInvokerServiceExporter.setService` method. As you can see, we need to specify the service interface also. XML configuration of the same bean looks like Listing 2-16.

Listing 2-16. HttpInvoker Server XML Configuration Example

```
<?xml version="1.0" encoding="UTF-8"?>
<beans xmlns="http://www.springframework.org/schema/beans"
  xmlns:xsi=http://www.w3.org/2001/XMLSchema-instance
  xmlns:context="http://www.springframework.org/schema/context"
  xsi:schemaLocation="http://www.springframework.org/schema/beans
    http://www.springframework.org/schema/beans/spring-beans.xsd
    http://www.springframework.org/schema/context
    http://www.springframework.org/schema/context/spring-context.xsd">
```

```xml
<context:component-scan base-package=
    "net.lkrnac.book.eiws.chapter02.httpinvoker.handlerservlet.xmlconfig" />

<bean name="barExporter" class=
    "org.springframework.remoting.httpinvoker.HttpInvokerServiceExporter">
  <property name="service" ref="barService" />
  <property name="serviceInterface" value=
  "net.lkrnac.book.eiws.chapter02.httpinvoker.handlerservlet.xmlconfig.shared.BarService" />
</bean>
</beans>
```

The next step is configuring an HttpRequestHandlerServlet. The Java servlet configuration look likes Listing 2-17.

Listing 2-17. HttpInvoker Servlet Descriptor Example

```java
package net.lkrnac.book.eiws.chapter02.httpinvoker.
         handlerservlet.javaconfig.server;

import javax.servlet.ServletContext;
import javax.servlet.ServletException;
import javax.servlet.ServletRegistration;
import org.springframework.web.WebApplicationInitializer;
import org.springframework.web.context.ContextLoaderListener;
import org.springframework.web.context.
         support.AnnotationConfigWebApplicationContext;
import org.springframework.web.context.support.HttpRequestHandlerServlet;

public class WebAppInitializer implements WebApplicationInitializer {
  @Override
  public void onStartup(ServletContext servletContext) throws ServletException {
    AnnotationConfigWebApplicationContext rootContext =
        new AnnotationConfigWebApplicationContext();
    rootContext.register(ServerConfiguration.class);
    rootContext.refresh();

    servletContext.addListener(new ContextLoaderListener(rootContext));
    ServletRegistration.Dynamic appServlet =
        servletContext.addServlet("barExporter",
            new HttpRequestHandlerServlet());
    appServlet.addMapping("/");
  }
}
```

WebApplicationInitializer is Spring's interface used for servlet configuration. It is used as an abstraction on top of the Servlet 3 Java API (javax.servlet.ServletContainerInitializer). Spring scans the implementation of WebApplicationInitializer and bootstraps it in SpringServletContainerInitializer (Spring's implementation of javax.servlet.ServletContainerInitializer). So WebApplicationInitializer can be used as a replacement for the web.xml configuration in Spring applications, or alongside the web.xml configuration. Such flexibility enables a smooth migration path from legacy XML configurations.

The WebApplicationInitializer.onStartup method is invoked by Spring during the servlet container initialization phase. Spring injects the javax.servlet.ServletContext instance, which is designed for interfacing with the underlying servlet container. So we can register our servlets into it. First of all, we create a Spring root context and register our ServerConfiguration. Now two boilerplate lines follow in Listing 2-17. The context needs to be refreshed after registering the configuration, and ContextLoaderListener needs to be registered also.

Finally, we register a new instance of HttpRequestHandlerServlet with a name matching the service exporter bean's name (barExporter) and map the servlet onto a URL (/ in this case). You will probably be more familiar with the web.xml style of configuration, as shown in Listing 2-18. It looks similar to WebAppInitializer in Listing 2-17.

Listing 2-18. HttpInvoker XML Servlet Description Example

```
<web-app ...>
  <display-name>0205-http-invoker-handler-servlet-xml-config</display-name>
  <context-param>
    <param-name>contextConfigLocation</param-name>
    <param-value>classpath:server-config.xml</param-value>
  </context-param>

  <listener>
    <listener-class>
      org.springframework.web.context.ContextLoaderListener
    </listener-class>
  </listener>

  <servlet>
    <servlet-name>barExporter</servlet-name>
    <servlet-class>
      org.springframework.web.context.support.HttpRequestHandlerServlet
    </servlet-class>
  </servlet>

  <servlet-mapping>
    <servlet-name>barExporter</servlet-name>
    <url-pattern>/</url-pattern>
  </servlet-mapping>
</web-app>
```

In this case, we used the spring-config.xml file as a Spring configuration from the example project 0205-http-invoker-handler-servlet-xml-config. But all other aspects of XML configuration follow the same concepts as in WebApplicationInitializer. Consistency of APIs across various technologies and configuration types is the beauty of Spring.

HttpRequestHandlerServlet is a lightweight alternative to DispatcherServlet, the backbone of the Spring MVC framework. So it is handy if we need to avoid the Spring MVC framework. But if your application already uses DispatcherServlet or you want to avoid unnecessary boilerplate configuration, the following approach is the way to go.

HttpInvoker Served via DispatcherServlet

DispatcherServlet is the central class of Spring's web support. It is extensively used by Spring MVC for building web applications and REST APIs. Its job is to route HTTP messages to controllers based on declarative URL mappings and map responses onto the appropriate views.

With DispatcherServlet, you can map the HttpInvokerServiceExporter bean directly to a URL. This is done by starting the bean name with a slash character, as shown in Listing 2-19.

Listing 2-19. HttpInvoker via DispatcherServlet Example (0206-http-invoker-bean)

```
package net.lkrnac.book.eiws.chapter02.httpinvoker.dispatcherservlet.server;

import net.lkrnac.book.eiws.chapter02.httpinvoker.
        dispatcherservlet.shared.BarService;
import org.springframework.boot.SpringApplication;
import org.springframework.boot.autoconfigure.EnableAutoConfiguration;
import org.springframework.context.annotation.Bean;
import org.springframework.context.annotation.ComponentScan;
import org.springframework.context.annotation.Configuration;
import org.springframework.remoting.httpinvoker.HttpInvokerServiceExporter;

@Configuration
@ComponentScan
@EnableAutoConfiguration
public class ServerConfiguration {
  public static void main(String... args) {
    SpringApplication.run(ServerConfiguration.class);
  }

  @Bean(name = "/BarService")
  public HttpInvokerServiceExporter exportBarService(BarService barService) {
    HttpInvokerServiceExporter httpInvokerServiceExporter =
        new HttpInvokerServiceExporter();
    httpInvokerServiceExporter.setService(barService);
    httpInvokerServiceExporter.setServiceInterface(BarService.class);
    return httpInvokerServiceExporter;
  }
}
```

Configuration of the exporter bean is similar to that in the "HttpInvoker Served via HttpRequestHandlerServlet" section. The only difference is the bean name, /BarService (notice the forward slash character at the beginning). A name with a slash character tells Spring that the bean should be served by DispatcherServlet from the URL endpoint defined by this name. No other configuration changes are needed if DispatcherServlet is already configured properly.

Configuring DispatcherServlet is covered in the Spring Web certification exam and is highlighted in Chapters 3 and 4. Therefore, I grabbed the chance and used a new approach to configure HttpInvoker via DispatcherServlet. As experienced Spring developers would recognize, Listing 2-19 uses an API that isn't part of the Spring Core framework (the EnableAutoConfiguration annotation and SpringApplication class). These are part of the new Spring Boot framework. Spring Boot promotes convention over configuration principles for a highly configurable Spring. This significantly helps decrease the amount of boilerplate configuration. But at the same time, conventions can be replaced with custom Spring configurations. This allows for rapid and flexible development with Spring family frameworks.

The EnableAutoConfiguration annotation tells Spring Boot to look at the classpath and apply the most appropriate Spring configuration based on found dependencies. Listing 2-20 contains Maven dependencies for this example.

Listing 2-20. Maven Dependencies (0206-http-invoker-bean)

```
<dependencies>
  <dependency>
    <groupId>org.springframework.boot</groupId>
    <artifactId>spring-boot-starter-web</artifactId>
  </dependency>
  <dependency>
      <groupId>org.springframework.boot</groupId>

      <artifactId>spring-boot-starter-tomcat</artifactId>
      <scope>provided</scope>
  </dependency>
</dependencies>
```

In this case, we have Tomcat on the classpath. So because we have a servlet container as a dependency, Spring Boot applies the most common servlet configuration with DispatcherServlet. This is handy for our example because it is, in fact, all the configuration needed if we are using Spring Boot JAR packaging.

If we need to use Spring Boot WAR packaging, one more class would be needed to cover servlet configuration, as shown in Listing 2-21.

Listing 2-21. Spring Boot Servlet Helper for WAR Packaging (example project 0206-http-invoker-bean)

```
package net.lkrnac.book.eiws.chapter02.httpinvoker.dispatcherservlet.server;

import org.springframework.boot.builder.SpringApplicationBuilder;
import org.springframework.boot.context.web.SpringBootServletInitializer;

public class WebInitializer extends SpringBootServletInitializer {
  @Override
  protected SpringApplicationBuilder configure(
      SpringApplicationBuilder application) {
    return application.sources(ServerConfiguration.class);
  }
}
```

SpringBootServletInitializer maps DispatcherServlet to "/" URL and uses ServerConfiguration class as main Spring context definition.

HttpInvoker Served via Simple Java HTTP Server

If the servlet container is overkill for our application, we could use a pure Java SE approach for exposing the service with HttpInvoker. The standard Java runtime contains a simple HTTP server implementation, which can be used by Spring to expose the service via HttpInvoker. The API details of this simple HTTP server are not relevant because we want to use Spring abstractions. Let's take a look at the Spring configuration in Listing 2-22.

Listing 2-22. HttpInvoker via Simple Java Server Configuration Example (0207-http-invoker-simple-service)

```java
package net.lkrnac.book.eiws.chapter02.httpinvoker.simple.server;

import java.util.HashMap;
import java.util.Map;
import net.lkrnac.book.eiws.chapter02.httpinvoker.simple.shared.BarService;
import org.springframework.boot.SpringApplication;
import org.springframework.context.annotation.Bean;
import org.springframework.context.annotation.ComponentScan;
import org.springframework.context.annotation.Configuration;
import org.springframework.remoting.
        httpinvoker.SimpleHttpInvokerServiceExporter;
import org.springframework.remoting.support.SimpleHttpServerFactoryBean;
import com.sun.net.httpserver.HttpHandler;

@Configuration
@ComponentScan
public class ServerConfiguration {
  @Bean
  public SimpleHttpInvokerServiceExporter barExporter(BarService barService) {
    SimpleHttpInvokerServiceExporter barExporter =
        new SimpleHttpInvokerServiceExporter();
    barExporter.setService(barService);
    barExporter.setServiceInterface(BarService.class);
    return barExporter;
  }

  @Bean
  public SimpleHttpServerFactoryBean httpServer(
      SimpleHttpInvokerServiceExporter barExporter) {
    SimpleHttpServerFactoryBean httpServer = new SimpleHttpServerFactoryBean();
    Map<String, HttpHandler> endpoints = new HashMap<>();
    endpoints.put("/BarService", barExporter);
    httpServer.setContexts(endpoints);
    httpServer.setPort(10207);
    return httpServer;
  }
}
```

ServerCondiguration.barExplorer bean is similar to the servlet HttpInvoker examples. The method creates an instance of SimpleHttpInvokerServiceExplorer. The service exporter has mandatory fields: the service and service interface. The service implementation instance is injected from Spring and represents the exposed logic. The service interface is the signature of the exposed service.

The second bean in our configuration configures a simple HTTP service. The exposed service needs to be bound to a URL endpoint. The second mandatory setting we need to provide is the port number where the simple HTTP server will be listening.

HttpInvoker Service Accessed from Client

The previous examples showed that we have various options for exposing a service via HttpInvoker, differentiated by the implementation of the web server/servlet. On the other side of the communication channel, we have two options for consuming the HttpInvoker protocol:

- Standard Java Development Kit (JDK) HTTP client—used by default

- Apache HttpComponents as the client library

Apache HttpComponents provides a few features that are not handled by the standard Java SE HTTP component:

- Basic HTTP authentication

- HTTP connection pooling

- HTTP state management

An example of Java configuration with a standard Java HTTP proxy is shown in Listing 2-23.

Listing 2-23. HttpInvoker Client Configuration Example (0204-http-invoker-handler-servlet-java-config)

```
package net.lkrnac.book.eiws.chapter02.httpinvoker.
        handlerservlet.javaconfig.client;

import net.lkrnac.book.eiws.chapter02.httpinvoker.
        handlerservlet.javaconfig.shared.BarService;
import org.springframework.context.annotation.Bean;
import org.springframework.context.annotation.Configuration;
import org.springframework.remoting.httpinvoker.HttpInvokerProxyFactoryBean;

@Configuration
public class ClientConfiguration {
  @Bean
  public HttpInvokerProxyFactoryBean httpInvokerProxy() {
    HttpInvokerProxyFactoryBean httpInvoker =
        new HttpInvokerProxyFactoryBean();
    httpInvoker.setServiceUrl("http://localhost:10204/BarService");
    httpInvoker.setServiceInterface(BarService.class);
    return httpInvoker;
  }
}
```

We need to register a bean of type `HttpInvokerProxyFactoryBean` into the Spring context. It is a factory bean, which indicates that it will be used for creating object(s). In this case, it will create a proxy bean, which will act as a local instance of the remote service. All requests to this bean will be serialized and sent through the wire to the server.

So the remote service will look like a local bean to the business logic. As the example highlights, the URL of the service location and service interface are needed to create an HttpInvoker tunnel. The server counterpart for this example is hosted on localhost on port 10204. Notice that no request executor instance is configured. This means we are using the standard Java HTTP client. Finally, we can use the `BarService` bean with standard autowiring, as shown in Listing 2-24.

Listing 2-24. Invoking HttpInvoker on the Client (0204-http-invoker-handler-servlet-java-config)

```
package net.lkrnac.book.eiws.chapter02.httpinvoker.
          handlerservlet.javaconfig.client;

import static org.testng.Assert.assertEquals;
import net.lkrnac.book.eiws.chapter02.httpinvoker.
          handlerservlet.javaconfig.shared.BarService;
import org.springframework.beans.factory.annotation.Autowired;
import org.springframework.test.context.ContextConfiguration;
import org.springframework.test.context.
          testng.AbstractTestNGSpringContextTests;
import org.testng.annotations.Test;

@ContextConfiguration(classes = { ClientConfiguration.class })
public class HttpInvokerServletJavaConfigITCase extends
    AbstractTestNGSpringContextTests {
  @Autowired
  private BarService barService;

  @Test
  public void testHttpInvoker() {
    // GIVEN - client context

    // WHEN
    String actualResult = barService.serveBar("0204 Integration test");

    // THEN
    assertEquals(actualResult,
        "Bar service 0204 response to parameter: 0204 Integration test");
  }
}
```

Listing 2-24 has a form of the TestNG integration test, but it is obvious that the same autowiring can be applied in our business logic bean. Neither the test nor the potential business bean has an idea that barService is a remote service exposed via HttpInvoker. This demonstrates how easy it is to expose and consume services via HttpInvoker without any change to the existing Spring application.

Now let's explore the second option of consuming HttpInvoker with the HttpComponents library. We would use this option if the features of the standard Java SE HTTP client are not enough for our use case. Basic HTTP authentication or HTTP connection pooling are common requirements for security or performance reasons.

To switch gears a little, we will use it in conjunction with XML Spring configuration, to show how to configure HttpInvoker via XML configuration as well. See Listing 2-25.

Listing 2-25. HttpInvoker XML Configuration Example (0205-http-invoker-handler-servlet-xml-config)

```xml
<?xml version="1.0" encoding="UTF-8"?>
<beans xmlns="http://www.springframework.org/schema/beans"
  xmlns:xsi="http://www.w3.org/2001/XMLSchema-instance"
  xsi:schemaLocation="http://www.springframework.org/schema/beans
    http://www.springframework.org/schema/beans/spring-beans.xsd">

  <bean id="httpInvokerProxy"
    class="org.springframework.remoting.httpinvoker.HttpInvokerProxyFactoryBean">
    <property name="serviceUrl" value="http://localhost:10205/BarService" />
    <property name="serviceInterface" value=
      "net.lkrnac.book.eiws.chapter02.httpinvoker.handlerservlet.xmlconfig.shared.BarService" />
    <property name="httpInvokerRequestExecutor">
      <bean class=
        "org.springframework.remoting.httpinvoker.HttpComponentsHttpInvokerRequestExecutor" />
    </property>
  </bean>
</beans>
```

This client is configured against the server on localhost with port 10205. It uses only a standard bean namespace to construct the proxy factory bean. The only difference here, compared to the Java configuration in Listing 2-24, is the `httpInvokerRequestExecutor` field. We explicitly configured it to use the Apache HttpComponents client library.

Summary

This chapter discussed remoting support of the Spring framework. In this synchronous communication, the client is blocked until the remote service finishes its job.

Serialization is needed for all classes involved in the communication (service method parameters and return type). Whether this is standard Java serialization, CORBA, or Caucho's XML binary serialization, it creates a significant constraint: the inability to version a server API. Each change to the client/server contract needs to be aligned on both sides. Therefore, these technologies should be avoided if we need to create a server API that has the following characteristics:

- Publicly facing.

- Not under our control.

- Consumed by a large number of clients. If the server contract is changed, all clients need to be changed also.

Each Spring remoting abstraction uses a different combination of transport protocol and serialization mechanism:

- RMI uses Java serialization and Java Remote Method Protocol.

- RMI-IIOP uses Java serialization and Internet Inter-Orb Protocol, which makes communication CORBA compatible.

- HttpInvoker uses Java serialization and HTTP.

- Hessian uses Caucho's binary XML serialization and HTTP.

- Burlap uses Caucho's textual XML serialization and HTTP.

The transport protocol and serialization mechanism can narrow architectural decisions when a remoting method needs to be chosen. For example, if communicating with non-Java applications is required, only Hessian or RMI-IIOP are suitable (Burlap should be avoided, because its Spring abstractions are deprecated since Spring 4). When we need to communicate via HTTP, only HttpInvoker and Hessian can fulfill this requirement.

Spring significantly simplifies transitions between remoting technologies, because it uses the same concepts for exposing and consuming services. While exposing a service, the notion of an exported service is used (`RmiServiceExporter`, `HttpInvokerServiceExporter`, `HessianServiceExporter`, `BurlapServiceExporter`). When consuming, a proxy factory bean mechanism penetrates all remoting abstractions (`RmiProxyFactoryBean`, `HttpInvokerProxyFactoryBean`, `HessianProxyFactoryBean`, `BurlapProxyFactoryBean`). All these abstractions have similar properties across different remoting technologies. Such API consistencies decrease the learning curve if we need to switch remoting technologies.

When using RMI, there are numerous benefits to using Spring abstractions instead of standard Java APIs. Benefits on the server are as follows:

- No need to throw checked exceptions

- No need to implement or extend invasive RMI types

- Allows for exposing business services without changes

- Handles creation of RMI registry if needed

Benefits on the client are as follows:

- Translating of checked exceptions into runtime

- Allows for consuming remote services without changing client code

While each remoting approach provides an easy way to implement distributed applications, they are rarely used in enterprise applications nowadays, because they create tight coupling between applications. So a certain remoting technology is not required or slightly lower performance is suitable, SOAP or especially RESTful web services likely will be considered for new projects.

CHAPTER 3

■ ■ ■

Web Services

This chapter covers the Spring Web Services project. SOAP web services can be considered as completely opposite to remote procedure calls (RPCs) in terms of decoupling and performance, because SOAP provides a very high level of decoupling but not for free. The cost of this variability is performance problems that can occur because of the bloated XML protocol SOAP uses. Implementation of SOAP services is also complex. We will dive into the Spring support provided in this field and show how Spring helps to simplify this process by leveraging best practices and reusing most modern approaches.

Introduction to Web Services

The software development world is like the fashion industry: it has trends. When it became clear that distributed systems would be powering modern web sites and that the disadvantages of remote procedure calls would push these technologies to the limits, the focus of software development turned to decoupling.

Web services are highly interconnected with service-oriented architecture (SOA), in which various pieces of functionality are separated into stand-alone service applications communicating with one another. These services are consumed by client-facing applications or other services. Such architecture allows for a separation of concerns and low coupling. On the other hand, it brings higher complexity, because a well-defined contract between the consumer and the producer of the web service needs to be specified. When all aspects of the contract are defined up front, services and applications can be developed, tested, and deployed in isolation.

RPC approaches may be considered also, but tight coupling of remoting technologies is a big problem for SOA, especially when the consumer of a web service is developed by a different team, department, or company. So communication needs to occur via a protocol that facilitates decoupling the client from the web service.

An important requirement of web services is the ability to handle different versions of the same service API. This is a killer for RPC technologies. Imagine a publicly facing API of an application and various clients consuming it. When a change or new feature needs to be implemented into the API, not all clients are keen to update—because of the additional cost for them. We may end up with two groups of clients using different contracts. Therefore, a protocol is needed, to handle versioning.

This protocol is SOAP (originally known as the Simple Object Access Protocol), which uses XML as its exchange format. SOAP is transport-protocol agnostic, so we can use HTTP, Simple Mail Transfer Protocol (SMTP), Transmission Control Protocol (TCP), User Datagram Protocol (UDP), Java Message Service (JMS), or Extensible Messaging and Presence Protocol (XMPP) as a transport protocol. Such variability doesn't tie up the underlying network architecture. The XML payload format is flexible, platform independent, and widely adopted. All major platforms such as Java, .NET, C++, Ruby, PHP, Python, and Perl support it. Therefore, it's a good candidate for an exchange format fulfilling SOA requirements.

The highest level of decoupling the client from the web service occurs when the client discovers the web-service capabilities and structure of the payload at runtime. XML Schema Definition (XSD) and Web Services Description Language (WSDL) can be used for this purpose. XSD defines the structure of the XML payload provided or consumed by the web service, complex types, and validation rules for certain data elements. So we can think of it as metadata for the web service payload. The web service can validate received payloads against XSD. WSDL is an XML-based description of the functionality provided by the web service. It gathers the name of the service, the service methods provided, and the signatures of the service methods (types of parameters and return values).

With this concept, the client doesn't need to know anything about the web service up front. The XML payload can be constructed based on XSD and WSDL files on the fly. But this approach also has downsides. Constructing an XML request based on XSD and WSDL files isn't trivial. Implementation of the web service is also more complex with such metadata rules. And when a payload is generated dynamically all the time, there are performance hits. Of course, we could omit the metadata contract of the web service and tie down the client to the static payload structure. But for such cases, there are less-verbose exchange formats (for example, JavaScript Object Notation, or JSON). Verbosity of the XML format is one of the problems pointed out by SOAP critics.

So let's summarize the most important SOAP advantages in comparison to remoting (RPC) technologies:

> *Decoupling*: Document-oriented communication allows for versioning and discoverability.

> *Interoperability*: Can connect various platforms easily and operate on top of various transport protocols.

And the disadvantages include the following:

> *Complexity*: SOAP is much more complicated to implement, because it requires knowledge of XSD, WSDL, XML marshalling, and the marshalling framework.

> *Performance*: The verbosity of XML and the need for marshalling and verification against the schema makes it perform less well.

Java Web Services

Java is not the only platform operating on top of the SOAP protocol. .NET is also a big player in this space. But Java EE is definitely the biggest adopter of SOAP web services concepts. Many libraries have evolved in the Java ecosystem to help with web services development. Because SOAP relies on XML, it's obvious that libraries for marshalling into XML and unmarshalling from XML are crucial for SOAP communication.

Let's look at the XML libraries for the major programming language platforms, starting with Java. These libraries are categorized according to their different approaches to XML processing:

- *Java*

  - Event-driven approach—application listens to events for certain XML elements: Simple API for XML (SAX)

  - DOM-based approach—application loads the whole XML and parses it as a tree structure: JDOM, XOM, dom4j, TrAX

  - Streaming API for XML (StAX): Introduces the concept of a cursor within an XML document that is used for reading forward and backward

  - Binding of XML to Java objects: Java Architecture for XML Binding (JAXB), Castor XML, XMLBeans, XStream, JiBX

- *.NET*: XmlSerializer, System.Xml, .NET XML parser

- *Python*: ElementTree, BeautifulSoup, MiniDom/PullDom

- *Ruby*: Builder, Nokogiri, REXML, XmlSimple

- *Perl*: Perl XML, XML::Simple

- *JavaScript*: LibXmlJs

It's obvious from this list that many possibilities exist for implementing XML-based web services. Let's focus only on Java web services for now. We have XML messages on one hand and Java objects on the other hand. The easiest way to accomplish XML conversion is direct binding to Java objects. But this approach is not suitable in every case. For example, if we have a really big XML message that can't be loaded into memory, we need to process it with a lower-level XML-processing library.

But for SOAP implementations, binding libraries are the best fit. Big messages in SOAP may indicate a design problem in communication. That is why most Java web services nowadays are implemented with Object to XML (OXM) binding libraries. JAXB is the main Java OXM player, because it is part of the Java EE standards. JAXB technology also is useful beyond SOAP, because it can handle JSON format.

As we described, XML marshalling and unmarshalling are happening within SOAP communication. SOAP messages have a specified high-level structure and need to conform to a formal contract (XSD/WSDL).

The mandatory high-level structure of a SOAP message used for exchanging data is as follows:

- Envelope

- Header: May contain metadata—for example, the data necessary for securing, routing, or business logic metadata

- Body: Contains the message itself, and may contain the target domain where the web service is located

A contract defines the exact format for interchanged XML messages. But how do we start developing such a web service? When we have Java objects on one side and XML messages on the other side, one side needs to conform to the other side via conversion. We have two possibilities to start developing a web service:

> *Contract Last*: Specify Java classes first and create a WSDL contract based on the Java classes' structure.

> *Contract First*: Create a WSDL contract up front and force the Java classes to conform to that contract.

You may expect us now to highlight the advantages and disadvantages of each approach—especially when both approaches nowadays have automatic conversion libraries. But SOA experiences show that the Contract Last approach can lead to various problems:

> *Performance*: Java object graphs can easily become very big. It is not suitable for a communication protocol to send huge XML messages that would be generated by big Java object graphs.

> *Type duplication*: Careful definition of XSD allows for reusability of XSD types. This is not possible when a contract is generated from Java.

> *Contract changes*:
>
> - The basic idea of decoupling is based on protecting the client from server changes. If XSD and WSDL are automatically generated from Java interfaces, the XML contract can be a target of frequent changes by the XSD/WSDL generation algorithm.

- When a contract is changed with the Contract Last approach, we can't support two versions of the contract. If we use the Contract First approach, we could handle changes between versions of the contract by XSLT transformations. When messages are converted by XSLT transformation, the same Java class representation can be used. So we can support various versions of the contract at the same time with Contract First.

Java to XML type conversion problems:

- It is easy to represent cyclic graphs in Java. But such a representation in XML is not trivial.

- XSD restrictions are a useful mechanism for restricting a group of possible data values (for example, regular expressions for strings). But the Java language doesn't contain such validation mechanisms out of the box.

- Some Java types have special constraints or semantics. These can be interpreted in XML, but this representation can be ambiguous. ArrayList can be represented on the client as LinkedList. The picture can become even more complicated when communication occurs between two programming languages.

In light of these arguments, Contract First is considered best practice. The Contract Last development style is considered easier, but Spring, in conjunction with existing XML libraries and tooling, makes the Contract First approach easy as well.

Spring Web Services

Spring supports web services development in two ways:

Support for JAX-WS (formerly JAX-RPC): JAX-WS is the Java EE standard for developing Contract First and Contract Last web services. It is part of Core Spring framework.

Spring Web Services project: Support for Contract First web services.

■ **Note** JAX-WS is beyond the scope of Enterprise Integration with Spring certification and thus also beyond the scope of this book.

The Spring Web Services project is by far the preferred way of implementing a web service. It is a stand-alone project within the Spring platform. As always, Spring Web Services doesn't try to reinvent the wheel, but rather takes advantage of existing technologies to provide convenient abstractions and features. Let's summarize some of these features:

Powerful routing of messages: We can map XML messages to endpoints via the payload root XML element, Web Services Addressing (WS-Addressing), or SOAPAction headers.

Wide support for XML converters: Supports DOM, SAX, StAX, JDOM, dom4j, XOM, and OXM technologies (for example, JAXB 2, Castor XML, XMLBeans, XStream, JiBX).

Integration with Spring Framework family: Developers use the same Inversion of Control (IoC) concepts as with all other Spring modules.

Support for WS-Security: Encryption, decryption of SOAP messages, and authentication for web service access are invaluable mechanisms for security.

■ **Note**   Support for WS-Security was removed from Enterprise Integration with Spring certification and therefore is beyond the scope of this book.

Contract Creation

Spring Web Services provides an excellent foundation for creating web services, because it facilitates only the Contract First approach. These well-defined steps indicate how to define a Spring Web Services contract:

1. Create a sample message payload.

2. Generate an XSD schema based on the sample message.

3. Enhance the generated XSD if needed:

    - Amend for the desired contract structure.

    - Change XSD types for elements.

    - Extract reusable XSD types.

    - Define XSD restrictions for elements.

4. Spring can dynamically generate WSDL based on XSD.

The first three steps are optional. A web service developer experienced with XSD may want to define a contract directly. But the simplest way is to generate it from sample messages. There is also a good chance that business experts will be able to provide sample messages with the desired XML structure.

Let's explain these steps with a simple example. Our example service will provide user details based on a requested e-mail address. This simple domain will be used across all web services examples. The request sample message looks like Listing 3-1.

■ **Note**   Source-code files explaining the creation of XSD contracts are stored in the example project `0301-ws-xmlconfig-service` in the directory `src/main/resources`.

Listing 3-1. Sample Request

```
<UserRequest>
  <Email>lubos.krnac@gmail.com</Email>
</UserRequest>
```

Based on this request, the service should provide user details. The sample payload for the user details response is highlighted in Listing 3-2.

Listing 3-2. Sample Response

```
<UserDetailsResponse>
  <FirstName>Lubos</FirstName>
  <LastName>Krnac</LastName>
</UserDetailsResponse>
```

When we have the request and response messages specified, we can generate the XSD contract draft. We have various options. Because this generation is a one-time step, there is no point in automating it into a continuous integration pipeline. So you can use any tool of your choice. Various types of tools with different levels of complexity and user interaction approaches are available. Some examples include the following:

XMLSpy: A comprehensive commercial XML IDE, useful for complicated XML modeling

Trang: A simple command-line JAR utility

DevUtilsOnline free XML-to-XSD generator: A free online generator (http://devutilsonline.com/xsd-xml/generate-xsd-from-xml)

Let's use the third option, because it doesn't require any installation nor downloads. This tool provides various design styles for a generated XSD structure. As we don't need reusable types, we can choose *Russian Doll Design.* Listing 3-3 was generated for the sample request, and Listing 3-4 for the sample response.

■ **Note** XSD and WSDL languages are used extensively in web services development, and are the topic of other books. Enterprise Integration with Spring Certification focuses on Spring-related abstractions and workflows. It doesn't dive deep into schema definitions nor web service descriptions. Therefore, detailed XSD and WSDL are beyond the scope of this book.

Listing 3-3. Generated XSDfrom Sample Request

```
<?xml version="1.0"?>
<xs:schema xmlns:xs="http://www.w3.org/2001/XMLSchema" attributeFormDefault="unqualified"
elementFormDefault="qualified">
  <xs:element name="UserRequest">
    <xs:complexType>
      <xs:sequence>
        <xs:element type="xs:string" name="Email"/>
      </xs:sequence>
    </xs:complexType>
  </xs:element>
</xs:schema>
```

Listing 3-4. Generated XSD from Sample Response

```
<?xml version="1.0"?>
<xs:schema xmlns:xs="http://www.w3.org/2001/XMLSchema" attributeFormDefault="unqualified"
elementFormDefault="qualified">
  <xs:element name="UserDetailsResponse">
    <xs:complexType>
```

```
    <xs:sequence>
      <xs:element type="xs:string" name="FirstName"/>
      <xs:element type="xs:string" name="LastName"/>
    </xs:sequence>
   </xs:complexType>
  </xs:element>
</xs:schema>
```

These generated results provide the basic foundation for our XSD contract. Developers may need to tweak this contract to cover input validation requirements and to enhance readability and code reusability. This example merges these two contracts into one file, because our contract isn't complicated and it's easier to work with one contract file. The enhanced contract is shown in Listing 3-5.

Listing 3-5. Manually Amended XSD Contract

```
<?xml version="1.0" encoding="UTF-8"?>
<xs:schema xmlns:xs="http://www.w3.org/2001/XMLSchema"
  attributeFormDefault="unqualified" elementFormDefault="qualified"
  targetNamespace="http://localhost:10301/0301-ws-xmlconfig-service">

  <xs:element name="UserDetailsResponse">
    <xs:complexType>
      <xs:sequence>
        <xs:element type="xs:NCName" name="FirstName" />
        <xs:element type="xs:NCName" name="LastName" />
      </xs:sequence>
    </xs:complexType>
  </xs:element>

  <xs:element name="UserRequest">
    <xs:complexType>
      <xs:attribute name="Email">
        <xs:simpleType>
          <xs:restriction base="xs:string">
            <xs:pattern value="[^@]+@[^\.]+\..+" />
          </xs:restriction>
        </xs:simpleType>
      </xs:attribute>
    </xs:complexType>
  </xs:element>

</xs:schema>
```

Let's sum up the manual changes introduced in Listing 3-5:

- Use xs:NCName types instead of xs:string for the first name and last name. This is useful because it excludes most special characters (which wouldn't make sense for a person's name).

- Narrow down e-mail values in the contract by using regular expression restriction.

- Specify the targetNamespace where the service will be hosted.

- Specify UTF-8 encoding for the XSD document.

The XSD contact is a crucial piece of web service interface specification. It is a single source of truth for the web service. Designing the XSD contract correctly is important, because its structural changes can later trigger refactoring in the Java code base. Therefore, we want to have the contract reviewed by as many stakeholders as possible up front.

The created XSD contract can be used for further generation of the following:

- Java model Plain Old Java Objects (POJOs) in case we are using a JAXB 2 XML marshaller

- Dynamic WSDL definition for the web service

Endpoint Mapping

When the request hits our application, we need to route it to certain Java logic. This binding is called *endpoint mapping* in the Spring world. The *endpoint* refers to the class where the web service logic is defined. This class is annotated with the @Endpoint annotation.

When the class is declared to hold web service logic, we need to route messages. Spring provides various declarative endpoint-mapping mechanisms in the form of these method-level annotations:

@PayloadRoot: Maps the method to the root element of the request payload

@Action: Maps the method to the WS-Addressing Action header

@SoapAction: Maps the method to the SOAPAction header

With these annotations, a web services developer can effectively route SOAP messages declaratively based on various message attributes.

@PayloadRoot routing is the most popular method-mapping mechanism. The top-level (root) XML element of the SOAP message drives the routing. The @PayloadRoot annotation has two parameters:

localPart: Specifies the name of the root element to map. This is a mandatory parameter.

namespace: Specifies the namespace of the payload root element. This is an optional parameter.

So to map the example message in Listing 3-6, localPart needs to have the value UserRequest, and namespace should have the value http://localhost:10301/0301-ws-xmlconfig-service.

Listing 3-6. Example SOAP Message

```
<SOAP-ENV:Envelope xmlns:SOAP-ENV="http://schemas.xmlsoap.org/soap/envelope/">
  <SOAP-ENV:Header />
  <SOAP-ENV:Body>
    <ns2:UserRequest xmlns:ns2="http://localhost:10301/0301-ws-xmlconfig-service"
      Email="lubos.krnac@gmail.com" />
  </SOAP-ENV:Body>
</SOAP-ENV:Envelope>
```

When a particular Java method is mapped, we need to map parameters and return the value of the Java method. Spring provides various options for signature mapping:

- Mapping XML parser types

  - @RequestPayload: Maps the request message to the method parameter; the parameter type is derived from the underlying XML marshaller, used for XML-to-Java conversion.

  - @ResponsePayload: Maps the response message to the method's return value; the return value type is derived from the underlying XML marshaller, used for XML-to-Java conversion.

- @XPathParam: Used for binding parameters based on XPath expressions

  - boolean or Boolean

  - double or Double

  - String

  - org.w3c.dom.Node

  - org.w3c.dom.NodeList

- Extracting message metadata into the method parameter (no annotation usage)

  - org.springframework.ws.context.MessageContext

  - Soap metadata (SoapMessage, SoapBody, SoapEnvelope, SoapHeader, SoapHeaderElements)

- Mapping parameters to a custom unmarshaller (this method requires the parameter to be annotated with @RequestPayload also)

The developer can decide which information from the message is relevant for the web service and needs to be injected into a method. This list of supported signature mappings provides huge variability. A handy Spring Web Services feature is the ability to choose an XML parsing mechanism. Table 3-1 presents the types of XML parsers that Spring can automatically map in the method signature. These types always have to be annotated by @RequestPayload or @ResponsePayload, respectively.

Table 3-1. *XML Parsers in Method Signature Mappings*

XML Parser	Method Signature Type
TrAX	javax.xml.transform.Source, DOMSource, SAXSource, StreamSource, and StAXSource
W3C DOM	org.w3c.dom.Element
dom4j	org.dom4j.Element
JDOM	org.jdom.Element
XOM	nu.xom.Element
StAX	javax.xml.stream.XMLStreamReader and javax.xml.stream.XMLEventReader (can be used only for method parameters and not for return values)

JAXB 2 Endpoint-Mapping Example

The most widely used marshaller is JAXB 2, which allows for generation of Java model classes from an XSD contract. Generated Java classes are annotated with special mapping annotations, which map XML elements onto POJO classes. This approach is called Object to XML Mapping (OXM). It is similar to the famous object-relational mapping (ORM), which maps SQL DB tables onto POJOs.

Examples in this book are based on the Maven 3 build system. So jaxb2-maven-plugin is used for Java model generation; the XJC binding compiler is used to generate Java classes from the XSD contract. More information about this plug-in can be found at http://mojo.codehaus.org/jaxb2-maven-plugin/xjc-mojo.html. The Maven plug-in configuration is shown in Listing 3-7.

Listing 3-7. Configurationof jsxb2-maven-plugin

```
<plugin>
  <groupId>org.codehaus.mojo</groupId>
  <artifactId>jaxb2-maven-plugin</artifactId>
  <version>1.6</version>
  <executions>
    <execution>
      <id>xjc</id>
      <goals>
        <goal>xjc</goal>
      </goals>
    </execution>
  </executions>
  <configuration>
    <schemaDirectory>${project.basedir}/src/main/resources/</schemaDirectory>
    <outputDirectory>${project.basedir}/src/main/java</outputDirectory>
    <clearOutputDir>false</clearOutputDir>
  </configuration>
</plugin>
```

This configuration reads all XSD schema files from the src/main/resources directory and its subfolders. It is crucial to know that it would pick up all XSD files present in the specified directory structure and convert the XSD types/elements into Java POJOs. Therefore, the number of POJO classes depends on the number of XSD types/elements defined. If one file has five XSD types, five POJO classes will be generated for these types. The conversion will fail if any name clashes occur.

When we run this configuration with Maven goals, JAXB POJOs will be generated based on the XSD schema into the src/main/java folder:

```
> clean install
```

The generated package structure follows the namespace of the XSD schema. In our case, it is localhost._10301._0301_ws_xmlconfig_service. These POJOs basically represent the domain model of the web service. For the XSD schema in Listing 3-5, three classes are created:

- UserRequest
- UserDetailsReponse
- ObjectFactory

The first two classes obviously represent the XSD elements from the contract. They contain getters and setters for subelements. The last class is a factory for creating contract elements. It can be used to create instances of POJO classes derived from XSD elements or types. It may not be needed, depending on the XSD contract. Listing 3-8 shows generated classes with their JAXB 2 annotations.

Listing 3-8. Generated JAXB 2 Model

```java
package localhost._10301._0301_ws_xmlconfig_service;

import javax.xml.bind.annotation.XmlAccessType;
import javax.xml.bind.annotation.XmlAccessorType;
import javax.xml.bind.annotation.XmlAttribute;
import javax.xml.bind.annotation.XmlRootElement;
import javax.xml.bind.annotation.XmlType;

@XmlAccessorType(XmlAccessType.FIELD)
@XmlType(name = "")
@XmlRootElement(name = "UserRequest")
public class UserRequest {
    @XmlAttribute(name = "Email")
    protected String email;

    /**
     * Gets the value of the email property.
     *
     * @return
     *     possible object is
     *     {@link String }
     *
     */
    public String getEmail() {
        return email;
    }

    /**
     * Sets the value of the email property.
     *
     * @param value
     *     allowed object is
     *     {@link String }
     *
     */
    public void setEmail(String value) {
        this.email = value;
    }
}

package localhost._10301._0301_ws_xmlconfig_service;

import javax.xml.bind.annotation.XmlAccessType;
import javax.xml.bind.annotation.XmlAccessorType;
import javax.xml.bind.annotation.XmlElement;
```

```java
import javax.xml.bind.annotation.XmlRootElement;
import javax.xml.bind.annotation.XmlSchemaType;
import javax.xml.bind.annotation.XmlType;
import javax.xml.bind.annotation.adapters.CollapsedStringAdapter;
import javax.xml.bind.annotation.adapters.XmlJavaTypeAdapter;

@XmlAccessorType(XmlAccessType.FIELD)
@XmlType(name = "", propOrder = {
    "firstName",
    "lastName"
    })
@XmlRootElement(name = "UserDetailsResponse")
public class UserDetailsResponse {
    @XmlElement(name = "FirstName", required = true)
    @XmlJavaTypeAdapter(CollapsedStringAdapter.class)
    @XmlSchemaType(name = "NCName")
    protected String firstName;
    @XmlElement(name = "LastName", required = true)
    @XmlJavaTypeAdapter(CollapsedStringAdapter.class)
    @XmlSchemaType(name = "NCName")
    protected String lastName;

    /**
     * Gets the value of the firstName property.
     *
     * @return
     *     possible object is
     *     {@link String }
     *
     */
    public String getFirstName() {
        return firstName;
    }

    /**
     * Sets the value of the firstName property.
     *
     * @param value
     *     allowed object is
     *     {@link String }
     *
     */
    public void setFirstName(String value) {
        this.firstName = value;
    }

    /**
     * Gets the value of the lastName property.
     *
     * @return
     *     possible object is
```

```java
 *      {@link String }
 *
 */
public String getLastName() {
    return lastName;
}

/**
 * Sets the value of the lastName property.
 *
 * @param value
 *     allowed object is
 *     {@link String }
 *
 */
public void setLastName(String value) {
    this.lastName = value;
}
}

package localhost._10301._0301_ws_xmlconfig_service;

import javax.xml.bind.annotation.XmlRegistry;

@XmlRegistry
public class ObjectFactory {
    /**
     * Create a new ObjectFactory that can be used to create new instances of schema derived
     * classes for package: localhost._10301._0301_ws_xmlconfig_service
     *
     */
    public ObjectFactory() {
    }

    /**
     * Create an instance of {@link UserDetailsResponse }
     *
     */
    public UserDetailsResponse createUserDetailsResponse() {
        return new UserDetailsResponse();
    }

    /**
     * Create an instance of {@link UserRequest }
     *
     */
    public UserRequest createUserRequest() {
        return new UserRequest();
    }
}
```

Bear in mind that this code is generated from an XSD contract. Therefore, when the contract is changed, the JAXB 2 model is regenerated. Any changes to POJO field names or types can trigger Java compiler issues in the code where they are used. This useful behavior of the Contract First approach for creating web services uses the advantages of Java's type-safety features. If the XSD contract were generated from a Java model, the change could be missed during development. And as we all know, the sooner an issue is discovered, the cheaper the damage is.

The class ObjectFactory is a factory for all other types involved. It had wider use in earlier versions of JAXB for creation of model instances. But in recent versions of JAXB 2, the use of this class is limited, because POJO constructors can be used to create model instances now. ObjectFactory may be needed depending on the complexity of the XSD schema. If you notice that your generated ObjectFactory contains factory methods returning JAXBElement<T> types, your schema may not be directly mapped to the Java class hierarchy. Another option is that your XSD restrictions can't be expressed by the Java type system. In such cases, you may need to create a meta-structure in the form of JAXBElement<T> types. But that is rare.

UserRequest and UserDetailResponse are domain model types that will be used in web service logic. Listing 3-9 shows an example of endpoint mapping that uses generated types in the method signature.

Listing 3-9. Endpoint Root Mapping (0301-ws-xmlconfig-service)

```java
package net.lkrnac.book.eiws.chapter03.ws.xmlconfig.server;

import localhost._10301._0301_ws_xmlconfig_service.UserDetailsResponse;
import localhost._10301._0301_ws_xmlconfig_service.UserRequest;
import org.springframework.ws.server.endpoint.annotation.Endpoint;
import org.springframework.ws.server.endpoint.annotation.PayloadRoot;
import org.springframework.ws.server.endpoint.annotation.RequestPayload;
import org.springframework.ws.server.endpoint.annotation.ResponsePayload;

@Endpoint
public class UserEndpoint {
  @PayloadRoot(namespace = "http://localhost:10301/0301-ws-xmlconfig-service",
        localPart = "UserRequest")
  @ResponsePayload
  public UserDetailsResponse getUserDetails(
      @RequestPayload UserRequest userRequest) {
    UserDetailsResponse userDetails = null;
    if ("lubos.krnac@gmail.com".equals(userRequest.getEmail())) {
      userDetails = new UserDetailsResponse();
      userDetails.setFirstName("Lubos");
      userDetails.setLastName("Krnac");
    }
    return userDetails;
  }
}
```

Developers can take advantage of the flexibility of the Spring Web Services binding mechanism and vary it with parameters.

Spring can also inject into our web service method the metadata of the message—for example, the SOAP header or message context. The message context contains all data involved in the service's current request:

- Request

- Repose

- Properties, which can be used to communicate with the interceptors and endpoint

Let's say we want to read the SOAP header role and use the message context in web service logic now. Listing 3-10 reflects this requirement.

Listing 3-10. Example of Payload Root Endpoint-Mapping Variations

```java
package net.lkrnac.book.eiws.chapter03.ws.xmlconfig.server;

import localhost._10301._0301_ws_xmlconfig_service.UserDetailsResponse;
import localhost._10301._0301_ws_xmlconfig_service.UserRequest;
import org.springframework.ws.context.MessageContext;
import org.springframework.ws.server.endpoint.annotation.Endpoint;
import org.springframework.ws.server.endpoint.annotation.PayloadRoot;
import org.springframework.ws.server.endpoint.annotation.RequestPayload;
import org.springframework.ws.server.endpoint.annotation.ResponsePayload;
import org.springframework.ws.soap.SoapHeaderElement;
import org.springframework.ws.soap.server.endpoint.annotation.SoapHeader;

@Endpoint
public class UserEndpoint {
  @PayloadRoot(namespace = "http://localhost:10301/0301-ws-xmlconfig-service",
  localPart = "UserRequest")
  @ResponsePayload
  public UserDetailsResponse getUserDetails(
      @RequestPayload UserRequest userRequest, @SoapHeader("role") SoapHeaderElement role,
      MessageContext messageContext) {

        ...
      }
    return userDetails;
  }
}
```

Routing SOAP messages based on the root XML element (@PayloadRoot) is most common. But routings also can be based on WS-Addressing (@Action) or the SOAPAction header (@SoapAction). Listing 3-11 shows a SOAPAction routing example. WS-Addressing would be similar.

Listing 3-11. SOAPAction Endpoint Mapping (0307-ws-soapaction-service)

```java
package net.lkrnac.book.eiws.chapter03.ws.soapaction.server;

import localhost._10307._0307_ws_soapaction_service.UserDetailsResponse;
import localhost._10307._0307_ws_soapaction_service.UserRequest;
import org.springframework.ws.server.endpoint.annotation.Endpoint;
import org.springframework.ws.server.endpoint.annotation.RequestPayload;
import org.springframework.ws.server.endpoint.annotation.ResponsePayload;
import org.springframework.ws.soap.server.endpoint.annotation.SoapAction;

@Endpoint
public class UserEndpoint {
  @SoapAction("getUserDetails")
  @ResponsePayload
```

```
  public UserDetailsResponse getUserDetails(
      @RequestPayload UserRequest userRequest) {
    UserDetailsResponse userDetails = null;
    if ("lubos.krnac@gmail.com".equals(userRequest.getEmail())) {
      userDetails = new UserDetailsResponse();
      userDetails.setFirstName("Lubos");
      userDetails.setLastName("Krnac");
    }
    return userDetails;
  }
}
```

Spring Context Configuration

The previous section highlighted how an XSD contract can be mapped to Java logic with the Spring Web Services framework. A class annotated with @Endpoint is a candidate for Spring component scanning. So this class can be treated as a Spring component. Various options exist for integrating it into Spring's IoC container.

The first option is to use the Spring XML configuration shown in Listing 3-12.

Listing 3-12. Web Service XML Context Configuration (File web-service-config.xml in Example Project 0301-ws-xmlconfig-service)

```xml
<?xml version="1.0" encoding="UTF-8"?>
<beans xmlns="http://www.springframework.org/schema/beans"
  xmlns:xsi="http://www.w3.org/2001/XMLSchema-instance"
  xmlns:context="http://www.springframework.org/schema/context"
  xmlns:ws="http://www.springframework.org/schema/web-services"
  xsi:schemaLocation="http://www.springframework.org/schema/web-services
        http://www.springframework.org/schema/web-services/web-services.xsd
        http://www.springframework.org/schema/beans
        http://www.springframework.org/schema/beans/spring-beans.xsd
        http://www.springframework.org/schema/context
        http://www.springframework.org/schema/context/spring-context.xsd">

  <context:component-scan
        base-package="net.lkrnac.book.eiws.chapter03.ws.xmlconfig.server" />

  <ws:annotation-driven />

  <ws:dynamic-wsdl id="userDetails" portTypeName="UserDetailsPort"
    locationUri="/"
    targetNamespace="http://localhost:10301/0301-ws-xmlconfig-service">
    <ws:xsd location="classpath:userDetailsSchema.xsd" />
  </ws:dynamic-wsdl>
</beans>
```

This configuration uses three namespaces from Spring's deck of XML schemas:

> web-services: For web services configuration

> beans: Basic Spring IoC namespace

> context: For component scanning

The XML element `<context:component-scan>` scans for an endpoint defined in Listing 3-9. The `<ws:annotation-driven>` configuration says to Spring that we want to use Web Services annotations. The last element is the most interesting: `<ws:dynamic-wsdl>` is used for dynamic generation of WSDL based on the XSD contract file located in our classpath. Spring scans the classpath for the XSD schema file specified. As we are using Maven in these examples, userDetailsSchema.xsd is located in the folder src/main/resources. The location URI specifies the URL endpoint from which the generated WSDL will be served. We used the root-level location for WSDL exposure. The parameter id specifies the exposed name of the WSDL file. So when we run the server on localhost and port 10301, the final WSDL location would be http://localhost:10301/0301-ws-xmlconfig-service/userDetails.wsdl.

Dynamic WSDL generation is useful during the development stage of our web service, as requirements may change a lot. But in production we want to make sure that contact with the web service is stable. Because the generation algorithm can sometimes bring in small changes, it's a good practice during production to use static WSDL (not generated). This configuration is shown in Listing 3-13.

Listing 3-13. Web Service XML Context Configuration with Static WSDL Exposure (File web-service-config.xml in Example Project 0301-ws-xmlconfig-service)

```xml
<?xml version="1.0" encoding="UTF-8"?>
<beans xmlns="http://www.springframework.org/schema/beans"
  xmlns:xsi="http://www.w3.org/2001/XMLSchema-instance"
  xmlns:context="http://www.springframework.org/schema/context"
  xmlns:ws="http://www.springframework.org/schema/web-services"
  xsi:schemaLocation="http://www.springframework.org/schema/web-services
    http://www.springframework.org/schema/web-services/web-services.xsd
           http://www.springframework.org/schema/beans
    http://www.springframework.org/schema/beans/spring-beans.xsd
           http://www.springframework.org/schema/context
    http://www.springframework.org/schema/context/spring-context.xsd">

  <context:component-scan base-package="net.lkrnac.book.eiws.chapter03.ws.xmlconfig.server" />

  <ws:annotation-driven />

  <ws:static-wsdl id="userDetails" location="classpath:userDetailsSchema.wsdl"/>
</beans>
```

The XML element `<ws:static-wsdl>` is used for static WSDL exposure. A prerequirement is the existence of a WSDL file in our project. In this case, the file userDetailsSchema.wsdl should be in the classpath. As we are using the Maven build system, the concrete file is src/main/resources. The parameter id is important for the final name of the exposed WSDL. In this case, it is userDetails. Therefore, if we run the server on localhost and port 10301, the final WSDL location would be http://localhost:10301/0301-ws-xmlconfig-service/userDetails.wsdl again.

This XML configuration is becoming less relevant these days because of a shift toward more-maintainable Java Spring configurations. An analogous Java configuration is shown in Listing 3-14.

Listing 3-14. Web Service Java Context Configuration (0302-ws-javaconfig-service)

```java
package net.lkrnac.book.eiws.chapter03.ws.javaconfig.server;

import org.springframework.context.annotation.Bean;
import org.springframework.context.annotation.ComponentScan;
import org.springframework.context.annotation.Configuration;
import org.springframework.core.io.ClassPathResource;
```

```
import org.springframework.ws.config.annotation.EnableWs;
import org.springframework.ws.wsdl.wsdl11.DefaultWsdl11Definition;
import org.springframework.xml.xsd.SimpleXsdSchema;
import org.springframework.xml.xsd.XsdSchema;

@EnableWs
@ComponentScan
@Configuration
public class ServerConfiguration {
  public static final String NAMESPACE =
      "http://localhost:10302/0302-ws-javaconfig-service";

  @Bean
  public DefaultWsdl11Definition userDetails(XsdSchema userDetailsSchema) {
    DefaultWsdl11Definition wsdlDefinition = new DefaultWsdl11Definition();
    wsdlDefinition.setTargetNamespace(NAMESPACE);
    wsdlDefinition.setSchema(userDetailsSchema);
    wsdlDefinition.setPortTypeName("UserDetailsPort");
    wsdlDefinition.setLocationUri("/");
    return wsdlDefinition;
  }

  @Bean
  public XsdSchema userDetailsSchema() {
    return new SimpleXsdSchema(new ClassPathResource("userDetailsSchema.xsd"));
  }
}
```

The class is annotated with the standard @Configuration annotation used for Java Spring configurations, and the framework scans the current package and subpackages for Spring components. This scanning will pick up @Endpoint if web services are enabled with @EnableWs, which is the Java annotation replacement for the <ws:annotation-driven> XML element. The bean registered by the userDetails method facilitates the dynamic WSDL creation. Here we are injecting the XSD bean registered by the userDetailSchema method. Listing 3-14 is, in fact, the exact mirror of the XML configuration in Listing 3-12. Only the namespace differs, because it is located in a different example project.

A static WSDL exposure with a Java configuration is shown in Listing 3-15.

Listing 3-15. Web Service Java Context Configuration with Static WSDL Exposure (0302-ws-javaconfig-service)

```
package net.lkrnac.book.eiws.chapter03.ws.javaconfig.server;

import org.springframework.context.annotation.Bean;
import org.springframework.context.annotation.ComponentScan;
import org.springframework.context.annotation.Configuration;
import org.springframework.core.io.ClassPathResource;
import org.springframework.ws.config.annotation.EnableWs;
import org.springframework.ws.wsdl.wsdl11.SimpleWsdl11Definition;

@EnableWs
@ComponentScan
@Configuration
```

```
public class ServerConfiguration {
  public static final String NAMESPACE =
      "http://localhost:10302/0302-ws-javaconfig-service";

  @Bean
  public SimpleWsdl11Definition userDetails() {
    return new SimpleWsdl11Definition(new ClassPathResource(
        "userDetailsSchema.wsdl"));
  }
}
```

Transports

There are various ways to configure the transport layer for Spring Web Services. Each transport protocol requires certain Spring abstractions to be registered.

HTTP/HTTPS

First, there is the servlet container:

- MessageDispatcherServlet: This is the easiest and most used mechanism.

- DispatcherServlet: This is useful when we need to provide a SOAP endpoint alongside REST or Spring MVC endpoints. WebServiceMessageReceiverHandlerAdapter and RequestMappingHandlerAdapter create a bridge from the web service endpoints to DispatcherServlet.

Alternatively, there is the simple HTTP server, with the following as receivers:

- SoapMessageDispatcher

- SimpleHttpServerFactoryBean

- SoapMessageDispatcher

JMS

With JMS, we use the following:

- SoapMessageDispatcher

- ActiveMQConnectionFactory

- DefaultMessageListenerContainer

E-mail

With e-mail, we use the following:

- SoapMessageDispatcher

- MailMessageReceiver

XMPP

With XMPP, we use the following:

- `SoapMessageDispatcher`
- `XmppConnectionFactoryBean`
- `XmppMessageReceiver`

As you may notice for nonservlet transports, there are a few common bean types:

- Message factory
- Message dispatcher
- Message receiver
- Connection factory (XMPP, JMS)

▪ **Note**   Details of nonservlet transport configuration are not covered in Enterprise Integration with Spring certification. Therefore, we focus on only `MessageDispatcherServlet`. Information about configuration of nonservlet web service transports can be found in Spring Web Services reference documentation.

Servlet Transports

Bear in mind that `MessageDispatcherServlet` and `DispatcherServlet` are different servlet implementations. One serves SOAP endpoints, and the other serves MVC or REST endpoints. Configuring `MessageDispatcherServlet` in a Spring application can be done in various ways. The Spring Framework and Spring Boot projects nowadays provide various servlet descriptor wrappers to simplify web container configuration. Listing 3-16 shows a classic XML-based servlet descriptor configuration in a web.xml file.

Listing 3-16. XML Servlet Descriptor Configuration with MessageDispatcherServlet (0301-ws-xmlconfig-client)

```xml
<?xml version="1.0" encoding="UTF-8"?>
<web-app xmlns:xsi="http://www.w3.org/2001/XMLSchema-instance"
  xmlns="http://xmlns.jcp.org/xml/ns/javaee"
  xsi:schemaLocation="http://java.sun.com/xml/ns/javaee
    http://java.sun.com/xml/ns/javaee/web-app.xsd">
  <display-name>0301-ws-xmlconfig-service</display-name>
  <servlet>
    <servlet-name>web-service</servlet-name>
    <servlet-class>org.springframework.ws.transport.http.MessageDispatcherServlet
    </servlet-class>
    <init-param>
      <param-name>contextConfigLocation</param-name>
      <param-value>classpath:web-service-config.xml</param-value>
    </init-param>
    <init-param>
      <param-name>transformWsdlLocations</param-name>
      <param-value>true</param-value>
    </init-param>
```

```
    <load-on-startup>1</load-on-startup>
  </servlet>
  <servlet-mapping>
    <servlet-name>web-service</servlet-name>
    <url-pattern>/*</url-pattern>
  </servlet-mapping>
</web-app>
```

This servlet configuration is pretty common. MessageDispatcherServlet is used as a servlet class. If we didn't specify the contextConfigurationLocation parameter, Spring would try to find the Spring configuration in the file {servlet-name}-servlet.xml. But in this case, we used the explicit approach with the web-service-config.xml context configuration from the classpath (located in the directory src/main/resources).

The parameter transformWsdlLocations is false by default. If it's true, Spring treats the location element in the WSDL as a relative address and transforms the WSDL location element according to the URL received from the client. So by default Spring does not do this transformation, and the WSDL location element is hard-coded. But hard-coding is not suitable for professional software development, in which the same application artifact is promoted to various environments (for example, development, QA, performance, and production environments). So we want to have transformWsdlLocations configured to true nearly always.

Listing 3-16 includes two remaining elements of servlet configuration. The load-on-startup configuration tells the servlet container that we don't want to use the lazy initialization feature. So our servlet is initialized at the start of the servlet container. Otherwise, the servlet would be initialized when the first request arrives. Finally, the servlet-mapping element specifies the relative root URL of the servlet.

In the Java world, a big shift is occurring from XML configuration toward annotations. The Spring Web Services project is no exception in this field. Enhanced support for Servlet 3.0 Java configuration was introduced in version 2.2.

The example in Listing 3-17 has a similar effect as the web.xml configuration in Listing 3-16.

Listing 3-17. Java Servlet Descriptor Configuration with MessageDispatcherServlet (0302-ws-javaconfig-service)

```java
package net.lkrnac.book.eiws.chapter03.ws.javaconfig.server;

import org.springframework.ws.transport.http.support.
        AbstractAnnotationConfigMessageDispatcherServletInitializer;

public class WsServletinitializer extends
  AbstractAnnotationConfigMessageDispatcherServletInitializer {

  @Override
  protected Class<?>[] getRootConfigClasses() {
    return null;
  }

  @Override
  protected Class<?>[] getServletConfigClasses() {
    return new Class[] { ServerConfiguration.class };
  }
```

```
  @Override
  protected String[] getServletMappings() {
    return new String[] { "/*" };
  }
}
```

The AbstractAnnotationConfigMessageDispatcherServletInitializer class is an abstract implementation of WebApplicationInitializer, which is the interface helping with programmatic servlet configuration in the Spring world. Spring automatically seeks WebApplicationInitializer implementations if a servlet container is in the classpath.

MessageDispatcherServlet is configured by Spring under the hood when the AbstractAnnotationConfigMessageDispatcherServletInitializer implementation is detected in the classpath. The Spring servlet context configuration is defined in the ServerConfiguration class, which uses the @Configuration annotation to define a Java-based Spring context. We don't need the root Spring context for this example, so we can return null from getRootConfigClasses(). The last piece of this servlet configuration is the servlet URL mapping, which defines the relative address where the servlet will be located. But the default AbstractAnnotationConfigMessageDispatcherServletInitializer uses the /services value defined in one of the servlet initializer parent classes. Our example uses /*.

Listing 3-17 highlights a relatively new approach for Spring Web Services servlet configuration. But an even more modern approach introduced by the Spring Boot project is shown in Listing 3-18.

Listing 3-18. Servlet Registration with Spring Boot(0303-ws-boot-service)

```
package net.lkrnac.book.eiws.chapter03.ws.boot.server;

import org.springframework.boot.autoconfigure.EnableAutoConfiguration;
import org.springframework.boot.context.embedded.ServletRegistrationBean;
import org.springframework.context.ApplicationContext;
import org.springframework.context.annotation.Bean;
import org.springframework.context.annotation.ComponentScan;
import org.springframework.context.annotation.Configuration;
import org.springframework.core.io.ClassPathResource;
import org.springframework.ws.config.annotation.EnableWs;
import org.springframework.ws.transport.http.MessageDispatcherServlet;
import org.springframework.ws.wsdl.wsdl11.SimpleWsdl11Definition;

@EnableWs
@Configuration
@ComponentScan
@EnableAutoConfiguration
public class ServerConfiguration {
  public static final String NAMESPACE =
      "http://localhost:10303/0303-ws-boot-service";

  @Bean
  public SimpleWsdl11Definition userDetails() {
    return new SimpleWsdl11Definition(new ClassPathResource("userDetails.wsdl"));
  }
```

```
@Bean
public ServletRegistrationBean dispatcherServlet(
    ApplicationContext applicationContext) {
  MessageDispatcherServlet servlet = new MessageDispatcherServlet();
  servlet.setApplicationContext(applicationContext);
  servlet.setTransformWsdlLocations(true);
  return new ServletRegistrationBean(servlet, "/*");
  }
}
```

The @ComponentScan, @Configuration annotation should already be familiar. This Spring configuration class scans the current package and subpackages for Spring components. @EnableWs turns on Spring Web Services support.

One additional annotation is @EnableAutoConfiguration. It's one line, but its impact is very big. Spring Boot takes a look at the set of dependencies used by our application and guesses the desired Spring configuration based on it. It creates a few default beans out of the box. In this case, we need it for autoconfiguration of the embedded servlet container.

A key class of this new mechanism is ServletRegistrationBean, which is effectively a wrapper for servlet configuration. So when it's registered into the Spring container, Spring registers the wrapped servlet into the servlet container. The effect of this API is that the developer feels that the servlet configuration is being registered into the Spring context, and not the other way around. It turns upside-down the integration mechanism of the servlet container and Spring context from the API point of view. In Listing 3-18, MessageDispatcherServlet is our desired servlet implementation. An important aspect of this concept is that we need to configure the applicationContext property. In this case, we use the application context injected by Spring, which is in fact the context where this bean is registered.

When we have Spring/servlet configuration turned upside-down, we can register this bean alongside other beans needed for serving web services. Listing 3-18 shows the least verbose Spring Web Services configuration, which uses static WSDL exposure (previously explained).

Web Service Client

The focus of the previous sections was exposing Spring Web Services. Spring also provides support for consuming web services. This approach to client-side development is also focused on Contract First. And again, there is no need to create a client-side Java model manually.

Spring's preferred XML marshaller on the client is JAXB 2, as well as on the server. As our examples are based on the Maven build system, Listing 3-19 shows how to generate JAXB 2 model classes from WSDL located on a remote server.

Listing 3-19. Client Model Generation from Remote WSDL (File pom.xml in Example Project 0301-ws-xmlconfig-client)

```
<plugin>
  <groupId>org.jvnet.jaxb2.maven2</groupId>
  <artifactId>maven-jaxb2-plugin</artifactId>
  <version>0.12.3</version>
  <executions>
    <execution>
      <goals>
        <goal>generate</goal>
      </goals>
    </execution>
  </executions>
```

```
    <configuration>
      <generatePackage>net.lkrnac.book.eiws.chapter03.ws.xmlconfig.model</generatePackage>
      <schemas>
        <schema>
          <url>http://localhost:10301/0301-ws-xmlconfig-service/wsdl/userDetails.wsdl</url>
        </schema>
      </schemas>
    </configuration>
  </plugin>
```

maven-jax2b-plugin is hooked to generate the Maven goal, part of the default life-cycle phase. The target package for the generated classes is specified by the generatePackage element in the plug-in configuration. This generation relies on a schema to be accessible at http://localhost:10301/0301-ws-xmlconfig-service/wsdl/userDetails.wsdl. So it's handy when the target web service is already live.

But when we are developing a web service alongside a client consumer, the WSDL is not necessarily online. A nonexistent remote schema causes problems when we want to automate the build as part of a continuous integration/delivery/deployment pipeline. Therefore, there is also an option to use a local WSDL file, as highlighted in Listing 3-20.

Listing 3-20. Client Model Generation from Local WSDL File

```
<plugin>
  <groupId>org.jvnet.jaxb2.maven2</groupId>
  <artifactId>maven-jaxb2-plugin</artifactId>
  <version>0.12.3</version>
  <executions>
    <execution>
      <goals>
        <goal>generate</goal>
      </goals>
    </execution>
  </executions>
  <configuration>
    <generatePackage>net.lkrnac.book.eiws.chapter03.ws.xmlconfig.model</generatePackage>
    <schemas>
      <schema>
        <fileset>
          <directory>${basedir}/src/main/schemas</directory>
          <includes>
            <include>userDetails.wsdl</include>
          </includes>
        </fileset>
      </schema>
    </schemas>
  </configuration>
</plugin>
```

Model classes are generated into the package net.lkrnac.book.eiws.chapter03.ws.xmlconfig.model. They are generated based on a WSDL schema located in the file userDetails.wsdl and the directory src/main/schemas. The client model looks just like classes generated on the server counterpart in Listing 3-8.

Similar to server model generation, we take advantage of type-safety Java features on the client as well. It is obvious that the most important part of the client/server interface is an XSD/WSDL contract from which models on both sides are generated.

The central class for client Spring Web Services support is WebServiceTemplate. It covers a lot of responsibilities:

- Sending and receiving messages

- Calling marshaller/unmarshaller for converting messages

- Can be configured to intercept messages

- Can be configured to translate errors generated on the server into client-side runtime exceptions

Apart from SOAP, WebServiceTemplate can work also with a Plain Old XML payload and can operate on top of the same transport protocols as the server: HTTP, e-mail, JMS, and XMPP. Similar to server transport Spring Web Services support, the client counterpart also provides a set of bean wrappers for each one. The central interface is WebServiceMessageSender, which defines the message sender implementation for each protocol:

- HTTP

    - Default configuration for HTTP protocol—HttpUrlConnectionMessageSender

    - Apache HttpComponents— HttpComponentsMessageSender

- JMS—JmsMessageSender and JMS message factory (for example, ActiveMQConnectionFactory)

- E-mail— MailMessageSender

- XMPP— XmppMessageSender and XmppConnectionFactoryBean

These can be created directly via a Java constructor and has three mandatory fields: defaultUri, marshaller, and unmarshaller.

In our examples, we will be focusing on HTTP, which is the most common protocol for web services. First, the client Spring context configuration example in Listing 3-21 shows an XML configuration.

Listing 3-21. XML Configuration of Spring Web Services Client Configuration (ws-client-config.xml in Example Project 0301-ws-xmlconfig-client)

```
<?xml version="1.0" encoding="UTF-8"?>
<beans xmlns="http://www.springframework.org/schema/beans"
  xmlns:xsi="http://www.w3.org/2001/XMLSchema-instance"
  xmlns:context="http://www.springframework.org/schema/context"
  xsi:schemaLocation="http://www.springframework.org/schema/beans
    http://www.springframework.org/schema/beans/spring-beans.xsd
    http://www.springframework.org/schema/context
    http://www.springframework.org/schema/context/spring-context.xsd">

<context:component-scan
  base-package="net.lkrnac.book.eiws.chapter03.ws.xmlconfig.client"/>

<bean id="marshaller" class="org.springframework.oxm.jaxb.Jaxb2Marshaller">
  <property name="contextPath"
    value="net.lkrnac.book.eiws.chapter03.ws.xmlconfig.model"/>
</bean>
```

```
  <bean id="webServiceTemplate"
     class="org.springframework.ws.client.core.WebServiceTemplate">
    <property name="marshaller" ref="marshaller"/>
    <property name="unmarshaller" ref="marshaller"/>
    <property name="defaultUri"
      value="http://localhost:10301/0301-ws-xmlconfig-service"/>
  </bean>
</beans>
```

Here we are using two Spring XML namespaces: context and beans. Context is used for component scanning the bean, using WebServiceTemplate in the package net.lkrnac.book.eiws.chapter03.ws .xmlconfig.client. Two beans are needed for web service consumption. One of the beans is our famous webServiceTemplate. It needs to have the defaultUri property specified, which is nothing other than the address where the web service is hosted. Two other mandatory properties of WebServiceTemplate are marshaller and unmarshaller. These are both served by the marshaller bean. It is registered as a separate bean and used for XML-to-Java POJOs conversion. We can observe from earlier POJOs generation that JAXB 2 is our marshaller of choice (the implementation class is Jaxb2Marshaller).

Nearly the same configuration written in Java is shown in Listing 3-22. The only differences are the web service URI and marshaller context path.

Listing 3-22. Java Configuration of Spring Web Services Client Configuration (0302-ws-javaconfig-client)

```java
package net.lkrnac.book.eiws.chapter03.ws.javaconfig.client;

import org.springframework.context.annotation.Bean;
import org.springframework.context.annotation.ComponentScan;
import org.springframework.context.annotation.Configuration;
import org.springframework.oxm.jaxb.Jaxb2Marshaller;
import org.springframework.ws.client.core.WebServiceTemplate;

@Configuration
@ComponentScan
public class WsClientConfiguration {
  @Bean
  public Jaxb2Marshaller marshaller() {
    Jaxb2Marshaller marshaller = new Jaxb2Marshaller();
    marshaller
        .setContextPath("net.lkrnac.book.eiws.chapter03.ws.javaconfig.model");
    return marshaller;
  }

  @Bean
  public WebServiceTemplate webServiceTemplate(Jaxb2Marshaller marshaller) {
    WebServiceTemplate webServiceTemplate = new WebServiceTemplate();
    webServiceTemplate.setMarshaller(marshaller);
    webServiceTemplate.setUnmarshaller(marshaller);
    webServiceTemplate
        .setDefaultUri("http://localhost:10302/0302-ws-javaconfig-service");
    return webServiceTemplate;
  }
}
```

This example is Spring's default client support for web services. WebServiceTemplate uses the HttpUrlConnectionMessageSender bean under the hood. This bean is created automatically by Spring and uses the standard Java SE HTTP client implementation from the java.net package. But some advanced use cases can force you to use the Apache HttpComponents project for client HTTP access. Additional features of Apache HttpComponents are as follows:

- Client-side authentication

- HTTP state management

- HTTP connection pooling

Listing 3-23 shows an example of an Apache HttpComponents client.

Listing 3-23. Spring Web Services Client Configuration with HttpComponents(0303-ws-boot-client)

```java
package net.lkrnac.book.eiws.chapter03.ws.boot.client;

import org.springframework.context.annotation.Bean;
import org.springframework.context.annotation.ComponentScan;
import org.springframework.context.annotation.Configuration;
import org.springframework.oxm.jaxb.Jaxb2Marshaller;
import org.springframework.ws.client.core.WebServiceTemplate;
import org.springframework.ws.transport.http.HttpComponentsMessageSender;

@Configuration
@ComponentScan
public class WsBootClientConfiguration {
  @Bean
  public Jaxb2Marshaller marshaller() {
    Jaxb2Marshaller marshaller = new Jaxb2Marshaller();
    marshaller.setContextPath("net.lkrnac.book.eiws.chapter03.ws.boot.model");
    return marshaller;
  }

  @Bean
  public WebServiceTemplate webServiceTemplate(Jaxb2Marshaller marshaller) {
    WebServiceTemplate webServiceTemplate = new WebServiceTemplate();
    webServiceTemplate.setMarshaller(marshaller);
    webServiceTemplate.setUnmarshaller(marshaller);
    webServiceTemplate
        .setDefaultUri("http://localhost:10303/0303-ws-boot-service");

    HttpComponentsMessageSender messageSender =
        new HttpComponentsMessageSender();
    messageSender.setConnectionTimeout(100);
    messageSender.setMaxTotalConnections(10);
    webServiceTemplate.setMessageSender(messageSender);
    return webServiceTemplate;
  }
}
```

The Apache HttpComponents wrapper (HttpComponentsMessageSender) needs to be configured as a messageSender property into WebServiceTemplate. A similar approach for registering special message senders would apply for non-HTTP protocols also.

So now that you know how to create WebServiceTemplate, let's take a look at its use in Listing 3-24.

Listing 3-24. WebServiceTemplate for Payload Root Routing(0303-ws-boot-client)

```
package net.lkrnac.book.eiws.chapter03.ws.boot.client;

import net.lkrnac.book.eiws.chapter03.ws.boot.model.UserDetailsResponse;
import net.lkrnac.book.eiws.chapter03.ws.boot.model.UserRequest;
import org.springframework.beans.factory.annotation.Autowired;
import org.springframework.stereotype.Component;
import org.springframework.ws.client.core.WebServiceTemplate;

@Component
public class WebServiceClient {
  private WebServiceTemplate webServiceTemplate;

  @Autowired
  public WebServiceClient(WebServiceTemplate webServiceTemplate) {
    this.webServiceTemplate = webServiceTemplate;
  }

  public UserDetailsResponse getUserDetails(String email) {
    UserRequest request = new UserRequest();
    request.setEmail(email);

    UserDetailsResponse userDetails =
        (UserDetailsResponse) webServiceTemplate.marshalSendAndReceive(request);
    return userDetails;
  }
}
```

The method getUserDetails uses an injected WebServiceTemplate to send request and receive response POJOs via the method marshalSendAndReceive. You may notice that this method has four responsibilities: it marshals the message, sends it to the client, waits for a response, and unmarshals it. For marshalling and unmarshalling, it uses the instance of un/marshaller we configured during the creation of WebServiceTemplate. Request and response POJOs were generated by maven-jax2b-plugin in Listing 3-19.

If we need to use a custom marshalling algorithm, we can use the WebServiceTemplate method sendAndReceive. This method sends a message and waits for a response, leaving the marshalling concerns to the caller logic.

Listing 3-24 covers routing based on the payload root XML element. In case of the SOAPAction header routing, we would need to specify the target SOAP action. It is highlighted in Listing 3-25.

Listing 3-25. WebServiceTemplate for SOAP Action Routing(0307-ws-soapaction-client)

```
package net.lkrnac.book.eiws.chapter03.ws.soapaction.client;

import net.lkrnac.book.eiws.chapter03.ws.soapaction.model.UserDetailsResponse;
import net.lkrnac.book.eiws.chapter03.ws.soapaction.model.UserRequest;
import org.springframework.beans.factory.annotation.Autowired;
```

```
import org.springframework.stereotype.Component;
import org.springframework.ws.client.core.WebServiceTemplate;
import org.springframework.ws.soap.client.core.SoapActionCallback;

@Component
public class WebServiceClient {
  private WebServiceTemplate webServiceTemplate;

  private static final SoapActionCallback messageCallback =
      new SoapActionCallback("getUserDetails");

  @Autowired
  public WebServiceClient(WebServiceTemplate webServiceTemplate) {
    this.webServiceTemplate = webServiceTemplate;
  }

  public UserDetailsResponse getUserDetails(String email) {
    UserRequest request = new UserRequest();
    request.setEmail(email);

    UserDetailsResponse userDetails =
        (UserDetailsResponse) webServiceTemplate.marshalSendAndReceive(request,
            messageCallback);
    return userDetails;
  }
}
```

To specify which SOAP action we want to execute on the server, SoapActionCallback with the action name is passed into WebServiceTemplate. In case of WS-Addressing, we would use ActionCallback instead of SoapActionCallback.

Intercepting Messages

Intercepting messages is a powerful mechanism for fulfilling various business requirements. Spring supports two types of interceptions:

- Server interception

- Client interception

Each one is composed of different phases. These types of interception touchpoints can be configured on the client as well as on the server (in the following order):

1. Handle request—occurs before the message is sent from the client or processed on the server

2. Handle response— occurs before sending a response from the server to the client

3. Handle fault— occurs on the server and client, but only when an error occurs in web service logic

4. After completion—is usually used for releasing resources, because it will occur under all circumstances

The first three intercepting phases can terminate further processing of a request by returning a false value. A false value indicates a problem in the processing chain, whereas a true value indicates success of the intercepting phase.

Developers using the Spring Web Services project can take advantage of existing interceptor implementations or can create custom implementations.

Server-Side Interception

Server-side interception is covered by the interface org.springframework.ws.server.EndpointInterceptor. Various implementations of this interface are offered by Spring Web Services out of the box:

- Logging interceptors—PayloadLoggingInterceptor, SoapEnvelopeLoggingInterceptor

- Payload-handling interceptors— PayloadValidatingInterceptor, PayloadTransformingInterceptor

- Security interceptors—XwsSecurityInterceptor, Wss4jSecurityInterceptor

Apart from built-in interceptors, we can create custom implementations of EndpointInterceptor. An example is shown in Listing 3-26.

Listing 3-26. Custom Server Interceptor (0305-ws-interceptor-service)

```
package net.lkrnac.book.eiws.chapter03.ws.interceptor.server;

import org.springframework.beans.factory.annotation.Autowired;
import org.springframework.stereotype.Component;
import org.springframework.ws.context.MessageContext;
import org.springframework.ws.server.EndpointInterceptor;

@Component
public class UserInterceptor implements EndpointInterceptor {
  @Override
  public boolean handleRequest(MessageContext messageContext, Object endpoint)
      throws Exception {
    System.out.println("Endpoint handleRequest");
    return true;
  }

  @Override
  public boolean handleResponse(MessageContext messageContext, Object endpoint)
      throws Exception {
    System.out.println("Endpoint handleResponse");
    return true;
  }

  @Override
  public boolean handleFault(MessageContext messageContext, Object endpoint)
      throws Exception {
    System.out.println("Endpoint handleFault");
    return true;
  }
```

```
@Override
public void afterCompletion(MessageContext messageContext, Object endpoint,
    Exception ex) throws Exception {
  System.out.println("Endpoint afterCompletion");
}
}
```

This interceptor is a normal Spring bean implementing EndpointInterceptor. Each intercepting method will be called according to the interception phases' life cycle explained at the beginning of this section. An abstract implementation of EndpointInterceptorAdapter also exists for convenience, when a developer doesn't need to use all interception touchpoints. This abstract implementation simply returns true for touchpoints that can interrupt processing.

An important aspect of this mechanism are injected parameters; via the messageContext parameter, we are able to inspect and manipulate the message. The second parameter is of type Object, because it represents a mapped endpoint bean that serves the message.

Let's explore how to configure interceptors in Listing 3-27.

Listing 3-27. XML Configurationof Server Interceptors (File web-service-config.xml in Example Project 0301-ws-xmlconfig-service)

```
<?xml version="1.0" encoding="UTF-8"?>
<beans xmlns="http://www.springframework.org/schema/beans"
  xmlns:xsi="http://www.w3.org/2001/XMLSchema-instance"
  xmlns:context="http://www.springframework.org/schema/context"
  xmlns:ws="http://www.springframework.org/schema/web-services"
  xsi:schemaLocation="http://www.springframework.org/schema/web-services
    http://www.springframework.org/schema/web-services/web-services.xsd
    http://www.springframework.org/schema/beans
    http://www.springframework.org/schema/beans/spring-beans.xsd
    http://www.springframework.org/schema/context
    http://www.springframework.org/schema/context/spring-context.xsd">

<context:component-scan base-package="net.lkrnac.book.eiws.chapter03.ws.xmlconfig.server" />
<ws:annotation-driven />
<ws:static-wsdl id="userDetails" location="classpath:userDetailsSchema.wsdl"/>

<ws:interceptors>
  <ref bean="globalInterceptor"/>
  <ws:payloadRoot namespaceUri=
      "http://localhost:10301/0301-ws-xmlconfig-service" localPart="UserRequest">
    <bean class="net.lkrnac.book.eiws.chapter03.ws.xmlconfig.server.UserInterceptor"/>
    <ref bean="loggingInterceptor"/>
  </ws:payloadRoot>
  <bean class=

  "org.springframework.ws.soap.server.endpoint.interceptor.SoapEnvelopeLoggingInterceptor"/>
  <bean class=

  "org.springframework.ws.soap.server.endpoint.interceptor.PayloadValidatingInterceptor">
    <property name="schema" value="classpath:userDetailsSchema.xsd"/>
    <property name="validateRequest" value="true"/>
    <property name="validateResponse" value="true"/>
  </bean>
</ws:interceptors>
```

```
<bean id="loggingInterceptor" class=
        "org.springframework.ws.server.endpoint.interceptor.PayloadLoggingInterceptor"/>
<bean id="globalInterceptor"  class=
        "net.lkrnac.book.eiws.chapter03.ws.xmlconfig.server.GlobalInterceptor" />
</beans>
```

This example shows an XML configuration of interceptors. Spring namespace registration, component scanning, and annotation declaration should already be familiar from earlier sections of this chapter.

The new part of this example is an element of the web-services namespace: <ws:interceptors>. It registers interceptors for web services. Under this XML element, we can register a reference (using the ref element) or declare a new bean (using the bean element) of the global interceptor. Such an interceptor will be applied for all endpoints belonging to this Spring context. In this case, we used GlobalInterceptor, which is a class just like UserInterceptor from Listing 3-27.

The nested element payloadRoot binds interceptor(s) to a concrete endpoint specified by namespaceUri and localPart parameters. This is handy when we need to have different interception logic for different endpoints. We would use the soapAction element instead of payloadRoot if we were using SOAPAction routing. In this case, we registered two interceptors for endpoints with the namespace http://localhost:10301/0301-ws-xmlconfig-service and the local part UserRequest. The first one is our custom UserInterceptor, and the second is loggingInterceptor, which is a bean of type PayloadLoggingInterceptor. Of course, we can use custom as well as built-in interceptor implementations within bean declarations or as bean references.

Finally, we registered two more interceptors: one for logging SOAP envelopes, and one for validating requests against the XSD contract. The last three interceptors are implementations provided by the Spring Web Services project out of the box. We just need to register them accordingly. For validation schema interceptors, we need to specify the location of the schema.

The Java configuration is shown in Listing 3-28.

Listing 3-28. Java Configuration of Server Interceptors (0305-ws-interceptor-service)

```
package net.lkrnac.book.eiws.chapter03.ws.interceptor.server;

import java.util.List;
import org.springframework.beans.factory.annotation.Autowired;
import org.springframework.boot.autoconfigure.EnableAutoConfiguration;
import org.springframework.boot.context.embedded.ServletRegistrationBean;
import org.springframework.context.ApplicationContext;
import org.springframework.context.annotation.Bean;
import org.springframework.context.annotation.ComponentScan;
import org.springframework.context.annotation.Configuration;
import org.springframework.core.io.ClassPathResource;
import org.springframework.ws.config.annotation.EnableWs;
import org.springframework.ws.config.annotation.WsConfigurerAdapter;
import org.springframework.ws.server.EndpointInterceptor;
import org.springframework.ws.server.endpoint.interceptor.PayloadLoggingInterceptor;
import org.springframework.ws.soap.server.endpoint.interceptor.
PayloadRootSmartSoapEndpointInterceptor;
import org.springframework.ws.soap.server.endpoint.interceptor.PayloadValidatingInterceptor;
import org.springframework.ws.soap.server.endpoint.interceptor.
SoapEnvelopeLoggingInterceptor;
import org.springframework.ws.transport.http.MessageDispatcherServlet;
import org.springframework.ws.wsdl.wsdl11.SimpleWsdl11Definition;
import org.springframework.xml.xsd.SimpleXsdSchema;
```

```java
@EnableWs
@Configuration
@ComponentScan
@EnableAutoConfiguration
public class ServerConfiguration extends WsConfigurerAdapter {
  public static final String NAMESPACE =
      "http://localhost:10305/0305-ws-interceptor-service";

  @Autowired
  private UserInterceptor userInterceptor;
  @Autowired
  private GlobalInterceptor globalInterceptor;

  @Bean
  public SimpleWsdl11Definition userDetails() {
    return new SimpleWsdl11Definition(new ClassPathResource(
        "userDetailsSchema.wsdl"));
  }

  @Bean
  public ServletRegistrationBean dispatcherServlet(
      ApplicationContext applicationContext) {
    MessageDispatcherServlet servlet = new MessageDispatcherServlet();
    servlet.setApplicationContext(applicationContext);
    servlet.setTransformWsdlLocations(true);
    return new ServletRegistrationBean(servlet, "/*");
  }

  @Override
  public void addInterceptors(List<EndpointInterceptor> interceptors) {
    interceptors.add(new PayloadRootSmartSoapEndpointInterceptor(
        userInterceptor, NAMESPACE, "UserRequest"));

    PayloadRootSmartSoapEndpointInterceptor smartLoggingInterceptor =
        new PayloadRootSmartSoapEndpointInterceptor(
            new PayloadLoggingInterceptor(), NAMESPACE, "UserRequest");
    interceptors.add(smartLoggingInterceptor);

    interceptors.add(globalInterceptor);
    interceptors.add(new SoapEnvelopeLoggingInterceptor());

    PayloadValidatingInterceptor validationInterceptor =
        new PayloadValidatingInterceptor();
    SimpleXsdSchema schema =
        new SimpleXsdSchema(new ClassPathResource("userDetailsSchema.xsd"));
    validationInterceptor.setXsdSchema(schema);
    validationInterceptor.setValidateRequest(true);
    validationInterceptor.setValidateResponse(true);
    interceptors.add(validationInterceptor);
  }
}
```

The UserInterceptor and GlobalInterceptor beans are component scanned and autowired into this configuration class. In the method addInterceptors, we are registering interceptors into an injected list. The first two interceptors are wrapped into PayloadRootSmartSoapEndpointInterceptor. This wrapper makes the given interceptor effective only for endpoints with the namespace http://localhost:10305/ 0305-ws-interceptor-service and the local part UserRequest. We registered our custom UserInterceptor and PayloadLoggingInterceptor this way.

The remaining interceptors are global, which means they apply to all endpoints handled in this service. In this case, we registered two custom, two logging, and one validation interceptor. Built-in interceptors sometimes have mandatory parameters. In this case, the validation interceptor needs to have access to the XSD schema. This configuration is effectively the same as the XML configuration in Listing 3-27.

Client-Side Interception

An interesting part of Spring Web Services interception support is on the client side. The main interface ClientInterceptor signature is similar to the server-side EndpointInterceptor. The only difference is the missing endpoint bean instance injection into the interception touchpoints, because there aren't any endpoints on the client. There isn't a convenient abstract implementation of this interface. So we need to implement all touchpoints in a custom client interceptor. The only out-of-the-box interceptor provided by Spring Web Services is PayloadValidatingInterceptor. Client interceptors are registered into the WebServiceTemplate bean.

Listing 3-29 shows an example of a custom client-side interceptor.

Listing 3-29. Custom Client Interceptor (0305-ws-interceptor-client)

```
package net.lkrnac.book.eiws.chapter03.ws.interceptor.client;

import org.springframework.beans.factory.annotation.Autowired;
import org.springframework.stereotype.Component;
import org.springframework.ws.client.WebServiceClientException;
import org.springframework.ws.client.support.interceptor.ClientInterceptor;
import org.springframework.ws.context.MessageContext;

@Component
public class UserInterceptor implements ClientInterceptor {
  @Override
  public boolean handleRequest(MessageContext messageContext)
      throws WebServiceClientException {
    System.out.println("Client handleRequest");
    return true;
  }

  @Override
  public boolean handleResponse(MessageContext messageContext)
      throws WebServiceClientException {
    System.out.println("Client handleResponse");
    return true;
  }
```

```
@Override
public boolean handleFault(MessageContext messageContext)
    throws WebServiceClientException {
  System.out.println("Client handleFault");
  return true;
}

@Override
public void afterCompletion(MessageContext messageContext, Exception ex)
    throws WebServiceClientException {
  System.out.println("Client afterCompletion");
}
}
```

Instead of using simple logging example logic, a developer can place into each interception touchpoint custom logic that matches the requirements of his web service. Listing 3-30 shows an example configuration.

Listing 3-30. Client-Side Interceptors Registration(0305-ws-interceptor-client)

```
package net.lkrnac.book.eiws.chapter03.ws.interceptor.client;

import org.springframework.context.annotation.Bean;
import org.springframework.context.annotation.ComponentScan;
import org.springframework.context.annotation.Configuration;
import org.springframework.oxm.jaxb.Jaxb2Marshaller;
import org.springframework.ws.client.core.WebServiceTemplate;
import org.springframework.ws.client.support.interceptor.ClientInterceptor;

@Configuration
@ComponentScan
public class WsInterceptorClientConfiguration {
  @Bean
  public Jaxb2Marshaller marshaller() {
    Jaxb2Marshaller marshaller = new Jaxb2Marshaller();
    marshaller
        .setContextPath("net.lkrnac.book.eiws.chapter03.ws.interceptor.model");
    return marshaller;
  }

  @Bean
  public WebServiceTemplate webServiceTemplate(Jaxb2Marshaller marshaller,
      UserInterceptor userInterceptor) {
    WebServiceTemplate webServiceTemplate = new WebServiceTemplate();
    webServiceTemplate.setMarshaller(marshaller);
    webServiceTemplate.setUnmarshaller(marshaller);
    webServiceTemplate.setDefaultUri("http://localhost:10305/0305-ws-interceptor-service");

    ClientInterceptor[] interceptors =
        new ClientInterceptor[] { userInterceptor };
    webServiceTemplate.setInterceptors(interceptors);
    return webServiceTemplate;
  }
}
```

We are registering the interceptors array into the `WebServiceTemplate` field called `interceptors`. The XML configuration would be similar, as we use standard Spring dependency injection XML elements such as bean, property, and ref. See Listing 3-31.

Listing 3-31. XML Configuration of Client Interceptor (File ws-client-config.xml in Example Project 0301-ws-xmlconfig-client)

```xml
<?xml version="1.0" encoding="UTF-8" ?>
<beans xmlns="http://www.springframework.org/schema/beans"
  xmlns:xsi="http://www.w3.org/2001/XMLSchema-instance"
  xmlns:context="http://www.springframework.org/schema/context"
  xsi:schemaLocation="http://www.springframework.org/schema/beans
    http://www.springframework.org/schema/beans/spring-beans.xsd
    http://www.springframework.org/schema/context
    http://www.springframework.org/schema/context/spring-context.xsd">

  <context:component-scan base-package=
      "net.lkrnac.book.eiws.chapter03.ws.xmlconfig.client" />

  <bean id="marshaller" class="org.springframework.oxm.jaxb.Jaxb2Marshaller">
      <property name="contextPath"
        value="net.lkrnac.book.eiws.chapter03.ws.xmlconfig.model" />
  </bean>

  <bean id="webServiceTemplate"
          class="org.springframework.ws.client.core.WebServiceTemplate">
      <property name="marshaller" ref="marshaller" />
      <property name="unmarshaller" ref="marshaller" />
      <property name="defaultUri"
        value="http://localhost:10301/0301-ws-xmlconfig-service" />
      <property name="interceptors">
        <array>
          <bean class="net.lkrnac.book.eiws.chapter03.ws.xmlconfig.config.UserInterceptor"/>
        </array>
      </property>
  </bean>
</beans>
```

Error Handling

The Spring Web Services project enables easy translation of errors penetrated from web service logic. Similar to interception support, error handling is divided into the server and client side also.

Server-Side Error Handling

Lax error handling is often a source of serious security vulnerabilities that expose implementation details of a web service. When an exception bubbles up from the web service logic to the servlet container, it commonly sends a failed message with information about the web server and stack trace as a response message. The attacker can analyze (based on such a message) the type of web server, version, platform the web service is running on, and the frameworks used. Such data can be further used to create more-targeted attacks. This problem is number 6 in the Open Web Application Security Project (OWASP) Top 10 list of security risks.

Translation of exceptions on the server is useful for hiding these implementation details. The idea is that Spring will use registered exception resolvers to create a generic response instead of exposing sensitive information to the client. MessageDispatcher scans the classpath for implementations of the EndpointExceptionResolver interface. It has only one method called resolveException. This interface can be used in various ways:

- A custom implementation fulfills special requirements of error translation.

- SoapFaultMappingExceptionResolver maps each exception to a particular SOAP fault with an explicit error message.

- SimpleSoapExceptionResolver translates all exceptions into the SOAP client error with an exception message as a response payload.

Last but not least is the @SoapFault exception. It is used to mark the exception type, so that the exception can be translated into a message. The SOAP fault is specified in annotation parameters in such a case. All these mechanisms allow for higher security standards, but at the same time for variability to inform the client about known problems.

There aren't any specific XML elements for error handling. Therefore, we will focus only on Java examples. With XML, we would use standard DI elements such as bean, property, and ref. Listing 3-32 shows how to register SoapFaultMappingExceptionResolver.

Listing 3-32. SoapFaultMappingExceptionResolver Registration Example (0306-ws-error-service)

```
package net.lkrnac.book.eiws.chapter03.ws.error.server;

import java.util.Properties;

import org.springframework.boot.autoconfigure.EnableAutoConfiguration;
import org.springframework.boot.context.embedded.ServletRegistrationBean;
import org.springframework.context.ApplicationContext;
import org.springframework.context.annotation.Bean;
import org.springframework.context.annotation.ComponentScan;
import org.springframework.context.annotation.Configuration;
import org.springframework.core.io.ClassPathResource;
import org.springframework.ws.config.annotation.EnableWs;
import org.springframework.ws.soap.server.endpoint.SoapFaultDefinition;
import org.springframework.ws.soap.server.endpoint.SoapFaultMappingExceptionResolver;
import org.springframework.ws.transport.http.MessageDispatcherServlet;
import org.springframework.ws.wsdl.wsdl11.SimpleWsdl11Definition;

@EnableWs
@Configuration
@ComponentScan
@EnableAutoConfiguration
public class ServerConfiguration {
  public static final String NAMESPACE =
      "http://localhost:10306/0306-ws-error-service";

  @Bean
  public SimpleWsdl11Definition userDetails() {
    return new SimpleWsdl11Definition(new ClassPathResource("userDetailsSchema.xsd"));
  }
```

```
@Bean
public ServletRegistrationBean dispatcherServlet(
    ApplicationContext applicationContext) {
  MessageDispatcherServlet servlet = new MessageDispatcherServlet();
  servlet.setApplicationContext(applicationContext);
  servlet.setTransformWsdlLocations(true);
  return new ServletRegistrationBean(servlet, "/*");
}

@Bean
public SoapFaultMappingExceptionResolver exceptionResolver() {
  SoapFaultMappingExceptionResolver exceptionResolver =
      new SoapFaultMappingExceptionResolver();

  SoapFaultDefinition defaultSoapFault = new SoapFaultDefinition();
  defaultSoapFault.setFaultCode(SoapFaultDefinition.SERVER);
  exceptionResolver.setDefaultFault(defaultSoapFault);

  Properties errorMappings = new Properties();
  errorMappings.put(IllegalStateException.class.getName(),
      SoapFaultDefinition.CLIENT.toString());
  exceptionResolver.setExceptionMappings(errorMappings);
  exceptionResolver.setOrder(1);

  return exceptionResolver;
}
}
```

The exception resolver is registered in the method exceptionResolver. We first create an object of type SoapFaultMappingExceptionResolver. Then we register the default SOAP fault. This is used for every error unless a more specific mapping exists. Specific mappings are registered as an array of Properties type into the field exceptionMappings of SoapFaultMappingExceptionResolver. In this case, we map IllegalStateException to the client SOAP error. Method setOrder specifies the order in which mappings are processed when an exception occurs.

If we prefer SimpleSoapExceptionResolver or a custom exception resolver implementation, it would be created via a constructor and registered as a Spring bean in a similar way.

Listing 3-33 shows how to use the @SoapFault annotation.

Listing 3-33. @SoapFault Annotation (0306-ws-error-service)

```
package net.lkrnac.book.eiws.chapter03.ws.error.server;

import org.springframework.ws.soap.server.endpoint.annotation.FaultCode;
import org.springframework.ws.soap.server.endpoint.annotation.SoapFault;

@SoapFault(faultCode = FaultCode.CLIENT)
public class CustomErrorException extends RuntimeException {
  private static final long serialVersionUID = 1L;

  public CustomErrorException(String message) {
    super(message);
  }
}
```

When this exception percolates to a Spring Web Services container, it's translated into a client SOAP fault. This is specified by the annotation parameter faultCode. In this case, we mapped CustomErrorException to the client SOAP error. The exception message field is used as a response payload. If we would like to explicitly specify a generic error message for an exception of this type, we would define the annotation parameter faultStringOrReason.

Client-Side Error Handling

Client-side error translation is in place for the translation of SOAP messages into exceptions in client code. The central interface is called FaultMessageResolver and needs to be registered as a property of WebServiceTemplate. There are two out-of-the-box implementations:

- SoapFaultMessageResolver translates the error into SoapFaultClientException.

- SimpleFaultMessageResolver translates the error message into WebServiceFaultException.

We can also provide a custom implementation of FaultMessageResolver, as shown in Listing 3-34.

Listing 3-34. Client Error Resolver Registration (0306-ws-error-client)

```java
package net.lkrnac.book.eiws.chapter03.ws.error.client;

import org.springframework.context.annotation.Bean;
import org.springframework.context.annotation.ComponentScan;
import org.springframework.context.annotation.Configuration;
import org.springframework.oxm.jaxb.Jaxb2Marshaller;
import org.springframework.ws.client.core.WebServiceTemplate;
import org.springframework.ws.soap.client.core.SoapFaultMessageResolver;

@Configuration
@ComponentScan
public class WsErrorClientConfiguration {
  @Bean
  public Jaxb2Marshaller marshaller() {
    Jaxb2Marshaller marshaller = new Jaxb2Marshaller();
    marshaller.setContextPath("net.lkrnac.book.eiws.chapter03.ws.error.model");
    return marshaller;
  }

  @Bean
  public WebServiceTemplate webServiceTemplate(Jaxb2Marshaller marshaller) {
    WebServiceTemplate webServiceTemplate = new WebServiceTemplate();
    webServiceTemplate.setMarshaller(marshaller);
    webServiceTemplate.setUnmarshaller(marshaller);
    webServiceTemplate.setDefaultUri("http://localhost:10306/0306-ws-error-service");

    webServiceTemplate.setFaultMessageResolver(new SoapFaultMessageResolver());
    return webServiceTemplate;
  }
}
```

Out-of-Container Testing

Various approaches exist for automatically testing web services. Unit tests usually don't create Spring's context instance. A class or group of classes are tested in isolation, and the test fakes dependencies. These tests are useful as documentation of a developer's intentions of how the module should work. Such testing is particularly useful for sanitizing the business logic of the web service or web service consumer.

In another type of testing, we automatically deploy the web service to a target environment and execute a test suite, which would perform or consume real requests. This is heading toward an end-to-end level of testing. Because deployment steps are needed in the build pipeline, these tests may take some time. Therefore, this type of testing is commonly not triggered as often as unit testing.

Slightly more suitable is simulating a deployment environment during the build process. Examples are `tomcat7-maven-plugin` or `gradle-maven-plugin`, which enable us to build a full artifact of our application and deploy it to an embedded servlet container.

Additionally, Spring Web Services provides support for integration testing of full or partial Spring configurations. It can be integrated with a unit-testing framework of your choice (most commonly JUnit or TestNG). This testing support is handy, because it covers integrated Spring configuration and doesn't need to use a servlet container (or other type of resource-intensive environment) at the same time.

Server-Side Testing Support

When we are testing a web service server, we need to send requests to the web service under test, receive the request, and verify a response. The Spring Web Services project provides helpers to fulfill these tasks easily:

- `MockWebServiceClient` is used to simulate the client and for sending requests.

- `org.springframework.ws.test.server.RequestCreator`/`org.springframework.ws.test.server.RequestCreators` helps with creation of request messages.

- `org.springframework.ws.test.server.ResponseActions`/`org.springframework.ws.test.server.ResponseMatchers` provides support for response verification.

In this example, we'll use a testing request from Listing 3-35 and a response located in Listing 3-36.

Listing 3-35. Request Used for Testing (File testRequest.xml in Example Project 0303-ws-boot-service)

```
<ns2:UserRequest xmlns:ns2="http://localhost:10303/0303-ws-boot-service"
    Email="lubos.krnac@gmail.com" />
```

Listing 3-36. Response Used for Testing (File testResponse.xml in Example Project 0303-ws-boot-service)

```
<ns2:UserDetailsResponse
  xmlns:ns2="http://localhost:10303/0303-ws-boot-service">
  <ns2:FirstName>Lubos</ns2:FirstName>
  <ns2:LastName>Krnac</ns2:LastName>
</ns2:UserDetailsResponse>
```

Let's explore service-side testing support in Listing 3-37.

Listing 3-37. Server-Side Testing (0303-ws-boot-service)

```java
package net.lkrnac.book.eiws.chapter03.ws.boot.client;

import java.io.IOException;
import net.lkrnac.book.eiws.chapter03.ws.boot.server.ServerConfiguration;
import org.springframework.beans.factory.annotation.Autowired;
import org.springframework.context.ApplicationContext;
import org.springframework.core.io.ClassPathResource;
import org.springframework.test.context.ContextConfiguration;
import org.springframework.test.context.testng.AbstractTestNGSpringContextTests;
import org.springframework.ws.test.server.MockWebServiceClient;
import org.springframework.ws.test.server.RequestCreator;
import org.springframework.ws.test.server.RequestCreators;
import org.springframework.ws.test.server.ResponseActions;
import org.springframework.ws.test.server.ResponseMatchers;
import org.testng.annotations.Test;

@ContextConfiguration(classes = ServerConfiguration.class)
public class WsJavaConfigServerITest extends AbstractTestNGSpringContextTests {
  @Autowired
  private ApplicationContext applicationContext;

  @Test
  public void testGetUserDetails() throws IOException {
    // GIVEN
    MockWebServiceClient wsClient =
        MockWebServiceClient.createClient(applicationContext);

    RequestCreator requestCreator =
        RequestCreators.withPayload(new ClassPathResource("testRequest.xml"));

    // WHEN
    ResponseActions response = wsClient.sendRequest(requestCreator);

    // THEN
    response.andExpect(ResponseMatchers.noFault()).andExpect(
        ResponseMatchers.payload(new ClassPathResource("testResponse.xml")));
  }
}
```

TestNG is a testing framework used for powering the test. To integrate it with the Spring context, we need to inherit the test class from AbstractTestNGSpringContextTests. This class is part of the Spring Core test module. We are testing the Spring configuration defined by the class ServerConfiguration from the example project 0303-ws-boot-service. This configuration was already explained in earlier sections of this chapter. To create the mock client, we can use an autowired application context instance.

The next step is the creation of the request. We create it based on the test file testRequest.xml with the help of RequestCreator and RequestCreators. Now we are ready to perform virtual requests. We do this by calling the method sendRequest on the mock client instance. It returns a virtual response. Finally, we verify that the web service responded with the expected result and message payload. The ResponseMatchers class has a lot of helper verification methods, so we are capable of testing complex behaviors.

Client-Side Testing Support

When we are testing a web service client, we need to use the test client to perform requests first. Then we receive responses from the fake server and verify that they are represented on the client as expected. The classes that help us with it are as follows:

- MockWebServiceServer is used to simulate the client and to send requests.

- org.springframework.ws.test.client.ResponseCreator/org.springframework.ws.test.client.ResponseCreators provides support recording the expected responses into the fake server. It will be used to send responses from the fake server.

- org.springframework.ws.test.client.RequestMatchers provides support recording the expected requests into the fake server. It will be used to verify that the client sent the correct payload in the request.

Let's explore the testing support in Listing 3-38.

Listing 3-38. Client-Side Testing (0303-ws-boot-client)

```
package net.lkrnac.book.eiws.chapter03.ws.boot.client;

import static org.testng.Assert.assertEquals;
import java.io.IOException;
import net.lkrnac.book.eiws.chapter03.ws.boot.model.UserDetailsResponse;
import org.springframework.beans.factory.annotation.Autowired;
import org.springframework.core.io.ClassPathResource;
import org.springframework.test.annotation.DirtiesContext;
import org.springframework.test.context.ContextConfiguration;
import org.springframework.test.context.testng.AbstractTestNGSpringContextTests;
import org.springframework.ws.client.core.WebServiceTemplate;
import org.springframework.ws.test.client.MockWebServiceServer;
import org.springframework.ws.test.client.RequestMatchers;
import org.springframework.ws.test.client.ResponseCreator;
import org.springframework.ws.test.client.ResponseCreators;
import org.testng.annotations.Test;

@ContextConfiguration(classes = WsBootClientConfiguration.class)
public class WsBootClientITest extends AbstractTestNGSpringContextTests {
  @Autowired
  private WebServiceClient webServiceClient;

  @Autowired
  private WebServiceTemplate webServiceTemplate;

  @Test
  public void testGetUserDetails() throws IOException {
    // GIVEN
    MockWebServiceServer mockWsServer =
        MockWebServiceServer.createServer(webServiceTemplate);

    ResponseCreator responseCreator =
        ResponseCreators.withPayload(new ClassPathResource("testResponse.xml"));
```

```
  mockWsServer.expect(
      RequestMatchers.payload(new ClassPathResource("testRequest.xml")))
      .andRespond(responseCreator);

  // WHEN
  UserDetailsResponse userDetails =
      webServiceClient.getUserDetails("lubos.krnac@gmail.com");

  // THEN
  assertEquals(userDetails.getFirstName(), "Lubos");
  assertEquals(userDetails.getLastName(), "Krnac");
  mockWsServer.verify();
  }
}
```

Similar to the server-side testing example in Listing 3-37, TestNG is used as a testing framework. The test uses WsBootClientConfiguration as a configuration under test. For creation of a fake server, we need to autowire an instance of WebServiceTemplate. Then we record requests that are expected from the client and responses provided by the fake server.

The testing client instance was injected from the Spring testing configuration. We perform the client call as it would be done from our client application. In the verification phase, we need to verify that the client correctly represented responses from the fake server. Last but not least, we need to verify that the requests sent from the test client to the fake server were correct. This is done by a method called verify on the fake server instance.

Summary

In this chapter, we briefly compared concepts for creating web services and distributed applications and the advantages that arise from decoupling services in comparison to remoting technologies. Then we presented XML marshalling technologies that can be integrated into Spring's ecosystem.

We also explored the benefits of a Contract First approach for building web services with the Spring Web Services project. This approach helps abstract away the complexity of developing web services and makes it much more approachable by providing APIs to follow best practices on top of existing libraries and protocols. It enables us to create SOAP-based web services that can communicate via HTTP, JMS, e-mail, and XMPP transport protocols.

We showed how to optimally start developing a web service contract based on communication requirements. The message payload is the starting line for generating an XSD contract draft. Subsequently, the JAXB 2 Java model can be generated based on this contract. Configuring a container environment and Spring configuration with use of XML and Java contexts was also covered.

Routing web service messages is the backbone of productive development with Spring. We can benefit from routing based on the payload root element, WS-Addressing, and the SOAPAction header.

Client-side support is a crucial part of Spring offerings because it allows us to generate a Java model from an XSD contract. Finally, the chapter explained how to intercept and handle errors and to test Spring configurations in isolation and more effectively.

CHAPTER 4

■ ■ ■

RESTful Web Services

This chapter explains the principles that conquer the enterprise integration world. It's about Representational State Transfer, or REST.

The evolution of distributed systems didn't stop with remoting and web services. SOAP allowed high decoupling, which solved a major problem of remoting technologies. As a successor of remoting technologies, SOAP web services were adopted by big enterprise companies. Cooperation between distributed development teams was enhanced, because SOAP web services rely on contracts. A well-defined XSD/WSDL contract can help avoid ambiguities or sanitize poor communication between developers on the client side and those on the server side.

But after some time, many people started to experience problems with SOAP web services. First, developing SOAP web services is not trivial. SOAP's complexity started to create a bigger and bigger bottleneck for developing enterprise applications. Even if SOAP provided rich possibilities for complex requirements, it turned out to be overkill in most cases. This slowed development and made maintenance more expensive.

The next highly criticized aspect of traditional web services is the XML payload it relies on. Even when computation capacities were multiplied every few years, users started to expect lower and lower latency. But XML is verbose, and SOAP completely relies on the XML exchange format. So when lightweight exchange formats started to pop up (most notably, JSON), SOAP couldn't take advantage of them.

Parallel to the SOAP web services track, a different school of web service development was evolving. This approach is REST (which is only two years younger than SOAP). Although SOAP gained a wider adoption at the beginning, people started to realize that REST has more advantages.

REST was born in a dissertation by Roy Fielding named "Architectural Styles and the Design of Network-Based Software Architectures." He codified a few architectural concepts for distributed computing based on the Hypertext Transfer Protocol and defined a new term for these concepts: Representational State Transfer (REST).

By definition, REST operates over HTTP. In fact, it promotes HTTP as an application protocol—as opposed to SOAP, which uses HTTP as a transport protocol only. The SOAP framework uses HTTP under the hood to transfer SOAP messages. A SOAP developer doesn't need to know about HTTP features, because that developer is using higher-level SOAP abstractions. REST uses an HTTP programming model, on the other hand; the developer needs to implement HTTP, because it drives the communication contract between the client and the server.

But *REST is not a protocol*; it's a set of architectural concepts. Therefore, these concepts can be used with other non-HTTP protocols.

REST gained popularity because it's much more lightweight than SOAP. No strict contract is involved. Without strict rules, developers have more space to fulfill business requirements. At the same time, they are dealing with a simpler programming model, because REST doesn't rely on schema.

A second big advantage is the ability to operate on top of various exchange formats. REST can take advantage of some lightweight XML alternatives. An extremely popular one nowadays is JavaScript Object Notation (JSON), invented by Douglas Crockford. As its name suggests, it was created primarily for the JavaScript language. But its simplicity and lightweight aspects quickly became popular across all major programming platforms.

Over time, it became clear that REST is a better approach than SOAP in most cases. Today, REST is the obvious winner. However, in some cases, using SOAP still makes perfect sense. For example, a need for statefulness or transactions would probably shift SOAP into a better position than REST. Keep in mind that SOAP and REST are not opposites. Each is useful in different cases.

REST Principles

As noted previously, Roy Fielding codified REST in his dissertation. This architectural style uses the following principles to simplify the development and operation of distributed systems.

Client/Server Separation

REST's basic principle is the decoupling of client/server communication and the separation of their concerns into manageable sets of requirements. For example, the client should be exclusively responsible for the presentation layer. Server concerns include persisting data and hiding persistence details from the client. When communication occurs via a unified interface, any side of the communication can be replaced. For example, you can replace the persistence storage type on the server without affecting the client side. Or you can replace the rendering engine on the client without affecting the server. This significantly enhances the modularity of an enterprise system.

CRUD Operations

Most SOAP services perform actions on top of resources (for example, booking a flight). So these services are designed to be verb-centric: both the type of resource (noun) and the type of action (verb) are important for the contract between the client and server.

Roy Fielding decided to simplify this verb-centric approach for REST web services. He recognized that we want to perform mostly create, read, update, and delete (CRUD) actions. And all of these are already contained in the Hypertext Transfer Protocol he helped to create: GET, POST, PUT, and DELETE. So he significantly simplified one dimension of the web services space because he removed the need to design verbs. This makes designing REST services easier, because we need to identify only the resources (or nouns) in our system. Actions are already defined by CRUD operations.

Uniform Interface

Identifying resources (or a domain model) within our application and exposing them via a constant set of actions creates a *uniform interface*. Manipulation of resources (the domain model) is done via the well-defined operations of HTTP. To be able to manipulate a resource, it has to have a unique identifier (for example, a URI). Not only does the resource itself need to be identifiable, but also the instance of certain resources. Fielding also goes further and specifies that messages about the resource need to contain all the information needed to manipulate the resource, regardless of any previous messages about it. So messages should contain all the information needed to perform any of the CRUD operations on top of the resource instance.

■ **Note** It is important to understand the difference between a uniform resource identifier (URI) and a uniform resource locator (URL). A URI is a text representation used to identify a resource (examples include `http://lkrnac.net/about`, `../../file.txt`, `file.txt`, and `/users`). A URL specifies the location of a resource on the network (for example, `http://lkrnac.net/about`). So a URL is also a URI, but not the other way around. In other words, a URL is a special type of URI.

Statelessness

Another crucial REST principle is strict *statelessness*. The server doesn't store any information about clients in sessions. We compensate for this lack of state on the server by including all needed user-specific data for each request. This simplifies implementation on the server side, because the server doesn't need to hold state in memory for all connected clients. Avoiding longer-lived sessions also saves a lot of server resources, because all objects needed to serve the request can be released immediately after the response is sent back to the server. This is a slight downside of REST communication, because sending all state transition information from the client to the server and back increases network bandwidth consumption.

Each request also has to contain data to perform authentication or authorization. Because the server doesn't know anything about the clients and their state, the client must fulfill authorization or authentication constraints in each request. On the other side, stateful communication is mostly implemented by generating session tokens after authentication occurs. If this token is stolen by an attacker, it can be abused for a limited amount of time, until the session is closed or times out. But with stateless communication, authentication credentials or authorization tokens don't expire in a short amount of time. The attacker has a wider window for performing serious attacks. This is a slight security downside of REST communication and shows how crucial it is to use encrypted HTTPS protocols instead of plain HTTP.

State not only consumes resources on the server (as Roy Fielding described in his dissertation), but also complicates clustering. When a user session isn't stored in any of the server nodes, it doesn't really matter to which server node user requests are routed, because any node can serve the request. Therefore, the stateless nature of web services is nowadays one of the main requirements.

To see how the presence of state in an application can complicate clustering, let's consider the scenario in Figure 4-1.

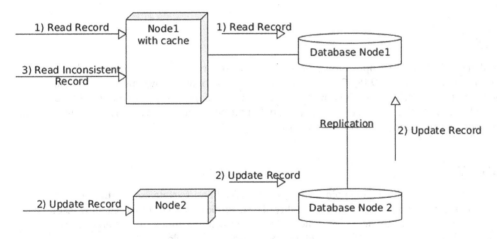

Figure 4-1. *Example of clustering problems with stateful application*

Let's consider that Node1 in our example has a cache for storing records in memory. It's not stateless, because it's storing data (even if for only a short time). The first request reads the record from Database Node1 via Node1 and stores the record into cache. The next request updates the same record via Node2 in Database Node2. Let's also consider that our database cluster is replicated across all database nodes, so the record also is updated in Database Node1. Finally, the third request reads the record from Node1 again, but this time it doesn't read the record from Database Node1, but rather from internal cache. In this case, the record doesn't reflect the change from request 2. Therefore, request 3 reads an inconsistent record.

Similar problems occur if we store state in a session on the server or we use Hibernate as a second-level cache in any of the nodes. Hibernate using a second-level cache expects that only our application is accessing the database. Therefore, if we want to cluster an application that relies on Hibernate's second-level cache, we need to host it on a separate server, and all nodes of our application need to be configured to use it as a second-level cache.

This problem of storing state is common in enterprise applications. Ideally, each application node should be stateless. But sometimes it makes sense to cache data when there isn't a strict requirement for data consistency. A good example is caching OAuth authentication tokens to save round-trips to the OAuth server. These tokens generally don't change. They expire after a certain time, so it is OK to cache them until they expire.

There also are ways to use clustering for server nodes that hold state in session. Load balancers can be configured to route traffic to a node where the session is stored. This mechanism is called a *sticky session*. But it complicates load balancer configuration and decreases the ability to effectively route traffic based on the actual load. The sticky session mechanism can be useful for persistent HTTP connections (keep-alive). These are used to boost latency of web services, because the HTTP connection remains open and the initial handshake doesn't need to occur for every request, which can be slightly more expensive in the case of HTTPS communication.

Layered Architecture

Statelessness also enables us to easily hide *layered architecture* from the client. Clients don't have a clue whether they're talking to one physical machine or a distributed cluster. This is a huge advantage for architects, because it allows them to iteratively scale toward a more robust, secure system without exposing these changes.

HATEOAS

Fielding's thinking about handling application state goes further, to a constraint called *hypermedia as the engine of application state*, or *HATEOAS*). For state transitions, the client uses only hypermedia contained in the payload from the server. The client's knowledge of the service infrastructure and the structure of resources should be minimalized. Therefore, it's expected that the client can discover most information from the server's responses (for example, via URIs to resources).

Cacheability

A further advantage of REST that Fielding points out is *cacheability*. Because stateless communication can be cached, we can boost the performance and scalability of web applications. Of course, caching resources doesn't always make sense, because doing so would make state transitions impossible. Therefore, it is crucial that the server can explicitly or implicitly mark a response as cacheable.

Flexibility

You may notice that these principles are generic and fairly limited. REST turned out to be a concise and maintainable approach for developing web services, because developers don't need to understand a lot of complicated details, as with the SOAP protocol. But it allows for similar interoperability, because HTTP and JSON (as the major REST transport format) have good support across all significant programming languages. A limited number of possible operations allowed for the creation of various frameworks, which can generate REST APIs based on the domain model. One example from the Spring world is Spring Data REST, where developers need to specify only JPA entities. The rest of the application, including the web layer, will be created using REST conventions.

When an application follows all REST principles, it is commonly called *RESTful*. But remember that REST is not a protocol, standard, or framework. So nothing can stop us from dropping any of its principles when there is a good reason to do so. But in that case, we can't call our application RESTful anymore.

Even though it may seem like REST is suitable for nearly everything, it's not. Using HTTP as an application protocol can improve performance, because we operate on lower layers. But we are forced to do one HTTP call per one CRUD operation for one resource instance. Sometimes use cases require various CRUD operations for various resource instances. Doing a lot of HTTP calls for such use cases can introduce performance problems for an application. Such situations are good candidates for dropping some REST principles.

For example, say a client needs to read user information (such as an e-mail address and name) alongside user actions. Following pure REST principles, we would design two resources: for example, user and userAction. But for performance reasons, we might want to consider aggregating these two resources into one response, so the client would need to perform only one HTTP call instead of two.

Another example is a requirement to implement a real-time chat feature into our REST application. In this case, we would probably use WebSockets to implement an endpoint fulfilling this non-CRUD bidirectional communication. But all other endpoints could still follow REST principles.

HTTP Overview

The *Hypertext Transfer Protocol* (HTTP) was designed for distributed systems to exchange hypertext data. It sits on the application layer of the Open Systems Interconnection (OSI) model.

■ **Note** The OSI model is a standardized, layered model for designing communication systems. It is beyond the scope of this book. A good place to start exploring it is its Wikipedia page: http://en.wikipedia.org/wiki/OSI_model.

HTTP is the main protocol that drives the World Wide Web (WWW), and therefore is probably the most widely used application protocol on the planet. As its name suggests, it was designed for exchanging *hyperlinks*, which are logical links between documents on the Web. Communication between the client and the server is initiated by the client sending an HTTP request message to the server. The server processes the request and sends back an HTTP response.

So there are two types of HTTP messages: request and response. Listing 4-1 and Listing 4-2 show examples of each one.

■ **Note** For testing HTTP applications (including REST), I find handy the Chrome plug-ins DHC - REST/HTTP API Client (https://chrome.google.com/webstore/detail/dhc-resthttp-api-client/aejoelaoggembcahagimdiliamlcdmfm) and Advanced REST Client (https://chrome.google.com/webstore/detail/advanced-rest-client/hgmloofddffdnphfgcellkdfbfbjeloo/). A more sophisticated tool often used for testing is SoapUI (www.soapui.org). The free version is powerful enough for testing REST endpoints, but the UI is not modern. A similar tool is Apache JMeter (https://jmeter.apache.org/), but it's targeted more toward performance testing. For troubleshooting and sniffing HTTP communication, including inspecting raw HTTP messages, I suggest Zed Attack Proxy, or ZAP, (www.owasp.org/index.php/OWASP_Zed_Attack_Proxy_Project). It is an Open Web Application Security Project (OWASP) subproject used for penetration testing, but is also useful for developing REST APIs.

Listing 4-1. HTTP Request Message

```
GET http://localhost:10403/users/1 HTTP/1.1
Proxy-Connection: keep-alive
Accept: text/html,application/xhtml+xml,application/xml;q=0.9,image/webp,*/*;q=0.8
User-Agent: Mozilla/5.0 (X11; Linux x86_64) AppleWebKit/537.36 (KHTML, like Gecko)
Chrome/41.0.2272.101 Safari/537.36
Accept-Encoding: sdch
Accept-Language: en-US,en;q=0.8,sk;q=0.6
Host: localhost:10403
```

Listing 4-2. HTTP Response Message

```
HTTP/1.1 200 OK
Server: Apache-Coyote/1.1
Content-Type: application/json;charset=UTF-8
Date: Tue, 31 Mar 2015 21:06:27 GMT

{"email": "lubos.krnac@gmail.com","name": "Lubos Krnac"}
```

The structures of the request and response messages are similar and effectively differ only in the first line. These are the parts of the HTTP message as described by the Hypertext Transfer Protocol:

- Initial line

    - In a request message, this is a request line containing the following:

        - HTTP method

        - Hostname with target URL

        - HTTP version

    - In a response message, this is a status line containing the following:

        - HTTP version

        - Status code

        - Status message

- Headers

- Empty line

- Optional body of the message

An important piece of information embedded in the response message is the HTTP status code. It has the form of a three-digit number and should inform the client about the result of processing the request. In some cases, the status is about server health. For convenience, status codes are separated into groups of a hundred:

100+ Informational: Informs the client that the service didn't finish processing the request and that a full response will come later.

200+ Success: Informs the client that the request was received, understood, accepted, and processed by the server.

300+ - Redirection: Informs the client that further action is needed to process the request. Such scenarios are commonly used for URL redirection.

400+ - Client errors: Informs the client that an error occurred, and it was most probably caused by the client sending an incorrect request. Such an error generally can be fixed by the client. The server must provide enough information about the error, so the client can figure out the problem.

500+ - Server errors: Informs the client about a server error that can't be fixed by client intervention. Such errors often indicate that the server application is down or irresponsible.

Not all the error codes within these intervals are occupied. Inventors of HTTP were thinking ahead and left enough space in the error codes for further revisions of the protocol—including future statuses that could be introduced, or custom statuses that could be introduced by an application using HTTP.

■ **Note** Listing HTTP status codes is beyond the scope of this book. A useful resource for inspecting these status codes and their contracts is at www.restapitutorial.com/httpstatuscodes.html. This resource contains citations from the HTTP specification as well as from Wikipedia.

Some groups of status codes require specific headers in the response. For example, when the status code is 201 Created (indicating that the resource was successfully created by request), the response should include the Location header, so the client knows where to find the created resource.

Headers of the HTTP message are optional. Various types of HTTP headers exist:

- Request headers (standard and nonstandard)

- Response headers (standard and nonstandard)

- Custom headers

The first two categories of headers are used by the server or client to control various aspects of communication. Some headers inform a counterpart (for example, what content type the user accepts or which browser type it is using). Other headers have a deeper function within communication (for example, can turn on compression of the payload or control caching).

■ **Note** A list of default HTTP headers is beyond the scope of this book. Wikipedia provides a nice overview of HTTP headers: http://en.wikipedia.org/wiki/List_of_HTTP_header_fields.

Custom headers are intended to be used by business logic.

HTTP Methods Used by REST

We mentioned that REST principles rely on a limited number of operations that can be performed against the resource instance. These operations are commonly called CRUD, as noted previously. HTTP (used as the application protocol in the REST world) contains methods for performing these operations.

An important parameter of HTTP methods is *idempotency*: the HTTP call will have the same effect if the same request is sent various times. This principle is not HTTP specific and can be applied to various use cases, including in mathematics. For example, multiplying any number by 1 is an idempotent operation, because any number can be multiplied by 1 many times with the same result. Another math example is logical OR with a true value. Examples from the computer world include reading a record from a database or updating a record in a database.

However, it is not guaranteed that a sequence of various idempotent actions will have the same result. For example, a sequence of DB reads of the same record can be nonidempotent if we also execute an update of the same record in the meantime.

The next important parameter of HTTP methods is *safety*. A safe method doesn't have side effects; It doesn't change the state of the application when an operation is performed. For example, reading a record from a database doesn't have any side effects because the persisted state in the database remains the same.

The following are HTTP methods used in REST services for performing CRUD operations:

GET:

- Used for reading the resource representation

- Idempotent operation, because recurrent reading should return the same result

- Safe operation, because reading the resource shouldn't change the state of the application

- Read-only nature of GET drives the fact that it is cacheable

- Request shouldn't contain a body

- Response should contain a representation of the resource in the message body

- Commonly used response success statuses:

    - 200 OK—resource read was successful

    - 204 No Content—resource does not exist

POST:

- Creates a new instance of the resource based on a generic resource URL

- Nonidempotent operation, because a recurrent request should create a new resource

- Should send back a Location header in response, to identify the created resource instance

- Unsafe operation, because recurrent creation changes the state, by creating new resource instances

- Request should contain a representation of the resource in the message body

- Response typically doesn't contain a body

- Commonly used response success statuses:

    - 201 Created—resource creation was successful

PUT:

- Used for updating or creating a resource instance specified by a concrete URI

- Idempotent operation, because it doesn't create a new resource instance every time. The first time, it creates a new instance; subsequently, it updates the same instance. So each request has the same effect.

- Unsafe operation, because it changes the state of the application

- Request should contain a representation of the resource in the message body

- Response typically doesn't contain a body

- Commonly used response success statuses:

  - 200 OK—resource was updated

  - 201 Created—resource was created

DELETE:

- Releases instance of the resource based on a given URI

- Idempotent operation, because all requests for deleting the same resource instance have the same result—the resource instance is released.

- Unsafe operation, because it changes the state of the application

- Request or response of this type shouldn't contain a body

- Commonly used response success statuses:

  - 200 OK—resource was deleted

  - 204 No Content—resource doesn't exist

HEAD:

- Similar to GET, but it reads headers without the body

- Idempotent and safe operation

- Is also cacheable

- Request or response of this type shouldn't contain body

- Commonly used response success statuses:

  - 200 OK—resource read was successful

  - 204 No Content—resource does not exist

■ **Note**   A full list of HTTP method types can be found on Wikipedia: en.wikipedia.org/wiki/Hypertext_ Transfer_Protocol#Request_methods.

Developers have to bear in mind that the safety and idempotency parameters of these HTTP methods are fulfilled only when the HTTP standard is followed. Unfortunately, a lot of applications are implemented without these parameters in mind or by breaking HTTP contract rules. Such applications break the HTTP contract and therefore can't be called RESTful.

Implementing all methods for each resource isn't necessary. For example, some resources are read-only based on application requirements, so the server doesn't need to handle POST/PUT/DELETE. Therefore, the server should send HTTP status code 405 Method Not Allowed, if such a request is performed against a read-only resource.

JAX-RS

Support for developing REST applications is represented in Java by a standard API, which is part of Java Enterprise Edition (JEE) standards. Its name is Java API for RESTful Web Services, or JAX-RS (https://jax-rs-spec.java.net). Like all APIs from JEE, JAX-RS is not an implementation of REST support. It's a standard abstraction. For running and using this API in production, a JEE-compliant application server or at least a server that conforms to the JAX-RS standard is needed.

A similar approach is used across all the APIs provided by JEE. Each API's abstraction can have various implementations. The JEE standard was created to unify the surface layers of Java application servers provided from different vendors. Migration from one JEE-compliant server to another is much easier when most of their APIs are the same. In addition, leveraging JEE APIs allows for reuse of experience and JEE API knowledge, which decreases the learning curve for developers migrating to a different application server.

JAX-RS Implementations

So when we want to use JAX-RS, we also need an application server or a lightweight runtime implementing this API. As JAX-RS is an abstraction on top of servlets, we have to use it with a servlet container. Here are the main application servers or runtimes implementing JAX-RS:

> *Jersey*: A reference implementation of JAX-RS APIs. Can be used alone and is also shipped by Oracle as part of the GlassFish JEE application server.

> *Apache CXF*: Framework for SOAP and REST web services with JMS, OSGi, and CORBA support.

> *RESTEasy*: Implementation of JAX-RS that can run on any servlet container. Can be used alone or with JBoss Application server.

> *Restlet*: Open source JAX-RS implementation, which can integrate with various Java technologies and frameworks.

> *WebSphere Application Server*: Full JEE-compliant commercial solution from IBM.

> *WebLogic Server*: Full JEE-compliant commercial solution from Oracle.

> *Apache Tuscany*: Provides REST support alongside wider support for the Service Component Architecture (SCA) specification.

JAX-RS API

The main surface of the JAX-RS API consists of various annotations for declaring Java REST endpoints. We have annotations for declaring the following:

- URL mapping—@Path

- HTTP method binding—@GET, @HEADER, @POST, @PUT, @DELETE

- Content type handling

  - @Produces: Content types being produced by endpoint

  - @Consumes: Content types that can be consumed by endpoint

- Data extraction from the HTTP message

  - @QueryParam: Parses the parameter value from the query part of the URI

  - @PathParam: Parses the parameter value from the URI

  - @HeaderParam: Parses the HTTP header

  - @DefaultValue: Specifies the default value if the parameter binding is not found

  - @Context: Retrieves the entire context of the request or response (for example, @Context HttpServletRequest httpRequest)

  - @CookieParam: Retrieves the cookie value into the method parameter

  - @FormParam: Retrieves the form value into the method parameter

With these annotations, we have powerful control over parsing and handling HTTP message metadata. For handling the HTTP message payload itself, JAX-RS integrates with various payload serialization libraries. So for converting Java objects into JSON, XML, and other formats and back, JAX-RS can integrate with main libraries such as Jackson (JSON serialization library) or JAXB 2 (XML serialization library). In the majority of cases, we don't need to call these libraries directly, because JAX-RS (or more precisely, the implementation of JAX-RS we are using) uses them under the hood.

Common Classes Used in Examples

Let's dive into a simple example. Because this book is about Spring, we are going to integrate JAX-RS with Spring. But first we need to introduce the domain for all the examples in this chapter. A simple model POJO is shown in Listing 4-3.

Listing 4-3. Model POJO Used in All REST Examples (0400-rest-common)

```
package net.lkrnac.book.eiws.chapter04.model;

import lombok.Data;
import lombok.EqualsAndHashCode;

@Data
@EqualsAndHashCode(of = { "email" })
public class User {
  private String email;
  private String name;
}
```

This is a simple class with simplified modeling of the User object. Properties of this simple POJO should store an e-mail address and user's name. Such a simplified model is enough to demonstrate REST API development.

In some examples, we will need to compare the equality of User objects. Historically, we would override Object.hashCode and Object.equals methods to fulfill the Java hash code and equality contract.

But our implementation uses the third-party library Lombok (https://projectlombok.org). Lombok is a handy productivity library that aims to eliminate some verbose parts of the Java language. The hashCode and equals methods are generated by the @EqualsAndHashCode annotation. Because we need to use only the email property in the equality contract, we specify it in the annotation parameter of. If we don't specify it explicitly, Lombok will use all the properties of User POJO in the hash/equality contract.

Moreover, Lombok helps us to generate getters and setters for all properties in the User class via the @Data annotation.

■ **Note** Object.equals and Object.hashCode are fundamental principles to understand in object-oriented Java programming: equal objects must have equal hash codes. Proper implementation ensures that objects are treated equally and handled properly in Java collections. Incorrect implementation can lead to confusing bugs. Implementation of hashCode and equals can be verbose and error prone; developers can introduce a lot of problems. Most of them are gathered in these Stack Overflow answers: http://stackoverflow. com/questions/27581/what-issues-should-be-considered-when-overriding-equals-and-hashcode-in-java. Therefore, I *strongly recommend* looking into the Lombok library (http://projectlombok.org/ features/EqualsAndHashCode.html) when overriding the Object.hashCode and Object.equals contract.

Listing 4-4 shows the second class that will be used in most of the REST examples.

Listing 4-4. User Repository Used in All REST Examples (0400-rest-common)

```java
package net.lkrnac.book.eiws.chapter04.persistence;

import java.util.Collection;
import java.util.Collections;
import java.util.HashMap;
import java.util.Map;
import java.util.stream.Collectors;
import net.lkrnac.book.eiws.chapter04.model.User;
import org.springframework.stereotype.Repository;

@Repository
public class UserRepository {
  private final Map<Integer, User> users = new HashMap<>();
  private int userSequence;

  public synchronized Collection<User> getAllUsers() {
    return Collections.unmodifiableCollection(users.values());
  }

  public synchronized User getUser(int identifier) {
    if (identifier == -1) {
      throw new UnsupportedOperationException("Identifier -1 is not supported.");
    }
    return users.get(identifier);
  }

  public synchronized int addUser(User user) {
    users.put(userSequence, user);
    return userSequence++;
  }
```

```java
public synchronized void updateOrAddUser(int identifier, User user) {
    users.put(identifier, user);
}

public synchronized User deleteUser(int identifier) {
    return users.remove(identifier);
}

public synchronized Collection<User> getUsersInterval(int lowerId, int upperId) {
    //@formatter:off
    Collection<User> usersInIdInterval = users.entrySet().stream()
        .filter(p -> p.getKey() >= lowerId && p.getKey() <= upperId)
        .collect(Collectors.toMap(p -> p.getKey(), p -> p.getValue()))
        .values();
    //@formatter:on
    return Collections.unmodifiableCollection(usersInIdInterval);
}
}
```

The UserRepository class is annotated with the @Repository annotation to indicate that it's a Spring bean sitting on the persistence layer. To simplify the examples, there is a simple in-memory cache for User objects defined as Map<Integer, User>. But such caching is not suitable for production use. Caching and persisting application state should be handled by specialized databases or in memory grids that are battle tested for such purposes. Also this particular usage breaks the stateless REST principle. But for simplicity, let's pretend that this class is calling a persistence layer for storing User objects. We are interested in the web layer anyway.

First, the getAllUsers method returns a map of all users stored in this cache. The returned map is encapsulated in an unmodifiable wrapper, so that we are sure its instance won't be replaced during the application run. The getUser method returns a single User object based on a given identifier. To highlight the error-handling features, we don't support -1 and the user identifier and throw UnsupportedOperationException.

The addUser method is little more complicated. It uses an identifier counter called userSequence to assign a unique identifier to the newly created User object and increases its value afterward. The updateOrAddUser method accepts the identifier and User parameters and replaces or adds this instance into the map slot represented by the identifier. The deleteUser method simply removes the object from the map.

The last method from this class is getUsersInterval. It reads a collection of users based on a given interval of identifiers. This isn't a realistic use case, but it helps demonstrate some features of Spring MVC mappings. The reading logic uses Java 8. First, we convert the map into a stream and apply filtering. Values filtering is based on a lower and upper bound of identifiers. After filtering, we collect the results into a map and wrap the values into an unmodifiable map. This gives us a filtered collection of users.

Another problem with this implementation is the singleton bean scope of UserService. Fields/cache/state in a singleton is always dangerous from a multithreading point of view. We can easily have various requests being handled by our application at the same time. These requests are served in separate threads. In this situation, various threads could be accessing this in-memory cache at the same time. We need to make this class thread-safe, so we made all access methods to our cache synchronized. It isn't an effective method of caching, but as we mentioned, it is just for example purposes.

You may ask, why not use ConcurrentHashMap as a map implementation and exclude synchronization?. But remember that the addUser method consists of two actions that should be atomic (adding to the map, and reading and increasing the sequence). With the ConcurrentHashMap approach without synchronization, this wouldn't be atomic and could lead to thread-unsafe scenarios. For example, two threads could use the same sequence number to store different objects, and thus we would lose one of them.

Listing 4-5 shows the next class heavily used in the examples.

Listing 4-5. User Repository Used in All REST Examples (0400-rest-common)

```
package net.lkrnac.book.eiws.chapter04.service;

import java.util.Collection;
import net.lkrnac.book.eiws.chapter04.model.User;
import net.lkrnac.book.eiws.chapter04.persistence.UserRepository;
import org.springframework.beans.factory.annotation.Autowired;
import org.springframework.stereotype.Service;

@Service
public class UserService {
  private final UserRepository userRepository;

  @Autowired
  public UserService(UserRepository userRepository) {
    super();
    this.userRepository = userRepository;
  }

  public Collection<User> getAllUsers() {
    return userRepository.getAllUsers();
  }

  public User getUser(int identifier) {
    return userRepository.getUser(identifier);
  }

  public int addUser(User user) {
    return userRepository.addUser(user);
  }

  public void updateOrAddUser(int identifier, User user) {
    userRepository.updateOrAddUser(identifier, user);
  }

  public User deleteUser(int identifier) {
    return userRepository.deleteUser(identifier);
  }

  public Collection<User> getUsersInterval(int lowerId, int upperId) {
    return userRepository.getUsersInterval(lowerId, upperId);
  }

}
```

This is a simple pass-through wrapper for UserRepository. We include it to follow the most common three-layer application model (web/service/persistence layer).

Listing 4-6 shows the last class we will use across all REST examples: a class holding the URL constant.

Listing 4-6. URL Constants Used in All REST Examples

```java
package net.lkrnac.book.eiws.chapter04;

public final class UrlConstants {
  private UrlConstants() {
  }

  public static final String USERS_URL = "/users";
}
```

This class is defined as final and has a private constructor for disallowing instantiation and inheritance of this class. It contains a constant that represents the root REST resource mapped in examples. The constant helps us reuse the same string literal various times.

JAX-RS Endpoint

After defining the service layer (pretending that it is reading/writing our User objects from/into the battle-tested and reliable persistence storage), we can jump into the REST API examples. Listing 4-7 shows the JAX-RS endpoint implementation.

Listing 4-7. JAX-RS Endpoint Implementation (0401-rest-jax-rs-server)

```java
package net.lkrnac.book.eiws.chapter04.jaxrs;

import java.net.URI;
import java.net.URISyntaxException;
import java.util.Collection;
import javax.ws.rs.Consumes;
import javax.ws.rs.DELETE;
import javax.ws.rs.GET;
import javax.ws.rs.POST;
import javax.ws.rs.PUT;
import javax.ws.rs.Path;
import javax.ws.rs.PathParam;
import javax.ws.rs.Produces;
import javax.ws.rs.WebApplicationException;
import javax.ws.rs.core.MediaType;
import javax.ws.rs.core.Response;
import net.lkrnac.book.eiws.chapter04.UrlConstants;
import net.lkrnac.book.eiws.chapter04.model.User;
import net.lkrnac.book.eiws.chapter04.service.UserService;
import org.springframework.beans.factory.annotation.Autowired;
import org.springframework.stereotype.Component;

@Path(UrlConstants.USERS_URL)
@Component
public class UserResource {
  private final UserService userService;
```

```java
@Autowired
public UserResource(UserService userService) {
  super();
  this.userService = userService;
}

@GET
@Produces(MediaType.APPLICATION_JSON)
public Collection<User> getUsers() {
  return userService.getAllUsers();
}

@GET
@Path("/{id}")
@Produces(MediaType.APPLICATION_JSON)
public User getUser(@PathParam("id") int identifier) {
  try {
    return userService.getUser(identifier);
  } catch (UnsupportedOperationException uoe) {
    throw new WebApplicationException(uoe, Response.Status.BAD_REQUEST);
  }
}

@POST
@Consumes(MediaType.APPLICATION_JSON)
public Response postUser(User user) throws URISyntaxException {
  int identifier = userService.addUser(user);
  URI uri = new URI(UrlConstants.USERS_URL + "/" + identifier);
  return Response.created(uri).build();
}

@PUT
@Path("/{id}")
@Consumes(MediaType.APPLICATION_JSON)
public Response putUser(@PathParam("id") int identifier, User user)
    throws URISyntaxException {
  userService.updateOrAddUser(identifier, user);
  return Response.ok().build();
}

@DELETE
@Path("/{id}")
public Response deleteUser(@PathParam("id") int identifier) {
  userService.deleteUser(identifier);
  return Response.ok().build();
}
}
```

The @Path annotation binds the UserResource class to the /users URI. When the request with the root URI /users hits our application, it will be served by this class. The @Component annotation declares the UserResource class as a Spring singleton bean. In the constructor, we inject UserService, which is used for persisting User objects.

Four methods handling the GET, POST, and DELETE HTTP methods follow. The getUsers() method reads the collection of all users and returns it to the consumer. It produces a JSON content type, which means the response will contain the HTTP header Content-Type equal to the value application/json. This header should inform the consumer about the payload format. The @Produces annotation also indicates to the underlying JAX-RS implementation (which in this case is Jersey) to use the Jackson JSON serialization library. It converts the collection of User objects into a JSON array payload structure.

Next, the getUser(int identifier) method reads the concrete User object with the @GET annotation also. This concrete object is identified by the URI path parameter identifier. So the URI /users/1 should perform a read operation of the user instance with identifier 1. To parse the identifier from the URI, we use the @PathParam annotation. A prerequirement for this parsing is the specification of the placeholder in the path binding, where the @Path annotation has the placeholder /{id} declared. Any URI part after /users/ will be mapped onto the parameter identifier, annotated by the @PathParam("id"). The annotation parameter id binds identifier to the path placeholder /{id}. The return value object User is converted to a JSON payload by the Jackson library under the hood.

The postUser method is bound to the POST HTTP method. The @Consumes annotation indicates that this endpoint expects a JSON payload. The message body is converted by the Jackson JSON serializer library into a User object and injected into the method as a parameter. After passing this object into the lower layer to store it, we need to send a message to the consumer with HTTP status code 201 Created and the Location header of the newly created object. For such an HTTP response creation, the javax.ws.rs.core.Response factory is used. It can cover most of the common HTTP responses as well as custom status codes. The Location header is defined as with a uri parameter of a response creation Response.created(uri).build() call.

The putUser method handles the PUT HTTP method. It is responsible for the creation or update of the given User record. This record is received as a JSON payload and converted into the method parameter User. The second parameter of this method is the identifier, which is extracted from the URL similarly to the getUser method. To perform the mentioned action, it delegates a request to the service layer via the userService.updateOrAddUser call. If everything goes well, it sends back HTTP status 400 OK.

The deleteUser method maps to the DELETE HTTP method with the help of the @DELETE annotation. It combines the mentioned approaches to parse the URL parameter and construct the response message with HTTP status code 200 OK. It calls the UserService.deleteUser method to release a given instance of the user.

Registering the UserResource bean into an Inversion of Control container is not enough for Spring and JAX-RS integration. Every such bean needs to be registered into a Jersey resource configuration, shown in Listing 4-8.

Listing 4-8. Registering JAX-RS/Spring Bean into Jersey Resource Configuration (0401-rest-jax-rs-server)

```
package net.lkrnac.book.eiws.chapter04.jaxrs;

import org.glassfish.jersey.server.ResourceConfig;
import org.springframework.stereotype.Component;

@Component
public class EndpointRegister extends ResourceConfig {
  public EndpointRegister() {
    super();
    register(UserResource.class);
  }
}
```

The EndpointRegister class is annotated with Spring's @Component annotation and extends org.glassfish.jersey.server.ResourceConfig. This represents the Spring and Jersey integration. The endpoint beans should be registered in the constructor of this class. In this case, it's only the UserResource bean.

Listing 4-9 is the main class responsible for starting this example as a Java application.

Listing 4-9. Main Class of JAX-RS Application (0401-rest-jax-rs-server)

```
package net.lkrnac.book.eiws.chapter04;

import org.springframework.boot.SpringApplication;
import org.springframework.boot.autoconfigure.SpringBootApplication;
import org.springframework.boot.context.web.SpringBootServletInitializer;

@SpringBootApplication
public class RestJaxrsApplication extends SpringBootServletInitializer {
  public static void main(String... args) {
    SpringApplication.run(RestJaxrsApplication.class, args);
  }
}
```

We use the Spring Boot project to easily host our application in an embedded Tomcat servlet container. This is a relatively new and convenient way to run Spring applications. The `@SpringBootApplication` annotation gathers various Spring annotations under one umbrella. It triggers component scanning in the package where the annotated class is declared and its subpackages (the equivalent of `@ComponentScan`). It also covers the `@EnableAutoConfiguration` Spring Boot annotation, which inspects the classpath for JAR dependencies and registers some sensible default beans . In this case, we are using the JAX-RS implementation, Jersey. Therefore, it starts the embedded Tomcat container. The class is extended from `SpringBootServlerInitializer`, which takes care of our servlet configuration. By default, it maps all endpoints to the root URL /. In the main method, we have the call `SpringApplication.run` with the Spring configuration class as a parameter. So the `RestJaxrsApplication` class is used as a Spring configuration and also the main class of our application.

Listing 4-10 covers the Spring Boot properties. These help us configure the embedded Tomcat container with port 10401 and initiate Spring's JAX-RS integration and configure Jersey for hosting servlets.

Listing 4-10. JAX-RS and Spring Boot Example Properties (File application.properties in Folder src/main/properties in Example Project 0401-rest-jax-rs-server)

```
server.port=10401
spring.jersey.type=servlet
```

After running the `RestJaxrsApplication` class from a Java application, we can execute the HTTP REST request against our server. We can use the Chrome plug-in DHC - REST/HTTP API Client (https://chrome.google.com/webstore/detail/dhc-resthttp-api-client/aejoelaoggembcahagimdiliamlcdmfm) for this purpose. Figure 4-2 shows the POST request executed against this running application.

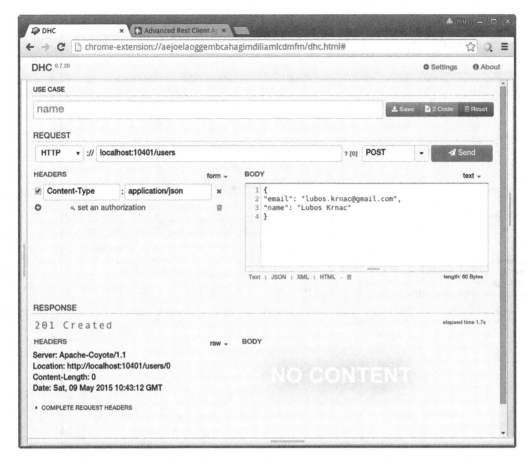

Figure 4-2. *HTTP POST request against JAX-RS example*

In the first half of the DHC - REST/HTTP API Client screen, we need to specify the request we want to send. In this case, we need to specify the URL of our REST endpoint, which is `http://localhost:10401/users`. Next we need to pick the HTTP method (`POST`, in this case), and finally, specify the JSON payload in the body section we want to send to the server.

After clicking the Send button, the response appears below if everything is configured properly. In this case, the server indicates that the resource instance was created and also sends us the `Location` HTTP header. This gives us a full URL of the created resource instance. It also shows us the ID assigned to this user. In this case, it is 0.

Figures 4-3, 4-4, and 4-5 show similar actions with the HTTP `GET`, `PUT`, and `DELETE` methods.

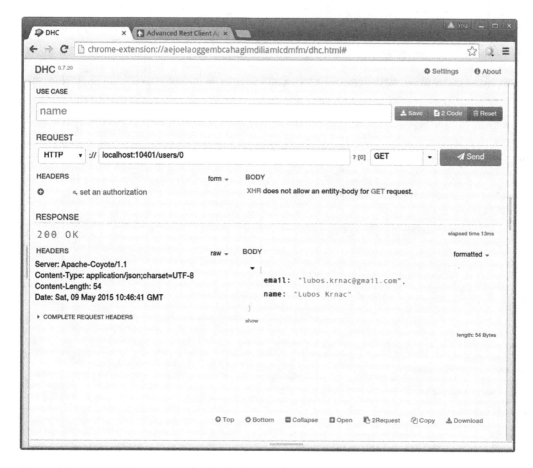

Figure 4-3. *HTTP GET request against JAX-RS example*

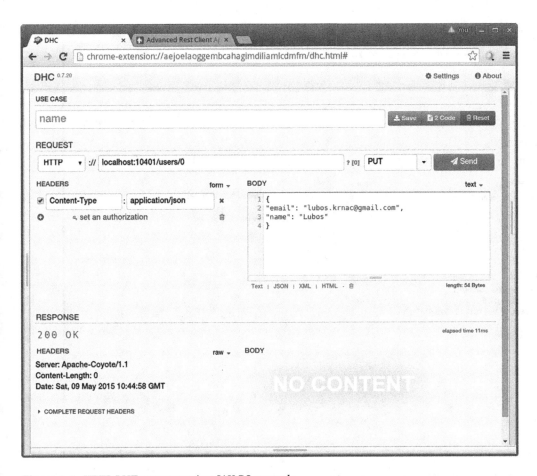

Figure 4-4. *HTTP PUT request against JAX-RS example*

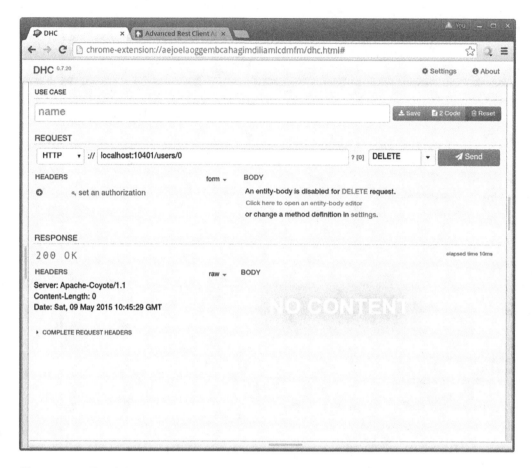

Figure 4-5. *HTTP DELETE request against JAX-RS example*

This Spring and JAX-RS integration provide a full-fledged approach to developing REST web services. It is supported by the Spring ecosystem even if Spring provides its own alternative APIs.

Spring MVC

Spring MVC is a central module for Spring web support. Its contracts are competitors to JAX-RS abstractions. As the name of this Spring module suggests, it wasn't originally designed for developing REST services. But APIs for the Model-View-Controller (MVC) style of architecture have been suitable enough to also cover REST concerns since Spring Framework version 3.0. It is a double win, because developers used to MVC APIs can easily switch to REST endpoint development, and vice versa.

JAX-RS is targeted toward application-to-application communication. So we can communicate with the REST server from a client developed in any major programming platform, including JavaScript in the browser. But sometimes we may need to use plain HTML as a consumer of our endpoint. An important fact about HTML is that it supports only GET (for example, when a user clicks a web page link) and POST (for example, when a user submits an HTML form) HTTP methods. The problem is the missing DELETE, PUT, and HEADER HTTP methods, in the case of plain HTML. This would be a significant problem for JAX-RS, as it doesn't expect such a restricted environment.

Spring MVC supports browsers as REST clients with a technique called *HTTP method conversion*. The main idea behind this concept is to use HTML forms to perform a POST with a hidden form parameter. This parameter should specify the desired HTTP method being performed, which may be DELETE, HEADER, or PUT instead of POST. On the server side, we can then register the servlet filter that will convert the HTML POST request into an HTTP request defined by the hidden form input parameter. But this feature is beyond the scope of this book.

Another difference between Spring MVC and JAX-RS is in client-side API support. JAX-RS introduced a client-side API in version 2.0. This version of JAX-RS is part of the standard Java EE 7. So if we are running older Java EE editions, we don't have native JAX-RS client API support. And enterprise companies often get stuck on Java EE 5 or 6, mainly because of the licence costs for expensive Java EE application servers, as an upgrade can be major investment for a company. With Spring MVC, you can use client-side APIs even within older Java EE application servers, because the Spring Framework is lightweight and easily pluggable into any Java EE platform.

A significant advantage of the Spring MVC module over JAX-RS is support for testing. The Spring MVC testing module provides powerful fake constructs that allow for the integration or unit testing of the server and client side. These constructs allow testing of mappings out of the servlet container. This is a huge benefit in continuous integration.

A significant feature that puts the Spring MVC API into a better position, when considering REST programming models, is content negotiation. With Spring MVC, this feature is embedded into the framework out of the box. But JAX-RS doesn't have standard support for content negotiation; therefore, developers need to rely on nonstandard JAX-RS implementations they are using or implement it explicitly.

Finally, JAX-RS has a disadvantage in the fact that it's standard, because Spring is able to iterate quicker and provide new features faster. Spring provides much richer possibilities for HTTP message mappings onto Java controllers and models. It also allows much wider possibilities for custom configurations (for example, message converters). These are possible reasons why the Spring MVC API adoption is higher than that of JAX-RS.

Configuring Spring MVC for REST

Spring MVC is an abstraction on top of Java servlets. So we need a servlet container in order to run the Spring MVC application. The most important class for integrating Java servlet technology is org.springframework.web.servlet.DispatcherServlet. This class is responsible for routing HTTP messages to the correct Java logic based on declarative mappings.

Spring MVC relies heavily on mapping annotations. To turn on this programming model, we need to declare in a Spring configuration that we are using Spring MVC. This can be done in two ways:

- <mvc:annotation-driven> XML element of Spring's namespace
  (www.springframework.org/schema/mvc)

- @EnableWebMvc annotation

■ **Note** The Spring MVC module covers a wide range of features for templating views, handling errors, using locales and themes, integrating with security frameworks, and more. All these features provide enough material for a book of its own (such as *Spring REST* by Balaji Varanasi and Sudha Belida, Apress, 2015). We highlight the main features useful for REST in this chapter. Anything else is beyond the scope of this book and can be found in the reference documentation (http://docs.spring.io/spring/docs/current/spring-framework-reference/htmlsingle/#mvc).

The XML configuration for enabling Spring MVC support is shown in Listing 4-11.

Listing 4-11. XML Spring MVC Configuration (File rest-service-config.xml in Example Project 0402-rest-xml-config-server)

```xml
<?xml version="1.0" encoding="UTF-8"?>
<beans xmlns="http://www.springframework.org/schema/beans"
  xmlns:xsi="http://www.w3.org/2001/XMLSchema-instance"
  xmlns:context="http://www.springframework.org/schema/context"
  xmlns:mvc="http://www.springframework.org/schema/mvc"
  xsi:schemaLocation="http://www.springframework.org/schema/mvc
    http://www.springframework.org/schema/mvc/spring-mvc.xsd
              http://www.springframework.org/schema/beans
    http://www.springframework.org/schema/beans/spring-beans.xsd
              http://www.springframework.org/schema/context
    http://www.springframework.org/schema/context/spring-context.xsd">

  <context:component-scan base-package="net.lkrnac.book.eiws.chapter04" />
  <mvc:annotation-driven />
</beans>
```

This configuration uses two namespaces: context and mvc. The first one is used for component scanning of Spring beans, including controllers that will be mapped to HTTP URLs. The second namespace is used for enabling MVC support. The equivalent Java configuration is shown in Listing 4-12.

Listing 4-12. Spring MVC Java Configuration (0403-rest-java-config-server)

```java
package net.lkrnac.book.eiws.chapter04;

import org.springframework.context.annotation.ComponentScan;
import org.springframework.context.annotation.Configuration;
import org.springframework.web.servlet.config.annotation.EnableWebMvc;

@Configuration
@ComponentScan
@EnableWebMvc
public class RestJavaConfigConfiguration {
}
```

The Spring context is configured with three annotations. The @Configuration annotation specifies the configuration bean. The @ComponentScan annotation orders Spring to do component scanning in the current package and subpackages. With this annotation, we don't need to specify the base package where the component scanning should be performed, because it starts from the current package. This is more maintainable; we can't forget to update the base package for component scanning if the package is renamed or moved. Finally, @EnableWebMvc turns on Spring MVC annotations and configures various default beans for Spring MVC support.

When we have a Spring configuration, it needs to be plugged into a servlet configuration. Listing 4-13 contains an example of an XML servlet descriptor configuration.

Listing 4-13. XML Servlet Descriptor for Spring MVC (File web.xml in Example Project 0402-rest-xml-config-server)

```xml
<?xml version="1.0" encoding="UTF-8"?>
<web-app xmlns:xsi="http://www.w3.org/2001/XMLSchema-instance"
  xmlns="http://xmlns.jcp.org/xml/ns/javaee"
  xsi:schemaLocation="http://java.sun.com/xml/ns/javaee
    http://java.sun.com/xml/ns/javaee/web-app_3_0.xsd"
  version="3.0">
  <display-name>0402-rest-xml-config-service</display-name>
  <servlet>
    <servlet-name>rest-service</servlet-name>
    <servlet-class>org.springframework.web.servlet.DispatcherServlet
    </servlet-class>
    <init-param>
      <param-name>contextConfigLocation</param-name>
      <param-value>classpath:rest-service-config.xml</param-value>
    </init-param>
    <load-on-startup>1</load-on-startup>
  </servlet>
  <servlet-mapping>
    <servlet-name>rest-service</servlet-name>
    <url-pattern>/</url-pattern>
  </servlet-mapping>
</web-app>
```

Here we specify a servlet with the name `rest-service` and the implementation class `DispatcherServlet`. This servlet implementation is provided by Spring and handles all the routing support (and much more). `DispatcherServlet` needs to know which Spring context should be bound to this servlet object. Therefore, we specify the servlet initialization parameter `contextConfigLocation`, and point it to the Spring configuration file `rest-service-config.xml`. If we didn't specify this parameter, Spring would try to find `[servlet-name]-servlet.xml` in the `WEB-INF` folder.

Next, the `load-on-startup` parameter tells the servlet container to load this servlet instance when the servlet container starts rather than wait for the first request. If we used lazy initialization, initializing the servlet would prolong the response time of the first request. Because the Spring load time can be measured in seconds, this is a significant performance hit for an initial request.

Finally, we map our servlet to the URL. In this case, it is the root-level URL /. A similar Java configuration looks like Listing 4-14.

Listing 4-14. Spring Java Servlet Configuration (0403-rest-java-config-server)

```java
package net.lkrnac.book.eiws.chapter04;

import org.springframework.web.servlet.support.
        AbstractAnnotationConfigDispatcherServletInitializer;

public class RestInitializer extends
    AbstractAnnotationConfigDispatcherServletInitializer {
```

```java
@Override
protected Class<?>[] getRootConfigClasses() {
  return null;
}

@Override
protected Class<?>[] getServletConfigClasses() {
  return new Class[] { RestJavaConfigConfiguration.class };
}

@Override
protected String[] getServletMappings() {
  return new String[] { "/" };
}
}
```

Spring tries to find implementations of the AbstractAnnotationConfigDispatcherServletInitializer class on the classpath and register it into the servlet container. This servlet initializer helper enables use of the DispatcherServlet out of the box. So our job is to override three methods to specify the servlet mapping, root, and servlet context. As we have only this servlet in our application and are not using separation in the servlet and context mapping, we specify the servlet configuration class and leave the root configuration class unused.

Running the Spring application within the servlet container would correctly initialize the servlet even without the web.xml configuration, as this mechanism is using Servlet 3.0 Java configuration under the hood.

The last configuration example in Listing 4-15 is a new and modern approach.

Listing 4-15. Spring Boot Application Configuration (0404-rest-boot-server)

```java
package net.lkrnac.book.eiws.chapter04;

import org.springframework.boot.SpringApplication;
import org.springframework.boot.autoconfigure.SpringBootApplication;
import org.springframework.boot.context.web.SpringBootServletInitializer;

@SpringBootApplication
public class RestBootApplication extends SpringBootServletInitializer {
  public static void main(String... args) {
    SpringApplication.run(RestBootApplication.class, args);
  }
}
```

This class uses the Spring Boot convention instead of the configuration approach to spin up the application as a JAR. The single SpringBootApplication annotation is powerful. It looks into JAR dependencies on the classpath and applies a common configuration based on these JAR dependencies. So when we have a spring-boot-starter-web library as a JAR dependency, Spring boot will do the following:

- Initialize embedded Tomcat

- Register a servlet with this Spring configuration mapped to the / URL

- Turn on MVC (@EnableWebMvc under the hood)

- Scan the package and subpackages for Spring components and register them into the Inversion of Control container

So with this configuration class, we can replace the servlet and Spring configuration. Simplifying the configuration is a significant advantage of the Spring Boot project. Such an application can be started from the command line via the standard Java command `java -jar 0404-rest-boot-server.jar`.

Spring MVC Mappings

The main Spring MVC concepts are similar to JAX-RS concepts, but annotations and their structures are slightly different. Spring MVC uses these annotations:

`@Controller`

- Is a class-level annotation

- Declares that the class is handling HTTP requests

- Creates a Spring bean, which is a candidate for component scanning

`@RequestMapping`

- As a class-level annotation, specifies the base HTTP mapping configuration for all methods handling HTTP requests within the class

- As a method-level annotation, specifies the method-level HTTP configuration narrowing down the base/class level `@RequestMapping` configuration

- Provides a flexible mapping of Spring beans and their methods onto the URL with the use of parameters. Each of these attributes can be used at the method as well as the class level:

    - `value`: Maps the method to a URI or URL pattern. If both class- and method-level annotations are used, the final mapping URI is concatenated.

    - `method`: Specifies the HTTP method being handled.

    - `consumes`: Specifies the content type that can be consumed.

    - `produces`: Specifies the content type that can be produced.

    - `headers`: Specifies the mapping based on headers. Supports wildcards for the headers `Accept` and `Content-Type`.

    - `params`: Specifies the mapping based on the query parameters of the request. Alongside equality mappings (`queryParam=value`), it also can use a nonequality mapping (`queryParam!=value`), or that parameter shouldn't be present in the request (`!queryParam`).

- Spring provides powerful mappings based on the following:

    - URI parameters (for example, `/users/{id}`)

    - URI patterns with regular expressions (for example, `/users/{id:\\d*}`)

    - URI patterns with wildcards (for example, `/users/**`)

@RequestBody

- Used for annotating method parameters in order to access the payload of the HTTP request

@PathVariable

- Maps the URI template variable onto the method parameter
- Annotation attribute is not necessary if the URI pattern name is the same as the annotated parameter

@RequestParam

- Maps the query parameter onto the method parameter
- Annotation attribue is not necessary if the query parameter name is the same as the annotated parameter

@RequestHeader

- Maps the HTTP header onto the method parameter

@ResponseBody

- Used for annotating methods. Specifies that the return value of the method will be converted into the body of the HTTP response.
- This annotation distinguishes between REST and MVC usage.
- Supports content negotiation (based on the Accept header); the client can request a certain format of the payload (for example, XML, JSON), and Spring will use the appropriate marshaler library (for example, JAXB 2, Jackson).

@RestController

- Convenience annotation combining the @Controller and @RequestBody annotations
- Introduced in Spring 4.0

@ResponseStatus

- Hard-codes the response of the method to a particular HTTP response status code

@ExceptionsHandler

- Is used for handling exceptions that bubble up to @Controller, where it is specified
- Exception types handled by exceptions handler are specified as annotation attributes
- Is handy for translating exceptions into specific HTTP status codes

Lower-level Abstraction Injection

With these annotations, we can inject various lower-level HTTP message abstractions into our controller methods. But Spring also provides annotation-free injections. If, for some reason, we need to access lower-level abstractions of the HTTP message, Spring can inject these types:

Servlet Message Abstractions

- Servlet doesn't necessarily need to use HTTP, so these abstractions don't contain HTTP-specific data.

- Most generic message abstractions conform to the Java Servlets API.

- `javax.servlet.ServletRequest` is the interface that represents an abstraction for the servlet request.

- `javax.servlet.ServletResponse` is the interface that represents an abstraction for the servlet request.

Java EE HTTP Message Abstractions

- HTTP subinterfaces of `javax.servlet.ServletRequest` and `javax.servlet.ServletResponse`.

- These interfaces provide a message payload in the form of `InputStream`.

- `javax.servlet.http.HttpServletRequest` is the interface that represents an abstraction for the HTTP request.

- `javax.servlet.http.HttpServletResponse` is the interface that represents an abstraction for the HTTP response.

Spring HTTP Message Abstractions

- These interfaces provide a message payload converted into generic type `T`.

- Generic type `T` specifies the Java type of the payload.

- `org.springframework.http.HttpEntity<T>` is the interface that represents an abstraction for the HTTP request provided by Spring.

- `org.springframework.http.ResponseEntity<T>` is the interface that represents an abstraction for the HTTP response provided by Spring. Contains fields for headers, body, and HTTP status.

- `org.springframework.http.RequestEntity<T>` is the interface that represents an abstraction for the HTTP request provided by Spring. Contains fields for HTTP headers, body, URI, and HTTP method.

To inject one of these HTTP message abstractions, we don't need to use any annotations. We just need to use them as parameters of the method handling the HTTP requests (annotated by `@RequestMapping`).

String MVC CRUD Example

Listing 4-16 provides an example of a simple HTTP mapping that uses Spring MVC annotation. This example uses the service and model POJO from Listings 4-3 and 4-4.

Listing 4-16. Spring MVC Mapping Example (0404-rest-boot-server)

```java
package net.lkrnac.book.eiws.chapter04.javaconfig;

import java.util.Collection;
import net.lkrnac.book.eiws.chapter04.UrlConstants;
import net.lkrnac.book.eiws.chapter04.model.User;
import net.lkrnac.book.eiws.chapter04.service.UserService;
import org.springframework.beans.factory.annotation.Autowired;
import org.springframework.http.HttpHeaders;
import org.springframework.http.HttpStatus;
import org.springframework.http.ResponseEntity;
import org.springframework.stereotype.Controller;
import org.springframework.web.bind.annotation.ExceptionHandler;
import org.springframework.web.bind.annotation.PathVariable;
import org.springframework.web.bind.annotation.RequestBody;
import org.springframework.web.bind.annotation.RequestMapping;
import org.springframework.web.bind.annotation.RequestMethod;
import org.springframework.web.bind.annotation.ResponseBody;
import org.springframework.web.bind.annotation.ResponseStatus;
import org.springframework.web.util.UriComponents;
import org.springframework.web.util.UriComponentsBuilder;

@Controller
@RequestMapping(UrlConstants.USERS_URL)
public class UserController {
  private final UserService userService;

  @Autowired
  public UserController(UserService userService) {
    super();
    this.userService = userService;
  }

  @RequestMapping(method = RequestMethod.GET)
  @ResponseBody
  public Collection<User> getUsers() {
    return userService.getAllUsers();
  }

  @RequestMapping(value = "/{id}", method = RequestMethod.GET)
  @ResponseBody
  public User getUser(@PathVariable("id") int identifier) {
    return userService.getUser(identifier);
  }
```

```
@RequestMapping(method = RequestMethod.POST)
@ResponseStatus(HttpStatus.CREATED)
public ResponseEntity<Void> postUser(@RequestBody User user,
    UriComponentsBuilder uriBuilder) {
  int identifier = userService.addUser(user);

  HttpHeaders httpHeaders = new HttpHeaders();
  String uri = UrlConstants.USERS_URL + "/{id}";
  UriComponents uriComponents =
      uriBuilder.path(uri).buildAndExpand(identifier);
  httpHeaders.setLocation(uriComponents.toUri());
  return new ResponseEntity<Void>(httpHeaders, HttpStatus.CREATED);
}

@RequestMapping(value = "/{id}", method = RequestMethod.PUT)
@ResponseStatus(HttpStatus.OK)
public void putUser(@PathVariable("id") int identifier, @RequestBody User user) {
  userService.updateOrAddUser(identifier, user);
}

@RequestMapping(value = "/{id}", method = RequestMethod.DELETE)
public void deleteUser(@PathVariable("id") int identifier) {
  userService.deleteUser(identifier);
}

@ExceptionHandler(UnsupportedOperationException.class)
public ResponseEntity<String> handleUnsupportedOperation(
    UnsupportedOperationException uoe) {
  return new ResponseEntity<String>(uoe.getMessage(), HttpStatus.BAD_REQUEST);
}
}
```

The @Controller annotation tells Spring that this class is handling HTTP requests. The @RequestMapping annotation maps this class to the base URI /users. In the constructor, we inject the UserService, which is the class from Listing 4-4.

The getUsers method is mapped to the HTTP GET method, because this is specified in its method-level @RequestMapping annotation. So getUsers will handle all GET requests for URI /users, because the value parameter is missing in the method-level @RequestMapping. Therefore, the basic URI specified in the class-level @RequestMapping annotation is used. The method itself reads all the User objects stored in UserService. The @ResponseBody annotation indicates that the return value should be serialized into HTTP transport format, which is a conversion from Collection<User> into a JSON array in this case. JSON is used by default because it is the most used transport format in HTTP messages nowadays. We will dive into an example that can narrow down this configuration later.

The second web method is getUser. As its name suggests, it should read a single user. Therefore, the consumer needs to specify which User object he is interested in. This is done via the URI parameter id specified as the parameter /{id} in the @RequestMapping annotation. The final URI mapping of this method will be /users/{id}, because the method-level @RequestMapping is combined with class level 1. With the help of the @PathVariable annotation, the placeholder value {id} from the URI is injected into the identifier parameter. The method reads the user based on the injected identifier and returns the User object. This object will be converted into JSON by default with the help of the @ResponseBody annotation.

The third method handling web requests is postUser. Similar to the getUsers method, postUser is mapped to the /users endpoint and handles the POST HTTP method. The HTTP message payload is converted into the User object. This is driven by the @RequestBody parameter annotation. The second parameter of this method is the UriComponentBuilder instance, which will help the user create the Location header to fulfill the HTTP contract, which indicates that the server should respond with the location of the created resource instance for the POST HTTP message. So the method creates the user, reads the created user identifier, creates the HTTP Location header, and constructs the response. To construct the HTTP response with a custom header and 201 Created HTTP status, we use the ResponseEntity<Void> Spring abstraction. The @ResponseStatus annotation also declaratively defines that the status of the response will always be 201 Created. The generic type Void is used to create the empty HTTP message body.

The putUser method handles the PUT HTTP method. The @ResponseStatus annotation ensures that it returns the HTTP status 200 OK, but only if no exception was thrown from underneath the logic. putUser uses the mentioned approaches to extract the identifier and user objects from the incoming request. The implementation calls the updateOrAddUser method of userService, which will create or replace the User object in our repository.

Next, the UserController method deletes the user. Again, we need to specify the ID of the user instance to delete it. The @RequestMapping annotation and placeholder mapping are similar to the getUser method. But in this case, we didn't need to specify the attribute of @PathVariable, because the name of the attribute is the same as the placeholder. The method doesn't return any value, which is by default translated into an HTTP response with an empty body and the status code 200 OK.

The last method represents an exception handler for all the UnsupportedOperationException errors. When such an error occurs and bubbles up to any of the @RequestMapping methods in UserController, this method would be invoked. This approach is useful for translating application exceptions into responses with specific HTTP status codes. In this case, we translated the UnsupportedOperationException into 400 Bad Request.

This example (0404-rest-boot-server) has the configuration file application.properties in the folder src/main/resources. There is only one configuration entry, server.port=10404, which tells Spring to bind the embedded Tomcat container to port 10404. Figure 4-6 shows the POST communication example, which uses DHC - REST/HTTP API Client again.

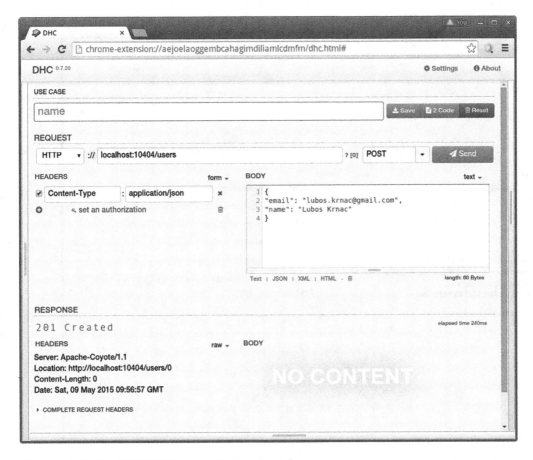

Figure 4-6. *Spring MVC POST communication example*

For the subsequent GET request for the resource /users/0, we get the output shown in Figure 4-7.

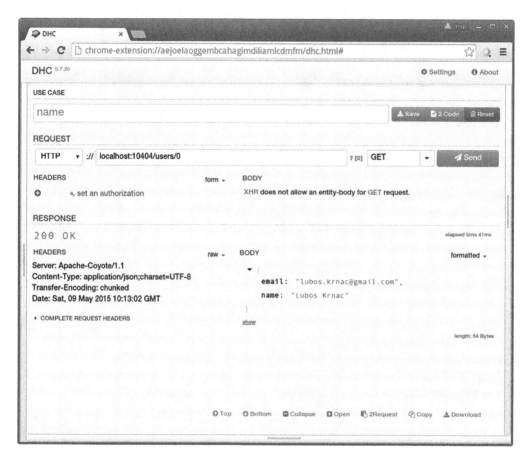

Figure 4-7. *Spring MVC valid GET communication example*

Next we explore the invalid GET request. If we try to read the resource /users/-1, UserRespository (from Listing 4-4), the system throws an UnsupportedOperationException. This exception is handled in UserController. handleUnsupportedOperation, because it is configured as @ExceptionHandler for the UnsupportedOperationException exception type. This is shown in Figure 4-8.

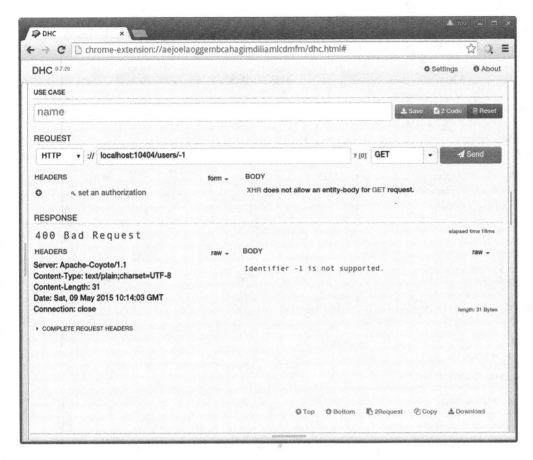

Figure 4-8. *Spring MVC invalid GET communication example*

Figures 4-9 and 4-10 show the PUT and DELETE requests and responses for our Spring MVC REST example.

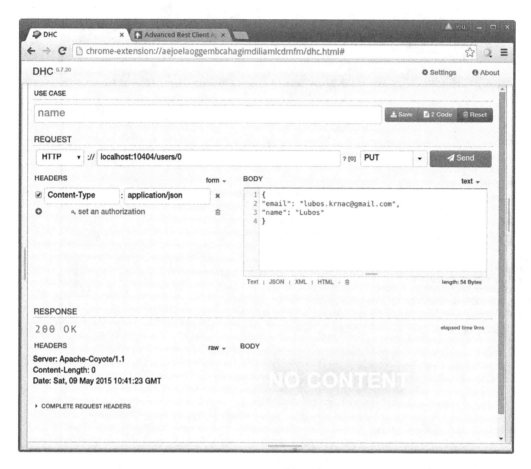

Figure 4-9. *Spring MVC PUT communication example*

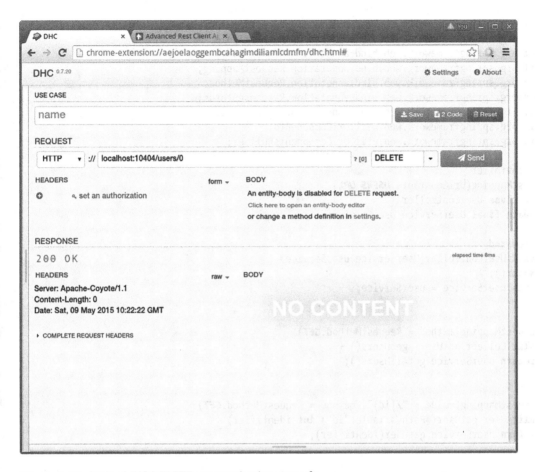

Figure 4-10. *Spring MVC DELETE communication example*

@RestController Example

Spring version 4.x introduced the new annotation @RestController. Use of this annotation is shown in Listing 4-17.

Listing 4-17. @RestController Example (0405-rest-restcontroller-server)

```
package net.lkrnac.book.eiws.chapter04.restcontroller;

import java.util.Collection;
import net.lkrnac.book.eiws.chapter04.UrlConstants;
import net.lkrnac.book.eiws.chapter04.model.User;
import net.lkrnac.book.eiws.chapter04.service.UserService;

import org.springframework.beans.factory.annotation.Autowired;
import org.springframework.http.HttpHeaders;
import org.springframework.http.HttpStatus;
import org.springframework.http.ResponseEntity;
```

```java
import org.springframework.web.bind.annotation.ExceptionHandler;
import org.springframework.web.bind.annotation.PathVariable;
import org.springframework.web.bind.annotation.RequestBody;
import org.springframework.web.bind.annotation.RequestMapping;
import org.springframework.web.bind.annotation.RequestMethod;
import org.springframework.web.bind.annotation.ResponseStatus;
import org.springframework.web.bind.annotation.RestController;
import org.springframework.web.util.UriComponents;
import org.springframework.web.util.UriComponentsBuilder;

@RestController
@RequestMapping(UrlConstants.USERS_URL)
public class UserController {
  private final UserService userService;

  @Autowired
  public UserController(UserService userService) {
    super();
    this.userService = userService;
  }

  @RequestMapping(method = RequestMethod.GET)
  public Collection<User> getUsers() {
    return userService.getAllUsers();
  }

  @RequestMapping(value = "/{id}", method = RequestMethod.GET)
  public User getUser(@PathVariable("id") int identifier) {
    return userService.getUser(identifier);
  }

  //remaining methods are the same as in Listing 4-16
  //...
}
```

If we compare this class to the controller in Listing 4-16, we would notice slight differences. The class is using the @RestController annotation instead of the @Controller annotation. The second difference is that we don't need to annotate return values from getUsers and getUser with the annotation @ResponseBody. By default, Spring MVC tries to find return values from the web methods view belonging to this controller. This is because Spring MVC was originally used for the Model-View-Controller style of web applications, where it also handles templating of views. As the functionality of the Spring MVC module was extended to handle REST concerns, we need to be able to specify that the return value should be converted into an HTTP payload.

So the @RestController annotation is a slight convenience shortcut for combining the @Controller and @ResponseBody annotations. But it significantly enhances the semantic characteristics of the web layer, because is clearly differentiates REST endpoints from MVC endpoints.

Spring MVC REST with Headers and Query Parameters

Let's shuffle our requirements a little bit and dive into Spring MVC mapping features:

- The first one was already mentioned in Listing 4-4, where we created the option to read users based on the interval of user identifiers.

- We want to version our REST API to be prepared for eventual breaking changes in the future. This version of the API will be stored in the HTTP header.

■ **Note** Versioning the REST API is a big topic, because it affects the API contract with the consumer and therefore needs to be carefully designed. The client can use various approaches to indicate the API version within the REST request: store the version in the URI, in the custom HTTP header, or in the content type. There is no clear winning approach because each has its advantages and disadvantages. This broad topic is beyond the scope of this book. In our example we used a custom header, because it allows us to highlight the Spring MVC HTTP header parsing and mapping features.

- The example covering these requirements would be more readable if it were split into various listings. The first part of this example is shown in Listing 4-18.

Listing 4-18. Initial Part of Spring MVC Example with Headers and Query Parameters (0406-rest-parameters-server)

```
package net.lkrnac.book.eiws.chapter04.parameters;

import java.util.Collection;
import java.util.List;
import net.lkrnac.book.eiws.chapter04.UrlConstants;
import net.lkrnac.book.eiws.chapter04.model.User;
import net.lkrnac.book.eiws.chapter04.service.UserService;
import org.springframework.beans.factory.annotation.Autowired;
import org.springframework.http.HttpHeaders;
import org.springframework.http.HttpStatus;
import org.springframework.http.MediaType;
import org.springframework.http.RequestEntity;
import org.springframework.http.ResponseEntity;
import org.springframework.web.bind.annotation.ExceptionHandler;
import org.springframework.web.bind.annotation.PathVariable;
import org.springframework.web.bind.annotation.RequestBody;
import org.springframework.web.bind.annotation.RequestHeader;
import org.springframework.web.bind.annotation.RequestMapping;
import org.springframework.web.bind.annotation.RequestMethod;
import org.springframework.web.bind.annotation.RequestParam;
import org.springframework.web.bind.annotation.RestController;
import org.springframework.web.util.UriComponents;
import org.springframework.web.util.UriComponentsBuilder;
```

```
@RestController
@RequestMapping(UrlConstants.USERS_URL)
public class UserController {
  private final UserService userService;

  @Autowired
  public UserController(UserService userService) {
    super();
    this.userService = userService;
  }

  @RequestMapping(value = "/{id}", method = RequestMethod.GET,
      produces = MediaType.APPLICATION_JSON_VALUE)
  public User getUser(@PathVariable("id") int identifier) {
    return userService.getUser(identifier);
  }
```

This listing shows the imports class signature with the constructor and method handling GET requests. Most of these constructs should already be familiar from previous examples. The only new element here is the new @RequestMapping attribute produces. It defines that the method will be mapped only to requests that expect a JSON response body format. This consumer's requirement involves HTTP content negotiation and is driven by the HTTP header Accept. The second part of the example is shown in Listing 4-19.

■ **Note**   Content negotiation is beyond the scope of this book. I suggest starting an investigation on this wiki page: https://en.wikipedia.org/wiki/Content_negotiation.

Listing 4-19. POST Part of Spring MVC Example with Headers and Query Parameters
(0406-rest-parameters-server)

```
@RequestMapping(method = RequestMethod.POST, consumes = MediaType.APPLICATION_JSON_VALUE,
    headers = "version=1")
public ResponseEntity<String> postUser(@RequestBody User user,
    UriComponentsBuilder uriBuilder,
    @RequestHeader(required = false) String version) {
  if ("1".equals(version)) {
    int identifier = userService.addUser(user);

    HttpHeaders httpHeaders = new HttpHeaders();
    String uri = UrlConstants.USERS_URL + "/{id}";
    UriComponents uriComponents =
        uriBuilder.path(uri).buildAndExpand(identifier);
    httpHeaders.setLocation(uriComponents.toUri());
    return new ResponseEntity<String>(httpHeaders, HttpStatus.CREATED);
  } else {
    return ResponseEntity.badRequest().body("Expected version is 1!");
  }
}
```

The @RequestMapping annotation has various attributes. The method attribute specifies the HTTP method that the annotated method is mapped to. The consumes attribute indicates that we are handling only JSON content. So the request must contain Content-Type: application/json in order to be routed to this method. The annotation attribute headers has the value version=1, which indicates that only requests with an API version equal to 1 will be routed to this logic.

postUser has three parameters. The first two, user and uriBuilder, were already covered in Listing 4-16. The last parameter, version, is annotated with @RequestHeader, which reads the HTTP header with the name version and injects it into this parameter.

The implementation verifies that the version of API is 1 and returns the HTTP status 400 Bad Request if not. If the version is 1, the implementation stores the User object and returns a response with the status 200 OK and the Location header. Checking the header in the implementation of the postUser method is not necessary, because the mapping annotation attribute headers is configured to consume only requests with version 1. But the code shows us how the @RequestHeader annotation can extract HTTP headers.

Listing 4-20 is the last piece of the Spring MVC server-side examples.

Listing 4-20. PUT and GET Interval Part of Spring MVC Example with Headers and Query Parameters (0406-rest-parameters-server)

```java
@RequestMapping(value = "/{id}", method = RequestMethod.PUT, headers = "version=1")
  public ResponseEntity<String> putUser(@PathVariable("id") int identifier,
      RequestEntity<User> request) {
    List<String> versions = request.getHeaders().get("version");
    boolean versionIsCorrect = versions != null && "1".equals(versions.get(0));
    if (versionIsCorrect) {
      userService.updateOrAddUser(identifier, request.getBody());
      return ResponseEntity.ok("");
    } else {
      return ResponseEntity.badRequest().body("Expected version is 1!");
    }
  }

  @RequestMapping(method = RequestMethod.GET, params = "lowerId",
      produces = MediaType.APPLICATION_JSON_VALUE)
  public Collection<User> getUsersInterval(@RequestParam int lowerId,
      @RequestParam("upperId") int upId) {
    return userService.getUsersInterval(lowerId, upId);
  }
}
```

The @RequestMapping annotation for the putUser method is annotated in a similar fashion as the putUser method from Listing 4-16. The difference is the headers attribute, which also ties this method to handle only requests with the HTTP header version: 1.

Parameters of the putUser method are also slightly different from Listing 4-16. Alongside the path variable extraction, there is also a new parameter called request of type RequestEntity<User>. This is the Spring representation of the HTTP request, where the body is marshaled into the type User. Spring converts the User type from the request body and wraps this object into RequestEntity<User> and injects it into the request parameter. We can use this object to inspect various attributes of the request, such as the HTTP method, headers, and URI.

In this case, we extracted the header version and used it to verify that the HTTP request with the correct version was routed into this logic. Again, such a check is not necessary, because the mapping based on headers="version-1" takes care of excluding other versions. But it shows an alternative to extracting the HTTP request metadata.

Testing Spring MVC REST APIs

Spring has a strong focus on testability. Because the Spring MVC is one of the most widely used Spring abstractions, it is of course not an exception. The concept behind testing the Spring MVC APIs is to perform fake HTTP requests to test the controller and verify the response. Even if this testing code is not running in a servlet container, the controller behaves the same way as it were registered to `DispatcherServlet`.

The central class of Spring MVC testing support is `org.springframework.test.web.servlet.MockMvc`. It is the final class used for sending fake requests and recording and verifying expected responses. With `MockMvc`, the developer doesn't need to create a lot of objects to fulfill complicated HTTP use cases, but rather can implement less-verbose chaining constructs.

perform

- The method defined in the class `org.springframework.test.web.servlet.MockMvc`

- Used for sending requests

- Uses the `MockMvcRequestBuilders` parameter as a helper for sending HTTP requests such as `GET`, `PUT`, `POST`, `PUT`, and `DELETE`

- The `MockMvcRequestBuilders` methods return helper `MockHttpServletRequestBuilder` for handling a wide-range of HTTP communication

  - HTTP headers

  - Content creation and negotiation

  - Query parameters

  - Encoding and locale handling

  - Session management (which is not targeted toward stateless REST)

andExpect

- Method defined in the interface `org.springframework.test.web.servlet.ResultActions`

- Provides support for chaining constructs during verification, because it also returns `ResultActions`

- Therefore, we can include as many expectations as needed for the following:

  - Verification of HTTP headers

  - Verification of the message body based on content parsing (for example, in XML/JSON format)

  - Verification of HTTP status code

andReturn

- Method defined in the interface `org.springframework.test.web.servlet.ResultActions`

- Provides support for returning the `MvcResult` object, which can be used for subsequent verifications outside the `andExpect` call chain

andDo

- Method in the interface `org.springframework.test.web.servlet.ResultActions`

- Uses `MockMvcResultHandlers.print()` for printing responses

MockMvc Instance Creation

The `MockMvc` instance can be created by the factory class `MockMvcBuilders` in two ways:

- Create the `MockMvc` instance based on Spring's context instance, `MockMvcBuilders.webAppContextSetup(WebApplicationContext context)`, which is handy for creating Spring integration tests. With this approach, we generally want to test Spring's configuration with all its dependencies together.

- Create the `MockMvc` instance based on one or more controller classes, `MockMvcBuilders.standaloneSetup(Object... controllers)`, which is handy for creating controller unit tests. This approach can test the controller or group of controllers in isolation by mocking their dependencies.

Spring testing support allows for extreme variability in our testing, but at the same time allows creation of a targeted unit or integration tests. We can have short tests focusing on important aspects of our HTTP REST communication. Such powerful support is missing for JAX-RS abstractions. This factor often simplifies the decision process when Spring MVC and JAX-RS abstractions are considered for REST-based projects.

MockMvc Integration Test Example

The Spring MVC integration test example for the application using the controller in Listing 4-16 is large, which makes it hard to present in one listing. Therefore, we split it. Listing 4-21 shows the imports and test class configuration.

Listing 4-21. Imports and Signature of REST Integration Test Example (0403-rest-java-config-server)

```
package net.lkrnac.book.eiws.chapter04;

import static org.springframework.test.web.servlet.request.MockMvcRequestBuilders.delete;
import static org.springframework.test.web.servlet.request.MockMvcRequestBuilders.get;
import static org.springframework.test.web.servlet.request.MockMvcRequestBuilders.post;
import static org.springframework.test.web.servlet.request.MockMvcRequestBuilders.put;
import static org.springframework.test.web.servlet.result.MockMvcResultHandlers.print;
import static org.springframework.test.web.servlet.result.MockMvcResultMatchers.content;
import static org.springframework.test.web.servlet.result.MockMvcResultMatchers.jsonPath;
import static org.springframework.test.web.servlet.result.MockMvcResultMatchers.status;
import static org.testng.Assert.assertEquals;
```

```
import org.springframework.beans.factory.annotation.Autowired;
import org.springframework.http.HttpStatus;
import org.springframework.http.MediaType;
import org.springframework.test.annotation.DirtiesContext;
import org.springframework.test.annotation.DirtiesContext.ClassMode;
import org.springframework.test.context.ContextConfiguration;
import org.springframework.test.context.testng.AbstractTestNGSpringContextTests;
import org.springframework.test.context.web.WebAppConfiguration;
import org.springframework.test.web.servlet.MockMvc;
import org.springframework.test.web.servlet.MvcResult;
import org.springframework.test.web.servlet.setup.MockMvcBuilders;
import org.springframework.web.context.WebApplicationContext;
import org.testng.annotations.BeforeMethod;
import org.testng.annotations.Test;

@WebAppConfiguration
@ContextConfiguration(classes = RestJavaConfigConfiguration.class)
@DirtiesContext(classMode = ClassMode.AFTER_EACH_TEST_METHOD)
public class RestApplicationContextTest extends
    AbstractTestNGSpringContextTests {

  private static final String FULL_USER_URL = "http://localhost:10403/users";
  private MockMvc mockMvc;

  @Autowired
  private WebApplicationContext webApplicationContext;

  @BeforeMethod
  public void init() {
    mockMvc = MockMvcBuilders.webAppContextSetup(webApplicationContext).build();
  }

  private static String createTestRecord(int identifier) {
    String testingRecordString =
        "{\"email\": \"user%d@gmail.com\", \"name\": \"User%d\"}";
    return String.format(testingRecordString, identifier, identifier,
        identifier);
  }
}
```

As you can see in the imports section, this example uses a lot of classes—primarily because of the variability that the Spring MVC test module provides. Design of this Spring module is not trivial. But as you will explore in subsequent examples, it is easy for developers to use. This is a good example of Spring's team member qualities. Testing HTTP possibilities is a complicated problem, but Spring solves it elegantly.

The test class is annotated by the WebAppConfiguration annotation, which indicates that we are using the WebApplicationContext implementation of the Spring ApplicationContext abstraction for testing. The ContextConfiguration annotation specifies which Spring configuration class is being tested.

By default, Spring keeps the testing context open in memory. So various tests can reuse the same context and speed up integration test suites by avoiding context initialization before each test. But remember that our UserService isn't truly stateless, and we don't want test methods affecting each other. Therefore, we need to initiate a fresh context for each method. This is ensured by the class-level annotation @DirtiesContext. By default, this annotation would create a Spring context from scratch for the whole test class. But with the ClassMode.AFTER_EACH_TEST_METHOD attribute, we initiate a new context for each test method.

The TestNG framework is used for testing. Therefore, for the Spring integration test, we need to use the AbstractTestNGSpringContextTests parent also provided by the Spring framework. The FULL_USER_URL constant enables test methods to not repeat the same String literal. The mockMvc variable is used in every test method for sending HTTP requests and verification.

Next, the class-level variable injects the Spring context instance created for the integration test. This instance is the one used by the application when running in the servlet container. The init method uses the MockMvcBuilders helper to initiate the mockMvc object before each test method, which is declared by the TestNG's BeforeMethod annotation.

The createTestRecord method helps us to create the JSON Spring representation of the user model used for sending requests. It will be used by various test methods in subsequent test example listings.

MockMvc Example for POST

Let's start with the POST version (see Listing 4-22).

Listing 4-22. Integration Testing HTTP POST (0403-rest-java-config-server)

```
@Test
public void testPost() throws Exception {
    // GIVEN
    String testingRecord = createTestRecord(0);

    // WHEN
    MvcResult mvcResult = mockMvc.perform(post(FULL_USER_URL)
        .contentType(MediaType.APPLICATION_JSON)
        .content(testingRecord))
        .andReturn();

    // THEN
    int httpStatus = mvcResult.getResponse().getStatus();
    assertEquals(httpStatus, HttpStatus.CREATED.value());
}
```

All testing methods are annotated with org.testng.annotations.Test, which marks the method as a test, similar to JUnit. In the method body, we create the testing record. Then we use the mockMvc class-level property to perform the POST operation against our URI. This is testing the URI mapping of the controller. We also use MockHttpServletRequestBuilder chaining for sending the JSON content type with the created JSON payload. This chained call will simulate the POST request against the controller in Listing 4-13. The result of this operation is stored in a local variable called mvcResult, which is used for retrieving and verifying the response status.

MockMvc Example for GET

The next test method covers testing of the GET request (see Listing 4-23).

Listing 4-23. Testing HTTP GET of Single Resource Instance (0403-rest-java-config-server)

```
@Test
public void testSingleGet() throws Exception {
  // GIVEN
  mockMvc.perform(post(FULL_USER_URL)
      .contentType(MediaType.APPLICATION_JSON)
      .content(createTestRecord(0)));

  // WHEN
  mockMvc.perform(get(FULL_USER_URL + "/{id}", 0)
      .accept(MediaType.APPLICATION_JSON)
    )

  // THEN
    .andDo(print())
    .andExpect(status().isOk())
    .andExpect(jsonPath("$.email").value("user0@gmail.com"))
    .andExpect(jsonPath("$.name").value("User0"));
}
```

At first, we use mockMvc to POST the testing record. This is needed because we use a clean sheet for each test method provided by the @DirtiesContext annotation. Testing the Spring context involves storing objects into UserService, so we need to POST the resource instance before testing GET. Next, the mockMvc call retrieves the testing resource instance. It specifies the URI with the identifier path variable and the Accept HTTP header to indicate that the client wants to consume JSON.

Then we chain-print the response to the console. Printing can be useful for troubleshooting purposes in case of continuous integration errors. The verification phase of the test is next. We make sure that the response status is correct and that the JSON payload contains the expected elements. The payload verification uses JSONPath Spring wrappers. JSONPath is a library for parsing the JSON payload. So it has to be on the classpath. This is another example of how Spring effectively uses third-party open source libraries to provide powerful APIs.

When we execute this test method, andDo(print()) prints the output shown in Listing 4-24.

Listing 4-24. The Results of Testing HTTP GET of Single Resource Instance (0403-rest-java-config-server)

```
MockHttpServletRequest:
        HTTP Method = GET
        Request URI = /users/0
         Parameters = {}
            Headers = {Accept=[application/json]}

            Handler:
               Type = net.lkrnac.book.eiws.chapter04.javaconfig.UserController
             Method = public net.lkrnac.book.eiws.chapter04.model.User net.lkrnac.book.
                      eiws.chapter04.javaconfig.UserController.getUser(int)
```

```
            Async:
  Was async started = false
        Async result = null

  Resolved Exception:
              Type = null

        ModelAndView:
          View name = null
               View = null
              Model = null

          FlashMap:

MockHttpServletResponse:
             Status = 200
      Error message = null
            Headers = {Content-Type=[application/json;charset=UTF-8]}
       Content type = application/json;charset=UTF-8
               Body = {"email":"user0@gmail.com","name":"User0"}
      Forwarded URL = null
     Redirected URL = null
            Cookies = []
```

Such output is handy for troubleshooting HTTP communication. The next method, in Listing 4-25, tests a multi GET request.

Listing 4-25. Integration Testing HTTP GET of Various Resource Instances (0403-rest-java-config-server)

```java
@Test
public void testMultiGet() throws Exception {
  // GIVEN
  mockMvc.perform(post(FULL_USER_URL)
      .contentType(MediaType.APPLICATION_JSON)
      .content(createTestRecord(0)));
  mockMvc.perform(post(FULL_USER_URL)
      .contentType(MediaType.APPLICATION_JSON)
      .content(createTestRecord(1)));

  // WHEN
  mockMvc.perform(get(FULL_USER_URL).accept(MediaType.APPLICATION_JSON))

  // THEN
    .andExpect(status().isOk())
    .andExpect(jsonPath("$[0].email").value("user0@gmail.com"))
    .andExpect(jsonPath("$[0].name").value("User0"))
    .andExpect(jsonPath("$[1].email").value("user1@gmail.com"))
    .andExpect(jsonPath("$[1].name").value("User1"));
}
```

Similar to the single GET test in Listing 4-23, we first POST the testing records. Then we use mockMvc to perform the GET method without the ID placeholder in the URI, which means we want to read all stored records. Then we use chained JSONPath verifications to ensure that the expected records were included in the response.

MockMvc Example for PUT

The PUT version is shown in Listing 4-26.

Listing 4-26. Integration Testing HTTP DELETE (0403-rest-java-config-server)

```
@Test
public void testPut() throws Exception {
  // GIVEN: test record

  // WHEN
  mockMvc.perform(put(FULL_USER_URL + "/0")
      .contentType(MediaType.APPLICATION_JSON)
      .content(createTestRecord(0)))

  // THEN
      .andExpect(status().isOk());
}
```

In this test, we send the PUT request to the URI /users/0 with the test record and expect the response 200 OK.

MockMvc Example for DELETE

The next part of the REST integration testing example covers HTTP DELETE. It is shown in Listing 4-27.

Listing 4-27. Integration Testing HTTP DELETE (0403-rest-java-config-server)

```
@Test
public void testDeleteUser() throws Exception {
  // GIVEN
  mockMvc.perform(post(FULL_USER_URL)
      .contentType(MediaType.APPLICATION_JSON)
      .content(createTestRecord(0)));

  // WHEN
  mockMvc.perform(delete(FULL_USER_URL + "/{id}", 0));

  // THEN
  mockMvc
      .perform(
          get(FULL_USER_URL + "/{id}", 0)
          .accept(MediaType.APPLICATION_JSON))
      .andExpect(status().isOk())
      .andExpect(content().string(""));
}
```

First, we post the testing record. Subsequently, we test the DELETE operation with the identifier path parameter. Next, the request against the controller is for verifying that the testing resource was deleted. We expect the body to be empty, because the null of the User object is translated into an empty string body.

MockMvc Negative Testing Example

MockMvc Spring constructs can be also used for negative testing, as shown in Listing 4-28.

Listing 4-28. Negative Integration REST Testing (0403-rest-java-config-server)

```
@Test
public void testClientError() throws Exception {
    // GIVEN

    // WHEN
    mockMvc.perform(get(FULL_USER_URL + "/{id}", -1)
        .accept(MediaType.APPLICATION_JSON)
      )

    // THEN
      .andExpect(status().isBadRequest())
      .andExpect(content().string("Identifier -1 is not supported."));
  }
}
```

We send the GET request to read /users/-1 resource. We know from Listing 4-16 that this user identifier should cause a 400 Bad Request response, which is verified accordingly.

This example highlights the abilities of the Spring MVC test module to perform integration tests against the whole application.

MockMvc Unit Test Example

It make also sense to test the Spring controller in isolation. Such unit testing is supported by the Spring MVC test module. The unit test example is split into various listings. The first part is shown in Listing 4-29.

Listing 4-29. Imports and Signature of REST Unit Test Example (0403-rest-java-config-server)

```
package net.lkrnac.book.eiws.chapter04;

import static org.mockito.Mockito.when;
import static org.springframework.test.web.servlet.request.MockMvcRequestBuilders.delete;
import static org.springframework.test.web.servlet.request.MockMvcRequestBuilders.get;
import static org.springframework.test.web.servlet.request.MockMvcRequestBuilders.post;
import static org.springframework.test.web.servlet.request.MockMvcRequestBuilders.put;
import static org.springframework.test.web.servlet.result.MockMvcResultHandlers.print;
import static org.springframework.test.web.servlet.result.MockMvcResultMatchers.content;
import static org.springframework.test.web.servlet.result.MockMvcResultMatchers.jsonPath;
import static org.springframework.test.web.servlet.result.MockMvcResultMatchers.status;
import static org.testng.Assert.assertEquals;
import java.util.ArrayList;
import java.util.Collection;
```

```
import net.lkrnac.book.eiws.chapter04.javaconfig.UserController;
import net.lkrnac.book.eiws.chapter04.model.User;
import net.lkrnac.book.eiws.chapter04.service.UserService;
import org.mockito.Mockito;
import org.springframework.http.HttpStatus;
import org.springframework.http.MediaType;
import org.springframework.test.web.servlet.MockMvc;
import org.springframework.test.web.servlet.MvcResult;
import org.springframework.test.web.servlet.setup.MockMvcBuilders;
import org.testng.annotations.Test;

public class UserControllerTest {
  private static final String DUMMY_ERROR_TEXT = "dummyErrorText";
  private static final int TESTING_ID = 0;
  private static final String FULL_USER_URL = "http://localhost:10403/users";

  private static User createTestUser(int identifier) {
    User user = new User();
    user.setEmail("user" + identifier + "@gmail.com");
    user.setName("User" + identifier);
    return user;
  }

  private static String createTestRecord(int identifier) {
    String testingRecordString =
        "{\"email\": \"user%d@gmail.com\", \"name\": \"User%d\"}";
    return String.format(testingRecordString, identifier, identifier,
        identifier);
  }
```

The TestNG unit test doesn't need to have any class-level annotations or Spring annotations. First, we declare constants for the repetitive literals. The createTestUser method creates an instance of the User object for testing, and the createTestRecord method creates a similar representation in plain JSON format.

MockMvc Example for POST

The test method in Listing 4-30 covers testing the POST request.

Listing 4-30. Unit Testing HTTP POST (0403-rest-java-config-server)

```
@Test
public void testPost() throws Exception {
  // GIVEN
  UserService userService = Mockito.mock(UserService.class);
  UserController userController = new UserController(userService);
  MockMvc mockMvc = MockMvcBuilders.standaloneSetup(userController).build();

  User testingUser = createTestUser(TESTING_ID);
  Mockito.when(userService.addUser(testingUser)).thenReturn(TESTING_ID);
```

```
// WHEN
MvcResult mvcResult = mockMvc.perform(post(FULL_USER_URL)
    .contentType(MediaType.APPLICATION_JSON)
    .content(createTestRecord(0)))
    .andReturn();

// THEN
int httpStatus = mvcResult.getResponse().getStatus();
assertEquals(httpStatus, HttpStatus.CREATED.value());

Mockito.verify(userService).addUser(testingUser);
Mockito.verifyNoMoreInteractions(userService);
}
```

The UserService mock is needed for verification of POST behavior in our controller. As the constructor injection is used for autowiring the UserController's dependencies, we just need to create a testing object via its constructor and pass in the UserService mock via the constructor's parameter. When we have our testing instance of UserController configured, we can create MockMvc based on the userController instance. This also helps test declarative annotation mappings of the controller.

Later in the test preparation phase, we record the desired behavior in the userService mock. In this case, we create a test User object and use it as a parameter for the userService.addUser() call. This call should return the identifier of the stored record assigned by the service.

The next statement performs the POST request in a similar way as in the integration test in Listing 4-22, with the content type JSON and payload created by the helper method createTestRecord. This fake POST request returns the MvcResult instance.

In the verification phase of the test, we make sure that the correct HTTP status code was returned and that interactions on the userService are as expected. An interesting verification is verifyNoMoreInteractions, which makes sure that there wasn't anything unexpected performed against our userService mock.

MockMvc Example for GET

Unit testing of a single GET is shown in Listing 4-31.

Listing 4-31. Unit Testing of Single GET (0403-rest-java-config-server)

```
@Test
public void testSingleGet() throws Exception {
    // GIVEN
    UserService userService = Mockito.mock(UserService.class);
    UserController userController = new UserController(userService);
    MockMvc mockMvc = MockMvcBuilders.standaloneSetup(userController).build();

    User testingUser = createTestUser(TESTING_ID);
    Mockito.when(userService.getUser(TESTING_ID)).thenReturn(testingUser);

    // WHEN
    mockMvc.perform(get(FULL_USER_URL + "/{id}", 0)
        .accept(MediaType.APPLICATION_JSON)
    )
```

```
    // THEN
      .andDo(print())
      .andExpect(status().isOk())
      .andExpect(jsonPath("$.email").value("user0@gmail.com"))
      .andExpect(jsonPath("$.name").value("User0"));
}
```

For a simple GET test, we also create the userService mock, and create the controller and MockMvc instance. The difference is in the expected behavior recorded in the userService mock. In this case, we expect to return the User object based on a given identifier. Sending a GET request and verification is the same as for the single GET integration test in Listing 4-23. Next, Listing 4-32 shows multi GET unit testing.

In this case, we can't use Mockito.verifyNoMoreInteractions(userService) for verification, because we're using a technique called *stubbing*. This means that we recorded the behavior of the userService. getUser(TESTING_ID) call into the mock. But we didn't verify that it really happened, because we verified the desired return value via andExpect verifications. Mockito keeps track of verifications, and in this case we have one unverified interaction. This is the reason we can't use Mockito.verifyNoMoreInteractions(userS ervice); otherwise, the test would fail.

Listing 4-32. Unit Testing of Multi GET (0403-rest-java-config-server)

```
@Test
public void testMultiGet() throws Exception {
    // GIVEN
    UserService userService = Mockito.mock(UserService.class);
    UserController userController = new UserController(userService);
    MockMvc mockMvc = MockMvcBuilders.standaloneSetup(userController).build();

    Collection<User> testingUsers = new ArrayList<>();
    testingUsers.add(createTestUser(TESTING_ID));
    testingUsers.add(createTestUser(1));
    Mockito.when(userService.getAllUsers()).thenReturn(testingUsers);

    // WHEN
    mockMvc.perform(get(FULL_USER_URL).accept(MediaType.APPLICATION_JSON))

    // THEN
      .andExpect(status().isOk())
      .andExpect(jsonPath("$[0].email").value("user0@gmail.com"))
      .andExpect(jsonPath("$[0].name").value("User0"))
      .andExpect(jsonPath("$[1].email").value("user1@gmail.com"))
      .andExpect(jsonPath("$[1].name").value("User1"));
}
```

Creation of the mock, controller, and mockMvc is similar to the previous examples. This UserService mock should return a collection of all testing records. Sending the request and verification was used the same way in the integration test.

We didn't use Mockito.verifyNoMoreInteractions(userService) for the same reason as in Listing 4-31.

MockMvc Example for PUT

Listing 4-33 shows the PUT version.

Listing 4-33. Unit Testing of PUT (0403-rest-java-config-server)

```java
@Test
public void testPut() throws Exception {
  // GIVEN
  UserService userService = Mockito.mock(UserService.class);
  UserController userController = new UserController(userService);
  MockMvc mockMvc = MockMvcBuilders.standaloneSetup(userController).build();

  User testingUser = createTestUser(TESTING_ID);

  // WHEN
  MvcResult mvcResult = mockMvc.perform(put(FULL_USER_URL + "/" + TESTING_ID)
      .contentType(MediaType.APPLICATION_JSON)
      .content(createTestRecord(0)))
      .andReturn();

  // THEN
  int httpStatus = mvcResult.getResponse().getStatus();
  assertEquals(httpStatus, HttpStatus.OK.value());

  Mockito.verify(userService).updateOrAddUser(TESTING_ID, testingUser);
  Mockito.verifyNoMoreInteractions(userService);
}
```

MockMvc Example for DELETE

The last unit test method, shown in Listing 4-34, is for DELETE.

Listing 4-34. Unit Testing HTTP DELETE (0403-rest-java-config-server)

```java
@Test
public void testDeleteUser() throws Exception {
  // GIVEN
  UserService userService = Mockito.mock(UserService.class);
  UserController userController = new UserController(userService);
  MockMvc mockMvc = MockMvcBuilders.standaloneSetup(userController).build();

  // WHEN
  mockMvc.perform(delete(FULL_USER_URL + "/{id}", 0));

  // THEN
  Mockito.verify(userService).deleteUser(TESTING_ID);
  Mockito.verifyNoMoreInteractions(userService);
}
```

To test DELETE, we need to make sure that the controller called userService.deleteUser() with the correct identifier as a parameter. Therefore, we don't need to record any behavior into the mock in this case. The behavior of the code under test is recorded in the mock instance, and it is enough to verify the UserService call. We also verify that there aren't any unexpected interactions with the userService mock.

MockMvc Negative Testing Example

Listing 4-35 shows the negative tsting example.

Listing 4-35. Negative Unit Testing (0403-rest-java-config-server)

```
@Test
  public void testClientError() throws Exception {
    // GIVEN
    UserService userService = Mockito.mock(UserService.class);
    UserController userController = new UserController(userService);
    MockMvc mockMvc = MockMvcBuilders.standaloneSetup(userController).build();

    when(userService.getUser(-1))
      .thenThrow(new UnsupportedOperationException(DUMMY_ERROR_TEXT));

    // WHEN
    mockMvc.perform(get(FULL_USER_URL + "/{id}", -1)
        .accept(MediaType.APPLICATION_JSON)
      )

    // THEN
      .andExpect(status().isBadRequest())
      .andExpect(content().string(DUMMY_ERROR_TEXT));
  }
}
```

The last server unit test shows a possible approach to testing error conditions of the server REST code. We create userController with the userService mock as a parameter again. Then we record in the userService mock to throw an exception when the consumer asks for identifier -1.

After performing the expected request with the -1 identifier in the URI, we expect the response to have the status 400 Bad Request and a dummy error message.

Consuming REST

So far, we have focused on the server side of REST communication. But Spring also supports client-side access from the Java client application. The main class for client access to REST services is org.springframework.web.client.RestTemplate. You should create its instance via the constructor. It contains methods for performing all the REST-related HTTP methods, as shown in Table 4-1.

Table 4-1. *RestTemplate Methods*

HTTP Method	RestTemplate Method	Explanation
DELETE	delete	Delete objects based on a given URI.
POST	postForLocation	Post object and read location of it.
	postForObject	Post object and expect its instance as a response.
	postForEntity	Post object and expect a response of ResponseEntity<T> type. Generic type T is the type of the response payload.
HEAD	headForHeaders	Read headers based on a given URL and return the HttpHeaders object.
GET	getForObject	Read the object based on a given URL.
	getForEntity	Read the ResponseEntity<T> instance based on a given URI. Generic type T is the type of the response payload.
OPTIONS	optionsForAllow	Return the value of the Allow header for a given URI.
PUT	put	Perform the PUT of a given object against a given URI.
Any HTTP method	exchange	Perform any HTTP method against a server and exchange HttpEntity<T> and ResponseEntity<T> instances.

For most of these methods, marshaling and unmarshalling is needed. RestTemplate abstracts out the marshalling libraries and provides a conversion directly into/from Java types. For this purpose, it uses message converters for major formats such as JSON, XML, GSON, and RSS. It is also able to detect converter libraries such as Jackson, JAXB, GSON, and Rome on the classpath and to register appropriate converters automatically.

If built-in converters are not enough, we can register custom converters with the RestTemplate.setMessageConverters(List<HttpMessageConverter<?>>) method. When there are various converters, RestTemplate uses the first appropriate one for the given content type. Such behavior enables handling content negotiation without much effort.

The last notable feature of the RestTemplate class is error handling. By default, the class translates server (HTTP status codes 5*xx*) and client (HTTP status codes 4*xx*) errors into checked exceptions on the client by default. But if we don't want this behavior, we can override the error handler with our implementation by using RestTemplate.setErrorHandler(ResponseErrorHandler).

We are going to explore basic use of this class in an example. But first we need to show the configuration of the client application in Listing 4-36.

Listing 4-36. Configuration of Client-Side Application (0404-rest-boot-client)

```
package net.lkrnac.book.eiws.chapter04.client;

import org.springframework.context.annotation.Bean;
import org.springframework.context.annotation.ComponentScan;
import org.springframework.context.annotation.Configuration;
import org.springframework.web.client.RestTemplate;

@Configuration
@ComponentScan
```

```java
public class ClientConfiguration {
  @Bean
  public RestTemplate restTemplate() {
    return new RestTemplate();
  }
}
```

The @Configuration and @ComponentScan annotations are standard for Spring. They declare the Spring configuration class that should perform a component scan for the current package and its subpackages. We register just one bean here, and that is the RestTemplate instance used for sending and receiving HTTP messages to the server. We register it in the configuration class as a separate bean because it will help us with testing in later examples. Listing 4-37 shows use of this REST client bean.

Listing 4-37. RestTemplate (0404-rest-boot-client)

```java
package net.lkrnac.book.eiws.chapter04.client;

import java.net.URI;
import java.net.URISyntaxException;
import java.util.Arrays;
import java.util.List;
import net.lkrnac.book.eiws.chapter04.model.User;
import org.springframework.beans.factory.annotation.Autowired;
import org.springframework.http.HttpMethod;
import org.springframework.http.RequestEntity;
import org.springframework.http.ResponseEntity;
import org.springframework.stereotype.Component;
import org.springframework.web.client.RestTemplate;

@Component
public class UsersClient {
  private static final String URL = "http://localhost:10404/users";
  private RestTemplate restTemplate;

  @Autowired
  public UsersClient(RestTemplate restTemplate) {
    super();
    this.restTemplate = restTemplate;
  }

  public URI createUser(User user) {
    return restTemplate.postForLocation(URL, user);
  }

  public User getUser(int identifier) {
    return restTemplate.getForObject(URL + "/" + identifier, User.class);
  }

  public List<User> getUsers() {
    User[] usersArray = restTemplate.getForObject(URL, User[].class);
    return Arrays.asList(usersArray);
  }
```

```
  public void updateOrCreateUser(int identifier, User user) {
    restTemplate.put(URL + "/" + identifier, user);
  }

  public void deleteUser(int identifier) {
    restTemplate.delete(URL + "/" + identifier);
  }

  public User getUserExchange(int identifier) throws URISyntaxException {
    RequestEntity<Void> request =
        new RequestEntity<Void>(HttpMethod.GET, new URI(URL + "/" + identifier));
    ResponseEntity<User> response = restTemplate.exchange(request, User.class);
    return response.getBody();
  }
}
```

The Component annotation marks this class as a Spring bean so it can be component scanned. The url constant defines the address of the REST server. Then we define the restTemplate property, which is used for constructor injection of the bean registered in Listing 4-36.

The createUser method uses the restTemplate.postForLocation call to perform a POST request against our REST server. In this call, we pass in the User object to be converted into the JSON payload of the message. The return value from this call is the URI object, which was returned from the server as the Location header of the created resource instance.

The getUser method performs the GET request for the concrete resource instance. The call restTemplate.getForObject takes two parameters: the URL of the resource to read, and the type that the response payload will be converted into. The created POJO is returned as the return value.

The getUsers method performs a GET request also, but in this case we read all the resource instances and convert the response payload into a collection of User objects. The restTemplate.getForObject call can handle only arrays, because the collection has a generic type, and it is impossible for the Spring framework to figure out this generic type because it is erased on runtime. So if we would like Spring to convert it into a List.class type, it can't cast it to List<User>.

The updateOrCreateUser method does exactly what its name suggests, based on a given identifier and User object. identifier is parsed from the URI, and user is converted from the HTTP request body.

The deleteUser method fires the DELETE request of the resource identified by the given identifier.

Finally, we use the RestTemplate.exchange call in the getUserExchange method. It effectively has same result as the getUser method. But it highlights how we can use RestTemplate to cover more-generic HTTP communication, where the HTTP method is passed as a parameter. We also need to pass a representation of the HTTP request of type RequestEntity<Void> as a parameter. The generic type Void represents the type of the body. Obviously, this means that the GET request doesn't have a body. As a return value, we receive from the server Spring's representation of the HTTP response of type ResponseEntity<User>. The generic type User again represents the type that the body of the message would be converted into.

If any of these methods receive HTTP status 4xx or 5xx, RestTemplate will throw an unchecked exception, which would penetrate into the code using this UserClient bean.

Custom Error Handler

By default, Spring translates 4xx HTTP status codes into HttpClientErrorException and 5xx status codes into HttpServerErrorException. Both are unchecked exceptions. We don't need to handle such exceptions explicitly, because they are children of RuntimeException.

But sometimes this default RestTemplate error-handling behavior might not fit our requirements. Fortunately, we can easily change the default exception handling and register a custom error handler with the RestTemplate.setErrorHandler call.

To explore it's use, let's pretend that we must translate all server errors into our custom exception. This example is shown in Listing 4-38.

Listing 4-38. Custom Exception (0406-rest-errorhandler-client)

```
package net.lkrnac.book.eiws.chapter04.client;

public class CustomException extends RuntimeException {
  private static final long serialVersionUID = 1L;

  public CustomException(String message) {
    super(message);
  }
}
```

We extend CustomException from RuntimeException to have the exception unchecked, as it is good Java practice. The constructor takes the error message and calls the parent constructor with the message parameter also. This is the simplest example of a custom application-specific exception. Configuration of the RestTemplate bean is shown in Listing 4-39.

Listing 4-39. Custom Error Handler for RestTemplate (0406-rest-errorhandler-client)

```
package net.lkrnac.book.eiws.chapter04.client;

import java.io.IOException;
import org.springframework.context.annotation.Bean;
import org.springframework.context.annotation.ComponentScan;
import org.springframework.context.annotation.Configuration;
import org.springframework.http.HttpStatus;
import org.springframework.http.client.ClientHttpResponse;
import org.springframework.web.client.ResponseErrorHandler;
import org.springframework.web.client.RestTemplate;

@Configuration
@ComponentScan
public class ClientConfiguration {
  @Bean
  public RestTemplate restTemplate() {
    RestTemplate restTemplate = new RestTemplate();
    restTemplate.setErrorHandler(new ResponseErrorHandler() {

      @Override
      public boolean hasError(ClientHttpResponse response) throws IOException {
        HttpStatus statusCode = response.getStatusCode();
        return statusCode.is5xxServerError();
      }
```

```
    @Override
    public void handleError(ClientHttpResponse response) throws IOException {
      throw new CustomException(response.getStatusText());
    }
  });
  return restTemplate;
  }
}
```

This time, we don't just create the RestTemplate instance with all the default dependencies. We use the RestTemplate.setErrorHandler method to implement our own custom error handler. This implementation is wrapped into an anonymous inner class of type ResponseErrorHandler.

Because the anonymous inner class is of type ResponseErrorHandler, it must implement two methods. The hasError method should indicate whether the ClientHttpResponse instance is erroneous. As this is our custom implementation, we should decide when the response should trigger an error. In this case, we decide to throw an exception when the HTTP response indicates server error 5xx.

The second method of the custom error handler is handleError. This one is designed to perform the desired action when an error happens. In this case, we want to throw our CustomException with the error message received from the server.

Client-Side Testing

The great testability story of the Spring Framework is also provided for the REST client-side code. The concept is to create a fake server based on the RestTemplate instance used for the REST client code. This mock server records expected requests and sends fake responses to the client-side code under test. The fake server is represented by the class org.springframework.test.web.client.MockRestServiceServer.

An instance of the mock server is created by the MockRestServiceServer.createServer factory method, which takes the RestTemplate bean as a parameter. It has to be the same RestTemplate instance as used for performing the REST request in the code under test.

MockRestServiceServer has two methods, expect and verify, which are used for testing. The expect method records the expected behavior in the fake server. It is used for chaining the request expectations and recording the expected response that will be returned to the testing client logic. expect returns instances of the ResponseActions interface, which provide two methods:

- andExpect

  - Takes org.springframework.test.web.client.RequestMatcher as a parameter, which allows for recording expected content, headers, the HTTP method, and URI.

  - org.springframework.test.web.client.match.MockRestRequestMatchers is the abstract class containing the factory methods requestTo, header, content, jsonPath, xpath, and anything that produces instances of RequestMatcher and can be used for constructing comprehensive request expectations.

- andRespond

  - Takes org.springframework.test.web.client.ResponseActions as a parameter, which allows for defining content, HTTP status, and headers for the response.

  - org.springframework.test.web.client.response.MockRestResponseCreators is an abstract class containing the factory methods withSuccess, withCreatedEntity, withNoContent, withBadRequest, withUnauthorizedRequest, withServerError, and withStatus that produce instances of ResponseCreators and can be used for recording comprehensive HTTP responses in the fake server.

The verify method is used to verify the behavior recorded by the expect method.

The example of this client-side testing concept is split into various listings to enhance readability. First, Listing 4-40 shows the imports, constants, and properties of the test.

Listing 4-40. First Part of Client-Side Test (0404-rest-boot-client)

```
package net.lkrnac.book.eiws.chapter04.client;

import static org.hamcrest.Matchers.is;
import static org.springframework.test.web.client.match.MockRestRequestMatchers.jsonPath;
import static org.springframework.test.web.client.match.MockRestRequestMatchers.method;
import static org.springframework.test.web.client.match.MockRestRequestMatchers.requestTo;
import static org.springframework.
        test.web.client.response.MockRestResponseCreators.withBadRequest;
import static org.springframework.
        test.web.client.response.MockRestResponseCreators.withCreatedEntity;
import static org.springframework.
        test.web.client.response.MockRestResponseCreators.withSuccess;
import static org.testng.Assert.assertEquals;
import java.net.URI;
import java.util.List;
import net.lkrnac.book.eiws.chapter04.model.User;
import org.springframework.beans.factory.annotation.Autowired;
import org.springframework.http.HttpMethod;
import org.springframework.http.MediaType;
import org.springframework.test.context.ContextConfiguration;
import org.springframework.test.context.testng.AbstractTestNGSpringContextTests;
import org.springframework.test.web.client.MockRestServiceServer;
import org.springframework.web.client.HttpClientErrorException;
import org.springframework.web.client.RestTemplate;
import org.testng.annotations.BeforeMethod;
import org.testng.annotations.Test;

@ContextConfiguration(classes = ClientConfiguration.class)
public class RestClientBootApplicationTest extends
    AbstractTestNGSpringContextTests {
  private static final String USER0_NAME = "User0";
  private static final String USER0_EMAIL = "user0@gmail.com";
  private static final String TEST_RECORD0 = "{\"email\": \"" + USER0_EMAIL
      + "\", \"name\": \"" + USER0_NAME + "\"}";
  private static final String TEST_RECORD1 = "{\"email\": "
      + "\"user1@gmail.com\", \"name\": \"User1\"}";
  private static final String USERS_URL = "http://localhost:10404/users";

  private MockRestServiceServer mockServer;

  @Autowired
  private RestTemplate restTemplate;

  @Autowired
  private UsersClient usersClient;
```

```
@BeforeMethod
public void init() {
  mockServer = MockRestServiceServer.createServer(restTemplate);
}
```

The ContextConfiguration annotation specifies which Spring configuration will be used for testing. In this case, we test the client side from Listing 4-37. The test class is extended from AbstractTestNGSpringContextTests, which is the Spring helper for TestNG integration testing.

In the test class, we first specify a few constants that will be used during testing, including two string payloads for representing the resource JSON representations. Two injected properties follow; one is restTemplate, created in the configuration class in Listing 4-37. The second injected bean is our testing client code UsersClient.

The fake server instance is declared in the mockServer variable and initiated in the init method by the MockRestServiceServer.createServer(restTemplate) call. Listing 4-41 shows testing of the POST request.

Listing 4-41. Client -Side POST Test (0404-rest-boot-client)

```
@Test
public void testPost() throws Exception {
  // GIVEN
  URI expectedUri = new URI(USERS_URL + "/0");
  mockServer.expect(requestTo(USERS_URL))
    .andExpect(method(HttpMethod.POST))
    .andExpect(jsonPath("$.email", is(USER0_EMAIL)))
    .andExpect(jsonPath("$.name", is(USER0_NAME)))
    .andRespond(withCreatedEntity(expectedUri));

  User user = new User();
  user.setName(USER0_NAME);
  user.setEmail(USER0_EMAIL);

  // WHEN
  URI location = usersClient.createUser(user);

  // THEN
  assertEquals(location, expectedUri);
  mockServer.verify();
}
```

First, we create the testing URI. Then we use mockServer to record the URI with the payload and HTTP method of the expected request message. We also record the fake server response with the location header and success HTTP status code. MockRestResponseCreators.withCreatedEntity is designed to simulate response 201 Created and send back the Location header. That is why you would see this construct mostly for testing POST requests.

Creation of the testing User object follows. This object is posted to the fake server by the testing logic usersClient.createUser. After we have set up for the test, we can execute this testing logic. It should return the URI location of the created object.

In the verification phase of the test, we compare the returned location with the expected one. We also need to use mockServer.verify() to make sure that the recorded request occurred as expected. The test in Listing 4-42 covers a single GET.

Listing 4-42. Client-Side Single GET Test (0404-rest-boot-client)

```
@Test
public void testSingleGet() throws Exception {
  // GIVEN
  int testingIdentifier = 0;
  mockServer.expect(requestTo(USERS_URL + "/" + testingIdentifier))
    .andExpect(method(HttpMethod.GET))
    .andRespond(withSuccess(TEST_RECORD0, MediaType.APPLICATION_JSON));

  // WHEN
  User user = usersClient.getUser(testingIdentifier);

  // THEN
  mockServer.verify();
  assertEquals(user.getName(), USER0_NAME);
  assertEquals(user.getEmail(), USER0_EMAIL);
}
```

The expected GET request against the URI /users/0 is recorded into the fake server. We also send back a JSON representation of the object belonging to the testing identifier 0. The testing logic usersClient.getUser should return the User object for the given testing identifier.

In the verification phase, we verify that the request was sent properly from the testing logic and also verify that the received object contains the fields we expect. Listing 4-43 tests GET of multiple records.

Listing 4-43. Client-Side Multi GET Test (0404-rest-boot-client)

```
@Test
public void testMultiGet() throws Exception {
  // GIVEN
  mockServer.expect(requestTo(USERS_URL))
    .andExpect(method(HttpMethod.GET))
    .andRespond(withSuccess("[ " + TEST_RECORD0 + ", " + TEST_RECORD1 + "]",
        MediaType.APPLICATION_JSON));

  // WHEN
  List<User> users = usersClient.getUsers();

  // THEN
  mockServer.verify();
  assertEquals(users.get(0).getName(), USER0_NAME);
  assertEquals(users.get(0).getEmail(), USER0_EMAIL);
  assertEquals(users.get(1).getName(), "User1");
  assertEquals(users.get(1).getEmail(), "user1@gmail.com");
}
```

We expect the GET request against the /users URI. The fake response is a JSON array of two records. The testing logic (usersClient.getUsers) doesn't take any parameters in this case. But it should return a collection of all User objects. *All* is, in this case, the two objects we sent in the fake JSON response.

Verification again includes a request check. Finally, we verify that the returned collection contains the expected User objects. Listing 4-44 tests for PUT method.

Listing 4-44. Client-Side PUT Test (0404-rest-boot-client)

```
@Test
public void testPut() throws Exception {
  // GIVEN
  mockServer.expect(requestTo(USERS_URL + "/0"))
    .andExpect(method(HttpMethod.PUT))
    .andExpect(jsonPath("$.email", is(USER0_EMAIL)))
    .andExpect(jsonPath("$.name", is(USER0_NAME)))
    .andRespond(withSuccess());

  User user = new User();
  user.setName(USER0_NAME);
  user.setEmail(USER0_EMAIL);

  // WHEN
  usersClient.updateOrCreateUser(0, user);

  // THEN
  mockServer.verify();
}
```

Similar to previous tests, we expect a PUT request with particular content in the request body against /users/0 URI. The expected response of the fake server is 200 OK.

The method under test is UsersClient.updateOrCreateUser. The identifier and User object are passed to the testing method as parameters.

At the end of the test, we need to call mockServer.verify, to make sure that the client logic behaves as we expect. Next, Listing 4-45 contains the HTTP DELETE client test.

Listing 4-45. Client-Side DELETE Test (0404-rest-boot-client)

```
@Test
public void testDeleteUser() throws Exception {
  // GIVEN
  //@formatter:off
  int testingIdentifier = 1;
  mockServer.expect(requestTo(USERS_URL + "/" + testingIdentifier))
    .andExpect(method(HttpMethod.DELETE))
    .andRespond(withSuccess());
  //@formatter:on

  // WHEN
  usersClient.deleteUser(testingIdentifier);

  // THEN
  mockServer.verify();
}
```

The recorded request in mockServer is now DELETE against the URI /users/0. The fake response is sent back with HTTP status 200 OK. The testing logic should remove the User object with ID 0. The verification phase checks that the request was sent according to our expectations.

The last test method in this integration test is testing error handling, in Listing 4-46.

Listing 4-46. Client-Side Error-Handling Test (0404-rest-boot-client)

```java
@Test(expectedExceptions = HttpClientErrorException.class)
  public void testClientError() throws Exception {
    // GIVEN
    //@formatter:off
    int testingIdentifier = -1;
    mockServer.expect(requestTo(USERS_URL + "/" + testingIdentifier))
      .andExpect(method(HttpMethod.GET))
      .andRespond(
          withBadRequest()
          .body("Identifier -1 is not supported.")
      );
    //@formatter:on

    // WHEN
    usersClient.getUser(testingIdentifier);

    // THEN
    mockServer.verify();
  }
}
```

We expect the GET request against the /users/-1 resource URI, and the response should be 400 Bad Request. After calling the testing method getUser, we expect HttpClientErrorException to be thrown.

Such testing can also be used for unit testing; the testing methods would be almost exactly the same. The only difference is in the construction of the testing object and class signature. This unit test is shown in Listing 4-47.

Listing 4-47. Client-Side Unit Test Signature (0404-rest-boot-client)

```java
package net.lkrnac.book.eiws.chapter04.client;

import static org.hamcrest.Matchers.is;
import static org.springframework.test.web.client.match.MockRestRequestMatchers.jsonPath;
import static org.springframework.test.web.client.match.MockRestRequestMatchers.method;
import static org.springframework.test.web.client.match.MockRestRequestMatchers.requestTo;
import static org.springframework.
        test.web.client.response.MockRestResponseCreators.withBadRequest;
import static org.springframework.
        test.web.client.response.MockRestResponseCreators.withCreatedEntity;
import static org.springframework.
        test.web.client.response.MockRestResponseCreators.withSuccess;
import static org.testng.Assert.assertEquals;
import java.net.URI;
import java.util.List;
import net.lkrnac.book.eiws.chapter04.model.User;
import org.springframework.http.HttpMethod;
import org.springframework.http.MediaType;
import org.springframework.test.web.client.MockRestServiceServer;
import org.springframework.web.client.HttpClientErrorException;
```

```java
import org.springframework.web.client.RestTemplate;
import org.testng.Assert;
import org.testng.annotations.BeforeMethod;
import org.testng.annotations.Test;

public class UserClientUnitTest {
  private static final String USER0_NAME = "User0";
  private static final String USER0_EMAIL = "user0@gmail.com";
  private static final String TEST_RECORD0 = "{\"email\": \"" + USER0_EMAIL
      + "\", \"name\": \"" + USER0_NAME + "\"}";
  private static final String TEST_RECORD1 = "{\"email\": "
      + "\"user1@gmail.com\", \"name\": \"User1\"}";
  private static final String USERS_URL = "http://localhost:10404/users";

  private MockRestServiceServer mockServer;
  private RestTemplate restTemplate = new RestTemplate();
  private UsersClient usersClient = new UsersClient(restTemplate);

  @BeforeMethod
  public void init() {
    mockServer = MockRestServiceServer.createServer(restTemplate);
  }
}
```

The rest of the client-side unit test example is the same as Listings 4-41 through 4-46.

Consuming REST Asynchronously

RestTemplate calls against the REST server block the caller thread on the client side. This may not be suitable sometimes. We might need to not block the caller thread on the client side. Such a requirement is often referred to as a *fire and forget scenario*.

In the days before Spring 4, Spring developers were forced to use explicit asynchronous programming for such use cases. Spring's @Async annotation is good for this. The Spring 4 release introduced a new class, AsyncRestTemplate, which handles these asynchronous scenarios by registering callbacks or using the Java Feature implementation ListenableFuture.

To explain this use in an example, we need to extend our domain. We still need to consume a remote REST API that provides user information, as in the previous examples. But let's have an additional requirement to read user actions from separate storage and aggregate them into one object. Listing 4-48 shows this aggregated model class.

Listing 4-48. Extended Model for Reading User Information with User Actions (0405-rest-async-client)

```java
package net.lkrnac.book.eiws.chapter04.model;

import java.util.Collection;
import lombok.Value;

@Value
public class UserInfo {
  private User user;
  private Collection<String> userActions;
}
```

We again use the Lombok project to generate boilerplate getters and a constructor with parameters. The aggregated model class UserInfo contains an instance to the User object and a collection of user actions. For simplicity, a user action is represented by the String type. Listing 4-49 shows an implementation of the user's action repository.

Listing 4-49. User's Action Repository (0405-rest-async-client)

```
package net.lkrnac.book.eiws.chapter04.client;

import java.util.Arrays;
import java.util.Collection;

import org.springframework.stereotype.Repository;

@Repository
public class UserActionsRepository {
  public Collection<String> getUserActions(int identifier) {
    return Arrays.asList(new String[] { "dummy action 1", "dummy action 2", });
  }
}
```

To keep the example simple, we return dummy values. This class is not of deep interest anyway. We want to explore an asynchronous REST call. This is present, because we need to perform an action while the REST API call is executed asynchronously. Listing 4-50 shows the Spring configuration of this asynchronous example.

Listing 4-50. Consuming REST Asynchronously (0405-rest-async-client)

```
package net.lkrnac.book.eiws.chapter04.client;

import java.util.concurrent.Executor;
import java.util.concurrent.Executors;
import org.springframework.context.annotation.Bean;
import org.springframework.context.annotation.ComponentScan;
import org.springframework.context.annotation.Configuration;
import org.springframework.scheduling.concurrent.ConcurrentTaskExecutor;
import org.springframework.web.client.AsyncRestTemplate;

@Configuration
@ComponentScan
public class ClientConfiguration {
  @Bean
  public AsyncRestTemplate asyncRestTemplate() {
    Executor executor = Executors.newFixedThreadPool(10);
    ConcurrentTaskExecutor taskExecutor = new ConcurrentTaskExecutor(executor);
    return new AsyncRestTemplate(taskExecutor);
  }
}
```

ClientConfiguration is annotated as a standard Spring configuration. @Configuration defines Spring's configuration class, and @ComponentScan performs a scan for Spring's beans within the current package and its subpackages.

This configuration registers only one bean of type AsyncRestTemplate. By default, Spring uses the SimpleAsyncTaskExecutor thread pool implementation for asynchronous beans. But this implementation doesn't reuse threads from the thread pool, and therefore it's not suitable for production usage.

We use the Java Executors factory to create a thread pool with a fixed number of threads in the pool. When we wrap this Executor implementation into ConcurrentTaskExecutor, we can register it as a thread pool used by our instance of AsyncRestTemplate. The AsyncRestTemplate instance will be reusing a thread instance from this thread pool for asynchronous REST calls. Listing 4-51 shows example usage of AsyncRestTemplate.

Listing 4-51. Consuming REST Asynchronously (0405-rest-async-client)

```java
package net.lkrnac.book.eiws.chapter04.client;

import java.util.Collection;

import net.lkrnac.book.eiws.chapter04.model.User;
import net.lkrnac.book.eiws.chapter04.model.UserInfo;

import org.slf4j.Logger;
import org.slf4j.LoggerFactory;
import org.springframework.beans.factory.annotation.Autowired;
import org.springframework.http.ResponseEntity;
import org.springframework.stereotype.Service;
import org.springframework.util.concurrent.ListenableFuture;
import org.springframework.util.concurrent.ListenableFutureCallback;
import org.springframework.web.client.AsyncRestTemplate;

@Service
public class UserInfoService {
  private static final Logger LOGGER = LoggerFactory
      .getLogger(UserInfoService.class);

  private static final String URL = "http://localhost:10405/users";
  private AsyncRestTemplate asyncRestTemplate;
  private UserActionsRepository userActionsRepository;

  @Autowired
  public UserInfoService(AsyncRestTemplate asyncRestTemplate,
      UserActionsRepository userActionsRepository) {
    super();
    this.asyncRestTemplate = asyncRestTemplate;
    this.userActionsRepository = userActionsRepository;
  }

  private void logElapsedTime(String messagePrefix, long start) {
    LOGGER.info("{} call took {} ms.", messagePrefix,
        System.currentTimeMillis() - start);
  }
```

```java
  private ListenableFuture<ResponseEntity<User>> getUserAsync(int identifier,
      final long start) {
    ListenableFuture<ResponseEntity<User>> futureResult =
        asyncRestTemplate.getForEntity(URL + "/" + identifier, User.class);

    futureResult
        .addCallback(new ListenableFutureCallback<ResponseEntity<User>>() {
          @Override
          public void onSuccess(ResponseEntity<User> result) {
            logElapsedTime("User Service", start);
          }

          @Override
          public void onFailure(Throwable ex) {
            logElapsedTime("User Service", start);
          }
        });
    return futureResult;
  }

  public UserInfo getUserInfo(int identifier) {
    final long start = System.currentTimeMillis();

    ListenableFuture<ResponseEntity<User>> futureResult =
        getUserAsync(identifier, start);

    Collection<String> userActions =
        userActionsRepository.getUserActions(identifier);
    logElapsedTime("User Actions repository", start);

    User user = null;
    try {
      user = futureResult.get().getBody();
    } catch (Exception e) {
      throw new IllegalStateException(e);
    }

    logElapsedTime("Overall", start);
    return new UserInfo(user, userActions);
  }
}
```

This Spring bean is annotated with @Service to indicate that it's sitting on the service layer. The first statement defines the SLF4J constant for logging. This is a standard construct for a Java application.

Then we specify the REST service URL that will be called from this service and define dependencies. We have two dependencies: UserActionsRepository and AsyncRestTemplate. These two beans will be used to asynchronously aggregate data into the UserInfo object. They are injected by constructor injection.

The first method is the private logElapsedTime, used for logging time measurements.

The second method, getUserAsync, is responsible for executing an asynchronous REST call by calling asyncRestTemplate.getForEntity. This call performs a GET request against the REST server and returns the ListenableFuture<ResponseEntity<User>> type. This call kicks off a REST call in a separate thread, and we can retrieve a response via this return value wrapped into the ListenableFuture abstraction.

As we are interested in timings of this call, we register a callback into the futureResult return value that logs elapsed time of the asynchronous REST call. The last statement in this method returns a futureResult instance so that it is used for retrieving the REST server response.

The last method, getUserInfo, is the main and the only public method of this service, where aggregation happens. First we store the start time for time measurements. Then we call the private method getUserAsync and pass parameters identifier and start time, so that it can retrieve the User object asynchronously and log the elapsed time. When we get the futureResult instance, the REST call is being performed in the background. Our thread can focus on retrieving user actions from userActionsRepository.

When we have the userActions collection, we can call futureResult.get. This call blocks this thread until the asynchronous REST call finishes if it is still progress. If the asynchronous REST call is already finished, futureResult.get returns a response immediately. When we have the User object and user actions, we can aggregate them into the UserInfo object.

To test this application, we need to run code from Listing 4-52.

Listing 4-52. Main Class and Testing Code of Asynchronous Client (0405-rest-async-client)

```
package net.lkrnac.book.eiws.chapter04;

import java.util.concurrent.ExecutionException;
import lombok.extern.slf4j.Slf4j;
import net.lkrnac.book.eiws.chapter04.client.ClientConfiguration;
import net.lkrnac.book.eiws.chapter04.client.UserInfoService;
import net.lkrnac.book.eiws.chapter04.model.User;
import net.lkrnac.book.eiws.chapter04.model.UserInfo;
import org.springframework.boot.SpringApplication;
import org.springframework.boot.autoconfigure.SpringBootApplication;
import org.springframework.context.ConfigurableApplicationContext;
import org.springframework.context.annotation.Import;
import org.springframework.http.HttpEntity;
import org.springframework.http.ResponseEntity;
import org.springframework.util.concurrent.ListenableFuture;
import org.springframework.web.client.AsyncRestTemplate;

@Slf4j
public class RestClientAsyncApplication {
  public static void main(String... args) throws InterruptedException,
      ExecutionException {
    ConfigurableApplicationContext context =
        SpringApplication.run(ClientConfiguration.class, args);

    AsyncRestTemplate asyncRestTemplate = context.getBean(AsyncRestTemplate.class);
    UserInfoService userInfoService = context.getBean(UserInfoService.class);

    User user = new User();
    user.setName("Lubos");
    HttpEntity<User> httpRequest = new HttpEntity<>(user);
    ListenableFuture<ResponseEntity<User>> httpResponse =
        asyncRestTemplate.postForEntity("http://localhost:10405/users",
            httpRequest, User.class);
    httpResponse.get();
```

```
    UserInfo userInfo = userInfoService.getUserInfo(0);
    log.info(userInfo.getUser().getName());
  }
}
```

Annotation @Slf4j is more of Lombok's "syntactic sugar" for defining logger instances. It uses the current class as a parameter for retrieving the logger from the logger factory. In the main method, we start ClientConfiguration as the Spring Boot application and get Spring's context instance as the return value.

The context instance is used for retrieving the AsyncRestTemplate and UserInfoService beans. We use the AsyncRestTemplate instance to create the testing user object on the server.

Then we execute our userInfoService.getUserInfo call and log the name we received from the server.

When we run this asynchronous example, we see results similar to Listing 4-53. Of course, a server needs to handle our requests for the endpoint http://localhost:10405/users. In this case, we can use project 0405-rest-restcontroller-server as the server, because it is handling all the requests we need to test client logic against.

Listing 4-53. Asynchronous REST Consumption Example Console Output

```
20:38:11.101 [main] INFO  n.l.b.e.c.client.UserInfoService - User Actions repository call took 4 ms.
20:38:11.121 [main] INFO  n.l.b.e.c.client.UserInfoService - Overall call took 25 ms.
20:38:11.121 [pool-1-thread-2] INFO  n.l.b.e.c.client.UserInfoService - User Service call took 25 ms.
20:38:11.121 [main] INFO  n.l.b.e.c.RestClientAsyncApplication - Lubos
```

As you can see, the User Service call was executed in a separate thread and took 25 milliseconds (ms). The User Actions repository call took 4 ms. And overall execution took 25 ms. So it is obvious that these two calls were executed in parallel.

Summary

This chapter explained the benefits of the REST architecture style as compared to remoting or SOAP. You learned about the main concepts of REST, such as its uniform interface, statelessness, hypermedia, resource representation, and caching.

This chapter also provided a quick overview of HTTP. We covered its message structure and the main HTTP methods suitable for REST communication. Next you explored the JAX-RS approach to developing REST services and learned how to integrate it with Spring in a short example.

Subsequently, the chapter presented Spring MVC features. Examples of how to configure and route messages should provide a decent foundation for REST development with Spring MVC. We also covered server-side integration and unit-testing support and examples. The last sections were about client-side support and how to test it.

CHAPTER 5

■ ■ ■

Java Message Service

The enterprise integration technology explained in this chapter is the Java Message Service (JMS). It is different from the technologies discussed in previous chapters, because it is an inherently asynchronous technology for exchanging messages.

In the remoting, REST, and SOAP web services approaches, a client sends a request and waits for a server response. Waiting for a response can be implemented synchronously (the client thread is blocked until a response is received or times out) or asynchronously (the client registers callback logic, which is executed when the response arrives or the communication times out). But the HTTP communication between them remains open, at least until the client receives a response.

JMS is different, because it doesn't follow this approach of request-response. Looking deeper, communication counterparts in JMS communication can't be characterized as a client/server relationship at all. JMS is a technology whereby a producer sends a message to a consumer. But the message is not directly sent to the consumer via a socket connection.

A special middle component is used in JMS communication, called a *destination*. We can think of it as storage for messages. The producer sends a message to this destination and then doesn't care about this message anymore. The message is stored in the destination and sits there until it gets attention from a consumer or consumers. When the consumer is ready, it reads the message from the destination. So the producer and consumer are *highly decoupled* from each other: they don't need to know anything about the other side of this communication. The only important aspect is to know how to send/receive the message to/from destination.

Such communication is *asynchronous*, because the producer doesn't wait for the consumer to receive the message. There is no guarantee that the message will be delivered at all. If there's no application consuming messages from the destination, the message could sit in the destination theoretically forever.

Another important attribute of this type of communication is *reliability*. As we mentioned, the destination stores messages. It is obvious that storing messages requires a specialized server that can store them. This server is often called a *message broker*. It is specialized middleware, which can provide various destinations and can store messages in persistent storage if needed.

The Java Message Service is part of the Java Enterprise Edition standard, and therefore each JEE-compliant application server can also perform the role of a message broker. But you may wonder now, what about lightweight Spring applications? These applications are often hosted only on servlet containers without message broker capabilities. In these cases, projects focusing only on a stand-alone JMS implementation could be embedded into the Spring application if needed. But for most architectures, it makes sense to host the JMS parts as separate components of the enterprise system.

The following are main JMS providers:

- Apache ActiveMQ

- HornetQ (JBoss)

- JBoss Messaging (JBoss)

- WebSphere MQ (IBM)

- WebSphere Application Server (IBM)

- SonicMQ (Progress Software)

- Oracle WebLogic

- Oracle Advanced Queuing (AQ)

- Open Message Queue (Oracle)

- FFMQ

- TIBCO Enterprise Message Service

- OpenJMS

All these JMS providers are often referred to as *message-oriented middleware* (*MOM*). Some of them are full JEE-compliant application servers, and others implement only the JMS part of the JEE standard. So another significant difference in comparison to client/server communication is operational overhead for managing the message broker in the middle of the communication. If we are using a full JEE application server, this operational overhead is not huge, because the message broker is hosted with the JEE application server on the same server. But if we are using a lightweight solution (which is the case with most Spring applications), we can host a JMS message broker as a stand-alone server instance or embed it into the Spring application.

JMS messaging is often useful when we need to throttle messages between a producer and consumer. Also it is often used as temporary storage for streamed data, because we can easily replay all the messages if needed. Its reliability as a storage system for messages makes it a popular choice for caching data that enters our enterprise system.

When the producer and consumer are decoupled via a JMS destination, we can easily change the infrastructure routing between them without triggering any changes to either side of the communication. Moreover, when the consumer and receiver don't know about each other, we can easily plug in some logic in between their communication channels—for example, filtering or transforming messages. All these aspects make JMS messaging an excellent choice for decoupling components in an enterprise system.

JMS Standard Overview

As part of Java Enterprise Edition, the Java Message Service provides a standardized API for message exchange. This is handy because it eliminates problems related to locking into a particular messaging middleware vendor and significantly decreases the cost of migrating to a different JMS provider. It also enables reuse of the developer's knowledge across various JMS providers.

These two messaging paradigms are supported by JMS:

- Point-to-point

  - The destination is in this case called the *message queue*.

  - Each message can have *exactly one consumer*.

  - When a message is successfully consumed from the message queue, it is discarded.

  - There are two types of point-to-point communication:

    - *Unidirectional (sending only)*—As JMS is highly decoupled, no special features are needed.

    - *Bidirectional (request-reply)*—Is supported via correlation IDs, contained within the request and response messages.

- Publish/subscribe

  - The destination is in this case called the *message topic*.

  - The message is consumed by *all subscribers* (consupmers).

  - The message is discarded from the JMS server only after all subscribers have successfully consumed the message.

These JMS messaging paradigms relate to the type of destination. But it is important to remember that there can be various producers sending messages as well as various consumers receiving messages. So it is a valid configuration to have various producers sending messages to a point-to-point queue. It is also valid to have various receivers consuming messages from a point-to-point queue, but a particular message typically would be consumed by only one of them randomly.

JMS messages can be consumed in two ways:

- *Asynchronously*: The consumer registers a special JMS component called a listener to the destination and is able to consume messages as they are processed by the destination. Typically no delay is involved in the message reception. The reception of messages by the listener is done in a separate thread.

- *Synchronously*: The consumer is responsible for initiating a read from the message queue or topic. When the consumers polls the destination for the next JMS message, there are two possible scenarios:

  - There is no message in the destination, and the consumer thread is blocked until a new message arrives. This waiting can be terminated by an optional time-out.

  - If the message arrives before the consumer reads it from the destination, it is read immediately. But this message has to wait to be consumed for some time on the destination.

In most cases, registering the listener makes much more sense than explicit synchronous reception, because it decreases delays in our enterprise systems.

Java JMS API

JMS is a Java API; therefore, the JMS standard contains Java types for JMS communication. This API was unchanged for a long time (since Java Enterprise Edition 1.4 was introduced in 2003) and got stuck on version JMS 1.1.

But a recent version of the Java Enterprise Edition 7 standard made a major revision of the JMS API and introduced version JMS 2.0. This version simplifies some highly verbose aspects of the JMS 1.1 API. But as JEE 7 is a relatively new standard, JMS 2.0 wasn't implemented by all JMS providers so far (for example, ActiveMQ doesn't support JMS 2.0 as of May 2015). The main concepts from JMS 1.1 remained unchanged in JMS 2.0, and therefore it makes sense to explain the components of both versions together.

JMS Message

The most fundamental piece of the JMS puzzle is of course abstraction for the JMS message. It is represented by the javax.jms.Message interface, which is composed of these three elements:

- *Message headers*: A set of predefined types used for identification, routing, and the delivery and reply strategy of the message. These are meant to be used mostly by the JMS infrastructure, but sometimes also by the application code.

- *Message properties*: Custom values stored in the message. They are often used as a compatibility layer between different messaging systems. Usage also includes filtering of messages by message selectors.

- *Message body*: Contains the actual message.

- Based on different body types, various JMS message subinterfaces are provided by the JMS API. All are located in the javax.jms package:

- TextMessage: JMS wrapper for java.lang.String.

- MapMessage: Name/value pairs, where names are String objects and values are Java primitive types. The order of names is not specified.

- BytesMessage: Stream of bytes.

- StreamMessage: Stream of Java primitive types, read sequentially.

- ObjectMessage: Serializable Java object.

These interfaces are used to transfer messages of different payload types. The best interoperability is often achieved by sending text messages, especially in the most common transport formats such as JSON and XML. Therefore, TextMessage is most often used.

JMS Infrastructure Abstractions

We have mentioned various basic concepts for JMS communication, including the JMS destination, producer, and consumer. All these JMS communication parties need to have certain abstractions so the JMS client can communicate in pure Java to the JMS server.

Because the consumer and producer need to communicate with the JMS destination again and again, it makes sense to keep the connection between them open. When the connection is open, the consumer or producer can perform actions as a unit of work commonly referred to as a *session*. One connection can have various sessions open, so that we can run numerous units of work at the same time.

As JMS stands for Java Message Service, these abstractions have these Java representations:

- javax.jms.Destination: Object that represents the JMS queue or topic.

- javax.jms.MessageProducer: Abstraction representing the object responsible for sending JMS messages.

- javax.jms.MessageConsumer: Abstraction responsible for a synchronous read of JMS messages.

- javax.jms.JMSProducer: Enhanced version of MessageProducer introduced in JMS 2.0.

- javax.jms.JMSConsumer: Enhanced version of MessageConsumer introduced in JMS 2.0.

- `javax.jms.MessageListener`: Abstraction responsible for asynchronous reception of JMS messages.

- `javax.jms.Session`: Single-threaded context abstraction responsible for sending and receiving messages.

- `javax.jms.Connection`: Represents a virtual connection to the JMS provider.

- `javax.jms.JMSContext`: JMS 2.0 syntactic sugar for reducing verbosity of JMS 1.1 API. It combines `Connection` and `Session` into a single object.

- `javax.jms.ConnectionFactory`: Main configuration class of JMS that is responsible for creating connections to the JMS provider. It is usually created at the start of the JMS application.

- So the usual workflow of a JMS 1.1 developer is to create JMS objects in this order: `ConnectionFactory` ➤ `Connection` ➤ `Session` ➤ `MessageProducer/MessageConsumer/Message`. With JMS 2.0, the situation is a little enhanced: `ConnectionFactory` ➤ `JMSContext` ➤ `JMSProducer/JMSConsumer/Message`. In the case of a full-blown JEE container, `ConnectionFactory` would likely be injected.

- As you may have noticed, this workflow of JMS objects doesn't include `Destination`. This object is created or injected separately and is used to create `Producer` or `Consumer`. `MessageListener` is designed to be registered into the `MessageConsumer` object.

■ **Note** This overview of the JMS API is limited, because this book focuses on Spring's abstractions built on top of a plain JMS API. Therefore, the deeper aspects and additional features are beyond the scope of this book. The best place to start exploring it is the JEE 7 tutorial here: `https://docs.oracle.com/javaee/7/tutorial/jms-concepts003.htm#BNCEH`.

Java JMS Examples

The most common open source JMS provider is ActiveMQ. But at the time of writing, ActiveMQ doesn't cover JMS 2.0. We chose HornetQ to show our plain Java JMS examples, because it already supports the new JMS 2.0 standard.

As mentioned, JMS providers are often hosted as separate instances to our application. This is the case for our Java JMS examples. We will be running the HornetQ instance server locally and assume that a recent Java version is installed on the target machine.

To download the HornetQ server, you need to download the ZIP or TAR.GZ bundle from `http://hornetq.jboss.org/downloads.html` and unpack it. Running the server is easy. Just run the `bin/run.sh` or `bin/run.bat` file from the command line. If the proper Java version is installed, the server should start without any problems. To stop the server, we need to execute `bin/stop.sh` or `bin/stop.bat`—an easy process.

For example purposes, we don't need to tweak the default HornetQ configuration, because the example projects are using JMS resources configured by HornetQ out of the box. These examples were tested against HornetQ version 2.4.0.Final.

Synchronous JMS 1.1 Example

- Our first Java JMS example uses an old JMS 1.1 API that was standardized in 2003. Listing 5-1 shows how to configure JMS 1.1 access.

Listing 5-1. JMS 1.1 HornetQ Configuration (0501-jms11-jndi)

```java
package net.lkrnac.book.eiws.chapter05.jms11jndi;

import java.util.Hashtable;
import javax.jms.Connection;
import javax.jms.ConnectionFactory;
import javax.jms.JMSException;
import javax.jms.Queue;
import javax.naming.InitialContext;
import javax.naming.NamingException;
import lombok.Getter;

public class JmsConfiguration implements AutoCloseable {
  private InitialContext initialContext;

  @Getter
  private Queue queue;
  @Getter
  private Connection connection;

  public void init() throws NamingException, JMSException {
    Hashtable<Object, Object> env = new Hashtable<Object, Object>();
    env.put("java.naming.factory.initial",
        "org.jnp.interfaces.NamingContextFactory");
    env.put("java.naming.factory.url.pkgs",
        "org.jboss.naming:org.jnp.interfaces");
    env.put("java.naming.provider.url", "jnp://localhost:1099");
    initialContext = new InitialContext(env);

    queue = (Queue) initialContext.lookup("queue/ExpiryQueue");
    ConnectionFactory connectionFactory =
        (ConnectionFactory) initialContext.lookup("/ConnectionFactory");
    connection = connectionFactory.createConnection();
  }

  public void close() throws NamingException, JMSException {
    if (initialContext != null) {
      initialContext.close();
    }
    if (connection != null) {
      connection.close();
    }
  }
}
```

The JmsConfiguration class encapsulates the JMS provider-specific configuration. It has three fields. The first one is of type InitialContext, which is the starting point for resolving JNDI names. HornetQ is a JBoss technology, which is part of the broader JBoss Application Server portfolio. Therefore, the easiest way to initialize stand-alone HornetQ access is to use JNDI naming abstractions.

The following two fields defined in the JmsConfiguration class are the JMS objects queue and connection. These are annotated by Lombok's @Getter annotation, which generates getters for these two variables. Lombok is handy when we want to avoid Java verbosity so often highlighted by Java opponents. So they are exposed via getters, and other classes can use them for JMS messaging.

The first method is called init. As its name suggests, it initializes the JMS configuration. We define the map for storing JNDI naming values. The first two JNDI naming values are created based on HornetQ manual instructions in the section "JNDI configuration": http://docs.jboss.org/hornetq/2.4.0.Final/docs/user-manual/html_single/index.html#d0e1265. The third value, with the key java.naming.provider.url, specifies the address of our HornetQ server. In this case, the server will be located on localhost and port 1099.

When we have the JNDI configuration in the map, we can create a JNDI InitialContext instance and use it to look up JMS resources. As previously mentioned, the default HornetQ configuration is used in our Java JMS examples, so we use the queue name queue/ExpiryQueue and the connection factory name /ConnectionFactory to create the queue and connectionFactory objects. connectionFactory is used to create a connection instance. A queue with the name queue/ExpiryQueue is configured by default in the HornetQ server; we are using it here for simplicity's sake.

These two instances are already JMS abstractions, so the method init is the only place in our example containing a HornetQ-specific configuration.

The next method is called close. As its name suggests, it is used for closing resources that need to be closed. In this case, we need to close connection and initialContext. But this close method is special, because it belongs to the java.lang.AutoCloseable interface. This interface was introduced in Java 7 as part of a feature often referred to as *try-with-resources*. It adds syntactic sugar for closing resources after a try block. We will show its use later in this example.

- Listing 5-2 shows how to send a message with the JMS 1.1 API.

Listing 5-2. Sending a JMS Message with the JMS 1.1 API (0501-jms11-jndi)

```
package net.lkrnac.book.eiws.chapter05.jms11jndi;

import javax.jms.Connection;
import javax.jms.JMSException;
import javax.jms.MessageProducer;
import javax.jms.Queue;
import javax.jms.Session;
import javax.jms.TextMessage;

public class SimpleMessageSender {
  private MessageProducer messageProducer;
  private Session session;

  public void init(Connection connection, Queue queue) throws JMSException {
    session = connection.createSession(false, Session.AUTO_ACKNOWLEDGE);
    messageProducer = session.createProducer(queue);
  }
```

```java
  public void sendMessage(String message) throws JMSException {
    TextMessage textMessage = session.createTextMessage(message);
    messageProducer.send(textMessage);
  }
}
```

This class is straightforward. The JMS Connection and Queue instances are passed into init and are used to create MessageProducer and Session instances. Notice that for session creation, AUTO_ACKNOWLEDGE mode is used. You'll learn more about this later in the chapter, when you explore JMS transaction features. For now, you just need to know that when we read a message from the queue via this session, the message will be discarded from the queue. But in this case, the session is used for sending, which is not affected by this setting.

The second method is called sendMessage. It is obvious that it will be used for sending message, passed as a parameter into it. In this simple example, we are sending a String message, which is wrapped into the textMessage object. Notice that we need the session object to create this message. Finally, the messageProducer object is used to perform the send.

Notice the checked JMSException in the signature of both methods. Listing 5-3 shows the synchronous reception.

Listing 5-3. Synchronous Message Reception with the JMS 1.1 API (0501-jms11-jndi)

```java
package net.lkrnac.book.eiws.chapter05.jms11jndi;

import javax.jms.Connection;
import javax.jms.JMSException;
import javax.jms.MessageConsumer;
import javax.jms.Queue;
import javax.jms.Session;
import javax.jms.TextMessage;

public class SimpleMessageReader {
  private MessageConsumer messageConsumer;

  public void init(Connection connection, Queue queue) throws JMSException {
    Session session = connection.createSession(false, Session.AUTO_ACKNOWLEDGE);
    messageConsumer = session.createConsumer(queue);
  }

  public String readMessage() throws JMSException {
    TextMessage messageReceived = (TextMessage) messageConsumer.receive(5000);
    return messageReceived.getText();
  }
}
```

Similar to SimpleMessageSender, the SimpleMessageReader class also has an init method that takes connection and queue objects as parameters and creates a session in AUTO_ACKNOWLEDGE mode. After being read, the message is discarded from queue. The second object created in the init method is messageConsumer.

The readMessage method is used for explicit reception of messages. This means that we ask the queue if there is a message. This is done via the messageConsumer.receive call. If the queue doesn't contain any unread messages, this call waits for the message to arrive to queue. Parameter 5000 specifies the maximum wait time-out in milliseconds. If we don't specify a time-out, we would block the caller thread potentially forever. Calling messageConsumer.receive returns an object of type Message. To retrieve text from this message, we need to cast it into TextMessage. This is a criticized aspect of the JMS 1.1 API, because explicit casting is considered bad practice.

Another criticized aspect of the JMS API is the need for handling JMSExceptions. The last class shown in Listing 5-4 (belonging to the synchronous JMS 1.1 example) is the main class that uses classes from Listings 5-1–5-3.

Listing 5-4. Main Class of Synchronous JMS 1.1 Example (0501-jms11-jndi)

```java
package net.lkrnac.book.eiws.chapter05.jms11jndi;

import javax.jms.Connection;
import javax.jms.JMSException;
import javax.jms.Queue;
import javax.naming.NamingException;
import lombok.extern.slf4j.Slf4j;

@Slf4j
public class Jms11JndiApplication {
  public static void main(String[] args) throws JMSException, NamingException {
    try (JmsConfiguration jmsConfiguration = new JmsConfiguration()) {
      jmsConfiguration.init();
      Queue queue = jmsConfiguration.getQueue();
      Connection connection = jmsConfiguration.getConnection();
      connection.start();

      SimpleMessageSender messageSender = new SimpleMessageSender();
      messageSender.init(connection, queue);
      messageSender.sendMessage("simple message");

      SimpleMessageReader messageReader = new SimpleMessageReader();
      messageReader.init(connection, queue);
      String message = messageReader.readMessage();

      log.info("Message Received: {}", message);
    }
  }
}
```

Jms11JndiApplication is the main class of the synchronous JMS 1.1 example. It is annotated by Lombok's annotation @Slf4j, which gives us a convenient way to define the SLF4J constant for logging. It will be used to output the received message.

The main method uses the Java 7 feature try-with-resources. This means that resources initialized in braces after the try block will be closed in the virtual finally block. This is nice syntactic sugar. The only requirement for this feature is that the resource needs to implement the AutoCloseable interface. The resource in this case is an instance of our class JmsConfiguration from Listing 5-1, and this class is implementing AutoCloseable to close JMS and JNDI resources.

In a try block, we first initialize the jmsConfiguration object and the retrieved connection and queue objects from it. Next we start the JMS connection.

The following phase is to create and initialize SimpleMessageSender and initialize it and send a simple text message. After that, we create a SimpleMessageReader instance, initialize it, and read the message. Finally, the message is written to the console. The output after running may look like Listing 5-5.

Listing 5-5. Output of Synchronous JMS 1.1 Example

```
21:50:37.038 [main] INFO  n.l.b.e.c.j.Jms11JndiApplication - Message Received:
simple message
```

Synchronous JMS 2.0 Example

Our example of the JMS 2.0 API usage also relies on a HornetQ server running on localhost. Listing 5-6 shows the HornetQ JMS configuration.

Listing 5-6. JMS 2.0 HornetQ Configuration (0502-jms2-jndi)

```java
package net.lkrnac.book.eiws.chapter05.jms2jndi;

import java.util.Hashtable;
import javax.jms.ConnectionFactory;
import javax.jms.JMSContext;
import javax.jms.Queue;
import javax.naming.InitialContext;
import javax.naming.NamingException;
import lombok.Getter;

public class JmsConfiguration implements AutoCloseable {
  private InitialContext initialContext;

  @Getter
  private JMSContext jmsContext;
  @Getter
  private Queue queue;

  public void init() throws NamingException {
    Hashtable<Object, Object> env = new Hashtable<Object, Object>();
    env.put("java.naming.factory.initial",
        "org.jnp.interfaces.NamingContextFactory");
    env.put("java.naming.factory.url.pkgs",
        "org.jboss.naming:org.jnp.interfaces");
    env.put("java.naming.provider.url", "jnp://localhost:1099");
    initialContext = new InitialContext(env);

    queue = (Queue) initialContext.lookup("queue/ExpiryQueue");
    ConnectionFactory cf =
        (ConnectionFactory) initialContext.lookup("/ConnectionFactory");
    jmsContext = cf.createContext();
  }

  @Override
  public void close() throws NamingException {
    if (initialContext != null) {
      initialContext.close();
    }
```

```
    if (jmsContext != null) {
      jmsContext.close();
    }
  }
}
```

This JMS 2.0 configuration is similar to the JMS 1.1 configuration in Listing 5-1. The only difference is that we create a JMSContext instance instead of a Connection instance. JMSContext is a new abstraction introduced in JMS 2.0. Listing 5-7 shows an example JMS 2.0 sender implementation.

Listing 5-7. Sending a JMS Message with the JMS 2.0 API (0502-jms2-jndi)

```
package net.lkrnac.book.eiws.chapter05.jms2jndi;

import javax.jms.JMSContext;
import javax.jms.Queue;

public class SimpleMessageSender {
  private JMSContext jmsContext;
  private Queue queue;

  public SimpleMessageSender(JMSContext jmsContext, Queue queue) {
    this.jmsContext = jmsContext;
    this.queue = queue;
  }

  public void sendMessage(String message) {
    jmsContext.createProducer().send(queue, message);
  }
}
```

In comparison to Listing 5-2, we don't need to initialize Session nor MessageProducer instances. Therefore, it's more suitable to accept jmsContext and queue via the constructor and store them into the class fields.

The sending message is also more concise, because we create JMSProducer via the jmsContext. createProducer call and use the queue object to chain the send call. Notice that the need to handle the checked JMSException disappeared with JMS 2.0 when sending the message. Listing 5-8 shows the implementation of the message reader.

Listing 5-8. Synchronous Message Reception with JMS 2.0 API (0502-jms2-jndi)

```
package net.lkrnac.book.eiws.chapter05.jms2jndi;

import javax.jms.JMSConsumer;
import javax.jms.JMSContext;
import javax.jms.JMSException;
import javax.jms.Message;
import javax.jms.Queue;

public class SimpleMessageReader {
  private JMSContext jmsContext;
  private Queue queue;
```

```java
    public SimpleMessageReader(JMSContext jmsContext, Queue queue) {
        this.jmsContext = jmsContext;
        this.queue = queue;
    }

    public String readMessage() throws JMSException {
        JMSConsumer jmsConsumer = jmsContext.createConsumer(queue);
        Message message = jmsConsumer.receive(5000);
        return message.getBody(String.class);
    }
}
```

In comparison to Listing 5-3, which uses the JMS 1.1 API, we again don't need to initialize. Instead, we accept the jmsContext and queue objects via the constructor. When reading the message, we first create a JMSConsumer instance from jmsContext based on the queue object and then perform a potentially blocking call. It is potentially blocking because if the message is already sitting in the queue, we may not need to wait at all. Time-out 5000 is again an optional parameter. If we don't specify it, we could wait forever.

Unlike with the JMS 1.1 API, there's no need to cast a message to TextMessage. But it's done anyway under the hood based on the String.class parameter we specify for the message.getBody() call. This call can throw a checked JMSException, so we are forced to handle it or bubble it up. In this case, the second option is used by the readMessage() method, so the caller of this method will need to take care of it also (see Listing 5-9).

Listing 5-9. Main Class of Synchronous JMS 2.0 Example (0502-jms2-jndi)

```java
package net.lkrnac.book.eiws.chapter05.jms2jndi;

import javax.jms.JMSContext;
import javax.jms.JMSException;
import javax.jms.Queue;
import javax.naming.NamingException;
import lombok.extern.slf4j.Slf4j;

@Slf4j
public class Jms2JndiApplication {
    public static void main(String[] args) throws JMSException, NamingException {
        try (JmsConfiguration jmsConfiguration = new JmsConfiguration()) {
            jmsConfiguration.init();
            JMSContext jmsContext = jmsConfiguration.getJmsContext();
            Queue queue = jmsConfiguration.getQueue();

            SimpleMessageSender messageSender =
                new SimpleMessageSender(jmsContext, queue);
            messageSender.sendMessage("simple message");

            SimpleMessageReader messageConsumer =
                new SimpleMessageReader(jmsContext, queue);
            String message = messageConsumer.readMessage();

            log.info("Message Received: {}", message);
        }
    }
}
```

Jms2JndiApplication is again similar to Jms11JndiApplication, but the JMS 2.0 API allowed us to reduce the init calls for messageSender and messageConsumer. Instead, we pass into their constructor the jmsContext and queue objects—nice improvements against the JMS 1.1 API. Listing 5-10 shows the output of this example after running this main class.

Listing 5-10. Output of Synchronous JMS 2.0 Example

```
23:27:41.859 [main] INFO  n.l.b.e.c.j.Jms2JndiApplication - Message Received: simple message
```

Asynchronous JMS Example

Our last pure Java example highlights how to receive JMS messages with an asynchronous listener. But before we dive into JMS constructs, we need to introduce the class that will be used across most examples in this chapter. It is shown in Listing 5-11.

Listing 5-11. Common Service for Processing Messages (0500-jms-common)

```java
package net.lkrnac.book.eiws.chapter05.text;

import lombok.extern.slf4j.Slf4j;
import org.springframework.stereotype.Service;

@Slf4j
@Service
public class SimpleService {
  public void processText(String message) {
    log.info("Message received: {}", message);
  }
}
```

Notice that this example is located in the common project 0500-jms-common. This is because we will use the same class in this pure Java example and in most of the Spring JMS examples. Its purpose is to be the class where we delegate JMS messages after asynchronous reception. It can then be used in integration test suite verification that the JMS message was received. As a responsible programmer, I want to make sure that code snippets in the book are working. But diving into JMS integration testing is beyond the scope of this book, so it's up to you to explore the testing strategies used to make sure that JMS examples are working.

The SimpleService class is annotated with Lombok's @Slf4j annotation, which is handy when we need to use the SLF4J logging façade. @Service may be confusing for a pure Java JMS example, but it will be used and scanned as a Spring bean in Spring JMS asynchronous examples. Implementation is trivial—the code just logs the received message to the console.

The next class explained in this example is the JMS listener implementation in Listing 5-12.

Listing 5-12. Asynchronous Message Reception with JMS 2.0 API (0503-async-jndi)

```java
package net.lkrnac.book.eiws.chapter05.asyncjndi;

import javax.jms.Message;
import javax.jms.MessageListener;

import lombok.extern.slf4j.Slf4j;
import net.lkrnac.book.eiws.chapter05.text.SimpleService;
```

```java
@Slf4j
public class SimpleMessageListener implements MessageListener {
  private SimpleService simpleService;

  public SimpleMessageListener(SimpleService simpleService) {
    super();
    this.simpleService = simpleService;
  }

  @Override
  public void onMessage(Message message) {
    try {
      simpleService.processText(message.getBody(String.class));
    } catch (Throwable t) {
      log.error("Error during message reception", t);
    }
  }
}
```

SimpleMessageListener expects an instance of SimpleService to be passed via the constructor.

Because it implements the JMS interface, MessageListener must implement the onMessage method. This method has a defined signature by JMS contract, where it has to accept a Message parameter. This is the method of the message listener that will be asynchronously executed when the JMS queue needs to send a new message. It is effectively an implementation of the observer pattern.

Because this method will be called in a separate thread, which is managed by a thread pool created by the HornetQ client library, it is good idea to handle all the exceptions. In this case, we log the stack trace. The message itself is delegated to the simpleService.processText() call after reception.

Listing 5-13 shows the HornetQ JMS configuration.

Listing 5-13. Asynchronous JMS HornetQ Configuration (0503-async-jndi)

```java
package net.lkrnac.book.eiws.chapter05.asyncjndi;

import java.util.Hashtable;
import javax.jms.ConnectionFactory;
import javax.jms.JMSConsumer;
import javax.jms.JMSContext;
import javax.jms.MessageListener;
import javax.jms.Queue;
import javax.naming.InitialContext;
import javax.naming.NamingException;
import lombok.Getter;
import net.lkrnac.book.eiws.chapter05.text.SimpleService;

public class JmsConfiguration implements AutoCloseable {
  private InitialContext initialContext;
  private SimpleService simpleService;

  @Getter
  private JMSContext jmsContext;
  @Getter
  private Queue queue;
```

```java
public JmsConfiguration(SimpleService simpleService) {
  super();
  this.simpleService = simpleService;
}

public void init() throws NamingException {
  Hashtable<Object, Object> env = new Hashtable<Object, Object>();
  env.put("java.naming.factory.initial",
      "org.jnp.interfaces.NamingContextFactory");
  env.put("java.naming.factory.url.pkgs",
      "org.jboss.naming:org.jnp.interfaces");
  env.put("java.naming.provider.url", "jnp://localhost:1099");
  initialContext = new InitialContext(env);

  queue = (Queue) initialContext.lookup("queue/ExpiryQueue");
  ConnectionFactory cf =
      (ConnectionFactory) initialContext.lookup("/ConnectionFactory");
  jmsContext = cf.createContext();

  JMSConsumer jmsConsumer = jmsContext.createConsumer(queue);
  MessageListener messageListener = new SimpleMessageListener(simpleService);
  jmsConsumer.setMessageListener(messageListener);
}

@Override
public void close() throws NamingException {
  if (initialContext != null) {
    initialContext.close();
  }
  if (jmsContext != null) {
    jmsContext.close();
  }
}
}
```

This JMS configuration is again similar to the configuration of the pure Java JMS 2.0 example in Listing 5-6. This JmsConfiguration expects an instance of SimpleService in the constructor. One additional piece is the creation and registration of the message listener.

First we need to create the JMSConsumer instance from the jmsContext object based on queue. To create the SimpleMessageListener instance, we need the SimpleService instance, as we already know from Listing 5-12. Next we register our listener into jmsConsumer, and the listener is registered. Listing 5-14 shows the main class of this example.

Listing 5-14. Main Class of Asynchronous JMS 2.0 Example (0503-async-jndi)

```java
package net.lkrnac.book.eiws.chapter05.asyncjndi;

import javax.jms.JMSContext;
import javax.jms.JMSException;
import javax.jms.Queue;
import javax.naming.NamingException;
import net.lkrnac.book.eiws.chapter05.text.SimpleService;
```

```java
public class AsyncJndiApplication {
  public static void main(String[] args) throws JMSException, NamingException {
    SimpleService simpleService = new SimpleService();
    try (JmsConfiguration jmsConfiguration =
        new JmsConfiguration(simpleService)) {
      jmsConfiguration.init();
      JMSContext jmsContext = jmsConfiguration.getJmsContext();
      Queue queue = jmsConfiguration.getQueue();

      SimpleMessageSender messageSender =
          new SimpleMessageSender(jmsContext, queue);
      messageSender.sendMessage("simple message");
    }
  }
}
```

The `main` method creates a `SimpleService` instance, and within the try-with-resources block, it initializes the JMS configuration and sends the message. The difference between this `main` method and the synchronous JMS examples is a lack of explicit reading from queue. In this case, it's not needed, because we registered the JMS listener against the queue.

The last piece used in this example is `SimpleMessageSender`, but its implementation is exactly the same as for synchronous JMS examples. Therefore, we skip this listing. When we execute this main class against running the HornetQ server, the message is sent to queue, received by `SimpleMessageListener`, and logged by `SimpleService` with output similar to Listing 5-15.

Listing 5-15. Output of Asynchronous JMS 2.0 Example

```
18:08:33.330 [Thread-0 (HornetQ-client-global-threads-114132791)] INFO n.l.b.e.chapter05.
text.SimpleService - Message received: simple message
```

Notice that the logged thread is not the main thread, as with the synchronous examples. This thread is managed by the HornetQ client library thread pool.

Spring JMS

Spring JMS support aims to simplify use, creation, and release of JMS resources. Similar to other Spring abstractions, it decouples the application code from details of the underlying JMS infrastructure and an invasive JMS API. Spring JMS features can be divided into these main areas:

- Support for creating or obtaining JMS resources
  - JNDI lookup of container-managed JMS resources via the `<jee:jndi-lookup>` XML element
  - Direct creation of `javax.jms.ConnectionFactory` and `javax.jms.Destination` objects
- Support for sending and synchronous reception of JMS messages via the `org.springframework.jms.core.JmsTemplate` class

- Support for asynchronous reception of JMS messages

  - @JmsListener annotation

  - <jms:listener-container> and <jms:listener> XML elements

  - Extraction of JMS message elements via the annotations @Payload, @Header, @Headers

  - To enable Spring JMS annotation configuration, Spring 4.1 introduced the @EnableJms annotation

- Rich conversion of JMS messages—allows for easy conversion of text messages

  - From/to various transport formats such as JSON or XML

  - Custom JMS message conversion via the interface org.springframework.jms. support.converter.MessageConverter

One important feature of Spring JMS is common for most of the above-mentioned features. It translates the checked javax.jmsJMSException into the unchecked exception org.springframework.jms. JmsException. This allows the application developer to completely decouple the application code from the underlying JMS communication constructs.

As each of the mentioned Spring JMS areas is a broader topic, we will cover them separately with various examples.

Configuring Spring JMS

Spring provides various possibilities for configuring the technologies it supports. The Spring JMS module isn't an exception.

When our application is hosted on the Java Enterprise Edition container, JMS resources such as ConnectionFactory or Destination typically are managed by the application server. It this case, the JEE standard provides a standard API to discover such managed JMS resources via the JNDI naming service. Spring enables integration with the underlying application service via JNDI by use of the <jee:jndi-lookup> XML element that belongs to the namespace www.springframework.org/schema/jee. Another option is to configure the JNDI service via registering the javax.naming.InitialContext instance.

If our application uses a lightweight container that doesn't provide JMS resources, or our application is running as a stand-alone Java application, we can use standard dependency injection constructs to register JMS resources into the Spring container.

A relatively new option for creating JMS resources such as Destination and ConnectionFactory is to use the Spring Boot project. It enables autoconfiguration of JMS access via the @EnableAutoConfiguration annotation. Based on this annotation, the Spring container inspects classpath dependencies, and if there is an implementation of the ActiveMQ or HornetQ JMS client, it creates JMS resources with the default configuration.

When we have an implementation of a HornetQ or ActiveMQ server between our classpath dependencies, Spring Boot also configures the embedded JMS server, which can simulate a configuration similar to a full-blown JEE application server with a JMS broker.

Spring Boot 1.2 introduced the @SpringBootApplication annotation, which is a convenient shortcut for the combination of @Configuration, @ComponentScan, and @EnableAutoConfiguration annotations under one umbrella.

Another new configuration option introduced in Spring 4.1 is the @EnableJms annotation. It enables the @JmsListener annotation and also creates a listener container factory that is responsible for managing the asynchronous JMS message reception.

Spring JMS APIs often use plain string names for the JMS destination when sending or receiving messages. But this is not compatible with the JMS API, which requires all the queues or topics to implement the javax.jms.Destination interface. So how can a resolution based on names work? For name resolution of the JMS destination, Spring uses a special bean of type org.springframework.jms.support. destination.DestinationResolver. The signature of this interface is shown in Listing 5-16.

Listing 5-16. DestinationResolver Signature

```
package org.springframework.jms.support.destination;

import javax.jms.Destination;
import javax.jms.JMSException;
import javax.jms.Session;

public interface DestinationResolver {
  Destination resolveDestinationName(Session session, String destinationName,
    boolean pubSubDomain) throws JMSException;
}
```

This interface is designed to resolve finding the JMS Destination instance based on the string name of the JMS destination and a given JMS session on the runtime. Spring provides various out-of-the-box implementations:

- BeanFactoryDestinationResolver: An implementation based on Spring's BeanFactory that resolves Spring-managed beans of type javax.jms.Destination based on their name.

- DynamicDestinationResolver: Creates JMS destination instances dynamically, based on given names. This implementation is used by default if not explicitly specified.

- JndiDestinationResolver: Resolved JMS destination based on given JNDI names.

All these features provide a lot of approaches and combinations for configuring JMS with Spring. Major approaches are covered in subsequent examples.

■ **Note** Java examples in earlier sections of this chapter use HornetQ as a JMS provider, because it allowed us to also explore the JMS 2.0 API. To keep the JMS provider consistent, HornetQ is used in most of the following examples. We use ActiveMQ only when Spring Boot support does not easily provide certain features.

Spring JMS XML Configuration Example

The first Spring JMS configuration example uses XML to configure JMS resources, as shown in Listing 5-17.

Listing 5-17. Spring JMS JNDI Lookup Configuration (File spring-jms-config.xml in Folder src/main/resources in Example Project 0504-async-jms-namespace)

```
<?xml version="1.0" encoding="UTF-8"?>
<beans xmlns="http://www.springframework.org/schema/beans"
  xmlns:xsi="http://www.w3.org/2001/XMLSchema-instance"
  xmlns:jee="http://www.springframework.org/schema/jee"
  xmlns:util="http://www.springframework.org/schema/util"
```

```
xsi:schemaLocation="http://www.springframework.org/schema/jee
    http://www.springframework.org/schema/jee/spring-jee.xsd
              http://www.springframework.org/schema/beans
    http://www.springframework.org/schema/beans/spring-beans.xsd
              http://www.springframework.org/schema/util
    http://www.springframework.org/schema/util/spring-util.xsd">

<util:map id="jndiProperties" map-class="java.util.Properties">
  <entry key="java.naming.factory.initial"
    value="org.jnp.interfaces.NamingContextFactory" />
  <entry key="java.naming.factory.url.pkgs"
    value="org.jboss.naming:org.jnp.interfaces" />
  <entry key="java.naming.provider.url" value="jnp://localhost:1099" />
</util:map>

<jee:jndi-lookup id="connectionFactory" jndi-name="/ConnectionFactory"
  environment-ref="jndiProperties" />
<jee:jndi-lookup id="queue" jndi-name="queue/ExpiryQueue"
  environment-ref="jndiProperties" />

<bean id="jmsTemplate" class="org.springframework.jms.core.JmsTemplate">
  <constructor-arg ref="connectionFactory" />
</bean>

<bean id="destinationResolver"
  class="org.springframework.jms.support.destination.JndiDestinationResolver">
  <property name="jndiEnvironment" ref="jndiProperties" />
</bean>
</beans>
```

This Spring XML configuration file uses three namespaces. bean is a standard dependency injection namespace, which is the backbone of any Spring XML configuration file. The jee namespace is meant for integration with Java Enterprise Edition application containers. The namespace util is used for various nonstandard XML configuration constructs.

In this case, we are using the util namespace to define the map of JNDI properties for the HornetQ configuration. We use the same values that are suggested by the HornetQ documentation here http://docs.jboss.org/hornetq/2.4.0.Final/docs/user-manual/html_single/index.html#d0e1265. The same values were used for the plain Java JMS examples. This configuration can talk to the HornetQ server with the default configuration running on localhost.

These properties are needed here because our example is not running on a JEE application server. If that were the case, we would exclude the jndiProperties part completely, as Spring would perform a JNDI lookup against the application server naming service.

The next section is the JNDI lookup itself. We use <jee:jndi-lookup> elements to obtain an instance of the JMS ConnectionFactory and Queue based on their JNDI names and jndiProperties map. Again we would be able to exclude the environment-ref attribute if the JNDI lookup were performed against the JEE container. The results of these operations are two registered beans in Spring's context with the names connectionFactory and queue. This is handy for abstracting out JNDI resources from the Spring application's point of view.

Next we create the jmsTemplate instance, which will use the connectionFactory bean as the constructor parameter. This demonstrates how we can use beans that were created by the JNDI lookup. The use of and features behind the JmsTemplate itself are explained later.

The last bean registered in this configuration file is destinationResolver. As we are doing a JNDI lookup for JMS resources, we want to use JndiDestinationResolver instead of DynamicDestinationResolver. This allows us to use the string name queue/ExpiryQueue of the JMS destination when we'll be sending or receiving JMS messages.

Spring JMS Java Configuration Example

Listing 5-18 shows a possible Java configuration of a Spring JMS application in which JMS resources are created explicitly.

Listing 5-18. Java Configuration with Explicit Creation of JMS Resources (0506-async-jms-java-config)

```java
package net.lkrnac.book.eiws.chapter05.text;

import java.util.Hashtable;
import javax.jms.ConnectionFactory;
import javax.jms.Queue;
import javax.naming.InitialContext;
import javax.naming.NamingException;
import org.springframework.context.annotation.Bean;
import org.springframework.context.annotation.Configuration;
import org.springframework.jms.annotation.EnableJms;
import org.springframework.jms.core.JmsTemplate;

@Configuration
@EnableJms
public class JmsConfiguration {
  @Bean
  public InitialContext initialContext() throws NamingException {
    Hashtable<Object, Object> env = new Hashtable<Object, Object>();
    env.put("java.naming.factory.initial",
        "org.jnp.interfaces.NamingContextFactory");
    env.put("java.naming.factory.url.pkgs",
        "org.jboss.naming:org.jnp.interfaces");
    env.put("java.naming.provider.url", "jnp://localhost:1099");
    return new InitialContext(env);
  }

  @Bean
  public ConnectionFactory connectionFactory(InitialContext initialContext)
      throws NamingException {
    return (ConnectionFactory) initialContext.lookup("/ConnectionFactory");
  }

  @Bean
  public Queue queue(InitialContext initialContext) throws NamingException {
    return (Queue) initialContext.lookup("/queue/ExpiryQueue");
  }
```

```
  @Bean
  public JmsTemplate jmsTemplate(ConnectionFactory connectionFactory) {
    return new JmsTemplate(connectionFactory);
  }
}
```

The JmsConfiguration class is annotated with @Configuration to define it as Spring's configuration class. The @EnableJms annotation is used for enabling JMS annotations and some supporting beans for asynchronous JMS message reception.

The first bean registered in this configuration class is the JNDI InitialContext instance with HornetQ access configuration. It will be used during creation of the JMS resources ConnectionFactory and Queue. These are also created in methods annotated with @Bean so that they will be registered in the context. We create them via a JNDI lookup against the initialContext instance, and therefore we need to explicitly cast them into relevant types. These three methods are the only use of the HornetQ-specific API within the 0506-async-jms-java-config example project.

Finally, we create and register an instance of JmsTemplate based on the injected connectionFactory created in this class also. JmsTemplate can be used for sending and synchronous reception of JMS messages.

Listing 5-19 shows a Spring Boot configuration example.

Listing 5-19. Example of Configuring JMS with Spring Boot (0507-sync-jms-java-config)

```
package net.lkrnac.book.eiws.chapter05.text;

import org.springframework.boot.SpringApplication;
import org.springframework.boot.autoconfigure.SpringBootApplication;
import org.springframework.scheduling.annotation.EnableScheduling;

@EnableScheduling
@SpringBootApplication
public class JavaConfigJmsSyncApplication {
  public static void main(String[] args) throws InterruptedException {
    SpringApplication.run(JavaConfigJmsSyncApplication.class, args);
  }
}
```

You may notice that this example has no sign of the org.springframework.jms package. Spring Boot is smart enough to recognize that we have Spring JMS dependencies on the classpath and therefore creates all the JMS resources automatically. It uses opinionated default configurations for the creation. If it finds HornetQ client dependencies on the classpath, it creates a ConnectionFactory out of the box. If we use destinations via String names and not as instances of the Destination interface, DynamicDestinationResolver will create them for us. This Spring Boot approach significantly reduces the amount of configuration needed to create modern enterprise-ready services.

The @EnableScheduling annotation is used because the example uses Spring Scheduling support for sending messages. This is shown in later examples.

Caching JMS Resources

As we mentioned, normal JMS flow is to create JMS resources in this order: ConnectionFactory ➤ Connection ➤ Session ➤ MessageProducer/MessageConsumer/Message. JMS 2.0 provided a little bit more convenience with use of JMSContext, JMSConsumer, and JMSProducer. But these are using older JMS 1.1 abstractions under the hood. Also Spring has its own JMS APIs, so these JMS 2.0 convenience abstractions are not used in Spring code at all. Therefore, when we are thinking about caching JMS resources, it is all about JMS 1.1 abstractions.

If instances from this chain are reused across our application, everything should be fine. But if we were creating all these objects every time we wanted to send or receive a message, performance of our application would suffer. Connection and Session are especially time-intensive to create.

Therefore, Spring provides two implementations of ConnectionFactory that can help cache these resources:

- SingleConnectionFactory: For every call, ConnectionFactory.createConnection() returns the same instance of Connection and ignores ConnectionFactory.close() calls.

- CachingConnectionFactory: Builds on top of SingleConnectionFactory functionality and adds caching of Session, MessageProducer, and MessageConsumer instances. The sessionCacheSize property is used to change cache size, which is by default 1. MessageConsumer and MessageProducer instances are cached within the Session instance.

Both implementations are used as wrappers for a JMS provider-specific connection factory. An example of such a configuration is shown in Listing 5-20.

■ **Note** As Spring Boot currently doesn't provide an easy way to combine CachingConnectionFactory with HornetQ (see Spring Boot issue https://github.com/spring-projects/spring-boot/issues/2956), this example uses an ActiveMQ embedded broker.

Listing 5-20. CachingConnectionFactory Usage (0511-jms-caching-connection-factory)

```
package net.lkrnac.book.eiws.chapter05.text;

import javax.jms.ConnectionFactory;
import org.apache.activemq.ActiveMQConnectionFactory;
import org.springframework.context.annotation.Bean;
import org.springframework.context.annotation.Configuration;
import org.springframework.jms.annotation.EnableJms;
import org.springframework.jms.connection.CachingConnectionFactory;

@Configuration
@EnableJms
public class JmsConfiguration {
  @Bean
  public ConnectionFactory connectionFactory() {
    ActiveMQConnectionFactory activeMqConnectionFactory =
        new ActiveMQConnectionFactory();
    activeMqConnectionFactory.setBrokerURL("vm://localhost");

    CachingConnectionFactory connectionFactory =
        new CachingConnectionFactory(activeMqConnectionFactory);
    connectionFactory.setSessionCacheSize(10);
    return connectionFactory;
  }
}
```

The @Configuration annotation makes a Spring configuration class from JmsConfiguration. The @EnableJms annotation is used to enable JMS-specific Spring annotations and create some JMS supporting beans.

In this class, we register a Spring bean of type ConnectionFactory. But we don't expose the ActiveMQ instance directly as usual. Instead, we wrap ActiveMQConnectionFactory into CachingConnectionFactory and expose its instance as a default connectionFactory bean. So everywhere JMS connectionFactory is used, JMS resources are reused to boost performance. Cache size is configured in this case to store 10 Session objects.

Using JmsTemplate

JmsTemplate is the most important class of the Spring JMS module. Its primary focus is on synchronous reception and sending JMS messages. For fine-grained control over these tasks, the JmsTemplate instance stores various configuration options. These are some of the most important:

- setSessionAcknowledgeMode or setSessionAcknowledgeModeName: Configures acknowledge mode. Possible values are as follows:

  - Session.AUTO_ACKNOWLEDGE or "AUTO_ACKNOWLEDGE"

  - Session.CLIENT_ACKNOWLEDGE or "CLIENT_ACKNOWLEDGE"

  - Session.DUPS_OK_ACKNOWLEDGE or "DUPS_OK_ACKNOWLEDGE"

- setSessionTransacted: Turns on transactional behavior. When turned on, overrides acknowledge mode configuration.

- setConnecionFactory: Mandatory connection factory instance as main entry class into JMS client access.

- Default JMS Destination it will be used against

  - setDefaultDestination: Sets the destination via the Destination/Queue/Topic instance.

  - setDefaultDestinationName: Sets the destination via the name.

- setReceiveTimeout: Changes the receive time-out for this JmsTemplate instance. It applies for synchronous reception of JMS messages. The value is in milliseconds, and the default value is 0, which means that receive calls will be waiting forever.

- setPubSubDomain: Switches between publish/subscribe and point-to-point communication. The default is false, which uses point-to-point.

- setDestinationDesolver: Specifies the class that will be responsible for translating JMS destination names into javax.jms.Destination instances. By default, it uses DynamicDestinationResolver. Spring also provides JndiDestinationResolver.

- setMessageConverter: Delegates the conversion of JMS messages to a separate bean. By default, it uses SimpleMessageConverter. Converters are further explained in later sections of this chapter.

Obviously, all this configuration stored in single object can raise questions about whether such an object/bean can be used in a multithreaded environment. An important aspect of the JmsTemplate class is that it is thread-safe: we can share and use the JmsTemplate instance across various threads.

When our instance is configured, we can use it to perform actions against the JMS destination or session. It covers various features for JMS message handling:

- Methods for *message sending*:

  - send: Sends the message to the default or given destination

  - convertAndSend: Converts the message with the use of MessageConverter first and sends it to the default or given destination

  - sendAndReceive: Sends the message to the default or given destination and receives a reply message asynchronously

- Methods for *synchronous message reception*—by default, these operations are blocking a caller thread without time-out:

  - receive: Receives the message synchronously.

  - receiveSelected: Receives the message synchronously with use of a given message selector. Message selectors are used to filter messages based on their filtering expression.

  - receiveAndConvert: Receives the message synchronously and converts it via MessageConverter.

  - receiveSelectedAndConvert: Combines the applied message selectors and message converter.

- Methods for *browsing messages*, which means to read messages without discarding them from the JMS destination:

  - browse: Used for browsing all messages.

  - browseSelected: Used for browsing selected messages; selected messages are narrowed down via BrowserCallback<T>.

- Methods for executing *custom actions* against the JMS session:

  - execute: Registers the action callback where the Session object will be passed. In this callback, we can perform custom actions against JMS Session.

Another important feature of JmsTemplate is that it translates the checked javax.jmsJMSException into the unchecked exception org.springframework.jms.JmsException.

Releasing JMS resources is also convenient. Connection and Session need to be closed when they are no longer needed by the application. With the JMS API, this has to be done manually by calling the close method of both JMS resources. But when we use JmsTemplate, this releasing of JMS resources is done automatically under the hood.

Listing 5-21 shows how to configure and register JmsTemplate as a Spring bean.

Listing 5-21. Configuring JmsTemplate (0507-sync-jms-java-config)

```
package net.lkrnac.book.eiws.chapter05.text;

import javax.jms.ConnectionFactory;
import org.springframework.context.annotation.Bean;
import org.springframework.context.annotation.Configuration;
import org.springframework.jms.core.JmsTemplate;
```

```java
@Configuration
public class JmsConfiguration {
  @Bean
  public JmsTemplate jmsTemplate(ConnectionFactory connectionFactory) {
    JmsTemplate jmsTemplate = new JmsTemplate(connectionFactory);
    jmsTemplate.setReceiveTimeout(1000);
    return jmsTemplate;
  }
}
```

In this case, we will be using JmsTemplate for sending messages and for synchronous message reception. Therefore, if we want to avoid eventual blocking of the thread reading the JMS messages, it is often a good idea to configure the receiveTimeout property. Listing 5-22 shows what the JMS message-sending implementation may look like.

Listing 5-22. Sending JMS Message (0507-sync-jms-java-config)

```java
package net.lkrnac.book.eiws.chapter05.text;

import lombok.extern.slf4j.Slf4j;
import org.springframework.beans.factory.annotation.Autowired;
import org.springframework.jms.core.JmsTemplate;
import org.springframework.scheduling.annotation.Scheduled;
import org.springframework.stereotype.Component;

@Slf4j
@Component
public class SimpleMessageSender {
  private static final String SIMPLE_MESSAGE = "simple message";
  private JmsTemplate jmsTemplate;

  @Autowired
  public SimpleMessageSender(JmsTemplate jmsTemplate) {
    super();
    this.jmsTemplate = jmsTemplate;
  }

  @Scheduled(fixedRate = 1000)
  public void send() {
    log.info("Sending message: {}", SIMPLE_MESSAGE);
    this.jmsTemplate.convertAndSend("queue/ExpiryQueue", SIMPLE_MESSAGE);
  }
}
```

The SimpleMessageSender class is a Spring bean, which is defined by the @Component annotation. @Slf4j is Lombok's convenient shortcut for creating the SLF4J logger constant. We inject in this Spring bean the jmsTemplate instance via constructor injection.

With the send method, we will be sending a simple JMS message every second. Recurring execution of the send method is ensured by the @Scheduled annotation. In the method body, we first log the message and call the jmsTemplate.convertAndSend method. Conversion is needed from Spring into the Message instance, which is done by SimpleMessageConverter.

Listing 5-23 shows a simple implementation of synchronous message reception.

Listing 5-23. Synchronous JMS Message Reception (0507-sync-jms-java-config)

```
package net.lkrnac.book.eiws.chapter05.text;

import org.springframework.beans.factory.annotation.Autowired;
import org.springframework.jms.core.JmsTemplate;
import org.springframework.scheduling.annotation.Scheduled;
import org.springframework.stereotype.Component;

@Component
public class SimpleMessageReader {
  private JmsTemplate jmsTemplate;
  private SimpleService simpleService;

  @Autowired
  public SimpleMessageReader(JmsTemplate jmsTemplate,
      SimpleService simpleService) {
    super();
    this.jmsTemplate = jmsTemplate;
    this.simpleService = simpleService;
    jmsTemplate.setReceiveTimeout(1000);
  }

  @Scheduled(fixedRate = 1200)
  public void readMessage() {
    String message = (String) jmsTemplate.receiveAndConvert("queue/ExpiryQueue");
    simpleService.processText(message);
  }
}
```

The SimpleMessageReader class is again a Spring component and injects two dependencies via constructor injection. The first one is the famous jmsTemplate instance. We make sure that synchronous reception wouldn't be blocked forever by configuring the receiveTimeout property for jmsTemplate. The second dependency is simpleService, which is responsible for processing messages (logging them).

The readMessage method is scheduled every 1.2 seconds to highlight delays when we use synchronous reception. The jmsTemplate.receiveAndConvert call returns Object, so we need to explicitly cast to String. Spring also converts the JMS Message instance under the hood. Finally, we pass the message in text form to simpleService.

The last class in this example is JavaConfigJmsSyncApplication (shown in Listing 5-19). When we run this class as a Java application, we get output similar to Listing 5-24.

Listing 5-24. Output of Synchronous JMS Reception Example

```
2015-05-30 20:44:47.417  INFO 23387 --- [pool-2-thread-1] n.l.b.e.c.text.SimpleMessageSender
: Sending message: simple message
2015-05-30 20:44:47.419  INFO 23387 --- [           main] n.l.b.e.c.t.JavaConfigJmsSync
Application : Started JavaConfigJmsSyncApplication in 1.828 seconds (JVM running for 2.367)
2015-05-30 20:44:47.651  INFO 23387 --- [pool-2-thread-1] n.l.b.eiws.chapter05.text.
SimpleService  : Message received: simple message
2015-05-30 20:44:48.417  INFO 23387 --- [pool-2-thread-1] n.l.b.e.c.text.SimpleMessageSender
: Sending message: simple message
```

```
2015-05-30 20:44:48.631  INFO 23387 --- [pool-2-thread-1] n.l.b.eiws.chapter05.text.
SimpleService  : Message received: simple message
2015-05-30 20:44:49.417  INFO 23387 --- [pool-2-thread-1] n.l.b.e.c.text.SimpleMessageSender
: Sending message: simple message
2015-05-30 20:44:49.834  INFO 23387 --- [pool-2-thread-1] n.l.b.eiws.chapter05.text.
SimpleService  : Message received: simple message
2015-05-30 20:44:50.417  INFO 23387 --- [pool-2-thread-1] n.l.b.e.c.text.SimpleMessageSender
: Sending message: simple message
2015-05-30 20:44:51.030  INFO 23387 --- [pool-2-thread-1] n.l.b.eiws.chapter05.text.
SimpleService  : Message received: simple message
2015-05-30 20:44:51.417  INFO 23387 --- [pool-2-thread-1] n.l.b.e.c.text.SimpleMessageSender
: Sending message: simple message
2015-05-30 20:44:52.230  INFO 23387 --- [pool-2-thread-1] n.l.b.eiws.chapter05.text.
SimpleService  : Message received: simple message
2015-05-30 20:44:52.417  INFO 23387 --- [pool-2-thread-1] n.l.b.e.c.text.SimpleMessageSender
: Sending message: simple message
2015-05-30 20:44:53.417  INFO 23387 --- [pool-2-thread-1] n.l.b.e.c.text.SimpleMessageSender
: Sending message: simple message
2015-05-30 20:44:53.435  INFO 23387 --- [pool-2-thread-1] n.l.b.eiws.chapter05.text.
SimpleService  : Message received: simple message
2015-05-30 20:44:54.417  INFO 23387 --- [pool-2-thread-1] n.l.b.e.c.text.SimpleMessageSender
: Sending message: simple message
2015-05-30 20:44:54.628  INFO 23387 --- [pool-2-thread-1] n.l.b.eiws.chapter05.text.
SimpleService  : Message received: simple message
```

Such message reception is also called *polling*. As we can see from the output, this synchronous message reception brings into the equation delays that might not be suitable for our requirements in most cases. Therefore, it is most common to use asynchronous JMS reception via registering JMS listeners.

Using the MessageCreator Callback

Sometimes we may need to construct a message based on the JMS Session object. In such a case, we need to use JmsTemplate with conjunction with the MessageCreator interface for sending messages. The signature of this interface is shown in Listing 5-25.

Listing 5-25. Signature of the MessageCreator Interface

```
package org.springframework.jms.core;

import javax.jms.JMSException;
import javax.jms.Message;
import javax.jms.Session;

public interface MessageCreator {
  Message createMessage(Session session) throws JMSException;
}
```

This callback interface expects that we implement the createMessage method and provide custom logic for the javax.jms.Message creation based on the javax.jms.Session object. Such custom message construction logic is then passed into JmsTemplate.send and JmsTemplate.sendAndReceive methods while sending the message.

185

This mechanism allows Spring to manage session instances (for example, for caching) and at the same time provides application developers full flexibility of lower-level JMS APIs. An example of this use is shown in Listing 5-26.

Listing 5-26. MessageCreator Usage (0512-jms-message-creator)

```java
package net.lkrnac.book.eiws.chapter05.text;

import javax.jms.JMSException;
import javax.jms.Message;
import javax.jms.Session;

import lombok.extern.slf4j.Slf4j;

import org.springframework.beans.factory.annotation.Autowired;
import org.springframework.jms.core.JmsTemplate;
import org.springframework.jms.core.MessageCreator;
import org.springframework.scheduling.annotation.Scheduled;
import org.springframework.stereotype.Component;

@Slf4j
@Component
public class SimpleMessageSender {
  private static final String SIMPLE_MESSAGE = "simple message";
  private JmsTemplate jmsTemplate;

  @Autowired
  public SimpleMessageSender(JmsTemplate jmsTemplate) {
    super();
    this.jmsTemplate = jmsTemplate;
  }

  @Scheduled(fixedRate = 1000)
  public void send() {
    log.info("Sending message: {}", SIMPLE_MESSAGE);
    jmsTemplate.send("queue/ExpiryQueue", new MessageCreator() {
      @Override
      public Message createMessage(Session session) throws JMSException {
        return session.createTextMessage(SIMPLE_MESSAGE);
      }
    });
  }
}
```

This variant of SimpleMessageSender is similar to Listing 5-20, except for the send method implementation. Here we use the jmsTemplate.send call with the name of the destination as its first parameter. The second parameter of type MessageCreator is created via an anonymous inner class.

To create a message in the MessageCreator callback, we use the JMS API call session.createTextMessage, which returns a TextMessage instance. This is then passed to Spring so that it can send the instance to the queue.

Listening to JMS Messages

Synchronous reception of JMS messages, which can be subject to delays, doesn't really fit into the current real-time demands from enterprise systems. Therefore, listening to JMS messages is a much more common approach for JMS message consumption. Spring uses the `MessageListenerContainer` interface to listen to new messages that appear on the JMS destination.

There are two out-of-the-box implementations that use opposite approaches for message reception:

- `SimpleMessageListenerContainer`: This implementation uses the standard JMS listener registration `MessageConsumer.setMessageListener()` under the hood, as we showed in the asynchronous JMS example in Listings 5-11 and 5-12. It is not able to participate in any distributed transactions. Also it is using a constant number of JMS `Session` objects, so it can't dynamically adapt to runtime spikes in the message load.

- `DefaultMessageListenerContainer`: This is a default implementation that uses a mechanism called *long polling*. This means that Spring uses `MessageConsumer. receive()` calls in a stand-alone thread to wait for messages. This thread is blocked, and when the message appears on the destination, it is immediately received and passed to the registered listener in a separate thread. We can configure the number of listener threads via the `concurrentConsumers` property. To avoid endless waiting, the `receive` call uses a time-out parameter in conjunction with an endless loop, which makes sure that this listener container is listening nearly all the time. There are various advantages to this approach:

  - The consumer can use transactional features of JMS reception and participate in distributed transactions.

  - It can easily recover from a temporary outage of the JMS destination.

  - We can optionally allow for dynamic adaptation to runtime demand by specifying a `maxConcurrentConsumers` property different from `concurrentConsumers`.

Various options exist for creating `MessageListenerContainer`:

- Using the `<jms:listener-container>` XML element

- Registering the `MessageListenerContainer` bean directly via the `@Bean` annotation or `<bean>` XML element

`MessageListenerContainer` manages the reception of messages, but we also need to register listeners into it. Again, various options are available for registering application logic that will be handling received messages:

- Using the `<jms:listener>` XML element

- Registering the `MessageListenerContainer` bean with a list of listener implementations

- Using the `@JmsListener` annotation

The @JmsListener annotation was introduced in Spring version 4.1. A method annotated with @JmsListener can be used for flexible injection of JMS message instances or their parts. Spring supports injections of the following:

- javax.jms.Message or any of its subclasses

- javax.jms.Session

- org.springframework.messaging.Message<T> as a generic Spring messaging abstraction for Spring messaging. This abstraction also can be used for other messaging types Spring supports (for example, by Spring Integration, WebSockets, AMQP)

- JMS message header with the @Header annotation

- All JMS message headers with the @Headers annotation

- JMS message payload with the @Payload annotation

- Let's demonstrate some of these constructs on simple examples.

Examples of Registering Listener with XML Configuration

Our first example of the Spring JMS listener implementation is shown in Listing 5-27.

Listing 5-27. Message Listener as a Subclass of javax.jms.MessageListener (0505-async-jms-xml)

```java
package net.lkrnac.book.eiws.chapter05.text;

import javax.jms.JMSException;
import javax.jms.Message;
import javax.jms.MessageListener;
import javax.jms.TextMessage;
import net.lkrnac.book.eiws.chapter05.text.SimpleService;
import org.springframework.beans.factory.annotation.Autowired;
import org.springframework.stereotype.Component;

@Component
public class SimpleMessageListener implements MessageListener {
  private SimpleService simpleService;

  @Autowired
  public SimpleMessageListener(SimpleService simpleService) {
    super();
    this.simpleService = simpleService;
  }

  @Override
  public void onMessage(Message message) {
    try {
      TextMessage textMessage = (TextMessage) message;
      simpleService.processText(textMessage.getText());
    } catch (JMSException ex) {
      ex.printStackTrace();
    }
  }
}
```

This listener implements the `javax.jms.MessageListener` interface. At the same time, it is also a Spring bean that injects the `simpleService` instance via constructor injection. This service instance is the same as in Listing 5-10.

`SimpleMessageListener` has to implement the `onMessage` method as per the JMS listener contract driven by the interface `javax.jms.MessageListener`. An instance of `javax.jms.Message` is passed into this method when the message is received via its JMS destination. To consume this message in our application, we need to cast it into `TextMessage` and pass it into our `simpleService` instance. Calling `textMessage.getTest()` forces us to handle `JMSException` because it is a checked one.

Listing 5-28 shows how to register this listener in Spring.

Listing 5-28. Listener Configured Without JMS Namespace (File spring-jms-listener.xml in Folder src/main/resources in Example Project 0505-async-jms-xml)

```xml
<?xml version="1.0" encoding="UTF-8"?>
<beans xmlns="http://www.springframework.org/schema/beans"
  xmlns:xsi="http://www.w3.org/2001/XMLSchema-instance"
  xsi:schemaLocation="http://www.springframework.org/schema/beans
    http://www.springframework.org/schema/beans/spring-beans.xsd">

  <bean
    class="org.springframework.jms.listener.DefaultMessageListenerContainer">
    <property name="connectionFactory" ref="connectionFactory" />
    <property name="destinationName" value="queue/ExpiryQueue" />
    <property name="messageListener" ref="simpleMessageListener" />
  </bean>
</beans>
```

This Spring XML configuration uses only the bean namespace for registering Spring beans. There is only one bean of type `DefaultMessageListenerContainer` registered. We need to configure the mandatory parameter `connectionFactory`, which was created in a similar way as we already explained earlier in this chapter.

The second mandatory parameter is `destinationName`. As this example is using Spring Boot as a convenience layer for configuring some boilerplate beans, we use the same queue name as in our other examples.

Finally, we register our `simpleMessageListener` instance, and the listener is configured.

As you can see, this approach has a downside because the invasive JMS API forces us to handle the checked `JMSException` and we need to implement the `javax.jms.MessageListener` interface. But there is better way, which can help us to avoid the invasive JMS API altogether.

One possible question arises: "What if we require an application with more than one listener?" In such a case, it is better to use the `<jms-listener>` namespace or the most modern `@JmsListener` annotation introduced in Spring 4.1. These are shown in subsequent examples.

Listing 5-29 shows a possible implementation of the message listener that wouldn't need to implement `javax.jms.MessageListener`.

Listing 5-29. JMS API Agnostic Listener Implementation (0504-async-jms-namespace)

```
package net.lkrnac.book.eiws.chapter05.text;

import org.springframework.beans.factory.annotation.Autowired;
import org.springframework.stereotype.Component;

@Component
public class SimpleMessageListener {
  private SimpleService simpleService;

  @Autowired
  public SimpleMessageListener(SimpleService simpleService) {
    super();
    this.simpleService = simpleService;
  }

  public void handleMessage(String message) {
    simpleService.processText(message);
  }
}
```

It is a Spring bean, which takes the `simpleService` instance via constructor injection. `SimpleService` is the bean from Listing 5-10. Listing 5-30 shows how to use XML configuration to configure this listener.

Listing 5-30. Listener Configured with JMS Namespace (File spring-jms-listener.xml in Folder src/main/resources in Example Project 0504-async-jms-namespace)

```
<?xml version="1.0" encoding="UTF-8"?>
<beans xmlns="http://www.springframework.org/schema/beans"
  xmlns:xsi="http://www.w3.org/2001/XMLSchema-instance"
  xmlns:jms="http://www.springframework.org/schema/jms"
  xsi:schemaLocation="http://www.springframework.org/schema/jms
    http://www.springframework.org/schema/jms/spring-jms.xsd
    http://www.springframework.org/schema/beans
    http://www.springframework.org/schema/beans/spring-beans.xsd">

  <jms:listener-container destination-resolver="destinationResolver">
    <jms:listener destination="queue/ExpiryQueue" ref="simpleMessageListener"
      method="handleMessage" />
  </jms:listener-container>
</beans>
```

This configuration uses the bean namespace to enable working with Spring beans, and the jms namespace for JMS container support. The root XML element `<jms:listener-container>` by default uses the `DefaultMessageListenerContainer` implementation of the listener container. The attribute `destination-resolver` uses the bean already shown in Listing 5-16.

The XML subelement `<jms:listener>` registers the listener instance `simpleMessageListener` for message reception via its method `handleMessage`. This method takes the `String` parameter, so Spring automatically converts the JMS message payload into the `String` type and injects it as a parameter.

`<jms:listener-container>` can have various `<jms-listener>` subelements registered for different JMS destinations.

Examples of Registering Listener with Java Configuration

Registering the listener with a Java configuration looks like Listing 5-31.

Listing 5-31. Listener Configured with Java Configuration (0506-async-jms-java-config)

```java
package net.lkrnac.book.eiws.chapter05.text;

import javax.jms.ConnectionFactory;
import javax.jms.Queue;
import org.springframework.context.annotation.Bean;
import org.springframework.context.annotation.Configuration;
import org.springframework.jms.listener.DefaultMessageListenerContainer;

@Configuration
public class JmsListenerConfiguration {
  @Bean
  public DefaultMessageListenerContainer defaultMessageListenerContainer(
      ConnectionFactory connectionFactory,
      SimpleMessageListener simpleMessageListener, Queue queue) {
    DefaultMessageListenerContainer listenerContainer =
        new DefaultMessageListenerContainer();
    listenerContainer.setConnectionFactory(connectionFactory);
    listenerContainer.setDestination(queue);
    listenerContainer.setMessageListener(simpleMessageListener);
    return listenerContainer;
  }
}
```

This Spring configuration class registers only the DefaultMessageListenerContainer bean. The method registering the bean injects three other Spring beans: containerFactory, queue, and simpleMessageListener. These are needed for configuring the listenerContainer instance after it's created via the constructor.

Spring 4.1 introduced a new JMS annotation, shown in Listing 5-32.

Listing 5-32. Listener Configured with @JmsListener Annotation (0508-async-listener-annotation)

```java
package net.lkrnac.book.eiws.chapter05.text;

import net.lkrnac.book.eiws.chapter05.text.SimpleService;

import org.springframework.beans.factory.annotation.Autowired;
import org.springframework.jms.annotation.JmsListener;
import org.springframework.stereotype.Component;

@Component
public class SimpleMessageListener {
  private SimpleService simpleService;
```

```
  @Autowired
  public SimpleMessageListener(SimpleService simpleService) {
    super();
    this.simpleService = simpleService;
  }

  @JmsListener(destination = "queue/ExpiryQueue")
  public void readMessage(String message) {
    simpleService.processText(message);
  }
}
```

The method handling messages is annotated with @JmsListener. Spring exposes this method as a JMS endpoint that listens to JMS messages. This annotation has the mandatory attribute destination, which defines the name of the destination it listens to. This is the preferred way of receiving messages nowadays.

Converting JMS Messages

A useful feature provided by the Spring JMS module is message conversion. Although plain JMS provides an option to send Serializable objects as a payload, it's not a popular solution because of lack of interoperability. So as JMS primary uses a text and sometimes binary payload format, conversion from/to some text-based formats is a pretty standard requirement. This may be a verbose and error-prone exercise with plain Java JMS APIs.

Fortunately, Spring JMS provides an elegant solution. We can convert messages on both sides of the communication channel, because both JmsTemplate (responsible for sending and for synchronous JMS message reception) and AbstractJmsListenerContainerFactory (responsible for listening to the JMS destination and the abstract parent of DefaultJmsListenerContainerFactory and SimpleJmsListenerContainerFactory) allows us to optionally register the MessageConverter interface as their property. Listing 5-33 shows the signature of this interface.

Listing 5-33. Signature of org.springframework.jms.support.converter.MessageConverter

```
package org.springframework.jms.support.converter;

import javax.jms.JMSException;
import javax.jms.Message;
import javax.jms.Session;

public interface MessageConverter {
  Message toMessage(Object object, Session session) throws JMSException,
    MessageConversionException;

  Object fromMessage(Message message) throws JMSException,
    MessageConversionException;
}
```

It's obvious that bidirectional conversion is expected. This message converter instance is used to convert any message that flows through JmsTemplate or AbstractJmsListenerContainerFactory where it was registered. So with this approach, we can easily plug into our JMS communication custom message conversion.

Furthermore, Spring provides a few out-of-the-box implementations for the most common transport formats:

- `org.springframework.jms.support.converter.`
  `MappingJackson2MessageConverter`: As a wrapper for Jackson library version 2, providing JSON to Java POJOs conversion.

- `MarshallingMessageConverter`: For XML marshaling/unmarshalling using `org.springframework.oxm.Marshaller` and `org.springframework.oxm.Unmarshaller`.

- `MessagingMessageConverter`: Is used in cases where we are also sending custom JMS headers alongside the payload that should be converted. Was introduced in Spring 4.1.

To demonstrate this support, we'll change the domain model. The domain model will be represented by the POJO shown in Listing 5-34.

Listing 5-34. User POJO (0500-jms-common)

```
package net.lkrnac.book.eiws.chapter05.user;

import lombok.Data;

@Data
public class User {
  private String email;
  private String name;
}
```

This is a simple Java type with two private fields: `email` and `name`. The Lombok annotation `@Data` will generate a constructor with these two parameters, and getters and setters for them.

Example of JSON Conversion

To demonstrate the out-of-the-box JSON conversion that Spring JMS provides, we need to register the `MessageConverter` bean, as shown in Listing 5-35.

Listing 5-35. JSON JMS Conversion Configuration (0509-jms-message-converter)

```
package net.lkrnac.book.eiws.chapter05.user;

import javax.jms.ConnectionFactory;

import org.springframework.context.annotation.Bean;
import org.springframework.context.annotation.Configuration;
import org.springframework.jms.annotation.EnableJms;
import org.springframework.jms.config.DefaultJmsListenerContainerFactory;
import org.springframework.jms.core.JmsTemplate;
import org.springframework.jms.support.converter.MappingJackson2MessageConverter;
import org.springframework.jms.support.converter.MessageConverter;
import org.springframework.jms.support.converter.MessageType;

@Configuration
@EnableJms
```

```java
public class JmsConfiguration {
  @Bean
  public MessageConverter messageConverter() {
    MappingJackson2MessageConverter messageConverter =
        new MappingJackson2MessageConverter();
    messageConverter.setTargetType(MessageType.TEXT);
    messageConverter.setTypeIdPropertyName("__type");
    return messageConverter;
  }

  @Bean
  public JmsTemplate jmsTemplate(ConnectionFactory connectionFactory,
      MessageConverter messageConverter) {
    JmsTemplate jmsTemplate = new JmsTemplate(connectionFactory);
    jmsTemplate.setMessageConverter(messageConverter);
    return jmsTemplate;
  }

  @Bean
  public DefaultJmsListenerContainerFactory jmsListenerContainerFactory(
      ConnectionFactory connectionFactory, MessageConverter messageConverter) {
    DefaultJmsListenerContainerFactory factory =
        new DefaultJmsListenerContainerFactory();
    factory.setConnectionFactory(connectionFactory);
    factory.setMessageConverter(messageConverter);
    return factory;
  }
}
```

The first bean registered in this configuration class is messageConverter. We use the MappingJackson2MessageConverter implementation that covers JSON conversion. In order to tell Spring that our target format is plain text, we need to configure the targetType property to MessageType.TEXT. The typeIdPropertyName property with the value __type is needed, because Spring needs to know that we are converting text-transport format into/from Java POJOs. The __type value is used as a special JMS header that holds the full Java name of the type being used for JSON conversion. Two underscores should ensure that this header won't conflict with the custom JMS header that the application may use.

The next two beans are already familiar to us. JmsTemplate is used for sending messages, and DefaultJmsListenerContainerFactory is used for message reception. The difference here is that we inject and set the messageConverter property for both.

Listing 5-36 shows how to send the User object to the JMS destination.

Listing 5-36. Sending JSON Formatted JMS Messages (0509-jms-message-converter)

```java
package net.lkrnac.book.eiws.chapter05.user;

import lombok.extern.slf4j.Slf4j;
import net.lkrnac.book.eiws.chapter05.user.User;

import org.springframework.beans.factory.annotation.Autowired;
import org.springframework.jms.core.JmsTemplate;
import org.springframework.scheduling.annotation.Scheduled;
import org.springframework.stereotype.Component;
```

```
@Slf4j
@Component
public class UserMessageSender {
  private JmsTemplate jmsTemplate;

  @Autowired
  public UserMessageSender(JmsTemplate jmsTemplate) {
    super();
    this.jmsTemplate = jmsTemplate;
  }

  @Scheduled(fixedRate = 1000)
  public void send() {
    User user = new User();
    user.setEmail("lubos.krnac@gmail.com");
    user.setName("Lubos Krnac");

    log.info("Sending message: {}", user);
    jmsTemplate.convertAndSend("queue/ExpiryQueue", user);
  }
}
```

In this class, the JMS message is sent every second, as defined by the @Scheduled annotation. First we create and initialize the User object and log the message about sending it. Next we call the jmsTemplate.convertAndSend() method with the message queue name and the user object as parameters. Spring will use the underlying MappingJackson2MessageConverter to convert our POJO into JSON and embed it into the JMS message payload.

Listing 5-37 shows how to listen to such a message.

Listing 5-37. Listening to JSON Formatted JMS Message (0509-jms-message-converter)

```
package net.lkrnac.book.eiws.chapter05.user;

import net.lkrnac.book.eiws.chapter05.user.User;
import net.lkrnac.book.eiws.chapter05.user.UserService;
import org.springframework.beans.factory.annotation.Autowired;
import org.springframework.jms.annotation.JmsListener;
import org.springframework.stereotype.Component;

@Component
public class UserMessageListener {
  private UserService userService;

  @Autowired
  public UserMessageListener(UserService userService) {
    super();
    this.userService = userService;
  }

  @JmsListener(destination = "queue/ExpiryQueue")
  public void readMessage(User user) {
    userService.processUser(user);
  }
}
```

The readMessage method is annotated with @JmsListener, so it listens to the JMS queue with the name queue/ExpiryQueue. The parameter of this method is of type User. Spring knows which converter to use to convert the JSON message into a User object. After conversion, it is injected into our logic.

The UserService bean implementation is shown in Listing 5-38.

Listing 5-38. UserService Bean Configuration (0500-jms-common)

```java
package net.lkrnac.book.eiws.chapter05.user;

import lombok.extern.slf4j.Slf4j;
import org.springframework.stereotype.Service;

@Slf4j
@Service
public class UserService {
  public void processUser(User user) {
    log.info("User object Received: {}", user);
  }
}
```

Handling of the message is simple: print the output to the console. The last class in this 0509-jms-message-converter example is the main class in Listing 5-39.

Listing 5-39. Main Class of the JSON Message Converter Example (0509-jms-message-converter)

```java
package net.lkrnac.book.eiws.chapter05.user;

import org.springframework.boot.SpringApplication;
import org.springframework.boot.autoconfigure.SpringBootApplication;
import org.springframework.scheduling.annotation.EnableScheduling;

@EnableScheduling
@SpringBootApplication
public class JmsMessageConverterApplication {
  public static void main(String[] args) throws InterruptedException {
    SpringApplication.run(JmsMessageConverterApplication.class, args);
  }
}
```

This is a standard Spring Boot main class. When we run it, the output looks like Listing 5-40.

Listing 5-40. Output of JSON Conversion Example

```
2015-05-30 19:50:28.076  INFO 22175 --- [pool-1-thread-1] n.l.b.e.c.user.UserMessageSender
: Sending message: User(email=lubos.krnac@gmail.com, name=Lubos Krnac)
2015-05-30 19:50:28.093  INFO 22175 --- [enerContainer-1] n.l.b.eiws.chapter05.user.
UserService    : User object Received: User(email=lubos.krnac@gmail.com, name=Lubos Krnac)
2015-05-30 19:50:29.076  INFO 22175 --- [pool-1-thread-1] n.l.b.e.c.user.UserMessageSender
: Sending message: User(email=lubos.krnac@gmail.com, name=Lubos Krnac)
2015-05-30 19:50:29.092  INFO 22175 --- [enerContainer-1] n.l.b.eiws.chapter05.user.
UserService    : User object Received: User(email=lubos.krnac@gmail.com, name=Lubos Krnac)
```

Note that listening to messages doesn't introduce any artificial delays into our communication.

Custom Conversion Example

The next example highlights how to transfer and convert messages with a custom conversion format. Listing 5-41 shows conversion into/from our custom payload format.

Listing 5-41. Custom Message Converter (0510-jms-custom-converter)

```java
package net.lkrnac.book.eiws.chapter05.user;

import javax.jms.JMSException;
import javax.jms.Message;
import javax.jms.Session;
import net.lkrnac.book.eiws.chapter05.user.User;
import org.springframework.jms.support.converter.MessageConversionException;
import org.springframework.jms.support.converter.MessageConverter;
import org.springframework.stereotype.Component;

@Component
public class UserMessageConverter implements MessageConverter {
  private static final String DELIMITER = ";";

  @Override
  public Message toMessage(Object object, Session session) throws JMSException,
      MessageConversionException {
    User user = (User) object;
    String userString = user.getEmail() + DELIMITER + user.getName();
    return session.createTextMessage(userString);
  }

  @Override
  public Object fromMessage(Message message) throws JMSException,
      MessageConversionException {
    String userMessage = message.getBody(String.class);
    String[] userStringChunks = userMessage.split(DELIMITER);
    User user = new User();
    user.setEmail(userStringChunks[0]);
    user.setName(userStringChunks[1]);
    return user;
  }
}
```

This class implements the `org.springframework.jms.support.converter.MessageConverter` interface. Its contract is driven by two methods: `toMessage` and `fromMessage`. In `toMessage`, we receive a Java object that should be converted into `javax.jms.Message`. We know that it will be of type `User`; therefore, we cast it into this type. Our custom format is a simple listing of `User` object properties in the order `email` and `name`, delimited by `;`. When we have the `userString` payload constructed, we call `session.createTextMessage()` to wrap `String` into `javax.jms.Message`. The session instance is injected into the `toMessage` conversion method via a parameter from Spring.

The second method, `fromMessage`, does the exact opposite. It extracts an injected message of type `javax.jms.Message` into the `String` representation `userMessage` and splits it into an array of values based on the delimiter. Subsequently, a user object is created based on these values and returned to the Spring framework.

197

This converter component is annotated by @Component, and therefore Spring can use it for configuring JmsTemplate and DefaultJmsListenerContainerFactory. This configuration is shown in Listing 5-42.

Listing 5-42. Custom JMS Converter Example Configuration (0510-jms-custom-converter)

```
package net.lkrnac.book.eiws.chapter05.user;

import javax.jms.ConnectionFactory;
import org.springframework.context.annotation.Bean;
import org.springframework.context.annotation.Configuration;
import org.springframework.jms.annotation.EnableJms;
import org.springframework.jms.config.DefaultJmsListenerContainerFactory;
import org.springframework.jms.core.JmsTemplate;
import org.springframework.jms.support.converter.MessageConverter;

@Configuration
@EnableJms
public class JmsConfiguration {
  @Bean
  public JmsTemplate jmsTemplate(ConnectionFactory connectionFactory,
      MessageConverter messageConverter) {
    JmsTemplate jmsTemplate = new JmsTemplate(connectionFactory);
    jmsTemplate.setMessageConverter(messageConverter);
    return jmsTemplate;
  }

  @Bean
  public DefaultJmsListenerContainerFactory jmsListenerContainerFactory(
      ConnectionFactory connectionFactory, MessageConverter messageConverter) {
    DefaultJmsListenerContainerFactory factory =
        new DefaultJmsListenerContainerFactory();
    factory.setConnectionFactory(connectionFactory);
    factory.setMessageConverter(messageConverter);
    return factory;
  }
}
```

This configuration is similar to Listing 5-35. The only difference is that the message converter is our custom converter UserMessageConverter instance.

Sending and listening to messages is exactly the same as in Listings 5-36 and 5-37 from the JSON conversion example.

MessagingMessageConverter Example

The last JMS message conversion example covers MessagingMessageConverter and the annotations for injecting JMS message parts when using the @JmsListener annotation. This message conversion is handy when we need to convert messages and send custom JMS headers alongside the converted message payload.

To explain these capabilities of the Spring 4.1 framework, we again need to amend the requirements. We keep the need to send the User object as a payload. The new requirement is sending the role or the user in the JMS header as a String value. Listing 5-43 shows an implementation of the message sender with this new requirement.

Listing 5-43. JMS Message Sender or User Object and Role (0514-jms-message-annotations)

```java
package net.lkrnac.book.eiws.chapter05.userwithrole;

import lombok.extern.slf4j.Slf4j;
import net.lkrnac.book.eiws.chapter05.user.User;
import org.springframework.beans.factory.annotation.Autowired;
import org.springframework.jms.core.JmsTemplate;
import org.springframework.messaging.Message;
import org.springframework.messaging.support.MessageBuilder;
import org.springframework.scheduling.annotation.Scheduled;
import org.springframework.stereotype.Component;

@Slf4j
@Component
public class UserMessageSender {
  private static final String ADMIN = "admin";
  private JmsTemplate jmsTemplate;

  @Autowired
  public UserMessageSender(JmsTemplate jmsTemplate) {
    super();
    this.jmsTemplate = jmsTemplate;
  }

  @Scheduled(fixedRate = 1000)
  public void send() {
    User user = new User();
    user.setEmail("lubos.krnac@gmail.com");
    user.setName("Lubos Krnac");

    log.info("Sending User: {} in role {}", user, ADMIN);
    Message<User> userMessage = MessageBuilder
     .withPayload(user)
     .setHeader("role", ADMIN)
     .build();

    jmsTemplate.convertAndSend("queue/ExpiryQueue", userMessage);
  }
}
```

The beginning of this UserMessageSender class should be familiar from previous examples. What's new is the constant defining the role of the user, which we want to send as the JMS header. The send method is again scheduled to run every second.

In the body of this method, we create the user object that will be sent to the JMS destination and the log data we want to send. Next we use MessageBuilder support that was introduced in Spring 4.0 for constructing JMS messages. The payload will be our user object, and the role header has the admin value. Finally, we call jmsTemplate to send the message we constructed.

Listing 5-44 covers the listener part of this example.

Listing 5-44. Injecting JMS Message Parts (0514-jms-message-annotations)

```java
package net.lkrnac.book.eiws.chapter05.userwithrole;

import java.util.Map;
import lombok.extern.slf4j.Slf4j;
import net.lkrnac.book.eiws.chapter05.user.User;
import org.springframework.beans.factory.annotation.Autowired;
import org.springframework.jms.annotation.JmsListener;
import org.springframework.messaging.handler.annotation.Header;
import org.springframework.messaging.handler.annotation.Headers;
import org.springframework.messaging.handler.annotation.Payload;
import org.springframework.stereotype.Component;

@Slf4j
@Component
public class UserMessageListener {
  private UserWithRoleService userWithRoleService;

  @Autowired
  public UserMessageListener(UserWithRoleService userWithRoleService) {
    super();
    this.userWithRoleService = userWithRoleService;
  }

  @JmsListener(destination = "queue/ExpiryQueue")
  public void readMessage(@Payload User user, @Header String role,
      @Headers Map<String, Object> headers) {
    log.info("Message with ID " + headers.get("id") + " received");
    userWithRoleService.processUser(user, role);
  }
}
```

In this case, the readMessage method doesn't take the String parameter of the message body anymore. When we annotate the user parameter with @Payload, we indicate to Spring that conversion of the JMS message into the User type should be performed. The second injection we do here is injection of the custom JMS header with the name role. This injection is possible via the @Header annotation. Spring is able to identify the header based on the parameter name. Both objects are later passed into the userWithRoleService.processUser() call.

Finally, we inject all the headers of the JMS message into the map and use the header with the name id in the log entry, indicating that the message was received. UserWithRoleService is defined in Listing 5-45.

Listing 5-45. Service for Processing User Message with Role (0500-jms-common)

```java
package net.lkrnac.book.eiws.chapter05.userwithrole;

import lombok.extern.slf4j.Slf4j;
import net.lkrnac.book.eiws.chapter05.user.User;
import org.springframework.stereotype.Service;
```

```
@Slf4j
@Service
public class UserWithRoleService {
  public void processUser(User user, String role) {
    log.info("User object Received: {} with role {}", user, role);
  }
}
```

Again, to simplify the example and at the same time allow our examples to be backed up by the integration test suite (as we want to make sure that code snippets in the book are working), we just log the data received. The interesting configuration difference for the Spring JMS resource beans is shown in Listing 5-46.

Listing 5-46. JMS Configuration of MessagingMessageConverter Example (0514-jms-message-annotations)

```
package net.lkrnac.book.eiws.chapter05.userwithrole;

import javax.jms.ConnectionFactory;
import org.springframework.context.annotation.Bean;
import org.springframework.context.annotation.Configuration;
import org.springframework.jms.annotation.EnableJms;
import org.springframework.jms.config.DefaultJmsListenerContainerFactory;
import org.springframework.jms.core.JmsTemplate;
import org.springframework.jms.support.converter.MappingJackson2MessageConverter;
import org.springframework.jms.support.converter.MessageConverter;
import org.springframework.jms.support.converter.MessageType;
import org.springframework.jms.support.converter.MessagingMessageConverter;

@Configuration
@EnableJms
public class JmsConfiguration {
  @Bean
  public JmsTemplate jmsTemplate(ConnectionFactory connectionFactory,
      MessageConverter messageConverter) {
    JmsTemplate jmsTemplate = new JmsTemplate(connectionFactory);
    jmsTemplate.setMessageConverter(messageConverter);
    return jmsTemplate;
  }

  @Bean
  public MessageConverter messageConverter() {
    MappingJackson2MessageConverter payloadConverter =
        new MappingJackson2MessageConverter();
    payloadConverter.setTargetType(MessageType.TEXT);
    payloadConverter.setTypeIdPropertyName("__type");

    MessagingMessageConverter messageConverter =
        new MessagingMessageConverter();
    messageConverter.setPayloadConverter(payloadConverter);
    return messageConverter;
  }
```

```
@Bean
public DefaultJmsListenerContainerFactory jmsListenerContainerFactory(
    ConnectionFactory connectionFactory, MessageConverter messageConverter) {
  DefaultJmsListenerContainerFactory factory =
      new DefaultJmsListenerContainerFactory();
  factory.setConnectionFactory(connectionFactory);
  factory.setMessageConverter(messageConverter);
  return factory;
  }
}
```

The noticeable difference in this snippet is in the messageConverter bean construction. Instead of returning MappingJackson2MessageConverter as our message converter, we wrap it into MessagingMessageConverter as the payload converter, which allows us to append the String value of the role to the messages. Without this construct, String would also try to convert our role from/to the User type. If we didn't wrap it this way, conversion would obviously fail. So this configuration is needed when we want to inject JMS message headers and at the same time use custom conversion for the JMS message payload.

All these Spring beans are again under the same umbrella of the main Spring Boot class shown in Listing 5-47.

Listing 5-47. Main Class of User with Role Example (0514-jms-message-annotations)

```
package net.lkrnac.book.eiws.chapter05.userwithrole;

import org.springframework.boot.SpringApplication;
import org.springframework.boot.autoconfigure.SpringBootApplication;
import org.springframework.scheduling.annotation.EnableScheduling;

@EnableScheduling
@SpringBootApplication
public class JmsMessageAnnotationsApplication {
  public static void main(String[] args) throws InterruptedException {
    SpringApplication.run(JmsMessageAnnotationsApplication.class, args);
  }
}
```

If you paid attention to the previous examples, there's no surprise here. Listing 5-48 shows the output from running this main class.

Listing 5-48. Output of User with Role Example

```
2015-06-19 20:10:14.156  INFO 10408 --- [pool-2-thread-1] n.l.b.e.c.u.UserMessageSender
: Sending User: User(email=lubos.krnac@gmail.com, name=Lubos Krnac) in role admin
2015-06-19 20:10:14.285  INFO 10408 --- [enerContainer-1] n.l.b.e.c.u.UserMessageListener
: Message with ID c742ee49-6234-5804-7b60-3f51ede3ed73 received
2015-06-19 20:10:14.286  INFO 10408 --- [enerContainer-1] n.l.b.e.c.u.UserWithRoleService
: User object Received: User(email=lubos.krnac@gmail.com, name=Lubos Krnac) with role admin
2015-06-19 20:10:15.148  INFO 10408 --- [pool-2-thread-1] n.l.b.e.c.u.UserMessageSender
: Sending User: User(email=lubos.krnac@gmail.com, name=Lubos Krnac) in role admin
2015-06-19 20:10:15.160  INFO 10408 --- [enerContainer-1] n.l.b.e.c.u.UserMessageListener
: Message with ID 39b06e8f-84f6-0f0b-71b9-d9a88867633e received
2015-06-19 20:10:15.161  INFO 10408 --- [enerContainer-1] n.l.b.e.c.u.UserWithRoleService
: User object Received: User(email=lubos.krnac@gmail.com, name=Lubos Krnac) with role admin
```

Using the Publish/Subscribe JMS Model

At the beginning of this chapter, we mentioned a communication paradigm for sending messages to various subscribers. This important JMS abstraction hasn't been covered by the examples so far. The following examples will fix that.

The first class introduced is the service where we delegate received messages. It's shown in Listing 5-49.

Listing 5-49. PubSubService (0515-publish-subscribe-java-config)

```java
package net.lkrnac.book.eiws.chapter05.pubsub;

import lombok.extern.slf4j.Slf4j;
import org.springframework.stereotype.Service;

@Slf4j
@Service
public class PubSubService {
  public void handleMessage(int listenerId, String message) {
    log.info("Message Received: {} via listener {}", message, listenerId);
  }
}
```

This logs the message received alongside the ID of the listener from which the message was received. Listing 5-50 shows the listener used in this example.

Listing 5-50. Listener for Publish/Subscribe (0515-publish-subscribe-java-config)

```java
package net.lkrnac.book.eiws.chapter05.pubsub;

import org.springframework.beans.factory.annotation.Autowired;
import org.springframework.jms.annotation.JmsListener;
import org.springframework.stereotype.Component;

@Component
public class SimpleMessageListener1 {
  private PubSubService pubSubService;

  @Autowired
  public SimpleMessageListener1(PubSubService pubSubService) {
    super();
    this.pubSubService = pubSubService;
  }

  @JmsListener(destination = "simpleTopic")
  public void readMessage(String message) {
    pubSubService.processText(1, message);
  }
}
```

SimpleMessageListener1 looks like a listener we've already seen. But notice that the JMS destination used here has the name simpleTopic. In the next section, you will see how this JMS destination of type javax.jms.Topic can be configured.

The most obvious difference compared to other listeners in this chapter is the number in the class name. This is intentional; to demonstrate reception of one message by two listeners, we have two listeners in this example project. To keep the examples simple and listings shorter, the second listener is named SimpleMessageListener2 and is an exact copy of SimpleMessageListener1, except 1 is changed to 2.

Configuring JMS Publish/Subscribe with Spring

So far we've used the JMS destination queue/ExpiryQueue, because this queue is configured by the HornetQ server by default. But for the publish/subscribe JMS communication model, we need to use the JMS topic instead of the queue. So we need to change the HornetQ default configuration to provide this capability.

At the beginning of this chapter, we explained how to run the HornetQ server with the bin/run.sh or bin/run.bat commands. For the same HornetQ server, we need to append the topic configuration at the end of the configuration file config/stand-alone/non-clustered/hornet-jms.xml, as shown in Listing 5-51.

Listing 5-51. HornetQ Topic Configuration

```
<!-- ... -->

<queue name="ExpiryQueue">
   <entry name="/queue/ExpiryQueue"/>
</queue>

<topic name="simpleTopic">
   <entry name="/topic/simpleTopic"/>
</topic>
</configuration>
```

As we mentioned, ExpiryQueue is configured by default in the HornetQ installation. Every JMS example so far has used this queue. To configure our simpleTopic, we append the <topic> XML element at the end of this configuration file.

The main Spring class is named JmsApplication. It uses the same constructs as the main classes already shown in the previous examples, so we don't list it. Also, the sender of the messages is similar to other sender classes from this chapter, except instead of queue/ExpiryQueue, we use simpleTopic.

Listing 5-52 shows the Java JMS configuration for the publish/subscribe model for the sender and listeners.

Listing 5-52. Java Configuration of Publish/Subscribe Model (0515-publish-subscribe-java-config)

```
package net.lkrnac.book.eiws.chapter05.pubsub;

import java.util.Hashtable;
import javax.jms.ConnectionFactory;
import javax.naming.InitialContext;
import javax.naming.NamingException;
import org.springframework.context.annotation.Bean;
import org.springframework.context.annotation.Configuration;
import org.springframework.jms.annotation.EnableJms;
import org.springframework.jms.config.DefaultJmsListenerContainerFactory;
import org.springframework.jms.core.JmsTemplate;

@Configuration
@EnableJms
```

```java
public class JmsConfiguration {
  @Bean
  public InitialContext initialContext() throws NamingException {
    Hashtable<Object, Object> env = new Hashtable<Object, Object>();
    env.put("java.naming.factory.initial",
        "org.jnp.interfaces.NamingContextFactory");
    env.put("java.naming.factory.url.pkgs",
        "org.jboss.naming:org.jnp.interfaces");
    env.put("java.naming.provider.url", "jnp://localhost:1099");
    return new InitialContext(env);
  }

  @Bean
  public ConnectionFactory connectionFactory(InitialContext initialContext)
      throws NamingException {
    return (ConnectionFactory) initialContext.lookup("/ConnectionFactory");
  }

  @Bean
  public JmsTemplate jmsTemplate(ConnectionFactory connectionFactory) {
    JmsTemplate jmsTemplate = new JmsTemplate(connectionFactory);
    jmsTemplate.setPubSubDomain(true);
    return jmsTemplate;
  }

  @Bean
  public DefaultJmsListenerContainerFactory jmsListenerContainerFactory(
      ConnectionFactory connectionFactory) {
    DefaultJmsListenerContainerFactory factory =
        new DefaultJmsListenerContainerFactory();
    factory.setConnectionFactory(connectionFactory);
    factory.setPubSubDomain(true);
    return factory;
  }
}
```

The HornetQ JNDI configuration with the connectionFactory bean is the same as for the point-to-point examples. The publish/subscribe model needs to be turned on for JmsTemplate and DefaultJmsListenerContainerFactory via the pubSubDomain flag on both beans. When we run the JmsApplication class, we will see output similar to Listing 5-53.

Listing 5-53. Output of Publish/Subscribe Example

```
2015-05-30 20:52:19.860  INFO 23740 --- [pool-1-thread-1] n.l.b.e.c.pubsub.
SimpleMessageSender     : Sending message: simple message
2015-05-30 20:52:19.869  INFO 23740 --- [enerContainer-1] n.l.b.e.chapter05.pubsub.
PubSubService    : Message Received: simple message via listener 2
2015-05-30 20:52:19.869  INFO 23740 --- [enerContainer-1] n.l.b.e.chapter05.pubsub.
PubSubService    : Message Received: simple message via listener 1
2015-05-30 20:52:20.860  INFO 23740 --- [pool-1-thread-1] n.l.b.e.c.pubsub.
SimpleMessageSender     : Sending message: simple message
```

```
2015-05-30 20:52:20.871  INFO 23740 --- [enerContainer-1] n.l.b.e.chapter05.pubsub.
PubSubService    : Message Received: simple message via listener 2
2015-05-30 20:52:20.872  INFO 23740 --- [enerContainer-1] n.l.b.e.chapter05.pubsub.
PubSubService    : Message Received: simple message via listener 1
```

Spring Boot JMS Publish/Subscribe Example

There is also a new way of configuring the embedded HornetQ or ActiveMQ JMS broker hosted alongside our application. This configuration can help us reduce the Spring configuration boilerplate to a bare minimum and focus on business logic.

So far, we've used HornetQ and our JMS provider. But the latest stable version of Spring Boot doesn't work with embedded HornetQ in publish/subscribe mode. Therefore, we switch to the embedded ActiveMQ JMS broker for this example. ActiveMQ by default creates the JMS destination if it's been configured before. Therefore, no special configuration targeted to ActiveMQ is needed.

The only crucial piece of configuration is in Listing 5-54.

Listing 5-54. Spring Boot Publish/Subscribe Configuration (File application.properties in Folder src/main/resources in Example Project 0515-publish-subscribe-spring-boot)

```
spring.jms.pub-sub-domain=true
```

This configuration enables publish/subscribe mode on the JMS provider used in this example. It is fair to mention that Spring Boot externalized a huge number of properties for configuring underlying technologies. This way, we can amend the opinionated default behavior of Spring Boot to fit our requirements. In this case, we switched from point-to-point JMS communication to publish/subscribe.

All other classes are the same as for the previous plain Spring Java configuration example, but in this case we don't need to specify any JMS configuration beans, because Spring will autoconfigure them for us.

Integrating JMS with Higher-Level Messaging Abstractions

The Spring framework introduced in version 4.0 uniform messaging abstractions that can be used across various protocols such as STOMP, WebSockets, AMQP, JMS, or SockJS. These abstractions are located under a new Spring module called `spring-messaging`. The central abstraction for this support is `org.springframework.messaging.Message<T>`, which aims to abstract all the messages for the mentioned protocols.

Spring 4.1 created a new `JmsMessagingTemplate` class, built on top of `JmsTemplate`, that provides integration with the generic messaging abstraction (see Listing 5-55). Similar to `JmsTemplate`, `JmsMessagingTemplate` is also used for synchronous reception and sending of messages. On the other hand, listening to generic messages can be also integrated with the `@JmsListener` annotation.

Listing 5-55. Configuration of JmsMessagingTemplate (0513-jms-messaging-template)

```java
package net.lkrnac.book.eiws.chapter05.userwithrole;

import javax.jms.ConnectionFactory;
import org.springframework.context.annotation.Bean;
import org.springframework.context.annotation.Configuration;
import org.springframework.jms.annotation.EnableJms;
import org.springframework.jms.config.DefaultJmsListenerContainerFactory;
import org.springframework.jms.core.JmsMessagingTemplate;
import org.springframework.jms.support.converter.MappingJackson2MessageConverter;
```

```java
import org.springframework.jms.support.converter.MessageConverter;
import org.springframework.jms.support.converter.MessageType;
import org.springframework.jms.support.converter.MessagingMessageConverter;

@Configuration
@EnableJms
public class JmsConfiguration {
  @Bean
  public JmsMessagingTemplate jmsMessagingTemplate(
      ConnectionFactory connectionFactory, MessageConverter messageConverter) {
    JmsMessagingTemplate jmsMessagingTemplate =
      new JmsMessagingTemplate(connectionFactory);
    jmsMessagingTemplate.setJmsMessageConverter(messageConverter);
    return jmsMessagingTemplate;
  }

  @Bean
  public MessageConverter messageConverter() {
    MappingJackson2MessageConverter payloadConverter =
      new MappingJackson2MessageConverter();
    payloadConverter.setTargetType(MessageType.TEXT);
    payloadConverter.setTypeIdPropertyName("__type");

    MessagingMessageConverter messageConverter =
      new MessagingMessageConverter();
    messageConverter.setPayloadConverter(payloadConverter);
    return messageConverter;
  }

  @Bean
  public DefaultJmsListenerContainerFactory jmsListenerContainerFactory(
      ConnectionFactory connectionFactory, MessageConverter messageConverter) {
    DefaultJmsListenerContainerFactory factory =
      new DefaultJmsListenerContainerFactory();
    factory.setConnectionFactory(connectionFactory);
    factory.setMessageConverter(messageConverter);
    return factory;
  }
}
```

This creates three beans. The construction of JmsMessaggingTemplate is similar to JmsTemplate, as it's using the connectionFactory and messageConverter beans. These two beans are created in exactly the same way as in Listing 5-46 from the example project 0514-jms-message-annotations. All other beans are similar to examples we already covered.

The question may come up: "What is the benefit of using JmsMessagingTemplate over JmsTemplate, when there isn't a big difference between their usage and configuration?" It's true that using JmsMessagingTemplate isn't much different and doesn't bring any syntactic sugar for us, but bear in mind that JmsMessagingTemplate represents integration with the new Spring 4.0 generic type for messaging, org.springframework.messaging.Message<T>. Therefore, it can be essential when we need to integrate JMS with other Spring-supported messaging. For example, imagine a requirement to receive a message from the JMS destination synchronously and push it to a browser via WebSockets. Reading the message from the JMS destination via `JmsMessagingTemplate` allows us to read it as type `org.springframework.messaging.Message<T>` and send it to a web socket without any conversion.

In addition, the Spring Integration module is highly dependent on using `org.springframework.messaging.Message<T>` for sending via its pipes. Therefore, `JmsMessagingTemplate` can be useful in some use cases involving Spring Integration and JMS.

Summary

This chapter explained how JMS messaging communication differs from other types of communication protocols and approaches. In a pure Java example, we explored how to use the older JMS 1.1 and newer JMS 2.0 APIs as well as synchronous vs. asynchronous reception. These Java examples enabled us to compare the advantages of Spring abstractions and the significant reduction of plain JMS API verbosity.

Various possible Spring JMS configurations were explained based on plain XML or the `jms` namespace. Java configuration and Spring Boot also were covered. Then we presented the features of `JmsTemplate` and how it can be used for synchronous JMS message reception as well as for sending messages.

To receive JMS messages from JMS destinations immediately, you learned about Spring's `MessageListener` abstractions and how to configure them with XML and Java configuration.

The important `MessageConverter` abstractions allow us to use various standard and custom transport formats. We also dived into various new Spring 4.1 features such as `@JmsListener`, `@Header`, `@Headers`, `@Payload`, and `JmsMessagingTemplate`.

Near the end of the chapter, we also showed how to use the publish/subscribe JMS model.

CHAPTER 6

■ ■ ■

JMS Transactions

This chapter explains how to reliably send and receive JMS messages with local JMS transactions and explicit or implicit acknowledge modes. While explaining the main messaging concepts in the preceding chapter, we skipped one of the most important aspects of messaging communication: *reliability*. The Java Message Service communicates in most cases via a network. And networks commonly fail. Therefore, if we rely on messaging communication, we need to make sure that this communication is *fault-tolerant*.

This concept is similar to data persistence, because persisting data needs to be reliable and fault-tolerant also. You may be familiar with *ACID principles* from the data persistence world. This acronym stands for these principles:

- *Atomicity*: The whole transaction is committed, or no change is performed.

- *Consistency*: A state transition is done from one valid state into another valid state.

- *Isolation*: A partial change by transaction doesn't affect any other transactions.

- *Durability*: A change by transaction, once completed, remains persistent.

All these principles come into play because we are storing state into a database. But the Java Message Service also stores state. In fact, JMS providers often also persist messages on hard drives and act like a special kind of temporary document store that sends or removes messages from a JMS destination. Therefore, ACID principles make perfect sense for JMS communication.

JMS Reliability Mechanisms

To achieve ACID parameters of messaging, the Java Message Service protocol provides various mechanisms. All of them are centered around javax.jms.Session. With JMS 2.0, this responsibility was transferred to the javax.jms.JMSContext abstraction. We can think of both abstractions as a *unit of work* that can keep track of all the actions performed against it.

For reliable delivery of messages to/from the JMS server, the JMS standard provides two supporting concepts: message acknowledgement and local transactions. Here is list of all the possible JMS reliability modes:

- *Acknowledge modes*: Make sense only for reception of messages and don't affect sending

    - AUTO_ACKNOWLEDGE: Messages are acknowledged automatically with sending or reception.

    - CLIENT_ACKNOWLEDGE: Client needs to explicitly call Message.acknowledge() to acknowledge sending or reception.

- DUPS_OK_ACKNOWLEDGE: Messages are acknowledged automatically in batches. Duplicates are possible, and the application needs to handle them.

- *Transaction support*: The application needs to explicitly call commit() or rollback() for javax.jms.Session or javax.jms.JMSContext. Transacted behavior applies to JMS message reception as well as to sending.

When a message is acknowledged on the JMS destination, it means that the client has finished its processing and that the action can be reflected in the JMS server. *Acknowledge message during read* marks the message as delivered and discards the message from the queue. So message reception is performed in these three steps:

- Client receives the message

- Client processes the message

- Client acknowledges the message (which can be done implicitly or explicitly, depending on the acknowledge mode)

Bear in mind that automatic acknowledging of messages doesn't work atomically across various messages. It is suitable only in scenarios where we can't rely on ACID characteristics for a batch of messages.

In CLIENT_ACKNOWLEDGE mode, the JMS client is responsible for acknowledging messages explicitly. This is done via a call to Message.acknowledge(). From this API, it may look like each message needs to be acknowledged separately, but that's not the case with this mode. The acknowledgement action is done against the session; therefore, the Message.acknowledge() call acknowledges all not-acknowledged messages consumed in the current session. So, for example, we can read 10 messages within the same session and acknowledge them with a single Message.acknowledge().

We may also consider using JMS local transactions, performing various actions against javax.jms. Session or javax.jms.JMSContext and at the end of our logical transaction explicitly committing or rolling back all the work done against them. This is a similar concept to transaction support of relational databases. Both JMS resources provide the explicit methods commit() and rollback() for this purpose.

JMS local transactions can be used as umbrellas for JMS message reception and sending, whereas acknowledging of messages is handled only during message reception.

Java JMS Transaction Examples

■ **Note**   Acknowledging javax.jms.Message would be the same for Spring as well as for pure Java JMS. Implicit acknowledge modes (AUTO_ACKNOWLEDGE and DUPS_OK_ACKNOWLEDGE) are handled automatically, and explicit CLIENT_ACKNOWLEDGE mode is handled by calling javax.jms.Message.acknowledge(). Therefore, we will not focus on pure Java JMS acknowledge examples.

Our first example covers the JMS 1.1 API with synchronous reception and transacted writing and reading of JMS messages. It also covers having to process various messages under one transaction. Listing 6-1 shows how we configure a connection against the JMS provider.

Listing 6-1. JMS 1.1 Configuration Class (0601-java-jms11-sync-tx)

```java
package net.lkrnac.book.eiws.chapter06.javasynctx;

import java.util.Hashtable;
import javax.jms.Connection;
import javax.jms.ConnectionFactory;
import javax.jms.JMSException;
import javax.jms.Queue;
import javax.naming.InitialContext;
import javax.naming.NamingException;
import lombok.Getter;

public class JmsConfiguration implements AutoCloseable {
  private InitialContext initialContext;

  @Getter
  private Queue queue;
  @Getter
  private Connection connection;

  public void init() throws NamingException, JMSException {
    Hashtable<Object, Object> env = new Hashtable<>();
    env.put("java.naming.factory.initial",
        "org.jnp.interfaces.NamingContextFactory");
    env.put("java.naming.factory.url.pkgs",
        "org.jboss.naming:org.jnp.interfaces");
    env.put("java.naming.provider.url", "jnp://localhost:1099");
    initialContext = new InitialContext(env);

    queue = (Queue) initialContext.lookup("/queue/ExpiryQueue");
    ConnectionFactory connectionFactory =
        (ConnectionFactory) initialContext.lookup("/ConnectionFactory");
    connection = connectionFactory.createConnection();
  }

  public void close() throws NamingException, JMSException {
    if (initialContext != null) {
      initialContext.close();
    }
    if (connection != null) {
      connection.close();
    }
  }
}
```

This configuration is the same as we used in the previous chapter to configure the JMS 1.1 example. It uses a HornetQ configuration of the JNDI initialContext instance to look up instances of queue and connection. These two are JMS objects suitable for connection to a JMS provider. queue is created based on JNDI lookup of the /queue/ExpiryQueue and connectionFactory instance based on /ConnectionFactory. These are configured by default for HornetQ server. This configuration is located in the file config/stand-alone/non-clustered/hornetq-jms.xml.

Private instances of queue and connection objects are exposed to the outside world via getters generated by Lombok. @Getter is responsible for that.

The close method will close resources that need to be released—namely, JNDI initialContext and JMS connection. The JmsConfigurable class participates in the AutoClosable contract, which represents the try-with-resources Java 7 feature. With a special try block, the close() method will be automatically called by Java as if it were part of the finally block.

Listing 6-2 shows configuration of the sender.

Listing 6-2. JMS 1.1 Sender with Transaction Example (0601-java-jms11-sync-tx)

```java
package net.lkrnac.book.eiws.chapter06.javasynctx;

import javax.jms.Connection;
import javax.jms.JMSException;
import javax.jms.MessageProducer;
import javax.jms.Queue;
import javax.jms.Session;
import javax.jms.TextMessage;

public class SimpleMessageSender {
  private MessageProducer messageProducer;
  private Session session;

  public void init(Connection connection, Queue queue) throws JMSException {
    session = connection.createSession(true, Session.SESSION_TRANSACTED);
    messageProducer = session.createProducer(queue);
  }

  public void sendMessages(String message1, String message2)
      throws JMSException {
    try {
      TextMessage textMessage1 = session.createTextMessage(message1);
      messageProducer.send(textMessage1);
      TextMessage textMessage2 = session.createTextMessage(message2);
      messageProducer.send(textMessage2);
      session.commit();
    } catch (Throwable throwable) {
      session.rollback();
    }
  }
}
```

This class has two properties of type javax.jmsSession and javax.jms.MessageProducer, which are initialized in the init() method based on the given parameters javax.jms.Connection and javax.jms.Queue. Notice that the session object is created from the connection instance by the connection.createSession() call. The first parameter in this method means that we are turning on transacted support, and the second means that we are going to use SESSION_TRANSACTED acknowledge mode.

The sendMessage method in this case takes two String parameters that should be sent to the JMS server. We create two TextMessage types from session and send them via messageProducer.send() calls. Before we commit, both messages are not visible to other JMS sessions opened against queue. Only call session.commit() commits the JMS transaction and makes it available for processing by other sessions opened against the JMS destination.

Sending messages and commits is backed up by the `try-catch` block. If an error occurs during the sending or commit phase, the transaction is rolled back by calling `session.rollback()`.

Listing 6-3 shows implementation of the reader class.

Listing 6-3. JMS 1.1 Reader with Transaction (0601-java-jms11-sync-tx)

```java
package net.lkrnac.book.eiws.chapter06.javasynctx;

import javax.jms.Connection;
import javax.jms.JMSException;
import javax.jms.MessageConsumer;
import javax.jms.Queue;
import javax.jms.Session;
import javax.jms.TextMessage;

public class SimpleMessageReader {
  private MessageConsumer messageConsumer;
  private Session session;

  public void init(Connection connection, Queue queue) throws JMSException {
    session = connection.createSession(true, Session.SESSION_TRANSACTED);
    messageConsumer = session.createConsumer(queue);
  }

  public String readMessage() throws JMSException {
    TextMessage messageReceived = (TextMessage) messageConsumer.receive(5000);
    return messageReceived.getText();
  }

  public void finishReading() throws JMSException {
    session.commit();
  }

  public void rollbackReading() throws JMSException {
    session.rollback();
  }
}
```

The reader class has two properties of type `javax.jms.Session` and `javax.jms.MessageConsumer` that are initialized via the `init()` call. Parameters of this method are the JMS objects `connection` and `queue`, similar to the reader example in Listing 6-2. These are used to create `messageConsumer` and the transacted session.

The `readMessage()` method reads `TextMessage` from the queue with a time-out and returns the received text. Again, after this call, the message can be used by JMS client logic, but the message isn't discarded from the queue until a `session.commit()` call is performed. Committing the transaction can be accomplished by the `finishReading()` method. Bear in mind that the sender and reader use separate sessions against our queue. So the messages are visible for the reader session only after the sender commits the messages for the sender session.

The last `rollbackReading()` call performs a rollback against the `session` object, in case we would like to revert all the reading against the queue.

This implementation obviously expects that the transaction will be handled by logic using this reader class. Listing 6-4 explores the main class of this example.

Listing 6-4. Main Class of JMS 1.1 Transacted Example (0601-java-jms11-sync-tx)

```java
package net.lkrnac.book.eiws.chapter06.javasynctx;

import javax.jms.Connection;
import javax.jms.JMSException;
import javax.jms.Queue;
import javax.naming.NamingException;

import lombok.extern.slf4j.Slf4j;

@Slf4j
public class JavaSyncTxApplication {
  public static void main(String[] args) throws JMSException, NamingException {
    try (JmsConfiguration jmsConfiguration = new JmsConfiguration()) {
      jmsConfiguration.init();
      Queue queue = jmsConfiguration.getQueue();
      Connection connection = jmsConfiguration.getConnection();
      connection.start();

      SimpleMessageSender messageSender = new SimpleMessageSender();
      messageSender.init(connection, queue);
      messageSender.sendMessages("simple message1", "simple message2");

      SimpleMessageReader messageReader = new SimpleMessageReader();
      messageReader.init(connection, queue);
      String message1 = messageReader.readMessage();
      log.info("Message Received: {}", message1);
      String message2 = messageReader.readMessage();
      log.info("Message Received: {}", message2);

      messageReader.rollbackReading();

      String message3 = messageReader.readMessage();
      log.info("Message Received: {}", message3);
      String message4 = messageReader.readMessage();
      log.info("Message Received: {}", message4);

      messageReader.finishReading();
    }
  }
}
```

This class has only a main method where all the work is done. It is uses the try-with-resources feature to make sure that the JMS connection will be properly released after the JMS execution. In the body, we first initialize the JMS connection and start it. Next we create and initialize a messageSender instance we already explored in Listing 6-2 and send two simple messages into the JMS queue. Notice that the commit is part of the messageSender.sendMessages() call; therefore, our transaction is applied to the queue after this call and messages are readable by other JMS sessions.

Subsequently, we create a messageReader instance and initialize it. Reading of the two messages that follow is reflected in this logic and logged into the console, but when we call messageReader.rollbackReading(), both messages remain in the queue and can be picked up by other transactions.

Therefore, the next two `messageReader.readMessage()` calls call the same values and log them to the console again. After this logic, we finally commit the transaction, and messages are discarded from the JMS queue. Listing 6-5 shows partial output of the console when we run this example.

Listing 6-5. Output of Transacted JMS 1.1 Example

```
20:44:31.643 [main] INFO  n.l.b.e.c.j.JavaSyncTxApplication - Message Received: simple message1
20:44:31.644 [main] INFO  n.l.b.e.c.j.JavaSyncTxApplication - Message Received: simple message2
20:44:31.647 [main] DEBUG org.hornetq.core.client - client ack messageID = 2147485517
20:44:31.652 [main] INFO  n.l.b.e.c.j.JavaSyncTxApplication - Message Received: simple message1
20:44:31.652 [main] INFO  n.l.b.e.c.j.JavaSyncTxApplication - Message Received: simple message2
20:44:31.652 [main] DEBUG org.hornetq.core.client - client ack messageID = 2147485517
```

We can see that after rollback, messages remain in the queue and are available for the next transacted read in the main method. This behavior is similar to the transacted behavior of relational databases. So we can easily group our messages into a unit of work, which will have ACID characteristics.

Our second pure Java JMS example combines the JMS 2.0 API with a message listener and local JMS transactions. The first class we explore from this example is the listener of the messages in Listing 6-6.

Listing 6-6. Transacted Listener (0602-java-jms20-async-tx)

```java
package net.lkrnac.book.eiws.chapter06.javaasynctx;

import javax.jms.JMSContext;
import javax.jms.Message;
import javax.jms.MessageListener;
import lombok.extern.slf4j.Slf4j;
import net.lkrnac.book.eiws.chapter05.text.SimpleService;

@Slf4j
public class SimpleMessageListener implements MessageListener {
  private SimpleService simpleService;
  private JMSContext jmsContext;

  public SimpleMessageListener(SimpleService simpleService,
      JMSContext jmsContext) {
    super();
    this.simpleService = simpleService;
    this.jmsContext = jmsContext;
  }

  @Override
  public void onMessage(Message message) {
    try {
      String textMessage = message.getBody(String.class);
      log.info("Message received: {}", textMessage);
      simpleService.processText(textMessage);
      jmsContext.commit();
    } catch (Throwable throwable) {
      jmsContext.rollback();
      log.error("Error during message reception", throwable);
    }
  }
}
```

This message listener again uses SimpleService to delegate the message. SimpleService was defined in example project 0500-jms-common in Listing 5-11 of the previous chapter. This class logs given text to the console.

An interesting fact is that an instance of JMSContext is passed via the constructor. This is because we expect this JMSContext instance to be transacted and we need to be able to perform a commit against it after the read. This is done in the onMessage() method by calling jmsContext.commit().

The logic in the onMessage() method is wrapped into a try-catch block, which rolls back via the jmsContext.rollback() call and logs the error message if any error occurs. The next class from this example covers the JMS configuration in Listing 6-7.

Listing 6-7. JMS 2.0 Configuration with Transacted JMSContext (0602-java-jms20-async-tx)

```java
package net.lkrnac.book.eiws.chapter06.javaasynctx;

import java.util.Hashtable;
import javax.jms.ConnectionFactory;
import javax.jms.JMSConsumer;
import javax.jms.JMSContext;
import javax.jms.MessageListener;
import javax.jms.Queue;
import javax.naming.InitialContext;
import javax.naming.NamingException;
import lombok.Getter;
import net.lkrnac.book.eiws.chapter05.text.SimpleService;

public class JmsConfiguration implements AutoCloseable {
  private InitialContext initialContext;
  private SimpleService simpleService;
  private JMSContext readContext;

  @Getter
  private JMSContext writeContext;
  @Getter
  private Queue queue;

  public JmsConfiguration(SimpleService simpleService) {
    super();
    this.simpleService = simpleService;
  }

  public void init() throws NamingException {
    Hashtable<Object, Object> env = new Hashtable<>();
    env.put("java.naming.factory.initial",
        "org.jnp.interfaces.NamingContextFactory");
    env.put("java.naming.factory.url.pkgs",
        "org.jboss.naming:org.jnp.interfaces");
    env.put("java.naming.provider.url", "jnp://localhost:1099");
    initialContext = new InitialContext(env);
```

```
    queue = (Queue) initialContext.lookup("/queue/ExpiryQueue");
    ConnectionFactory cf =
        (ConnectionFactory) initialContext.lookup("/ConnectionFactory");
    readContext = cf.createContext(JMSContext.SESSION_TRANSACTED);
    writeContext = cf.createContext(JMSContext.SESSION_TRANSACTED);

    JMSConsumer jmsConsumer = readContext.createConsumer(queue);
    MessageListener messageListener =
        new SimpleMessageListener(simpleService, readContext);
    jmsConsumer.setMessageListener(messageListener);
  }

  @Override
  public void close() throws NamingException {
    if (initialContext != null) {
      initialContext.close();
    }
    if (readContext != null) {
      readContext.close();
    }
    if (writeContext != null) {
      writeContext.close();
    }
  }
}
```

This JMS configuration class is created via a constructor that takes a SimpleService instance via the constructor and stores it in a class-level variable. It will be used for creation of the SimpleMessageListener instance.

The init() method is used for initializing JMS resources. First of all, we create a JNDI initialContext instance with HornetQ JNDI properties. This instance is used to look up JMS resources, queue and ConnectionFactory. Again, their values are already configured for the HornetQ server by default.

JMS 2.0 allows creation of JMSContext out of the ConnectionFactory object. To separate the sender and listener contexts, we create two transacted instances called readContext and writeContext. readContext will be used for asynchronous reading from the JMS destination, and writeContext will be used for sending messages. Both are stored in class-level variables, because we need to use them or close them later. At the end of the init() method, we create SimpleMessageListener and register it into readContext as the listener.

The last method of this class is close(). It is part of the try-with-resources contract of Autoclosable and releases the JNDI initialContext and both JMS contexts. The sender part of this example is shown in Listing 6-8.

Listing 6-8. Sender Part of Transacted JMS 2.0 Example (0602-java-jms20-async-tx)

```
package net.lkrnac.book.eiws.chapter06.javaasynctx;

import javax.jms.JMSContext;
import javax.jms.Queue;
import lombok.extern.slf4j.Slf4j;
```

```
@Slf4j
public class SimpleMessageSender {
  private JMSContext jmsContext;
  private Queue queue;

  public SimpleMessageSender(JMSContext jmsContext, Queue queue) {
    super();
    this.jmsContext = jmsContext;
    this.queue = queue;
  }

  public void sendMessage(String message) {
    log.info("Sending message: {}", message);
    try {
      jmsContext.createProducer().send(queue, message);
      jmsContext.commit();
    } catch (Throwable throwable) {
      jmsContext.rollback();
    }
  }
}
```

The class is similar to the pure Java JMS 2.0 example in the previous chapter. The difference is the sendMessage() method, which uses the jmsContext.commit() call to confirm the transacted unit of work, which in this case is sending one message. Sending and committing the message is wrapped into the try-catch block, which ensures that the transaction is rolled back if an error occurs. The last class of this example is shown in Listing 6-9.

Listing 6-9. Main Class of Transacted JMS 2.0 Example (0602-java-jms20-async-tx)

```
package net.lkrnac.book.eiws.chapter06.javaasynctx;

import javax.jms.JMSContext;
import javax.jms.Queue;
import javax.naming.NamingException;
import net.lkrnac.book.eiws.chapter05.text.SimpleService;

public class JavaAsyncTxApplication {
  public static void main(String[] args) throws NamingException,
      InterruptedException {
    SimpleService simpleService = new SimpleService();
    try (JmsConfiguration jmsConfiguration =
        new JmsConfiguration(simpleService)) {
      jmsConfiguration.init();
      JMSContext jmsContext = jmsConfiguration.getWriteContext();
      Queue queue = jmsConfiguration.getQueue();

      SimpleMessageSender messageSender =
          new SimpleMessageSender(jmsContext, queue);
      messageSender.sendMessage("simple message");
    }
  }
}
```

This class creates `JmsConfiguration` in the try-with-resources block, to ensure that the JNDI and JMS resources are released. It also is used for initialization and retrieving the JMS resources. Last, we call `messageSender.sendMessage()` to send a simple message to the listener. Listing 6-10 shows the output we can see when we run this application.

Listing 6-10. Output of Plain JMS 2.0 Example

```
21:29:59.693 [main] INFO  n.l.b.e.c.j.SimpleMessageSender - Sending message: simple message
21:29:59.723 [Thread-0 (HornetQ-client-global-threads-114132791)]
INFO  n.l.b.e.c.j.SimpleMessageListener - Message received: simple message
21:29:59.723 [Thread-0 (HornetQ-client-global-threads-114132791)]
INFO  n.l.b.e.chapter05.text.SimpleService - Message received: simple message
21:29:59.723 [Thread-0 (HornetQ-client-global-threads-114132791)]
DEBUG org.hornetq.core.client - client ack messageID = 2147486104
```

Common Classes for Spring JMS Examples

The following sections show examples of various JMS configurations, with success and failure scenarios to highlight how we can easily get into trouble with JMS. At the end, we mention standard and recommended usage of Spring JMS reliability mechanisms. Therefore, the following examples shouldn't be used as templates without understanding the consequences.

Before we start diving into JMS transactional support, we should explain the classes that are used in the Spring JMS examples in this chapter. To highlight how Spring JMS cooperates with database access, we will be using a relational database. To keep the example simple and focused, we will be using the H2 database engine. It is often used for testing Spring applications accessing relational storage.

Listing 6-11 shows a simple repository class.

Listing 6-11. Repository Class Used in Spring JMS Examples (0600-jms-tx-common)

```java
package net.lkrnac.book.eiws.chapter06.text;

import javax.annotation.PostConstruct;

import org.springframework.beans.factory.annotation.Autowired;
import org.springframework.jdbc.core.JdbcTemplate;
import org.springframework.stereotype.Repository;

@Repository
public class SimpleRepository {
  private final JdbcTemplate jdbcTemplate;
  private static final String SELECT_COUNT =
      "select count(*) from TEXT_TABLE where text = ?";

  @Autowired
  public SimpleRepository(JdbcTemplate jdbcTemplate) {
    super();
    this.jdbcTemplate = jdbcTemplate;
  }
```

```java
@PostConstruct
public void initDbTable() {
    jdbcTemplate.execute("drop table TEXT_TABLE if exists");
    jdbcTemplate.execute("create table TEXT_TABLE(TEXT varchar(30))");
}

public void persistText(String text) {
    jdbcTemplate.update("insert into TEXT_TABLE values (?)", text);
}

public boolean containsText(String text) {
    long count = jdbcTemplate.queryForObject(SELECT_COUNT, Long.class, text);
    return count != 0;
}
}
```

We mark this Spring bean with the @Repository annotation to highlight that it sits on the persistence layer and is used as a data access object. This class depends on the standard Spring JdbcTemplate bean. This is Spring's standard mechanism for JDBC access. The JdbcTemplate bean will be created by each example and injected into this common bean.

Examples are Spring Boot–based. When we use @EnableAutoConfiguration or @SpringBootApplication annotations, Spring Boot will automatically try to configure defaults of our application. The difference between these two annotations is that @SpringBootApplication is a shortcut annotation covering @EnableAutoConfiguration, @Configuration, and @ComponentScan.

So with one or the other, if we have an H2 database engine dependency on the classpath, Spring Boot automatically creates DataSource and JdbcTemplate beans and registers them into its IoC container. So we aren't going to see any other database-related bean in the Spring examples of this chapter because Spring Boot configures JdbcTemplate for us. This is a relatively new and convenient way of configuring modern Spring applications: just use Spring Boot defaults and change them only if requirements force us to.

When we have JdbcTemplate injected via constructor injection, we need to initialize the database table. The @PostConstruct annotation ensures that the initDbTable() method will be called at the end of the initialization phase of the application, after all the Spring beans are created and properly injected into each other. So it is a convenient place to initialize our database table. In this case, we drop the old table and re-create a fresh one.

This obviously isn't something we would do in production, but initialization of the DB schema for our Spring application isn't within the scope of this book. Therefore, let's swallow this strange initialization for explanatory purposes.

The database table used for storing our data will have the name TEXT_TABLE and will contain only one text column, TEXT. Again, we keep it simple, because we are interested in DB transactions and their cooperation with JMS transactions or acknowledge modes.

The persistText() method stores the given text into the database, and the containsText() method performs a check of whether the given text is present in the database. Listing 6-12 shows the service-layer bean belonging to SimpleRepository.

Listing 6-12. Service Class Used in Spring JMS Examples (0600-jms-tx-common)

```java
package net.lkrnac.book.eiws.chapter06.text;

import lombok.extern.slf4j.Slf4j;
import org.springframework.beans.factory.annotation.Autowired;
import org.springframework.stereotype.Service;

@Slf4j
@Service
public class SimpleService {
  private final SimpleRepository simpleRepository;

  @Autowired
  public SimpleService(SimpleRepository simpleRepository) {
    super();
    this.simpleRepository = simpleRepository;
  }

  public void processText(String text) {
    log.info("Process Message: {}", text);
    simpleRepository.persistText(text);
  }

  public boolean isProcessed(String text) {
    return simpleRepository.containsText(text);
  }
}
```

SimpleService uses Lombok's @Slf4j annotation for logging purposes. It generates the logger constant log entry for us. @Service enables component scanning of this class as a Spring bean and also highlights its presence on the service layer of the application. There is a single dependency for this class injected via constructor injection. It is our SimpleRepository for DB access.

This service bean provides only two methods, processText() and isProcessed(), which are used by simpleRepository.persistText() and simpleRepository.containsText() because processing the message would persist it into our DB store within the examples.

The last class, common to all the Spring JMS examples in this chapter, is the JMS sender in Listing 6-13.

Listing 6-13. JMS Sender (0600-jms-tx-common)

```java
package net.lkrnac.book.eiws.chapter06.text;

import javax.annotation.PostConstruct;
import lombok.extern.slf4j.Slf4j;
import org.springframework.beans.factory.annotation.Autowired;
import org.springframework.jms.core.JmsTemplate;
import org.springframework.stereotype.Component;

@Slf4j
@Component
public class SimpleMessageSender {
  private static final String SIMPLE_MESSAGE = "simple message";
  private JmsTemplate jmsTemplate;
```

```
@Autowired
public SimpleMessageSender(JmsTemplate jmsTemplate) {
  super();
  this.jmsTemplate = jmsTemplate;
}

@PostConstruct
public void send() {
  log.info("Sending message: {}", SIMPLE_MESSAGE);
  jmsTemplate.convertAndSend("ExpiryQueue", SIMPLE_MESSAGE);
}
}
```

This JMS sender class is similar to what we saw in the previous chapter. It just injects a jmsTemplate instance via constructor injection.

The message is sent to the messageQueue destination via the send() method. The difference from the Chapter 5 Spring JMS examples is usage of the @PostConstruct annotation. Previously, we used scheduling for sending messages as it was handy for describing delays in synchronous reception in the previous chapter.

This chapter focuses on the reliability of JMS message delivery. @PostConstruct is a better fit for sending a single message after the Spring context is initialized, which is better suited to highlighting acknowledge and transactional characteristics.

AUTO_ACKNOWLEDGE Mode

We already mentioned that one of the mechanisms for ensuring reliable JMS message delivery is JMS acknowledge modes. The first one is called AUTO_ACKNOWLEDGE, whereby JMS message action reception is immediately reflected in the JMS destination and changes are immediately visible to other JMS sessions open against the related JMS destination. It is the default JMS acknowledge mode, so it is used if we don't configure JMS resources otherwise.

So with successful reception, the message is *immediately marked as delivered* and discarded from the JMS destination. Reception is considered successful after return from the MessageConsumer.receive() call or after successful completion of the MessageListener.onMessage() call. The only exception to the three-phase JMS message reception (receive/process/acknowledge) is synchronous reception via JMS 2.0 JMSContext in AUTO_ACKNOWLEDGE mode. This reception merges receiving and acknowledging into one step, which is followed by processing on the client.

But with Spring, there is an important gotcha when we use JMS listeners. To remind Spring constructs of JMS message listening, there are two types of listener containers: SimpleJmsListenerContainerFactory and DefaultJmsListenerContainerFactory.

SimpleJmsListenerContainerFactory, introduced in Spring 4.1, is used for creating the SimpleMessageListenerContainer bean. This listener container type uses standard JMS asynchronous features under the hood and registers a direct JMS listener against the JMS destination. Therefore, AUTO_ACKNOWLEDGE mode has behavior as defined by the JMS standard: the message is acknowledged/discarded from the destination *after a successful call of the listener method.*

On the other hand, DefaultJmsListenerContainerFactory is a factory class for DefaultMessageListenerContainer. It also was introduced in Spring 4.1. For reception of JMS messages, it uses a long-polling mechanism. Under the hood, Spring uses synchronous reception with a time-out in an infinite loop. When time-out occurs, Spring immediately performs another MessageConsumer.receive() call. This emulates asynchronous JMS message processing. In fact, this reception can be better performing;

therefore, this type of listener container is used by default by Spring and Spring Boot. But the downside of this approach is *immediate acknowledgement of the JMS message before execution enters the listener method.* Therefore, DefaultJmsListenerContainerFactory is better suited for use with transactions (which will be explained later).

Interestingly, with these two listener containers, we get totally opposite AUTO_ACKNOWLEDGE behavior when listening to JMS messages.

With a successful send, the message is *immediately available for reception.* Sending of the message is considered successful after completion of the MessageProducer.send() call.

The JMS client implementation acknowledges each message one by one under the hood. So it is automatic that an additional action is performed against the JMS destination. Therefore, this acknowledge mode *can be slower than other modes,* because they typically perform acknowledge calls less often.

As this is the default acknowledge mode, it was used in all the examples in the previous chapter describing nontransacted features of Spring JMS. The following example is similar to examples in Chapter 5, but in this case we will also be storing messages in the H2 database. Listing 6-14 shows the main class of this example.

Listing 6-14. Main Class (0603-auto-acknowledge-listener-success)

```
package net.lkrnac.book.eiws.chapter06.text;

import org.springframework.boot.SpringApplication;
import org.springframework.boot.autoconfigure.SpringBootApplication;

@SpringBootApplication
public class JmsApplication {
  public static void main(String[] args) throws Exception {
    SpringApplication.run(JmsApplication.class, args);
  }
}
```

The @SpringBootApplication annotation is a convenient shortcut for the group of @Configuration, @ComponentScan, and @EnableAutoConfiguration annotations. @Configuration marks this class as a Spring configuration.

@ComponentScan performs scans of the current package and its subpackages for Spring beans. Because the 0600-jms-tx-common project is a dependency of this example project (0603-auto-acknowledge-listener-success), this scan will also load and register SimpleRepository and SimpleService beans from Listings 6-12 and 6-13 into our context.

@EnableAutoConfiguration will make Spring Boot scan the classpath for known dependencies and apply a common default opinionated configuration based on libraries present on the classpath. In this case, (example project 0603-auto-acknowledge-listener-success), we have the H2 database engine on the classpath, so Spring Boot automatically configures the DataSource bean as a connection gateway to the H2 DB engine and JdbcTemplate bean for performing JDBC operations against it. This JdbcTemplate bean is then injected into SimpleRepository.

The second support initialized by @EnableAutoConfiguration is JMS. Because project 0603-auto-acknowledge-listener-success contains the HornetQ broker dependency on the classpath, Spring Boot automatically initializes the embedded instance of this JMS provider and configured access to it via the JmsTemplate bean. We just need to inject JmsTemplate in our beans and use it.

This configuration approach will be used by all Spring examples in this chapter. In the main method, we just call SpringApplication.run() to execute this Spring Boot configuration as a Java application.

Success Scenario

Listing 6-15 shows the JMS listener for this example.

Listing 6-15. JMS Listener of AUTO_ACKNOWLEDGE Example (0603-auto-acknowledge-listener-success)

```
package net.lkrnac.book.eiws.chapter06.text;

import org.springframework.beans.factory.annotation.Autowired;
import org.springframework.jms.annotation.JmsListener;
import org.springframework.stereotype.Component;

@Component
public class SimpleMessageListener {
  private SimpleService simpleService;

  @Autowired
  public SimpleMessageListener(SimpleService simpleService) {
    super();
    this.simpleService = simpleService;
  }

  @JmsListener(destination = "ExpiryQueue")
  public void readMessage(String message) {
    simpleService.processText(message);
  }
}
```

This class should be familiar, because all of the constructs were already described in the previous chapter. We cover it here because this implementation ensures the correct reception of the message. It is important to remember that Spring Boot creates DefaultJmsListenerContainerFactory for this listener automatically; therefore, when we are about to call simpleService.processText(), the JMS message is already being acknowledged and discarded from the JMS destination.

To explore this JMS reception scenario, we use the sequence diagram in Figure 6-1.

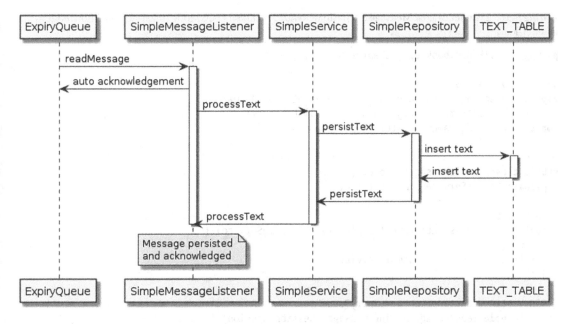

Figure 6-1. *Sequence diagram of* AUTO_ACKNOWLEDGE *scenario with DefaultJmsListenerContainerFactory (file sequence.uml in folder uml-Diagrams of example project 0603-auto-acknowledge-listener-success)*

This sequence diagram shows that the acknowledgement is done before the SimpleMessageListener. readMessage() method is called, because DefaultJmsListenerContainerFactory is using long polling. With this mechanism, the message is acknowledged before Spring calls the listener method.

After entering the listener method code, the success scenario flows through SimpleService, SimpleRepository and stores the message in our database table, TEXT_TABLE.

■ **Note** All the sequence diagrams in this chapter were created by an excellent open source project called PlantUML (plantuml.com). It provides an easy-to-grasp domain-specific language (DSL) for creating various UML diagrams. It's a different approach from classical UML editors (UMLet, Enterprise Architect, Visio), which enable higher productivity, because we developers are more efficient at writing code than dragging, resizing, and connecting rectangles and arrows. It also has good integration with most IDEs and editors as well as different programming tools (see plantuml.com/running.html for more info).

Lost Message with Listener

Success behavior is what each developer strives for when implementing JMS with database support. But the real world isn't always so friendly to our good intentions. With AUTO_ACKNOWLEDGE mode, messages can easily get lost if we use DefaultJmsListenerContainerFactory with the same main and sender class as we showed for the success scenario. The long polling mechanism this listener container factory uses forces it to acknowledge the message right after the reception.

As Spring Boot's default implementation of a listener container factory is DefaultJmsListenerContainerFactory with AUTO_ACKNOWLEDGE mode configured, we don't need to register special beans as a JMS configuration. The listener is shown in Listing 6-16.

Listing 6-16. Listener of Lost Message Scenario with AUTO_ACKNOWLEDGE Mode (0605-auto-acknowledge-listener-lost)

```java
package net.lkrnac.book.eiws.chapter06.text;

import javax.jms.Session;
import org.springframework.beans.factory.annotation.Autowired;
import org.springframework.jms.annotation.JmsListener;
import org.springframework.stereotype.Component;

@Component
public class SimpleMessageListener {
  private SimpleService simpleService;

  @Autowired
  public SimpleMessageListener(SimpleService simpleService) {
    super();
    this.simpleService = simpleService;
  }

  @JmsListener(destination = "ExpiryQueue")
  public void readMessage(String message, Session session) {
    preprocess(message);
    simpleService.processText(message);
  }

  private void preprocess(String message) {
    // simulate error
    throw new IllegalArgumentException(message);
  }
}
```

In this case, we don't simulate an error after persisting the message. We simulate it in a method called `preprocess()` before the `simpleService.processText()` call. Figure 6-2 shows the behavior after running this example.

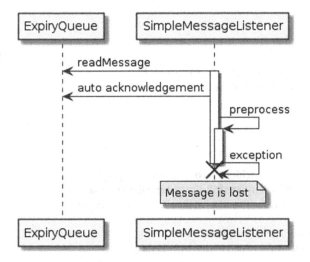

Figure 6-2. *Sequence diagram of message lost scenario with listener and* AUTO_ACKNOWLEDGE *mode (file sequence.uml in folder uml-diagrams of example project 0605-auto-acknowledge-listener-lost)*

As Spring uses long polling, synchronous reception with a time-out is used in an infinite loop under the hood to simulate asynchronous behavior. Synchronous reception is by JMS definition autoacknowledged straight after the return from the MessageConsumer.receive() call. This is because we are using a DefaultJmsListenerContainerFactory implementation for the listener container.

Therefore, when our listener calls the preprocess() method, the message is already acknowledged. The exception in preprocess() stops processing in the listener before the message is persisted. But the message was already discarded from the destination and is lost.

Lost Message with Synchronous Reception

Example 0606-auto-acknowledge-sync-lost explains how AUTO_ACKNOWLEDGE mode in combination with synchronous reception can also lead to message loss. Again, the main and sender classes of this example are exactly the same as in Listings 6-13 and 6-14. Listing 6-17 shows the JMS configuration.

Listing 6-17. JMS Configuration of Synchronous AUTO_ACKNOWLEDGE Mode (0606-auto-acknowledge-sync-lost)

```
package net.lkrnac.book.eiws.chapter06.text;

import javax.jms.ConnectionFactory;
import org.springframework.context.annotation.Bean;
import org.springframework.context.annotation.Configuration;
import org.springframework.jms.core.JmsTemplate;
import org.springframework.scheduling.annotation.EnableScheduling;
```

```java
@Configuration
@EnableScheduling
public class JmsConfiguration {
  @Bean
  public JmsTemplate jmsTemplate(ConnectionFactory connectionFactory) {
    JmsTemplate jmsTemplate = new JmsTemplate(connectionFactory);
    jmsTemplate.setReceiveTimeout(1000);
    return jmsTemplate;
  }
}
```

This configuration class registers the JmsTemplate bean, which has one nondefault property, receiveTimeout. By default, the receive time-out is 0, which means infinite waiting if no messages are available for read. We should specify the receive time-out, if we want to make sure that our reading thread won't be stuck, forever waiting for a message.

The JmsConfiguration class also enables scheduling via the @EnableScheduling annotation, which will be used to initialize a synchronous read of the JMS message, which is shown in Listing 6-18.

Listing 6-18. Synchronous Reader of AUTO_ACKNOWLEDGE Scenario with Lost Message (0604-auto-acknowledge-sync-lost)

```java
package net.lkrnac.book.eiws.chapter06.text;

import lombok.extern.slf4j.Slf4j;
import org.springframework.beans.factory.annotation.Autowired;
import org.springframework.jms.core.JmsTemplate;
import org.springframework.scheduling.annotation.Scheduled;
import org.springframework.stereotype.Component;

@Slf4j
@Component
public class SimpleMessageReader {
  private JmsTemplate jmsTemplate;
  private SimpleService simpleService;

  @Autowired
  public SimpleMessageReader(JmsTemplate jmsTemplate,
      SimpleService simpleService) {
    super();
    this.jmsTemplate = jmsTemplate;
    this.simpleService = simpleService;
  }

  @Scheduled(fixedRate = Long.MAX_VALUE)
  public void readMessage() {
    String message = (String) jmsTemplate.receiveAndConvert("messageQueue");
    log.info("Message read: {}", message);
```

```
    preprocess(message);
    simpleService.processText(message);
}

  private void preprocess(String message) {
    // simulate error
    throw new IllegalArgumentException(message);
  }
}
```

This reader class is similar to synchronous examples from the previous chapter. It defines a Spring component with the Lombok logging capability enabled by the @Slf4j annotation. It injects two dependencies via constructor injection. JmsTemplate is used for reception of messages, and SimpleService is our bean for processing and persisting messages.

Message reception is done by the readMessage() method, which is kicked off by the Spring scheduling feature. We picked a long fixed rate of scheduling because we want the read to occur once. Notice that the preprocess() call is placed between the jmsTemplate.receiveAndConvert() call and simpleService. processText() to simulate errors that can occur between synchronous reception and persisting the message. Figure 6-3 shows this behavior with a sequence diagram.

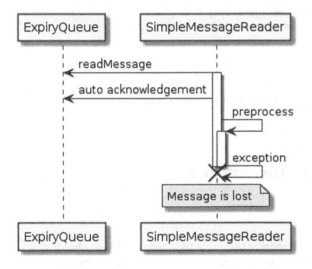

Figure 6-3. *Sequence diagram of message lost scenario with synchronous reception and* AUTO_ACKNOWLEDGE *mode (file sequence.uml in folder uml-diagrams of example project 0606-auto-acknowledge-sync-lost)*

The behavior is similar to the previous example. The only difference is that we explicitly ask to receive, and in the previous example, Spring did it for us under the DefaultJmsListenerContainerFactory hood. In fact, from the JMS provider point of view, both examples are synchronous.

CLIENT_ACKNOWLEDGE Mode

As we have mentioned, with CLIENT_ACKNOWLEDGE mode, the client is responsible for explicitly acknowledging one or a batch of messages. If we use client acknowledging in batches, we decrease the number of calls against the JMS provider server, and therefore can save some bandwidth.

But Spring's design of JmsTemplate acknowledges the message before is it returned to our logic. Therefore, CLIENT_ACKNOWLEDGE mode works for synchronous message reception with Spring exactly the same way as if we were using AUTO_ACKNOWLEDGE. Therefore, it doesn't make practical sense to configure JmsTemplate with this mode. Spring's documentation doesn't explicitly state why such behavior is in place, so we avoid any speculation about it.

Success Scenario

The first Spring example using CLIENT_ACKNOWLEDGE mode highlights a success scenario. Our common main and listener classes are in use again. Listing 6-19 shows the JMS configuration.

Listing 6-19. JMS Configuration of CLIENT_ACKNOWLEDGE Success Scenario (0607-client-acknowledge-listener-success)

```
package net.lkrnac.book.eiws.chapter06.text;

import javax.jms.ConnectionFactory;
import javax.jms.Session;

import org.springframework.context.annotation.Bean;
import org.springframework.context.annotation.Configuration;
import org.springframework.jms.config.DefaultJmsListenerContainerFactory;

@Configuration
public class JmsConfiguration {
  @Bean
  public DefaultJmsListenerContainerFactory jmsListenerContainerFactory(
      ConnectionFactory connectionFactory) {
    DefaultJmsListenerContainerFactory factory =
        new DefaultJmsListenerContainerFactory();
    factory.setConnectionFactory(connectionFactory);
    factory.setSessionAcknowledgeMode(Session.CLIENT_ACKNOWLEDGE);
    return factory;
  }
}
```

In this configuration class, we register the jmsListenerContainerFactory bean for defining listener behavior. The instance of it needs to be based on the injected connectionFactory, created automatically by Spring Boot features, and to have CLIENT_ACKNOWLEDGE mode configured. Listing 6-20 shows the implementation of the listener.

Listing 6-20. Listener Class for Success Scenario with CLIENT_ACKNOWLEDGE Mode (0607-client-acknowledge-listener-success)

```
package net.lkrnac.book.eiws.chapter06.text;

import javax.jms.JMSException;
import javax.jms.Message;
import lombok.extern.slf4j.Slf4j;
import org.springframework.beans.factory.annotation.Autowired;
import org.springframework.jms.annotation.JmsListener;
import org.springframework.stereotype.Component;
```

```
@Slf4j
@Component
public class SimpleMessageListener {
  private SimpleService simpleService;

  @Autowired
  public SimpleMessageListener(SimpleService simpleService) {
    super();
    this.simpleService = simpleService;
  }

  @JmsListener(destination = "ExpiryQueue")
  public void readMessage(String messageText, Message message)
      throws JMSException {
    simpleService.processText(messageText);
    log.info("Acknowledging reception: " + messageText);
    message.acknowledge();
  }
}
```

In the listener, we acknowledge the message after the processing/persisting to indicate success. The behavior of this success is described in Figure 6-4. This diagram shows smooth and straightforward calls down to the persistence layer and successful acknowledgement.

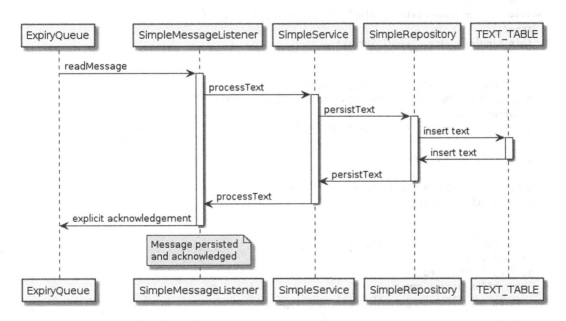

Figure 6-4. *Sequence diagram of success scenario with* CLIENT_ACKNOWLEDGE *mode (file sequence.uml in folder uml-diagrams of example project 0607-client-acknowledge-listener-success)*

Duplicate Message Scenario

A failure scenario with CLIENT_ACKNOWLEDGE will show how it is possible to process the same message twice. All the classes have the same implementation as from the CLIENT_ACKNOWLEDGE success scenario, except for the listener class shown in Listing 6-21.

Listing 6-21. Listener Class for Duplicate Message Scenario in CLIENT_ACKNOWLEDGE Mode (0607-client-acknowledge-listener-success)

```java
package net.lkrnac.book.eiws.chapter06.text;

import javax.jms.JMSException;
import javax.jms.Message;
import lombok.extern.slf4j.Slf4j;
import org.springframework.beans.factory.annotation.Autowired;
import org.springframework.jms.annotation.JmsListener;
import org.springframework.stereotype.Component;

@Slf4j
@Component
public class SimpleMessageListener {
  private SimpleService simpleService;
  private boolean errorSimulated = false;

  @Autowired
  public SimpleMessageListener(SimpleService simpleService) {
    super();
    this.simpleService = simpleService;
  }

  @JmsListener(destination = "messageQueue")
  public void readMessage(String messageText, Message message)
      throws JMSException {
    simpleService.processText(messageText);

    postprocess(messageText);

    log.info("Acknowledging reception: " + messageText);
    message.acknowledge();
  }

  private void postprocess(String message) {
    //simulate error
    if (!errorSimulated) {
      errorSimulated = true;
      throw new IllegalArgumentException(message);
    }
  }
}
```

This listener class looks familiar, as it is similar to listeners used in the previous chapter.

One unusual property in this class is errorSimulated. This variable is used for highlighting erroneous behavior, which could happen in the real world for various reasons. In this case, we store it in this singleton bean (which should ring a bell for every responsible developer). Of course, storing state in a singleton bean shouldn't be used for production purposes, because it represents a global state that is not thread safe.

But for our purposes, it is essential, because we want to fail the message reception to highlight what would happen with JMS and database integration. errorSimulated is used in the private method postprocess() to simulate an error for the first received message. The first hit of this method also further disables error simulation. It is useful for highlighting a scenario in which processing the first message can fail and the second attempt could be successful.

This pattern will be used for error simulation across various failure examples in this chapter.

In this message reception logic, we simulate an error in the private method postprocess(), which is called right after persisting the message but before the explicit message.acknowledge() call. After execution of this example, the sequence shown in Figure 6-5 will happen.

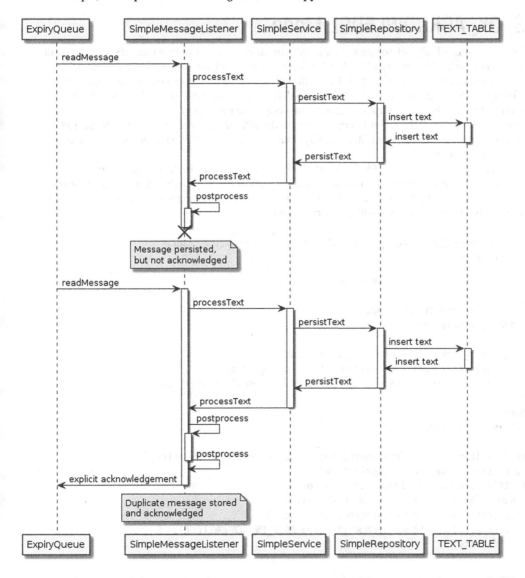

Figure 6-5. *Sequence diagram of duplicate message scenario in CLIENT_ACKNOWLEDGE mode (file sequence.uml in folder uml-diagrams of example project 0608-client-acknowledge-listener-duplicate)*

The message is received and persisted, but not acknowledged, because the postprocess() method throws an error. So the JMS destination makes sure that according to the JMS contract, this message will be redelivered. After the second persistence call, postprocess() won't throw a second error as per our example and will let the message be explicitly acknowledged.

Obviously, this is behavior we don't want to have in our application, unless our persistent store is idempotent. Idempotency was described in Chapter 4. In this case, if the database would insert the message when it doesn't exist and update it when it already exists, we could perform any of the simpleService. processText() duplicate calls without affecting the consistency of state in the database.

But storage in our example is not idempotent; therefore, a duplicate simpleService.processText() call is a problem.

DUPS_OK_ACKNOWLEDGE Mode

This acknowledge mode lazily acknowledges messages automatically. This means that JMS is in charge of doing so. The downside of this approach is that the client can get duplicate messages while using this mode, because messages are acknowledged in bulk by the JMS server. So when acknowledgement is not in the client's hands, there's no guarantee that the message will be delivered exactly once. Therefore, this mode is most suitable when the client is idempotent (can handle duplicate messages).

If a message is redelivered a second time, it will have the JMSRedelivered message header set to true. So we can ask whether a message was redelivered by calling Message.getJMSRedelivered() and acting according to our requirements.

As the acknowledgement with DUPS_OK_ACKNOWLEDGE mode is specific to the JMS provider implementation, it is hard to reproduce a duplicate scenario for our example. Therefore, we cover only a success scenario, in which we show only the JMS configuration class in Listing 6-22. Other classes are exactly the same as for the success scenarios, without error simulation.

Listing 6-22. Listener Class for Success Scenario in DUPS_OK_ACKNOWLEDGE Mode (0609-dups-ok-acknowledge)

```
package net.lkrnac.book.eiws.chapter06.text;

import javax.jms.ConnectionFactory;
import javax.jms.Session;

import org.springframework.context.annotation.Bean;
import org.springframework.context.annotation.Configuration;
import org.springframework.jms.config.DefaultJmsListenerContainerFactory;

@Configuration
public class JmsConfiguration {
  @Bean
  public DefaultJmsListenerContainerFactory jmsListenerContainerFactory(
      ConnectionFactory connectionFactory) {
    DefaultJmsListenerContainerFactory factory =
        new DefaultJmsListenerContainerFactory();
    factory.setConnectionFactory(connectionFactory);
    factory.setSessionAcknowledgeMode(Session.DUPS_OK_ACKNOWLEDGE);
    return factory;
  }
}
```

In this case, `jmsListenerContainerFactory` uses `DUPS_OK_ACKNOWLEDGE` mode. The sequence diagram of this example is shown in Figure 6-6.

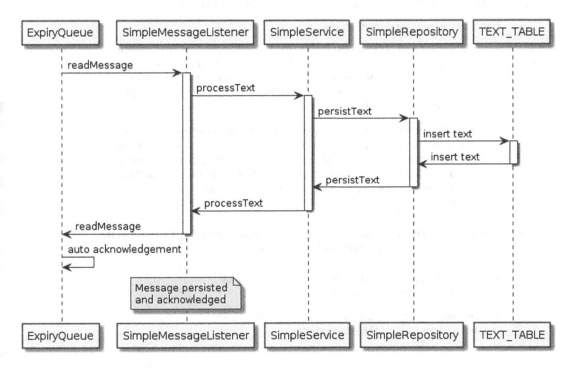

Figure 6-6. *Sequence diagram of success scenario with DULS_OK_ACKNOWLEDGE mode (file sequence.uml in folder uml-diagrams of example project 0609-dups-ok-acknowledge)*

After receiving and persisting the message, the JMS provider acknowledges it at a point convenient to the JMS provider. This option is useful for enabling various JMS destination handling optimizations that the JMS provider might want to put in place in order to make JMS communication more efficient.

Local JMS Transactions with Spring

Acknowledge modes are not the only way to make sure that our messages are delivered reliably. The JMS standard allows us to use transacted features, similar to ACID transactions common for relational databases.

We already covered how to use local JMS transactions with pure Java JMS APIs. Now we are going to explore how to use them with Spring. This support can be turned on `JmsTemplate` by setting `setSessionTransacted()` to `true` and `setSessionAcknowledgeMode()` to `Session.SESSION_TRANSACTED`.

For this support, Spring expects the presence of a transaction manager bean. Therefore, it doesn't make sense to use `JmsTemplate` (for message sending and synchronous message reception) with transacted behavior without the transaction manager. Use of the transaction manager will be shown later in this book.

But we can use local JMS transactions without any transaction manager while listening to messages. In this case, we can configure setSessionTransacted() to true and setSessionAcknowledgeMode() to Session.SESSION_TRANSACTED for any of these JMS listener supporting beans:

- Container listener implementations

    - SimpleMessageListenerContainer—Creates a listener container, with pure asynchronous JMS reception, where the listener is registered to the JMS destination and the JMS server initiates the reception of the message. It is handy if we plan to use a listener with CLIENT_ACKNOWLEDGE or AUTO_ACKNOWLEDGE mode.

    - DefaultMessageListenerContainer—Creates a listener container, where Spring makes synchronous calls with a time-out in a loop under the hood, so that the message is read as soon as it appears at the JMS destination. This mechanism is handy when we are using JMS transaction support and is the only support that can work with distributed transactions (covered in the next chapter).

- Container listener factory implementations, introduced in Spring 4.1 and enables annotating JMS listener methods with @JmsListener

    - SimpleJmsListenerContainerFactory—Factory for SimpleMessageListenerContainer

    - DefaultJmsListenerContainerFactory—Factory for DefaultMessageListenerContainer

Success Scenario

To show use of local JMS transactions with Spring, we can reuse the main and sender classes common in the Spring JMS examples in this chapter. We can also have the same listener implementation as that of the success scenarios in this chapter (for example, in Listing 6-14). The only difference is the JMS configuration shown in Listing 6-23.

Listing 6-23. JMS Configuration of Success Scenario with Local Transaction (0610-transacted-listener-success)

```
package net.lkrnac.book.eiws.chapter06.text;

import javax.jms.ConnectionFactory;
import javax.jms.Session;
import org.springframework.context.annotation.Bean;
import org.springframework.context.annotation.Configuration;
import org.springframework.jms.config.DefaultJmsListenerContainerFactory;

@Configuration
public class JmsConfiguration {
  @Bean
  public DefaultJmsListenerContainerFactory jmsListenerContainerFactory(
      ConnectionFactory connectionFactory) {
    DefaultJmsListenerContainerFactory factory =
        new DefaultJmsListenerContainerFactory();
```

```
    factory.setConnectionFactory(connectionFactory);
    factory.setSessionTransacted(true);
    factory.setSessionAcknowledgeMode(Session.SESSION_TRANSACTED);
    return factory;
  }
}
```

This registers the DefaultJmsListenerContainerFactory bean with the name jmsListenerContainerFactory and sets the sessionTransacted property to true and sessionAcknowledgeMode to Session.SESSION_TRANSACTED to enable local JMS local transaction support. Similar support can be achieved with XML configuration, as shown in Listing 6-24.

Listing 6-24. XML JMS Configuration of Success Scenario with Local Transaction (File spring-jms-config. xml in Folder src/main/resources in Example Project 0612-transacted-xml)

```xml
<?xml version="1.0" encoding="UTF-8"?>
<beans xmlns="http://www.springframework.org/schema/beans"
  xmlns:xsi="http://www.w3.org/2001/XMLSchema-instance"
  xmlns:jms="http://www.springframework.org/schema/jms"
  xsi:schemaLocation="http://www.springframework.org/schema/jms
    http://www.springframework.org/schema/jms/spring-jms.xsd
    http://www.springframework.org/schema/beans
    http://www.springframework.org/schema/beans/spring-beans.xsd">

  <jms:listener-container acknowledge="transacted"
      connection-factory="jmsConnectionFactory">
    <jms:listener destination="messageQueue" ref="simpleMessageListener"
      method="readMessage" />
  </jms:listener-container>
</beans>
```

In this case, we use Spring's XML namespace, jms, to specify the listener container. The local JMS transaction is enabled by setting the acknowledge attribute to the transacted value. The rest of this configuration should be familiar from the previous chapter. The connection-factory reference is mandatory. The listener points to the JMS destination with the name messageQueue, and the listener method simpleMessageListener.readMessage(). The behavior of this example is shown in Figure 6-7.

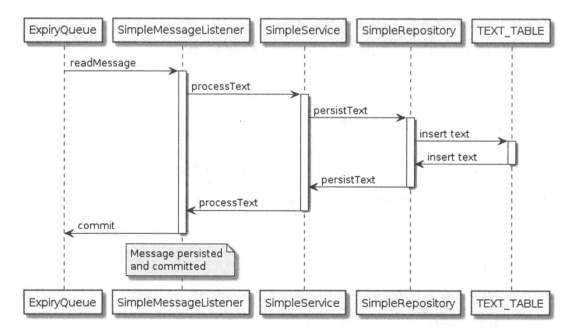

Figure 6-7. *Sequence diagram of success scenario with SESSION_TRANSACTED mode (file sequence.uml in folder uml-diagrams of example project 0610-transacted-listener-success)*

This is straightforward. Spring commits the message for us automatically, after the listener finishes execution. Therefore, we can't receive various messages in a single transaction with the local JMS transaction + Spring combination.

Duplicate Message Scenario

As with acknowledge modes, reception of a local JMS transaction can go wrong. Imagine the main and sender classes from the Spring JMS examples in this chapter combined with the JMS configuration from the previous example (Listing 6-24) and the listener from Listing 6-25.

Listing 6-25. Listener Class for Duplicate Message Scenario with SESSION_TRANSACTED Mode (0611-transacted-listener-duplicate)

```java
package net.lkrnac.book.eiws.chapter06.text;

import javax.jms.JMSException;
import org.springframework.beans.factory.annotation.Autowired;
import org.springframework.jms.annotation.JmsListener;
import org.springframework.stereotype.Component;

@Component
public class SimpleMessageListener {
  private SimpleService simpleService;
  private boolean errorSimulated = false;

  @Autowired
  public SimpleMessageListener(SimpleService simpleService) {
    super();
    this.simpleService = simpleService;
  }

  @JmsListener(destination = "messageQueue")
  public void readMessage(String message) throws JMSException {
    simpleService.processText(message);
    postprocess(message);
  }

  private void postprocess(String message) {
    // simulate error
    if (!errorSimulated) {
      errorSimulated = true;
      throw new IllegalArgumentException(message);
    }
  }
}
```

In fact, we've seen such a listener in Listing 6-21, in the duplicate scenario listener in AUTO_ACKNOWLEDGE mode. The behavior is shown in Figure 6-8.

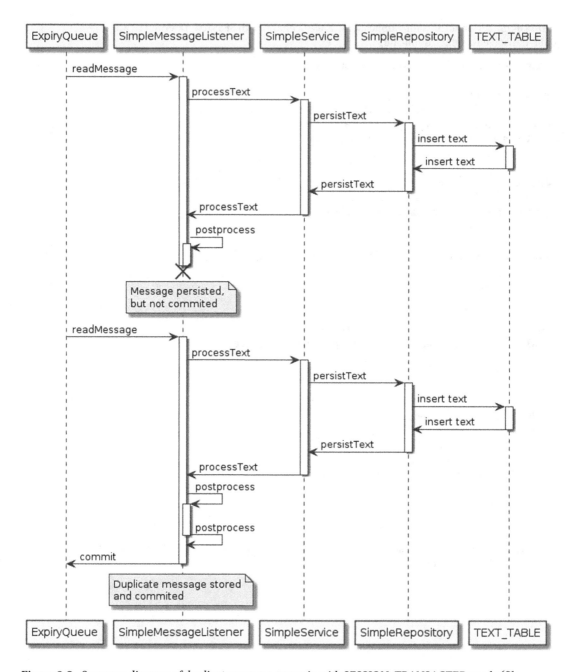

Figure 6-8. *Sequence diagram of duplicate message scenario with SESSION_TRANSACTED mode (file sequence.uml in folder uml-diagrams of example project 0611-transacted-listener-duplicate)*

The problem is that the message is stored into the DB, and after that, postprocess throws an exception before committing the first message. On redelivery, the same message is stored into the database a second time.

JmsTransactionManager

Spring also provides the possibility of handling JMS transactions via its transaction demarcation features, using the @Transactional annotation. Such support is possible when we register the JmsTransactionManager bean as a manager for Spring transactions. In such a case, Spring ignores JMS native acknowledge modes and transactional configuration. This support works for JMS 1.1 as well as for JMS 2.0.

JmsTransactionManager can be used for a single ConnectionFactory, as it binds JMS Connection/Session/JMSContext to the thread. This configuration can be handy for a thread-bound Session per ConnectionFactory.

It is recommended to combine this transaction manager with CachingConnectionFactory, which was shown in the previous chapter.

An example of JmsTransactionManager that starts with JMS configuration is shown in Listing 6-26.

Listing 6-26. JMS Configuration with JmsConfigurationManager (0613-jms-transaction-manager)

```java
package net.lkrnac.book.eiws.chapter06.text;

import javax.jms.ConnectionFactory;
import org.springframework.context.annotation.Bean;
import org.springframework.context.annotation.Configuration;
import org.springframework.jms.config.DefaultJmsListenerContainerFactory;
import org.springframework.jms.connection.JmsTransactionManager;

@Configuration
public class JmsConfiguration {
  @Bean
  public JmsTransactionManager transactionManager(
      ConnectionFactory connectionFactory) {
    return new JmsTransactionManager(connectionFactory);
  }

  @Bean
  public DefaultJmsListenerContainerFactory jmsListenerContainerFactory(
      ConnectionFactory connectionFactory,
      JmsTransactionManager transactionManager) {
    DefaultJmsListenerContainerFactory factory =
        new DefaultJmsListenerContainerFactory();
    factory.setConnectionFactory(connectionFactory);
    factory.setTransactionManager(transactionManager);
    return factory;
  }
}
```

First of all, we create and register the JmsTransactionManager bean based on a connectionFactory instance injected by Spring. The second bean is DefaultJmsListenerContainerFactory, also based on the same connectionFactory object as shown in the previous examples. But now we also inject and configure transactionManager into the listener container factory to enable Spring transactional features on top of this listener container factory.

Listing 6-27 shows a listener implementation for this example.

Listing 6-27. Listener Class for JmsConfigurationManager Example (0613-jms-transaction-manager)

```java
package net.lkrnac.book.eiws.chapter06.text;

import javax.jms.JMSException;
import org.springframework.beans.factory.annotation.Autowired;
import org.springframework.jms.annotation.JmsListener;
import org.springframework.stereotype.Component;
import org.springframework.transaction.annotation.Transactional;

@Component
public class SimpleMessageListener {
  private SimpleService simpleService;
  private boolean errorSimulated = false;

  @Autowired
  public SimpleMessageListener(SimpleService simpleService) {
    super();
    this.simpleService = simpleService;
  }

  @Transactional
  @JmsListener(destination = "messageQueue")
  public void readMessage(String messageText) throws JMSException {
    preprocess(messageText);
    simpleService.processText(messageText);
  }

  private void preprocess(String message) {
    // simulate error
    if (!errorSimulated) {
      errorSimulated = true;
      throw new IllegalArgumentException(message);
    }
  }
}
```

We used a transaction demarcation feature for the listener method readMessage(). The preprocess() method called before simpleService.processText() simulated an error for the first received message. For subsequent messages, no error is simulated. The sequence diagram for this behavior after running the example is shown in Figure 6-9.

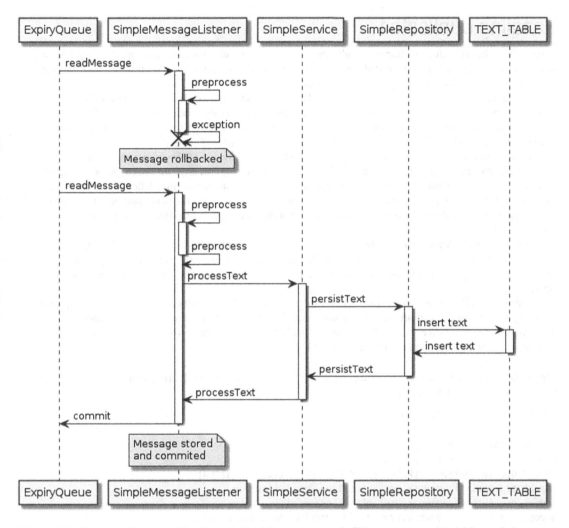

Figure 6-9. *Sequence diagram of JmsTransactionManager example (file sequence.uml in folder uml-diagrams of example project 0613-jms-transaction-manager)*

When the first message is received and an exception from preprocess() is thrown, JmsTransactionManager rolls back the transaction created on message reception. That causes redelivery of the message. The second preprocess() call doesn't throw an exception, and the message is, on second attempt, persisted and committed afterward.

Notice that if we simulated an error in postprocess() after message persistence, the result would be a duplicate message in the database again. But we'll skip this example because we already covered a duplicate scenario with JMS transactions.

Handling Duplicates

Even with all the reliability mechanisms we've mentioned, some scenarios can still cause message loss or duplication. Spring can't abstract out all the problems of JMS integration with other transactional storage options, but tries to decrease the possibility of failure.

Therefore, using SimpleMessageListenerContainer or SimpleJmsListenerContainerFactory is recommended if our JMS message reception is based on acknowledge modes, especially AUTO_ACKNOWLEDGE. If we use transactions for JMS for message reception, the best-suited implementation is DefaultMessageListenerContainer or DefaultJmsListenerContainerFactory.

There is another option that we haven't mentioned, which provides ACID characteristics across various transacted data stores. Based on distributed JTA transactions, this option is described in the next chapter. However, it is resource intensive and widely considered a significant performance killer. Therefore, every programmer should try to avoid it if possible. Fortunately, options exist for ensuring that no lost messages or duplicates occur without distributed transactions. But first, we need to take into account various considerations.

First, we need to know whether the target storage is idempotent—whether it can handle duplicate messages without creating an inconsistent state. When storage is idempotent, we can use any of the duplicate scenario examples from this chapter, and your integration between JMS and the database would be safe.

A more complicated situation arises when we don't have such smart storage that can detect duplicates. Handling this scenario is explained in the next example. We reuse the common main and sender implementations and JMS configuration based on JmsTransactionManager from the previous example in Listing 6-27. The listener of this example is shown in Listing 6-28.

Listing 6-28. Listener Class for Handling Duplicates Covering Scenario with Error after Message Persistence (0614-handle-duplicates-error-after)

```java
package net.lkrnac.book.eiws.chapter06.text;

import javax.jms.JMSException;
import javax.jms.Message;
import org.springframework.beans.factory.annotation.Autowired;
import org.springframework.jms.annotation.JmsListener;
import org.springframework.stereotype.Component;
import org.springframework.transaction.annotation.Transactional;

@Component
public class SimpleMessageListener {
  private SimpleService simpleService;

  @Autowired
  public SimpleMessageListener(SimpleService simpleService) {
    super();
    this.simpleService = simpleService;
  }
```

```
@Transactional
@JmsListener(destination = "messageQueue")
public void readMessage(String messageText, Message message)
    throws JMSException {
  if (message.getJMSRedelivered()) {
    processIfNeeded(messageText);
  } else {
    simpleService.processText(messageText);
    postprocess(messageText);
  }
}

private void processIfNeeded(String messageText) {
  if (!simpleService.isProcessed(messageText)) {
    simpleService.processText(messageText);
  }
}

private void postprocess(String messageText) {
  // simulate error
  throw new IllegalArgumentException(messageText);
}
}
```

Into the transacted listener method readMessage, we inject the text of the message and the javax.jms.Message instance. A message instance is needed for a call to message.getJMSRedelivered(), which is used to find out whether this message is a redelivery. There is also a new private method called processIfNeeded().This method first verifies whether the message is already processed; if not, the method would call simpleMessage.processText() to persist it.

So here is the full logic: If the message is redelivered, process it only if needed; if not, just process it. You may ask: "Why don't we always call processIfNeeded() without bothering about the message.getJMSRedelivered() check?" The reason is simple. Checking whether the message was already processed is one additional, usually *expensive*, call to the external system, and message redelivery is so rare that we can eliminate wasting the majority of these calls by simply checking whether the message was redelivered before checking whether it was processed/persisted.

Let's explore the behavior in the sequence diagram in Figure 6-10.

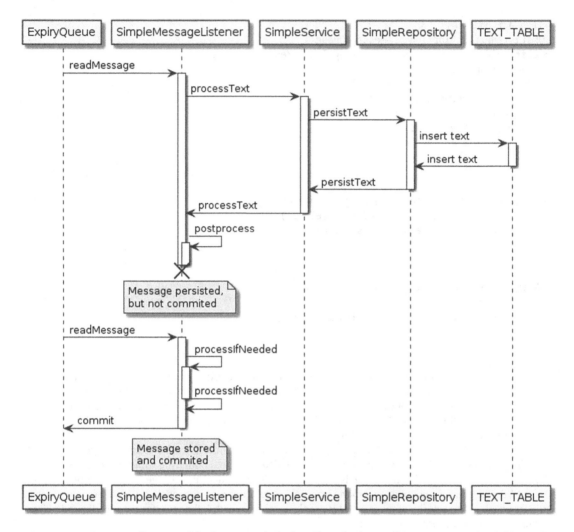

Figure 6-10. *Sequence diagram of the first example for handling duplicates (file sequence.uml in folder uml-diagrams of example project 0614-handle-duplicates-error-after)*

If a message is being delivered for the first time, message.getJMSRedelivered() returns false and sends execution to the else section where it's persisted. Next, the postprocess() method is called, which simulates an error. At this stage, the message is processed, but not committed to the JMS destination.

Therefore, the message is redelivered again to our listener. But in this case, message.getJMSRedelivered() is true, so our logic calls processIfNeeded(). The message was already processed, so persisting is skipped, the message listener call finishes, and the message is committed.

Let's also check what would happen if the error were simulated before persisting the message. Consider Listing 6-29.

Listing 6-29. Listener Class for Handling Duplicates Covering Scenario with Error Before Message Persistence (0615-handle-duplicates-error-before)

```java
package net.lkrnac.book.eiws.chapter06.text;

import javax.jms.JMSException;
import javax.jms.Message;
import org.springframework.beans.factory.annotation.Autowired;
import org.springframework.jms.annotation.JmsListener;
import org.springframework.stereotype.Component;
import org.springframework.transaction.annotation.Transactional;

@Component
public class SimpleMessageListener {
  private SimpleService simpleService;

  @Autowired
  public SimpleMessageListener(SimpleService simpleService) {
    super();
    this.simpleService = simpleService;
  }

  @Transactional
  @JmsListener(destination = "messageQueue")
  public void readMessage(String messageText, Message message)
      throws JMSException {
    if (message.getJMSRedelivered()) {
      processIfNeeded(messageText);
    } else {
      preprocess(messageText);
      simpleService.processText(messageText);
    }
  }

  private void processIfNeeded(String messageText) {
    if (!simpleService.isProcessed(messageText)) {
      simpleService.processText(messageText);
    }
  }

  private void preprocess(String messageText) {
    // simulate error
    throw new IllegalArgumentException(messageText);
  }
}
```

Notice that the error is in this case simulated before the simpleService.processText() call in the listener method readMessage(). The sequence diagram of this scenario is shown in Figure 6-11.

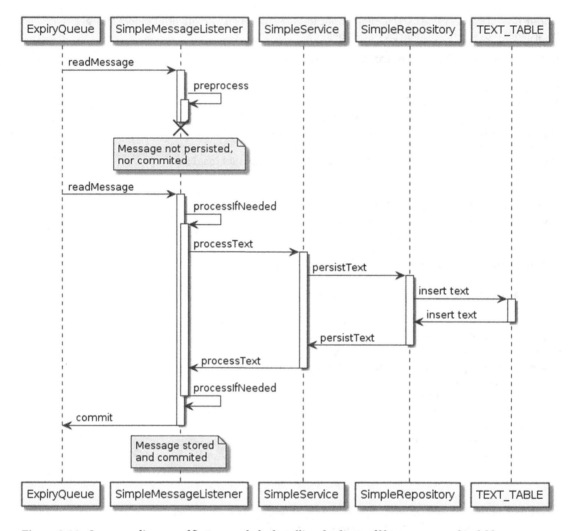

Figure 6-11. *Sequence diagram of first example for handling duplicates (file sequence.uml in folder uml-diagrams of example project 0615-handle-duplicates-error-before)*

After receiving the message for the first time, message.getJMSRedelivered() returns false; preprocess() in the else section then throws the message. Processing of the readMessage() method is unsuccessful, and the message is rolled back without persisting.

After redelivery of the message, message.getJMSRedelivered() returns true, so the processIfNeeded() method is called. In this case, we check that simpleService.isProcessed() is false; we then call simpleService.processText(). At the end, we also have exactly one message persisted, as desired.

Summary

This chapter explained that JMS messaging has various mechanisms for handling secure message delivery. We listed all the delivery acknowledgment and transactional modes offered by the JMS API and highlighted how verbose the use of this API can be.

Than we explored how to use these with Spring and covered various success and failure scenarios, because if we are not careful, messages can easily become lost or duplicated in the system we are integrating JMS with.

We also highlighted that we can't get ACID characteristics across various transactional systems without use of distributed transactions. But we also explained how this can be elegantly handled without them. Therefore, we now know how to handle JMS integration with other transactional storage, reliably avoiding resource-expensive distributed transactions.

CHAPTER 7

■ ■ ■

Distributed Transactions

Chapter 6 covered ACID characteristics (atomicity, consistency, isolation, and durability) that Java and the Spring platform provide for transactional data sources (for example, relational databases) or JMS providers. Such a transaction against a single data source is often referred to as *a local transaction*. But a single data source is not where this support ends. Sometimes we can have requirements to ensure a single ACID transaction across various types of storage.

Java (and Spring abstractions) provide support for single transactions across multiple data sources. This is called a *distributed transaction*, or sometimes a *global transaction*. Such a transaction typically exceeds the boundaries of one server or network host and has to be synchronized across these data stores or JMS servers.

Understanding Distributed Transactions

So let's say we have a PostgreSQL database and HornetQ JMS server. When we distribute the transaction on top of these stores, we can start reading messages from the HornetQ JMS destination and start inserting them via JDBC into the PostgreSQL storage. If one of the insert statements fails, we can be sure that our messages won't get lost, because the transaction manager will ensure that the JMS operations performed in this global transaction are rolled back.

As you can imagine, this support is not trivial to implement; various mechanisms need to be in place for distributed transactions to be possible. First, a special *global transaction manager* needs to coordinate the distributed transaction across various transactional stores. This transaction manager needs to conform to the *Java Transaction API (JTA)*. This API defines mechanisms for distributed transaction demarcation.

We also need to make sure that each store involved in the global transaction supports the *XA standard* (eXtended Architecture standard). This standard was developed by The Open Group (formerly X/Open), a consortium of several member organizations specializing in open Unix system standards (`www.opengroup.org`).

The XA standard specifies an *interface between the global and local transaction managers* to be able to participate in an ACID global transaction. An XA-compliant local transaction manager needs to have a JTA-compliant global transaction manager to cooperate with. You can think of XA as bridge between the local transaction manager (the manager handling transactions for a single data source) and the JTA global transaction manager (the manager coordinating local managers to cooperate in a global transaction).

So, long story short, *XA needs JTA* in order to work properly. Cooperation between these standards is ensured via a *two-phase commit algorithm/protocol*, which works in the following phases:

1. Commit request phase (voting phase)

   a. The global transaction manager (also called the *coordinator*) asks all the XA local transaction managers (also called *XA stores* or *participants*) to decide whether a commit or rollback needs to be performed.

   b. If the participant decides to commit the transaction, the participant should then wait for orders from the global transaction manager and not perform any additional actions against the underlying storage.

   c. The participant may decide to roll back the transaction and disclose this intention to the global transaction manager.

2. Commit phase

   d. The global transaction manager decides, based on all the responses, whether all participants (local transaction managers) need to commit or roll back.

   e. The local transaction managers perform the chosen action (commit or rollback) that was ordered by the global transaction manager.

This algorithm involves various steps and can be hard to imagine. Figures 7-1 and 7-2 provide sequence diagrams for success and failure scenarios for this algorithm.

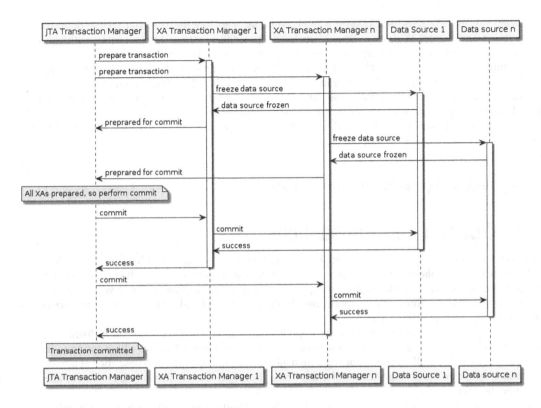

Figure 7-1. *Success scenario for a JTA transaction*

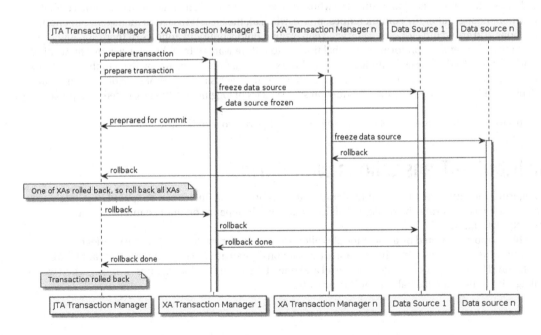

Figure 7-2. *Failure scenario for a JTA transaction*

It is obvious that this algorithm involves a lot of ceremony to achieve the ACID transaction boundary across various data sources. We have to emphasize that the preceding figures depict scenarios with only two data sources. The amount of ceremony would multiply if we were to add more data sources.

It is important to remember that JTA is a standard that is part of Java Enterprise Edition. Therefore, various implementations of JTA and global transaction managers exist. These implementations can be stand-alone or part of a Java EE application server. In fact, if we are using Java EE transaction management embedded with an application server, we get this support out of the box.

So the list of JTA providers would include every Java EE–compliant application server. Additionally, the main stand-alone providers are as follows:

- Atomikos (`www.atomikos.com`)

- Bitronix JTA (`https://github.com/bitronix/btm`)

Cons of Distributed Transactions

Distributed transactions are powerful. We can imagine that it is able to magically solve all the possible problems (including duplicate data and lost data) described in the previous chapter. But this mechanism has significant performance overhead; if we bring into the equation a two-phase commit, which covers various data sources (two, three, or even more) and the various phases involved in it, the performance of this distributed transaction may be very slow.

This often means a huge problem for the high-performance requirements demanded in distributed systems. Therefore, the architects of these systems often try to avoid the need for two-phase commits. It is often much smarter to handle commits for separate data sources with the approach described at the end of Chapter 6, where we did an explicit check for duplicates. But sometimes requirements force us to use distributed transactions.

Reduced performance is the biggest, but not the only, problem of the two-phase commit algorithm. Too many parts are involved in such transactions, and the failure of any local transaction managers or global transaction managers can destroy the whole transaction. In addition, imagine a failure of a global transaction manager after the commit request phase, when all the local transaction managers can't perform any actions and are waiting for him. They will keep waiting until a time-out appears (if there are any).

Another problem is monitoring the global transaction. If we want to troubleshoot, a common way is to log the sides involved in the communication. But three sides, at a minimum, are involved in the distributed transaction (a global and two local transaction managers), and each side creates at least one log entry for each phase. If logging is enabled for a production system, a lot of logging overhead is added, and processing slows even more.

So we can see there are a lot of reasons that we should strive to avoid distributed transactions.

Distributed Transactions with Spring

Configuring and implementing distributed transactions is not trivial. But we can be spared from this complexity by using Spring abstractions. This approach highly depends on understanding Spring transactional support.

This support is covered by a core module called `spring-tx`. It provides the generic interface `PlatformTransactionManager`, which enables transaction demarcation based on the `@Transactional` annotation. The `spring-tx` module is powerful and one of the main flagship features of Spring when we are dealing with transactional databases or JMS providers.

> ■ **Note** Spring transactional support is not part of the Enterprise Integration with Spring certification. Therefore, it is beyond the scope of this book. But this knowledge is crucial for understanding distributed transactions with Spring and is part of the Spring Core certification. I will mention the simple golden rule here: a Spring managed transaction starts on a class or public method wrapped into the `@Transactional` annotation and ends when code escapes this wrapped logic. But bear in mind that the `@Transactional` annotation has various attributes that can significantly change transaction boundaries.

In fact, the same APIs are able to work with distributed transactions. Spring provides implementation of `JtaTransactionManager` of the `PlatformTransactionManager` interface, which enables this support. But bear in mind that `JtaTransactionManager` itself doesn't give us full JTA-compliant implementation of a global transaction manager. It is just a wrapper that operates on top of Java EE or a stand-alone JTA transaction manager implementation (for example, Atomikos or Bitronix JTA). So Spring alone doesn't give us this support. This is smart, because why would Spring reinvent the wheel when it's not necessary? Spring takes advantage of existing implementations and uses them under the `JtaTransactionManager` wrapper umbrella.

The main implication of this interface is that our transacted business code doesn't need to know we are using a distributed transaction when it is marked as `@Transactional`. We just need to configure `JtaTransactionManager`, backed up by a JTA implementation and use various XA data sources to get ACID transaction characteristics across them.

Java EE servers have disadvantages when they force the presence of a JTA transaction manager on the platform. With Spring, we can simply change the configuration and turn this support on or off. The `@Transactional` annotation boundary specifies the start of a transaction, whether it is a global or local one. This will be seen in the examples of this chapter.

Common Classes for JTA Examples

To demonstrate ACID characteristics of distributed transactions across various data sources with Spring, we will apply a JTA transaction manager on examples similar to those in the preceding chapter that had problems with duplicating or losing messages. We will use a few common classes across all examples in this chapter. The first one, in Listing 7-1, is a repository sitting on the DAO layer.

Listing 7-1. Repository Class Used for JTA Examples (0700-jta-common)

```java
package net.lkrnac.book.eiws.chapter07;

import javax.annotation.PostConstruct;
import org.springframework.beans.factory.annotation.Autowired;
import org.springframework.jdbc.core.JdbcTemplate;
import org.springframework.stereotype.Repository;

@Repository
public class SimpleRepository {
  private final JdbcTemplate jdbcTemplate;

  @Autowired
  public SimpleRepository(JdbcTemplate jdbcTemplate) {
    super();
    this.jdbcTemplate = jdbcTemplate;
  }
```

```
@PostConstruct
public void initDbTable() {
    jdbcTemplate.execute("drop table TEXT_TABLE if exists");
    jdbcTemplate.execute("create table TEXT_TABLE(TEXT varchar(30))");
}

public void persistText(String text) {
    jdbcTemplate.update("insert into TEXT_TABLE values (?)", text);
}
}
```

This class is similar to the DAO from Chapter 6. The only difference is a lack of querying for the number of stored text entries. The @Repository annotation marks this class as a Spring bean sitting on the persistence layer. For executing JDBC queries, it injects the JdbcTemplate instance via the constructor.

The initDbTable() method creates a fresh table after the Spring context is initialized. Its execution at this stage is ensured by the @PostConstruct annotation. This construct is obviously not typical for relational databases, but in this case we are using an in-memory database and want to have it empty for the examples, for each application to run.

The persistText() method is used to insert given text into the in-memory database. Listing 7-2 shows the service-layer class used for processing text messages.

Listing 7-2. Service Class Used for JTA Examples (0700-jta-common)

```
package net.lkrnac.book.eiws.chapter07;

import lombok.extern.slf4j.Slf4j;
import org.springframework.beans.factory.annotation.Autowired;
import org.springframework.stereotype.Service;

@Slf4j
@Service
public class SimpleService {
    private final SimpleRepository simpleRepository;

    @Autowired
    public SimpleService(SimpleRepository simpleRepository) {
        super();
        this.simpleRepository = simpleRepository;
    }

    public void processText(String text) {
        log.info("Process Message: {}", text);
        simpleRepository.persistText(text);
    }
}
```

Again this service is similar to that in the preceding chapter. The only difference is the missing method for reading the count of stored text records. The @Service annotation places this Spring bean at the service layer. The @Slf4j annotation is a Lombok feature for enabling easy access to the SLF4J logger. Constructor injection of the SimpleRepository instance enables use of the DAO bean instance.

Notice that we didn't use the @Transactional annotation for any of these classes, because we plan to also include the JMS data source in the global transaction boundary. So the JMS data source will be used in components using SimpleService.

The processText() method is used in the examples to process text messages by logging the given message and persisting via the simpleRepository bean. The last class shared across the JTA examples is shown in Listing 7-3.

Listing 7-3. JMS Message Sender Used by JTA Examples (0700-jta-common)

```java
package net.lkrnac.book.eiws.chapter07;
import javax.jms.ConnectionFactory;
import lombok.extern.slf4j.Slf4j;
import org.springframework.beans.factory.annotation.Autowired;
import org.springframework.beans.factory.annotation.Qualifier;
import org.springframework.jms.core.JmsTemplate;
import org.springframework.scheduling.annotation.Scheduled;
import org.springframework.stereotype.Component;

@Slf4j
@Component
public class SimpleMessageSender {
  private static final String SIMPLE_MESSAGE = "simple message";
  private final JmsTemplate jmsTemplate;

  @Autowired
  public SimpleMessageSender(
      @Qualifier("nonXaJmsConnectionFactory") ConnectionFactory nonXaConnectionFactory) {
    super();
    jmsTemplate = new JmsTemplate(nonXaConnectionFactory);
  }

  @Scheduled(initialDelay = 1000, fixedRate = Long.MAX_VALUE)
  public void send() {
    log.info("Sending message: {}", SIMPLE_MESSAGE);
    jmsTemplate.convertAndSend("ExpiryQueue", SIMPLE_MESSAGE);
  }
}
```

As you may notice, this sender is similar to that in the preceding chapter, with a few differences. First, we are not using the @PostConstruct annotation to trigger the sending of the message. This is because JTA configuration is sometimes not initiated fast enough after creating this SimpleMessageSender bean, so sending the message must wait for the configuration in this example. In a real-life application, this sending would be triggered by the external system consuming our application. Therefore, for this example, we can rely on scheduling with initialDelay, which will delay sending of the example message after context creation. The scheduling attribute fixedRate is configured to Long.MAX_VALUE to ensure that the second message won't be sent during execution of the JTA example.

The second difference as compared to the example in the previous chapter, is injection of nonXaConnectionFactory instead of the jmsTemplate bean. This is needed because we want to have the sender of the message be independent of the JTA transaction. Therefore, in upcoming examples, we will create alongside the XA-compliant JMS connectionFactory, a nonXaConnectionFactory bean, which bypasses JTA ceremonies. Bear in mind that in real life this sender wouldn't be placed in our message consumer application.

Other constructs should be familiar. The constructor injection of JmsTemplate enables use of the Spring bean for sending messages. The send() method itself first logs the fact that the message is being sent and performs this action.

Spring JTA Example with XML Configuration

Our first example of JTA integration with Spring is based mainly on XML configuration. There is no need to introduce a new XML namespace for it, because we operate in a non-JEE environment. If our application were deployed into a JEE container, we would use the jee namespace. First, we need to configure Atomikos as the JTA transaction manager for the Spring application. Listing 7-4 shows this XML configuration.

Listing 7-4. XML Configuration of JTA-Related Beans (File spring-jta-config.xml in Folder src/main/ resources in Example Project 0701-jta-xml-config)

```
<?xml version="1.0" encoding="UTF-8"?>
<beans xmlns="http://www.springframework.org/schema/beans"
  xmlns:xsi="http://www.w3.org/2001/XMLSchema-instance"
  xmlns:tx="http://www.springframework.org/schema/tx"
  xsi:schemaLocation="http://www.springframework.org/schema/beans
    http://www.springframework.org/schema/beans/spring-beans.xsd
    http://www.springframework.org/schema/tx
    http://www.springframework.org/schema/tx/spring-tx.xsd">

  <tx:annotation-driven transaction-manager="transactionManager"/>

  <bean id="userTransactionManager" class="com.atomikos.icatch.jta.UserTransactionManager"
      init-method="init" destroy-method="close"/>

  <bean id="transactionManager"
      class="org.springframework.transaction.jta.JtaTransactionManager">
    <property name="transactionManager" ref="userTransactionManager"/>
    <property name="userTransaction" ref="userTransactionManager"/>
  </bean>
</beans>
```

In this configuration, we use the tx namespace to enable the @Transactional annotation under the umbrella of the JTA transaction manager. The JTA bean definition follows with use of the bean namespace. The first bean we need to create is com.atomikos.icatch.jta.UserTransactionManager as the global transaction manager. We already mentioned that Spring doesn't have JTA capability built in, so we need help of an external JTA framework.

To integrate the Atomikos global transaction manager into the Spring application as PlatformTransactionManager, we need to wrap it into Spring's JtaTransactionManager. This allows us to take advantage of Spring's transaction JTA support on top of the Atomikos implementation. An important configuration step is creation of com.atomikos.icatch.jta.UserTransactionImp, which starts the Atomikos transaction service. Configuring this for the Java SE environment is important. For a Java EE drive application, we would use com.atomikos.icatch.jta.J2eeUserTransaction.

Listing 7-5 shows configuration of the JDBC data source.

Listing 7-5. XML Configuration of JDBC XA Data Source (File spring-jdbc-config.xml in Folder src/main/ resources in Example Project 0701-jta-xml-config)

```xml
<?xml version="1.0" encoding="UTF-8"?>
<beans xmlns="http://www.springframework.org/schema/beans"
  xmlns:xsi="http://www.w3.org/2001/XMLSchema-instance"
  xsi:schemaLocation="http://www.springframework.org/schema/beans
    http://www.springframework.org/schema/beans/spring-beans.xsd">

  <bean id="dataSource" class="com.atomikos.jdbc.AtomikosDataSourceBean">
    <property name="uniqueResourceName" value="jdbcDataSource" />
    <property name="xaDataSource">
      <bean class="org.h2.jdbcx.JdbcDataSource">
        <property name="url"
          value="jdbc:h2:mem:testdb"/>
        <property name="user" value="sa"/>
      </bean>
    </property>
  </bean>

  <bean id="jdbcTemplate" class="org.springframework.jdbc.core.JdbcTemplate">
    <property name="dataSource" ref="dataSource"/>
  </bean>
</beans>
```

Here we use only the bean Spring XML namespace for defining Spring beans. First, we create an XA data source bean based on the com.atomikos.jdbc.AtomikosDataSourceBean implementation that Atomikos provides. This implementation is needed to properly work with the JTA global transaction manager. uniqueResourceName is a mandatory parameter, which needs to be unique in case we have various XA data sources of this type in the application. So the value jdbcDataSource is just fine for our example.

In the xaDataSource property, we wrap the local data source implementation. This wrapper is needed to allow the classical JDBC data source to participate in a global transaction. In this case, we are using an in-memory H2 database engine, as mentioned in the classical JDBC data source. We also need to wrap this bean into the JdbcTemplate bean to enable Spring JDBC support on top of this XA data source. So the JdbcTemplate doesn't have a clue that it is dealing with an XA data source. Listing 7-6 shows the JMS configuration.

Listing 7-6. XML Configuration of JMS XA Data Source (File spring-jms-config.xml in Folder src/main/ resources in Example Project 0701-jta-xml-config)

```xml
<?xml version="1.0" encoding="UTF-8"?>
<beans xmlns="http://www.springframework.org/schema/beans"
  xmlns:xsi="http://www.w3.org/2001/XMLSchema-instance"
  xmlns:jee="http://www.springframework.org/schema/jee"
  xmlns:util="http://www.springframework.org/schema/util"
  xmlns:jms="http://www.springframework.org/schema/jms"
  xsi:schemaLocation="http://www.springframework.org/schema/jms
    http://www.springframework.org/schema/jms/spring-jms.xsd
    http://www.springframework.org/schema/jee
    http://www.springframework.org/schema/jee/spring-jee.xsd
    http://www.springframework.org/schema/beans
    http://www.springframework.org/schema/beans/spring-beans.xsd
```

```
    http://www.springframework.org/schema/util
    http://www.springframework.org/schema/util/spring-util.xsd">

  <util:map id="jndiProperties" map-class="java.util.Properties">
    <entry key="java.naming.factory.initial"
      value="org.jnp.interfaces.NamingContextFactory" />
    <entry key="java.naming.factory.url.pkgs"
      value="org.jboss.naming:org.jnp.interfaces" />
    <entry key="java.naming.provider.url" value="jnp://localhost:1099" />
  </util:map>

  <jee:jndi-lookup id=" " jndi-name="/ConnectionFactory"
    environment-ref="jndiProperties" />
  <jee:jndi-lookup id="connectionFactory" jndi-name="/XAConnectionFactory"
    environment-ref="jndiProperties" />
  <jee:jndi-lookup id="queue" jndi-name="/queue/ExpiryQueue"
    environment-ref="jndiProperties" />

  <bean id="jmsTemplate" class="org.springframework.jms.core.JmsTemplate">
    <constructor-arg ref="connectionFactory" />
  </bean>

  <bean id="destinationResolver"
    class="org.springframework.jms.support.destination.JndiDestinationResolver">
    <property name="jndiEnvironment" ref="jndiProperties" />
  </bean>

  <jms:listener-container transaction-manager="transactionManager" acknowledge="transacted"
      destination-resolver="destinationResolver">
    <jms:listener destination="/queue/ExpiryQueue" ref="simpleMessageListener"
      method="readMessage" />
  </jms:listener-container>
</beans>
```

In this case, we use various Spring XML namespaces. The util namespace helps us define necessary JNDI properties for the HornetQ connection, and the jee namespace is needed for JNDI lookup of these properties. We already saw this configuration in the preceding chapter. But this example uses connector factory beans; notice that the default HornetQ configuration contains XAConfigurationFactory and also plain ConfigurationFactory. Use of XAConnectionFactory ensures that the connectionFactory JMS data source will be XA compliant and thus can participate in a global transaction. The nonXaJmsConnectionFactory bean is used by the SimpleMessageSender bean to send a message for the JTA example. This connection factory doesn't participate in the JTA transaction, as it would confuse the example's behavior.

The HornetQ JMS server has both connection factories specified in its default configuration. Chapter 6, explained how easy it is to download and start the HornetQ server. So if you are interested, the default configuration for XAConnectionFactory and ConnectionFactory can be found in the configuration file <hornet>/config/stand-alone/non-clustered/hornetq-jms.xml.

The next step is wrapping this connection factory into the JmsTemplate bean. This allows us to send (or synchronously receive) JMS messages. The DestinationResolver bean is needed to work with JNDI lookup properties to find the JMS destination we are planning to send and read from.

Last, we use the jms Spring namespace to configure the JMS listener plug-in's JMS listener bean. Notice that we are using transactionManager as an attribute for this listener container. This allows the listener container to offer global transaction support. Another important attribute is enabling of transacted acknowledge mode in the acknowledge attribute. Without this configuration, the listener wouldn't be transacted and therefore would ignore all transaction managers. This configuration is also the reason we don't need to turn on <tx:transaction-driven> to enable the @Transactional annotation on SimpleMessageSender. We are not using this annotation in this case.

As the listener method is configured, readMessage() is implemented in the simpleMessageListener bean shown in Listing 7-7.

Listing 7-7. JMS Listener Simulating Processing Error to Highlight JTA Support (0701-jta-xml-config)

```
package net.lkrnac.book.eiws.chapter07;

import org.springframework.beans.factory.annotation.Autowired;
import org.springframework.stereotype.Component;

@Component
@Transactional
public class SimpleMessageListener {
  private SimpleService simpleService;
  private boolean errorSimulated = false;

  @Autowired
  public SimpleMessageListener(SimpleService simpleService) {
    super();
    this.simpleService = simpleService;
  }

  public void readMessage(String message) {
    simpleService.processText(message);
    postprocess(message);
  }

  private void postprocess(String message) {
    // simulate error
    if (!errorSimulated) {
      errorSimulated = true;
      throw new IllegalArgumentException(message);
    }
  }
}
```

The @Component annotation registers this class as a Spring bean. It injects the SimpleService bean via constructor injection. The readMessage() method is used for listening to JMS messages in the JMS configuration from Listing 7-6. The JMS listener container from this listing is configured to participate in a global transaction, so we have this bean covered by the @Transactional annotation, which is participating in the global JTA transaction (including JMS and the underlying JDBC data source).

This method first calls SimpleService to process the message, which means persisting it into the H2 in-memory database. After that, we simulate an error, but only for the first received message.

Notice that a similar implementation was already shown in Chapter 6, in Listing 6-28, as we discussed potential duplicates if an error occurs for a transacted JMS listener. In that case, the behavior was shown in Figure 6-9, and we ended up with a duplicate message being persisted in the database.

Listing 7-8 shows the main class of this example.

Listing 7-8. Main Class of XML Configuration Example (0701-jta-xml-config)

```
package net.lkrnac.book.eiws.chapter07;

import org.springframework.boot.SpringApplication;
import org.springframework.context.annotation.ComponentScan;
import org.springframework.context.annotation.Configuration;
import org.springframework.context.annotation.ImportResource;
import org.springframework.jms.annotation.EnableJms;
import org.springframework.scheduling.annotation.EnableScheduling;
import org.springframework.transaction.annotation.EnableTransactionManagement;

@Configuration
@ComponentScan
@EnableJms
@EnableScheduling
@ImportResource(value = { "classpath:spring-jdbc-config.xml",
    "classpath:spring-jta-config.xml", "classpath:spring-jms-config.xml" })
public class JtaApplication {
  public static void main(String[] args) throws Exception {
    SpringApplication.run(JtaApplication.class, args);
  }
}
```

This class takes advantage of Spring Boot constructs to start the application based on the `main` method. It allows us to use this example as an executable JAR, something Spring Boot introduced. But we don't use the autoconfiguration feature in this case, because we want to highlight plain Spring configuration with JTA.

Therefore, we have to enable each Spring feature separately:

- Component scanning in the current package and its subpackages by the @ComponentScan annotation

- Enabling Spring JMS via the @EnableJms annotation

- Enabling Spring scheduling support via the @EnableScheduling annotation, used for sending messages (see Listing 7-3)

- Importing all XML configurations explained for this example

After running this example, we can observe the output in Listing 7-9.

Listing 7-9. Output of XML JTA Example

```
2015-09-05 16:44:08.260  INFO 4151 --- [          main] n.l.book.eiws.chapter07.
JtaApplication    : Started JtaApplication in 1.905 seconds (JVM running for 2.582)
2015-09-05 16:44:08.272  INFO 4151 --- [erContainer#0-1] c.a.icatch.imp.
BaseTransactionManager    : createCompositeTransaction ( 10000 ): created new ROOT
transaction with id 127.0.1.1.tm0000100060
```

```
2015-09-05 16:44:09.254  INFO 4151 --- [pool-1-thread-1] n.l.b.e.chapter07.
SimpleMessageSender    : Sending message: simple message
2015-09-05 16:44:09.343  INFO 4151 --- [erContainer#0-1] n.l.book.eiws.chapter07.
SimpleService    : Process Message: simple message
2015-09-05 16:44:09.347  INFO 4151 --- [erContainer#0-1] c.atomikos.jdbc.
AbstractDataSourceBean    : AtomikosDataSoureBean 'jdbcDataSource': getConnection ( null )
2015-09-05 16:44:09.348  INFO 4151 --- [erContainer#0-1] c.atomikos.jdbc.
AbstractDataSourceBean    : AtomikosDataSoureBean 'jdbcDataSource': init...
2015-09-05 16:44:09.359  INFO 4151 --- [erContainer#0-1] c.a.icatch.imp.
CompositeTransactionImp    : addParticipant ( XAResourceTransaction: 3132372E302E312E312E746D
30303030313030303630:3132372E302E312E312E746D31 ) for transaction 127.0.1.1.tm0000100060
2015-09-05 16:44:09.359  INFO 4151 --- [erContainer#0-1] c.a.datasource.
xa.XAResourceTransaction    : XAResource.start ( 3132372E302E312E312E746D30303030303031303030303630
:3132372E302E312E312E746D31 , XAResource.TMNOFLAGS ) on resource jdbcDataSource represented
by XAResource instance xads0: conn0: url=jdbc:h2:mem:testdb user=SA
2015-09-05 16:44:09.360  INFO 4151 --- [erContainer#0-1] c.a.icatch.imp.
CompositeTransactionImp    : registerSynchronization ( com.atomikos.jdbc.AtomikosConnectionPr
oxy$JdbcRequeueSynchronization@e947e942 ) for transaction 127.0.1.1.tm0000100060
2015-09-05 16:44:09.361  INFO 4151 --- [erContainer#0-1] c.atomikos.jdbc.
AtomikosConnectionProxy    : atomikos connection proxy for conn1: url=jdbc:h2:mem:testdb
user=SA: calling prepareStatement(insert into TEXT_TABLE values (?))...
2015-09-05 16:44:09.370  INFO 4151 --- [erContainer#0-1] c.a.icatch.imp.
CompositeTransactionImp    : setRollbackOnly() called for transaction 127.0.1.1.tm0000100060
2015-09-05 16:44:09.378  WARN 4151 --- [erContainer#0-1] o.s.j.l.DefaultMessageListenerConta
iner  : Execution of JMS message listener failed, and no ErrorHandler has been set.

org.springframework.jms.listener.adapter.ListenerExecutionFailedException: Listener method
'readMessage' threw exception; nested exception is java.lang.IllegalArgumentException:
simple message
        at org.springframework.jms.listener.adapter.MessageListenerAdapter.invokeListenerMet
        hod(MessageListenerAdapter.java:309)
        at org.springframework.jms.listener.adapter.MessageListenerAdapter.onMessage(Message
        ListenerAdapter.java:230)
        ...
        at java.lang.Thread.run(Thread.java:745)
Caused by: java.lang.IllegalArgumentException: simple message
        at net.lkrnac.book.eiws.chapter07.SimpleMessageListener.postprocess(SimpleMessageLi
        stener.java:28)
        at net.lkrnac.book.eiws.chapter07.SimpleMessageListener.readMessage(SimpleMessageLi
        stener.java:21)
        ...
        at org.springframework.jms.listener.adapter.MessageListenerAdapter.invokeListenerMet
        hod(MessageListenerAdapter.java:301)
        ... 10 common frames omitted

2015-09-05 16:44:09.383  INFO 4151 --- [erContainer#0-1] c.atomikos.jdbc.
AtomikosConnectionProxy    : atomikos connection proxy for conn1: url=jdbc:h2:mem:testdb
user=SA: close()...
2015-09-05 16:44:09.384  INFO 4151 --- [erContainer#0-1] c.a.datasource.
xa.XAResourceTransaction    : XAResource.end ( 3132372E302E312E312E746D30303030303031303030303630:
```

3132372E302E312E312E746D31 , XAResource.TMSUCCESS) on resource jdbcDataSource represented by XAResource instance xads0: conn0: url=jdbc:h2:mem:testdb user=SA
2015-09-05 16:44:09.390 INFO 4151 --- [erContainer#0-1] c.a.datasource.
xa.XAResourceTransaction : XAResource.rollback (3132372E302E312E312E746D30303030313030
303630:3132372E302E312E312E746D31) on resource jdbcDataSource represented by XAResource instance xads0: conn0: url=jdbc:h2:mem:testdb user=SA
2015-09-05 16:44:09.398 INFO 4151 --- [erContainer#0-1] c.a.icatch.imp.
CompositeTransactionImp   : rollback() done of transaction 127.0.1.1.tm0000100060
2015-09-05 16:44:09.411 INFO 4151 --- [erContainer#0-1] c.a.icatch.imp.
BaseTransactionManager   : createCompositeTransaction (10000): created new ROOT transaction with id 127.0.1.1.tm0000200060
2015-09-05 16:44:09.429 INFO 4151 --- [erContainer#0-1] n.l.book.eiws.chapter07.
SimpleService   : Process Message: simple message
2015-09-05 16:44:09.430 INFO 4151 --- [erContainer#0-1] c.atomikos.jdbc.
AbstractDataSourceBean   : AtomikosDataSoureBean 'jdbcDataSource': getConnection (null)...
2015-09-05 16:44:09.430 INFO 4151 --- [erContainer#0-1] c.atomikos.jdbc.
AbstractDataSourceBean   : AtomikosDataSoureBean 'jdbcDataSource': init...
2015-09-05 16:44:09.430 INFO 4151 --- [erContainer#0-1] c.a.icatch.imp.
CompositeTransactionImp   : addParticipant (XAResourceTransaction: 3132372E302E312E312E746D
30303030323030303630:3132372E302E312E312E746D32) for transaction 127.0.1.1.tm0000200060
2015-09-05 16:44:09.431 INFO 4151 --- [erContainer#0-1] c.a.datasource.
xa.XAResourceTransaction : XAResource.start (3132372E302E312E312E746D30303030323030303630
:3132372E302E312E312E746D32 , XAResource.TMNOFLAGS) on resource jdbcDataSource represented by XAResource instance xads0: conn0: url=jdbc:h2:mem:testdb user=SA
2015-09-05 16:44:09.431 INFO 4151 --- [erContainer#0-1] c.a.icatch.imp.
CompositeTransactionImp   : registerSynchronization (com.atomikos.jdbc.AtomikosConnectionPr
oxy$JdbcRequeueSynchronization@eafcc1e1) for transaction 127.0.1.1.tm0000200060
2015-09-05 16:44:09.431 INFO 4151 --- [erContainer#0-1] c.atomikos.jdbc.
AtomikosConnectionProxy   : atomikos connection proxy for conn1: url=jdbc:h2:mem:testdb
user=SA: calling prepareStatement(insert into TEXT_TABLE values (?))...
2015-09-05 16:44:09.433 INFO 4151 --- [erContainer#0-1] c.atomikos.jdbc.
AtomikosConnectionProxy   : atomikos connection proxy for conn1: url=jdbc:h2:mem:testdb
user=SA: close()...
2015-09-05 16:44:09.434 INFO 4151 --- [erContainer#0-1] c.a.datasource.
xa.XAResourceTransaction : XAResource.end (3132372E302E312E312E746D30303030323030303630:31
32372E302E312E312E746D32 , XAResource.TMSUCCESS) on resource jdbcDataSource represented by XAResource instance xads0: conn0: url=jdbc:h2:mem:testdb user=SA
2015-09-05 16:44:09.434 INFO 4151 --- [erContainer#0-1] c.a.icatch.imp.
CompositeTransactionImp   : commit() done (by application) of transaction
127.0.1.1.tm0000200060
2015-09-05 16:44:09.494 INFO 4151 --- [erContainer#0-1] c.a.datasource.
xa.XAResourceTransaction : XAResource.commit (3132372E302E312E312E746D30303030323030303630
:3132372E302E312E312E746D32 , true) on resource jdbcDataSource represented by XAResource instance xads0: conn0: url=jdbc:h2:mem:testdb user=SA

We can see various log entries from JTA and XA transaction managers, which demonstrates how resource intensive JTA transactions are. The behavior is best explained in Figure 7-3.

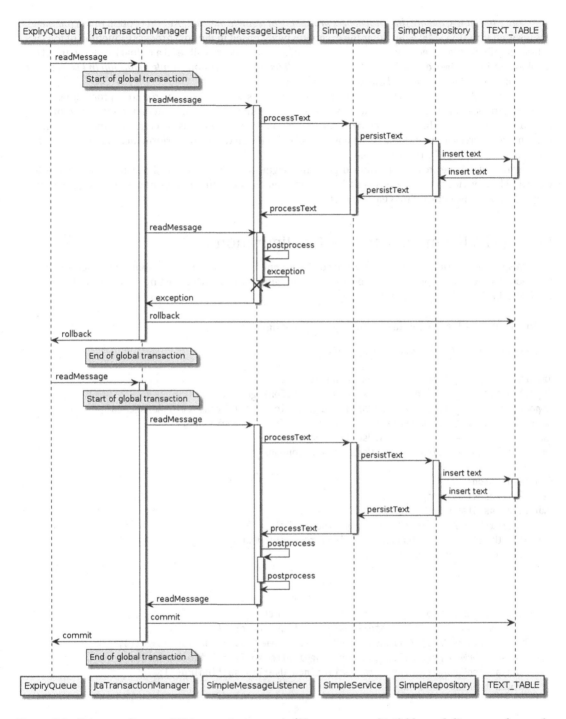

Figure 7-3. *Sequence diagram JTA transaction example (file sequence.uml in folder uml-diagrams of example project 0701-jta-xml-config)*

Notice that this sequence diagram covers processing of a single message. After reception of the message, it is inserted into TEXT_TABLE. But after the exception being raised in the postprocess() method of the JMS listener for the first received message, the global transaction manager will send a rollback order to the H2 database and to the JMS queue ExpiryQueue. *This is different from the same implementation in Listener 6-28, where the H2 database committed the local transaction.*

After the rollback is sent to the JMS queue, the message is sent for a second round of processing. Again, the global transaction is started and the message is inserted into TEXT_TABLE. But on second reception, postprocess() doesn't throw an exception, and our global transaction ends successfully, sending a commit to both data sources. Happy global ACID days. We can sleep well when our performance characteristics for our application using JTA are acceptable.

But notice that we are using a point-to-point messaging paradigm here. Dealing with JMS topics, where we would have various consumers, would involve an even more careful (and resource-intensive) approach to handle JTA transactions across each of them.

Spring JTA Example with Java Configuration

Every responsible Spring developer has noticed movement from XML to Java configuration. Therefore, this section covers how Spring JTA support can be configured without XML. Listing 7-10 shows a JTA configuration.

Listing 7-10. Java JTA Configuration (0702-jta-java-config)

```
package net.lkrnac.book.eiws.chapter07;

import org.springframework.context.annotation.Bean;
import org.springframework.context.annotation.Configuration;
import org.springframework.transaction.annotation.EnableTransactionManagement;
import org.springframework.transaction.jta.JtaTransactionManager;
import com.atomikos.icatch.jta.UserTransactionImp;
import com.atomikos.icatch.jta.UserTransactionManager;

@Configuration
@EnableTransactionManagement
public class JtaConfiguration {
  @Bean(initMethod = "init", destroyMethod = "close")
  public UserTransactionManager atomikosTransactionManager() {
    return new UserTransactionManager();
  }

  @Bean
  public JtaTransactionManager transactionManager(
      UserTransactionManager atomikosTransactionManager) {
    JtaTransactionManager transactionManager = new JtaTransactionManager();
    transactionManager.setTransactionManager(atomikosTransactionManager);
    transactionManager.setUserTransaction(new UserTransactionImp());
    return transactionManager;
  }
}
```

This configuration class enables Spring transactional support via the @EnableTransactionManagement annotation. As with XML configuration, we need to register the com.atomikos.icatch.jta. UserTransactionManager bean as an implementation of global transactional manager. We use the initMethod and destroyMethod attributes of this @Bean annotation to tell Spring how to instantiate and destroy this bean.

The second bean wraps the Atomikos transaction manager into JtaTransactionManager, which is an implementation of PlatformTransactionManager, and enables Spring transactional support for this application. Again we need to configure the userTransaction property to an instance of com.atomikos. icatch.jta.UserTransactionImp so that Atomikos will work fine for this non–Java EE application. Listing 7-11 dives into JDBC configuration of the XA data source.

Listing 7-11. Java Configuration of JDBC XA Data Source (0702-jta-java-config)

```
package net.lkrnac.book.eiws.chapter07;

import javax.sql.DataSource;
import org.h2.jdbcx.JdbcDataSource;
import org.springframework.boot.jta.atomikos.AtomikosXADataSourceWrapper;
import org.springframework.context.annotation.Bean;
import org.springframework.context.annotation.Configuration;
import org.springframework.jdbc.core.JdbcTemplate;

@Configuration
public class JdbcConfiguration {
  @Bean
  public DataSource dataSource() throws Exception {
    JdbcDataSource h2DataSource = new JdbcDataSource();
    h2DataSource.setUrl("jdbc:h2:mem:testdb");
    h2DataSource.setUser("sa");
    AtomikosXADataSourceWrapper wrapper = new AtomikosXADataSourceWrapper();
    return wrapper.wrapDataSource(h2DataSource);
  }

  @Bean
  public JdbcTemplate jdbcTemplate(DataSource dataSource) {
    return new JdbcTemplate(dataSource);
  }
}
```

Similar to JTA XML configuration, we need to wrap our H2 data source into AtomikosXADataSourceWrapper. This allows the H2 database to participate in global transactions. To enable use of handy Spring JDBC abstractions, we define the JdbcTemplate based on this XA data source. Listing 7-12 shows the JMS configuration.

Listing 7-12. Java Configuration of JMS XA Data Source (0702-jta-java-config)

```
package net.lkrnac.book.eiws.chapter07;

import java.util.Hashtable;
import javax.jms.ConnectionFactory;
import javax.jms.Session;
import javax.naming.InitialContext;
```

267

```java
import javax.naming.NamingException;
import org.springframework.context.annotation.Bean;
import org.springframework.context.annotation.Configuration;
import org.springframework.jms.annotation.EnableJms;
import org.springframework.jms.config.DefaultJmsListenerContainerFactory;
import org.springframework.jms.core.JmsTemplate;

@Configuration
@EnableJms
public class JmsConfiguration {
  @Bean
  public InitialContext initialContext() throws NamingException {
    Hashtable<Object, Object> env = new Hashtable<Object, Object>();
    env.put("java.naming.factory.initial",
        "org.jnp.interfaces.NamingContextFactory");
    env.put("java.naming.factory.url.pkgs",
        "org.jboss.naming:org.jnp.interfaces");
    env.put("java.naming.provider.url", "jnp://localhost:1099");
    return new InitialContext(env);
  }

  @Bean
  public ConnectionFactory connectionFactory(InitialContext initialContext)
      throws NamingException {
    return (ConnectionFactory) initialContext.lookup("/XAConnectionFactory");
  }

  @Bean
  public JmsTemplate jmsTemplate(ConnectionFactory connectionFactory) {
    return new JmsTemplate(connectionFactory);
  }

  @Bean
  public DefaultJmsListenerContainerFactory jmsListenerContainerFactory(
      ConnectionFactory connectionFactory) {
    DefaultJmsListenerContainerFactory factory =
        new DefaultJmsListenerContainerFactory();
    factory.setConnectionFactory(connectionFactory);
    factory.setSessionTransacted(true);
    factory.setSessionAcknowledgeMode(Session.SESSION_TRANSACTED);
    return factory;
  }
}
```

This configuration class enables JMS via the @EnableJms annotation and defines the InitialContext bean necessary for HornetQ access. The ConnectionFactory bean retrieves the XAConnectionFactory implementation from this HornetQ context. JmsTemplate and DefaultJmsListenerContainerFactory are standard Spring JMS beans explained in the previous chapter. *The important configuration is enabling transacted mode of the listener container; otherwise, this listener container wouldn't be plugged into the JTA infrastructure.* The main class of this example is highlighted in Listing 7-13.

Listing 7-13. Main Class Java Configuration JTA Example (0702-jta-java-config)

```java
package net.lkrnac.book.eiws.chapter07;

import org.springframework.boot.SpringApplication;
import org.springframework.context.annotation.ComponentScan;
import org.springframework.context.annotation.Configuration;
import org.springframework.scheduling.annotation.EnableScheduling;

@Configuration
@ComponentScan
@EnableScheduling
public class JtaApplication {
  public static void main(String[] args) throws Exception {
    SpringApplication.run(JtaApplication.class, args);
  }
}
```

The main class uses the Spring Boot main method mechanism to start the application via the main method. Again, we avoid using autoconfiguration, as we want to highlight plain Spring configuration for JTA. @EnableScheduling turns on scheduling used by the message sender, as shown in Listing 7-13. @ComponentScan allows us to use Spring configurations and common classes we already described as well as the listener in Listing 7-14.

Listing 7-14. JMS Listener Used by Java Configuration JTA Example (0702-jta-java-config)

```java
package net.lkrnac.book.eiws.chapter07;

import org.springframework.beans.factory.annotation.Autowired;
import org.springframework.jms.annotation.JmsListener;
import org.springframework.stereotype.Component;
import org.springframework.transaction.annotation.Transactional;

@Component
@Transactional
public class SimpleMessageListener {
  private SimpleService simpleService;
  private boolean errorSimulated = false;

  @Autowired
  public SimpleMessageListener(SimpleService simpleService) {
    super();
    this.simpleService = simpleService;
  }

  @JmsListener(destination = "ExpiryQueue")
  public void readMessage(String message) {
    simpleService.processText(message);
    postprocess(message);
  }
```

```
private void postprocess(String message) {
  // simulate error
  if (!errorSimulated) {
    errorSimulated = true;
    throw new IllegalArgumentException(message);
  }
 }
}
}
```

This listener is similar to the one in Listing 7-7, in the XML JTA example. The difference is that we have to specify that this bean is going to participate in a global transaction. This is done via the @Transactional annotation. The second difference is the @JmsListener annotation, which marks the method listening to the JMS messages. It is needed because there isn't any separate XML configuration that would configure it for Spring.

When we run this example, we get exactly same behavior as that shown in Figure 7-1, and similar output as for the same example 0701-jta-xml-config in Listing 7-9. (I believe you don't want to see that Mordor again.) But in this case, the configuration and code is more readable and maintainable than in the XML configuration example.

Spring Boot JTA Example

An even more readable and maintainable application can be based on Spring Boot autoconfiguration support, because it registers all the necessary configuration beans for us. We specify the HornetQ configuration in Listing 7-15.

Listing 7-15. HornetQ Spring Boot Configuration (File application.properties in Folder src/main/resources of Example Project 0703-jta-spring-boot)

```
spring.hornetq.mode=embedded
spring.hornetq.embedded.enabled=true
spring.hornetq.embedded.queues=ExpiryQueue
```

This configuration file enables an embedded instance of the HornetQ JMS server with a JMS destination called ExpiryQueue. The main class is shown in Listing 7-16.

Listing 7-16. Spring Boot Main Class for JTA Examples (0703-jta-spring-boot)

```
package net.lkrnac.book.eiws.chapter07;

import org.springframework.boot.SpringApplication;
import org.springframework.boot.autoconfigure.SpringBootApplication;
import org.springframework.scheduling.annotation.EnableScheduling;

@SpringBootApplication
@EnableScheduling
public class JtaApplication {
  public static void main(String[] args) throws Exception {
    SpringApplication.run(JtaApplication.class, args);
  }
}
```

This Spring Boot main class uses the @SpringBootApplication annotation to enable a Spring Boot scan for opinionated configuration of the Spring application. It does a component scan of the current package plus subpackages and scans classpath dependencies to enable features provided by these libraries. In this case, it creates the necessary Spring infrastructure for the following:

- Atomikos JTA transaction manager

- Embedded HornetQ JMS server and JmsTemplate with XA support

- H2 embedded database and JdbcTemplate with XA support

These are defined in a Maven configuration for this example, which can be found on GitHub. And that's all the configuration needed. It also uses common classes shown in Listing 7-1, 7-2, and 7-3 plus exactly the same implementation as the listener in Listing 7-14. This example nicely highlights why every Spring developer should look into Spring Boot, as it significantly reduces configuration for JTA support.

Again, when we run this example, the behavior is the same as in Figure 7-1. The same is true for the output, as you can see in Listing 7-9 (example 0701-jta-xml-config).

Summary

This chapter explored how JTA/XA protocols can help us cover various transactional data sources by global distributed transaction and enable ACID characteristics on top of them. Even when such support is compelling and easy to use with Spring, every smart developer should strive to avoid distributed transactions wherever possible.

Examples showed how easy it is to configure global transaction managers with XML and Java configuration and even easier with new mechanisms of Spring Boot. We also compared this support to plain transactional support and how it can help us target possible problems of using separate data sources within one application.

CHAPTER 8

■ ■ ■

Spring Integration

This book covers two of the most fundamental paradigms of an enterprise system: the request-response model (for example, REST, SOAP) and messaging (JMS). The first one can be synchronous (the caller of the service is blocked until the response arrives) or asynchronous (the caller registers a callback to execute or Future to fill in when the response arrives). The second one is, by definition, asynchronous; the sender of the massage doesn't wait until the consumer processes the message.

These mechanisms are essential for providing communication between distributed applications: *integrating them together*. But in a modern enterprise, hundreds or thousands of applications need to be integrated. Of course, enterprise architects need to keep them decoupled as much as possible, but in order to provide functionality and value to the customer, such an enterprise system will have some level of coupling. It is easy to imagine how complex a flow diagram of such a complicated distributed system can become over time.

For requirements like these, request-response and messaging integration are too granular as building blocks and abstractions. As bigger and bigger enterprise systems were produced, various architectural patterns started popping up. Gregor Hohpe and Bobby Woolf gathered them into their famous book, *Enterprise Integration Patterns* (Addison-Wesley Professional, 2003). These patterns provided higher-level abstractions than those in the request-response or messaging model, but often used them as partial building blocks.

Around the same time, David Chappell published *Enterprise Service Bus* (O'Reilly Media, 2004). Its goal was to simplify integration and communication of services within a service-oriented architecture (SOA). The central concept is a bus (similar to a hardware bus), which should control routing and flow of requests or messages exchanged between services.

After these patterns and principles were codified, a lot of companies and open source developers recognized that these patterns and principles could be implemented into generic frameworks, commonly referred to as Enterprise Service Bus (ESB) frameworks. Nowadays they are sometimes split into categories of lightweight integration frameworks, medium ESB frameworks, and ESB distributed systems.

Major players in this ESB software product space are as follows:

- Open source

  - Spring Integration framework

  - Apache Camel

  - Mule ESB (Community Edition)

  - Talend ESB

  - Petals ESB

  - Apache ServiceMix

  - WSO2 ESB

  - JBoss ESB

- Commercial

    - WebSphere Message Broker (IBM)

    - WebSphere ESB (IBM)

    - Oracle ESB

    - Mule ESB (Enterprise Edition)

Spring Integration Introduction

As a book about Enterprise Integration with Spring, it will obviously focus on the Spring Integration (SI) framework. It all started when Mark Fisher read the book *Enterprise Integration Patterns* and started implementing these patterns. Over the years, it emerged into a project, which is now considered a leader in the ESB framework market (along with Apache Camel, to be fair).

SI is a separate project in the Spring portfolio, but uses Spring Framework concepts such as dependency injection and inversion of control. Therefore, it requires Spring Framework as a dependency.

Spring Integration provides two killer features:

- Implementation of enterprise integration patterns in the form of in-memory messaging

- Powerful integration with various technologies and external applications in the form of pluggable adapters

APIs from the same portfolio of projects don't typically compete with each other, but SI is an exception. Its adapters provide alternative APIs to Spring modules such as Spring JDBC, Spring MVC, Spring JMS, Spring ORM, Spring WS, and various Spring Data and Spring Social projects. This is because SI aims for pluggable implementation of enterprise integration patterns with easy mapping to these external APIs. In fact SI, often uses these modules and projects under the hood in order to avoid reinventing the wheel.

Messages or requests from external systems are converted into in-memory messages (Java POJOs) with use of powerful Spring conversion mechanisms. This ensures extreme interoperability with pretty much all modern (for example, WebSockets) or traditional (for example, FTP) protocols or popular third-party services (for example, Twitter).

This messaging nature ensures that the flow of data is separated into small, composable units that exchange messages between each other synchronously or asynchronously. Such an approach ensures a high level of decoupling, modularity, and testability. Separation of concerns between business logic and integration (often referred to as *plumbing*) logic is a key goal of SI.

Another major feature is the easy switch between synchronous and asynchronous processing: SI abstractions allow for plugging of asynchronous executors, schedulers, and pollers into the message flow without need for changing processing logic. When using synchronous message flows, we can easily propagate exceptions and transactions across SI components.

Because the Spring framework's major configuration approach was originally targeted toward XML configuration, SI has followed this habit since its beginning. In the meantime, the Spring framework has shifted its configuration focus to approaches based on Java annotations. This shift also affected the SI framework, and most of the components can now be configured with Java annotations as well as integration flow. But modeling integration flow XML remains the preferred approach because of the following:

- A lot of adapters for external protocols or technologies can be exclusively provided in XML.

- ESB flow tends to be hard to follow when spread to various Java classes with annotations.

- SI flow can be visualized with the help of the Spring Tools Suite (STS) IDE. We'll explore these diagrams later in the chapter.

■ **Note**   If you are or want to be a Spring developer and are not familiar with STS, it is time to download it from http://spring.io/tools/sts and try it. It is based on Eclipse, so all the features from this popular IDE are available for STS. In addition to the Eclipse offerings, STS contains a lot of features tailored for Spring development. The quality guarantee of STS is that it is maintained by the Spring team.

Spring Integration's Main Concepts

A programming model is all about sending, routing, and consuming messages between message endpoints. Spring Integration contains a lot of components, and most of them are configurable. Each falls into one of these three categories:

- Message
- Message channel
- Message endpoint

Messages are exchanged between *message endpoints* via *message channels*. A single message channel connects two message endpoints. But a message endpoint can have any number of (even zero) input and output message channels.

When a message endpoint consumes messages from a message channel, it can *passively receive them* (listen) or *actively read them* (poll). Message channels can *pass through messages* (direct channel) or *temporarily store them in memory* (queue channel).

When we are modeling SI flow, it's important to understand whether the flow is *bidirectional* (of a request-response nature) or *unidirectional* (of a messaging or fire-and-forget nature). Based on these requirements, we may want to use specialized SI components designed for our case or use specialized mechanisms for replying to the originator of the message. Sometimes this flow can be combined (for example, read the value from the DB, expose it via the REST API, and send a message about this interaction into the tracking subsystem).

■ **Note**   Spring Integration provides a lot of basic in-memory components and many adapters for external systems, protocols, or technologies in order to enable extreme configurability and flexibility. Neither this book nor Enterprise Integration with Spring certification can detail each adapter that SI provides or attributes provided by SI components. Such a deep dive requires a book of its own. We cover major SI components and features that allow for a quick start with the framework so you can grasp the idea of the programming model. These principles and mechanisms can then be reused for additional components with the help of the SI reference documentation.

Common Classes Used in SI Examples

Before we start diving into concrete SI features, let's introduce some simple classes and interfaces used across a lot of our examples. Because the SI topic is broad, we'll go with Hello World–like examples. Trying to map these examples to a simple use case would make the examples bloated. The first common interface is shown in Listing 8-1.

Listing 8-1. Bidirectional Wrapper Interface for SI Flows (0800-integration-common)

```
package net.lkrnac.book.eiws.chapter08.in;

public interface SiWrapperService {
  boolean processText(String text);
}
```

This simple interface is designed to process a given text parameter and return the result of that action. It will be used for wrapping SI bidirectional flow. So we won't implement this interface, but instead will be using SI message flow as an implementation of this interface. The second interface is shown in Listing 8-2.

Listing 8-2. Unidirectional Wrapper Interface for SI Flows (0800-integration-common)

```
package net.lkrnac.book.eiws.chapter08.in;

public interface SiWrapperServiceVoid {
  void processText(String text);
}
```

This interface is similar to SiWrapperService, but in this case no result is returned to the caller. This one will be also be used to wrap SI flow, in this case unidirectional. Next we introduce the repository class in Listing 8-3.

Listing 8-3. Repository Class Used in Most Examples (0800-integration-common)

```
package net.lkrnac.book.eiws.chapter08.out;
import lombok.extern.slf4j.Slf4j;
import org.springframework.stereotype.Repository;

@Slf4j
@Repository
public class WriteRepository {
  public int persist(String text) {
    log.info("Text persisted: " + text);
    return 1;
  }
}
```

For this example's simplicity, this repository class will be fake. It will log the given message parameter and return a count of written records hard-coded to 1. It uses the @Repository annotation so that we can plug it into the Spring container via a component scan. The @Slf4j annotation was already mentioned and serves as an easy logger configuration. The last class from our common deck is shown in Listing 8-4.

Listing 8-4. Service Class Used in Most Examples (0800-integration-common)

```
package net.lkrnac.book.eiws.chapter08.out;
import org.springframework.beans.factory.annotation.Autowired;
import org.springframework.stereotype.Service;

@Service                    ˙
public class WriteService {
  private WriteRepository writeRepository;
```

```
  @Autowired
  public WriteService(WriteRepository writeRepository) {
    super();
    this.writeRepository = writeRepository;
  }

  public void write(String message) {
    writeRepository.persist(message);
  }

  public boolean writeAndIndicateSuccess(String message) {
    return writeRepository.persist(message) == 1;
  }
}
```

The class is called WriteService, because its Hello World–type concern is to persist the message with the help of WriteRepository. It uses the @Service annotation, so we can use it as a Spring bean. The WriteRepository bean is injected via constructor injection.

It provides two methods. The write() method persists the message without indicating the result of that operation to the caller. This method will often be used as target/output logic for unidirectional SI flows. The second method, writeAndIndicateSuccess(), also persists the message and returns a Boolean value about the result of that operation. You probably already guessed that it will be used as target logic of bidirectional SI flows in the examples.

The SI flow mostly starts where messages/requests are received. Think about this endpoint as input to the SI flow. We will place Spring beans or interfaces belonging to the input part of the SI flow into the package net.lkrnac.book.eiws.chapter08.in. The common interfaces SiWrapperService and SiWrapperServiceVoid also belong to this bucket.

On the other hand, the SI flow also has an output part. Classes or interfaces belonging to the output part of the SI flow will be placed in the net.lkrnac.book.eiws.chapter08.out package. The common classes WriteService and WriteRepository belong here.

Message

The message interface used by the SI framework is defined in the Spring Core framework. It is represented by the Java interface, and its definition is shown in Listing 8-5.

Listing 8-5. Message Interface

```
package org.springframework.messaging;

public interface Message<T> {
  T getPayload();
  MessageHeaders getHeaders();
}
```

The message is composed from headers and message payloads. The signature of this interface uses generics to enable users to handle any type as the payload of the message. The org.springframework.messaging.MessageHeaders type is a special implementation of Map<String, Object>. So we can store a header of any type into a message based on its header name.

By default, when any SI component needs to produce a message, it uses the implementation org.springframework.messaging.support.GenericMessage<T>. Notice that both the interface and implementation are not part of the SI framework, but part of the Spring framework and its messaging module. They were moved from SI into Spring Core since the 4.x versions of both frameworks, because the Spring team is trying to enhance interoperability of various messaging Spring abstractions.

The GenericMessage<T> message is *immutable*. After creation, we can't change the message payload or message headers. So if we need to amend the payload or headers, we would have to create a new message and send this new one instead of the original.

This is important because it ensures that the message cannot be manipulated by threads running in the background of our logic. When developers can rely on messages not being changed randomly under the hood, they can focus on the higher-level abstractions of message flow and easily switch between synchronous (single-threaded) and asynchronous (multithreaded) flow.

But the immutability of GenericMessage<T> is shallow. Even when we can't change the reference stored in the message payload nor the header value references, we can still change the fields of objects stored as the payload or as the header value if its class definition allows it. This fact can cause problems if we don't take care, but there is nothing SI can do about it, as the payload and header values can be of any type.

Message headers are meant to store message metadata. We can store our custom business logic headers in the message, but there are also headers that SI creates or understands. All messages by default have the id or timestamp of the message.

Headers can be added to a message to amend SI behavior or change message flow. For example, we can use the header priority (so messages with higher priority can surpass messages with lower priority) or replyChannel (so the message can specify which channel will be used when the reply is sent to the caller component). We discuss these headers in detail later in examples.

SI messages can be created in two major ways:

- Automatically by the SI framework

  - By SI adapter conversion from a transport format (for example, XML, JSON, file)

  - When SI generic components need to create a new message from an old message (for example, enriching headers, transforming message)

- Programmatically

Programmatic Creation of Messages

Readers familiar with Java concepts understand that in order to achieve immutability of GenericMessage<T>, its payload and headers fields must be marked as final. So creation of such a message cannot be achieved via setters. We could use constructors provided by the GenericMessage<T> class, but the SI framework provides a much more convenient way, with the help of org.springframework.integration.support.MessageBuilder<T>.

With this class, we can use fluent APIs to do the following:

- Create a message from scratch

- Create a message from an existing message

- Set default headers via specialized methods

- Copy headers from other messages

- Add/remove custom headers

If you are not familiar with the term *fluent API*, it will be described in a subsequent example. Notice that the Spring Core framework introduced in version 4 a messaging module with org.springframework.messaging.support.MessageBuilder<T>. It is a slightly different implementation from `org.springframework.integration.support.MessageBuilder<T>`, but produces messages of the same type. With SI, we should use `org.springframework.integration.support.MessageBuilder<T>`, because it can create various message headers tailored to SI communication.

Bear in mind that the focus of this example is the creation of messages, not their processing. The processing part of this example will be hidden in this example and explained later in the chapter. This example will use a wrapper for SI flow, shown in Listing 8-6.

Listing 8-6. SI Wrapper Interface for Programmatic Message Creation Example (0801-programmatic-message-creation)

```
package net.lkrnac.book.eiws.chapter08.in;
import org.springframework.messaging.Message;

public interface SiWrapperServiceMessage {
  public void processMessage(Message<String> message);
}
```

This SI flow wrapper interface is slightly different from the common wrapper interfaces in Listings 8-1 and 8-2, because it accepts a full message object instead of just the payload of the message. This is because we want to pass the message with headers to the SI flow to highlight the `MessageBuilder<T>` features. Listing 8-7 shows the message creation.

Listing 8-7. Programmatic Message Creation Example (0801-programmatic-message-creation)

```
package net.lkrnac.book.eiws.chapter08;
import net.lkrnac.book.eiws.chapter08.in.SiWrapperServiceMessage;
import org.springframework.boot.SpringApplication;
import org.springframework.boot.autoconfigure.SpringBootApplication;
import org.springframework.context.ApplicationContext;
import org.springframework.context.annotation.ImportResource;
import org.springframework.integration.support.MessageBuilder;
import org.springframework.messaging.Message;

@SpringBootApplication
@ImportResource("classpath:si-config.xml")
public class SiApplication {
  public static void main(String[] args) throws InterruptedException {
    ApplicationContext ctx = SpringApplication.run(SiApplication.class, args);

    SiWrapperServiceMessage wrapperService =
        ctx.getBean(SiWrapperServiceMessage.class);

    Message<String> message1 = MessageBuilder.withPayload("message1")
            .setHeader("simpleHeader", "simple header")
            .build();
    wrapperService.processMessage(message1);

    Message<String> message2 = MessageBuilder.fromMessage(message1)
        .setPriority(10)
        .setCorrelationId(System.currentTimeMillis())
        .build();
    wrapperService.processMessage(message2);
```

```
    Message<String> message3 = MessageBuilder.withPayload("message3")
        .copyHeaders(message2.getHeaders())
        .removeHeader("simpleHeader")
        .build();
    wrapperService.processMessage(message3);

    Message<String> message4 = MessageBuilder.withPayload("message4")
        .setPriority(5)
        .copyHeadersIfAbsent(message2.getHeaders())
        .build();
    wrapperService.processMessage(message4);
  }
}
```

This is a Java class with the main method using Spring Boot to start the application based on @SpringBootApplication and the SpringApplication.run() method. It imports the XML SI flow configuration located in the file si-config.xml. The SI flow hidden behind this SI configuration is not important for this message creation example and therefore we won't focus on it now. The SI building blocks located in the si-config.xml XML configuration are explained in later examples. The only important fact here is that it configures the simple SI flow, which only logs the message behind the scenes.

After the SpringApplication.run(), the SI application is initiated and configured, and we can start using it. First we read the SiWrapperServiceMessage bean, so that we have an entry point for sending messages. You might be confused about how we can inject this bean without registering its implementation into the Spring context. We just mention here that implementation of this interface is configured in si-config.xml and consists of SI components.

The logic following this call will be explained after we execute this class as a Java application. We can observe similar output as in Listing 8-8.

Listing 8-8. Output of Programmatic Message Creation Example

```
2015-08-21 21:39:12.353  INFO 30700 --- [         main] n.l.b.e.c.out.WriteServiceMessage
: Message: GenericMessage [payload=message1, headers={simpleHeader=simple header,
id=9779333f-b352-eb83-afdf-a52f7f4fed01, timestamp=1440189552345}]
2015-08-21 21:39:12.366  INFO 30700 --- [         main] n.l.b.e.c.out.WriteServiceMessage
: Message: GenericMessage [payload=message1, headers={simpleHeader=simple header,
correlationId=1440189552365, id=c46ff29f-c743-90dd-11b2-4c64e36a3d0b, priority=10,
timestamp=1440189552365}]
2015-08-21 21:39:12.367  INFO 30700 --- [         main] n.l.b.e.c.out.WriteServiceMessage
: Message: GenericMessage [payload=message3, headers={correlationId=1440189552365,
id=1fbbf243-0cc5-9d35-a8d1-f2d97a54d63d, priority=10, timestamp=1440189552366}]
2015-08-21 21:39:12.367  INFO 30700 --- [         main] n.l.b.e.c.out.WriteServiceMessage
: Message: GenericMessage [payload=message4, headers={simpleHeader=simple header,
correlationId=1440189552365, id=b91e5386-9151-0c94-cc6f-361bb688f480, priority=5,
timestamp=1440189552367}]
```

With MessageBuilder<T> help, we create a message with the payload message1, header simpleHeader, and value simple header. Calls against MessageBuilder<T>, where we chain methods via dot calls, is the *fluent API* we mentioned. This chain (fluent API) can continue until we are finished with message creation. Creation is finished by calling MessageBuilder<T>.build(). This call at the end is needed because the created message is immutable and the build() method calls all the necessary constructors for Message<T> and MessageHeaders to create our message based on the recorded configuration.

After we create the message, we call the `wrapperService` bean to initiate the SI flow, which in this simple case logs the message.

The second message is created from `message1` and adds some SI default headers via specialized methods. In this case, we configure `priority`, which can be used to amend message consumption ordering in the SI flow, and `correlationId`, which can be used to aggregate various messages into one message. We don't need to worry about these SI features now, as they are explained later in this chapter. The feature highlighted here is the fact that we can use specialized methods to create message headers that SI understands and can use them to affect the flow of messages.

The third message copies all headers from `message2`. This is handy when we want to slightly amend the SI message. In this case, the mentioned amendment is removal of the `simpleHeader` header.

The last message is created with the payload `message4` and configured with the priority value 5. Next we copy all the missing headers from `message2`. We are specifically interested in header `simpleHeader`, but because `message4` should have higher priority, we use the `copyHeadersIfAbsent()` method, because `message2` had lower priority with value 10 and we want to it to have priority with value 5.

Parsing Message Headers

We managed to explain programmatic message creation with headers for SI flow. The next feature, which is not specific to the SI framework but is a useful mechanism for SI message processing, is parsing of message headers. It's good to highlight that this feature of the Spring framework was already shown in Chapter 5.

So without too much buzz, we'll jump straight to the point and show an example of parsing headers of a message in Listing 8-9. We will use the same constructs as in the previous example, but still hide the SI flow. We will get there; don't worry.

Listing 8-9. Parsing Headers of Message (0802-parsing-headers)

```java
package net.lkrnac.book.eiws.chapter08.out;
import java.util.Date;
import java.util.Map;
import lombok.extern.slf4j.Slf4j;
import org.springframework.beans.factory.annotation.Autowired;
import org.springframework.messaging.handler.annotation.Header;
import org.springframework.messaging.handler.annotation.Headers;
import org.springframework.stereotype.Service;

@Slf4j
@Service
public class WriteServiceWithHeaders {
  private WriteRepository writeRepository;

  @Autowired
  public WriteServiceWithHeaders(WriteRepository writeRepository) {
    super();
    this.writeRepository = writeRepository;
  }

  public void write(String message, @Header("timestamp") long creationTime,
      @Headers Map<String, Object> headers) {
    log.info("Message received with payload: {}; Created: {}; Headers: {}",
        message, new Date(creationTime), headers);
    writeRepository.persist(message);
  }
}
```

Here the @Service class injects via constructor injection WriteRepository, belonging to the common deck of classes for this chapter. We are interested in the write method, where we accept the message payload as the string parameter message. The second parameter is annotated by @Header, which defines interest in the timestamp header (based on the annotation attribute) of the message and injects it into the creationTime variable. The annotation attribute is not mandatory if the parameter name matches the header name. The last parameter injects all the headers of the message into a map, which is defined by the @Headers annotation. These injected parameters are logged, and writeRepository is called to persist a message payload afterward.

We still keep the SI flow hidden for now; later examples will reveal SI features. The main class of this example looks exactly the same as the main class from the programmatic message creation example in Listing 8-7. The WriteServiceWithHeaders class is executed from the SI flow defined in si-config.xml. When we run the main class for this example, we get output similar to Listing 8-10.

Listing 8-10. Output of Message-Parsing Example

```
2015-08-22 12:57:38.045  INFO 12517 --- [           main] n.l.b.e.c.out.
WriteServiceWithHeaders    : Message received with payload: message1; Created:
Sat Aug 22 12:57:37 IST 2015; Headers: {simpleHeader=simple header,
id=a8e4193c-8b4a-def6-4c6f-16a5a04d368e, timestamp=1440244657998}
2015-08-22 12:57:38.059  INFO 12517 --- [           main]
n.l.b.e.chapter08.out.WriteRepository    : Text persisted: message1
2015-08-22 12:57:38.065  INFO 12517 --- [           main]
n.l.b.e.c.out.WriteServiceWithHeaders    : Message received with payload: message1; Created:
Sat Aug 22 12:57:38 IST 2015; Headers: {simpleHeader=simple header,
correlationId=1440244658059, id=2a8bfcc8-c950-f5c9-c01a-cf3048f6eebd, priority=10,
timestamp=1440244658059}
2015-08-22 12:57:38.065  INFO 12517 --- [           main]
n.l.b.e.chapter08.out.WriteRepository    : Text persisted: message1
2015-08-22 12:57:38.068  INFO 12517 --- [           main]
n.l.b.e.c.out.WriteServiceWithHeaders    : Message received with payload: message3; Created:
Sat Aug 22 12:57:38 IST 2015; Headers: {correlationId=1440244658059,
id=78d366ae-8aaa-dd7a-bcbf-ce9bacc1edfa, priority=10, timestamp=1440244658066}
2015-08-22 12:57:38.068  INFO 12517 --- [           main]
n.l.b.e.chapter08.out.WriteRepository    : Text persisted: message3
2015-08-22 12:57:38.069  INFO 12517 --- [           main]
n.l.b.e.c.out.WriteServiceWithHeaders    : Message received with payload: message4; Created:
Sat Aug 22 12:57:38 IST 2015; Headers: {simpleHeader=simple header,
correlationId=1440244658059, id=c41ee6ce-a319-60e5-e595-7fb276efdff1, priority=5,
timestamp=1440244658068}
2015-08-22 12:57:38.070  INFO 12517 --- [           main]
n.l.b.e.chapter08.out.WriteRepository    : Text persisted: message4
```

As we can see, logged messages have the same structure as messages in Listing 8-8, but they're logged in a different format to highlight the header parsing features.

Message Endpoint

The message endpoint is probably the most diverse SI component. The SI reference documentation refers to it as a *filter* from the pipes-and-filters architecture. We already mentioned that in order to send or receive messages, the endpoint has to be connected to one or more message channels. Its primary role is to encapsulate application logic and decouple it from the SI messaging infrastructure. Our application code often doesn't even know that it's part of the SI flow. A good example is `WriteService`, shown previously in Listing 8-4. From a first look at this class, we can't say whether it's a standard Spring bean or part of the SI flow.

As we mentioned, it makes sense to model SI flow in an XML configuration. The message endpoint, as a generic component, doesn't have any XML tag representation, because each type of specific component has its own XML tag. But some parts of the SI flow can be configured via Java annotations. In such a case generic annotations are required for message endpoint configuration.

The first, most important, annotation from the SI framework is `@EnableIntegration`. It enables the declaration of standard SI beans when we use Spring's `@Configuration` annotation. The same effect can be achieved with Spring Boot's `@EnableAutoConfiguration` annotation or `@SpringBootApplication`. So when we use Spring Boot with autoconfiguration, we can skip `@EnableIntegration`, because it will be configured automatically for us.

Another generic SI annotation is `@IntegrationComponentScan`. As the name suggests, it scans the classpath for SI message endpoints. It works similarly to the `@ComponentScan` we are used to from the Spring framework for SI-specific components. So it has to be used with the `@MessageEndpoint` or `@MessagingGateway` annotations (we explain these annotations later in the chapter), which register SI-specific beans into the Spring context. This annotation is needed for registering SI-specific components even if we are using Spring Boot with autoconfiguration enabled (`@EnableAutoConfiguration` or `@SpringBootApplication`).

The last generic annotation is `@MessageEndpoint`, which marks the class participating in SI flow, where some of its methods will be annotated with more-specific SI annotations. These specific annotations are explained later, when we discuss concrete types of message endpoints.

Use of these annotations is shown as part of specific SI component examples.

Message Endpoint Types

We can categorize message endpoints in various ways, detailed in the following subsections.

Message Flow Direction

- *Unidirectional*: The component can participate in fire-and-forget scenarios.

- *Bidirectional*: The component can participate in request-response scenarios. This flow involves sending a response to the upstream consumer via `replyChannel`.

Placement in the Message Flow

- *Input component*: Connects the SI flow to the upstream external application or internal Java logic. Messages enter the SI flow via this component.

- *Output component*: Connects the SI flow to the downstream external application or internal Java logic. Messages are sent out of the SI flow via this component.

- *Middle component*: Capable of operating in the middle of the flow. This component can participate in unidirectional as well as bidirectional message flow.

Triggering Activity of the Component

- *Passive*: The component waits until the message is pushed to it via the input channel. This mode is usually part of synchronous execution and is able to propagate transactions to the output channel or bubble up exceptions to the originator of the message.

- *Active*: The component actively reads messages from the input channel based on internal triggering. This triggering can be achieved with a special subcomponent called a *poller* (configured via the <poller> XML tag or the @Poller annotation). An important requirement for this mode is that the input channel needs to be capable of temporarily storing messages flowing into it. We discuss this channel type later in this chapter.

Component Purpose

Generic component

- Maps the message channel to the Java interface or class. If it's mapped to the Java interface, the implementation is covered by SI abstractions.

- Handles the message endpoint concern (for example, routing, message transformation) on top of standard Java classes or interfaces.

Technology-specific component

- Connects the SI flow to an external system or transport protocol (for example, FTP, HTTP, JMS). SI provides many of these connector components, which are gathered in this table: http://docs.spring.io/spring-integration/docs/latest-ga/reference/htmlsingle/#endpoint-summary.

- Handles message endpoint concerns on top of a specific technology (for example, XML message conversion, filtering XML messages based on XPath expressions).

List of Message Endpoints

It's important to understand that each particular message endpoint can operate in various modes, based on its configuration. But once the component is configured, we can't switch these modes at runtime.

The following is a list of the major message endpoints that SI provides and the modes they can operate in. They are also divided into three major functional categories.

- *Messaging components*: Used to connect the SI flow with external technology or Java logic

  - *Channel adapter*: Unidirectional, input/output, passive/active, generic/specific

  - *Service activator*: Unidirectional/bidirectional, output/middle, passive/active, generic

  - *Messaging gateway*: Unidirectional/bi-directional, input/output, passive, generic/specific

- *Transformation components*: Their function is to convert the message payload or headers to a different format. They are middle components that can participate in unidirectional as well as bidirectional message flow.

  - *Transformer*: Passive/active, generic/specific

  - *Content enricher*: Passive/active, generic/specific

- *Routing components*: Their function is to control the flow of messages. They are middle components that can participate in unidirectional as well as bidirectional message flow.

  - *Filter*: Passive/filter, generic/specific

  - *Router*: Passive, generic/specific

  - *Bridge*: Passive/active, generic

  - *Chain*: Passive, generic

  - *Splitter*: Passive/active, generic/specific

  - *Aggregator*: Passive, generic

■ **Note** This is not a complete list of SI message endpoints. This list covers the major endpoints you are most likely to use in practice for standard integration use cases. Special endpoints for various corner use cases are beyond the scope of Enterprise Integration with Spring certification and thus also beyond the scope of this book. For a full list of message endpoints, refer to the SI reference documentation at `http://docs.spring.io/spring-integration/docs/latest-ga/reference/htmlsingle/`.

Channel Adapter

The channel adapter is an SI endpoint component for unidirectional message flow. So it is suitable for fire-and-forget scenarios. From a triggering point of view, it can act as a passive as well as active component (if the poller subcomponent is configured). As each unidirectional message flow needs to have input and output, we have two types of channel adapters:

- *Input channel adapter*: Sits on the input side of the SI flow, where it passively listens or actively reads messages

- *Output channel adapter*: Sits on the output side of SI flow, where it sends messages to the Java class or external system or protocol

The term *adapter* suggests that it maps the message channel to a non-SI system or subsystem. From this point of view, we can divide channel adapters into these two categories:

- *Generic Java adapters*: Map the message channel to the Java interface or class. If the adapter is mapped to the Java interface, implementation is covered by SI abstractions. Can be configured via the XML tag `<int:inbound-channel-adapter>` or `<int:outbound-channel-adapter>`, where it uses the core SI XML namespace. The inbound channel adapter can be also configured via the @InboundChannelAdapter. This annotation is not available for the outbound channel adapter as of SI version 4.1.6.RELEASE.

- *Technology-specific adapters*: Connect the message channel to an external system or transport protocol (for example, FTP, HTTP, JMS). SI provides numerous implementations of these adapters for different technologies, which can be configured via only XML tags. For each technology, we need to use specific XML namespaces (for example, `<int-http:inbound-channel-adapter>`, `<int-amqp:inbound-channel-adapter>`, `<int-mail:outbound-channel-adapter>`, `<int-jms:outbound-channel-adapter>`). External adapters don't have any SI annotations available, so we have to use XML configuration for them. A concise table presenting channel adapter implementations for external technologies can be found at `http://docs.spring.io/spring-integration/docs/latest-ga/reference/htmlsingle/#endpoint-summary`.

Generic Inbound and Outbound Channel Adapters Example Configured with XML

The following generic channel adapter examples are the only examples in this chapter not using Spring Boot, in order to highlight how to configure SI applications with pure Spring and SI frameworks.

This example covers generic inbound and outbound channel adapters based on XML configuration. The first class, shown in Listing 8-11, is a service we will be actively polling.

Listing 8-11. Service Used for Reading Messages via Inbound Channel Adapter (0803-channel-adapter-generic-xml)

```
package net.lkrnac.book.eiws.chapter08.in;
import org.springframework.stereotype.Service;

@Service
public class ReadService {
  public String read() {
    return "simple message";
  }
}
```

This Spring service bean has just one simple method that returns a simple string message. Listing 8-12 shows the XML configuration of the SI flow.

Listing 8-12. XML Configuration of SI Flow for Generic Channel Adapters Example (File si-config.xml in Folder src/main/resources of Example Project 0803-channel-adapter-generic-xml)

```
<?xml version="1.0" encoding="UTF-8"?>
<beans xmlns="http://www.springframework.org/schema/beans"
  xmlns:xsi="http://www.w3.org/2001/XMLSchema-instance"
  xmlns:int="http://www.springframework.org/schema/integration"
  xmlns:context="http://www.springframework.org/schema/context"
  xsi:schemaLocation="http://www.springframework.org/schema/beans
    http://www.springframework.org/schema/beans/spring-beans.xsd
            http://www.springframework.org/schema/context
    http://www.springframework.org/schema/context/spring-context.xsd
            http://www.springframework.org/schema/integration
    http://www.springframework.org/schema/integration/spring-integration.xsd">
```

```
<context:component-scan base-package="net.lkrnac.book.eiws.chapter08" />

<int:inbound-channel-adapter ref="readService" method="read" channel="inChannel">
  <int:poller fixed-rate="1000" max-messages-per-poll="1"/>
</int:inbound-channel-adapter>

<int:channel id="inChannel" />

<int:outbound-channel-adapter channel="inChannel" ref="writeService" method="write" />
</beans>
```

SI provides various XML namespaces for generic SI components and separate namespaces for particular technology we want the SI flow to hook on. In this case, we use only a generic SI namespace aliased to int. Alongside this SI namespace, we also use the standard Spring namespaces context and a default one for handling Spring beans.

The first XML tag <context:component-scan> performs classpath scanning for Spring components in the base package net.lkrnac.book.eiws.chapter08 and its subpackages. This scan includes ReadService and our common beans WriteService and WriteRepository.

Next we can use the SI tag <int:inbound-channel-adapter>, which will be connected to the readService bean. We also have to specify the attribute method, which maps this inbound channel adapter to readService.read(). As ReadService is a passive bean not sending any messages, we need to configure the <int:poller> subelement for this adapter. With attributes for this poller, we define a 1-second fixed-rate poll interval and we will read only one message per poll. Under the hood, SI uses a standard Spring scheduler with the fixed rate of 1 second in this case. So every second, this channel adapter will call readService.read(),and create an SI message out of its return value.

This message is then handed to another inChannel, which is defined by the mandatory attribute channel. inChannel also has to be configured for SI flow, and this is done via the separate XML element <int:channel>. On the other side of inChannel, we connect the outbound channel adapter via the XML tag <int:outbound-channel-adapter>. This adapter is mapped to our common bean, writeService, and the write method.

The main class of this example is shown in Listing 8-13.

Listing 8-13. Main Class of Generic Channel Adapters Example Based on XML Configuration (0803-channel-adapter-generic-xml)

```
package net.lkrnac.book.eiws.chapter08;
import org.springframework.context.support.GenericXmlApplicationContext;
import org.springframework.core.io.ClassPathResource;

public class SiApplication {
  public static void main(String[] args) throws InterruptedException {
    new GenericXmlApplicationContext(new ClassPathResource("si-config.xml"));
  }
}
```

This class starts the Spring context defined in si-config.xml. When we run this main class as a Java application, we get the output shown in Listing 8-14.

Listing 8-14. Output of XML Generic Channel Adapters Example

```
20:35:49.774 [task-scheduler-1] INFO  n.l.b.e.c.out.WriteRepository - Text persisted: simple
message
20:35:50.760 [task-scheduler-1] INFO  n.l.b.e.c.out.WriteRepository - Text persisted: simple
message
20:35:51.758 [task-scheduler-2] INFO  n.l.b.e.c.out.WriteRepository - Text persisted: simple
message
20:35:52.758 [task-scheduler-1] INFO  n.l.b.e.c.out.WriteRepository - Text persisted: simple
message
20:35:53.758 [task-scheduler-3] INFO  n.l.b.e.c.out.WriteRepository - Text persisted: simple
message
```

The flow is executed in the task scheduler threads instead of the main thread. This is because we specified a poller for the inbound channel adapter, which reads a new message each second and sends it to `writerService`. This is also why this Spring context remains open and would run indefinitely until we forcibly stop the application.

We need to bear in mind that the types of Java POJO on input and output of this flow must match. In this case, it is of type `String`, which is used as a payload of `GenericMessage<String>` flowing. It is also important to understand that SI components register Spring beans into the Spring context. For example, the `<int:channel>` tag created a Spring bean with the name `inChannel` and the type `DirectChannel`. This channel type is explained later in the "Message Channel" section.

Figure 8-1 shows one more interesting thing about this example.

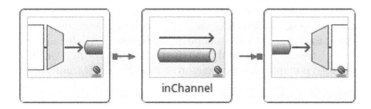

Figure 8-1. *Visualization of generic channel's adapter SI flow*

Figure 8-1 depicts our SI flow. It is nice, because it effectively shows a live diagram of our SI application—something every architect dreams of. This visualization can be found in the STS writer window of the `si-config.xml` file, between the bottom tabs. From my experience, a lot of developers don't even know where these tabs are located in Eclipse/STS, so let's show it visually in Figure 8-2.

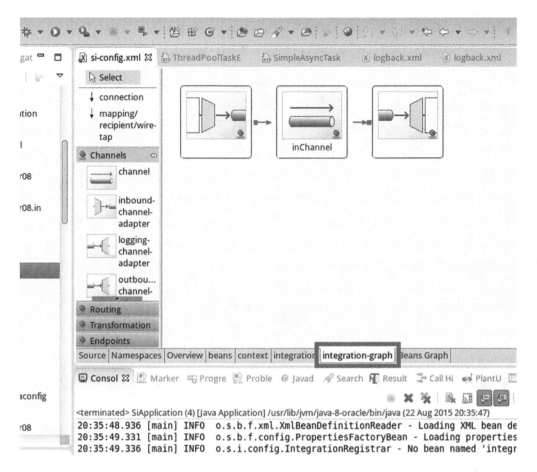

***Figure 8-2.** Location of integration-graph tab*

But this is not only a visualization. We can also create SI flows based on this integration-graph tab. As you can see, on left side of the writer window are available SI components, and we can drag them into our flow. When the component is located on our graph, we can double-click it, and STS will open the Properties window, where we can edit properties of this component. This is shown in Figure 8-3.

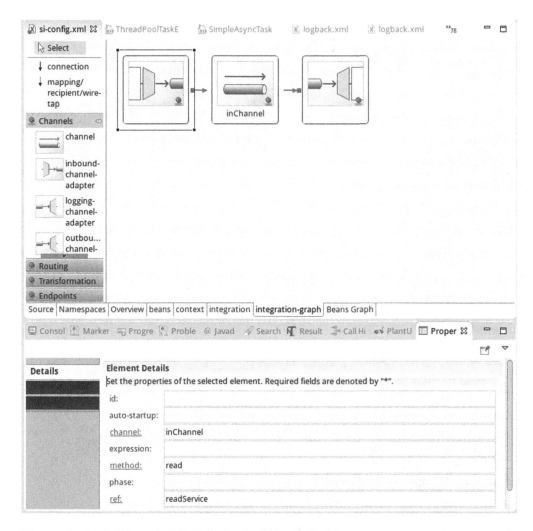

Figure 8-3. *Editing SI component attributes via the Properties tab*

As we can see, all the possible attributes for a particular SI component are listed. Mandatory attributes are underlined.

Generic Inbound Channel Adapter Example Configured with Java Annotation

Next we will show how to configure the same flow with a Java configuration. Listing 8-15 shows a partial XML configuration of SI flow, because so far there isn't an annotation for the outbound channel adapter.

Listing 8-15. Partial XML Configuration of Outbound Channel Adapter (File si-config.xml in Folder src/main/resources of Example Project 0804-channel-adapter-generic-javaconfig)

```
<?xml version="1.0" encoding="UTF-8"?>
<beans xmlns="http://www.springframework.org/schema/beans"
  xmlns:xsi="http://www.w3.org/2001/XMLSchema-instance"
```

```
xmlns:int="http://www.springframework.org/schema/integration"
xmlns:context="http://www.springframework.org/schema/context"
xsi:schemaLocation="http://www.springframework.org/schema/beans
   http://www.springframework.org/schema/beans/spring-beans.xsd
              http://www.springframework.org/schema/integration
   http://www.springframework.org/schema/integration/spring-integration.xsd">

<int:channel id="inChannel"/>

<int:outbound-channel-adapter channel="inChannel" ref="writeService" method="write"/>
</beans>
```

This configuration of an outbound channel adapter was already shown in a previous example. The channel could be configured with a Java configuration, but we show that configuration later in the examples. Listing 8-16 shows a Java configuration of an inbound channel adapter.

Listing 8-16. Java Configuration of Inbound Channel Adapter (0804-channel-adapter-generic-javaconfig)

```
package net.lkrnac.book.eiws.chapter08.in;
import org.springframework.integration.annotation.InboundChannelAdapter;
import org.springframework.integration.annotation.Poller;
import org.springframework.stereotype.Service;

@Service
public class ReadServiceAnnotated {
  @InboundChannelAdapter(value = "inChannel",
      poller = @Poller(fixedRate = "1000", maxMessagesPerPoll = "1"))
  public String read() {
    return "simple message";
  }
}
```

In this case, the read service method read() is annotated with @InboundChannelAdapter, which makes it an SI message endpoint. We need to specify the mandatory value attribute of this annotation to connect it to the message channel inChannel.

Because we also want to have this component active (which means it will be actively polling an annotated method), we configure @Poller with a fixed rate of 1 second for this adapter. This annotation will create a Spring scheduler under the hood to perform active polling. With the maxMessagesPerPoll attribute, we define that only one message should be read per poll.

Listing 8-17 shows the main class of this example.

Listing 8-17. Main Application of Channel Adapters Example with Java Configuration (0804-channel-adapter-generic-javaconfig)

```
package net.lkrnac.book.eiws.chapter08;
import org.springframework.context.annotation.AnnotationConfigApplicationContext;
import org.springframework.context.annotation.ComponentScan;
import org.springframework.context.annotation.Configuration;
import org.springframework.context.annotation.ImportResource;
import org.springframework.integration.config.EnableIntegration;
```

```
@Configuration
@ComponentScan
@EnableIntegration
@ImportResource("classpath:si-config.xml")
public class SiApplication {
  public static void main(String[] args) throws InterruptedException {
    new AnnotationConfigApplicationContext(SiApplication.class);
  }
}
```

This main class also acts as a Spring configuration class (@Configuration annotation) and scans the current package with subpackages for Spring beans. The @ImportResource annotation also plugs into this Spring context the XML part of the SI flow. The last annotation, @EnableIntegration, turns on the SI features. After running this class, we would see similar output as in Listing 8-14 for the 0803-channel-adapter-generic-xml example.

The downside of the Java configuration is that the SI flow can't be visualized or edited via the integration-graph editor of STS.

Nongeneric Channel Adapters Example

Now it's time to explore adapters for external technologies. In this case, we expose our SI flow as a REST service on the input side and connect it to a JDBC data source on the output side. As a database, we use the H2 database engine. When Spring Boot autoconfiguration detects it on the classpath, it configures the jdbcTeamplate bean automatically. Listing 8-18 shows the SI configuration.

Listing 8-18. SI Configuration for Nongeneric Channel Adapters (File si-config.xml in Folder src/main/resources of Example Project 0805-channel-adapter-non-generic)

```xml
<?xml version="1.0" encoding="UTF-8"?>
<beans xmlns="http://www.springframework.org/schema/beans"
  xmlns:xsi="http://www.w3.org/2001/XMLSchema-instance"
  xmlns:int="http://www.springframework.org/schema/integration"
  xmlns:int-http="http://www.springframework.org/schema/integration/http"
  xmlns:int-jdbc="http://www.springframework.org/schema/integration/jdbc"
  xsi:schemaLocation="http://www.springframework.org/schema/integration/jdbc
    http://www.springframework.org/schema/integration/jdbc/spring-integration-jdbc.xsd
    http://www.springframework.org/schema/beans
    http://www.springframework.org/schema/beans/spring-beans.xsd
    http://www.springframework.org/schema/integration/http
    http://www.springframework.org/schema/integration/http/spring-integration-http.xsd
    http://www.springframework.org/schema/integration
    http://www.springframework.org/schema/integration/spring-integration.xsd">

  <int-http:inbound-channel-adapter path="/" channel="inChannel" supported-methods="POST" />
  <int:channel id="inChannel" />

  <int-jdbc:outbound-channel-adapter data-source="dataSource" channel="inChannel"
    query="insert into TEXT_TABLE values (:payload)"/>
</beans>
```

We use the beans and context Spring namespaces and the generic SI int namespace again. New namespaces are int-http and int-jdbc to allow the use of adapters for these technologies. The first XML element is <int-http:inbound-channel-adapter>. It exposes inChannel as a REST endpoint, which listens to POST messages on the root URL. The payload will be a simple string.

On the other side of inChannel, we configured the connected SI to the JDBC data source via <int-jdbc:outbound-channel-adapter>. This component needs to know which data-source bean to use for JDBC access. In this case, we refer it to the bean with the name dataSource, which is created in the Spring context (creation of it is discussed later in this section). Of course, when we are accessing the database, we need to have a query to execute. In this case, we use the inline query attribute to define it. It is a simple insert into TEXT_TABLE, where the stored value will be used from the SI message payload. This payload is received from the REST endpoint.

Listing 8-19 shows initialization of the TEXT_TABLE table.

Listing 8-19. Initialization of DB Table (0805-channel-adapter-non-generic)

```
package net.lkrnac.book.eiws.chapter08;
import javax.annotation.PostConstruct;
import org.springframework.beans.factory.annotation.Autowired;
import org.springframework.jdbc.core.JdbcTemplate;
import org.springframework.stereotype.Repository;

@Repository
public class SimpleDatabasePopulator {
  private JdbcTemplate jdbcTemplate;

  @Autowired
  public SimpleDatabasePopulator(JdbcTemplate jdbcTemplate) {
    super();
    this.jdbcTemplate = jdbcTemplate;
  }

  @PostConstruct
  public void initDbTable() {
    jdbcTemplate.execute("drop table TEXT_TABLE if exists");
    jdbcTemplate.execute("create table TEXT_TABLE(TEXT varchar(30))");
  }
}
```

This component will initialize the in-memory database based on the injected jdbcTemplate bean it autowires. The JdbcTemplate instance is created automatically by Spring Boot. Listing 8-20 shows the Spring Boot configuration of the server port for HTTP access.

Listing 8-20. Configuration of Server Port (File application.properties in Folder src/main/resources of Example Project 0805-channel-adapter-non-generic)

```
server.port=18080
```

Finally, Listing 8-21 shows the main class of the application in this example.

Listing 8-21. Main Class of Nongeneric Channel Adapters Example (0805-channel-adapter-non-generic)

```
package net.lkrnac.book.eiws.chapter08;
import org.springframework.boot.SpringApplication;
import org.springframework.boot.autoconfigure.SpringBootApplication;
import org.springframework.context.annotation.ImportResource;

@SpringBootApplication
@ImportResource("classpath:si-config.xml")
public class SiApplication {
  public static void main(String[] args) throws InterruptedException {
    SpringApplication.run(SiApplication.class, args);
  }
}
```

We use Spring Boot here to initialize everything with autoconfiguration by the using @SpringBootApplication annotation. As we have the JAR dependencies needed for running the embedded servlet container as well as in-memory database support on the classpath, Spring automatically configures for us the servlet container and jdbcTemplate and dataSource bean to access this in-memory database. This annotation also scans the current package and subpackages for Spring beans, and of course initializes SI. You can think of it as having @EnableIntegration under the hood, because @SpringBootApplication turns on this feature via autoconfiguration.

The next annotation imports our XML SI configuration. In the main method, we run the Spring Boot application via the SpringApplication.run() call. When we run it, the application listens on address http://localhost:18080. Any text POSTed to this address will be persisted into TEXT_TABLE. Chapter 4 already covered REST and how to send payloads via HTTP. We used the Advanced REST Client Chrome plug-in for this purpose, so please refer to chapter 4 if you are unsure about sending HTTP messages.

Visualization of the SI flow looks similar to the XML generic channel adapters example in Figure 8-1.

Service Activator

A *service activator* is a generic SI message endpoint, which maps a message channel onto a Spring bean and invokes a specified method. The message received by this endpoint will try to be converted (if needed) into a parameter or various parameters of the mapped method. Similarly, the eventual return value from the method will try to be converted into a new message (if needed). If any of these conversions fail, an exception will be thrown.

The service activator can be plugged into the middle of the SI flow or as an output component; therefore, the input channel attribute is mandatory. This fact also means that the method mapped to the service activator must have at least one parameter, so that the message can be passed to the service. It can participate in a unidirectional as well as a bidirectional message flow. The difference in these flows depends on the signature of the method mapped into the service activator.

If the mapped method is void (it doesn't return any value), it can act as a unidirectional output message endpoint. This mode is pretty much the same as that of the generic outbound channel adapter.

If the mapped method returns a value, the service activator can act as follows:

An output component in bidirectional SI flow.

- A middle component in bidirectional or unidirectional SI flow. In this configuration, it is similar to a message transformer endpoint (will have its own section) in the sense that it receives a message and returns a different message. The fundamental difference here is that the message transformer is designed to convert messages, whereas the service activator is designed to invoke a method on the Spring bean and optionally gather a return value into the message.

If the mapped method returns null and an upstream SI component requires a response (for example, an upstream message gateway has request-reply configured to true), an exception is thrown in the SI flow.

For configuring the service activator, we use the <int:service-activator> XML tag or @ServiceActivator annotation.

Service Activator Example with XML Configuration

Listing 8-22 shows the XML SI configuration.

Listing 8-22. XML Configuration for Service Activator Example (File si-config.xml in Folder src/main/resources of Example Project 0806-service-activator-xml)

```xml
<?xml version="1.0" encoding="UTF-8"?>
<beans xmlns="http://www.springframework.org/schema/beans"
  xmlns:xsi="http://www.w3.org/2001/XMLSchema-instance"
  xmlns:int="http://www.springframework.org/schema/integration"
  xmlns:context="http://www.springframework.org/schema/context"
  xsi:schemaLocation="http://www.springframework.org/schema/beans
    http://www.springframework.org/schema/beans/spring-beans.xsd
    http://www.springframework.org/schema/integration
    http://www.springframework.org/schema/integration/spring-integration.xsd">

  <int:inbound-channel-adapter ref="readService" method="read" channel="inChannel">
    <int:poller fixed-rate="1000" />
  </int:inbound-channel-adapter>

  <int:channel id="inChannel" />

  <int:service-activator input-channel="inChannel" ref="writeService" method="write" />
</beans>
```

The input part of the SI message flow is identical to 0803-channel-adapter-generic-xml from Listing 8-12. In fact, we are using the same readService bean for message creation. The difference is in the output part of the SI flow, which uses <int:service-activator> to map the writeService.write() method to our message flow. As you may remember, this method is void, so no response will be generated and it is compatible with the input channel adapter's unidirectional nature. The main class of this example is shown in Listing 8-23.

Listing 8-23. Main Class of XML Service Activator Example (0806-service-activator-xml)

```java
package net.lkrnac.book.eiws.chapter08;
import org.springframework.boot.SpringApplication;
import org.springframework.boot.autoconfigure.SpringBootApplication;
import org.springframework.context.annotation.ImportResource;

@SpringBootApplication
@ImportResource("classpath:si-config.xml")
public class SiApplication {
  public static void main(String[] args) throws InterruptedException {
    SpringApplication.run(SiApplication.class, args);
  }
}
```

This is the Spring Boot configuration class and the main class, which executes itself as the Spring Boot application. This is a common pattern with Spring Boot. The @ImportResource annotation includes the XML SI flow into this Spring context. @SpringBootApplication also covers component scanning for Spring beans. That is why references to readService and writeService are available for us in the si-config.xml file.

Running this example results in output similar to Listing 8-14 for the 0803-channel-adapter-generic-xml example. Visualization of this SI flow is shown in Figure 8-4.

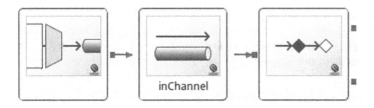

Figure 8-4. Visualization of SI flow for XML channel adapter example

Service Activator Example with Java Configuration

Listing 8-24 shows the Java SI configuration.

Listing 8-24. Java Configuration of Message Channel (0807-service-activator-javaconfig)

```
package net.lkrnac.book.eiws.chapter08;
import org.springframework.context.annotation.Bean;
import org.springframework.context.annotation.Configuration;
import org.springframework.integration.channel.DirectChannel;
import org.springframework.messaging.MessageChannel;

@Configuration
public class SiConfiguration {
  @Bean
  public MessageChannel inChannel() {
    return new DirectChannel();
  }
}
```

This standard Spring configuration class defines one bean of type MessageChannel and name inChannel. The DirectChannel implementation is used in this case. This channel type is explained later, in the "Message Channel" section. Listing 8-25 shows the Java configuration of the service activator.

Listing 8-25. Java Configuration of Service Activator (0807-service-activator-javaconfig)

```
package net.lkrnac.book.eiws.chapter08.out;
import net.lkrnac.book.eiws.chapter08.out.WriteRepository;
import org.springframework.beans.factory.annotation.Autowired;
import org.springframework.integration.annotation.ServiceActivator;
import org.springframework.stereotype.Service;
```

```
@Service
public class WriteServiceAnnotated {
  private WriteRepository writeRepository;

  @Autowired
  public WriteServiceAnnotated(WriteRepository writeRepository) {
    super();
    this.writeRepository = writeRepository;
  }

  @ServiceActivator(inputChannel = "inChannel")
  public void write(String message) {
    writeRepository.persist(message);
  }
}
```

This service class injects the WriteRepository bean via constructor injection, so that we can call it in order to process the received message. The message is received via WriteServiceAnnotated.write(), which is annotated with @ServiceActivator, and this is participating in a unidirectional SI flow. The inputChannel attribute is mandatory and refers to inChannel from Listing 8-24.

Another bean included in this example is ReadServiceAnnotated from Listing 8-16, which is an annotated version of the inbound channel adapter. The main class of this example is shown in Listing 8-26.

Listing 8-26. Main Class of Service Activator Example with Java Configuration (0807-service-activator-javaconfig)

```
package net.lkrnac.book.eiws.chapter08;

import org.springframework.boot.SpringApplication;
import org.springframework.boot.autoconfigure.SpringBootApplication;

@SpringBootApplication
public class SiApplication {
  public static void main(String[] args) throws InterruptedException {
    SpringApplication.run(SiApplication.class, args);
  }
}
```

This standard Spring Boot pattern runs an autoconfigured application that scans for beans in the current package and subpackages. Running it results in output similar to Listing 8-14 for the 0803-channel-adapter-generic-xml example, because the inbound channel adapter mapped to ReadServiceAnnotated reads a message each second and sends it to the service activator.

Messaging Gateway

The *messaging gateway* is a passive component that can participate in unidirectional or bidirectional message flows. So it inherently handles request-response concerns. We can divide gateways into two categories:

- *Generic messaging gateway*: Wraps SI message flow into the Java interface as input to the message infrastructure. Therefore, the method wrapping the flow must have a return value. We can think of it as a proxy between Java and the SI flow. It can be configured via the XML element `<int:gateway>`. The Java configuration uses two annotations: `@MessagingGateway` marks the interface as a gateway wrapper, and `@Gateway` maps a particular method as an entrance to SI messaging. Notice that we can annotate various methods in the same class with the `@Gateway` annotation and in this way have various entry points to our SI flow. Therefore, we need to scan the annotated inbound gateway with `@IntegrationComponentScan`.

- *Technology-specific messaging gateway*: Can handle communication with an external technology or protocol (for example, HTTP, JDBC, SOAP Web Services). This type of gateway can be inbound or outbound in relation to SI flow. To configure a technology-specific gateway with XML, we need to use special XML namespaces (for example, `<int-file:outbound-gateway>`, `<int-http:inbound-gateway>`, `<int-ws:outbound-gateway>`). A technology-specific gateway doesn't have any SI annotations available, so only an XML configuration is possible. A concise table listing messaging gateway implementations for external technologies is available at `http://docs.spring.io/spring-integration/docs/latest-ga/reference/htmlsingle/#endpoint-summary`.

If we want to have an inbound messaging gateway participating in bidirectional flow of messages, there has to be a mechanism for sending reply messages back to the gateway in place. We can handle this in various ways:

- *Temporary reply channel*: By default, the inbound messaging gateway creates a temporary channel, which will be used when the downstream output endpoint replies with a message. This channel is created for each message flowing through the SI flow.

- *Reply channel specified on the message*: The message can have the special header `replyChannel` defined, which will be used when the downstream output endpoint replies with a message

- *Default reply channel defined on the inbound gateway*: If the gateway has specified the attribute `default-reply-channel` (`reply-channel` with technology-specific gateways), the reply message from the downstream output component will be passed to this channel.

- *Output channel specified on downstream output endpoint*: If the output endpoint of the SI flow specifies the `output-channel` attribute, this channel will be used for sending a reply message.

Generic Messaging Gateway Example Based on XML Configuration

Listing 8-27 shows the XML configuration of the SI flow.

Listing 8-27. XML Configuration of Generic Messaging Gateway Example (File si-config.xml in Folder src/main/resources of Example Project 0808-gateway-generic-xml)

```xml
<?xml version="1.0" encoding="UTF-8"?>
<beans xmlns="http://www.springframework.org/schema/beans"
  xmlns:xsi="http://www.w3.org/2001/XMLSchema-instance"
  xmlns:int="http://www.springframework.org/schema/integration"
  xsi:schemaLocation="http://www.springframework.org/schema/beans
    http://www.springframework.org/schema/beans/spring-beans.xsd
    http://www.springframework.org/schema/integration
    http://www.springframework.org/schema/integration/spring-integration.xsd">

  <int:gateway default-request-channel="inChannel"
    service-interface="net.lkrnac.book.eiws.chapter08.in.SiWrapperService" />

  <int:channel id="inChannel" />

  <int:service-activator input-channel="inChannel" ref="writeService"
    method="writeAndIndicateSuccess">
  </int:service-activator>
</beans>
```

The first XML element specifies the generic inbound gateway. We need to define the mandatory default-request-channel, which specifies the channel where inbound messages will be passed in (in this case, inChannel). The service-interface attribute is also mandatory and specifies the Java interface, which will be used for hiding SI flow from caller. In this case, we use our common interface SiWrapperService. Notice that when the request arrives to the gateway and is converted into a message, a temporary reply channel is created for this message. The gateway will be expecting a response message via this temporary reply channel.

Messages received by this gateway will be passed to the service activator endpoint, which is mapped to the writeService.writeAndIndicateSuccess() method. This method returns the result of the write operation; therefore, we are dealing with bidirectional message flow. To send a reply message back to the gateway, the temporary reply channel created for the request will be used automatically. When a value is returned from WriteService.writeAndIndicateSuccess(), the service activator converts this value into a reply message and sends it to the temporary reply channel. The gateway receives this response message via the temporary reply channel and converts it to a return value of the service interface SiWrapperService.

Listing 8-28 shows the main class of this application.

Listing 8-28. Main Class of Generic Messaging Gateway Example with XML Configuration (0808-gateway-generic-xml)

```java
package net.lkrnac.book.eiws.chapter08;
import lombok.extern.slf4j.Slf4j;
import net.lkrnac.book.eiws.chapter08.in.SiWrapperService;
import org.springframework.boot.SpringApplication;
import org.springframework.boot.autoconfigure.SpringBootApplication;
import org.springframework.context.ApplicationContext;
import org.springframework.context.annotation.ImportResource;
```

```
@Slf4j
@SpringBootApplication
@ImportResource("classpath:si-config.xml")
public class SiApplication {
  public static void main(String[] args) throws InterruptedException {
    ApplicationContext ctx = SpringApplication.run(SiApplication.class, args);

    SiWrapperService wrapperService = ctx.getBean(SiWrapperService.class);
    boolean result = wrapperService.processText("simple message");
    log.info("Result: " + result);
  }
}
```

We are dealing with a Spring Boot application that scans for Spring beans. In this case, we need to have WriteService scanned. @ImportResource includes your XML SI flow into this application context. @Slf4j enables logging for this class. In the main method, we execute the Spring configuration defined by this class. Remember this Spring configuration, because it will be used alongside most subsequent examples, so we won't need to explain it again and again.

After the Spring context with SI flow is up, we retrieve the SiWrapperService bean from the Spring context. You may wonder where the implementation of this interface is defined. So notice that the gateway defined in the XML configuration represents the implementation of this interface. So by executing wrapperService.processText(), we send a message to the gateway. After the reception of the response, we just log it. Running this example results in the output shown in Listing 8-29.

Listing 8-29. Output of XML Generic Gateway Example

```
2015-08-23 17:43:26.798  INFO 21994 --- [           main]
n.l.b.e.chapter08.out.WriteRepository    : Text persisted: simple message
2015-08-23 17:43:26.799  INFO 21994 --- [           main]
n.l.book.eiws.chapter08.SiApplication    : Result: true
```

As expected, the input message is logged in WriteRepository, and the response of this operation is logged in the main class. Visualization of this SI flow is shown in Figure 8-5.

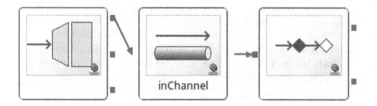

Figure 8-5. *Visualization of SI flow for generic inbound gateway example*

Generic Messaging Gateway Example Based on Java Configuration

Listing 8-30 covers the SI configuration class.

Listing 8-30. Java Configuration for Generic Inbound Gateway Example (0809-gateway-generic-javaconfig)

```
package net.lkrnac.book.eiws.chapter08;
import org.springframework.context.annotation.Bean;
import org.springframework.context.annotation.Configuration;
```

```
import org.springframework.integration.annotation.IntegrationComponentScan;
import org.springframework.integration.channel.DirectChannel;
import org.springframework.messaging.MessageChannel;

@Configuration
@IntegrationComponentScan
public class SiConfiguration {
  @Bean
  public MessageChannel inChannel() {
    return new DirectChannel();
  }
}
```

Alongside the standard Spring @Configuration annotation, we also use the @IntegrationComponentScan annotation. It is needed to scan the current package and its subpackages for SI components. In addition, the inChannel bean is configured as an SI channel. Listing 8-31 shows the output of the service activator configuration.

Listing 8-31. Output Service Activator for Generic Messaging Gateway Example (0809-gateway-generic-javaconfig)

```
package net.lkrnac.book.eiws.chapter08.out;
import org.springframework.beans.factory.annotation.Autowired;
import org.springframework.integration.annotation.ServiceActivator;
import org.springframework.stereotype.Service;

@Service
public class WriteServiceAnnotated {
  private WriteRepository writeRepository;

  @Autowired
  public WriteServiceAnnotated(WriteRepository writeRepository) {
    super();
    this.writeRepository = writeRepository;
  }

  @ServiceActivator(inputChannel = "inChannel")
  public boolean writeAndIndicateSuccess(String message) {
    return writeRepository.persist(message) == 1;
  }
}
```

This service activator is different from the previous examples, because it returns the result of the write operation from the mapped method WriteServiceAnnotated.writeAndIndicateSuccess() and thus is able to participate in bidirectional message flow. As we already know, bidirectional flow involves automatic creation of a temporary reply channel, which is used to send a reply back to the upstream consumer. Listing 8-32 covers the inbound gateway configuration.

Listing 8-32. Messaging Gateway Java Configuration (0809-gateway-generic-javaconfig)

```
package net.lkrnac.book.eiws.chapter08.in;
import org.springframework.integration.annotation.Gateway;
import org.springframework.integration.annotation.MessagingGateway;

@MessagingGateway
public interface SiWrapperServiceAnnotated {
  @Gateway(requestChannel = "inChannel")
  public boolean processText(String text);
}
```

The @MessagingGateway annotation is needed to mark this interface as an SI inbound gateway. The wrapper method is annotated by @Gateway, where requestChannel is a mandatory attribute. This interface doesn't have any implementation defined, because SI creates an implementation based on the SI flow definition. Notice that this method returns a Boolean value, which will be converted into a reply message of bidirectional message flow, where a temporary reply channel is created under the hood automatically. Listing 8-33 shows the main class of this example.

Listing 8-33. Main Class of Inbound Gateway Example Configured with Java (0809-gateway-generic-javaconfig)

```
package net.lkrnac.book.eiws.chapter08;

import lombok.extern.slf4j.Slf4j;
import net.lkrnac.book.eiws.chapter08.in.SiWrapperServiceAnnotated;

import org.springframework.boot.SpringApplication;
import org.springframework.boot.autoconfigure.SpringBootApplication;
import org.springframework.context.ApplicationContext;

@Slf4j
@SpringBootApplication
public class SiApplication {
  public static void main(String[] args) throws InterruptedException {
    ApplicationContext ctx = SpringApplication.run(SiApplication.class, args);

    SiWrapperServiceAnnotated wrapperService =
        ctx.getBean(SiWrapperServiceAnnotated.class);
    boolean result = wrapperService.processText("simple message");
    log.info("Result: " + result);
  }
}
```

@ImportResource is not needed in this case, as we have a pure Java configuration. After the Spring Boot application is started via the main method, we read our service interface from the Spring context, send the message to the SI flow, and log the result. The output from running this main class looks similar to the output of the previous example, 0808-gateway-generic-xml in Listing 8-29.

Technology-Specific Gateway Example

This example uses an HTTP inbound gateway and JDBC outbound gateway to handle bidirectional SI flow. Listing 8-34 shows the XML SI configuration.

Listing 8-34. SI Flow XML Configuration for Technology-Specific Gateways Example (File si-config.xml in Folder src/main/resources of Example Project 0810-gateway-non-generic)

```xml
<?xml version="1.0" encoding="UTF-8"?>
<beans xmlns="http://www.springframework.org/schema/beans"
  xmlns:xsi="http://www.w3.org/2001/XMLSchema-instance"
  xmlns:int="http://www.springframework.org/schema/integration"
  xmlns:int-http="http://www.springframework.org/schema/integration/http"
  xmlns:int-jdbc="http://www.springframework.org/schema/integration/jdbc"
  xsi:schemaLocation="http://www.springframework.org/schema/integration/jdbc
http://www.springframework.org/schema/integration/jdbc/spring-integration-jdbc.xsd
    http://www.springframework.org/schema/beans
    http://www.springframework.org/schema/beans/spring-beans.xsd
    http://www.springframework.org/schema/integration/http
    http://www.springframework.org/schema/integration/http/spring-integration-http.xsd
    http://www.springframework.org/schema/integration
    http://www.springframework.org/schema/integration/spring-integration.xsd">

  <int-http:inbound-gateway path="/" request-channel="inChannel" supported-methods="POST"/>

  <int:channel id="inChannel" />

  <int-jdbc:outbound-gateway data-source="dataSource" request-channel="inChannel"
    update="insert into TEXT_TABLE values (:payload)" />
</beans>
```

We use two technology-specific XML namespaces here: int-http and int-jdbc. The input part uses an HTTP inbound gateway, which is mapped to the root URL assigned by the servlet container and consumes only POST HTTP requests. After conversion, the message is passed to inChannel.

In the output part of the SI flow, we have a JDBC outbound gateway, using the dataSource bean to access an in-memory DB. The query used to insert the message into TEXT_TABLE should already be familiar from Listing 8-18, the 0805-channel-adapter-non-generic example. SimpleDatabasePopulator, which initializes the DB table, is also taken from the same example (see Listing 8-19). The main class is also the same as in the 0805-channel-adapter-non-generic example (Listing 8-21). It executes the Spring Boot application and leaves it listening for POST requests. Chapter 4 covered how to send HTTP messages.

Transformer

A message *transformer* is a message endpoint that sits in the middle of the SI flow. Like all middle SI components, it can participate in unidirectional as well as bidirectional flow. It can operate in passive mode. It also can have a poller subcomponent and thus act as an active component. These types of transformers are possible:

- *Generic message transformer*: Transforms the received Java object into another Java object. A new message is created because, by default, all the messages are immutable. So a generic transformer is a good candidate for using MessageBuilder<T> to create a converted message from the original received message. The XML configuration uses the <int:transformer> tag. When we want to configure it via Java configuration, we need to annotate the Transformer class with @MessageEndpoint and annotate the transformation method with @Transformer. To scan this bean into the Spring context, we need to use @IntegrationComponentScan somewhere in the Java configuration classes.

- *Technology-specific transformer*: Converts the received message between various standard Java types (for example, Map, Object) and various common formats (for example, JSON, XML). These transformers can be configured only via XML tags (for example, <int:json-to-object-transformer>, <int:map-to-object-transformer>, <int:object-to-json-transformer>).

- *Header filter*: A subset of the message transformer that removes specified headers. Can be configured via <int:header-filter>.

Generic Transformer Example with XML Configuration

Listing 8-35 shows the transformation class.

Listing 8-35. Transformation Class for XML Transformer Example (0811-transformer-generic-xml)

```
package net.lkrnac.book.eiws.chapter08;

public class SimpleMessageTransformer {
  public String transformMessage(String message) {
    return new String(message + " transformed");
  }
}
```

This class is not even a Spring bean and has one method that appends a string to the message payload. It's easy to imagine that any transformation logic could be present here. As long as the method returns a value that can be represented or converted into an SI message and parameters that SI can inject values in (for example, a payload or headers marked with @Header/@Headers annotations), it can be used in the SI flow.

Listing 8-36 covers the SI flow configuration.

Listing 8-36. XML SI Flow Configuration for Generic Transformer Example (File si-config.xml in Folder src/main/resources of Example Project 0811-transformer-generic-xml)

```
<?xml version="1.0" encoding="UTF-8"?>
<beans xmlns="http://www.springframework.org/schema/beans"
  xmlns:xsi="http://www.w3.org/2001/XMLSchema-instance"
  xmlns:int="http://www.springframework.org/schema/integration"
  xsi:schemaLocation="http://www.springframework.org/schema/beans
    http://www.springframework.org/schema/beans/spring-beans.xsd
    http://www.springframework.org/schema/integration
    http://www.springframework.org/schema/integration/spring-integration.xsd">

  <int:gateway default-request-channel="inChannel"
    service-interface="net.lkrnac.book.eiws.chapter08.in.SiWrapperService" />
  <int:channel id="inChannel" />

  <int:transformer input-channel="inChannel" output-channel="transformedChannel">
    <bean class="net.lkrnac.book.eiws.chapter08.SimpleMessageTransformer" />
  </int:transformer>
  <int:channel id="transformedChannel" />
```

```
  <int:service-activator input-channel="transformedChannel" ref="writeService"
    method="writeAndIndicateSuccess">
  </int:service-activator>
</beans>
```

The inbound gateway is already a familiar component from the previous examples. Again, it maps our common service interface SiWrapperService and sends messages into inChannel. This channel is then connected to the transformer. The <int:transformer> tag specifies input-channel, output-channel. The transformation bean is created via the <bean> subelement, which is a normal Spring construct for creating beans.

The output channel of the transformer is then connected to the service activator mapped to our common WriteService.writeAndIndicateSuccess(). As this method returns a value, we are dealing with bidirectional flow, and a response is sent back to the gateway component via a temporary reply channel. Listing 8-37 shows the main class of this example.

Listing 8-37. Main Class of Generic Transformer Example (0811-transformer-generic-xml)

```
package net.lkrnac.book.eiws.chapter08;
import lombok.extern.slf4j.Slf4j;
import net.lkrnac.book.eiws.chapter08.in.SiWrapperService;
import org.springframework.boot.SpringApplication;
import org.springframework.boot.autoconfigure.SpringBootApplication;
import org.springframework.context.ApplicationContext;
import org.springframework.context.annotation.ImportResource;


@Slf4j
@SpringBootApplication
@ImportResource("classpath:si-config.xml")
public class SiApplication {
  public static void main(String[] args) throws InterruptedException {
    ApplicationContext ctx = SpringApplication.run(SiApplication.class, args);

    SiWrapperService wrapperService = ctx.getBean(SiWrapperService.class);
    String text = "simple message";
    log.info("Sending message: " + text);
    boolean result = wrapperService.processText(text);
    log.info("Result: " + result);
  }
}
```

Before sending a message to the SI gateway via its service interface SiWrapperService, we first log it as well as the result returned from it. Listing 8-38 shows the output of this example if we run the main class as a Java application.

Listing 8-38. Output of XML Generic Transformer Example

```
2015-08-23 22:10:39.437  INFO 29551 --- [              main]
n.l.book.eiws.chapter08.SiApplication     : Sending message: simple message
2015-08-23 22:10:39.580  INFO 29551 --- [              main]
n.l.b.e.chapter08.out.WriteRepository     : Text persisted: simple message transformed
2015-08-23 22:10:39.595  INFO 29551 --- [              main]
n.l.book.eiws.chapter08.SiApplication     : Result: true
```

The WriteRepository bean logs the transformed message. Figure 8-6 shows this SI flow.

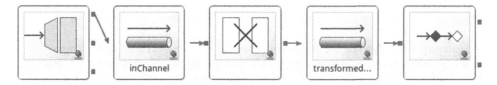

Figure 8-6. *Visualization of generic transformer flow*

Generic Transformer Example with Java Configuration

Let's now dive into the same flow based on Java annotations. Listing 8-39 shows the transformer configuration.

Listing 8-39. Generic Transformer with Java Configuration (0812-transformer-generic-javaconfig)

```
package net.lkrnac.book.eiws.chapter08;
import org.springframework.integration.annotation.MessageEndpoint;
import org.springframework.integration.annotation.Transformer;

@MessageEndpoint
public class SimpleMessageTransformer {
  @Transformer(inputChannel = "inChannel", outputChannel = "transformedChannel")
  public String transformMessage(String message) {
    return new String(message + " transformed");
  }
}
```

The transformer logic is the same as in the previous example, 0811-transformer-generic-xml in Listing 8-35, but in this case we annotate the class with @MessagingEndpoint, which makes it eligible for integration component scanning. The conversion method is annotated with @Transformer, and we also have to specify the mandatory attributes inputChannel and outputChannel. Listing 8-40 shows the SI configuration class.

Listing 8-40. SI Configuration Class for Generic Transformer Example (0812-transformer-generic-javaconfig)

```
package net.lkrnac.book.eiws.chapter08;
import org.springframework.context.annotation.Bean;
import org.springframework.context.annotation.Configuration;
import org.springframework.integration.annotation.IntegrationComponentScan;
import org.springframework.integration.channel.DirectChannel;
import org.springframework.messaging.MessageChannel;

@Configuration
@IntegrationComponentScan
public class SiConfiguration {
  @Bean
  public MessageChannel inChannel() {
    return new DirectChannel();
  }
```

```
@Bean
public MessageChannel transformedChannel() {
  return new DirectChannel();
}
}
```

This configuration class enables the SI component scan based on the @IntegrationComponentScan annotation, which is needed to scan SimpleMessageTransformer. It registers two channels used in our SI flow: inChannel and transformedChannel. Listing 8-41 shows the annotated service activator configuration.

Listing 8-41. Service Activator Used in Generic Transformer Example (0812-transformer-generic-javaconfig)

```
package net.lkrnac.book.eiws.chapter08.out;
import net.lkrnac.book.eiws.chapter08.out.WriteRepository;
import org.springframework.beans.factory.annotation.Autowired;
import org.springframework.integration.annotation.ServiceActivator;
import org.springframework.stereotype.Service;

@Service
public class WriteServiceAnnotated {
  private WriteRepository writeRepository;

  @Autowired
  public WriteServiceAnnotated(WriteRepository writeRepository) {
    super();
    this.writeRepository = writeRepository;
  }

  @ServiceActivator(inputChannel = "transformedChannel")
  public boolean writeAndIndicateSuccess(String message) {
    return writeRepository.persist(message) == 1;
  }
}
```

This service activator is similar to the service activator in example 0809-gateway-generic-javaconfig (Listing 8-31), with one difference. The service activator input channel is in this case transformedChannel. We also borrowed the class from SiWrapperServiceAnnotated of the same example and Listing 8-32.

So the integration component scan has the chain SiWrapperServiceAnnotated ➤ SimpleMessageTransformer ➤ WriteServiceAnnotated. Listing 8-42 covers the main class of this example.

Listing 8-42. Main Class of Generic Transformer Based on Java Configuration (0812-transformer-generic-javaconfig)

```
package net.lkrnac.book.eiws.chapter08;
import lombok.extern.slf4j.Slf4j;
import net.lkrnac.book.eiws.chapter08.in.SiWrapperServiceAnnotated;
import org.springframework.boot.SpringApplication;
import org.springframework.boot.autoconfigure.SpringBootApplication;
import org.springframework.context.ApplicationContext;
```

```
@Slf4j
@SpringBootApplication
public class SiApplication {
  public static void main(String[] args) throws InterruptedException {
    ApplicationContext ctx = SpringApplication.run(SiApplication.class, args);

    SiWrapperServiceAnnotated wrapperService =
        ctx.getBean(SiWrapperServiceAnnotated.class);
    String text = "simple message";
    log.info("Sending message: " + text);
    boolean result = wrapperService.processText(text);
    log.info("Result: " + result);
  }
}
```

After we read the service interface from the context, we create the message, log it, and send it to the SI flow. Finally, we log the result of this operation. As it returns a value, it is a bidirectional request-response type of flow. The output looks the same as for 0809-gateway-generic-javaconfig (Listing 8-38). Visualization of the flow is not possible, as annotated SI flows are not currently being visualized in STS.

JSON Transformer Example

We are also going to show a technology-specific example of the transformer. Because one of the most common concerns nowadays is conversion of JSON into Java objects, we are going to cover it. Obviously, we need an object to convert JSON into. So Listing 8-43 shows the User class.

Listing 8-43. User Class Used in JSON Transformer Example (0813-transformer-json)

```
package net.lkrnac.book.eiws.chapter08.model;
import lombok.Data;

@Data
public class User {
  private String email;
  private String name;
}
```

It is a simple Java POJO, where getters and setters are generated by the Lombok annotation @Data. Listing 8-44 shows a fake repository for User objects.

Listing 8-44. Fake Repository for User Objects (0813-transformer-json)

```
package net.lkrnac.book.eiws.chapter08.out;
import lombok.extern.slf4j.Slf4j;
import net.lkrnac.book.eiws.chapter08.model.User;
import org.springframework.stereotype.Repository;
```

```java
@Slf4j
@Repository
public class UserRepository {
  public void persistUser(User user) {
    log.info("Object received: " + user);
  }
}
```

Similar to the common WriteRepository class we use in nearly every example, this repository is also faking the persistence of the given parameter, which is the User object in this case. Listing 8-45 shows the service bean calling this fake repository.

Listing 8-45. Service Bean for Processing User Objects (0813-transformer-json)

```java
package net.lkrnac.book.eiws.chapter08.out;
import net.lkrnac.book.eiws.chapter08.model.User;
import org.springframework.beans.factory.annotation.Autowired;
import org.springframework.stereotype.Service;

@Service
public class UserService {
  private UserRepository userRepository;

  @Autowired
  public UserService(UserRepository userRepository) {
    super();
    this.userRepository = userRepository;
  }

  public void processUser(User user) {
    userRepository.persistUser(user);
  }
}
```

This service bean autowires a UserRepository instance as a dependency. The processUser method takes the User object as a parameter, and passes it to UserRepository to persist it. This is a similar pattern as with WriteRepository.write(). Listing 8-46 finally shows the SI flow of this example.

Listing 8-46. SI Flow of JSON Transformer Example (File si-config.xml in Folder src/main/resources of Example Project 0813-transformer-json)

```xml
<?xml version="1.0" encoding="UTF-8"?>
<beans xmlns="http://www.springframework.org/schema/beans"
  xmlns:xsi="http://www.w3.org/2001/XMLSchema-instance"
  xmlns:int="http://www.springframework.org/schema/integration"
  xmlns:int-http="http://www.springframework.org/schema/integration/http"
  xsi:schemaLocation="http://www.springframework.org/schema/beans
    http://www.springframework.org/schema/beans/spring-beans.xsd
    http://www.springframework.org/schema/integration/http
    http://www.springframework.org/schema/integration/http/spring-integration-http.xsd
    http://www.springframework.org/schema/integration
    http://www.springframework.org/schema/integration/spring-integration.xsd">
```

```xml
<int-http:inbound-gateway path="/" request-channel="jsonChannel"
  supported-methods="POST"/>
<int:channel id="jsonChannel" />

<int:json-to-object-transformer input-channel="jsonChannel"
  output-channel="objectChannel" type="net.lkrnac.book.eiws.chapter08.model.User"/>
<int:channel id="objectChannel" />

<int:service-activator input-channel="objectChannel" ref="userService"
  method="processUser" />
</beans>
```

If we are converting JSON to a Java object, a good example would be to use an HTTP inbound gateway for it. So we include the int-http namespace into our XML configuration. This inbound gateway is mapped to the POST HTTP method of the root URL and sends the received JSON payload as a text message to jsonChannel.

This channel is connected to the specific transformer <int:json-to-object-transformer>. We need to specify the type attribute into which the text message with the JSON payload should be converted. In this case, it is our User class. Spring Integration uses standard Jackson converters under the hood, as it would with Spring MVC conversion. The output-channel attribute is also mandatory. The new transformed message with the User payload is sent to it.

Finally, we map the service activator to UserService.processUser(). Listing 8-47 shows the Spring Boot configuration file.

Listing 8-47. Spring Boot Configuration File for JSON Transformer Example (File application.properties in Folder src/main/resource of Example Project 0813-transformer-json)

```
server.port=18080
```

This specifies the port on which the HTTP gateway will be listening to POST requests. Listing 8-48 shows the main class of this example.

Listing 8-48. Main Class of JSON Transformer Example (0813-transformer-json)

```java
package net.lkrnac.book.eiws.chapter08;
import org.springframework.boot.SpringApplication;
import org.springframework.boot.autoconfigure.SpringBootApplication;
import org.springframework.context.annotation.ImportResource;

@SpringBootApplication
@ImportResource("classpath:si-config.xml")
public class SiApplication {
  public static void main(String[] args) throws InterruptedException {
    SpringApplication.run(SiApplication.class, args);
  }
}
```

This is the Spring Boot configuration and main class that executes our SI flow. When we start it, the application remains open and will be waiting for POST requests on the URL http://localhost:18080. So to initiate this request, let's use the simple tool curl. This command is shown in Listing 8-49.

Listing 8-49. curl Command for JSON Transformer Example

```
curl -i -X POST -H "Content-Type: application/json" -d '{"name": "Lubos Krnac", "email":
"lubos.krnac@gmail.com"}' http://localhost:18080
```

Parameter –i includes a header in the message; the -X parameter specifies the HTTP method used; -H defines the HTTP header to include; and the –d parameter specifies the payload. After executing this command, we get the response shown in Listing 8-50.

Listing 8-50. HTTP Response for JSON Transformer Example

```
HTTP/1.1 200 OK
Server: Apache-Coyote/1.1
Content-Length: 0
Date: Mon, 24 Aug 2015 23:05:54 GMT
```

This indicates a successful processing of the message we sent. Of course, our server is not fully HTTP compliant, because it should reply with the location URL of the created resource, but let's ignore this fact so as not to complicate this example. Listing 8-51 shows the output logged by the application.

Listing 8-51. Output of JSON Transformer Example

```
2015-08-25 00:05:53.791  INFO 17254 --- [io-18080-exec-1]
n.l.b.eiws.chapter08.out.UserRepository  : Object received: User(email=lubos.krnac@gmail.com,
name=Lubos Krnac)
```

The UserRepository bean has received the converted User object from the JSON payload. Notice that for this example, it is not possible to create a Java configuration mirror, because the `<int-http:inbound-gateway>` SI component doesn't have a Java annotation counterpart.

Content Enricher

A *content enricher* is similar to a transformer in messaging endpoint characteristics. It can participate in unidirectional or bidirectional communication, can be passive or active, and fits into the middle of the SI flow. From a functional point of view, these types of content enrichers are possible:

- *Generic header enricher*: Most common use of this endpoint, which adds a new header to the message. Of course, the message is by default immutable, so a generic context enricher creates a new message instance out of the original one with an enriched header(s). It doesn't have any SI annotation available, so it can be configured only via the XML element `<int:header-enricher>`.

- *Generic payload enricher*: This is effectively a special type of message transformer, enriching the payload of the received message by adding information. This enricher can be configured only via the XML element `<int:enricher>`.

- *Technology-specific header enricher*: Enriches headers for three technologies: Mail, XPath, and XMPP (Jabber protocol). These configurations are possible only via XML configuration, which uses special technology-specific XML namespaces: `<int-xml:xpath-header-enricher>`, `<int-xmpp:header-enricher>`, and `<int-mail:header-enricher>`.

Header Enricher Example

Listing 8-52 shows header enricher logic.

Listing 8-52. Header Enricher Logic (0814-header-enricher-xml)

```
package net.lkrnac.book.eiws.chapter08;
import org.springframework.stereotype.Component;

@Component
public class SimpleHeaderEnricher {
  public String addHeader(String message) {
    return message.contains("1") ? "header1" : "header2";
  }
}
```

This Spring bean checks whether the received message contains 1 and returns a header value based on the result. The return value will be used in the SI flow to enrich the message. Listing 8-53 shows the SI flow configuration.

Listing 8-53. SI Flow of Header Enricher Example (File si-config.xml in Folder src/main/resources of Example Project 0814-header-enricher-xml)

```
<?xml version="1.0" encoding="UTF-8"?>
<beans xmlns="http://www.springframework.org/schema/beans"
  xmlns:xsi="http://www.w3.org/2001/XMLSchema-instance"
  xmlns:int="http://www.springframework.org/schema/integration"
  xmlns:context="http://www.springframework.org/schema/context"
  xsi:schemaLocation="http://www.springframework.org/schema/beans
    http://www.springframework.org/schema/beans/spring-beans.xsd
    http://www.springframework.org/schema/integration
    http://www.springframework.org/schema/integration/spring-integration.xsd">

  <int:gateway default-request-channel="inChannel"
    service-interface="net.lkrnac.book.eiws.chapter08.in.SiWrapperServiceVoid" />
  <int:channel id="inChannel"/>

  <int:header-enricher input-channel="inChannel" output-channel="enrichedChannel">
    <int:header name="simpleHeader" ref="simpleHeaderEnricher" method="addHeader"/>
  </int:header-enricher>
  <int:channel id="enrichedChannel"/>

  <int:outbound-channel-adapter channel="enrichedChannel" ref="writeServiceWithHeaders"
    method="write"/>
</beans>
```

The inbound gateway is configured to use our common service interface SiWrapperServiceVoid, convert its parameter into a message, and pass it to inChannel.

From this channel, the message is picked up by the header enricher, which defines the input-channel and output-channel mandatory attributes on the top-level XML element <int:header-enricher>. Now we can define one or more headers to enrich. This is done via the XML sub-element <int:header>. For a single header, we need to specify name, which will become a key in the headers map, and the ref and method of the bean that contains header enricher logic. In this case, it is `SimpleHeaderEnricher.addHeader()`. In the `<int:header>` tag, we can also use Spring Expression Language (SpEL) to define enricher logic inline. Use of SpEL is shown later in the chapter.

The last element in our flow is the outbound channel adapter, which encapsulates the logic shown in Listing 8-54.

Listing 8-54. Write Service Used in Header Enricher Example (0814-header-enricher-xml)

```java
package net.lkrnac.book.eiws.chapter08.out;
import lombok.extern.slf4j.Slf4j;
import org.springframework.beans.factory.annotation.Autowired;
import org.springframework.messaging.handler.annotation.Header;
import org.springframework.stereotype.Service;

@Slf4j
@Service
public class WriteServiceWithHeaders {
  private WriteRepository writeRepository;

  @Autowired
  public WriteServiceWithHeaders(WriteRepository writeRepository) {
    super();
    this.writeRepository = writeRepository;
  }

  public void write(String message, @Header String simpleHeader) {
    log.info("Writing message: {}; simpleHeader: {}", message, simpleHeader);
    writeRepository.persist(message);
  }
}
```

This service injects our common `WriteRepository` to persist the received message payload. It also logs this payload with `simpleHeader` that was enriched earlier in the flow. Listing 8-55 covers the main class of this example.

Listing 8-55. Main Class of Header Enricher Example (0814-header-enricher-xml)

```java
package net.lkrnac.book.eiws.chapter08;
import net.lkrnac.book.eiws.chapter08.in.SiWrapperServiceVoid;
import org.springframework.boot.SpringApplication;
import org.springframework.boot.autoconfigure.SpringBootApplication;
import org.springframework.context.ApplicationContext;
import org.springframework.context.annotation.ImportResource;

@SpringBootApplication
@ImportResource("classpath:si-config.xml")
public class SiApplication {
  public static void main(String[] args) throws InterruptedException {
    ApplicationContext ctx = SpringApplication.run(SiApplication.class, args);
```

```
    SiWrapperServiceVoid wrapperService =
        ctx.getBean(SiWrapperServiceVoid.class);
    wrapperService.processText("message1");
    wrapperService.processText("message2");
  }
}
```

After running the Spring Boot application, we retrieve the wrapperService bean from the context and send two messages with the payload message1 and message2 to the SI flow. Again, SiWrapperServiceVoid is the entry point to the SI flow. The output after running it is similar to Listing 8-56.

Listing 8-56. Output of Header Enricher Example

```
2015-08-25 20:23:03.934  INFO 27342 --- [          main]
n.l.b.e.c.out.WriteServiceWithHeaders   : Writing message: message1; simpleHeader: header1
2015-08-25 20:23:03.950  INFO 27342 --- [          main]
n.l.b.e.chapter08.out.WriteRepository   : Text persisted: message1
2015-08-25 20:23:03.952  INFO 27342 --- [          main]
n.l.b.e.c.out.WriteServiceWithHeaders   : Writing message: message2; simpleHeader: header2
2015-08-25 20:23:03.953  INFO 27342 --- [          main]
n.l.b.e.chapter08.out.WriteRepository   : Text persisted: message2
```

The header enricher logic is applied: message1 is enriched with the header1 value, and message2 is enriched with the header2 value. Figure 8-7 shows this header enricher SI flow.

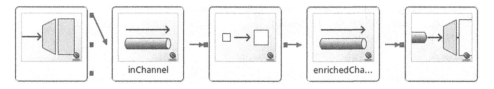

Figure 8-7. *Visualization of header enricher flow*

Filter

A *filter* is another middle SI message endpoint that can participate in bidirectional and unidirectional flows. It can act as a passive as well as an active component. Its purpose is to decide whether the received message should or shouldn't be passed to the downstream flow. This decision can be based on generic logic, which can be configured via the <int:filter> XML element or the @Filter annotation. The annotation configuration doesn't provide the flexibility of XML, which can be based on the following:

- *Custom Java logic*: Should implement the interface MessageSelector and can be defined via the <beans:bean> subelement of the <int:filter> tag or its ref attribute.

- *SpEL expression*: Can be configured via the <int:expression> XML subelement or the expression attribute of the <int:filter> XML tag.

- *Custom script*: Supports Ruby and Groovy via the <int-script:script> subelement of the <int:filter> XML tag.

Alongside these generic filter types, we can also configure special filters for these technologies:

- *XPath filter*: `<int-xml:xpath-filter>`
- *XML validation filter*: `<int-xml:validating-filter>`

The filter's decision to pass the message to the next component in the SI flow is represented by the Boolean value returned by the filter logic (whether it is Java logic, SpEL, or scripting). If the value is `false`, the filter gives us the opportunity to discard the message or throw an exception in the SI flow. If we discard the message, we can specify `discardChannel` to route the message.

An important fact is that by default the filter silently discards messages.

A filter can also be embedded into unidirectional flow as the channel adapter's attribute (for example, `local-filter` for `<int-ftp:inbound-channel-adapter>` or `mail-filter-expression` for `<int-mail:imap-idle-channel-adapter>`).

Filter Example Based on XML Configuration

Listing 8-57 shows custom filter logic.

Listing 8-57. Custom Filter Logic for XML Configuration Example (0815-filter-xml-ref)

```
package net.lkrnac.book.eiws.chapter08;
import org.springframework.integration.core.MessageSelector;
import org.springframework.messaging.Message;
import org.springframework.stereotype.Component;

@Component
public class SimpleFilter implements MessageSelector {
  @Override
  public boolean accept(Message<?> message) {
    String stringPayload = (String) message.getPayload();
    return !stringPayload.contains("corrupt");
  }
}
```

This Spring bean, which implements the `MessageSelector` interface, can be used as filter logic in the SI flow. It needs to implement the `MessageSelector.accept()` method. In this case, we inspect the `String` payload of the message and refuse it if it contains the `corrupt` substring. Listing 8-58 dives into the SI flow configuration for this example.

Listing 8-58. SI Flow Configuration for XML Filter Example (File si-config.xml in Folder src/main/resources of Example Project 0815-filter-xml-ref)

```
<?xml version="1.0" encoding="UTF-8"?>
<beans xmlns="http://www.springframework.org/schema/beans"
  xmlns:xsi="http://www.w3.org/2001/XMLSchema-instance"
  xmlns:int="http://www.springframework.org/schema/integration"
  xmlns:context="http://www.springframework.org/schema/context"
  xmlns:int-http="http://www.springframework.org/schema/integration/http"
  xsi:schemaLocation="http://www.springframework.org/schema/beans
    http://www.springframework.org/schema/beans/spring-beans.xsd
    http://www.springframework.org/schema/integration
    http://www.springframework.org/schema/integration/spring-integration.xsd">
```

```xml
    <int:gateway default-request-channel="inChannel"
      service-interface="net.lkrnac.book.eiws.chapter08.in.SiWrapperServiceVoid" />
    <int:channel id="inChannel"/>

    <int:filter input-channel="inChannel" output-channel="filteredChannel"
      ref="simpleFilter" />
    <int:channel id="filteredChannel"/>

    <int:service-activator input-channel="filteredChannel" ref="writeService"
      method="write"/>
</beans>
```

The inbound gateway uses our common SiWrapperServiceVoid bean to hide the SI flow, which indicates unidirectional message handling. Messages are handled in inChannel, where the filter comes into play. It has to define mandatory input-channel and output-channel attributes and one of the expression or ref attributes. In this case, it is a reference to our filter bean simpleFilter.

The message is then sent to filteredChannel and passed to the service activator, which executes another common bean, WriteService.write(). To highlight that filtering works, take a look at Listing 8-59.

Listing 8-59. Main Class of XML Filter Example (0815-filter-xml-ref)

```java
package net.lkrnac.book.eiws.chapter08;
import net.lkrnac.book.eiws.chapter08.in.SiWrapperServiceVoid;
import org.springframework.boot.SpringApplication;
import org.springframework.boot.autoconfigure.SpringBootApplication;
import org.springframework.context.ApplicationContext;
import org.springframework.context.annotation.ImportResource;

@SpringBootApplication
@ImportResource("classpath:si-config.xml")
public class SiApplication {
  private static final String SIMPLE_MESSAGE = "simple message";

  public static void main(String[] args) throws InterruptedException {
    ApplicationContext ctx = SpringApplication.run(SiApplication.class, args);

    SiWrapperServiceVoid wrapperService =
        ctx.getBean(SiWrapperServiceVoid.class);
    wrapperService.processText(SIMPLE_MESSAGE);
    wrapperService.processText("corrupted message");
    wrapperService.processText(SIMPLE_MESSAGE);
  }
}
```

We sent three messages to the SI flow, one of which is corrupted. So in Listing 8-60 we expect to see only two messages.

Listing 8-60. Output of XML Filter Example

```
2015-08-25 22:51:12.143  INFO 30904 --- [            main]
n.l.b.e.chapter08.out.WriteRepository   : Text persisted: simple message
2015-08-25 22:51:12.147  INFO 30904 --- [            main]
n.l.b.e.chapter08.out.WriteRepository   : Text persisted: simple message
```

As we can observe, the example works as expected. Figure 8-8 shows this SI flow.

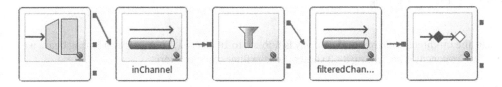

Figure 8-8. Visualization of filter example flow

Filter Example Based on Java Configuration

Let's now dive into the Java configuration of the filter component. Listing 8-61 shows the Java configuration.

Listing 8-61. Java Configuration for Filter Example (0816-filter-javaconfig)

```
package net.lkrnac.book.eiws.chapter08;
import org.springframework.context.annotation.Bean;
import org.springframework.context.annotation.Configuration;
import org.springframework.integration.annotation.IntegrationComponentScan;
import org.springframework.integration.channel.DirectChannel;
import org.springframework.messaging.MessageChannel;

@Configuration
@IntegrationComponentScan
public class SiConfiguration {
  @Bean
  public MessageChannel inChannel() {
    return new DirectChannel();
  }

  @Bean
  public MessageChannel filteredChannel() {
    return new DirectChannel();
  }
}
```

This Spring configuration class uses @IntegrationComponentScan to scan for SI Java annotated components and defines two SI channels: inChannel and filteredChannel. Listing 8-62 shows the Java configuration of the inbound gateway interface.

Listing 8-62. Java Configuration of Inbound Gateway for Filter Example (0816-filter-javaconfig)

```
package net.lkrnac.book.eiws.chapter08.in;
import org.springframework.integration.annotation.Gateway;
import org.springframework.integration.annotation.MessagingGateway;

@MessagingGateway
public interface SiWrapperServiceVoidAnnotated {
  @Gateway(requestChannel = "inChannel")
  public void processText(String text);
}
```

In this case, the unidirectional inbound gateway is hooked to inChannel. To scan it as a Spring bean, we use @IntegrationComponentScan. Listing 8-63 shows the Java filter configuration.

Listing 8-63. Java Filter Configuration (0816-filter-javaconfig)

```
package net.lkrnac.book.eiws.chapter08;
import org.springframework.integration.annotation.Filter;
import org.springframework.integration.annotation.MessageEndpoint;

@MessageEndpoint
public class SimpleFilter {
  @Filter(inputChannel = "inChannel", outputChannel = "filteredChannel")
  public boolean accept(String message) {
    return !message.contains("corrupt");
  }
}
```

With @MessageEndpoint, we can register it as a Spring bean. The @Filter annotation marks the method accepted as filtering logic. Notice that we don't need to implement the MessageSelector interface. But we need to define the input and output channel. The filtering logic again refuses messages with a payload containing a corrupted string. Listing 8-64 shows the service activator configuration, which sits on the output side of the SI flow.

Listing 8-64. Service Activator for Filter Java Configuration Example (0816-filter-javaconfig)

```
package net.lkrnac.book.eiws.chapter08.out;
import org.springframework.beans.factory.annotation.Autowired;
import org.springframework.integration.annotation.ServiceActivator;
import org.springframework.stereotype.Service;

@Service
public class WriteServiceAnnotated {
  private WriteRepository writeRepository;

  @Autowired
  public WriteServiceAnnotated(WriteRepository writeRepository) {
    super();
    this.writeRepository = writeRepository;
  }
```

```
@ServiceActivator(inputChannel = "filteredChannel")
public void write(String message) {
  writeRepository.persist(message);
}
}
```

We've seen such configurations before. Listing 8-65 shows the main class of this example.

Listing 8-65. Main Class of Java Configured Filter Example (0816-filter-javaconfig)

```
package net.lkrnac.book.eiws.chapter08;
import net.lkrnac.book.eiws.chapter08.in.SiWrapperServiceVoidAnnotated;
import org.springframework.boot.SpringApplication;
import org.springframework.boot.autoconfigure.SpringBootApplication;
import org.springframework.context.ApplicationContext;

@SpringBootApplication
public class SiApplication {
  private static final String SIMPLE_MESSAGE = "simple message";

  public static void main(String[] args) throws InterruptedException {
    ApplicationContext ctx = SpringApplication.run(SiApplication.class, args);

    SiWrapperServiceVoidAnnotated wrapperService =
        ctx.getBean(SiWrapperServiceVoidAnnotated.class);
    wrapperService.processText(SIMPLE_MESSAGE);
    wrapperService.processText("corrupted message");
    wrapperService.processText(SIMPLE_MESSAGE);
  }
}
```

The only difference from the previous example is the lack of si-config.xml import, which is understandable as we use Java configuration. When we run it, output is similar to the output of the 0815-filter-xml-ref example in Listing 8-60.

SpEL-Based Filter Example Based on XML Configuration

Now it's time for a filter example, which includes filtering logic inline into the SI flow. This can be done via SpEL, which can be embedded into various SI components including the filter. In fact, this example uses all the same classes from the XML filter example 0815-filter-xml-ref except SI flow configuration, which is shown in Listing 8-66.

Listing 8-66. SI Flow Configuration of Filter with SpEL (File si-config.xml in Folder src/main/resources of Example Project 0817-filter-xml-spel)

```
<?xml version="1.0" encoding="UTF-8"?>
<beans xmlns="http://www.springframework.org/schema/beans"
  xmlns:xsi="http://www.w3.org/2001/XMLSchema-instance"
  xmlns:int="http://www.springframework.org/schema/integration"
  xmlns:context="http://www.springframework.org/schema/context"
  xmlns:int-http="http://www.springframework.org/schema/integration/http"
```

```
  xsi:schemaLocation="http://www.springframework.org/schema/beans
    http://www.springframework.org/schema/beans/spring-beans.xsd
    http://www.springframework.org/schema/integration
    http://www.springframework.org/schema/integration/spring-integration.xsd">

  <int:gateway default-request-channel="inChannel"
    service-interface="net.lkrnac.book.eiws.chapter08.in.SiWrapperServiceVoid" />
  <int:channel id="inChannel"/>

  <int:filter input-channel="inChannel" output-channel="filteredChannel"
    expression="!payload.contains('corrupt')" />
  <int:channel id="filteredChannel"/>

  <int:service-activator input-channel="filteredChannel" ref="writeService"
    method="write">
  </int:service-activator>
</beans>
```

The only difference is in the `<int:filter>` XML tag, which uses the `expression` attribute instead of `ref`. As you can see, we can define a simple Java-like scripting condition, which effectively has the same functionality as the `simpleFilter` bean from the `0815-filter-xml-ref` example. Even the output and SI graph are similar to the previous example.

Router

A *router* is an SI component that can fork your message flow. In other words, it represents a decision component within SI. It applies routing logic and decides into which channel or various channels the message should be passed further. Notice that it should be OK to pass the same instance of the message to various channels, as the message is immutable. Routing logic can be defined in numerous ways, based on the following:

- Generic routing

  - *Custom Java logic*: A Spring bean is used to route a message into a target channel or various channels. Can be configured via the XML element `<int:router>` or via the SI annotation @Router. This Java logic needs to return one of the types `MessageChannel`, `List<MessageChannel>`, `String`, `Listing<String>`, which specifies the channel instance(s) or channel name(s) to send messages to.

  - *Payload type*: Can be configured via `<int:payload-type-router>`.

  - *Header value*: Can be configured via `<int:header-value-router>`.

  - *Exception type*: Can handle routing of messages, which have `Throwable` as a payload type. It is, in fact, a special type of payload type handler. Can be configured via `<int:exception-type-router>`.

  - *Recipient list router*: Special type of router that sends messages to a static list of channels. It can be configured via `<int:recipient-list-router>`.

  - *SpEL expression*: Inline SpEL expression can be configured via an expression attribute of the `<int:router>` XML element.

- Technology-specific routing

  - *XPath expression*: Can be configured via `<int-xml:xpath-router>`.

A router is a passive middle component and thus can participate in unidirectional or bidirectional flows.

Generic Router Example Based on XML Configuration

Listing 8-67 shows a `WriterService` implementation for the router example.

Listing 8-67. Output Service of Generic XML Router Example (0818-router-xml-generic)

```
package net.lkrnac.book.eiws.chapter08.out;
import lombok.extern.slf4j.Slf4j;
import net.lkrnac.book.eiws.chapter08.out.WriteRepository;
import org.springframework.beans.factory.annotation.Autowired;
import org.springframework.stereotype.Service;

@Slf4j
@Service
public class WriteService {
  private WriteRepository writeRepository;

  @Autowired
  public WriteService(WriteRepository writeRepository) {
    super();
    this.writeRepository = writeRepository;
  }

  public boolean writeRoute1(String message) {
    log.info("Route 1 hit with message: " + message);
    return writeRepository.persist(message) == 1;
  }

  public boolean writeRoute2(String message) {
    log.info("Route 2 hit with message: " + message);
    return writeRepository.persist(message) == 1;
  }
}
```

This service is plugged into the output of the SI flow. It uses our common `WriteRepository` to persist messages. But the difference from previous examples is the use of the two methods `writeRoute1()` and `writeRoute2()` for consuming messages. They are used to split the message flow into two routes. Listing 8-68 shows the SI flow configuration.

Listing 8-68. SI Flow Configuration of Generic XML Router Example (File si-config.xml in Folder src/main/ resources of Example Project 0818-router-xml-generic)

```
<?xml version="1.0" encoding="UTF-8"?>
<beans xmlns="http://www.springframework.org/schema/beans"
  xmlns:xsi="http://www.w3.org/2001/XMLSchema-instance"
  xmlns:int="http://www.springframework.org/schema/integration"
```

```
  xsi:schemaLocation="http://www.springframework.org/schema/beans
    http://www.springframework.org/schema/beans/spring-beans.xsd
    http://www.springframework.org/schema/integration
    http://www.springframework.org/schema/integration/spring-integration.xsd">

  <int:gateway default-request-channel="inChannel"
    service-interface="net.lkrnac.book.eiws.chapter08.in.SiWrapperService" />
  <int:channel id="inChannel"/>

  <int:router input-channel="inChannel" expression="payload">
    <int:mapping channel="route1Channel" value="message1"/>
    <int:mapping channel="route2Channel" value="message2"/>
  </int:router>
  <int:channel id="route1Channel"/>
  <int:channel id="route2Channel"/>

  <int:service-activator input-channel="route1Channel" ref="writeService"
    method="writeRoute1"/>
  <int:service-activator input-channel="route2Channel" ref="writeService"
    method="writeRoute2"/>
</beans>
```

After the SI flow consumes the message via the inbound gateway, it is passed to the router component via inChannel. The router endpoint uses expression to inspect the payload of the message. If the payload is message1, it's routed to route1Channel, and if the payload is message2, it is routed to route2Channel. These two channels are connected to service activators, which map them to the WriteService.writeRoute1() and WriteService.writeRoute2() Java methods. This is a simple fork of SI flow based on the payload value. Listing 8-69 shows the main class of this example.

Listing 8-69. Main Class of Generic XML Router Example (0818-router-xml-generic)

```
package net.lkrnac.book.eiws.chapter08;
import lombok.extern.slf4j.Slf4j;
import net.lkrnac.book.eiws.chapter08.in.SiWrapperService;
import org.springframework.boot.SpringApplication;
import org.springframework.boot.autoconfigure.SpringBootApplication;
import org.springframework.context.ApplicationContext;
import org.springframework.context.annotation.ImportResource;

@Slf4j
@SpringBootApplication
@ImportResource("classpath:si-config.xml")
public class SiApplication {
  public static void main(String[] args) throws InterruptedException {
    ApplicationContext ctx = SpringApplication.run(SiApplication.class, args);

    SiWrapperService wrapperService = ctx.getBean(SiWrapperService.class);
    boolean result1 = wrapperService.processText("message1");
    log.info("Result:" + result1);
    boolean result2 = wrapperService.processText("message2");
    log.info("Result:" + result2);
  }
}
```

After creating the Spring context with the included SI flow, we read the `SiWrapperService` bean. Then we send two messages with payloads `message1` and `message2` to the SI flow and log the returned value. So we are now dealing with bidirectional message flow with a temporary reply channel. Listing 8-70 covers the output when we run this main class.

Listing 8-70. Output of Generic XML Router Example

```
2015-08-26 21:41:20.504  INFO 8057 --- [          main] n.l.b.eiws.chapter08.out.WriteService
: Route 1 hit with message: message1
2015-08-26 21:41:20.516  INFO 8057 --- [          main] n.l.b.e.chapter08.out.WriteRepository
: Text persisted: message1
2015-08-26 21:41:20.518  INFO 8057 --- [          main] n.l.book.eiws.chapter08.SiApplication
: Result:true
2015-08-26 21:41:20.519  INFO 8057 --- [          main] n.l.b.eiws.chapter08.out.WriteService
: Route 2 hit with message: message2
2015-08-26 21:41:20.519  INFO 8057 --- [          main] n.l.b.e.chapter08.out.WriteRepository
: Text persisted: message2
2015-08-26 21:41:20.519  INFO 8057 --- [          main] n.l.book.eiws.chapter08.SiApplication
: Result:true
```

The routing works as expected. We also get back return values, as if the SI flow is just a single service call. Figure 8-9 shows the SI graph for this example.

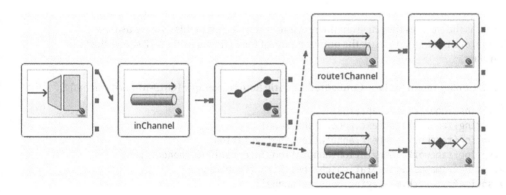

Figure 8-9. *Visualization of SI flow for generic XML router*

Generic Router Example Based on Java Configuration

Now let's configure the same logic with Java. Listing 8-71 shows the output service.

Listing 8-71. Output Service of Java-Configured Generic Router (0819-router-javaconfig)

```java
package net.lkrnac.book.eiws.chapter08.out;
import lombok.extern.slf4j.Slf4j;
import net.lkrnac.book.eiws.chapter08.out.WriteRepository;
import org.springframework.beans.factory.annotation.Autowired;
import org.springframework.integration.annotation.ServiceActivator;
import org.springframework.stereotype.Service;
```

```
@Slf4j
@Service
public class WriteServiceAnnotated {
  private WriteRepository writeRepository;

  @Autowired
  public WriteServiceAnnotated(WriteRepository writeRepository) {
    super();
    this.writeRepository = writeRepository;
  }

  @ServiceActivator(inputChannel = "route1Channel")
  public boolean writeRoute1(String message) {
    log.info("Route 1 hit with message: " + message);
    return writeRepository.persist(message) == 1;
  }

  @ServiceActivator(inputChannel = "route2Channel")
  public boolean writeRoute2(String message) {
    log.info("Route 2 hit with message: " + message);
    return writeRepository.persist(message) == 1;
  }
}
```

This service is the same as the one from the previous example, but in this case we use the @ServiceActivator annotation to mark the output points of the SI flow. Listing 8-72 shows the SI configuration class.

Listing 8-72. SI Configuration for Java-Configured Generic Router Example (0819-router-javaconfig)

```
package net.lkrnac.book.eiws.chapter08;
import org.springframework.context.annotation.Bean;
import org.springframework.context.annotation.Configuration;
import org.springframework.integration.annotation.IntegrationComponentScan;
import org.springframework.integration.channel.DirectChannel;
import org.springframework.messaging.MessageChannel;

@Configuration
@IntegrationComponentScan
public class SiConfiguration {
  @Bean
  public MessageChannel inChannel() {
    return new DirectChannel();
  }

  @Bean
  public MessageChannel route1Channel() {
    return new DirectChannel();
  }
```

```
  @Bean
  public MessageChannel route2Channel() {
    return new DirectChannel();
  }
}
```

Alongside SI component scanning, we register all the channels needed to fork the flow. Listing 8-73 shows the input service interface.

Listing 8-73. Service Interface for Java-Configured Generic Router Example (0819-router-javaconfig)

```
package net.lkrnac.book.eiws.chapter08.in;
import org.springframework.integration.annotation.Gateway;
import org.springframework.integration.annotation.MessagingGateway;

@MessagingGateway
public interface SiWrapperServiceAnnotated {
  @Gateway(requestChannel = "inChannel")
  public boolean processText(String text);
}
```

The interface is marked as an inbound messaging gateway connected to inChannel. It returns a value, so again we have a request-response scenario of the flow. Listing 8-74 shows the routing logic.

Listing 8-74. Routing Logic with Java Configuration (0819-router-javaconfig)

```
package net.lkrnac.book.eiws.chapter08;
import org.springframework.beans.factory.annotation.Autowired;
import org.springframework.integration.annotation.MessageEndpoint;
import org.springframework.integration.annotation.Router;
import org.springframework.messaging.MessageChannel;

@MessageEndpoint
public class SimpleRouter {
  private MessageChannel route1Channel;
  private MessageChannel route2Channel;

  @Autowired
  public SimpleRouter(MessageChannel route1Channel,
      MessageChannel route2Channel) {
    super();
    this.route1Channel = route1Channel;
    this.route2Channel = route2Channel;
  }

  @Router(inputChannel = "inChannel")
  public MessageChannel route(String message) {
    return (message.contains("1") ? route1Channel : route2Channel);
  }
}
```

The router class is annotated by the SI @MessageEndpoint annotation to be component scanned by the SI framework. We need to inject both channel instances we will route to. The routing method needs to be annotated by @Router and has to specify the inputChannel attribute so that we can consume messages from it. The routing logic itself is based on the presence of the substring 1 in the message. The channel instance we return will be used for passing the message further in the flow. Listing 8-75 shows the main class of this example.

Listing 8-75. Main Class of Java-Configured Router Example (0819-router-javaconfig)

```java
package net.lkrnac.book.eiws.chapter08;
import lombok.extern.slf4j.Slf4j;
import net.lkrnac.book.eiws.chapter08.in.SiWrapperServiceAnnotated;
import org.springframework.boot.SpringApplication;
import org.springframework.boot.autoconfigure.SpringBootApplication;
import org.springframework.context.ApplicationContext;

@Slf4j
@SpringBootApplication
public class SiApplication {
  public static void main(String[] args) throws InterruptedException {
    ApplicationContext ctx = SpringApplication.run(SiApplication.class, args);

    SiWrapperServiceAnnotated wrapperService =
        ctx.getBean(SiWrapperServiceAnnotated.class);
    boolean result1 = wrapperService.processText("message1");
    log.info("Result:" + result1);
    boolean result2 = wrapperService.processText("message2");
    log.info("Result:" + result2);
  }
}
```

The logic is similar to that in the 0818-router-xml-generic example in Listing 8-69, but in this case we don't include an XML configuration because the flow is configured purely in Java. The second difference is in the type of bean we use as the service interface for the SI gateway, because this time it is an annotated version. The output is the same as for the 0818-router-xml-generic example from Listing 8-70, and as we don't use an XML configuration, an integration graph can't be visualized via STS.

Message Type Router Example

This example uses routing based on payload type. Listing 8-76 shows the output service.

Listing 8-76. Output Service for Message Type Router Example (0820-router-xml-message-type)

```java
package net.lkrnac.book.eiws.chapter08.out;
import lombok.extern.slf4j.Slf4j;
import net.lkrnac.book.eiws.chapter08.out.WriteRepository;
import org.springframework.beans.factory.annotation.Autowired;
import org.springframework.stereotype.Service;
```

```
@Slf4j
@Service
public class WriteService {
  private WriteRepository writeRepository;

  @Autowired
  public WriteService(WriteRepository writeRepository) {
    super();
    this.writeRepository = writeRepository;
  }

  public boolean writeRoute1(String message) {
    log.info("Route 1 hit with message: " + message);
    return writeRepository.persist(message) == 1;
  }

  public boolean writeRoute2(int message) {
    log.info("Route 2 hit with message: " + message);
    return writeRepository.persist("message" + message) == 1;
  }
}
```

Again, this is a similar output service with two methods as targets for routing. The difference is in the parameter of writeRouter2(), which consumes the int message. Notice that the integer parameter is concatenated to the string value message, so that it can be passed to WriterRepository. Listing 8-77 shows the service interface, which will be used as input to the SI flow.

Listing 8-77. Service Interface for Message Type Router Example (0820-router-xml-message-type)

```
package net.lkrnac.book.eiws.chapter08.in;

public interface SiWrapperService {
  public boolean processMessage(Object message);
}
```

Notice that the processMessage() method takes the Object type as a parameter. Listing 8-78 shows the SI flow's XML configuration.

Listing 8-78. SI Flow Configuration for Message Type Router Example (File si-config.xml in Folder src/main/resources of Example Project 0820-router-xml-message-type)

```xml
<?xml version="1.0" encoding="UTF-8"?>
<beans xmlns="http://www.springframework.org/schema/beans"
  xmlns:xsi="http://www.w3.org/2001/XMLSchema-instance"
  xmlns:int="http://www.springframework.org/schema/integration"
  xsi:schemaLocation="http://www.springframework.org/schema/beans
    http://www.springframework.org/schema/beans/spring-beans.xsd
    http://www.springframework.org/schema/integration
    http://www.springframework.org/schema/integration/spring-integration.xsd">

  <int:gateway default-request-channel="inChannel"
    service-interface="net.lkrnac.book.eiws.chapter08.in.SiWrapperService" />
  <int:channel id="inChannel"/>
```

```
<int:payload-type-router input-channel="inChannel">
  <int:mapping channel="route1Channel" type="java.lang.String"/>
  <int:mapping channel="route2Channel" type="java.lang.Integer"/>
</int:payload-type-router>
<int:channel id="route1Channel"/>
<int:channel id="route2Channel"/>

<int:service-activator input-channel="route1Channel" ref="writeService"
  method="writeRoute1"/>
<int:service-activator input-channel="route2Channel" ref="writeService"
  method="writeRoute2"/>
</beans>
```

In this case, we use the <int:payload-type-router> XML element instead of <int:router>. To pick the target channel, we use the <int:mapping> element with the type attribute specified, which binds the payload Java type to a particular channel. Listing 8-79 shows the main class of this example.

Listing 8-79. Main Class of Payload Type Router Example (0820-router-xml-message-type)

```
package net.lkrnac.book.eiws.chapter08;
import lombok.extern.slf4j.Slf4j;
import net.lkrnac.book.eiws.chapter08.in.SiWrapperService;
import org.springframework.boot.SpringApplication;
import org.springframework.boot.autoconfigure.SpringBootApplication;
import org.springframework.context.ApplicationContext;
import org.springframework.context.annotation.ImportResource;

@Slf4j
@SpringBootApplication
@ImportResource("classpath:si-config.xml")
public class SiApplication {
  public static void main(String[] args) throws InterruptedException {
    ApplicationContext ctx = SpringApplication.run(SiApplication.class, args);

    SiWrapperService wrapperService = ctx.getBean(SiWrapperService.class);
    boolean result1 = wrapperService.processMessage("message1");
    log.info("Result:" + result1);
    boolean result2 = wrapperService.processMessage(2);
    log.info("Result:" + result2);
  }
}
```

First we send message1 to the message flow. The second message consists of value 2. The output of this example is shown in Listing 8-80.

Listing 8-80. Output of Payload Type Router Example

```
2015-08-26 22:47:08.840  INFO 9922 --- [            main]
n.l.b.eiws.chapter08.out.WriteService    : Route 1 hit with message: message1
2015-08-26 22:47:08.854  INFO 9922 --- [            main]
n.l.b.e.chapter08.out.WriteRepository    : Text persisted: message1
2015-08-26 22:47:08.859  INFO 9922 --- [            main]
```

```
n.l.book.eiws.chapter08.SiApplication      : Result:true
2015-08-26 22:47:08.861  INFO 9922 --- [          main]
n.l.b.eiws.chapter08.out.WriteService      : Route 2 hit with message: 2
2015-08-26 22:47:08.861  INFO 9922 --- [          main]
n.l.b.e.chapter08.out.WriteRepository      : Text persisted: message2
2015-08-26 22:47:08.862  INFO 9922 --- [          main]
n.l.book.eiws.chapter08.SiApplication      : Result:true
```

As expected, the second message received by WriterService has the value 2.

Bridge

A *bridge* is simple routing endpoint that connects two message channels or channel adapters. It is therefore used as a middle component, which can obviously participate in unidirectional and bidirectional flows. It can be configured via the XML element <int:bridge> or via the @BridgeFrom or @BridgeTo annotations, where it is used to mark channel beans. Use includes passive as well as active mode. In active mode, it needs to use the <int:poller> or @Poller subelement.

We may, for example, use it when we need to consume messages in a passive component from a channel designed for an active consumer (PollableChannel is described later in the chapter). In this case, the channel and component are incompatible, and the active bridge component will help us bridge this gap. Another use case is to connect two SI flows or systems where data conversion is not needed.

Bridge Example with XML Configuration

Listing 8-81 shows the SI flow of the XML bridge example.

Listing 8-81. SI Configuration of XML Bridge Example (File si-config.xml in Folder src/main/resources of Example Project 0821-bridge-xml)

```xml
<?xml version="1.0" encoding="UTF-8"?>
<beans xmlns="http://www.springframework.org/schema/beans"
  xmlns:xsi="http://www.w3.org/2001/XMLSchema-instance"
  xmlns:int="http://www.springframework.org/schema/integration"
  xmlns:context="http://www.springframework.org/schema/context"
  xsi:schemaLocation="http://www.springframework.org/schema/beans
    http://www.springframework.org/schema/beans/spring-beans.xsd
    http://www.springframework.org/schema/integration
    http://www.springframework.org/schema/integration/spring-integration.xsd">

  <int:gateway default-request-channel="inChannel"
    service-interface="net.lkrnac.book.eiws.chapter08.in.SiWrapperServiceVoid" />

  <int:channel id="inChannel" >
    <int:queue capacity="10" />
  </int:channel>

  <int:bridge input-channel="inChannel" output-channel="outputChannelAdapter" >
    <int:poller fixed-rate="100" />
  </int:bridge>
```

```
    <int:outbound-channel-adapter id="outputChannelAdapter"
      ref="writeService" method="write">
    </int:outbound-channel-adapter>
</beans>
```

Messages will be passed to the SI infrastructure via the inbound message gateway, which uses our common SiWrapperServiceVoid as a service interface and sends messages to inChannel. In this case, inChannel is configured as a temporary store of 10 messages. This type of channel is explained in detail later, in the "QueueChannel" section.

This channel is connected to the bridge component, which is in this case active, and polls inChannel every 100 ms. The output side of the bridge is connected directly to the outbound channel adapter. The output-channel attribute of the bridge and id of the channel adapter match, which means that these components are interconnected. The output channel adapter is mapped to our common method WriteService.write(). Listing 8-82 shows the main class of this example.

Listing 8-82. Main Class of XML Bridge Example (0821-bridge-xml)

```
package net.lkrnac.book.eiws.chapter08;
import net.lkrnac.book.eiws.chapter08.in.SiWrapperServiceVoid;
import org.springframework.boot.SpringApplication;
import org.springframework.boot.autoconfigure.SpringBootApplication;
import org.springframework.context.ApplicationContext;
import org.springframework.context.annotation.ImportResource;

@SpringBootApplication
@ImportResource("classpath:si-config.xml")
public class SiApplication {
  public static void main(String[] args) throws InterruptedException {
    ApplicationContext ctx = SpringApplication.run(SiApplication.class, args);

    SiWrapperServiceVoid wrapperService =
        ctx.getBean(SiWrapperServiceVoid.class);
    wrapperService.processText("message1");
    wrapperService.processText("message2");
  }
}
```

This starts the Spring context and sends two messages to the SI flow via the SiWrapperServiceVoid bean. Listing 8-83 covers the output when we run this main class.

Listing 8-83. Output of XML Bridge Example

```
2015-08-27 19:12:54.862  INFO 21268 --- [ask-scheduler-1]
n.l.b.e.chapter08.out.WriteRepository    : Text persisted: message1
2015-08-27 19:12:54.864  INFO 21268 --- [ask-scheduler-1]
n.l.b.e.chapter08.out.WriteRepository    : Text persisted: message2
```

As expected, both messages are being persisted. Notice that this happens in the task scheduler thread, which is created by the <int:poller> subcomponent of the bridge. Figure 8-10 shows the SI graph for this SI flow.

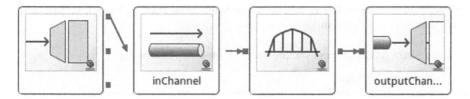

Figure 8-10. *SI graph of XML bridge example*

@BridgeFrom Example

Listing 8-84 shows the service interface sitting on the input side of the flow.

Listing 8-84. Service Interface for @BridgeFrom Example (0822-bridge-from-javaconfig)

```
package net.lkrnac.book.eiws.chapter08.in;
import org.springframework.integration.annotation.Gateway;
import org.springframework.integration.annotation.MessagingGateway;

@MessagingGateway
public interface SiWrapperServiceAnnotated {
  @Gateway(requestChannel = "inChannel")
  public boolean processText(String text);
}
```

This bidirectional service interface is configured as an inbound gateway. Listing 8-85 shows the output bean of the SI flow.

Listing 8-85. Output of SI Flow for @BridgeFrom Example (0822-bridge-from-javaconfig)

```
package net.lkrnac.book.eiws.chapter08.out;
import net.lkrnac.book.eiws.chapter08.out.WriteRepository;
import org.springframework.beans.factory.annotation.Autowired;
import org.springframework.integration.annotation.ServiceActivator;
import org.springframework.stereotype.Service;

@Service
public class WriteServiceAnnotated {
  private WriteRepository writeRepository;

  @Autowired
  public WriteServiceAnnotated(WriteRepository writeRepository) {
    super();
    this.writeRepository = writeRepository;
  }

  @ServiceActivator(inputChannel = "bridgedChannel")
  public boolean writeAndIndicateSuccess(String message) {
    return writeRepository.persist(message) == 1;
  }
}
```

WriterServiceAnnotated is configured as a service activator listening on bridgedChannel. Listing 8-86 shows the Java SI configuration in which the bridge is configured.

Listing 8-86. SI Configuration of @BridgeFrom Example (0822-bridge-from-javaconfig)

```java
package net.lkrnac.book.eiws.chapter08;
import org.springframework.context.annotation.Bean;
import org.springframework.context.annotation.Configuration;
import org.springframework.integration.annotation.BridgeFrom;
import org.springframework.integration.annotation.IntegrationComponentScan;
import org.springframework.integration.annotation.Poller;
import org.springframework.integration.channel.DirectChannel;
import org.springframework.integration.channel.QueueChannel;
import org.springframework.messaging.MessageChannel;
import org.springframework.messaging.PollableChannel;

@Configuration
@IntegrationComponentScan
public class SiConfiguration {
  @Bean
  public PollableChannel inChannel() {
    return new QueueChannel();
  }

  @Bean
  @BridgeFrom(value = "inChannel", poller = @Poller(fixedDelay = "100"))
  public MessageChannel bridgedChannel() {
    return new DirectChannel();
  }
}
```

After a component scan for SI components, this defines two channels: inChannel and bridgedChannel. These channels are bridged via the value attribute of the @BridgeFrom annotation. The @Poller annotation turns this bridge to an active component. Listing 8-87 shows the main class of this example.

Listing 8-87. Main Class of @BridgeFrom Example (0822-bridge-from-javaconfig)

```java
package net.lkrnac.book.eiws.chapter08;
import lombok.extern.slf4j.Slf4j;
import net.lkrnac.book.eiws.chapter08.in.SiWrapperServiceAnnotated;
import org.springframework.boot.SpringApplication;
import org.springframework.boot.autoconfigure.SpringBootApplication;
import org.springframework.context.ApplicationContext;

@Slf4j
@SpringBootApplication
public class SiApplication {
  public static void main(String[] args) throws InterruptedException {
    ApplicationContext ctx = SpringApplication.run(SiApplication.class, args);
```

```
    SiWrapperServiceAnnotated wrapperService =
        ctx.getBean(SiWrapperServiceAnnotated.class);
    boolean result = wrapperService.processText("simple message");
    log.info("Result: " + result);
  }
}
```

After running the Spring context, we send the message via the SiWrapperServiceAnnotated service interface and log the result returned by the SI flow. Listing 8-88 shows the output after running this example.

Listing 8-88. Output of @BridgeFrom Example

```
2015-08-27 19:36:10.635  INFO 22768 --- [ask-scheduler-1]
n.l.b.e.chapter08.out.WriteRepository    : Text persisted: simple message
2015-08-27 19:36:10.637  INFO 22768 --- [            main]
n.l.book.eiws.chapter08.SiApplication    : Result: true
```

The message is persisted in the task scheduler thread, and the result is handled in the main thread.

@BridgeTo Example

This example is similar to the @BridgeFrom example. The only difference between these two examples is shown in Listing 8-89.

Listing 8-89. SI Configuration of @BridgeTo Example (0823-bridge-to-javaconfig)

```java
package net.lkrnac.book.eiws.chapter08;

import org.springframework.context.annotation.Bean;
import org.springframework.context.annotation.Configuration;
import org.springframework.integration.annotation.BridgeTo;
import org.springframework.integration.annotation.IntegrationComponentScan;
import org.springframework.integration.annotation.Poller;
import org.springframework.integration.channel.DirectChannel;
import org.springframework.integration.channel.QueueChannel;
import org.springframework.messaging.MessageChannel;
import org.springframework.messaging.PollableChannel;

@Configuration
@IntegrationComponentScan
public class SiConfiguration {
  @Bean
  @BridgeTo(value = "bridgedChannel", poller = @Poller(fixedDelay = "100"))
  public PollableChannel inChannel() {
    return new QueueChannel();
  }

  @Bean
  public MessageChannel bridgedChannel() {
    return new DirectChannel();
  }
}
```

The @BridgeTo annotation is on inChannel in this case. The output of this example is also the same as for the @BridgeFrom example. As we can see, @BridgeTo annotates the source channel or component—the opposite of @BridgeFrom, which annotates the target channel or component.

Chain

A *chain* is a passive middle component, which also means it can participate in unidirectional and bidirectional message flows. As its name suggests, it is used for chaining message endpoints together without the need to specify channels to connect them. Messages are most commonly passed sequentially through chain subelements.

This component can wrap a set of message endpoints into one message endpoint. In fact, we can use a chain as a component in a higher-level chain and thus create a complex structure of SI flow chunks connected on various chain levels. Such nested chains need to be defined with use of the messaging gateway.

A chain can be configured via the XML element <int:chain>. Notice that there is no Java annotation equivalent for a chain definition. It requires only one mandatory attribute: input-channel. Components used in chains have various restrictions as compared to their use outside the chain. For example, components in a chain shouldn't specify input-channel. In addition, the following are restrictions for the last element in the chain in relation to the output channel:

- If the chain is connected to a downstream message endpoint, the last element in the chain must specify output-channel, or the message should have the replyChannel header defined.

- If the last element is a channel adapter or service activator, it doesn't need to specify the output channel.

Another restriction is that each endpoint in a chain must produce a message (can't return null) and thus terminate the flow. Only the last element can discard the message. Elements in a chain can't be active (can't have poller).

Chain Example

This example borrows all the classes from the 0814-header-enricher-xml example:

- SimpleHeaderEnricher (Listing 8-52)

- WriteServiceWithHeaders (Listing 8-54)

- SiApplication (Listing 8-55)

Listing 8-90 shows the SI flow with the chain.

Listing 8-90. SI Flow for Chain Example (File si-config.xml in Folder src/main/resources of Example Project 0824-chain-xml)

```
<?xml version="1.0" encoding="UTF-8"?>
<beans xmlns="http://www.springframework.org/schema/beans"
  xmlns:xsi="http://www.w3.org/2001/XMLSchema-instance"
  xmlns:int="http://www.springframework.org/schema/integration"
  xmlns:context="http://www.springframework.org/schema/context"
  xsi:schemaLocation="http://www.springframework.org/schema/beans
    http://www.springframework.org/schema/beans/spring-beans.xsd
    http://www.springframework.org/schema/integration
    http://www.springframework.org/schema/integration/spring-integration.xsd">
```

```
<int:gateway default-request-channel="inChannel"
  service-interface="net.lkrnac.book.eiws.chapter08.in.SiWrapperServiceVoid" />
<int:channel id="inChannel"/>

<int:chain input-channel="inChannel">
  <int:header-enricher>
    <int:header name="simpleHeader" ref="simpleHeaderEnricher" method="addHeader"/>
  </int:header-enricher>
  <int:outbound-channel-adapter ref="writeServiceWithHeaders" method="write"/>
</int:chain>
</beans>
```

As compared to the 0814-header-enricher-xml example, we don't need to define enrichedChannel, because the header enricher and outbound channel adapter are wrapped in a chain. The output of this example is also the same as the output of the header enricher example in Listing 8-56. The SI graph for this flow is shown in Figure 8-11.

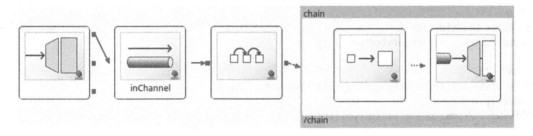

Figure 8-11. *SI graph for chain example*

Splitter

A *splitter* is a middle component (can participate in unidirectional or bidirectional flows) that can operate in passive or active mode. It has a unique function in the SI framework, splitting the received message into various messages based on these mechanisms:

- *Custom Java logic*: Generic component, which can be configured via the <int:splitter> XML element or @Splitter annotation

- *XPath*: XML payload specific, which can be configured via <int-xml:xpath-splitter>

Each message produced by the splitter will be filled with these headers:

- correlationId: By default, messages created from a single message will have the same correlationId.

- sequenceSize: By default, the number of messages created from the original.

- sequenceNumber: By default, the order of the message created from the original.

These headers are explained in detail in the upcoming "Aggregator" section. An aggregator is commonly used with a splitter in message flows.

Splitter XML Example

Listing 8-91 shows the output service from the SI flow.

Listing 8-91. Output Service from Message Flow (0825-splitter-delimiters-xml)

```java
package net.lkrnac.book.eiws.chapter08.out;
import static org.springframework.integration.IntegrationMessageHeaderAccessor.CORRELATION_ID;
import static org.springframework.integration.IntegrationMessageHeaderAccessor.SEQUENCE_NUMBER;
import static org.springframework.integration.IntegrationMessageHeaderAccessor.SEQUENCE_SIZE;
import java.util.Map;
import java.util.UUID;
import lombok.extern.slf4j.Slf4j;
import org.springframework.beans.factory.annotation.Autowired;
import org.springframework.messaging.handler.annotation.Headers;
import org.springframework.stereotype.Service;

@Slf4j
@Service
public class WriteService {
  private WriteRepository writeRepository;

  @Autowired
  public WriteService(WriteRepository writeRepository) {
    super();
    this.writeRepository = writeRepository;
  }

  public boolean writeAndIndicateSuccess(String message,
      @Headers Map<String, Object> headers) {
    logHeaders(headers);

    boolean result = writeRepository.persist(message) == 1;
    if ("messageFail".equals(message)) {
      return false;
    }
    return result;
  }

  public void logHeaders(Map<String, Object> headers) {
    UUID correlationId = (UUID) headers.get(CORRELATION_ID);
    int sequenceSize = (int) headers.get(SEQUENCE_SIZE);
    int sequenceNumber = (int) headers.get(SEQUENCE_NUMBER);

    log.info("Received message headers: correlationId={}, "
        + "sequenceSize={}, sequenceNumber={}", correlationId, sequenceSize,
        sequenceNumber);
  }
}
```

The `writeAndIndicateSuccess()` method is used to consume messages in the SI flow. Into the first parameter we inject the `String` payload, and into the second parameter we inject the `Map` headers of the message. Messages are injected in order to log the default headers created by the splitter. The payload is passed to `WriteRepository` to persist it. At the end of the method, we return a `false` value if the message payload equals `messageFail`. This is useful to show which forked messages will be used to construct the reply message. Listing 8-92 shows the SI flow configuration.

Listing 8-92. SI Configuration for XML Splitter Example (File si-config.xml in Folder src/main/resources of Example Project 0825-splitter-delimiters-xml)

```xml
<?xml version="1.0" encoding="UTF-8"?>
<beans xmlns="http://www.springframework.org/schema/beans"
  xmlns:xsi="http://www.w3.org/2001/XMLSchema-instance"
  xmlns:int="http://www.springframework.org/schema/integration"
  xsi:schemaLocation="http://www.springframework.org/schema/beans
    http://www.springframework.org/schema/beans/spring-beans.xsd
    http://www.springframework.org/schema/integration
    http://www.springframework.org/schema/integration/spring-integration.xsd">

  <int:gateway default-request-channel="inChannel"
    service-interface="net.lkrnac.book.eiws.chapter08.in.SiWrapperService" />
  <int:channel id="inChannel" />

  <int:splitter input-channel="inChannel" output-channel="splitChannel" delimiters=";"/>
  <int:channel id="splitChannel" />

  <int:service-activator input-channel="splitChannel" ref="writeService"
    method="writeAndIndicateSuccess">
  </int:service-activator>
</beans>
```

The input part of the flow is covered by the inbound gateway with our common `SiWrapperService` interface and connects it to the splitter via `inChannel`. The splitter uses the `delimiters` attribute as splitting logic, which means the messages will be split based on a semicolon in this case. The splitter's `output-channel` continues into the service activator mapped to `WriteService.writeAndIndicateSuccess()` from Listing 8-91. Listing 8-93 shows the main class of this example.

Listing 8-93. Main Class of XML Splitter Example (0825-splitter-delimiters-xml)

```java
package net.lkrnac.book.eiws.chapter08;
import lombok.extern.slf4j.Slf4j;
import net.lkrnac.book.eiws.chapter08.in.SiWrapperService;
import org.springframework.boot.SpringApplication;
import org.springframework.boot.autoconfigure.SpringBootApplication;
import org.springframework.context.ApplicationContext;
import org.springframework.context.annotation.ImportResource;

@Slf4j
@SpringBootApplication
@ImportResource("classpath:si-config.xml")
```

```
public class SiApplication {
  public static void main(String[] args) throws InterruptedException {
    ApplicationContext ctx = SpringApplication.run(SiApplication.class, args);

    SiWrapperService wrapperService = ctx.getBean(SiWrapperService.class);
    boolean resultSuccess =
        wrapperService.processText("messageSuccess;messageFail;messageSuccess");
    log.info("Result: " + resultSuccess);

    boolean resultFail =
        wrapperService.processText("messageSuccess;messageFail;");
    log.info("Result: " + resultFail);
  }
}
```

After we run the Spring context and retrieve the service interface from the context, we send two messages to the SI infrastructure. The first one has two semicolons, and messageFail is in the middle; the second one has only one semicolon, and messageFail is at the end of the string message. So in the first case, we expect the message to be split into three messages, and the second one into two. Let's show the output of this example in Listing 8-94.

Listing 8-94. Output of XML Splitter Example

```
2015-08-28 20:57:32.928  INFO 2794 --- [        main]
n.l.b.eiws.chapter08.out.WriteService    : Received message headers:
correlationId=5b3c3226-3d40-0db2-645c-213dd638126f, sequenceSize=3, sequenceNumber=1
2015-08-28 20:57:32.945  INFO 2794 --- [        main]
n.l.b.e.chapter08.out.WriteRepository    : Text persisted: messageSuccess
2015-08-28 20:57:32.976  INFO 2794 --- [        main]
n.l.b.eiws.chapter08.out.WriteService    : Received message headers:
correlationId=5b3c3226-3d40-0db2-645c-213dd638126f, sequenceSize=3, sequenceNumber=2
2015-08-28 20:57:32.977  INFO 2794 --- [        main]
n.l.b.e.chapter08.out.WriteRepository    : Text persisted: messageFail
2015-08-28 20:57:32.978  INFO 2794 --- [        main]
n.l.b.eiws.chapter08.out.WriteService    : Received message headers:
correlationId=5b3c3226-3d40-0db2-645c-213dd638126f, sequenceSize=3, sequenceNumber=3
2015-08-28 20:57:32.979  INFO 2794 --- [        main]
n.l.b.e.chapter08.out.WriteRepository    : Text persisted: messageSuccess
2015-08-28 20:57:32.979  INFO 2794 --- [        main]
n.l.book.eiws.chapter08.SiApplication    : Result: true
2015-08-28 20:57:32.982  INFO 2794 --- [        main]
n.l.b.eiws.chapter08.out.WriteService    : Received message headers:
correlationId=41a2d47e-9dab-3c11-48c2-6507eac3bd49, sequenceSize=2, sequenceNumber=1
2015-08-28 20:57:32.982  INFO 2794 --- [        main]
n.l.b.e.chapter08.out.WriteRepository    : Text persisted: messageSuccess
2015-08-28 20:57:32.983  INFO 2794 --- [        main]
n.l.b.eiws.chapter08.out.WriteService    : Received message headers:
correlationId=41a2d47e-9dab-3c11-48c2-6507eac3bd49, sequenceSize=2, sequenceNumber=2
2015-08-28 20:57:32.984  INFO 2794 --- [        main]
n.l.b.e.chapter08.out.WriteRepository    : Text persisted: messageFail
2015-08-28 20:57:32.984  INFO 2794 --- [        main]
n.l.book.eiws.chapter08.SiApplication    : Result: false
```

We can observe that the first three messages have the same correlationId, sequenceSize=3, and are split as we expect with sequenceNumber in the order that we expect. The same is true for the second group of messages. An interesting fact is that the return value from the service activator is sent back via a temporary reply channel only for the last message from each group. This is because there is only one temporary reply channel for all split messages, and obviously there can be only one return value from the service interface SiWrapperService. Other reply messages are discarded. Figure 8-12 shows the SI graph for this flow.

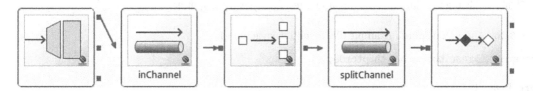

Figure 8-12. *SI graph for splitter example*

Splitter Example with Java Configuration

This example will use similar constructs to those in the previous example, 0825-splitter-delimiters-xml. To avoid presenting the same long code listing, we'll list the similar classes:

- WriteServiceAnnotated: A Java implementation, like WriteService in Listing 8-91, *with only one difference:* WriteServiceAnnotated.writeAndIndicateSuccess() is annotated with @ServiceActivator and connected to splitChannel.

- SiWrapperServiceAnnotated: The same interface signature as the common SiWrapperService, but annotated with @Gateway and @MessageEndpoint.

- SiApplication: The same as the SiApplication class in Listing 8-93. The only difference is the missing import of the si-config.xml file, as this is a Java-configured example.

Listing 8-95 shows the SI configuration.

Listing 8-95. SI Configuration of Annotated Splitter Example (0826-splitter-javaconfig)

```java
package net.lkrnac.book.eiws.chapter08;
import org.springframework.context.annotation.Bean;
import org.springframework.context.annotation.Configuration;
import org.springframework.integration.annotation.IntegrationComponentScan;
import org.springframework.integration.channel.DirectChannel;
import org.springframework.messaging.MessageChannel;

@Configuration
@IntegrationComponentScan
public class SiConfiguration {
  @Bean
  public MessageChannel inChannel() {
    return new DirectChannel();
  }
```

```
  @Bean
  public MessageChannel splitChannel() {
    return new DirectChannel();
  }
}
```

This configuration class with an SI component scan registers two channels: inChannel and splitChannel. Listing 8-96 finally shows an annotated example of the splitter.

Listing 8-96. Annotated Splitter Example (0826-splitter-javaconfig)

```
package net.lkrnac.book.eiws.chapter08;

import java.util.Arrays;
import java.util.List;

import org.apache.commons.lang3.StringUtils;
import org.springframework.integration.annotation.MessageEndpoint;
import org.springframework.integration.annotation.Splitter;

@MessageEndpoint
public class SimpleSplitter {
  @Splitter(inputChannel = "inChannel", outputChannel = "splitChannel")
  public List<String> splitMessage(String message) {
    return Arrays.asList(StringUtils.split(message, ";"));
  }
}
```

The class needs to be annotated by @MessageEndpoint to mark it as a bean for SI endpoints. @Splitter annotates the splitting method with two mandatory parameters: inputChannel and outputChannel. The splitting method needs to return the List<String> of the object, which will be represented as payloads for split messages. The output is also the same as for the 0825-splitter-delimiters-xml example in Listing 8-94.

Aggregator

An aggregator is a passive middle component, so it can be integrated into bidirectional and unidirectional SI flows. As we already mentioned, an aggregator's function is the opposite of a splitter's. An aggregator aggregates various messages into one message and can be configured via the XML element <int:aggregator> or via the annotation @Aggregator. An aggregation is performed based on these two mechanisms:

- CorrelationStrategy: A mechanism used to group incoming messages, so that they can be aggregated together. A custom CorrelationStrategy can be configured via the correlation-strategy-method or correlation-strategy-expression XML attributes or the @CorrelationStrategy annotation with a Java configuration.

- ReleaseStrategy: A mechanism to decide when the group of input messages is complete, so that they can be aggregated. The custom ReleaseStrategy can be configured via the release-strategy-method or release-strategy-expression attributes or the @ReleaseStrategy annotation with a Java configuration.

By default, aggregation is performed based on these message headers:

- `correlationId`: Tells the aggregator that messages with the same `correlationId` should be merged (`CorrelationStrategy` based on `correlationId`).

- `sequenceSize`: Tells the aggregator how big the group of messages is to aggregate.

- `sequenceNumber`: Tells the aggregator the order of the current message within the group to aggregate.

So, by default, the aggregator's `ReleaseStrategy` works based on gathering messages, and then inspecting their `sequenceSize`, `sequenceNumber`, and `correlationId`. Messages are released when we have a full group of correlated messages.

We can also configure a time-out for the aggregator component, whereby a group of messages will be released/aggregated after a defined time. In this case, we have to specify whether we want to aggregate a partial message or discard a partial group of messages.

The aggregator obviously must first temporarily store messages before it can aggregate them. Therefore, it is a much more complex component than a splitter, as it implements internal storage for partial message groups.

Custom Aggregator Example with XML Configuration

Listing 8-97 shows the service interface used by the inbound gateway on entrance to the SI flow.

Listing 8-97. Service Interface for Custom XML Aggregator Example (0827-aggregator-xml)

```
package net.lkrnac.book.eiws.chapter08.in;
import java.util.concurrent.Future;

public interface SiWrapperServiceFuture {
  Future<Boolean> processText(String text);
}
```

Notice that the return value is wrapped into `Future<T>`. It represents the result of an asynchronous operation that will be filled in the future when the operation finishes. We will use it to highlight how an aggregator in a bidirectional flow can end up blocking the caller. Listing 8-98 shows the SI flow's XML configuration.

Listing 8-98. SI Configuration for Custom Aggregator Example (File si-config.xml in Folder src/main/ resources of Example Project 0827-aggregator-xml)

```
<?xml version="1.0" encoding="UTF-8"?>
<beans xmlns="http://www.springframework.org/schema/beans"
  xmlns:xsi="http://www.w3.org/2001/XMLSchema-instance"
  xmlns:int="http://www.springframework.org/schema/integration"
  xsi:schemaLocation="http://www.springframework.org/schema/beans
    http://www.springframework.org/schema/beans/spring-beans.xsd
    http://www.springframework.org/schema/integration
    http://www.springframework.org/schema/integration/spring-integration.xsd">

  <int:gateway default-request-channel="inChannel"
    service-interface="net.lkrnac.book.eiws.chapter08.in.SiWrapperServiceFuture" />
  <int:channel id="inChannel" />
```

```
  <int:aggregator input-channel="inChannel" output-channel="aggregatedChannel"
    correlation-strategy-expression="payload.substring(7)"
    release-strategy-expression="size() > 1"/>
  <int:channel id="aggregatedChannel" />

  <int:service-activator input-channel="aggregatedChannel" ref="writeService"
    method="writeAndIndicateSuccess" />
</beans>
```

The inbound gateway uses the SiWrapperServiceFuture service interface and is connected to the aggregator via inChannel. The aggregator needs to specify the input-channel and output-channel attributes. In this case, we also specify the custom correlation and release strategy via inline SpEL expressions. Correlation of messages is based on the eighth character in the message. So if this character matches, messages should be aggregated together. The release strategy is based on the message group size. As soon as we have two correlated messages, we release them. By default, string messages are aggregated by concatenation with a comma.

This aggregator is connected to the service activator, which invokes our common WriteService.writeAndIndicateSuccess() method. Listing 8-99 shows the asynchronous sender of the messages.

Listing 8-99. Asynchronous Sender of Messages for XML Aggregator Example (0827-aggregator-xml)

```
package net.lkrnac.book.eiws.chapter08.in;
import java.util.concurrent.Future;
import java.util.concurrent.TimeUnit;
import lombok.extern.slf4j.Slf4j;
import org.springframework.beans.factory.annotation.Autowired;
import org.springframework.scheduling.annotation.Async;
import org.springframework.stereotype.Component;

@Slf4j
@Component
public class AsyncMessageSender {
  private SiWrapperServiceFuture wrapperService;

  @Autowired
  public AsyncMessageSender(SiWrapperServiceFuture wrapperService) {
    super();
    this.wrapperService = wrapperService;
  }

  @Async("customExecutor")
  public void sendMessage(String message) throws Exception {
    Future<Boolean> resultFuture = wrapperService.processText(message);
    boolean result = resultFuture.get(1, TimeUnit.SECONDS);
    log.info("Result for " + message + ": " + result);
  }
}
```

This Spring bean injects SiWrapperServiceFuture, which is the service interface used in the gateway, and encapsulates SI flow. The sendMessage() method is annotated with @Async, so it will be executed in a separate thread when called. Notice that we use customExecutor as an annotation attribute, which specifies the name of the executor bean used to execute this asynchronous logic.

In this method, we call the service interface to pass the message to the SI flow. The returned resultFuture is then used to wait for the resulting Boolean value that will eventually be returned. To be make sure it won't stay hanging in the resultFuture.get() call forever, we configure a 1-second time-out for this operation. Finally, we log the returned result. Listing 8-100 shows the main class of this example.

Listing 8-100. Main Class of Custom XML Aggregator Example (0827-aggregator-xml)

```java
package net.lkrnac.book.eiws.chapter08;
import java.util.concurrent.Executor;
import net.lkrnac.book.eiws.chapter08.in.AsyncMessageSender;
import org.springframework.boot.SpringApplication;
import org.springframework.boot.autoconfigure.SpringBootApplication;
import org.springframework.context.ApplicationContext;
import org.springframework.context.annotation.Bean;
import org.springframework.context.annotation.ImportResource;
import org.springframework.scheduling.annotation.EnableAsync;
import org.springframework.scheduling.concurrent.ThreadPoolTaskExecutor;


@EnableAsync
@SpringBootApplication
@ImportResource("classpath:si-config.xml")
public class SiApplication {
  @Bean
  public Executor customExecutor() {
    ThreadPoolTaskExecutor threadPool = new ThreadPoolTaskExecutor();
    threadPool.setCorePoolSize(10);
    return threadPool;
  }

  public static void main(String[] args) throws Exception {
    ApplicationContext ctx = SpringApplication.run(SiApplication.class, args);

    AsyncMessageSender messageSender = ctx.getBean(AsyncMessageSender.class);
    messageSender.sendMessage("message1");
    messageSender.sendMessage("message2");
    messageSender.sendMessage("message2");
    messageSender.sendMessage("message1");
  }
}
```

This Spring Boot main class enables asynchronous Spring features alongside XML SI flow configuration. This is also a Spring configuration class, so we take advantage of that fact and register the customExecutor thread pool with pool size 10, to have enough threads available for our example.

After we start the Spring Boot application, we retrieve AsyncMessageSender from the Spring context and send four messages to the SI flow via this asynchronous sender. Notice the order of messages. Bear in mind that our correlation logic should correlate message1 with message1, and message2 with message2. When we run this example, we get the output in Listing 8-101.

Listing 8-101. Output of Custom XML Aggregator Example

```
2015-08-29 11:49:23.588  INFO 22149 --- [cTaskExecutor-4]
n.l.b.e.chapter08.out.WriteRepository     : Text persisted: message2,message2
2015-08-29 11:49:23.589  INFO 22149 --- [ustomExecutor-2]
n.l.b.e.chapter08.in.AsyncMessageSender   : Result for message2: true
2015-08-29 11:49:23.590  INFO 22149 --- [cTaskExecutor-3]
n.l.b.e.chapter08.out.WriteRepository     : Text persisted: message1,message1
2015-08-29 11:49:23.590  INFO 22149 --- [ustomExecutor-4]
n.l.b.e.chapter08.in.AsyncMessageSender   : Result for message1: true
2015-08-29 11:49:24.524 ERROR 22149 --- [ustomExecutor-3]
.a.i.SimpleAsyncUncaughtExceptionHandler : Unexpected error occurred invoking async method
'public void net.lkrnac.book.eiws.chapter08.in.AsyncMessageSender.sendMessage(java.lang.
String) throws
java.lang.Exception'.

java.util.concurrent.TimeoutException: null
        at java.util.concurrent.FutureTask.get(FutureTask.java:205)
        ...

2015-08-29 11:49:24.526 ERROR 22149 --- [ustomExecutor-1]
.a.i.SimpleAsyncUncaughtExceptionHandler : Unexpected error occurred invoking async method
'public void net.lkrnac.book.eiws.chapter08.in.AsyncMessageSender.sendMessage(java.lang.
String) throws
java.lang.Exception'.

java.util.concurrent.TimeoutException: null
        at java.util.concurrent.FutureTask.get(FutureTask.java:205)
        ...
```

There are some problems, so let's explain. When we send four messages into the asynchronous sender, the main thread is not blocked. The four new threads are kicked off (with the names customExecutor-1 .. customExecutor-4), executing logic in AsyncMessageSender.sendMessage() asynchronously.

So we send four messages in four separate concurrent threads into the aggregator component. These messages should be aggregated into two messages, which happens as expected in the first and third log entries. Notice the thread names for these log entries. Log entry Text persisted: message1,message1 is logged from AsyncTaskExecutor-3, and Text persisted: message2,message2 is logged from AsyncTaskExecutor-4. So as you can see, the aggregator uses a separate thread pool to aggregate the messages together internally.

Now let's focus on responses from the aggregator. The gateway component creates four temporary reply channels and expects four replies. Two of the temporary reply channels get a successful response (in threads customExecutor-2 and customExecutor-4)—one for each aggregated message. But the remaining two temporary reply channels (in threads customExecutor-1 and customExecutor-3) timed out in the AsyncMessageSender.sendMessage() logic. So if we didn't set up a time-out for resultFuture.get(), the thread would be hanging forever, waiting for a response from the aggregator, which obviously wouldn't come back.

This highlights how tricky it can be to configure bidirectional flow with an aggregator. Therefore, it's much better suited for unidirectional flows, or in conjunction with a splitter.

Figure 8-13 shows the SI graph for this example.

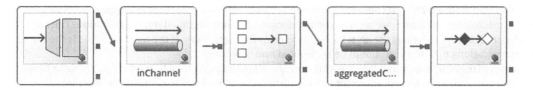

Figure 8-13. *Visualization of SI configuration for XML aggregator example*

Custom Aggregator Example with Java Configuration

This example borrows some classes from the previous example, 0827-aggregator-xml:

- SiWrapperServiceFuture (Listing 8-97)
- AsyncMessageSender (Listing 8-99)
- SiApplication (Listing 8-100)

Listing 8-102 shows the Java configuration of the aggregator component.

Listing 8-102. Java Configuration of Aggregator (0828-aggregator-javaconfig)

```java
package net.lkrnac.book.eiws.chapter08;
import java.util.List;
import org.springframework.integration.annotation.Aggregator;
import org.springframework.integration.annotation.CorrelationStrategy;
import org.springframework.integration.annotation.MessageEndpoint;
import org.springframework.integration.annotation.ReleaseStrategy;

@MessageEndpoint
public class SimpleAggregator {
  @Aggregator(inputChannel = "inChannel", outputChannel = "aggregatedChannel")
  public String aggregate(List<String> messages) {
    return messages.stream().reduce((m1, m2) -> m1 + "," + m2).get();
  }

  @ReleaseStrategy
  public boolean releaseChecker(List<String> messages) {
    return messages.size() == 2;
  }

  @CorrelationStrategy
  public String correlateBy(String message) {
    return message.substring(7);
  }
}
```

The class is annotated with @MessageEndpoint to mark it as an SI component for the integration component scan. The first method, aggregate(), joins messages. We used the Java 8 Stream API for this purpose. It converts the message collection into the Java 8 stream and uses the reduce() feature to concatenate two elements of the stream into one. Finally, it again converts the stream into the collection via the get() method. The @Aggregator annotation requires the inputChannel and outputChannel attributes to be defined.

The second method, releaseChecker(), defines a custom release strategy for the aggregator. When the group reaches two messages, we return true to inform SI about the fulfilled release condition. The last method, correlateBy(), defines the correlation strategy for this aggregator. If the returned value is the same, the messages belong together and should be aggregated into one group.

The rest of the SI flow is defined via the XML configuration in Listing 8-103—partially to highlight how to combine XML and Java configurations for an SI application, and partially to decrease the number of listings needed for this example.

Listing 8-103. SI Configuration for Java Aggregator Example (File si-config.xml in Folder src/main/resources of Example Project 0828-aggregator-javaconfig)

```xml
<?xml version="1.0" encoding="UTF-8"?>
<beans xmlns="http://www.springframework.org/schema/beans"
  xmlns:xsi="http://www.w3.org/2001/XMLSchema-instance"
  xmlns:int="http://www.springframework.org/schema/integration"
  xmlns:task="http://www.springframework.org/schema/task"
  xsi:schemaLocation="http://www.springframework.org/schema/beans
    http://www.springframework.org/schema/beans/spring-beans.xsd
    http://www.springframework.org/schema/integration
    http://www.springframework.org/schema/integration/spring-integration.xsd">

  <int:annotation-config/>

  <int:gateway default-request-channel="inChannel"
    service-interface="net.lkrnac.book.eiws.chapter08.in.SiWrapperServiceFuture" />

  <int:channel id="inChannel" />
  <int:channel id="aggregatedChannel" />

  <int:service-activator input-channel="aggregatedChannel" ref="writeService"
    method="writeAndIndicateSuccess" />
</beans>
```

The element <int:annotation-config> is the XML equivalent of the @IntegrationComponentScan annotation, so it performs a scan for the @MessageEndpoint components. Better placement of this configuration would be on the main Spring configuration class, but we want to highlight this XML configuration feature of the SI framework. The inbound gateway, service activators, and two channels are constructs we've already seen in previous examples.

When we run this example via the main SiApplication class, we get similar output similar to that of the 0827-aggregator-xml example in Listing 8-101.

Aggregator with Default Headers Example

This example is configured purely with Java. Listing 8-104 shows the inbound gateway.

Listing 8-104. Inbound Gateway for Default Headers Aggregation Example (0829-aggregator-default-headers)

```java
package net.lkrnac.book.eiws.chapter08.in;
import java.util.concurrent.Future;
import org.springframework.integration.annotation.Gateway;
import org.springframework.integration.annotation.MessagingGateway;
import org.springframework.messaging.Message;
```

346

```
@MessagingGateway
public interface SiWrapperServiceFutureAnnotated {
  @Gateway(requestChannel = "inChannel")
  Future<Boolean> processText(Message<String> text);
}
```

This bidirectional gateway returns Future<Boolean> and accepts Message<String> connected to inChannel. Listing 8-105 shows the aggregator connected to inChannel on the other side.

Listing 8-105. Aggregator with Default Headers Example (0829-aggregator-default-headers)

```
package net.lkrnac.book.eiws.chapter08;
import java.util.List;
import org.springframework.integration.annotation.Aggregator;
import org.springframework.integration.annotation.MessageEndpoint;

@MessageEndpoint
public class SimpleAggregator {
  @Aggregator(inputChannel = "inChannel", outputChannel = "aggregatedChannel")
  public String aggregate(List<String> messages) {
    return messages.stream().reduce((m1, m2) -> m1 + "," + m2).get();
  }
}
```

In this case, we don't specify a custom correlation or release strategy. So the defaults are used, based on the correlationId, sequenceSize, and sequenceNumber headers. Listing 8-106 shows the configuration of the service activator.

Listing 8-106. Service Activator for Default Headers Aggregation Example (0829-aggregator-default-headers)

```
package net.lkrnac.book.eiws.chapter08.out;
import net.lkrnac.book.eiws.chapter08.out.WriteRepository;
import org.springframework.beans.factory.annotation.Autowired;
import org.springframework.integration.annotation.ServiceActivator;
import org.springframework.stereotype.Service;

@Service
public class WriteServiceAnnotated {
  private WriteRepository writeRepository;

  @Autowired
  public WriteServiceAnnotated(WriteRepository writeRepository) {
    super();
    this.writeRepository = writeRepository;
  }

  @ServiceActivator(inputChannel = "aggregatedChannel")
  public boolean writeAndIndicateSuccess(String message) {
    return writeRepository.persist(message) == 1;
  }
}
```

The class uses the common WriteRepository to persist the received messages. The @ServiceActivator annotation connects this component to the output of the aggregator. Listing 8-107 shows the asynchronous logic used for sending messages.

Listing 8-107. Asynchronous Sender of Messages Used in Default Headers Aggregation Example (0829-aggregator-default-headers)

```java
package net.lkrnac.book.eiws.chapter08.in;
import java.util.concurrent.Future;
import java.util.concurrent.TimeUnit;
import lombok.extern.slf4j.Slf4j;
import org.springframework.beans.factory.annotation.Autowired;
import org.springframework.integration.support.MessageBuilder;
import org.springframework.messaging.Message;
import org.springframework.scheduling.annotation.Async;
import org.springframework.stereotype.Component;

@Slf4j
@Component
public class AsyncMessageSender {
  private SiWrapperServiceFutureAnnotated wrapperService;

  @Autowired
  public AsyncMessageSender(SiWrapperServiceFutureAnnotated wrapperService) {
    super();
    this.wrapperService = wrapperService;
  }

  @Async("customExecutor")
  public void sendMessage(String stringMessage, int correlationId)
      throws Exception {
    Message<String> message =
        MessageBuilder.withPayload(stringMessage).setSequenceSize(2)
            .setCorrelationId(correlationId).build();

    Future<Boolean> resultFuture = wrapperService.processText(message);
    boolean result = resultFuture.get(1, TimeUnit.SECONDS);
    log.info("Result for " + stringMessage + ": " + result);
  }
}
```

We inject SiWrapperServiceFutureAnnotated, which can consume Message<String> message types, and return a Future<Boolean> result. The asynchronous method sendMessage() constructs messages based on the given stringMessage payload and correlationId parameters using MessageBuilder. The sequenceSize header is hard-coded to value 2, so the aggregator will aggregate the two messages into one. One more header is needed for aggregation: sequenceNumber, which defines the order of messages in the sequence so that aggregator can release all messages from the sequence when they arrive. This header is injected into messages by default.

The rest of the logic should be familiar. We send messages to the SI flow and read the Future<Boolean> result. Subsequently, we wait for the SI flow to respond or time out. Listing 8-108 shows the main class of this example.

Listing 8-108. Main Class of Default Headers Aggregation Example (0829-aggregator-default-headers)

```java
package net.lkrnac.book.eiws.chapter08;
import java.util.concurrent.Executor;
import net.lkrnac.book.eiws.chapter08.in.AsyncMessageSender;
import org.springframework.boot.SpringApplication;
import org.springframework.boot.autoconfigure.SpringBootApplication;
import org.springframework.context.ApplicationContext;
import org.springframework.context.annotation.Bean;
import org.springframework.integration.annotation.IntegrationComponentScan;
import org.springframework.scheduling.annotation.EnableAsync;
import org.springframework.scheduling.concurrent.ThreadPoolTaskExecutor;

@EnableAsync
@SpringBootApplication
@IntegrationComponentScan
public class SiApplication {
  @Bean
  public Executor customExecutor() {
    ThreadPoolTaskExecutor threadPool = new ThreadPoolTaskExecutor();
    threadPool.setCorePoolSize(10);
    return threadPool;
  }

  public static void main(String[] args) throws Exception {
    ApplicationContext ctx = SpringApplication.run(SiApplication.class, args);

    AsyncMessageSender messageSender = ctx.getBean(AsyncMessageSender.class);
    messageSender.sendMessage("message1", 1);
    messageSender.sendMessage("message2", 2);
    messageSender.sendMessage("message2", 2);
    messageSender.sendMessage("message1", 1);
  }
}
```

This performs the SI scan, enables asynchronous processing, configures customExecutor, and starts the Spring Boot application. Notice that we didn't register the channels inChannel and aggregatedChannel anywhere. SI can sometimes figure out wiring without explicit definition of channels. It creates DirectChannels under the hood in such a case (as discussed in the following "Message Channel" section).

After everything is configured, we retrieve the AsyncMessageSender bean and send four messages with correlation IDs. The output after running this class is similar to that of the 0827-aggregator-xml example in Listing 8-101.

Message Channel

The *message channel* is the last category of SI components (alongside the message and message endpoint). It is used to connect message endpoints. A message channel is a simple Spring bean, so no additional infrastructure is needed to fulfill its task. But if needed, messages temporarily stored in a channel can be persisted with JMS or JDBC.

To understand various channel types and their characteristics, it is good to review their inheritance structure, shown in Figure 8-14.

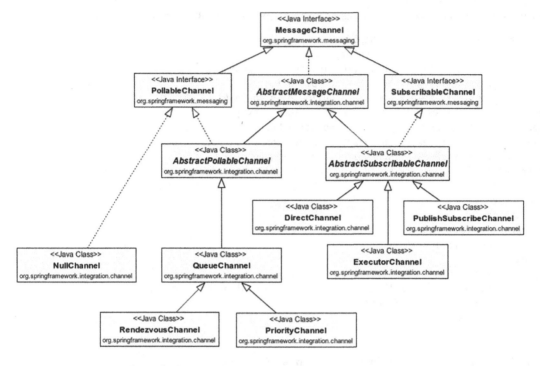

Figure 8-14. *Message channel inheritance structure*

Notice that the interfaces (MessageChannel, PollableChannel, SubscribableMessageChannel) are part of the org.springframework.messaging package, which is located in the spring-messaging module of the Spring Core framework. All the implementations are located in the SI framework itself (the package org.springframework.integration.channel).

Two types of channels are possible in terms of the number of consumers:

- *Point-to-point channel*: Each message is consumed by exactly one endpoint. Can be configured via the XML element <int:channel> or registered as a Java bean. All channel implementations except PublishSubscribeChannel belong here.

- *Publish/subscribe channel*: Each message is sent to all subscribed consumers. Can be configured via the XML element <int:publish-subscribe-channel> or by registering PublishSubscribeChannel as a Spring bean.

From a message hand-off point of view, a message channel can participate in the following:

- Synchronous message passingThe consumer is triggered immediately by using a caller thread.

- If the SI flow contains only synchronous passive components, the caller is blocked until the downstream component replies to the reply channel.

- The channel can propagate transactions or exceptions between the caller and consumer.

- The consumer can use the security context of the caller.

- Implementations: DirectChannel, synchronous PublishSubscribeChannel.

- Asynchronous message passing

  - Consumption is done in a different thread from that of the sending of the message.

  - The consumer can't use the transaction or security context from the sender.

  - The consumer can't propagate exceptions to the sender.

  - Implementations: `QueueChannel`, `PriorityChannel`, `ExecutorChannel`, `RendezvousChannel`, asynchronous `PublishSubscribeChannel`.

DirectChannel

`DirectChannel` is the simplest implementation of a channel. It is a synchronous, point-to-point channel. The consumer needs to subscribe to it, so it will be triggered immediately after the sender sends the message. Because it is synchronous, the caller and sender share the same thread as if their interaction were done via a simple Java call.

The showcase of this channel will refer to previous examples as all of them were using this channel implementation. We can configure it via the following:

- The XML element `<int:channel>` which doesn't use `<int:queue>`, `<int:priority-queue>`, or `<int:dispatcher>` subelements. An example of this configuration is `inChannel` or `aggregatedChannel` in the `0828-aggregator-javaconfig` example project, seen in Listing 8-103.

- Use one of the constructors to create an instance of `DirectChannel` and register it as a Spring bean via the @Bean annotation. The name of this bean then can be used as the channel name in the message endpoint configurations. A Java configuration example can be seen in Listing 8-95 as `inChannel` or `splitChannel` in example project `0826-splitter-javaconfig`.

QueueChannel

`QueueChannel` is the second most used channel implementation. It is an asynchronous, point-to-point channel, whereby the consumer needs to actively poll against it to verify whether the new message arrived. This message passing is done in a separate thread and can cause delays in communication. The consumer component needs to be active (needs to configure the poller).

As it's asynchronous, the transaction and security contexts are not populated from the sender to the consumer. Additionally, the consumer exceptions are not propagated back to the sender.

Because the consumer is polling for messages, the channel obviously needs to be able to temporarily store messages. Internally, it uses the standard Java BlockingQueue to store them. So it uses first-in/first-out (FIFO) ordering of messages. When we configure QueueChannel, you have the option to configure the queue capacity. If the capacity of the messages is reached, the sender will be blocked until room is available or the time-out is reached. By default, this queue has the capacity `Integer.MAX_VALUE`.

To configure QueueChannel, you can do the following:

- Use the XML element `<int:channel>` with the `<int:queue>` subelement. The capacity can be defined via the `capacity` attribute of `<int:queue>`. An example of this configuration is `inChannel` in the `0821-bridge-xml` example project, seen in Listing 8-81.

- Use one of constructors to create an instance of QueueChannel and register it as a Spring bean via the @Bean annotation. The queue capacity can be passed to the constructor as a parameter. The name of this bean can then be used as the channel name in the message endpoint configurations. A Java configuration example can be seen in Listing 8-89 as `inChannel` in example project `0823-bridge-to-javaconfig`.

PriorityChannel

PriorityChannel is the child class of QueueChannel. Therefore, they are similar and share most characteristics. The only difference is that PriorityChannel does not use FIFO for message ordering in the underlying queue storage. With PriorityChannel, we are able to specify the order in which messages will be consumed from the channel. This order can be configured in two ways:

- Based on the message header priority. Messages with a higher-priority value will be consumed first. This mechanism is used by default when comparator is not configured for PriorityChannel.

- Based on the Comparator<Message<T>> implementation, using custom logic for message comparison.

PriorityChannel can be configured via the following:

- The XML element <int:channel> with the <int:priority-queue> subelement.

- Use one of constructors to create an instance of PriorityChannel and register it as a Spring bean via the @Bean annotation. The comparator or queue capacity can be configured as constructor parameters. The name of this bean can then be used as the channel name in the message endpoint configurations.

PriorityChannel Example

This example implements our own comparator to order messages in PriorityChannel. It is an XML-based configuration. Listing 8-109 shows the comparator implementation.

Listing 8-109. Comparator for PriorityChannel Example (0830-channel-priority-xml)

```
package net.lkrnac.book.eiws.chapter08;
import java.util.Comparator;
import org.springframework.messaging.Message;
import org.springframework.stereotype.Component;

@Component
public class SimpleMessageComparator implements Comparator<Message<String>> {
  @Override
  public int compare(Message<String> o1, Message<String> o2) {
    return -1 * o1.getPayload().compareTo(o2.getPayload());
  }
}
```

It's worth remembering the Comparator<T>.compare() contract here. The comparator will decide that o1 in comparison to o2 is less than/equal to/greater than based on the returned value negative integer/zero/positive integer. Lesser objects will be consumed first from the channel.

In this case, we use reverse natural ordering of the String message payload. Natural ordering is in String's case alphabetical. So if our messages should be consumed from the channel in reverse alphabetical order, we use this comparator. Listing 8-110 shows the XML SI configuration.

Listing 8-110. XML SI Configuration for PriorityChannel Example (File si-config.xml in Folder src/main/resources of Example Project 0830-channel-priority-xml)

```xml
<?xml version="1.0" encoding="UTF-8"?>
<beans xmlns="http://www.springframework.org/schema/beans"
  xmlns:xsi="http://www.w3.org/2001/XMLSchema-instance"
  xmlns:int="http://www.springframework.org/schema/integration"
  xmlns:context="http://www.springframework.org/schema/context"
  xsi:schemaLocation="http://www.springframework.org/schema/beans
    http://www.springframework.org/schema/beans/spring-beans.xsd
    http://www.springframework.org/schema/integration
    http://www.springframework.org/schema/integration/spring-integration.xsd">

  <int:gateway default-request-channel="inChannel"
    service-interface="net.lkrnac.book.eiws.chapter08.in.SiWrapperServiceVoid" />

  <int:channel id="inChannel">
    <int:priority-queue capacity="10" comparator="simpleMessageComparator"/>
  </int:channel>

  <int:outbound-channel-adapter channel="inChannel" ref="writeService" method="write">
    <int:poller receive-timeout="1" fixed-delay="100" max-messages-per-poll="1"/>
  </int:outbound-channel-adapter>
</beans>
```

On the input side of the SI flow, we use the inbound gateway mapped to our common service interface SiWrapperServiceVoid and connected to inChannel. This in channel is configured as the priority channel with capacity 10 and SimpleMessageComparator bean as comparator.

The outbound channel adapter (connected to inChannel) is configured as an active component with a polling interval of 100 ms. It will also read only one message per poll cycle (attribute max-messages-per-poll) and will time out after 1 ms when reading from inChannel. The latter configuration is needed to highlight the changed ordering of the priority channel. If we didn't configure such a short interval, the outbound channel adapter would eagerly wait to consume the first message that appears in the channel queue, and we wouldn't have a chance to gather at least two messages.

Listing 8-111 shows the main class of this example.

Listing 8-111. Main Class of PriorityChannel Example (0830-channel-priority-xml)

```java
package net.lkrnac.book.eiws.chapter08;
import lombok.extern.slf4j.Slf4j;
import net.lkrnac.book.eiws.chapter08.in.SiWrapperServiceVoid;
import org.springframework.boot.SpringApplication;
import org.springframework.boot.autoconfigure.SpringBootApplication;
import org.springframework.context.ApplicationContext;
import org.springframework.context.annotation.ImportResource;

@Slf4j
@SpringBootApplication
@ImportResource("classpath:si-config.xml")
public class SiApplication {
  private static final String MESSAGE2 = "message2";
  private static final String MESSAGE1 = "message1";
```

```java
public static void main(String[] args) throws InterruptedException {
  ApplicationContext ctx = SpringApplication.run(SiApplication.class, args);

  SiWrapperServiceVoid wrapperService =
      ctx.getBean(SiWrapperServiceVoid.class);
  log.info("Starting to send messages...");
  wrapperService.processText(MESSAGE1);
  log.info(MESSAGE1 + " sent");
  wrapperService.processText(MESSAGE2);
  log.info(MESSAGE2 + " sent");
  }
}
```

After running the application with the XML SI configuration we described, we read the service interface bean SiWrapperServiceVoid from the Spring context to send messages. We also log the information that the message was sent to the SI flow already. Listing 8-112 shows the output when we run this main class.

Listing 8-112. Output of PriorityChannel Example (0830-channel-priority-xml)

```
2015-08-30 14:36:35.149  INFO 16162 --- [            main]
n.l.book.eiws.chapter08.SiApplication    : Starting to send messages...
2015-08-30 14:36:35.160  INFO 16162 --- [            main]
n.l.book.eiws.chapter08.SiApplication    : message1 sent
2015-08-30 14:36:35.160  INFO 16162 --- [            main]
n.l.book.eiws.chapter08.SiApplication    : message2 sent
2015-08-30 14:36:35.272  INFO 16162 --- [ask-scheduler-1]
n.l.b.e.chapter08.out.WriteRepository    : Text persisted: message2
2015-08-30 14:36:35.375  INFO 16162 --- [ask-scheduler-2]
n.l.b.e.chapter08.out.WriteRepository    : Text persisted: message1
```

Information about sending both messages is printed first. This means that the caller (main thread) isn't blocked with the wrapperService.processText() call. When both messages are gathered in the priority channel, the output channel adapter reads them in reverse alphabetical order, as we configured.

RendezvousChannel

RendezvousChannel is also a child class of QueueChannel, but it uses SynchronousQueue as the queue implementation (it's BlockingQueue configured with zero capacity). So it is able to perform synchronously (via direct handoff) but at the same time act as an active component (consumer is polling for messages). The sender of the message is blocked until the active consumer reads the message from RendezvousChannel.

RendezvousChannel can be configured via the following:

- The XML element <int:channel> with the <int:rendezvous-queue/> subelement.

- Use one of the constructors to create an instance of RendezvousChannel and register it as a Spring bean via the @Bean annotation. The name of this bean can be then used as the channel name in the message endpoint configuration.

RendezvousChannel Example

Listing 8-113 shows the XML SI configuration.

Listing 8-113. SI Configuration for RendezvousChannel Example (File si-config.xml in Folder src/main/resources of Example Project 0831-channel-rendezvous-xml)

```xml
<?xml version="1.0" encoding="UTF-8"?>
<beans xmlns="http://www.springframework.org/schema/beans"
  xmlns:xsi="http://www.w3.org/2001/XMLSchema-instance"
  xmlns:int="http://www.springframework.org/schema/integration"
  xmlns:context="http://www.springframework.org/schema/context"
  xsi:schemaLocation="http://www.springframework.org/schema/beans
    http://www.springframework.org/schema/beans/spring-beans.xsd
    http://www.springframework.org/schema/integration
    http://www.springframework.org/schema/integration/spring-integration.xsd">

  <int:gateway default-request-channel="inChannel"
    service-interface="net.lkrnac.book.eiws.chapter08.in.SiWrapperServiceVoid" />

  <int:channel id="inChannel">
    <int:rendezvous-queue/>
  </int:channel>

  <int:outbound-channel-adapter channel="inChannel" ref="writeService" method="write">
      <int:poller fixed-delay="1000" max-messages-per-poll="1"/>
  </int:outbound-channel-adapter>
</beans>
```

The inChannel channel is configured as RendezvousChannel and is connected to the inbound gateway and outbound channel adapter. In this case, the outbound channel adapter polls at 1-second intervals and reads one message at the per poll cycle. This polling was chosen to highlight RendezvousChannel features in the output from Listing 8-114. The main class is the same as in the 0830-channel-priority-xml example in Listing 8-111.

Listing 8-114. Output of RendezvousChannel Example (0831-channel-rendezvous-xml)

```
2015-08-30 14:38:55.215  INFO 16238 --- [          main]
n.l.book.eiws.chapter08.SiApplication    : Starting to send messages...
2015-08-30 14:38:55.224  INFO 16238 --- [          main]
n.l.book.eiws.chapter08.SiApplication    : message1 sent
2015-08-30 14:38:55.250  INFO 16238 --- [ask-scheduler-1]
n.l.b.e.chapter08.out.WriteRepository    : Text persisted: message1
2015-08-30 14:38:56.252  INFO 16238 --- [          main]
n.l.book.eiws.chapter08.SiApplication    : message2 sent
2015-08-30 14:38:56.254  INFO 16238 --- [ask-scheduler-1]
n.l.b.e.chapter08.out.WriteRepository    : Text persisted: message2
```

Notice the timing on these log entries. The handoff of message1 happens nearly immediately as it's sent to the SI flow. This is because the outbound channel adapter is already waiting for the message to arrive to inChannel. But the second handoff of message2 happens approximately 1 second after the handoff of message1. This is because the main thread is blocked in the wrapperService.processText(MESSAGE2) call until the channel adapter poller triggers reading of message2.

ExecutorChannel

ExecutorChannel is a subscribable channel, so the consumer is a passive component waiting to be triggered by the received message. But as opposed to DirectChannel, the message is passed from the sender to the consumer in a separate thread. The dispatch of the message is delegated to the TaskExecutor instance configured for ExecutorChannel.

It can be configured via the following:

- The XML element <int:channel> with the <int:dispatcher task-executor="..."/> subelement.

- Use one of constructors to create an instance of ExecutorChannel and register it as a Spring bean via the @Bean annotation. The name of this bean can then be used as the channel name in the message endpoint configurations.

ExecutorChannel Example

Listing 8-115 shows the SI configuration.

Listing 8-115. SI Configuration for ExecutorsChannel Example (File si-config.xml in Folder src/main/resources of Example Project 0832-channel-executor-xml)

```xml
<?xml version="1.0" encoding="UTF-8"?>
<beans xmlns="http://www.springframework.org/schema/beans"
  xmlns:xsi="http://www.w3.org/2001/XMLSchema-instance"
  xmlns:int="http://www.springframework.org/schema/integration"
  xmlns:context="http://www.springframework.org/schema/context"
  xmlns:task="http://www.springframework.org/schema/task"
  xsi:schemaLocation="http://www.springframework.org/schema/task
    http://www.springframework.org/schema/task/spring-task.xsd
    http://www.springframework.org/schema/beans
    http://www.springframework.org/schema/beans/spring-beans.xsd
    http://www.springframework.org/schema/context
    http://www.springframework.org/schema/context/spring-context.xsd
    http://www.springframework.org/schema/integration
    http://www.springframework.org/schema/integration/spring-integration.xsd">

  <int:gateway default-request-channel="inChannel"
    service-interface="net.lkrnac.book.eiws.chapter08.in.SiWrapperServiceVoid" />

  <task:executor id="executor" pool-size="10"/>

  <int:channel id="inChannel">
    <int:dispatcher task-executor="executor"/>
  </int:channel>

  <int:outbound-channel-adapter channel="inChannel" ref="writeService" method="write" />
</beans>
```

The inChannel channel is configured as ExecutorChannel, using the TaskExecutor bean with the name executor. This TaskExecutor bean is also created in this configuration file by the XML element <task:executor>. inChannel is connected to the inbound gateway with our common service interface SiWrapperServiceVoid. The consumer of inChannel is in this case the passive outbound channel adapter mapped to the common WriteService.write().

We again use the same main class as for 0830-channel-priority-xml from Listing 8-111. When we run this main class, we can observe the output in Listing 8-116.

Listing 8-116. Output of ExecutorChannel Example

```
2015-08-30 15:42:48.844  INFO 18377 --- [            main]
n.l.book.eiws.chapter08.SiApplication    : Starting to send messages...
2015-08-30 15:42:48.858  INFO 18377 --- [            main]
n.l.book.eiws.chapter08.SiApplication    : message1 sent
2015-08-30 15:42:48.859  INFO 18377 --- [            main]
n.l.book.eiws.chapter08.SiApplication    : message2 sent
2015-08-30 15:42:48.877  INFO 18377 --- [      executor-1]
n.l.b.e.chapter08.out.WriteRepository    : Text persisted: message1
2015-08-30 15:42:48.877  INFO 18377 --- [      executor-2]
n.l.b.e.chapter08.out.WriteRepository    : Text persisted: message2
```

Notice that the handoff occurs immediately and in separate threads (using the executor thread pool) without blocking the caller (main) thread.

PublishSubscribeChannel

PublishSubscribeChannel uses the publish/subscribe model of messaging, whereby all the subscribers will receive message sent to it. So our message can have multiple consumers.

PublishSubscribeChannel can be configured via the following:

- The XML element <int:publish-subscribe-channel>.

- Use one of the constructors to create an instance of PublishSubscribeChannel and register it as a Spring bean via the @Bean annotation. The name of this bean can then be used as the channel name in the message endpoint configurations.

We can configure PublishSubscribeChannel to handle message passing as follows:

- Synchronously

  - Default configuration

  - Processing of all consumers is done sequentially in the sender's thread, so each consumer needs to wait for other consumers.

  - *Can* propagate transaction, security context, and exceptions between consumers and sender.

- Asynchronously

  - Can be configured with the `task-executor` attribute of `<int:publish-subscribe-channel>`, whereby we specify the reference to the `TaskExecutor` instance.

  - Each consumer processing can be done in a separate thread and thus they occur concurrently.

  - Transaction propagation, passing the security context, and bubbling exceptions between consumers and sender *doesn't work in this mode.*

PublishSubscribeChannel example

Listing 8-117 shows the SI configuration.

Listing 8-117. SI Configuration of PublishSubscribeChannel Example (File si-config.xml in Folder src/ main/resources of Example Project 0833-channel-pub-sub-xml)

```xml
<?xml version="1.0" encoding="UTF-8"?>
<beans xmlns="http://www.springframework.org/schema/beans"
  xmlns:xsi="http://www.w3.org/2001/XMLSchema-instance"
  xmlns:int="http://www.springframework.org/schema/integration"
  xmlns:context="http://www.springframework.org/schema/context"
  xsi:schemaLocation="http://www.springframework.org/schema/beans
    http://www.springframework.org/schema/beans/spring-beans.xsd
    http://www.springframework.org/schema/integration
    http://www.springframework.org/schema/integration/spring-integration.xsd">

  <int:gateway default-request-channel="inChannel"
    service-interface="net.lkrnac.book.eiws.chapter08.in.SiWrapperServiceVoid" />

  <int:publish-subscribe-channel id="inChannel" />

  <int:outbound-channel-adapter channel="inChannel" ref="writeService" method="write"/>
  <int:outbound-channel-adapter channel="inChannel" ref="writeService" method="write"/>
</beans>
```

We use in this case the synchronous `PublishSubscribeChannel` with the name `inChannel`, consuming messages from the inbound gateway with the common service interface `SiWrapperServiceVoid`. Two outbound channel adapters are configured to listen to `inChannel`, delegating messages to our common `WriteService.write()`.

This example reuses the same main class as for 0830-channel-priority-xml in Listing 8-111. When we run it, we get the output in Listing 8-118.

Listing 8-118. Output of PublishSubscribeChannel Example

```
2015-08-30 18:20:05.017  INFO 21389 --- [            main]
n.l.book.eiws.chapter08.SiApplication    : Starting to send messages...
2015-08-30 18:20:05.092  INFO 21389 --- [            main]
n.l.b.e.chapter08.out.WriteRepository    : Text persisted: message1
2015-08-30 18:20:05.093  INFO 21389 --- [            main]
```

```
n.l.b.e.chapter08.out.WriteRepository     : Text persisted: message1
2015-08-30 18:20:05.093  INFO 21389 --- [          main]
n.l.book.eiws.chapter08.SiApplication     : message1 sent
2015-08-30 18:20:05.119  INFO 21389 --- [          main]
n.l.b.e.chapter08.out.WriteRepository     : Text persisted: message2
2015-08-30 18:20:05.120  INFO 21389 --- [          main]
n.l.b.e.chapter08.out.WriteRepository     : Text persisted: message2
2015-08-30 18:20:05.120  INFO 21389 --- [          main]
n.l.book.eiws.chapter08.SiApplication     : message2 sent
```

This whole communication occurs sequentially in a single main thread. Each message is persisted twice, because two consumers are configured for each message (two output channel adapters connected to inChannel).

NullChannel

NullChannel is a special type of channel used for discarding messages. SI creates this channel by default, so we can use it by specifying nullChannel as the channel name.

Channel Interceptor

As its name suggests, a *channel interceptor* is used for intercepting channels. We can implement the interface org.springframework.messaging.support.ChannelInterceptor and register it as a Spring bean and use this custom logic when on these interception points: preSend, postSend, afterSendCompletion, preReceive, postReceive, afterReceiveCompletion.

If the intercepted channel is AbstractSubscribableChannel, only the preSend, postSend, and afterSendCompletion interception points are relevant, because the consumer is triggered by the channel and is not executing the receive action. If the intercepted channel is AbstractPollableChannel, all interception points are relevant, because it has the send action as well as receive available.

The interception points afterSendCompletion and afterReceiveCompletion are executed only after the related action (send/receive) is successful.

A channel interceptor can be configured as follows:

- *Global interceptor*: The top-level XML element <int:channel-interceptor>, where we can specify the pattern attribute for channel names we want to intercept. The bean implementing the org.springframework.messaging.support. ChannelInterceptor interface can be configured via the ref attribute or via the <bean> subelement.

- *Local interceptor*: The channel XML subelement <int:interceptors>, where we can specify the list of interceptors for a particular channel. The bean implementing the ChannelInterceptor interface can be configured via the <ref> subelement of the <int:interceptors> tag.

Channel Interceptor Example

Listing 8-119 shows a simple implementation of ChannelInterceptor.

Listing 8-119. Interceptor Implementation Example (0834-channel-interceptor-xml)

```java
package net.lkrnac.book.eiws.chapter08;
import lombok.extern.slf4j.Slf4j;
import org.springframework.messaging.Message;
import org.springframework.messaging.MessageChannel;
import org.springframework.messaging.support.ChannelInterceptor;
import org.springframework.stereotype.Component;

@Slf4j
@Component
public class SimpleInterceptor implements ChannelInterceptor {
  @Override
  public Message<?> preSend(Message<?> message, MessageChannel channel) {
    log.info("Going to send message {} to channel {}", message.getPayload(),
        channel);
    return message;
  }

  @Override
  public void postSend(Message<?> message, MessageChannel channel, boolean sent) {
    log.info("Sending of message {} to channel {} finished",
        message.getPayload(), channel);
  }

  @Override
  public void afterSendCompletion(Message<?> message, MessageChannel channel,
      boolean sent, Exception ex) {
    log.info("Message {} was successfully send to channel {}",
        message.getPayload(), channel);
  }

  @Override
  public boolean preReceive(MessageChannel channel) {
    log.info("Going to receive message from channel {}", channel);
    return true;
  }

  @Override
  public Message<?> postReceive(Message<?> message, MessageChannel channel) {
    log.info("Receiving of message {} from channel {} finished",
        message.getPayload(), channel);
    return message;
  }
```

```
@Override
public void afterReceiveCompletion(Message<?> message,
    MessageChannel channel, Exception ex) {
  log.info("Message {} was successfully received from channel {}",
    message.getPayload(), channel);
  }
}
```

On each interception point that we need to implement as a contract for the ChannelInterceptor interface, we log information about hitting it. Notice that the preSend and postReceive intercept points have an option to return the message instance as a return value, and thus replace the message if needed. Also, the preReceive method returns a Boolean value, which may stop the receive action if false is returned. Listing 8-120 shows the SI configuration.

Listing 8-120. SI Configuration of Channel Interceptor Example (File si-config.xml in Folder src/main/resources of Example Project 0834-channel-interceptor-xml)

```xml
<?xml version="1.0" encoding="UTF-8"?>
<beans xmlns="http://www.springframework.org/schema/beans"
  xmlns:xsi=http://www.w3.org/2001/XMLSchema-instance
  xmlns:int="http://www.springframework.org/schema/integration"
  xmlns:context="http://www.springframework.org/schema/context"
  xsi:schemaLocation="http://www.springframework.org/schema/beans
    http://www.springframework.org/schema/beans/spring-beans.xsd
    http://www.springframework.org/schema/integration
    http://www.springframework.org/schema/integration/spring-integration.xsd">

  <int:gateway default-request-channel="inChannel"
    service-interface="net.lkrnac.book.eiws.chapter08.in.SiWrapperServiceVoid" />

  <int:channel-interceptor pattern="in*" ref="simpleInterceptor"/>

  <int:channel id="inChannel">
    <int:queue capacity="10"/>
  </int:channel>

  <int:outbound-channel-adapter channel="inChannel" ref="writeService" method="write">
    <int:poller fixed-rate="100" max-messages-per-poll="1"/>
  </int:outbound-channel-adapter>
</beans>
```

The configuration of the input and output component is common in our examples. We use the QueueChannel implementation, whereby the outbound channel adapter polls against inChannel. The channel interceptor configuration is interesting; the SimpleInterceptor bean is configured as the interceptor for all channels whose name starts with the in prefix.

The main class is again reused from 0830-channel-priority-xml (Listing 8-111). When we run it, we get the output in Listing 8-121.

Listing 8-121. Output of Channel Interceptor Example

```
2015-08-30 20:05:00.379  INFO 24624 --- [            main]
n.l.book.eiws.chapter08.SiApplication    : Starting to send messages...
2015-08-30 20:05:00.390  INFO 24624 --- [            main]
n.l.b.eiws.chapter08.SimpleInterceptor   : Going to send message GenericMessage
[payload=message1, headers={id=a1f4c8ca-c227-3315-646c-e14820558db7,
timestamp=1440961500390}]
to channel inChannel
2015-08-30 20:05:00.391  INFO 24624 --- [            main]
n.l.b.eiws.chapter08.SimpleInterceptor   : Message GenericMessage [payload=message1,
headers={id=a1f4c8ca-c227-3315-646c-e14820558db7, timestamp=1440961500390}] was successfully
send to channel inChannel
2015-08-30 20:05:00.391  INFO 24624 --- [ask-scheduler-1]
n.l.b.eiws.chapter08.SimpleInterceptor   : Message GenericMessage [payload=message1,
headers={id=a1f4c8ca-c227-3315-646c-e14820558db7, timestamp=1440961500390}] was successfully
received to channel inChannel
2015-08-30 20:05:00.392  INFO 24624 --- [ask-scheduler-1]
n.l.b.eiws.chapter08.SimpleInterceptor   : Message GenericMessage [payload=message1,
headers={id=a1f4c8ca-c227-3315-646c-e14820558db7, timestamp=1440961500390}] was received to
channel inChannel
2015-08-30 20:05:00.392  INFO 24624 --- [            main]
n.l.b.eiws.chapter08.SimpleInterceptor   : Message GenericMessage [payload=message1,
headers={id=a1f4c8ca-c227-3315-646c-e14820558db7, timestamp=1440961500390}] was send to
channel inChannel
2015-08-30 20:05:00.392  INFO 24624 --- [            main]
n.l.book.eiws.chapter08.SiApplication    : message1 sent
...
```

We include log entries for only one message. The second message would have similar log entries. All the interception points were executed because the consumer needs to poll (explicitly execute `AbstractPollableChannel.receive()`) against inChannel.

Wire Tap

A *wire tap* is one of the original enterprise integration patterns and, in fact, is a special type of interceptor. It sends a message to another channel without affecting the original flow. This behavior is especially useful for monitoring and debugging.

It can be configured as follows:

- *Global wire tap*: Can be configured as a top-level XML element `<int:wire-tap>`. It can specify a pattern for channel names to intercept.

- *Local wire tap*: Can be configured as part of the `<int:interceptors>` list for the channel and uses the `<int:wire-tap>` XML subelement.

Wire Tap Example

Listing 8-122 shows the SI configuration.

Listing 8-122. SI Configuration of Wire Tap Example (File si-config.xml in Folder src/main/resources of
Example Project 0835-channel-wire-tap-xml)

```xml
<?xml version="1.0" encoding="UTF-8"?>
<beans xmlns="http://www.springframework.org/schema/beans"
  xmlns:xsi="http://www.w3.org/2001/XMLSchema-instance"
  xmlns:int="http://www.springframework.org/schema/integration"
  xmlns:context="http://www.springframework.org/schema/context"
  xsi:schemaLocation="http://www.springframework.org/schema/beans
    http://www.springframework.org/schema/beans/spring-beans.xsd
    http://www.springframework.org/schema/integration
    http://www.springframework.org/schema/integration/spring-integration.xsd">

  <int:gateway default-request-channel="inChannel"
    service-interface="net.lkrnac.book.eiws.chapter08.in.SiWrapperServiceVoid" />

  <int:channel id="inChannel">
    <int:interceptors>
        <int:wire-tap channel="logChannel"/>
    </int:interceptors>
  </int:channel>

  <int:outbound-channel-adapter channel="inChannel" ref="writeService" method="write"/>

  <int:channel id="logChannel"/>
  <int:logging-channel-adapter channel="logChannel" level="INFO"/>
</beans>
```

The inChannel channel is configured with the interceptors list, and only the wire tap is configured. This
wire tap sends messages to logChannel, which is connected to the logging channel adapter. It will log the
message payload if the correct logging level is configured (in this case, at least INFO).

The main message flow is untouched, so the message is received by the inbound gateway with
the service interface SiWrapperServiceVoid and handed to the outbound channel adapter mapped to
WriteService.write().

We again borrow the main class from Listing 8-111 of the 0830-channel-priority-xml example project.
When we run it, we get the output in Listing 8-123.

Listing 8-123. Output of Wire Tap Example

```
2015-08-30 20:55:48.647  INFO 26516 --- [            main]
n.l.book.eiws.chapter08.SiApplication    : Starting to send messages...
2015-08-30 20:55:48.656  INFO 26516 --- [            main]
o.s.integration.handler.LoggingHandler   : message1
2015-08-30 20:55:48.673  INFO 26516 --- [            main]
n.l.b.e.chapter08.out.WriteRepository    : Text persisted: message1
2015-08-30 20:55:48.674  INFO 26516 --- [            main]
n.l.book.eiws.chapter08.SiApplication    : message1 sent
2015-08-30 20:55:48.675  INFO 26516 --- [            main]
```

```
o.s.integration.handler.LoggingHandler    : message2
2015-08-30 20:55:48.676  INFO 26516 --- [          main]
n.l.b.e.chapter08.out.WriteRepository     : Text persisted: message2
2015-08-30 20:55:48.677  INFO 26516 --- [          main]
n.l.book.eiws.chapter08.SiApplication     : message2 sent
```

As we expect, the main flow happens correctly. In addition, we have the message payload logged by the SI internal `LoggingHandler`.

Error Handling

Reliable error handling is an important part of each production-ready application. An SI application is no exception. Therefore, SI provides various mechanisms to simplify error-handling implementations. We can divide these mechanisms as follows:

- *Synchronous error handling*: When an error happens during synchronous message passing, it is wrapped into `org.springframework.messaging.MessageHandlingException` and propagated back to the sender of the message.

- *Asynchronous error handling*

  - *Unidirectional flow*: In the case of an asynchronous handoff, the exception can't be propagated to the sender. So SI in this case creates `org.springframework.messaging.support.ErrorMessage` from the exception and sends this message to a suitable `errorChannel`.

  - *Bidirectional flow*: The error is propagated to the sender of the messages even if we are dealing with an asynchronous message handoff.

We mentioned that `errorChanel` is used to send `ErrorMessage` in case an exception is thrown in a unidirectional asynchronous message flow. But SI enables us to configure `errorChannel` in various ways:

- *Message-specific error channel*: If a message has a specified header with the name `errorChannel`, errors caused by this message will be sent to the channel specified by this header.

- *Component-specific error channel*: If the component that initiated the asynchronous message dispatch has the specified `error-channel`, the error message that occurs in its thread will be sent to the channel specified by this attribute (notice that it has to be an asynchronous dispatch, because a synchronous dispatch represents a synchronous message passing where the error is propagated to the sender).

- *Global error channel*: If none of the preceding mechanisms is matched, the global error channel will be used to handle error messages. SI creates by default the publish/subscribe `errorChannel`, which sends error messages to the logging component. So, by default, all error messages are at least logged by the logging library used in the project. If needed, we can override this default global error channel by explicit definition of the channel with the name `errorChannel`.

It's also worth mentioning that SI provides a special type of router only for routing `ErrorMessage` messages based on the type of `Exception` raised. It can be configured via the `<int:exception-type-router>` XML element.

Custom Class in Error-Handling Examples

Before we jump to error-handling examples, let's introduce the class in Listing 8-124, which will be used for error simulation.

Listing 8-124. Common Class for Error-Handling Examples

```java
package net.lkrnac.book.eiws.chapter08.out;
import org.springframework.stereotype.Service;

@Service
public class WriteServiceWithError {
  public boolean writeAndIndicateSuccess(String message) {
    throw new IllegalStateException("error occurred");
  }

  public void write(String message) {
    throw new IllegalStateException("error occurred");
  }
}
```

This Spring service bean throws an exception when the write() or writeAndIndicateSuccess() method is executed.

Synchronous Error Propagation Example

Listing 8-125 shows the SI configuration for this example.

Listing 8-125. SI Configuration for Synchronous Error Propagation Example (File si-config.xml in Folder src/main/resources of Example Project 0836-error-handling-sync)

```xml
<?xml version="1.0" encoding="UTF-8"?>
<beans xmlns="http://www.springframework.org/schema/beans"
  xmlns:xsi="http://www.w3.org/2001/XMLSchema-instance"
  xmlns:int="http://www.springframework.org/schema/integration"
  xsi:schemaLocation="http://www.springframework.org/schema/beans
    http://www.springframework.org/schema/beans/spring-beans.xsd
    http://www.springframework.org/schema/integration
    http://www.springframework.org/schema/integration/spring-integration.xsd">

  <int:gateway default-request-channel="inChannel"
    service-interface="net.lkrnac.book.eiws.chapter08.in.SiWrapperServiceVoid" />

  <int:channel id="inChannel" />

  <int:outbound-channel-adapter channel="inChannel"  ref="writeServiceWithError"
    method="write" />
</beans>
```

The inbound gateway is mapped to our common service interface `SiWrapperServiceVoid`, so we are dealing with a unidirectional flow. The message is sent from the inbound gateway into the outbound channel adapter mapped to the `WriteServiceWithError.write()` method. Listing 8-126 shows the main class of this example.

Listing 8-126. Main Class of Synchronous Error Propagation Example (0836-error-handling-sync)

```
package net.lkrnac.book.eiws.chapter08;
import lombok.extern.slf4j.Slf4j;
import net.lkrnac.book.eiws.chapter08.in.SiWrapperServiceVoid;
import org.springframework.boot.SpringApplication;
import org.springframework.boot.autoconfigure.SpringBootApplication;
import org.springframework.context.ApplicationContext;
import org.springframework.context.annotation.ImportResource;

@Slf4j
@SpringBootApplication
@ImportResource("classpath:si-config.xml")
public class SiApplication {
  public static void main(String[] args) throws InterruptedException {
    ApplicationContext ctx = SpringApplication.run(SiApplication.class, args);

    try {
      SiWrapperServiceVoid wrapperService =
          ctx.getBean(SiWrapperServiceVoid.class);
      wrapperService.processText("simple message");
    } catch (IllegalStateException ise) {
      log.info("Exception thrown from SI flow", ise);
    }
  }
}
```

This Spring Boot application includes the `si-config.xml` SI flow and starts the Spring context. After that, we retrieve the service interface from the context and send the message. The sending logic is in the `try-catch` block, because we are expecting `IllegalStateException` here. Listing 8-127 shows the output of this example after running the main class.

Listing 8-127. Output of Synchronous Error Propagation Example

```
2015-08-31 20:30:57.294  INFO 13445 --- [          main]
n.l.book.eiws.chapter08.SiApplication    : Exception thrown from SI flow

java.lang.IllegalStateException: error occurred
        at
net.lkrnac.book.eiws.chapter08.out.WriteServiceWithError.write(WriteServiceWithError.java:12)
        at sun.reflect.NativeMethodAccessorImpl.invoke0(Native Method)
        ...
        at
org.springframework.aop.framework.JdkDynamicAopProxy.invoke(JdkDynamicAopProxy.java:207)
        at com.sun.proxy.$Proxy31.processText(Unknown Source)
        at net.lkrnac.book.eiws.chapter08.SiApplication.main(SiApplication.java:21)
```

An error is thrown in `WriteServiceWithError.write()` and bubbles up to `SiApplication.main()` via a lot of SI and Spring calls (represented by three dots in the listing). So this covers the synchronous message-passing scenario, whereby an error is propagated back to the sender of the message.

Asynchronous Bidirectional Flow

Listing 8-128 shows the SI configuration.

Listing 8-128. SI Configuration for Asynchronous Bidirectional Flow Error Propagation Example (File si-config.xml in Folder src/main/resources of Example Project 0837-error-propagated-async)

```xml
<?xml version="1.0" encoding="UTF-8"?>
<beans xmlns="http://www.springframework.org/schema/beans"
  xmlns:xsi="http://www.w3.org/2001/XMLSchema-instance"
  xmlns:int="http://www.springframework.org/schema/integration"
  xsi:schemaLocation="http://www.springframework.org/schema/beans
    http://www.springframework.org/schema/beans/spring-beans.xsd
    http://www.springframework.org/schema/integration
    http://www.springframework.org/schema/integration/spring-integration.xsd">

  <int:gateway default-request-channel="inChannel"
    service-interface="net.lkrnac.book.eiws.chapter08.in.SiWrapperService" />

  <int:channel id="inChannel">
    <int:queue capacity="10"/>
  </int:channel>

  <int:service-activator input-channel="inChannel" ref="writeServiceWithError"
    method="writeAndIndicateSuccess">
    <int:poller fixed-delay="100"/>
  </int:service-activator>
</beans>
```

The inbound gateway uses the `SiWrapperService` service interface, which indicates a bidirectional flow. `inChannel` is `QueueChannel` with capacity 10, which is connected to the service activator component mapped to `WriteServiceWithError.writeAndIndicateSuccess()`. It is an active component polling for messages every 100 ms. Listing 8-129 shows the main class of this example.

Listing 8-129. Main Class of Asynchronous Bidirectional Flow Error Propagation Example (0837-error-propagated-async)

```java
package net.lkrnac.book.eiws.chapter08;
import lombok.extern.slf4j.Slf4j;
import net.lkrnac.book.eiws.chapter08.in.SiWrapperService;
import org.springframework.boot.SpringApplication;
import org.springframework.boot.autoconfigure.SpringBootApplication;
import org.springframework.context.ApplicationContext;
import org.springframework.context.annotation.ImportResource;

@Slf4j
@SpringBootApplication
@ImportResource("classpath:si-config.xml")
```

```java
public class SiApplication {
  public static void main(String[] args) throws InterruptedException {
    ApplicationContext ctx = SpringApplication.run(SiApplication.class, args);

    SiWrapperService wrapperService = ctx.getBean(SiWrapperService.class);
    try {
      boolean result = wrapperService.processText("simple message");
      log.info("Result: " + result);
    } catch (IllegalStateException ise) {
      log.info("Exception thrown from SI flow", ise);
    }
  }
}
```

This Spring Boot main class uses the bidirectional service interface SiWrapperService bean to send a message into the SI flow. The message is sent in the try-catch block to prove that SI will propagate an exception to the main thread even when it's thrown in a separate thread. When we run this example, we can observe the output in Listing 8-130.

Listing 8-130. Output of Asynchronous Bidirectional Flow Error Propagation Example

```
2015-08-31 20:42:40.139  INFO 14052 --- [          main]
n.l.book.eiws.chapter08.SiApplication    : Exception thrown from SI flow

java.lang.IllegalStateException: error occurred
        at
net.lkrnac.book.eiws.chapter08.out.WriteServiceWithError.writeAndIndicateSuccess(
WriteServiceWithError.java:8)
        at sun.reflect.NativeMethodAccessorImpl.invoke0(Native Method)
        ...
        at java.util.concurrent.ThreadPoolExecutor$Worker.run(ThreadPoolExecutor.java:617)
        at java.lang.Thread.run(Thread.java:745)
```

As we can see, SI with Spring asynchronous support ensures that the error will be propagated into the main thread.

Asynchronous Unidirectional Flow

Let's now switch to unidirectional flow. Listing 8-131 shows the SI configuration.

Listing 8-131. SI Configuration of Asynchronous Unidirectional Flow Error Propagation Example (File si-config.xml in Folder src/main/resources of Example Project 0838-error-not-propagated-async)

```xml
<?xml version="1.0" encoding="UTF-8"?>
<beans xmlns="http://www.springframework.org/schema/beans"
  xmlns:xsi="http://www.w3.org/2001/XMLSchema-instance"
  xmlns:int="http://www.springframework.org/schema/integration"
  xsi:schemaLocation="http://www.springframework.org/schema/beans
    http://www.springframework.org/schema/beans/spring-beans.xsd
    http://www.springframework.org/schema/integration
    http://www.springframework.org/schema/integration/spring-integration.xsd">
```

```xml
<int:gateway default-request-channel="inChannel"
    service-interface="net.lkrnac.book.eiws.chapter08.in.SiWrapperServiceVoid" />

<int:channel id="inChannel">
    <int:queue capacity="10"/>
</int:channel>

<int:service-activator input-channel="inChannel" ref="writeServiceWithError"
    method="write">
    <int:poller fixed-delay="100"/>
</int:service-activator>
</beans>
```

This flow is similar to that in the previous example, 0837-error-propagated-async, but in this case we are dealing with unidirectional flow. This is because SiWrapperServiceViod.processText() and WiteServiceWithError.write() don't return a value.

The main class is reused from the 0836-error-handling-sync example (Listing 8-126). Listing 8-132 shows the output after running this method.

Listing 8-132. Output of Asynchronous Unidirectional Flow Error Propagation Example

```
2015-08-31 20:51:48.798  INFO 14484 --- [                main]
n.l.book.eiws.chapter08.SiApplication  : Started SiApplication in 2.059 seconds (JVM running for 2.573)
2015-08-31 20:51:48.821 ERROR 14484 --- [ask-scheduler-1]
o.s.integration.handler.LoggingHandler    :
org.springframework.messaging.MessageHandlingException: ; nested exception is
java.lang.IllegalStateException: error occurred
        at
org.springframework.integration.handler.MethodInvokingMessageProcessor.processMessage
(MethodInvokingMessageProcessor.java:78)
        ...
        at java.util.concurrent.ThreadPoolExecutor$Worker.run(ThreadPoolExecutor.java:617)
        at java.lang.Thread.run(Thread.java:745)
Caused by: java.lang.IllegalStateException: error occurred
        at
net.lkrnac.book.eiws.chapter08.out.WriteServiceWithError.write(WriteServiceWithError.java:12)
        at sun.reflect.NativeMethodAccessorImpl.invoke0(Native Method)
        ...
        at
org.springframework.integration.handler.MethodInvokingMessageProcessor.processMessage
(MethodInvokingMessageProcessor.java:75)
        ... 22 more
```

The main thread isn't affected by the error that happens in the downstream SI flow. But it is caught by SI, converted into ErrorMessage, and sent to the global errorChannel and then to LoggingHandler to be logged.

Global Error Handler Overriding

This example shows how to create a custom handler for errorChannel. We use the same classes and SI flow from the previous example. Listing 8-133 shows our custom global error handler.

Listing 8-133. Custom Global Error Handler Example (0839-error-channel-global)

```
package net.lkrnac.book.eiws.chapter08.out;
import lombok.extern.slf4j.Slf4j;
import org.springframework.integration.annotation.ServiceActivator;
import org.springframework.stereotype.Component;


@Slf4j
@Component
public class ErrorHandler {
  @ServiceActivator(inputChannel = "errorChannel")
  public void handleException(Throwable throwable) {
    log.error("Error occurred: ", throwable);
  }
}
```

This normal service activator is configured with a Java annotation to listen on errorChannel. It logs the error for this example's simplicity, but we could place any custom logic here. errorChannel by default consumes all the error messages from the SI flow that aren't handled otherwise. When we run the main class of this example, we get the output in Listing 8-134.

Listing 8-134. Output of Custom Global Error Handler

```
2015-08-31 21:07:41.510 ERROR 14942 --- [ask-scheduler-1]
n.l.b.eiws.chapter08.out.ErrorHandler    : Error occurred:

org.springframework.messaging.MessageHandlingException: ; nested exception is
java.lang.IllegalStateException: error occurred
        at org.springframework.integration.handler.MethodInvokingMessageProcessor.
processMessage(
MethodInvokingMessageProcessor.java:78)
        ...
```

The error is caught by SI and sent to errorChannel, where our ErrorHandler is listening. So the error is logged from this class.

Custom Error Channel Example

The last error-handling example shows how to configure a custom error channel for a particular poller. Listing 8-135 shows our custom handler.

Listing 8-135. Custom Error Handler Example (0840-error-channel-async)

```
package net.lkrnac.book.eiws.chapter08.out;
import lombok.extern.slf4j.Slf4j;
import org.springframework.integration.annotation.ServiceActivator;
import org.springframework.stereotype.Component;
```

```
@Slf4j
@Component
public class ErrorHandler {
  @ServiceActivator(inputChannel = "customErrorChannel")
  public void handleException(Throwable throwable) {
    log.error("Error occurred: ", throwable);
  }
}
```

This Java-configured service activator is connected to customErrorChannel, which logs the error. Listing 8-136 shows the SI configuration for this example.

Listing 8-136. SI Configuration for Custom Error Handler Example (File si-config.xml in Folder src/main/ resources of Example Project 0840-error-channel-async)

```xml
<?xml version="1.0" encoding="UTF-8"?>
<beans xmlns="http://www.springframework.org/schema/beans"
  xmlns:xsi="http://www.w3.org/2001/XMLSchema-instance"
  xmlns:int="http://www.springframework.org/schema/integration"
  xsi:schemaLocation="http://www.springframework.org/schema/beans
    http://www.springframework.org/schema/beans/spring-beans.xsd
    http://www.springframework.org/schema/integration
    http://www.springframework.org/schema/integration/spring-integration.xsd">

  <int:gateway default-request-channel="inChannel"
    service-interface="net.lkrnac.book.eiws.chapter08.in.SiWrapperServiceVoid" />

  <int:channel id="inChannel">
    <int:queue capacity="10"/>
  </int:channel>

  <int:service-activator input-channel="inChannel" ref="writeServiceWithError"
    method="write">
    <int:poller fixed-delay="100" error-channel="customErrorChannel"/>
  </int:service-activator>
  <int:channel id="customErrorChannel"/>
</beans>
```

The poller on the service activator is configured with error-channel equal to customErrorChannel, and ErrorHandler is listening. So this error handler is exclusive for this poller in this case, and the global errorChannel uses the default SI error handler. The main class for this example is the same as for the 0836-error-handling-sync example in Listing 8-126. The output is the same as for the previous example, 0839-error-channel-global, in Listing 8-134.

Transaction Handling

Propagation of transactions across the SI flow has slightly different boundaries than propagation of exceptions. As we've already shown, exceptions sometimes can be propagated back to the caller even when we are dealing with asynchronous message passing. But this is not true for transaction propagation. *Transactions can be propagated in the SI flow only when the entire flow is synchronous.* To configure transaction support, we can use standard Spring mechanisms (for example, @Transactional annotation).

But there is an option to have the transaction present for an asynchronous message subflow, whereby the transaction boundary starts in an active component. When we specify <int:poller> for any of the active components, we can define the XML poller subelement <int:transactional>. This element tells SI that we want to start a transaction for every new thread started by poller triggering. This mechanism is called *transacted polling*.

Transaction Propagation Example

To explore transaction propagation, we are going to persist the message into the in-memory database and simulate the error to roll back the transaction. Listing 8-137 shows the service simulating the mentioned error.

Listing 8-137. Service Simulating Error for Transaction Propagation Example (0841-transaction-propagation)

```
package net.lkrnac.book.eiws.chapter08.out;
import java.util.Map;
import org.springframework.stereotype.Service;

@Service
public class ServiceWithError {
  public boolean handleJdbcResult(Map<String, Object> jdbcResult) {
    throw new IllegalStateException("error occurred");
  }
}
```

When this Spring service bean is called, it throws IllegalStateException to simulate the error. The method call handleJdbcResult() takes an argument of type Map<String, Object>, because it will be passed from the SI component defined later in this example. Listing 8-138 shows the service interface used in this example.

Listing 8-138. Service Interface for Transaction Propagation Example (0841-transaction-propagation)

```
package net.lkrnac.book.eiws.chapter08.in;
import org.springframework.transaction.annotation.Transactional;

@Transactional
public interface SiWrapperServiceTransacted {
  boolean processText(String text);
}
```

This service interface is annotated with @Transactional, which wraps this call and all processing behind it into the Spring transaction. Listing 8-139 shows the configuration class that initializes the table for the in-memory database.

Listing 8-139. Initialization of DB Table for Transaction Propagation Example (0841-transaction-propagation)

```
package net.lkrnac.book.eiws.chapter08;
import javax.annotation.PostConstruct;
import org.springframework.beans.factory.annotation.Autowired;
import org.springframework.jdbc.core.JdbcTemplate;
import org.springframework.stereotype.Repository;

@Repository
public class SimpleDatabasePopulator {
  private JdbcTemplate jdbcTemplate;

  @Autowired
  public SimpleDatabasePopulator(JdbcTemplate jdbcTemplate) {
    super();
    this.jdbcTemplate = jdbcTemplate;
  }

  @PostConstruct
  public void initDbTable() {
    jdbcTemplate.execute("drop table TEXT_TABLE if exists");
    jdbcTemplate.execute("create table TEXT_TABLE(TEXT varchar(30))");
  }
}
```

This component initializes an in-memory database based on the injected jdbcTemplate bean it autowires. The JdbcTemplate instance is created automatically by Spring Boot. Listing 8-140 shows the SI XML configuration.

Listing 8-140. SI Configuration for Transaction Propagation Example (File si-config.xml in Folder src/main/resources of Example Project 0841-transaction-propagation)

```
<?xml version="1.0" encoding="UTF-8"?>
<beans xmlns="http://www.springframework.org/schema/beans"
  xmlns:xsi="http://www.w3.org/2001/XMLSchema-instance"
  xmlns:int="http://www.springframework.org/schema/integration"
  xmlns:int-http="http://www.springframework.org/schema/integration/http"
  xmlns:int-jdbc="http://www.springframework.org/schema/integration/jdbc"
  xsi:schemaLocation="http://www.springframework.org/schema/integration/jdbc
    http://www.springframework.org/schema/integration/jdbc/spring-integration-jdbc.xsd
    http://www.springframework.org/schema/beans
    http://www.springframework.org/schema/beans/spring-beans.xsd
    http://www.springframework.org/schema/integration
    http://www.springframework.org/schema/integration/spring-integration.xsd">

<int:gateway default-request-channel="inChannel"
  service-interface="net.lkrnac.book.eiws.chapter08.in.SiWrapperServiceTransacted" />
<int:channel id="inChannel" />

<int-jdbc:outbound-gateway
  data-source="dataSource"
  update="insert into TEXT_TABLE values (:payload)"
  request-channel="inChannel"
```

```
  reply-channel="replyChannel" >
 </int-jdbc:outbound-gateway>
 <int:channel id="replyChannel" />

 <int:service-activator input-channel="replyChannel" ref="serviceWithError"
   method="handleJdbcResult" />
</beans>
```

This flow starts with the inbound gateway mapped to the transacted service interface SiWrapperServiceTransacted and is connected to the outbound JDBC gateway via inChannel. This gateway uses the dataSource bean to run a query against the in-memory database, which inserts a message within the transaction into TEXT_TABLE.

The reply channel from this component is connected to the service activator, which invokes ServiceWithError.handleJdbcResult(). As we've seen, this logic simulates an error. Listing 8-141 shows the main class of this example.

Listing 8-141. Main Class of Transaction Propagation Example (0841-transaction-propagation)

```java
package net.lkrnac.book.eiws.chapter08;
import lombok.extern.slf4j.Slf4j;
import net.lkrnac.book.eiws.chapter08.in.SiWrapperServiceTransacted;
import org.springframework.boot.SpringApplication;
import org.springframework.boot.autoconfigure.SpringBootApplication;
import org.springframework.context.ApplicationContext;
import org.springframework.context.annotation.ImportResource;
import org.springframework.jdbc.core.JdbcTemplate;

@Slf4j
@SpringBootApplication
@ImportResource("classpath:si-config.xml")
public class SiApplication {
  private static final String SELECT_COUNT = "select count(*) from TEXT_TABLE";

  public static void main(String[] args) throws InterruptedException {
    ApplicationContext ctx = SpringApplication.run(SiApplication.class, args);

    try {
      SiWrapperServiceTransacted wrapperService =
          ctx.getBean(SiWrapperServiceTransacted.class);
      wrapperService.processText("simple message");
    } catch (IllegalStateException ise) {
      JdbcTemplate jdbcTemplate = ctx.getBean(JdbcTemplate.class);
      int recordCount =
          jdbcTemplate.queryForObject(SELECT_COUNT, Integer.class);
      log.info("Record count: " + recordCount);
    }
  }
}
```

After the Spring Boot application is started with the XML flow we defined, we retrieve the SiWrapperServiceTransacted bean. This is used for sending messages into the SI flow. As we expect an error to be thrown from it, this call is in the try-catch block. In the catch block, we read and log the number of persisted records in the DB. This will help highlight the transaction propagation feature. Listing 8-142 shows the possible output after running this main class.

Listing 8-142. Output of Transaction Propagation Example

```
2015-09-01 21:53:58.885  INFO 28736 --- [          main]
n.l.book.eiws.chapter08.SiApplication    : Record count: 0
```

No record is persisted into the database, because after the error is thrown from SiWrapperServiceTransacted (which is our transaction boundary), Spring rolls back the whole transaction. If we were to remove the @Transactional annotation from SiWrapperServiceTransacted, we would observe the record count equal to 1, despite the error that occurs afterward. This is because without the transaction, the insert from the outbound JDBC gateway would be committed immediately.

Transacted Polling Example

Now let's explore an example of transactional behavior within asynchronous SI threads. As we mentioned, a transaction can't pass an asynchronous boundary of SI flow, but we can start the transaction in the thread that handled the asynchronous SI subflow. Listing 8-143 shows the SI configuration.

Listing 8-143. SI Configuration for Transacted Polling Example (File si-config.xml in Folder src/main/resources of Example Project 0842-transacted-polling)

```xml
<?xml version="1.0" encoding="UTF-8"?>
<beans xmlns="http://www.springframework.org/schema/beans"
  xmlns:xsi="http://www.w3.org/2001/XMLSchema-instance"
  xmlns:int="http://www.springframework.org/schema/integration"
  xmlns:int-http="http://www.springframework.org/schema/integration/http"
  xmlns:int-jdbc="http://www.springframework.org/schema/integration/jdbc"
  xsi:schemaLocation="http://www.springframework.org/schema/integration/jdbc
    http://www.springframework.org/schema/integration/jdbc/spring-integration-jdbc.xsd
    http://www.springframework.org/schema/beans
    http://www.springframework.org/schema/beans/spring-beans.xsd
    http://www.springframework.org/schema/integration
    http://www.springframework.org/schema/integration/spring-integration.xsd">

  <int:gateway default-request-channel="inChannel"
    service-interface="net.lkrnac.book.eiws.chapter08.in.SiWrapperServiceVoid" />
  <int:channel id="inChannel">
    <int:queue capacity="10"/>
  </int:channel>

  <int-jdbc:outbound-gateway
    data-source="dataSource"
    update="insert into TEXT_TABLE values (:payload)"
    request-channel="inChannel"
    reply-channel="replyChannel" >
```

```xml
    <int:poller fixed-delay="100">
      <int:transactional/>
    </int:poller>
  </int-jdbc:outbound-gateway>
  <int:channel id="replyChannel" />

  <int:service-activator input-channel="replyChannel" ref="serviceWithError"
    method="handleJdbcResult">
  </int:service-activator>
</beans>
```

This SI configuration uses an inbound gateway with our common service interface SiWrapperServiceVoid and is connected to the outbound JDBC gateway via inChannel. But inChannel is of type QueueChannel, which means it needs to be consumed by an active SI endpoint. Therefore, the outbound JDBC gateway uses a poller to consume messages from inChannel every 100 ms in a separate thread. More important, this poller component is defined with the <int:transactional> XML subelement, which defines the transactional boundary for each poller thread.

The reply channel of the outbound JDBC gateway is connected to the service activator via DirectChannel. This endpoint is mapped to ServiceWithError.handleJdbcResult(), which is same as in the example project 0841-transaction-propagation in Listing 8-137. It simulates the error by throwing an IllegalStateException. Listing 8-144 shows the main class of this example.

Listing 8-144. Main Class of Transacted Polling Example (0842-transacted-polling)

```java
package net.lkrnac.book.eiws.chapter08;
import lombok.extern.slf4j.Slf4j;
import net.lkrnac.book.eiws.chapter08.in.SiWrapperServiceVoid;
import org.springframework.boot.SpringApplication;
import org.springframework.boot.autoconfigure.SpringBootApplication;
import org.springframework.context.ApplicationContext;
import org.springframework.context.annotation.ImportResource;
import org.springframework.jdbc.core.JdbcTemplate;

@Slf4j
@SpringBootApplication
@ImportResource("classpath:si-config.xml")
public class SiApplication {
  private static final String SELECT_COUNT = "select count(*) from TEXT_TABLE";

  public static void main(String[] args) throws InterruptedException {
    ApplicationContext ctx = SpringApplication.run(SiApplication.class, args);

    SiWrapperServiceVoid wrapperService =
        ctx.getBean(SiWrapperServiceVoid.class);
    wrapperService.processText("simple message");

    Thread.sleep(500);
    JdbcTemplate jdbcTemplate = ctx.getBean(JdbcTemplate.class);
    int recordCount = jdbcTemplate.queryForObject(SELECT_COUNT, Integer.class);
    log.info("Record count: " + recordCount);
  }
}
```

After we start the Spring Boot application with the SI configuration we described, we send the message to the SI flow via SiWrapperServiceVoid. It is not in the try-catch block in this case, because the error is not propagated to this code anyway. A sleep call is used to wait enough time to make sure that the asynchronous poller inserts the message and simulates the error afterward. After waiting, we look into the database table to see how many records were stored. Listing 8-145 shows the output when we run this main class.

Listing 8-145. Output of Transacted Polling Example

```
2015-09-01 22:22:33.252 ERROR 29589 --- [ask-scheduler-1]
o.s.integration.handler.LoggingHandler   :
org.springframework.messaging.MessageHandlingException: ; nested exception is
java.lang.IllegalStateException: error occurred
        ...
2015-09-01 22:22:33.724  INFO 29589 --- [           main]
n.l.book.eiws.chapter08.SiApplication    : Record count: 0
```

The error is simulated in a separate thread, which is the thread covered in the transactional boundary. Therefore, we observe a zero record count after, in the main thread. If we were to remove <int:transactional> from the SI configuration, the record count would be 1, because the insert wouldn't be covered by the transaction and rolled back after the error simulation.

MessagingTemplate

Use of the messaging gateway or inbound channel adapters is not necessary to send messages into an SI flow. SI provides the special abstraction org.springframework.integration.core.MessagingTemplate for sending and receiving messages to/from any channel in the SI flow. This mechanism can be more convenient, for example, in testing code or when we want to send a custom message to the SI flow.

We can think of this class as the SI equivalent of JmsTemplate or RestTemplate.

MessagingTemplate Example

This example uses exactly the same SI flow configuration as in Listing 8-27 (example 0808-gateway-generic-xml). To remind you, a messaging gateway is used to send a message via inChannel to the outbound channel adapter mapped to our common bean WriteService.writeAndIndicateSuccess(). Listing 8-146 shows the configuration of MessagingTemplate.

Listing 8-146. MessagingTemplate Configuration (0843-messaging-template)

```
package net.lkrnac.book.eiws.chapter08;
import org.springframework.context.annotation.Bean;
import org.springframework.context.annotation.Configuration;
import org.springframework.integration.core.MessagingTemplate;

@Configuration
public class SiConfiguration {
  @Bean
  public MessagingTemplate messagingTemplate() {
    MessagingTemplate messagingTemplate = new MessagingTemplate();
    messagingTemplate.setReceiveTimeout(1000);
    return messagingTemplate;
  }
}
```

In this Spring configuration class, we register the messageTemplate bean with the receive time-out of 1 second. Listing 8-147 shows how we would use it.

Listing 8-147. Use of MessagingTemplate (0843-messaging-template)

```java
package net.lkrnac.book.eiws.chapter08;
import org.springframework.boot.SpringApplication;
import org.springframework.boot.autoconfigure.SpringBootApplication;
import org.springframework.context.ConfigurableApplicationContext;
import org.springframework.context.annotation.ImportResource;
import org.springframework.integration.core.MessagingTemplate;
import lombok.extern.slf4j.Slf4j;

@Slf4j
@SpringBootApplication
@ImportResource("classpath:si-config.xml")
public class SiApplication {
  public static void main(String[] args) throws InterruptedException {
    ConfigurableApplicationContext context =
        SpringApplication.run(SiApplication.class, args);

    MessagingTemplate messagingTemplate = context.getBean(MessagingTemplate.class);
    boolean result = messagingTemplate.convertSendAndReceive(
        "inChannel", "simple message", Boolean.class);
    log.info("Result: " + result);
    context.close();
  }
}
```

After we create and start the Spring context via the Spring Boot constructs, we retrieve the messagingTemplate bean from it and send simple message. Next we log the result received from inChannel and close the context instance. After running this main class, we can observe the output in Listing 8-148.

Listing 8-148. Output of MessagingTemplate Example

```
2015-10-10 08:38:37.602  INFO 26721 --- [           main]
n.l.b.e.chapter08.out.WriteRepository    : Text persisted: simple message
2015-10-10 08:38:37.605  INFO 26721 --- [           main]
n.l.book.eiws.chapter08.SiApplication    : Result: true
```

The messaging gateway defined in the SI flow isn't used at all, and we send the message directly to inChannel via messagingTemplate. It is persisted, and the response is sent back to messagingTemplate.

Summary

This chapter introduced the benefits of higher-level integration frameworks and the need to abstract more-complicated message flows into a concise framework such as Spring Integration. We focused on SI's main concepts and killer features. SI is lightweight, because it doesn't need any special runtime environment.

We covered the three main SI building blocks (message, message endpoint, and message channel) and covered the various types of each component. We showed how to programmatically create message components if needed and emphasized the immutability of the default message type.

Most notably, we covered a lot of message endpoint types for message routing, transformation, and connecting SI flow to third-party technologies or Java classes and interfaces. These components were explained in passive (synchronous) and active (asynchronous with poller) mode. We also covered which components can participate in unidirectional (fire-and-forget scenarios) and bidirectional (request-response scenarios) flows.

We also looked at message channel types and characteristics. We covered how they behave and why they are useful for different scenarios in relation to active vs. passive message endpoints.

Last, we covered error handling, and error and transaction propagation in relation to synchronous vs. asynchronous message flow.

CHAPTER 9

Spring Batch

So far our focus has been tailored toward enterprise technologies, which process requests or messages from upstream applications. Such abstractions are crucial for handling real-time processing of a small amount of data, mostly representing one action against our enterprise system. But real-world enterprises also need to perform background tasks, whereby an often large amount of data needs to be processed, migrated, copied, or converted from one system to another on a regular basis.

Such processing is often referred to as *batch processing*, because data is processed in large amounts that usually can't fit into memory or a single transaction. This amount of data needs to be divided and processed in manageable chunks. This processing is often executed on a regular basis (for example, daily, weekly, or monthly) and may be long running. Batch processing typically doesn't involve user interaction.

Use cases for batch processing include the following:

- Sending subscription e-mails

- Sending monthly invoices

- Synchronizing a data warehouse

- Performing business reporting

- Processing orders

The first chapter covered scheduling support, which can be used for scheduling background tasks. But it isn't handy in real life, because a lot of problems can occur in background processing. Low-level scheduling support based on a fixed rate, fixed delay, or CRON expressions simply isn't advanced enough to cover handling errors, restarting, distributing work to other machines, chunking of data processing, or controlling the flow of batch actions without a lot of custom code.

Fortunately, the Spring portfolio contains the *Spring Batch* (SB) project, which fills the gap of advanced abstractions for enterprise batch-processing needs. SB was a unique project within the Java platform until Java Enterprise Edition version 7 (JEE 7) was introduced. This major revision of Java Enterprise standards introduced APIs for batch processing that were significantly influenced by Spring Batch constructs. Michael Minella (SB project lead) was heavily involved in the expert group defining JSR-352, which covers batch processing for the Java platform (https://jcp.org/en/jsr/detail?id=352). SB also remains the flagship implementation project of this Java standard.

Spring Batch Domain

The SB project philosophy tries to achieve the Spring family's overall goal of minimizing necessary boilerplate code, so that developers can concentrate on business logic. Therefore, it introduces various abstractions that are unique to the batch-processing domain, shown in Figure 9-1.

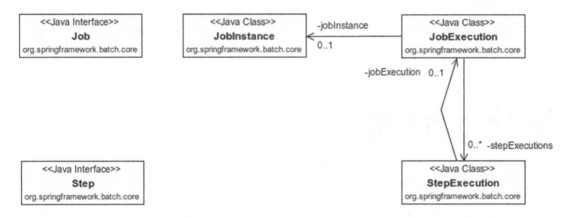

Figure 9-1. *Spring Batch domain*

The first and major abstraction is Job. It represents a unit of work that needs to be processed. Job is constructed of one or more steps. Step represents this partial processing of work performed by Job. Every time the Job is executed, the SB framework creates a new JobInstance, so one Job can have one or more JobInstances.

One job instance can be executed various times (for example, when JobInstance needs to be restarted), so it can have various JobExecutions. Because each Job needs to have at least one Step, it also needs to create a StepExecution for each JobExecution. One StepExecution can be executed various times within one JobExecution (for example, when we want to restart or retry Step), so there is a one-to-many relationship between them.

Developers need to define Job and Steps for batch processing. All the other objects are created by the SB framework. SB takes care of execution when Job is triggered and handles errors that can occur during execution according to the Job and Step definitions. This way, the developer can granulate work into various Steps and logically separate batch processing into smaller pieces and leave the hard work of coordinating execution for SB. We will dive into these definitions later in this chapter.

Chunk-Oriented Processing

The most common use case for the SB framework is processing large amounts of data in chunks. This is called *chunk-oriented processing,* and it happens in one Step. Step is composed of one mandatory ItemReader<T>, one optional ItemProcessor<T, S>, and one mandatory ItemWriter<S>. These Step parts are Java interfaces, which can be implemented by our custom logic. Notice that in the following text, we don't use generic types when these interfaces are discussed.

SB also provides some commonly used implementations out of the box for reading/writing from/to the following:

- JDBC/Hibernate/stored procedure

    - Cursor-based item readers—the cursor is a DB construct in which rows are streamed from a database

    - Paging-based item readers—uses a distinct where clause for each chunk of data (page)

    - Item writers

- Flat files

- XML

- JMS

Figure 9-2 shows a sequence diagram of this mechanism.

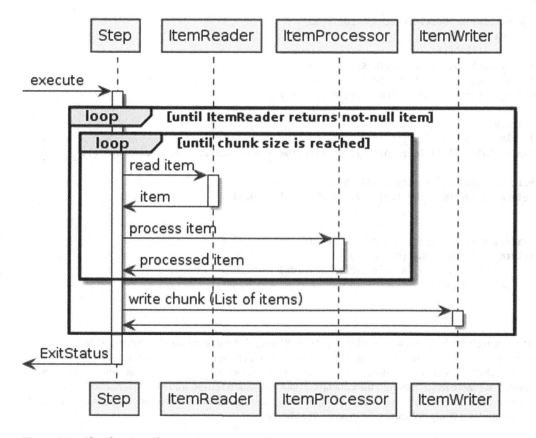

Figure 9-2. *Chunk-oriented processing sequence diagram*

When Step is executed, SB starts the loop of chunk processing. The Step definition has to have a chunk size defined; one chunk consists of various ItemReader and ItemProcessor calls to read and process one item at a time until the chunk size is reached. When the chunk is read and processed, Step calls ItemWriter to write the whole chunk and then continues with the next chunk. The looping ends when ItemReader returns null, which means that there's no more data to process and this partial chunk is the last one in the current StepExecution.

Common Classes for Chunk-Oriented Processing Examples

Before we dive into chunk-oriented examples, we'll introduce a few classes that are shared across those examples in this chapter. As in the previous chapter, we won't highlight SB features in real-life examples, because SB is also a highly configurable framework. The simplicity of the examples will better illustrate SB features. Listing 9-1 shows a simple repository for reading records of the String type.

Listing 9-1. Read Repository Used to Read Records for Chunk-Oriented Processing Examples
(0900-batch-common)

```java
package net.lkrnac.book.eiws.chapter09.read;
import java.util.Iterator;
import java.util.List;
import java.util.stream.Collectors;
import java.util.stream.IntStream;
import org.springframework.stereotype.Repository;

@Repository
public class ReadRepository {
  private static final Iterator<String> ITERATOR = generateRecords(15).iterator();

  public synchronized String readNext() {
    return (ITERATOR.hasNext()) ? ITERATOR.next() : null;
  }

  private static List<String> generateRecords(int count) {
    return IntStream.range(0, count)
        .mapToObj(idx -> "simple record " + idx)
        .collect(Collectors.toList());
  }
}
```

This Spring bean is annotated with @Repository. When this bean is initiated by Spring, it generates
simple records by using the Java 8 Stream API. The IntStream.range method generates a stream of
15 integers, which are converted into String records and collected into List. When this collection of records
is generated, we store its iterator into the constant ITERATOR, which is used for reading records via the
readNext method. This method is synchronized, because reading can occur in various threads. This is handy
in some examples. Listing 9-2 shows the custom ItemReader.

Listing 9-2. Custom ItemReader for Chunk-Oriented Processing Examples (0900-batch-common)

```java
package net.lkrnac.book.eiws.chapter09.read;
import org.springframework.batch.item.ItemReader;
import org.springframework.beans.factory.annotation.Autowired;
import org.springframework.stereotype.Component;

@Component
public class SimpleRecordReader implements ItemReader<String> {
  private ReadRepository readRepository;

  @Autowired
  public SimpleRecordReader(ReadRepository readRepository) {
    super();
    this.readRepository = readRepository;
  }
```

```
  @Override
  public String read() {
    return readRepository.readNext();
  }
}
```

This `ItemReader` implementation is also a Spring bean, which injects the `ReadRepository` bean to read from. The generic `String` defines the type of item we are reading. The `read` method needs to be implemented to read one item for processing. Listing 9-3 shows the custom `ItemProcessor` used in chunk-oriented examples.

Listing 9-3. Custom ItemProcessor for Chunk-Oriented Processing Examples (0900-batch-common)

```
package net.lkrnac.book.eiws.chapter09.process;
import org.springframework.batch.item.ItemProcessor;
import org.springframework.stereotype.Component;

@Component
public class SimpleRecordProcessor implements ItemProcessor<String, String> {
  @Override
  public String process(String item) throws Exception {
    return item + " processed";
  }
}
```

This is also a Spring bean, which appends the string `processed` to the processing record. In the real world, this would be the place where we convert items from read format/POJO into write format/POJO. Generic types of the `ItemProcessor` interface define the type of item before and after processing. In this simplistic example, both are of type `String`. Listing 9-4 shows the simple write repository.

Listing 9-4. Write Repository Used to Read Records for Chunk-Oriented Processing Examples (0900-batch-common)

```
package net.lkrnac.book.eiws.chapter09.write;
import java.util.List;
import lombok.extern.slf4j.Slf4j;
import org.springframework.stereotype.Repository;

@Slf4j
@Repository
public class WriteRepository {
  public void writeRecords(List<? extends String> records) {
    records.stream()
        .map(record -> "Writing record: " + record)
        .forEach(log::info);
  }
}
```

This Spring bean logs a given collection of records and pretends some type of processing. For logging, we use the Lombok annotation `@Slf4j`. For looping through records, we again use the Java 8 Stream API. Listing 9-5 shows the custom `ItemWriter`.

Listing 9-5. Custom ItemWriter for Chunk-Oriented Processing Examples (0900-batch-common)

```java
package net.lkrnac.book.eiws.chapter09.write;
import java.util.List;
import org.springframework.batch.item.ItemWriter;
import org.springframework.beans.factory.annotation.Autowired;
import org.springframework.stereotype.Component;

@Component
public class SimpleRecordWriter implements ItemWriter<String> {
  private WriteRepository writeRepository;

  @Autowired
  public SimpleRecordWriter(WriteRepository writeRepository) {
    super();
    this.writeRepository = writeRepository;
  }

  @Override
  public void write(List<? extends String> items) throws Exception {
    writeRepository.writeRecords(items);
  }
}
```

This Spring bean implements the `ItemWriter` interface; the item type is `String`. `WriteRepository` is injected, so we can write records via the `write()` method.

■ **Note** You might ask why we have `ReadRepository` and `WriteRepository` in place at all when we want to keep the example as simple as possible. The reason is testability. I want to make sure that the examples are working as described, so the SB configuration is covered by simple integrations tests. `ReadRepository` and `WriteRepository` are often faked in these tests and used for verification. But this testing is beyond the scope of this book. Tests alongside the book examples can be found in the GitHub repository (`https://github.com/lkrnac/book-eiws-code-samples`).

Chunk-Oriented Processing Example with XML Configuration

The chunk-oriented processing examples use Spring Boot, but you'll see that configuring SB applications with the plain Spring Framework is similar. Our first SB example, shown in Listing 9-6, uses XML configuration.

Listing 9-6. XML Configuration of Chunk-Oriented Processing Example (File batch-config.xml in Folder src/main/resources of Example Project 0901-chunk-processing-generic-xml)

```xml
<?xml version="1.0" encoding="UTF-8"?>
<beans:beans xmlns:beans="http://www.springframework.org/schema/beans"
  xmlns:xsi="http://www.w3.org/2001/XMLSchema-instance"
  xmlns="http://www.springframework.org/schema/batch"
```

```
xsi:schemaLocation="http://www.springframework.org/schema/batch
    http://www.springframework.org/schema/batch/spring-batch.xsd
    http://www.springframework.org/schema/beans
    http://www.springframework.org/schema/beans/spring-beans.xsd">

<job id="simpleRecordsJob">
  <step id="simpleRecordsStep">
    <tasklet>
      <chunk reader="simpleRecordReader" writer="simpleRecordWriter"
        processor="simpleRecordProcessor" commit-interval="4" />
    </tasklet>
  </step>
</job>
</beans:beans>
```

We don't use the beans namespace by default, because using the batch namespace (we don't need to use the <batch: prefix for batch XML tags) makes the SB configurations much more readable. We use this approach for SB configurations in this chapter.

The configuration itself contains the definition of one Job with one Step, which uses our common reader, processor, and writer. The <job> and <step> XML tags create Spring beans with names defined by the id attribute. The last attribute in the Step definition is commit-interval, which specifies the chunk size for this step. Listing 9-7 shows how the XML configuration is loaded into the Spring context.

Listing 9-7. BatchConfiguration Class for Chunk-Oriented Processing Example with XML Configuration (0901-chunk-processing-generic-xml)

```
package net.lkrnac.book.eiws.chapter09;

import org.springframework.batch.core.configuration.annotation.EnableBatchProcessing;
import org.springframework.context.annotation.Configuration;
import org.springframework.context.annotation.ImportResource;

@Configuration
@EnableBatchProcessing
@ImportResource("classpath:batch-config.xml")
public class BatchConfiguration {
}
```

This is a standard Spring configuration class, importing the XML configuration from Listing 9-6. The last annotation is @EnableBatchProcessing, which enables SB features and creates default beans needed for batch processing. We will dive into these beans later in the chapter. For now, we just need to know it's necessary for SB configuration. Notice that this configuration class is often used in examples involving XML configuration of SB, so we will be referring to this listing often.

Listing 9-8 presents the last part of this example.

Listing 9-8. Main Class for Chunk-Oriented Processing Example with XML Configuration (0901-chunk-processing-generic-xml)

```
package net.lkrnac.book.eiws.chapter09;

import org.springframework.boot.SpringApplication;
import org.springframework.boot.autoconfigure.SpringBootApplication;
```

```
@SpringBootApplication
public class BatchApplication {
  public static void main(String[] args) throws InterruptedException {
    SpringApplication.run(BatchApplication.class);
  }
}
```

This is the standard Spring Boot main application class. The @SpringBootApplication annotation executes Spring Boot's autoconfiguration and component scan in the current package and subpackages. This configuration is then executed in the main method via a call to SpringApplication.run().

This main Spring Boot class is used often in examples based on Spring Boot, so we will be referring to this listing later. It is important to remember that if the Spring Boot application uses @EnableBatchProcessing, all the jobs are executed by default at the application's start.

Running this main configuration class results in the output in Listing 9-9.

Listing 9-9. Output of XML Chunk-Oriented Processing Example

```
2015-09-26 14:49:32.829  INFO 25566 --- [           main] o.s.b.c.l.support.
SimpleJobLauncher     : Job: [FlowJob: [name=simpleRecordsJob]] launched with the following
parameters: [{}]
2015-09-26 14:49:32.858  INFO 25566 --- [           main] o.s.batch.core.job.
SimpleStepHandler      : Executing step: [simpleRecordsStep]
2015-09-26 14:49:32.955  INFO 25566 --- [           main] n.l.b.e.chapter09.write.
WriteRepository  : Writing record: simple record 0 processed
2015-09-26 14:49:32.955  INFO 25566 --- [           main] n.l.b.e.chapter09.write.
WriteRepository  : Writing record: simple record 1 processed
2015-09-26 14:49:32.955  INFO 25566 --- [           main] n.l.b.e.chapter09.write.
WriteRepository  : Writing record: simple record 2 processed
2015-09-26 14:49:32.956  INFO 25566 --- [           main] n.l.b.e.chapter09.write.
WriteRepository  : Writing record: simple record 3 processed
2015-09-26 14:49:32.961  INFO 25566 --- [           main] n.l.b.e.chapter09.write.
WriteRepository  : Writing record: simple record 4 processed
2015-09-26 14:49:32.962  INFO 25566 --- [           main] n.l.b.e.chapter09.write.
WriteRepository  : Writing record: simple record 5 processed
2015-09-26 14:49:32.962  INFO 25566 --- [           main] n.l.b.e.chapter09.write.
WriteRepository  : Writing record: simple record 6 processed
2015-09-26 14:49:32.962  INFO 25566 --- [           main] n.l.b.e.chapter09.write.
WriteRepository  : Writing record: simple record 7 processed
2015-09-26 14:49:32.967  INFO 25566 --- [           main] n.l.b.e.chapter09.write.
WriteRepository  : Writing record: simple record 8 processed
2015-09-26 14:49:32.967  INFO 25566 --- [           main] n.l.b.e.chapter09.write.
WriteRepository  : Writing record: simple record 9 processed
2015-09-26 14:49:32.967  INFO 25566 --- [           main] n.l.b.e.chapter09.write.
WriteRepository  : Writing record: simple record 10 processed
2015-09-26 14:49:32.967  INFO 25566 --- [           main] n.l.b.e.chapter09.write.
WriteRepository  : Writing record: simple record 11 processed
2015-09-26 14:49:32.971  INFO 25566 --- [           main] n.l.b.e.chapter09.write.
WriteRepository  : Writing record: simple record 12 processed
2015-09-26 14:49:32.972  INFO 25566 --- [           main] n.l.b.e.chapter09.write.
WriteRepository  : Writing record: simple record 13 processed
```

```
2015-09-26 14:49:32.972  INFO 25566 --- [            main] n.l.b.e.chapter09.write.
WriteRepository  : Writing record: simple record 14 processed
2015-09-26 14:49:32.986  INFO 25566 --- [            main] o.s.b.c.l.support.
SimpleJobLauncher     : Job: [FlowJob: [name=simpleRecordsJob]] completed with the
following parameters: [{}] and the following status: [COMPLETED]
```

Chunk-Oriented Processing Example with Java Configuration

Now let's configure the same behavior with a Java configuration. Listing 9-10 shows the Java batch configuration.

Listing 9-10. Java Configuration of Chunk-Oriented Processing Example (0902-chunk-processing-generic-javaconfig)

```java
package net.lkrnac.book.eiws.chapter09;
import net.lkrnac.book.eiws.chapter09.process.SimpleRecordProcessor;
import net.lkrnac.book.eiws.chapter09.read.SimpleRecordReader;
import net.lkrnac.book.eiws.chapter09.write.SimpleRecordWriter;
import org.springframework.batch.core.Job;
import org.springframework.batch.core.Step;
import org.springframework.batch.core.configuration.annotation.EnableBatchProcessing;
import org.springframework.batch.core.configuration.annotation.JobBuilderFactory;
import org.springframework.batch.core.configuration.annotation.StepBuilderFactory;
import org.springframework.context.annotation.Bean;
import org.springframework.context.annotation.Configuration;

@Configuration
@EnableBatchProcessing
public class BatchConfiguration {
  @Bean
  public Step simpleRecordsStep(StepBuilderFactory stepBuilderFactory,
      SimpleRecordReader simpleRecordReader,
      SimpleRecordProcessor simpleRecordProcessor,
      SimpleRecordWriter simpleRecordWriter) {
    return stepBuilderFactory.get("simpleRecordsStep")
        .<String, String> chunk(4)
        .reader(simpleRecordReader)
        .processor(simpleRecordProcessor)
        .writer(simpleRecordWriter)
        .build();
  }

  @Bean
  public Job simpleRecordsJob(JobBuilderFactory jobBuilderFactory,
      Step simpleRecordsStep) {
    return jobBuilderFactory.get("simpleRecordsJob")
        .start(simpleRecordsStep)
        .build();
  }
}
```

The @Configuration annotation is typically used for Spring Java configuration, and @EnableBatchProcessing was discussed in the previous example. The Step bean is created via the simpleRecordsStep() method, which is annotated by @Bean. Spring injects instances of the reader, writer, and processor alongside the instance of StepBuilderFactory. As its name suggests, it is used for building steps. Its creation was initiated by the @EnableBatchProcessing annotation.

When we have all the necessary beans injected, we can create the step. SB provides fluent APIs for defining batch flows. The stepBuilderFactory.get() method takes the name of the Step as a parameter, but notice that the Spring bean name can be different from the Step name. So we can't confuse the Step name with the Spring bean name of the Step instance.

The next call in the chain is the specification of the chunk size via the chunk() method. In this call, we need to define generic types of the items handled by the writer, reader, and processor. The Step creation chain then continues—defining the reader, writer, and processor in this step—and is finalized by the build() call, which applies the recorded configuration and creates the Step instance.

The second @Bean definition creates the Job instance. We need an instance of the Step and JobBuilderFactory, which is for Job instance creation. Similar to the Step creation chain, the Job creation chain needs to call JobBuilderFactory.get() to name the Job. Again, notice that the Job name can be different from the name of the bean specified by method. This Job will start only the Step we created, so we need to call start to define the Step method and build the job. In this case, we use only one step. Jobs with various steps are shown later in the chapter.

The main class of this application is the standard Spring Boot main class (shown previously in Listing 9-8). When we run it, we can see output similar to that in Listing 9-9.

Example with File Reader and JDBC Writer

First, we define the model class used for this example in Listing 9-11.

Listing 9-11. Model Class for File to DB Chunk-Oriented Example (0903-chunk-processing-non-generic)

```
package net.lkrnac.book.eiws.chapter09.model;
import lombok.Data;

@Data
public class User {
  private String email;
  private String name;
}
```

We've already seen this class in previous chapters. This POJO has two parameters, email and name, and uses Lombok's annotation @Data to generate getters and setters. Listing 9-12 shows the database initialization bean.

Listing 9-12. Bean Populating In-Memory Database on Application Start (0903-chunk-processing-non-generic)

```
package net.lkrnac.book.eiws.chapter09;
import javax.annotation.PostConstruct;
import org.springframework.beans.factory.annotation.Autowired;
import org.springframework.jdbc.core.JdbcTemplate;
import org.springframework.stereotype.Component;
```

```
@Repository
public class SimpleDatabasePopulator {
  private JdbcTemplate jdbcTemplate;

  @Autowired
  public SimpleDatabasePopulator(JdbcTemplate jdbcTemplate) {
    super();
    this.jdbcTemplate = jdbcTemplate;
  }

  @PostConstruct
  public Integer initDbTable() {
    jdbcTemplate.execute("drop table USERS if exists");
    jdbcTemplate.execute("create table USERS(NAME varchar(50), EMAIL varchar(50))");
    return null;
  }
}
```

Spring Boot initializes the JdbcTemplate and DataSource by default if autoconfiguration is turned on and the relevant database libraries are on the classpath. In this case, we have an H2 in-memory database configured on the classpath. This Spring bean injects the JdbcTemplate instance to initiate the schema of the in-memory database. The initDbTable() method is annotated by @PostConstruct, so it will be executed right after the Spring context is initialized.

Next, Listing 9-13 shows the input file we are using as a data source for reading.

Listing 9-13. Input File for File to DB Chunk-Oriented Example (File users.txt in Folder src/main/resources for Example Project 0903-chunk-processing-non-generic)

```
Lubos Krnac,lubos.krnac@gmail.com
Cade Mckee,massa.rutrum@magnaNam.ca
Melvin Boone,enim.Nunc@Sedcongue.co.uk
Thane Flowers,vulputate.velit@dignissimlacus.org
Mohammad Salas,convallis@malesuada.ca
Upton Ewing,tincidunt.nibh@natoque.org
```

The delimiter for this file is a comma. Listing 9-14 shows the configuration of the file reader and JDBC writer.

Listing 9-14. Reader and Writer Configuration for File to DB Chunk-Oriented Example (0903-chunk-processing-non-generic)

```
package net.lkrnac.book.eiws.chapter09;
import javax.sql.DataSource;
import net.lkrnac.book.eiws.chapter09.model.User;
import org.springframework.batch.item.ItemReader;
import org.springframework.batch.item.ItemWriter;
import org.springframework.batch.item.database.BeanPropertyItemSqlParameterSourceProvider;
import org.springframework.batch.item.database.JdbcBatchItemWriter;
import org.springframework.batch.item.file.FlatFileItemReader;
import org.springframework.batch.item.file.mapping.BeanWrapperFieldSetMapper;
import org.springframework.batch.item.file.mapping.DefaultLineMapper;
import org.springframework.batch.item.file.transform.DelimitedLineTokenizer;
import org.springframework.context.annotation.Bean;
```

```java
import org.springframework.context.annotation.Configuration;
import org.springframework.core.io.ClassPathResource;

@Configuration
public class ChunkConfiguration {
  @Bean
  public ItemReader<User> fileItemReader() {
    FlatFileItemReader<User> flatFileItemReader = new FlatFileItemReader<>();
    flatFileItemReader.setResource(new ClassPathResource("users.txt"));

    BeanWrapperFieldSetMapper<User> fieldSetMapper = new BeanWrapperFieldSetMapper<>();
    fieldSetMapper.setTargetType(User.class);

    DelimitedLineTokenizer lineTokenizer = new DelimitedLineTokenizer();
    lineTokenizer.setDelimiter(",");
    lineTokenizer.setNames(new String[] { "name", "email" });

    DefaultLineMapper<User> lineMapper = new DefaultLineMapper<>();
    lineMapper.setFieldSetMapper(fieldSetMapper);
    lineMapper.setLineTokenizer(lineTokenizer);

    flatFileItemReader.setLineMapper(lineMapper);
    return flatFileItemReader;
  }

  @Bean
  public ItemWriter<User> jdbcItemWriter(DataSource dataSource) {
    JdbcBatchItemWriter<User> writer = new JdbcBatchItemWriter<>();
    writer.setItemSqlParameterSourceProvider(
        new BeanPropertyItemSqlParameterSourceProvider<>());
    writer.setSql("insert into USERS (NAME, EMAIL) values (:name, :email)");
    writer.setDataSource(dataSource);
    return writer;
  }
}
```

This Spring configuration class defines two beans. The first one is used as Spring's implementation of ItemReader for reading from flat files: FlatFileItemReader<User>. First, we need to configure the source file location. In this case, we expect it on the classpath with the name users.txt (the file in Listing 9-13). Next we need to configure the target type for the conversion from one line into BeanWrapperFieldSetMapper<User>. In our case, we use the User class. DelimitedLineTokenizer is used for parsing the file based on the comma delimiter and maps the parsed values into the User object fields. Finally, we configure the created line tokenizer and field set mapper into the flatFileItemReader object, and the item reader is configured.

The second bean creates Spring's item writer implementation JdbcBatchItemWriter<User>, used for writing into databases. The generic type specifies the type of the items to be written. In order to use the User field names as parameters in the JDBC query, we need to configure the BeanPropertyItemSqlParameter SourceProvider<User> implementation as a SQL parameter provider. Apart from that, we need to also configure the JDBC data source instance and the SQL query to execute into the writer.

■ **Note**   The SB framework provides a lot of possibilities for out-of-the-box implementations of `ItemReader` and `ItemWriter`. Full coverage of these APIs and implementations is beyond the scope of this book. Refer to SB reference documentation for further details.

Listing 9-15 shows the batch configuration of Step and Job.

Listing 9-15. Batch Configuration of File to DB Chunk-Oriented Example (0903-chunk-processing-non-generic)

```java
package net.lkrnac.book.eiws.chapter09;
import net.lkrnac.book.eiws.chapter09.model.User;
import org.springframework.batch.core.Job;
import org.springframework.batch.core.Step;
import org.springframework.batch.core.configuration.annotation.EnableBatchProcessing;
import org.springframework.batch.core.configuration.annotation.JobBuilderFactory;
import org.springframework.batch.core.configuration.annotation.StepBuilderFactory;
import org.springframework.batch.item.ItemReader;
import org.springframework.batch.item.ItemWriter;
import org.springframework.context.annotation.Bean;
import org.springframework.context.annotation.Configuration;

@Configuration
@EnableBatchProcessing
public class BatchConfiguration {
  @Bean
  public Step simpleRecordsStep(StepBuilderFactory stepBuilderFactory,
      ItemReader<User> fileItemReader,
      ItemWriter<User> simpleRecordWriter) {
    return stepBuilderFactory.get("simpleRecordsStep")
        .<User, User> chunk(4)
        .reader(fileItemReader)
        .writer(simpleRecordWriter)
        .build();
  }

  @Bean
  public Job simpleRecordsJob(JobBuilderFactory jobBuilderFactory,
      Step simpleRecordsStep) {
    return jobBuilderFactory.get("simpleRecordsJob")
        .start(simpleRecordsStep)
        .build();
  }
}
```

This configuration is similar to the previous example. We create the Step and Job instance based on the file item reader and the JDBC item writer in Listing 9-14. In this case, we don't use a processor. It is an optional component of chunk-oriented processing. The main class of this example is also a standard Spring Boot main class. When we execute it as a Java application, we see the output in Listing 9-16.

Listing 9-16. Output of File to DB Chunk-Oriented Example

```
2015-09-26 21:25:35.320  INFO 2906 --- [            main] o.s.b.c.l.support.SimpleJobLauncher
: Job: [SimpleJob: [name=simpleRecordsJob]] launched with the following parameters: [{}]
2015-09-26 21:25:35.345  INFO 2906 --- [            main] o.s.batch.core.job.
SimpleStepHandler       : Executing step: [simpleRecordsStep]
2015-09-26 21:25:35.391  INFO 2906 --- [            main] o.s.b.c.l.support.SimpleJobLauncher
: Job: [SimpleJob: [name=simpleRecordsJob]] completed with the following parameters: [{}]
and the following status: [COMPLETED]
```

The status *completed* means that all the records were successfully copied from the file into the in-memory DB.

Tasklet Step

Chunk-oriented processing is not the only type of step we need to cover for enterprise application use cases. Sometimes we need to perform a single action as part of a bigger flow. For example, we might need to send a notification at the end of a job or perform a single stored procedure call. SB provides the Tasklet interface. It has only one method, execute, where we can place our custom logic. This instance can then be wrapped into the TaskletStep class and used as a Step in the SB flow.

Common Classes for Tasklet Examples

Various examples in this chapter use simple Tasklet steps to highlight Spring Batch features that control job execution flow. Listing 9-17 shows this class, which is used often in this chapter.

Listing 9-17. Simple Executable Point (0900-batch-common)

```
package net.lkrnac.book.eiws.chapter09.step;
import lombok.extern.slf4j.Slf4j;
import org.springframework.stereotype.Component;

@Slf4j
@Component
public class SimpleExecutablePoint {
  public void execute(String message) {
    log.info(message);
  }
}
```

This simple Spring bean uses Lombok to log a given message into the execute() method.

■ **Note** SimpleExecutablePoint is useless for real-world applications, but it is handy for the examples in this chapter, because we can fake this bean and verify that the SB configuration works as expected. Tests alongside the book examples can be found in the GitHub repository (https://github.com/lkrnac/book-eiws-code-samples).

Our domain for the Tasklet type of batch flows used in our examples is the preparing of tea. When we want to prepare tea, we need to perform a few steps to get a tasty result. For example, we might need to Boil Water, Add Tea to cup, and Add Water to cup. Listing 9-18 shows the class simulating the Boil Water step.

Listing 9-18. Class Simulating the Boil Water step (0900-batch-common)

```java
package net.lkrnac.book.eiws.chapter09.step.tea;
import net.lkrnac.book.eiws.chapter09.step.SimpleExecutablePoint;
import org.springframework.batch.core.StepContribution;
import org.springframework.batch.core.scope.context.ChunkContext;
import org.springframework.batch.core.step.tasklet.Tasklet;
import org.springframework.batch.repeat.RepeatStatus;
import org.springframework.beans.factory.annotation.Autowired;
import org.springframework.stereotype.Component;

@Component
public class BoilWater implements Tasklet {
  private SimpleExecutablePoint simpleExecutableStep;

  @Autowired
  public BoilWater(SimpleExecutablePoint simpleExecutableStep) {
    super();
    this.simpleExecutableStep = simpleExecutableStep;
  }

  @Override
  public RepeatStatus execute(StepContribution contribution,
      ChunkContext chunkContext) throws Exception {
    simpleExecutableStep.execute("Boil Water");
    return RepeatStatus.FINISHED;
  }
}
```

This simple Spring component autowires SimpleExecutablePoint. In the execute method, we call simpleExecutableStep.execute() to simulate the Boil Water step. SB injects the StepContribution and ChunkContext instances into this method and expects a return value of type RepeatStatus. Use of these types is explained in later sections. For this example, we just need to know that RepeatStatus.FINISHED indicates to the DB a successful completion of Step.

We won't list the AddTea and AddWater classes, because they are similar to BoilWater; we're only simulating the tea preparation step with a different text message.

Tasklet Step Example with XML Configuration

Now that we've sketched the domain, we can take a look at the SB configuration in Listing 9-19.

Listing 9-19. XML Configuration of XML Tasklet Step Example (File batch-config.xml in Folder src/main/resources of Example Project 0904-tasklet-step-xml)

```xml
<?xml version="1.0" encoding="UTF-8"?>
<beans:beans xmlns:beans="http://www.springframework.org/schema/beans"
  xmlns:xsi="http://www.w3.org/2001/XMLSchema-instance"
  xmlns="http://www.springframework.org/schema/batch"
```

```
  xsi:schemaLocation="http://www.springframework.org/schema/batch
    http://www.springframework.org/schema/batch/spring-batch.xsd
    http://www.springframework.org/schema/beans
    http://www.springframework.org/schema/beans/spring-beans.xsd">

  <job id="prepareTeaJob">
    <step id="boilWaterStep" next="addTeaStep">
      <tasklet ref="boilWater"/>
    </step>
    <step id="addTeaStep" next="addWaterStep">
      <tasklet ref="addTea"/>
    </step>
    <step id="addWaterStep">
      <tasklet ref="addWater"/>
    </step>
  </job>
</beans:beans>
```

Job in this case consists of three steps; each one refers to the Tasklet instance of BoilWater, AddTea, and AddWater. Each step has to have a unique name and needs to specify which step should go next after its completion. The main class BatchApplication and BatchConfiguration are exactly the same as for XML chunk-oriented examples in Listings 9-7 and 9-8. When we run BatchApplication as a Java application, we see the output in Listing 9-20.

Listing 9-20. Output of Tasklet Step Example

```
2015-09-26 23:23:04.933  INFO 6564 --- [          main] o.s.b.c.l.support.SimpleJobLauncher
: Job: [FlowJob: [name=prepareTeaJob]] launched with the following parameters: [{}]
2015-09-26 23:23:04.971  INFO 6564 --- [          main] o.s.batch.core.job.
SimpleStepHandler      : Executing step: [boilWaterStep]
2015-09-26 23:23:04.986  INFO 6564 --- [          main] n.l.b.e.c.step.
SimpleExecutablePoint      : Boil Water
2015-09-26 23:23:05.013  INFO 6564 --- [          main] o.s.batch.core.job.
SimpleStepHandler      : Executing step: [addTeaStep]
2015-09-26 23:23:05.019  INFO 6564 --- [          main] n.l.b.e.c.step.
SimpleExecutablePoint      : Add Tea
2015-09-26 23:23:05.045  INFO 6564 --- [          main] o.s.batch.core.job.
SimpleStepHandler      : Executing step: [addWaterStep]
2015-09-26 23:23:05.050  INFO 6564 --- [          main] n.l.b.e.c.step.
SimpleExecutablePoint      : Add Water
2015-09-26 23:23:05.067  INFO 6564 --- [          main] o.s.b.c.l.support.SimpleJobLauncher
: Job: [FlowJob: [name=prepareTeaJob]] completed with the following parameters: [{}] and the
following status: [COMPLETED]
```

Figure 9-3 depicts the SB job.

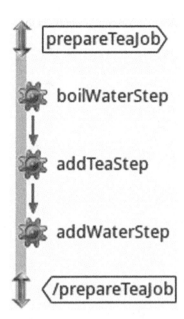

Figure 9-3. *Batch graph of tasklet example batch job*

With SB, we can also visualize batching flows in Spring Tools Suite (STS), similarly to Spring Integration. We can also use the STS Batch Graph Editor to create SB flows. Figure 9-4 shows the location of the editor in STS.

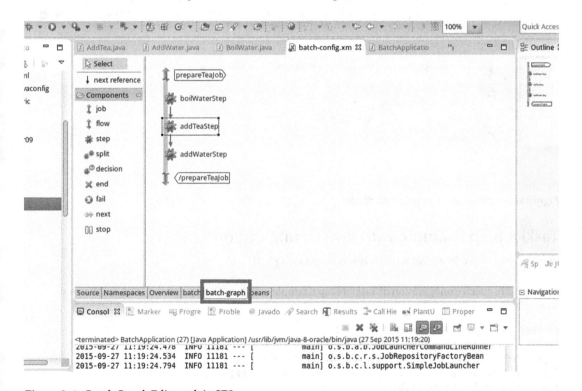

Figure 9-4. *Batch Graph Editor tab in STS*

By double-clicking SB components in the graph, we can change attributes of those components via the Properties tab. This is shown in Figure 9-5.

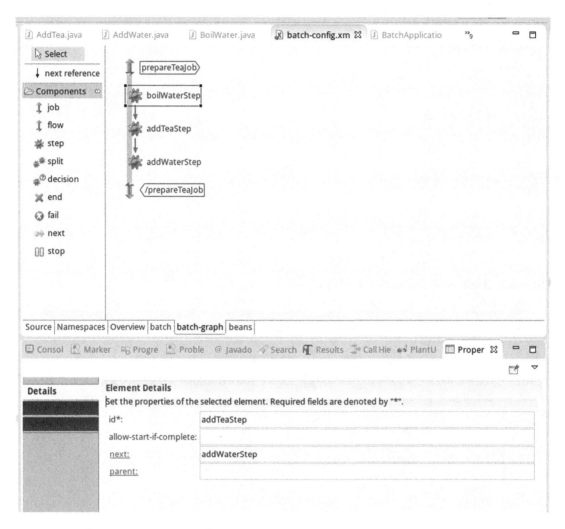

Figure 9-5. *Editing SB component attributes*

Tasklet Step Example with Java Configuration

Preparing tea with a Java configuration is shown in Listing 9-21.

Listing 9-21. Batch Configuration of Tasklet Step Example with Java Configuration (0905-tasklet-step-javaconfig)

```
package net.lkrnac.book.eiws.chapter09;
import net.lkrnac.book.eiws.chapter09.step.tea.AddTea;
import net.lkrnac.book.eiws.chapter09.step.tea.AddWater;
import net.lkrnac.book.eiws.chapter09.step.tea.BoilWater;
import org.springframework.batch.core.Job;
```

```java
import org.springframework.batch.core.Step;
import org.springframework.batch.core.configuration.annotation.EnableBatchProcessing;
import org.springframework.batch.core.configuration.annotation.JobBuilderFactory;
import org.springframework.batch.core.configuration.annotation.StepBuilderFactory;
import org.springframework.beans.factory.annotation.Qualifier;
import org.springframework.context.annotation.Bean;
import org.springframework.context.annotation.Configuration;

@Configuration
@EnableBatchProcessing
public class BatchConfiguration {
  @Bean
  public Step boilWaterStep(StepBuilderFactory stepFactory, BoilWater boilWater) {
    return stepFactory.get("boilWaterStep").tasklet(boilWater).build();
  }

  @Bean
  public Step addTeaStep(StepBuilderFactory stepFactory, AddTea addTea) {
    return stepFactory.get("addTeaStep").tasklet(addTea).build();
  }

  @Bean
  public Step addWaterStep(StepBuilderFactory stepFactory, AddWater addWater) {
    return stepFactory.get("addWaterStep").tasklet(addWater).build();
  }

  @Bean
  public Job prepareTeaJob(JobBuilderFactory jobBuilderFactory,
      @Qualifier("boilWaterStep") Step boilWaterStep,
      @Qualifier("addTeaStep") Step addTeaStep,
      @Qualifier("addWaterStep") Step addWaterStep) {
    return jobBuilderFactory.get("prepareTeaJob")
        .start(boilWaterStep)
        .next(addTeaStep)
        .next(addWaterStep)
        .build();
  }
}
```

Each custom Tasklet (BoilWater, AddTea, AddWater) needs to be wrapped into TaskletStep so that we can use it as part of the Job. We create a Step instance for each Tasklet by using StepBuilderFactory. The get() method creates an instance of StepBuilder based on the given name of the Step, the tasklet() method creates a TaskletStepBuilder instance based on the given Tasklet, and finally, the build() call creates the Step instance. We register this instance as a Spring bean.

When we create Job in the prepareTeaJob() method, we need to autowire each Step via the bean name instead of the type, because we have three beans of type Step in the Spring context. This is a little bit of annoying boilerplate code when we define an SB configuration with Java. After we inject all the steps and JobBuilderFactory, we create the Job instance and also register it as a Spring bean.

The main class for this example is the standard Spring Boot main class. When we run it, we see output similar to that of the previous example (Listing 9-20).

JobLauncher

JobLauncher is the interface used to execute SB jobs registered in the Spring context. Spring provides a SimpleJobLauncher implementation of this interface out of the box.

So far, we haven't needed to use it, because every Job was executed immediately after the Spring context was initialized by Spring Boot. We also didn't need to create the JobLauncher instance, as the @EnableBatchProcessing annotation created it for us. But automatic execution at the application's start is not always suitable, and we may need to explicitly execute a particular job.

Listing 9-22 shows the signature of the JobLauncher interface.

Listing 9-22. JobLauncher Interface

```
package org.springframework.batch.core.launch;
import org.springframework.batch.core.Job;
import org.springframework.batch.core.JobExecution;
import org.springframework.batch.core.JobParameters;
import org.springframework.batch.core.JobParametersInvalidException;
import org.springframework.batch.core.repository.JobExecutionAlreadyRunningException;
import org.springframework.batch.core.repository.JobInstanceAlreadyCompleteException;
import org.springframework.batch.core.repository.JobRestartException;

public interface JobLauncher {
  public JobExecution run(Job job, JobParameters jobParameters)
     throws JobExecutionAlreadyRunningException, JobRestartException,
            JobInstanceAlreadyCompleteException, JobParametersInvalidException;
}
```

JobLauncher declares only one method, run(), which returns an instance of JobExecution. When the client executes this method, the execution is by default synchronous; the caller is blocked until the job finishes. In such a case, the resulting status of the job is indicated by JobExecution.getExitStatus(). When we use synchronous execution, the exit status is typically ExitStatus.COMPLETED or ExitStatus.FAILED.

But in some cases, we don't want to block the caller. For these cases, implementation of SimpleJobLauncher can be configured with TaskExecutor. With this configuration, the SimpleJobLauncher.run() call doesn't block, and the existing status may configured to ExitStatus.UNKNOWN, ExitStatus.STARTING, or ExitStatus.STARTED, until the Job is finished.

JobLauncher Example with XML Configuration

In this case, we don't use Spring Boot. Listing 9-23 shows the XML configuration.

Listing 9-23. XML Configuration of JobLauncher Example (File batch-beans-config.xml in Folder src/main/resources of Example Project 0906-job-launcher-xml)

```
<?xml version="1.0" encoding="UTF-8"?>
<beans xmlns="http://www.springframework.org/schema/beans"
  xmlns:xsi="http://www.w3.org/2001/XMLSchema-instance"
  xmlns:context="http://www.springframework.org/schema/context"
  xsi:schemaLocation="http://www.springframework.org/schema/beans
    http://www.springframework.org/schema/beans/spring-beans.xsd
    http://www.springframework.org/schema/context
    http://www.springframework.org/schema/context/spring-context.xsd">
```

```
<context:component-scan base-package="net.lkrnac.book.eiws.chapter09" />

<bean id="transactionManager"
  class="org.springframework.batch.support.transaction.ResourcelessTransactionManager" />

<bean id="jobRepository"
  class="org.springframework.batch.core.repository.support.MapJobRepositoryFactoryBean">
  <property name="transactionManager" ref="transactionManager" />
</bean>

<bean id="jobLauncher"
  class="org.springframework.batch.core.launch.support.SimpleJobLauncher">
  <property name="jobRepository" ref="jobRepository" />
</bean>
</beans>
```

We configure the Spring components scan in the net.lkrnac.book.eiws.chapter09 package, which will configure the common Tasklet "tea" steps into our context. Next we need to configure two mandatory beans. For transactionManager, we use ResourcelessTransactionManager. This implementation of a transaction manager doesn't start a transaction; it is supposed to be used for testing purposes only. In our case, we don't use any transactions, but we need to configure a transaction manager for the JobRepository bean.

JobRepository is the second mandatory bean for SB configuration. We will dive into its function later in the chapter. We just quickly mention now that it is used to store SB processing metadata. In this case, we aren't using a real data store, but instead will store metadata into an in-memory map. This implementation of JobRepository is provided by MapJobRepositoryFactoryBean. Next we configure the JobLauncher bean. The SimpleJobLauncher implementation requires configuring the mandatory parameter jobRepository.

This example uses the same SB flow as the TaskletStep XML example in Listing 9-19. The main class of this example is shown in Listing 9-24.

Listing 9-24. Main Class of JobLauncher XML Example (0906-job-launcher-xml)

```java
package net.lkrnac.book.eiws.chapter09;
import lombok.extern.slf4j.Slf4j;
import org.springframework.batch.core.Job;
import org.springframework.batch.core.JobExecution;
import org.springframework.batch.core.JobParameters;
import org.springframework.batch.core.launch.JobLauncher;
import org.springframework.context.support.GenericApplicationContext;
import org.springframework.context.support.GenericXmlApplicationContext;
import org.springframework.core.io.ClassPathResource;

@Slf4j
public class BatchApplication {
  public static void main(String[] args) throws Exception {
    ClassPathResource batchConfig = new ClassPathResource("batch-config.xml");
    ClassPathResource batchBeansConfig = new ClassPathResource("batch-beans-config.xml");
    GenericApplicationContext context = new GenericXmlApplicationContext(
        batchConfig, batchBeansConfig);
```

```
  JobLauncher jobLauncher = (JobLauncher) context.getBean(JobLauncher.class);
  Job job = (Job) context.getBean("prepareTeaJob");
  JobExecution execution = jobLauncher.run(job, new JobParameters());
  log.info("Exit Status : {}", execution.getStatus());
  context.close();
 }
}
```

@Slf4j is Lombok's convenience annotation to define the Log4j logger instance. Notice that this main class is not a Spring configuration in this case. This is because we create the Spring context based on two XML configurations already mentioned in the previous listings.

When the Spring context instance is created, the JobLauncher and Job instances can be retrieved via the getBean() method. The next call is execution of Job itself. JobLauncher.run() also needs to take a parameter of type JobParameters. In this case, we create an empty instance of it, which means our Job doesn't take any parameters. We show the use of this feature later in the chapter.

The last statements in the main method print out the existing status and close the Spring context. Listing 9-25 shows the output when we run this main class.

Listing 9-25. Output of JobLauncher XML Example

```
16:15:58.829 [main] INFO  o.s.b.c.l.support.SimpleJobLauncher - Job: [FlowJob:
[name=prepareTeaJob]] launched with the following parameters: [{}]
16:15:58.865 [main] INFO  o.s.batch.core.job.SimpleStepHandler - Executing step: [boilWaterStep]
16:15:58.879 [main] INFO  n.l.b.e.c.step.SimpleExecutablePoint - Boil Water
16:15:58.919 [main] INFO  o.s.batch.core.job.SimpleStepHandler - Executing step: [addTeaStep]
16:15:58.923 [main] INFO  n.l.b.e.c.step.SimpleExecutablePoint - Add Tea
16:15:58.956 [main] INFO  o.s.batch.core.job.SimpleStepHandler - Executing step: [addWaterStep]
16:15:58.959 [main] INFO  n.l.b.e.c.step.SimpleExecutablePoint - Add Water
16:15:58.974 [main] INFO  o.s.b.c.l.support.SimpleJobLauncher - Job: [FlowJob:
[name=prepareTeaJob]] completed with the following parameters: [{}] and the following
status: [COMPLETED]
16:15:58.974 [main] INFO  n.l.b.e.chapter09.BatchApplication - Exit Status: COMPLETED
```

JobLauncher Example with Java Configuration

Listing 9-26 shows the Java configuration of the mandatory SB beans.

Listing 9-26. Java Configuration of JobLauncher Example (0907-job-launcher-javaconfig)

```
package net.lkrnac.book.eiws.chapter09;
import org.springframework.batch.core.launch.JobLauncher;
import org.springframework.batch.core.launch.support.SimpleJobLauncher;
import org.springframework.batch.core.repository.JobRepository;
import org.springframework.batch.core.repository.support.MapJobRepositoryFactoryBean;
import org.springframework.batch.support.transaction.ResourcelessTransactionManager;
import org.springframework.context.annotation.Bean;
import org.springframework.context.annotation.Configuration;
import org.springframework.transaction.PlatformTransactionManager;
```

```
@Configuration
public class BatchBeansConfiguration {
  @Bean
  public PlatformTransactionManager transactionManager() {
    return new ResourcelessTransactionManager();
  }

  @Bean
  public JobRepository jobRepository(PlatformTransactionManager transactionManager)
      throws Exception {
    return new MapJobRepositoryFactoryBean(transactionManager).getObject();
  }

  @Bean
  public JobLauncher jobLauncher(JobRepository jobRepository) {
    SimpleJobLauncher simpleJobLauncher = new SimpleJobLauncher();
    simpleJobLauncher.setJobRepository(jobRepository);
    return simpleJobLauncher;
  }
}
```

Readers familiar with Spring Core features shouldn't be surprised. This Java configuration is the exact mirror of the XML configuration in the previous example (Listing 9-23). The @Bean annotation and <bean> XML tag can be interchanged one to one in most cases for Spring configurations. The only difference is when FactoryBean is used, because XML configuration calls getObject() automatically, whereas the Java configuration needs to call this method explicitly. In this case, we need to create JobRepository by the factory method MapJobRepositoryFactoryBean.getObject().

The next class of this example defines the SB Job with Steps. We use the same tea preparation configuration as in Listing 9-21 from the TaskletStep example. The main class of this example is shown in Listing 9-27.

Listing 9-27. Main Class of JobLauncher Example with Java Configuration (0907-job-launcher-javaconfig)

```
package net.lkrnac.book.eiws.chapter09;
import lombok.extern.slf4j.Slf4j;
import org.springframework.batch.core.Job;
import org.springframework.batch.core.JobExecution;
import org.springframework.batch.core.JobParameters;
import org.springframework.batch.core.launch.JobLauncher;
import org.springframework.context.annotation.AnnotationConfigApplicationContext;
import org.springframework.context.annotation.ComponentScan;
import org.springframework.context.annotation.Configuration;
import org.springframework.context.support.GenericApplicationContext;

@Slf4j
@Configuration
@ComponentScan
public class BatchApplication {
  public static void main(String[] args) throws Exception {
    GenericApplicationContext context =
        new AnnotationConfigApplicationContext(BatchApplication.class);
```

```
JobLauncher jobLauncher = (JobLauncher) context.getBean(JobLauncher.class);
Job job = (Job) context.getBean("prepareTeaJob");
JobExecution execution = jobLauncher.run(job, new JobParameters());
log.info("Exit Status : {}", execution.getStatus());
context.close();
  }
}
```

This code is similar to the previous example. The only difference is that this class is also a Spring configuration doing a component scan in the current package with subpackages, and we use it to create the Spring context. The output after running this main class is also similar to the previous example in Listing 9-25.

Asynchronous JobLauncher Example

Let's dive into a case where the caller of the SB job can't be blocked. Listing 9-28 shows the SB beans configured to execute Job asynchronously.

Listing 9-28. Asynchronous Configuration of JobLauncher (0908-job-launcher-async)

```
package net.lkrnac.book.eiws.chapter09;
import org.springframework.batch.core.launch.JobLauncher;
import org.springframework.batch.core.launch.support.SimpleJobLauncher;
import org.springframework.batch.core.repository.JobRepository;
import org.springframework.batch.core.repository.support.MapJobRepositoryFactoryBean;
import org.springframework.batch.support.transaction.ResourcelessTransactionManager;
import org.springframework.context.annotation.Bean;
import org.springframework.context.annotation.Configuration;
import org.springframework.core.task.TaskExecutor;
import org.springframework.scheduling.concurrent.ThreadPoolTaskExecutor;
import org.springframework.transaction.PlatformTransactionManager;

@Configuration
public class BatchBeansConfiguration {
  @Bean
  public PlatformTransactionManager transactionManager() {
    return new ResourcelessTransactionManager();
  }

  @Bean
  public JobRepository jobRepository(PlatformTransactionManager transactionManager)
      throws Exception {
    return new MapJobRepositoryFactoryBean(transactionManager).getObject();
  }

  @Bean
  public TaskExecutor customTaskExecutor() {
    ThreadPoolTaskExecutor threadPool = new ThreadPoolTaskExecutor();
    threadPool.setCorePoolSize(10);
    return threadPool;
  }
```

```
@Bean
public JobLauncher jobLauncher(JobRepository jobRepository, TaskExecutor taskExecutor) {
  SimpleJobLauncher simpleJobLauncher = new SimpleJobLauncher();
  simpleJobLauncher.setJobRepository(jobRepository);
  simpleJobLauncher.setTaskExecutor(taskExecutor);
  return simpleJobLauncher;
  }
}
```

In this configuration, we introduce the new Spring bean TaskExecutor, which is used for JobLauncher bean creation. This setup ensures that Job is executed asynchronously by JobLauncher. This example also uses the tea preparation Job configuration from Listing 9-19. The main class of this example is in Listing 9-29.

Listing 9-29. Main Class of Asynchronous JobLauncher Example (0908-job-launcher-async)

```
package net.lkrnac.book.eiws.chapter09;
import lombok.extern.slf4j.Slf4j;
import org.springframework.batch.core.Job;
import org.springframework.batch.core.JobExecution;
import org.springframework.batch.core.JobParameters;
import org.springframework.batch.core.launch.JobLauncher;
import org.springframework.context.annotation.AnnotationConfigApplicationContext;
import org.springframework.context.annotation.ComponentScan;
import org.springframework.context.annotation.Configuration;
import org.springframework.context.support.GenericApplicationContext;

@Slf4j
@Configuration
@ComponentScan
public class BatchApplication {
  public static void main(String[] args) throws Exception {
    GenericApplicationContext context =
        new AnnotationConfigApplicationContext(BatchApplication.class);

    JobLauncher jobLauncher = (JobLauncher) context.getBean(JobLauncher.class);
    Job job = (Job) context.getBean("prepareTeaJob");
    JobExecution execution = jobLauncher.run(job, new JobParameters());
    log.info("Exit Status: {}", execution.getStatus());
    Thread.sleep(10);
    log.info("Exit Status: {}", execution.getStatus());
    Thread.sleep(500);
    log.info("Exit Status: {}", execution.getStatus());
    context.close();
  }
}
```

After we execute prepareTeaJob, we log the exit status immediately, after 10 ms and also after 500 ms. As Job is running, we should observe the exit status changing in these log entries. Listing 9-30 shows the output after running this main class.

Listing 9-30. Output of Asynchronous JobLauncher Example

```
17:37:46.318 [customTaskExecutor-1] INFO  o.s.b.c.l.support.SimpleJobLauncher - Job:
[SimpleJob: [name=prepareTeaJob]] launched with the following parameters: [{}]
17:37:46.317 [main] INFO  n.l.b.e.chapter09.BatchApplication - Exit Status: STARTING
17:37:46.330 [main] INFO  n.l.b.e.chapter09.BatchApplication - Exit Status: STARTED
17:37:46.359 [customTaskExecutor-1] INFO  o.s.batch.core.job.SimpleStepHandler - Executing
step: [boilWaterStep]
17:37:46.373 [customTaskExecutor-1] INFO  n.l.b.e.c.step.SimpleExecutablePoint - Boil Water
17:37:46.400 [customTaskExecutor-1] INFO  o.s.batch.core.job.SimpleStepHandler - Executing
step: [addTeaStep]
17:37:46.404 [customTaskExecutor-1] INFO  n.l.b.e.c.step.SimpleExecutablePoint - Add Tea
17:37:46.435 [customTaskExecutor-1] INFO  o.s.batch.core.job.SimpleStepHandler - Executing
step: [addWaterStep]
17:37:46.438 [customTaskExecutor-1] INFO  n.l.b.e.c.step.SimpleExecutablePoint - Add Water
17:37:46.453 [customTaskExecutor-1] INFO  o.s.b.c.l.support.SimpleJobLauncher - Job:
[SimpleJob: [name=prepareTeaJob]] completed with the following parameters: [{}] and the
following status: [COMPLETED]
17:37:46.830 [main] INFO  n.l.b.e.chapter09.BatchApplication - Exit Status: COMPLETED
```

The exit status immediately after we kick off the Job is STARTING, and after 10 ms it changes to STARTED. Notice that Job execution log entries are done from the customTaskExecutor thread pool. After 500 ms, the job also is COMPLETED in the caller thread.

JobParameters

There is often a requirement to pass parameters into a batch Job. Imagine we need to process data with an attribute-created date. We may want to specify a date parameter for batch processing, so that only data created on the specified date will be processed.

SB provides this support via the JobParameters class, which can be passed into the JobLauncher.run() method. This class encapsulates parameters into Map<String, JobParameter>. So each parameter has its name (key), and the value can be any Java type. Notice that the value in the map is the type JobParameter (singular), which represents a single batch Job parameter. JobParameters (plural) represents all parameters for one JobInstance.

In the JobParameters example, we slightly change the tea preparation process. Let's add sugar into our cup of tea. Listing 9-31 shows Tasklet using JobParameter.

Listing 9-31. JobParameter retrieval (0909-job-parameters)

```
package net.lkrnac.book.eiws.chapter09.step.tea;
import net.lkrnac.book.eiws.chapter09.step.SimpleExecutablePoint;
import org.springframework.batch.core.StepContribution;
import org.springframework.batch.core.scope.context.ChunkContext;
import org.springframework.batch.core.step.tasklet.Tasklet;
import org.springframework.batch.repeat.RepeatStatus;
import org.springframework.beans.factory.annotation.Autowired;
import org.springframework.stereotype.Component;
```

```
@Component
public class AddTeaWithParameter implements Tasklet {
  private SimpleExecutablePoint simpleExecutableStep;

  @Autowired
  public AddTeaWithParameter(SimpleExecutablePoint simpleExecutableStep) {
    super();
    this.simpleExecutableStep = simpleExecutableStep;
  }

  @Override
  public RepeatStatus execute(StepContribution contribution,
      ChunkContext chunkContext) throws Exception {
    String sugarAmount = chunkContext.getStepContext().getStepExecution()
        .getJobParameters().getString("sugarAmount");
    String stepSuffix = (sugarAmount == null) ? "" : " with " + sugarAmount;
    simpleExecutableStep.execute("Add Tea" + stepSuffix);
    return RepeatStatus.FINISHED;
  }
}
```

In this tea preparation Tasklet, we use the chunkContext instance to access the JobParameters instance and retrieve the parameter with the name sugarAmount. This specifies how much sugar the caller wants to add to a cup of tea. Again, we simulate the action by executing the simpleExecutableStep instance. After we are finished, we mark Step as FINISHED. Listing 9-32 shows the batch configuration.

Listing 9-32. Batch Configuration of JobParameters Example (0909-job-parameters)

```
package net.lkrnac.book.eiws.chapter09;
import net.lkrnac.book.eiws.chapter09.step.tea.AddTeaWithParameter;
import net.lkrnac.book.eiws.chapter09.step.tea.AddWater;
import net.lkrnac.book.eiws.chapter09.step.tea.BoilWater;
import org.springframework.batch.core.Job;
import org.springframework.batch.core.Step;
import org.springframework.batch.core.configuration.annotation.EnableBatchProcessing;
import org.springframework.batch.core.configuration.annotation.JobBuilderFactory;
import org.springframework.batch.core.configuration.annotation.StepBuilderFactory;
import org.springframework.beans.factory.annotation.Qualifier;
import org.springframework.context.annotation.Bean;
import org.springframework.context.annotation.Configuration;

@Configuration
@EnableBatchProcessing
public class BatchConfiguration {
  @Bean
  public Step boilWaterStep(StepBuilderFactory stepFactory, BoilWater boilWater) {
    return stepFactory.get("boilWaterStep").tasklet(boilWater).build();
  }
```

```java
@Bean
public Step addTeaStep(StepBuilderFactory stepFactory, AddTeaWithParameter addTea) {
  return stepFactory.get("addTeaStep").tasklet(addTea).build();
}

@Bean
public Step addWaterStep(StepBuilderFactory stepFactory, AddWater addWater) {
  return stepFactory.get("addWaterStep").tasklet(addWater).build();
}

@Bean
public Job prepareTeaJob(JobBuilderFactory jobBuilderFactory,
    @Qualifier("boilWaterStep") Step boilWaterStep,
    @Qualifier("addTeaStep") Step addTeaStep,
    @Qualifier("addWaterStep") Step addWaterStep) {
  return jobBuilderFactory.get("prepareTeaJob")
      .start(boilWaterStep)
      .next(addTeaStep)
      .next(addWaterStep)
      .build();
}
}
```

In this batch flow, we use AddTeaWithParameter instead of AddTea. Otherwise, the batch flow is exactly the same as in previous examples. Listing 9-33 shows the main class of this example.

Listing 9-33. Main Class of JobParameters Example (0909-job-parameters)

```java
package net.lkrnac.book.eiws.chapter09;
import lombok.extern.slf4j.Slf4j;
import org.springframework.batch.core.Job;
import org.springframework.batch.core.JobExecution;
import org.springframework.batch.core.JobParameters;
import org.springframework.batch.core.JobParametersBuilder;
import org.springframework.batch.core.launch.JobLauncher;
import org.springframework.boot.SpringApplication;
import org.springframework.boot.autoconfigure.SpringBootApplication;
import org.springframework.context.ConfigurableApplicationContext;

@Slf4j
@SpringBootApplication
public class BatchApplication {
  public static void main(String[] args) throws Exception {
    ConfigurableApplicationContext context =
        SpringApplication.run(BatchApplication.class, args);

    JobLauncher jobLauncher = (JobLauncher) context.getBean(JobLauncher.class);
    Job job = (Job) context.getBean("prepareTeaJob");

    JobParameters jobParameters1 = createJobParameters("no sugar");
    JobExecution execution1 = jobLauncher.run(job, jobParameters1);
    log.info("Exit Status: {}", execution1.getStatus());
```

```
    JobParameters jobParameters2 = createJobParameters("two spoons of sugar");
    JobExecution execution2 = jobLauncher.run(job, jobParameters2);
    log.info("Exit Status: {}", execution2.getStatus());
    context.close();
}

public static JobParameters createJobParameters(String sugarAmountValue) {
    return new JobParametersBuilder()
        .addString("sugarAmount", sugarAmountValue)
        .toJobParameters();
}
}
```

When we create the Spring context instance and retrieve JobLauncher and Job, we execute the prepareTeaJob job various times. The createJobParameters method helps us create the JobParameters instance with the parameter called sugarAmount. The first execution is done without sugar, and the second cup of tea is prepared with two spoonfuls of sugar. Each execution status is printed, and the Spring context is closed at the end of the program. Listing 9-34 shows the Spring Boot configuration file.

Listing 9-34. Turn Off Default Execution of SB Job by Spring Boot (File application.properties in Folder src/main/properties of Example Project 0909-job-parameters)

```
spring.batch.job.enabled=false
```

By default, Spring Boot with autoconfiguration enables executing all the SB Jobs it finds. But in this case, we don't want to run a default job without parameters, because we want to execute them explicitly with parameters. Therefore, this configuration is needed to disable automatic execution of SB jobs by Spring Boot autoconfiguration. Listing 9-35 shows the output when we run this example.

Listing 9-35. Output of JobParameters Example

```
2015-09-27 19:44:00.980  INFO  --- [          main] o.s.b.c.l.support.SimpleJobLauncher
: Job: [SimpleJob: [name=prepareTeaJob]] launched with the following parameters:
[{sugarAmount=no sugar}]
2015-09-27 19:44:01.014  INFO  --- [          main] o.s.batch.core.job.SimpleStepHandler
: Executing step: [boilWaterStep]
2015-09-27 19:44:01.038  INFO  --- [          main] n.l.b.e.c.step.SimpleExecutablePoint
: Boil Water
2015-09-27 19:44:01.070  INFO  --- [          main] o.s.batch.core.job.SimpleStepHandler
: Executing step: [addTeaStep]
2015-09-27 19:44:01.078  INFO  --- [          main] n.l.b.e.c.step.SimpleExecutablePoint
: Add Tea with no sugar
2015-09-27 19:44:01.100  INFO  --- [          main] o.s.batch.core.job.SimpleStepHandler
: Executing step: [addWaterStep]
2015-09-27 19:44:01.104  INFO  --- [          main] n.l.b.e.c.step.SimpleExecutablePoint
: Add Water
2015-09-27 19:44:01.126  INFO  --- [          main] o.s.b.c.l.support.SimpleJobLauncher
: Job: [SimpleJob: [name=prepareTeaJob]] completed with the following parameters:
[{sugarAmount=no sugar}] and the following status: [COMPLETED]
2015-09-27 19:44:01.128  INFO  --- [          main] n.l.b.eiws.chapter09.BatchApplication
: Exit Status: COMPLETED
```

```
2015-09-27 19:44:01.139  INFO  --- [            main] o.s.b.c.l.support.SimpleJobLauncher
: Job: [SimpleJob: [name=prepareTeaJob]] launched with the following parameters:
[{sugarAmount=two spoons of sugar}]
2015-09-27 19:44:01.154  INFO  --- [            main] o.s.batch.core.job.SimpleStepHandler
: Executing step: [boilWaterStep]
2015-09-27 19:44:01.162  INFO  --- [            main] n.l.b.e.c.step.SimpleExecutablePoint
: Boil Water
2015-09-27 19:44:01.205  INFO  --- [            main] o.s.batch.core.job.SimpleStepHandler
: Executing step: [addTeaStep]
2015-09-27 19:44:01.214  INFO  --- [            main] n.l.b.e.c.step.SimpleExecutablePoint
: Add Tea with two spoons of sugar
2015-09-27 19:44:01.240  INFO  --- [            main] o.s.batch.core.job.SimpleStepHandler
: Executing step: [addWaterStep]
2015-09-27 19:44:01.246  INFO  --- [            main] n.l.b.e.c.step.SimpleExecutablePoint
: Add Water
2015-09-27 19:44:01.260  INFO  --- [            main] o.s.b.c.l.support.SimpleJobLauncher
: Job: [SimpleJob: [name=prepareTeaJob]] completed with the following parameters:
[{sugarAmount=two spoons of sugar}] and the following status: [COMPLETED]
2015-09-27 19:44:01.260  INFO  --- [            main] n.l.b.eiws.chapter09.BatchApplication
: Exit Status: COMPLETED
```

CommandLineJobRunner

A lot of enterprises use some kind of scheduling system and monitoring system for batch processing. These systems often require running the execute batch processing logic from the command line. Therefore, SB provides easy execution of batch jobs via the command-line interface (CLI). This support is allowed via the CommandLineJobRunner class, where we can explicitly specify which Job should be executed as well as which parameters should be passed into it.

Of course, the SB application needs to indicate the exit status of the job execution when it is run from the CLI. This support uses a standard numeric exit code mechanism for processes within the operating system. When the operating system process returns a 0 exit code, it indicates success. If this exit code is nonzero, an error occurred. Therefore, SB assigns to each ExitStatus a numeric value, where COMPLETED has value 0. Every other ExitStatus is erroneous from the operating system point of view. FAILED status, for example, has value 5.

Execute Thin JAR from the Command Line

A Java application can be packaged in various ways. For example, Maven will build a thin JAR by default. This means that our application will be packaged into a single JAR without all the dependencies this JAR uses. This JAR packaging expects to have all the dependency locations provided in the CLASSPATH system variable.

This application structure is covered by the 0907-job-launcher-javaconfig example we already explained. This project needs to be first built with Maven. In the root directory of this project is the Maven configuration file pom.xml. If we have Maven installed, we can run the command mvn clean install, and the project will be built packaged as a thin JAR. After the project is packaged, we can run the SB Job from the command line by using the command in Listing 9-36. In this case, this command is executed on the Linux operating system, but the Windows or Mac command line would look the same.

Listing 9-36. Executing SB thin JAR from command line (File runFromCli.sh in Example Project 0907-job-launcher-javaconfig)

```
java -cp "target/dependency-jars/*:target/0907-job-launcher-javaconfig-0.0.2-SNAPSHOT.jar"
org.springframework.batch.core.launch.support.CommandLineJobRunner net.lkrnac.book.eiws.
chapter09.BatchApplication prepareTeaJob
```

This command is one line. The java command kicks off the installation of JRE in the operating system. The –cp parameter defines where to find CLASSPATH dependencies. Next, we need to specify the Java class to run. Of course, in this case, we want to run CommandLineJobRunner. Java expects the main method in this class, which is provided by SB. The last parameter is the name of the job we intend to run. After running this command, we can observe the same output as in Listing 9-30.

Execute Fat Spring Boot JAR from the Command Line

Another type of Java packaging type is often referred to as a *fat JAR*: all the JAR dependencies are packaged into the JAR file itself. This packaging can be easily achieved with Maven by using spring-boot-maven-plugin. The 0902-chunk-processing-generic-javaconfig example is configured this way, so when we build this project via the Maven command mvn clean install, we can execute the batch job via the command in Listing 9-37.

Listing 9-37. Executing SB Thin JAR from Command Line (File runFromCli.sh in Example Project 0902-chunk-processing-generic-javaconfig)

```
java -jar target/0902-chunk-processing-generic-javaconfig-0.0.2-SNAPSHOT.jar
```

Again, java kicks off the JRE installation on the local machine. The –jar parameter defines which JAR to execute—in this case, the Maven artifact created for this example. Spring Boot automatically runs all Jobs covered by this SB application, because we use autoconfiguration here. Running this command results in the same output as in Listing 9-9.

Execute XML Job from the Command Line

When we use XML configuration, execution from the command line looks like Listing 9-38.

Listing 9-38. Executing XML-Configured Job from Command Line (File runFromCli.sh in Example Project 0901-chunk-processing-generic-xml)

```
java -Dloader.main=org.springframework.batch.core.launch.support.CommandLineJobRunner -jar
target/0901-chunk-processing-generic-xml-0.0.2-SNAPSHOT.jar batch-config.xml
simpleRecordsJob
```

Instead of the main configuration class, we use the XML configuration file as a parameter for CommandLineJobRunner. The output after running this command again looks like Listing 9-9.

Execute Job with Parameters from the Command Line

Of course, it is possible to pass parameters into Job executed from the command line. This example is Spring Boot based. We use our common tea Tasklets with AddTeaWithParameter from the previous example in Listing 9-31, so that JobParameters can be applied. Listing 9-39 shows the batch configuration.

Listing 9-39. Batch Configuration for Example that runs Job from SLI with Parameters (0910-job-parameters-cli)

```
package net.lkrnac.book.eiws.chapter09;

import net.lkrnac.book.eiws.chapter09.step.tea.AddTeaWithParameter;
import net.lkrnac.book.eiws.chapter09.step.tea.AddWater;
import net.lkrnac.book.eiws.chapter09.step.tea.BoilWater;

import org.springframework.batch.core.Job;
import org.springframework.batch.core.Step;
import org.springframework.batch.core.configuration.annotation.EnableBatchProcessing;
import org.springframework.batch.core.configuration.annotation.JobBuilderFactory;
import org.springframework.batch.core.configuration.annotation.StepBuilderFactory;
import org.springframework.beans.factory.annotation.Qualifier;
import org.springframework.context.annotation.Bean;
import org.springframework.context.annotation.Configuration;

@Configuration
@EnableBatchProcessing
public class BatchConfiguration {
  @Bean
  public Step boilWaterStep(StepBuilderFactory stepFactory, BoilWater boilWater) {
    return stepFactory.get("boilWaterStep").tasklet(boilWater).build();
  }

  @Bean
  public Step addTeaStep(StepBuilderFactory stepFactory, AddTeaWithParameter addTea) {
    return stepFactory.get("addTeaStep").tasklet(addTea).build();
  }

  @Bean
  public Step addWaterStep(StepBuilderFactory stepFactory, AddWater addWater) {
    return stepFactory.get("addWaterStep").tasklet(addWater).build();
  }

  @Bean
  public Job prepareTeaJob(JobBuilderFactory jobBuilderFactory,
      @Qualifier("boilWaterStep") Step boilWaterStep,
      @Qualifier("addTeaStep") Step addTeaStep,
      @Qualifier("addWaterStep") Step addWaterStep) {
    return jobBuilderFactory.get("prepareTeaJob")
      .start(boilWaterStep)
      .next(addTeaStep)
      .next(addWaterStep)
      .build();
  }
```

```
    @Bean
    public Job prepareStrongTeaJob(JobBuilderFactory jobBuilderFactory,
        @Qualifier("boilWaterStep") Step boilWaterStep,
        @Qualifier("addTeaStep") Step addTeaStep,
        @Qualifier("addWaterStep") Step addWaterStep) {
      return jobBuilderFactory.get("prepareStrongTeaJob")
          .start(boilWaterStep)
          .next(addTeaStep)
          .next(addTeaStep)
          .next(addWaterStep)
          .build();
    }
}
```

We create two Jobs for tea preparation. The first one, prepareTeaJob, uses only one AddTeaWithParameter Tasklet. The second one adds tea twice (has two steps with AddTeaWithParameter), so that we can have stronger tea. Two jobs are defined to highlight Spring Boot features to specify which Job should be run from the command line. Listing 9-40 shows the main class of this application.

Listing 9-40. Main Class of Example that Runs Job from SLI with Parameters (0910-job-parameters-cli)

```
package net.lkrnac.book.eiws.chapter09;
import org.springframework.boot.SpringApplication;
import org.springframework.boot.autoconfigure.SpringBootApplication;

@SpringBootApplication
public class BatchApplication {
  public static void main(String[] args) throws Exception {
    SpringApplication.run(BatchApplication.class, args);
  }
}
```

Notice that this main class is different from the standard Spring Boot main class in Listing 9-8, because it passes command-line arguments from the main method to the SpringApplication.run() method as a second parameter. After we build the artifact of the fat JAR, we can execute the job or various jobs from the CLI. Listing 9-41 shows the CLI command whereby all the jobs will run with parameters passed from the command line.

Listing 9-41. Executing SB Jobs with Parameters from Command Line (File runFromCli.sh in Example Project 0910-job-parameters-cli)

```
java -jar target/0910-job-parameters-cli-0.0.2-SNAPSHOT.jar sugarAmount="no sugar"
```

In this command, we don't specify a job name to execute. Therefore, Spring Boot by default executes all jobs. Running this command provides the output in Listing 9-42.

Listing 9-42. Output of Running all Jobs with Parameters

```
2015-09-28 21:57:12.410  INFO 1869 --- [          main] o.s.b.c.l.support.SimpleJobLauncher
: Job: [SimpleJob: [name=prepareTeaJob]] launched with the following parameters:
[{sugarAmount=no sugar}]
2015-09-28 21:57:12.434  INFO 1869 --- [          main] o.s.batch.core.job.
SimpleStepHandler     : Executing step: [boilWaterStep]
```

```
2015-09-28 21:57:12.450  INFO 1869 --- [            main] n.l.b.e.c.step.
SimpleExecutablePoint      : Boil Water
2015-09-28 21:57:12.479  INFO 1869 --- [            main] o.s.batch.core.job.
SimpleStepHandler      : Executing step: [addTeaStep]
2015-09-28 21:57:12.486  INFO 1869 --- [            main] n.l.b.e.c.step.
SimpleExecutablePoint      : Add Tea with no sugar
2015-09-28 21:57:12.516  INFO 1869 --- [            main] o.s.batch.core.job.
SimpleStepHandler      : Executing step: [addWaterStep]
2015-09-28 21:57:12.520  INFO 1869 --- [            main] n.l.b.e.c.step.
SimpleExecutablePoint      : Add Water
2015-09-28 21:57:12.548  INFO 1869 --- [            main] o.s.b.c.l.support.SimpleJobLauncher
: Job: [SimpleJob: [name=prepareTeaJob]] completed with the following parameters:
[{sugarAmount=no sugar}] and the following status: [COMPLETED]
2015-09-28 21:57:12.565  INFO 1869 --- [            main] o.s.b.c.l.support.SimpleJobLauncher
: Job: [SimpleJob: [name=prepareStrongTeaJob]] launched with the following parameters:
[{sugarAmount=no sugar}]
2015-09-28 21:57:12.576  INFO 1869 --- [            main] o.s.batch.core.job.
SimpleStepHandler      : Executing step: [boilWaterStep]
2015-09-28 21:57:12.579  INFO 1869 --- [            main] n.l.b.e.c.step.
SimpleExecutablePoint      : Boil Water
2015-09-28 21:57:12.606  INFO 1869 --- [            main] o.s.batch.core.job.
SimpleStepHandler      : Executing step: [addTeaStep]
2015-09-28 21:57:12.610  INFO 1869 --- [            main] n.l.b.e.c.step.
SimpleExecutablePoint      : Add Tea with no sugar
2015-09-28 21:57:12.646  INFO 1869 --- [            main] o.s.batch.core.job.
SimpleStepHandler      : Duplicate step [addTeaStep] detected in execution of
job=[prepareStrongTeaJob]. If either step fails, both will be executed again on restart.
2015-09-28 21:57:12.653  INFO 1869 --- [            main] o.s.batch.core.job.
SimpleStepHandler      : Executing step: [addTeaStep]
2015-09-28 21:57:12.657  INFO 1869 --- [            main] n.l.b.e.c.step.
SimpleExecutablePoint      : Add Tea with no sugar
2015-09-28 21:57:12.687  INFO 1869 --- [            main] o.s.batch.core.job.
SimpleStepHandler      : Executing step: [addWaterStep]
2015-09-28 21:57:12.691  INFO 1869 --- [            main] n.l.b.e.c.step.
SimpleExecutablePoint      : Add Water
2015-09-28 21:57:12.700  INFO 1869 --- [            main] o.s.b.c.l.support.SimpleJobLauncher
: Job: [SimpleJob: [name=prepareStrongTeaJob]] completed with the following parameters:
[{sugarAmount=no sugar}] and the following status: [COMPLETED]
```

As you can see, both jobs were executed, and the addSugar parameter was applied for both of them. During execution of prepareStrongTeaJob, there is a log entry about duplicate step execution, as the SB framework detected duplicate use of addTeaStep. By default, each Step is meant to be executed only once for Job. In this case, we used the same Step in one Job twice. Step was executed anyway.

There are ways to highlight for the SB framework that we want to execute the same Step twice. We focus on them later in the chapter. This log message also mentions a restart; the restart mechanism is covered in upcoming sections.

Listing 9-43 shows the command indicating that only the specified job will run.

Listing 9-43. Executing SB Single Job with Parameters from the Command Line (File runOneJobFromCli.sh in Example Project 0910-job-parameters-cli)

```
java -Dspring.batch.job.names=prepareTeaJob -jar target/0910-job-parameters-cli-0.0.2-
SNAPSHOT.jar  sugarAmount="no sugar"
```

With the system property definition -Dspring.batch.job.names=prepareTeaJob, we specify that only prepareTeaJob should be executed by Spring Boot. Properties for the Spring Boot framework can be specified via the command line as well as via the application.properties configuration file shown earlier. This way, we can also specify various jobs when we enter their names as comma delimited. Listing 9-44 shows the output that confirms that only one job was executed with parameters.

Listing 9-44. Output of Running One Job with Parameters

```
2015-09-28 21:59:40.187  INFO 1981 --- [            main] o.s.b.c.l.support.SimpleJobLauncher
: Job: [SimpleJob: [name=prepareTeaJob]] launched with the following parameters:
[{sugarAmount=no sugar}]
2015-09-28 21:59:40.214  INFO 1981 --- [            main] o.s.batch.core.job.
SimpleStepHandler     : Executing step: [boilWaterStep]
2015-09-28 21:59:40.234  INFO 1981 --- [            main] n.l.b.e.c.step.
SimpleExecutablePoint     : Boil Water
2015-09-28 21:59:40.261  INFO 1981 --- [            main] o.s.batch.core.job.
SimpleStepHandler     : Executing step: [addTeaStep]
2015-09-28 21:59:40.266  INFO 1981 --- [            main] n.l.b.e.c.step.
SimpleExecutablePoint     : Add Tea with no sugar
2015-09-28 21:59:40.291  INFO 1981 --- [            main] o.s.batch.core.job.
SimpleStepHandler     : Executing step: [addWaterStep]
2015-09-28 21:59:40.296  INFO 1981 --- [            main] n.l.b.e.c.step.
SimpleExecutablePoint     : Add Water
2015-09-28 21:59:40.312  INFO 1981 --- [            main] o.s.b.c.l.support.SimpleJobLauncher
: Job: [SimpleJob: [name=prepareTeaJob]] completed with the following parameters:
[{sugarAmount=no sugar}] and the following status: [COMPLETED]
```

JobRepository

We already mentioned that SB needs to have the JobRepository bean configured. This bean ensures that every JobExecution and StepExecution states (or other states SB uses) are persisted into a data store. This data store can be any type of SQL database Spring can use. This access is based on the DataSource bean defined in the Spring context.

SB uses a defined database schema to store its metadata and provides SQL scripts to create or drop the schema for the most commonly used relational databases. These schemas are located in the spring-batch-core library in the org/springframework/batch/core folder. So, for example, if we want to create a schema for the PostgreSQL database, we can use the SQL script classpath:/org/springframework/batch/core/schema-postgresql.sql to create the SB schema and the script classpath:/org/springframework/batch/core/schema-drop-postgresql.sql to erase it.

This mechanism is powerful, because the developer doesn't need to care about persisting the state of batch execution. SB persists execution states automatically, so it is easy to handle scenarios in which, for example, Job is killed in the middle of execution and we want to continue execution from the point where the DB execution was left behind.

Configuring JobRepository with XML Configuration

This example does not use Spring Boot. Listing 9-45 shows the SB bean configuration needed for this example.

Listing 9-45. Beans Needed for JobRepository Configuration (File batch-beans-config.xml in Folder src/main/resources of Example Project 0911-job-repository-xml)

```xml
<?xml version="1.0" encoding="UTF-8"?>
<beans xmlns="http://www.springframework.org/schema/beans"
  xmlns:xsi="http://www.w3.org/2001/XMLSchema-instance"
  xmlns:batch="http://www.springframework.org/schema/batch"
  xmlns:context="http://www.springframework.org/schema/context"
  xmlns:jdbc="http://www.springframework.org/schema/jdbc"
  xsi:schemaLocation="http://www.springframework.org/schema/batch
    http://www.springframework.org/schema/batch/spring-batch.xsd
    http://www.springframework.org/schema/jdbc
    http://www.springframework.org/schema/jdbc/spring-jdbc.xsd
    http://www.springframework.org/schema/beans
    http://www.springframework.org/schema/beans/spring-beans.xsd
    http://www.springframework.org/schema/context
    http://www.springframework.org/schema/context/spring-context.xsd">

  <context:component-scan base-package="net.lkrnac.book.eiws.chapter09" />

  <bean id="transactionManager"
    class="org.springframework.batch.support.transaction.ResourcelessTransactionManager" />

  <bean id="jobLauncher"
    class="org.springframework.batch.core.launch.support.SimpleJobLauncher">
    <property name="jobRepository" ref="jobRepository" />
  </bean>

  <jdbc:embedded-database id="dataSource" type="H2">
    <jdbc:script
      location="classpath:/org/springframework/batch/core/schema-h2.sql" />
  </jdbc:embedded-database>

  <bean id="jdbcTemplate" class="org.springframework.jdbc.core.JdbcTemplate">
    <property name="dataSource" ref="dataSource"/>
  </bean>

  <batch:job-repository id="jobRepository" data-source="dataSource"
    transaction-manager="transactionManager" table-prefix="BATCH_"
    max-varchar-length="1000" />
</beans>
```

We use four namespaces that the Spring and SB frameworks provide: beans, jdbc, context, and batch. The default namespace here is beans, as we don't have a lot of batch XML tags. <context:component-scan>, transactionManager, and jobLauncher were already covered in previous examples. The component scan registers all the beans from the defined package into the Spring context. The transaction manager is needed to handle transactions, and JobLauncher is used for execution of batch jobs.

The `<jdbc:embedded-database>` XML tag configures the in-memory database we use in this example. This data source will be handling only storage of SB states, so we create a schema for it via the SQL script `classpath:/org/springframework/batch/core/schema-h2.sql`.

`JdbcTemplate` enables us to easily query the SB `JobRepository` data store. Finally, we create the `JobRepository` bean via the SB XML tag `<batch:job-repository>`. We need to specify the mandatory attributes `transaction-manager` and `data-source`, where we use the bean instances created earlier in this XML configuration. We can also define a prefix for all the SB tables in the database, which is handy for avoiding possible DB table name conflicts. The last attribute we use is the length of `VARCHAR` types in the DB. This can be handy if our `Job` or `Step` names are too long.

For SB `Job` configuration, we reuse the same `prepareTeaJob` flow from Listing 9-19. Listing 9-46 shows the main class of this example.

Listing 9-46. Main Class of JobRepository XML Example (0911-job-repository-xml)

```java
package net.lkrnac.book.eiws.chapter09;
import lombok.extern.slf4j.Slf4j;
import org.springframework.batch.core.Job;
import org.springframework.batch.core.JobExecution;
import org.springframework.batch.core.JobParameters;
import org.springframework.batch.core.launch.JobLauncher;
import org.springframework.context.annotation.AnnotationConfigApplicationContext;
import org.springframework.context.annotation.Configuration;
import org.springframework.context.annotation.ImportResource;
import org.springframework.context.support.GenericApplicationContext;
import org.springframework.jdbc.core.JdbcTemplate;

@Slf4j
@Configuration
@ImportResource({ "classpath:batch-config.xml", "classpath:batch-beans-config.xml" })
public class BatchApplication {
  public static void main(String[] args) throws Exception {
    GenericApplicationContext context =
        new AnnotationConfigApplicationContext(BatchApplication.class);

    JobLauncher jobLauncher = (JobLauncher) context.getBean(JobLauncher.class);
    Job job = (Job) context.getBean("prepareTeaJob");
    JobExecution execution = jobLauncher.run(job, new JobParameters());
    log.info("Exit Status: {}", execution.getStatus());

    JdbcTemplate jdbcTemplate = (JdbcTemplate) context.getBean(JdbcTemplate.class);
    long stepExecutionCount =
        jdbcTemplate.queryForObject("select count(*) from BATCH_STEP_EXECUTION",
            Long.class);
    log.info("Number of steps executed: {}", stepExecutionCount);
    context.close();
  }
}
```

This main class includes both XML configurations we mentioned. Creation of the Spring context is done via plain Spring constructs, which is in this case the `AnnotationConfigApplicationContext` constructor, and context configuration is defined by this class also. After the context instance is created, we retrieve the `JobLauncher` and `Job` instances to execute the job.

When the job is finished and the exit status is logged, we retrieve the JdbcTemplate instance from the Spring context, so that we can query the H2 in-memory database. In this case, we read how many job executions happened so far against this JobRepository.

■ **Note** Structure of the SB metadata schema is beyond the scope of this book. Curious readers can find the full schema metadata information in the SB reference documentation at http://docs.spring.io/spring-batch/trunk/reference/htmlsingle/#metaDataSchema.

After we run this main class, we can observe the output in Listing 9-47.

Listing 9-47. Output of XML JobRepository Example

```
19:43:00.206 [main] INFO  o.s.b.c.l.support.SimpleJobLauncher - Job: [FlowJob:
[name=prepareTeaJob]] completed with the following parameters: [{}] and the following
status: [COMPLETED]
19:43:00.206 [main] INFO  n.l.b.e.chapter09.BatchApplication - Exit Status: COMPLETED
19:43:00.209 [main] INFO  n.l.b.e.chapter09.BatchApplication - Number of steps executed: 3
```

Configuring JobRepository with Java Configuration

The Java configuration of JobRepository looks like Listing 9-48.

Listing 9-48. Java Configuration of JobRepository (0912-job-repository-javaconfig)

```java
package net.lkrnac.book.eiws.chapter09;
import javax.sql.DataSource;
import org.springframework.batch.core.launch.JobLauncher;
import org.springframework.batch.core.launch.support.SimpleJobLauncher;
import org.springframework.batch.core.repository.JobRepository;
import org.springframework.batch.core.repository.support.JobRepositoryFactoryBean;
import org.springframework.batch.support.transaction.ResourcelessTransactionManager;
import org.springframework.context.annotation.Bean;
import org.springframework.context.annotation.Configuration;
import org.springframework.jdbc.core.JdbcTemplate;
import org.springframework.jdbc.datasource.embedded.EmbeddedDatabaseBuilder;
import org.springframework.jdbc.datasource.embedded.EmbeddedDatabaseType;
import org.springframework.transaction.support.AbstractPlatformTransactionManager;

@Configuration
public class BatchBeansConfiguration {
  @Bean
  public AbstractPlatformTransactionManager transactionManager() {
    return new ResourcelessTransactionManager();
  }
```

```java
@Bean
public DataSource dataSource() {
  return new EmbeddedDatabaseBuilder()
      .setType(EmbeddedDatabaseType.H2)
      .addScript("classpath:/org/springframework/batch/core/schema-h2.sql")
      .build();
}

@Bean
public JdbcTemplate jdbcTemplate(DataSource dataSource) {
  return new JdbcTemplate(dataSource);
}

@Bean
public JobRepository jobRepository(
    AbstractPlatformTransactionManager transactionManager,
    DataSource dataSource) throws Exception {
  JobRepositoryFactoryBean jobRepositoryFactory =
      new JobRepositoryFactoryBean();
  jobRepositoryFactory.setTransactionManager(transactionManager);
  jobRepositoryFactory.setDataSource(dataSource);
  jobRepositoryFactory.setDatabaseType("h2");
  jobRepositoryFactory.setTablePrefix("BATCH_");
  jobRepositoryFactory.setMaxVarCharLength(10);
  return jobRepositoryFactory.getObject();
}

@Bean
public JobLauncher jobLauncher(JobRepository jobRepository) {
  SimpleJobLauncher simpleJobLauncher = new SimpleJobLauncher();
  simpleJobLauncher.setJobRepository(jobRepository);
  return simpleJobLauncher;
}
}
```

This Java configuration is an exact mirror of the XML configuration from the previous example (Listing 9-45). We just need to replace the <jdbc:embedded-database> and <batch:job-repository> XML tags with explicit construction of these beans and register them with the @Bean annotation. For creation of the H2 in-memory database, we use EmbeddedDatabaseBuilder. For the JobRepository instance creation, we use the JobRepositoryFactoryBean.getObject() call. Other beans are exact Java counterparts of the <bean> XML tag.

For this example, we also use BatchConfiguration from Listing 9-21, which creates prepareTeaJob with three common tea Steps. For the main class, we use a similar class as for the previous example in Listing 9-46. The only difference is replacement of the @ImportResource annotation with the @ComponentScan annotation, because we don't have XML configuration files on the classpath. Instead, we have the Java configuration classes BatchConfiguration and BatchBeansConfiguration, which are component scanned by this annotation. As this is a pretty straightforward main class, we won't list it. After running it, we can see the same output as for the previous example (Listing 9-47).

Stateful Job and Step Execution

There is often a need to pass state between Jobs or Steps, which can be any Java object. For example, one Step or Job might be processing records, and a subsequent Job or Step needs to send notification of how many records were processed.

Normally, Java developers would create some kind of in-memory cache, which needs to be thread safe. But fortunately, SB provides various mechanisms for passing state in a clean and thread-safe manner.

ExecutionContext

The first option for state transition can be done via the ExecutionContext class. This class encapsulates a map of type Map<String, Object>. So we are able to store any type of state that needs to be transferred between steps or chunk-oriented item handlers. This can be handy if we need to store partial results during batch processing. But, of course, this instance needs to be somehow injected into the place we need to use it. Luckily, SB provides a lot of ways to access ExecutionContext from any part of the SB application.

As we mentioned, when Step is executed, a StepExecution instance is created, and when Job is executed, an instance of JobExecution is created. Via StepExecution.getJobExecution(), we can access the JobExecution instance, and via JobExecution.getExecutionContext(), we can access the ExecutionContext instance.

The StepExecution instance can be injected into any chunk-oriented ItemProcessor, ItemWriter, and ItemReader via the initialization method annotated with @BeforeStep. For Tasklet, there is an even easier mechanism, whereby SB injects the ChunkContext instance as a second parameter of Tasklet.execute(). The StepExecution instance can be accessed and then ChunkContext.getStepContext().getStepExecution().

So via all these context instances, we can access the ExecutionContext instance in any part of the SB flow.

Accessing ExecutionContext from Tasklet Example

Listing 9-49 shows Tasklet, which stores state into the ExecutionContext instance. In this example, we are counting how many times we prepared tea in the previous Job runs. Based on this information, we amend our behavior of one Step. Therefore, our tea Tasklets will have the suffix WithCounter.

Listing 9-49. Tasklet That Stores State into ExecutionContext (0913-execution-context-tasklet)

```
package net.lkrnac.book.eiws.chapter09.step.tea;
import net.lkrnac.book.eiws.chapter09.step.SimpleExecutablePoint;
import org.springframework.batch.core.StepContribution;
import org.springframework.batch.core.scope.context.ChunkContext;
import org.springframework.batch.core.step.tasklet.Tasklet;
import org.springframework.batch.item.ExecutionContext;
import org.springframework.batch.repeat.RepeatStatus;
import org.springframework.beans.factory.annotation.Autowired;
import org.springframework.stereotype.Component;

@Component
public class BoilWaterWithCounter implements Tasklet {
  private SimpleExecutablePoint simpleExecutableStep;

  @Autowired
  public BoilWaterWithCounter(SimpleExecutablePoint simpleExecutableStep) {
    super();
    this.simpleExecutableStep = simpleExecutableStep;
  }
```

```
  @Override
  public RepeatStatus execute(StepContribution contribution,
      ChunkContext chunkContext) throws Exception {
    simpleExecutableStep.execute("Boil Water");
    ExecutionContext jobExecutionContext =
        chunkContext.getStepContext().getStepExecution().getJobExecution()
            .getExecutionContext();
    int teaCount = jobExecutionContext.getInt("teaCount", 0);
    teaCount++;
    jobExecutionContext.putInt("teaCount", teaCount);
    return RepeatStatus.FINISHED;
  }
}
```

Every time this Tasklet is executed, it increments the teaCount value stored in the ExecutionContext instance that is retrieved via the chunkContext.getStepContext().getStepExecution(). getJobExecution().getExecutionContext() call. Listing 9-50 shows how this state is used.

Listing 9-50. Tasklet That Retrieves State from ExecutionContext (0913-execution-context-tasklet)

```
package net.lkrnac.book.eiws.chapter09.step.tea;
import net.lkrnac.book.eiws.chapter09.step.SimpleExecutablePoint;
import org.springframework.batch.core.StepContribution;
import org.springframework.batch.core.scope.context.ChunkContext;
import org.springframework.batch.core.step.tasklet.Tasklet;
import org.springframework.batch.item.ExecutionContext;
import org.springframework.batch.repeat.RepeatStatus;
import org.springframework.beans.factory.annotation.Autowired;
import org.springframework.stereotype.Component;

@Component
public class AddWaterWithCounter implements Tasklet {
  private SimpleExecutablePoint simpleExecutableStep;

  @Autowired
  public AddWaterWithCounter(SimpleExecutablePoint simpleExecutableStep) {
    super();
    this.simpleExecutableStep = simpleExecutableStep;
  }

  @Override
  public RepeatStatus execute(StepContribution contribution,
      ChunkContext chunkContext) throws Exception {
    String message = "Add Water";
    ExecutionContext jobExecutionContext =
        chunkContext.getStepContext().getStepExecution().getJobExecution()
            .getExecutionContext();
    int teaCount = jobExecutionContext.getInt("teaCount");
    if (teaCount > 2) {
      message = "Add Dirty Water (you should clean kettle with citric acid)";
    }
```

```
    simpleExecutableStep.execute(message);
    return RepeatStatus.FINISHED;
  }
}
```

This is the Tasklet where the state from ExecutionContext will be used to amend the behavior of the step. Every time SB executes this Tasklet, it also retrieves ExecutionContext of the Job via calling chunkContext.getStepContext().getStepExecution().getJobExecution().getExecutionContext() to look for the teaCount value stored in it. If teaCount is more than 2, it simulates execution with a different message to highlight its reaction to the state in ExecutionContext. Listing 9-51 shows the batch configuration of this example.

Listing 9-51. Batch Configuration of Example Accessing ExecutionContext from Tasklet (0913-execution-context-tasklet)

```
package net.lkrnac.book.eiws.chapter09;
import net.lkrnac.book.eiws.chapter09.step.tea.AddTea;
import net.lkrnac.book.eiws.chapter09.step.tea.AddWaterWithCounter;
import net.lkrnac.book.eiws.chapter09.step.tea.BoilWaterWithCounter;
import org.springframework.batch.core.Job;
import org.springframework.batch.core.Step;
import org.springframework.batch.core.configuration.annotation.EnableBatchProcessing;
import org.springframework.batch.core.configuration.annotation.JobBuilderFactory;
import org.springframework.batch.core.configuration.annotation.StepBuilderFactory;
import org.springframework.beans.factory.annotation.Qualifier;
import org.springframework.context.annotation.Bean;
import org.springframework.context.annotation.Configuration;

@Configuration
@EnableBatchProcessing
public class BatchConfiguration {
  @Bean
  public Step boilWaterStep(StepBuilderFactory stepFactory, BoilWaterWithCounter boilWater)
{
    return stepFactory.get("boilWaterStep").tasklet(boilWater)
        .allowStartIfComplete(true).build();
  }

  @Bean
  public Step addTeaStep(StepBuilderFactory stepFactory, AddTea addTea) {
    return stepFactory.get("addTeaStep").tasklet(addTea)
        .allowStartIfComplete(true).build();
  }

  @Bean
  public Step addWaterStep(StepBuilderFactory stepFactory, AddWaterWithCounter addWater) {
    return stepFactory.get("addWaterStep").tasklet(addWater)
        .allowStartIfComplete(true).build();
  }
```

```
@Bean
public Job prepareTeaJob(JobBuilderFactory jobBuilderFactory,
    @Qualifier("boilWaterStep") Step boilWaterStep,
    @Qualifier("addTeaStep") Step addTeaStep,
    @Qualifier("addWaterStep") Step addWaterStep) {
  return jobBuilderFactory.get("prepareTeaJob")
      .start(boilWaterStep)
      .next(addTeaStep)
      .next(addWaterStep)
      .build();
}
}
```

It's obvious that one difference from the previous example is use of our stateful Tasklets. The second difference is enabling steps to be executed various times with the same JobParameters. If we didn't allow starting the Step various times, we couldn't highlight how we transition state between various Job runs. This feature is discussed later in this chapter. Listing 9-52 shows the main class of this example.

Listing 9-52. Main Class of Example Accessing ExecutionContext from Tasklets (0913-execution-context-tasklet)

```
package net.lkrnac.book.eiws.chapter09;
import org.springframework.batch.core.Job;
import org.springframework.batch.core.JobParameters;
import org.springframework.batch.core.launch.JobLauncher;
import org.springframework.boot.autoconfigure.SpringBootApplication;
import org.springframework.context.annotation.AnnotationConfigApplicationContext;
import org.springframework.context.support.GenericApplicationContext;

@SpringBootApplication
public class BatchApplication {
  public static void main(String[] args) throws Exception {
    GenericApplicationContext context =
        new AnnotationConfigApplicationContext(BatchApplication.class);

    JobLauncher jobLauncher = (JobLauncher) context.getBean(JobLauncher.class);
    Job job = (Job) context.getBean("prepareTeaJob");

    jobLauncher.run(job, new JobParameters());
    jobLauncher.run(job, new JobParameters());
    jobLauncher.run(job, new JobParameters());
    context.close();
  }
}
```

To highlight the stateful feature we included, we execute the batch job three times. As you may remember, each job increments teaCount, and in the third execution, the Boil Water step simulates the action with a different message. Listing 9-53 shows the output of this example.

Listing 9-53. Output of Example Accessing ExecutionContext from Tasklets

```
22:24:32.187 [main] INFO  o.s.b.c.l.support.SimpleJobLauncher - Job: [SimpleJob:
[name=prepareTeaJob]] launched with the following parameters: [{}]
22:24:32.217 [main] INFO  o.s.batch.core.job.SimpleStepHandler - Executing step: [boilWaterStep]
22:24:32.230 [main] INFO  n.l.b.e.c.step.SimpleExecutablePoint - Boil Water
22:24:32.251 [main] INFO  o.s.batch.core.job.SimpleStepHandler - Executing step: [addTeaStep]
22:24:32.257 [main] INFO  n.l.b.e.c.step.SimpleExecutablePoint - Add Tea
22:24:32.276 [main] INFO  o.s.batch.core.job.SimpleStepHandler - Executing step: [addWaterStep]
22:24:32.280 [main] INFO  n.l.b.e.c.step.SimpleExecutablePoint - Add Water
22:24:32.296 [main] INFO  o.s.b.c.l.support.SimpleJobLauncher - Job: [SimpleJob:
[name=prepareTeaJob]] completed with the following parameters: [{}] and the following
status: [COMPLETED]
22:24:32.409 [main] INFO  o.s.b.c.l.support.SimpleJobLauncher - Job: [SimpleJob:
[name=prepareTeaJob]] launched with the following parameters: [{}]
22:24:32.430 [main] INFO  o.s.batch.core.job.SimpleStepHandler - Executing step: [boilWaterStep]
22:24:32.435 [main] INFO  n.l.b.e.c.step.SimpleExecutablePoint - Boil Water
22:24:32.456 [main] INFO  o.s.batch.core.job.SimpleStepHandler - Executing step: [addTeaStep]
22:24:32.461 [main] INFO  n.l.b.e.c.step.SimpleExecutablePoint - Add Tea
22:24:32.481 [main] INFO  o.s.batch.core.job.SimpleStepHandler - Executing step: [addWaterStep]
22:24:32.486 [main] INFO  n.l.b.e.c.step.SimpleExecutablePoint - Add Water
22:24:32.501 [main] INFO  o.s.b.c.l.support.SimpleJobLauncher - Job: [SimpleJob: [name=prepareTeaJob]]
completed with the following parameters: [{}] and the following status: [COMPLETED]
22:24:32.513 [main] INFO  o.s.b.c.l.support.SimpleJobLauncher - Job: [SimpleJob:
[name=prepareTeaJob]] launched with the following parameters: [{}]
22:24:32.528 [main] INFO  o.s.batch.core.job.SimpleStepHandler - Executing step: [boilWaterStep]
22:24:32.533 [main] INFO  n.l.b.e.c.step.SimpleExecutablePoint - Boil Water
22:24:32.556 [main] INFO  o.s.batch.core.job.SimpleStepHandler - Executing step: [addTeaStep]
22:24:32.561 [main] INFO  n.l.b.e.c.step.SimpleExecutablePoint - Add Tea
22:24:32.582 [main] INFO  o.s.batch.core.job.SimpleStepHandler - Executing step: [addWaterStep]
22:24:32.587 [main] INFO  n.l.b.e.c.step.SimpleExecutablePoint - Add Dirty Water (you should
clean kettle with citric acid)
22:24:32.604 [main] INFO  o.s.b.c.l.support.SimpleJobLauncher - Job: [SimpleJob: [name=prepareTeaJob]]
completed with the following parameters: [{}] and the following status: [COMPLETED]
```

Notice that the third job run prints the desired stateful message when we add water to our tea.

Accessing ExecutionContext in Chunk-Oriented Processing

Listing 9-54 shows ItemWriter, which is stateful.

Listing 9-54. Stateful ItemWriter (0914-execution-context-chunk-processing)

```java
package net.lkrnac.book.eiws.chapter09.write;
import java.util.ArrayList;
import java.util.List;
import org.springframework.batch.core.StepExecution;
import org.springframework.batch.core.annotation.BeforeStep;
import org.springframework.batch.item.ExecutionContext;
import org.springframework.batch.item.ItemWriter;
import org.springframework.beans.factory.annotation.Autowired;
import org.springframework.stereotype.Component;
```

```java
@Component
public class SimpleRecordWriterDiscard implements ItemWriter<String> {
  private static final String CHUNK_COUNT = "chunkCount";
  private WriteRepository writeRepository;
  private ExecutionContext executionContext;

  @Autowired
  public SimpleRecordWriterDiscard(WriteRepository writeRepository) {
    super();
    this.writeRepository = writeRepository;
  }

  @BeforeStep
  public void storeExecutionContext(StepExecution stepExecution) {
    this.executionContext = stepExecution.getExecutionContext();
    executionContext.put(CHUNK_COUNT, 0);
  }

  @Override
  public void write(List<? extends String> items) throws Exception {
    int chunkCount = executionContext.getInt(CHUNK_COUNT);
    List<String> filteredItems = new ArrayList<>();
    if (chunkCount % 2 == 0) {
      filteredItems.add(items.get(0));
    } else {
      filteredItems.addAll(items);
    }
    executionContext.put(CHUNK_COUNT, chunkCount + 1);

    writeRepository.writeRecords(filteredItems);
  }
}
```

This `ItemWriter` uses the `@BeforeStep` annotation to retrieve `ExecutionContext` via the `StepExecution` instance and to initiate the map entry chunkCount to 0. During processing, it writes only the first record of the even chunk it is writing and increases chunkCount to maintain state in `ExecutionContext`. For the odd chunk, it writes all items. Listing 9-55 shows the batch configuration.

Listing 9-55. Batch Configuration of Stateful Chunk-Oriented Processing Example (0914-execution-context-chunk-processing)

```java
package net.lkrnac.book.eiws.chapter09;
import net.lkrnac.book.eiws.chapter09.process.SimpleRecordProcessor;
import net.lkrnac.book.eiws.chapter09.read.SimpleRecordReader;
import net.lkrnac.book.eiws.chapter09.write.SimpleRecordWriterDiscard;
import org.springframework.batch.core.Job;
import org.springframework.batch.core.Step;
import org.springframework.batch.core.configuration.annotation.EnableBatchProcessing;
import org.springframework.batch.core.configuration.annotation.JobBuilderFactory;
import org.springframework.batch.core.configuration.annotation.StepBuilderFactory;
import org.springframework.context.annotation.Bean;
import org.springframework.context.annotation.Configuration;
```

```
@Configuration
@EnableBatchProcessing
public class BatchConfiguration {
  @Bean
  public Step simpleRecordsStep(StepBuilderFactory stepBuilderFactory,
      SimpleRecordReader simpleRecordReader,
      SimpleRecordProcessor simpleRecordProcessor,
      SimpleRecordWriterDiscard simpleRecordWriter) {
    return stepBuilderFactory.get("simpleRecordsStep")
      .<String, String> chunk(4)
      .reader(simpleRecordReader)
      .processor(simpleRecordProcessor)
      .writer(simpleRecordWriter)
      .build();
  }

  @Bean
  public Job simpleRecordsJob(JobBuilderFactory jobBuilderFactory,
      Step simpleRecordsStep) {
    return jobBuilderFactory.get("simpleRecordsJob")
      .start(simpleRecordsStep)
      .build();
  }
}
```

This configuration was already shown in the chunk-oriented example, but in this case we use our stateful writer SimpleRecordWriterDiscard. The main class in this example is the common main batch class we reuse across examples. Listing 9-56 shows the output when we run it.

Listing 9-56. Output of Stateful Chunk-Oriented Processing Example

```
2015-09-29 23:15:23.082  INFO 17535 --- [           main] o.s.b.c.l.support.
SimpleJobLauncher      : Job: [SimpleJob: [name=simpleRecordsJob]] launched with the
following parameters: [{}]
2015-09-29 23:15:23.109  INFO 17535 --- [           main] o.s.batch.core.job.
SimpleStepHandler      : Executing step: [simpleRecordsStep]
2015-09-29 23:15:23.152  INFO 17535 --- [           main] n.l.b.e.chapter09.write.
WriteRepository  : Writing record: simple record 0 processed
2015-09-29 23:15:23.157  INFO 17535 --- [           main] n.l.b.e.chapter09.write.
WriteRepository  : Writing record: simple record 4 processed
2015-09-29 23:15:23.157  INFO 17535 --- [           main] n.l.b.e.chapter09.write.
WriteRepository  : Writing record: simple record 5 processed
2015-09-29 23:15:23.157  INFO 17535 --- [           main] n.l.b.e.chapter09.write.
WriteRepository  : Writing record: simple record 6 processed
2015-09-29 23:15:23.158  INFO 17535 --- [           main] n.l.b.e.chapter09.write.
WriteRepository  : Writing record: simple record 7 processed
2015-09-29 23:15:23.162  INFO 17535 --- [           main] n.l.b.e.chapter09.write.
WriteRepository  : Writing record: simple record 8 processed
2015-09-29 23:15:23.168  INFO 17535 --- [           main] n.l.b.e.chapter09.write.
WriteRepository  : Writing record: simple record 12 processed
2015-09-29 23:15:23.168  INFO 17535 --- [           main] n.l.b.e.chapter09.write.
WriteRepository  : Writing record: simple record 13 processed
```

```
2015-09-29 23:15:23.168  INFO 17535 --- [          main] n.l.b.e.chapter09.write.
WriteRepository  : Writing record: simple record 14 processed
2015-09-29 23:15:23.184  INFO 17535 --- [          main] o.s.b.c.l.support.
SimpleJobLauncher     : Job: [SimpleJob: [name=simpleRecordsJob]] completed with the
following parameters: [{}] and the following status: [COMPLETED]
```

Notice that the chunk size is 4. As expected, only the first record of each even chunk is written alongside all odd chunk records. Therefore, records 1, 2, 3, 9, 10, and 11 are missing in the output.

Batch Scopes

Every Spring developer should be familiar with the concept of bean scopes. Each Spring bean has by default a singleton scope, which means there is only one instance of that in the Spring context. Every time we inject this bean into our code, Spring provides the same object.

Another useful scope is request scope, in which the bean uses the @Scope(WebApplicationContext. SCOPE_REQUEST) annotation. In this case, a new instance is created when the web request is served by our application, and Spring creates a new instance of this bean for each request. So when we inject the bean into our code, we will get a different instance for each request. This mechanism can be useful for sharing state in our code within boundaries of the request thread. For example, we can store some information into the local variable of this bean in the controller and retrieve this information in the repository.

SB provides similar mechanisms for Job and Step. We can create beans with StepScope or JobScope, and SB makes sure that every new StepExecution will have a fresh instance of a bean with StepScope. Similarly for different JobExecutions, SB will inject fresh instances of a bean with JobScope.

To define StepScope, we can annotate beans with @StepScope or via the standard Spring annotation @Scope(value = "step", proxyMode = ScopedProxyMode.TARGET_CLASS). The @JobScope annotation defines the JobScope. It is also a convenience shortcut for @Scope(value = "job", proxyMode = ScopedProxyMode. TARGET_CLASS). With XML configuration, we can define the scope attribute with the job or scope values of the XML tag <bean>.

These scopes are also useful for late binding of references from the SB context. This can be done by using the placeholders #{...}.

Batch Scopes XML Example

In this example, we prepare tea and process records. Listing 9-57 shows the class, which will be used with StepScope.

Listing 9-57. Class Used for StepScope Bean (0915-batch-scopes-xml)

```
package net.lkrnac.book.eiws.chapter09;
import lombok.Getter;
import lombok.Setter;

@Getter
public class ReadCountRestricter {
  private long countToProcess;

  @Setter
  private long readCount;
```

```
  public ReadCountRestricter(long countToProcess) {
    super();
    this.countToProcess = countToProcess;
  }
}
```

This class will be used as a bean with StepScope. This configuration will be applied in the XML context we show later in this example. Lombok's annotation @Getter specifies that all fields of this class will be accessible via getters, and the @Setter annotation specifies that only the readCount field will have a setter. The purpose of this class is to configure how many records can be read, and for this we use the countToProcess variable. The second variable, readCount, is used to track how many records were actually read. Listing 9-58 presents StatefulRecordReader.

Listing 9-58. ItemReader Implementation Using Bean with StepScope (0915-batch-scopes-xml)

```
package net.lkrnac.book.eiws.chapter09.read;
import net.lkrnac.book.eiws.chapter09.ReadCountRestricter;
import org.springframework.batch.item.ItemReader;
import org.springframework.batch.item.NonTransientResourceException;
import org.springframework.batch.item.ParseException;
import org.springframework.batch.item.UnexpectedInputException;
import org.springframework.beans.factory.annotation.Autowired;
import org.springframework.stereotype.Component;

@Component
public class StatefulRecordReader implements ItemReader<String> {
  private ReadRepository readRepository;
  private ReadCountRestricter readCountRestricter;

  @Autowired
  public StatefulRecordReader(ReadRepository readRepository,
      ReadCountRestricter readCountRestricter) {
    super();
    this.readRepository = readReposi tory;
    this.readCountRestricter = readCountRestricter;
  }

  @Override
  public String read() throws Exception, UnexpectedInputException,
      ParseException, NonTransientResourceException {
    long previousReadCount = readCountRestricter.getReadCount();
    if (readCountRestricter.getCountToProcess() <= previousReadCount) {
      return null;
    }
    String nextRecord = readRepository.readNext();
    if (nextRecord != null) {
      readCountRestricter.setReadCount(previousReadCount + 1);
    }
    return nextRecord;
  }
}
```

This Spring component autowires the common bean ReadRepository, but also the step-scoped bean ReadCountRestricter shown in the previous listing. In the read() method, we retrieve readCount from the ReadCountRestricter bean and quit further reading if we reach the desired read count (readCountRestricter.getCountToProcess()). Of course, if we don't reach this limit, we continue reading new records and increment the read counter. Notice that if we run this step twice and configure this bean with StepScope, SB will inject a new instance of ReadCountRestricter. So it effectively resets the counter for each job.

Next we also include the JobScope bean in this example, which also will be configured in XML. But first, Listing 9-59 shows the class we will use for storing state while processing records.

Listing 9-59. Class Used for JobScope Bean (0915-batch-scopes-xml)

```java
package net.lkrnac.book.eiws.chapter09;
import lombok.Data;

@Data
public class WrittenRecordsCounter {
  private int processedCount;
}
```

This class stores the count of jobs executed. Lombok's @Data annotation will generate getters and setters for us. This class will be used for beans with JobScope. Listing 9-60 covers ItemWriter by using the WrittenRecordsCounter bean.

Listing 9-60. ItemWriter Implementation Using Bean with JobScope (0915-batch-scopes-xml)

```java
package net.lkrnac.book.eiws.chapter09.write;
import java.util.List;
import net.lkrnac.book.eiws.chapter09.WrittenRecordsCounter;
import org.springframework.batch.item.ItemWriter;
import org.springframework.beans.factory.annotation.Autowired;
import org.springframework.stereotype.Component;

@Component
public class StatefulRecordWriter implements ItemWriter<String> {
  private WriteRepository writeRepository;
  private WrittenRecordsCounter recordsCounter;

  @Autowired
  public StatefulRecordWriter(WriteRepository writeRepository,
      WrittenRecordsCounter recordsCounter) {
    super();
    this.writeRepository = writeRepository;
    this.recordsCounter = recordsCounter;
  }

  @Override
  @SuppressWarnings("unchecked")
  public void write(List<? extends String> items) throws Exception {
    writeRepository.writeRecords((List<String>) items);
```

```
  int previousRecordsCount = recordsCounter.getProcessedCount();
  recordsCounter.setProcessedCount(previousRecordsCount + items.size());
 }
}
```

This ItemWriter is autowired alongside our common WriteRepository and WrittenRecordsCounter. It is used to track the number of written records. If we set WrittenRecordsCounter in the XML configuration to have the JobScope bean, SB will create a new instance for each job and effectively reset the counter. Listing 9-61 shows Tasklet using the WrittenRecordsCounter bean.

Listing 9-61. Tasklet Using Bean with JobScope (0915-batch-scopes-xml)

```
package net.lkrnac.book.eiws.chapter09.step.tea;
import net.lkrnac.book.eiws.chapter09.WrittenRecordsCounter;
import net.lkrnac.book.eiws.chapter09.step.SimpleExecutablePoint;
import org.springframework.batch.core.StepContribution;
import org.springframework.batch.core.scope.context.ChunkContext;
import org.springframework.batch.core.step.tasklet.Tasklet;
import org.springframework.batch.repeat.RepeatStatus;
import org.springframework.beans.factory.annotation.Autowired;
import org.springframework.stereotype.Component;

@Component
public class BoilWaterStateful implements Tasklet {
  private SimpleExecutablePoint simpleExecutableStep;
  private WrittenRecordsCounter recordsCounter;

  @Autowired
  public BoilWaterStateful(SimpleExecutablePoint simpleExecutableStep,
      WrittenRecordsCounter recordsCounter) {
    super();
    this.simpleExecutableStep = simpleExecutableStep;
    this.recordsCounter = recordsCounter;
  }

  @Override
  public RepeatStatus execute(StepContribution contribution,
      ChunkContext chunkContext) throws Exception {
    simpleExecutableStep.execute("After we processed "
        + recordsCounter.getProcessedCount() + " records, let's have a tea");
    simpleExecutableStep.execute("Boil Water");
    return RepeatStatus.FINISHED;
  }
}
```

This Tasklet is similar to our common one for tea preparation, BoilWater. In this case, we also inject the WrittenRecordsCounter bean, so that we can output a specific message and highlight how the JobScope bean has transferred state between two Steps of the same Job. Listing 9-62 shows the XML configuration of the SB beans.

Listing 9-62. XML Configuration of SB Beans for Batch Scopes (File batch-beans-config.xml in Folder src/main/resource of Example Project 0915-batch-scopes-xml)

```xml
<?xml version="1.0" encoding="UTF-8"?>
<beans xmlns="http://www.springframework.org/schema/beans"
  xmlns:xsi="http://www.w3.org/2001/XMLSchema-instance"
  xsi:schemaLocation="http://www.springframework.org/schema/beans
    http://www.springframework.org/schema/beans/spring-beans.xsd">

  <bean id="readCountRestricter" scope="step"
    class="net.lkrnac.book.eiws.chapter09.ReadCountRestricter">
    <constructor-arg name="countToProcess" value="#{jobParameters[recordCountToProcess]}"/>
  </bean>

  <bean id="writtenRecordsCounter" scope="job"
    class="net.lkrnac.book.eiws.chapter09.WrittenRecordsCounter"/>

  <bean class="org.springframework.batch.core.scope.StepScope">
    <property name="proxyTargetClass" value="true"/>
  </bean>

  <bean class="org.springframework.batch.core.scope.JobScope">
    <property name="proxyTargetClass" value="true"/>
  </bean>
</beans>
```

The ReadCountRestricter bean is configured with step scope. Its parameter is initiated via late binding from the job parameter recordCountToProcess. This late binding wouldn't work with a singleton scope, for example, because in that case Spring most probably would create this bean during initialization of the Spring context, but JobParameters are not configured at that time.

WrittenRecordsCounter uses the job scope. When we use XML configuration, we need to enable batch scopes by configuring them as beans with the proxyTargetClass enabled. If we didn't configure these beans, Spring wouldn't know about SB scopes at all.

Listing 9-63 shows the XML configuration of the SB flow.

Listing 9-63. XML Configuration of Batch Scopes Example (File batch-beans-config.xml in Folder src/main/resource of Example Project 0915-batch-scopes-xml)

```xml
<?xml version="1.0" encoding="UTF-8"?>
<beans:beans xmlns:beans="http://www.springframework.org/schema/beans"
  xmlns:xsi="http://www.w3.org/2001/XMLSchema-instance"
  xmlns="http://www.springframework.org/schema/batch"
  xsi:schemaLocation="http://www.springframework.org/schema/batch
  http://www.springframework.org/schema/batch/spring-batch.xsd
  http://www.springframework.org/schema/beans
  http://www.springframework.org/schema/beans/spring-beans.xsd">

  <job id="combinedJob">
    <step id="simpleRecordsStep" next="boilWaterStep">
      <tasklet>
```

```
        <chunk reader="statefulRecordReader" writer="statefulRecordWriter"
          processor="simpleRecordProcessor" commit-interval="4" />
      </tasklet>
    </step>

    <step id="boilWaterStep" next="addTeaStep">
      <tasklet ref="boilWaterStateful" />
    </step>
    <step id="addTeaStep" next="addWaterStep">
      <tasklet ref="addTea" />
    </step>
    <step id="addWaterStep">
      <tasklet ref="addWater" />
    </step>
  </job>
</beans:beans>
```

This job will be called combinedJob, because we combine the processing of records and tea preparation steps into one Job. Listing 9-64 covers the main class of this example.

Listing 9-64. Main Class of XML Batch Scopes Example (0915-batch-scopes-xml)

```java
package net.lkrnac.book.eiws.chapter09;
import org.springframework.batch.core.Job;
import org.springframework.batch.core.JobParameters;
import org.springframework.batch.core.JobParametersBuilder;
import org.springframework.batch.core.configuration.annotation.EnableBatchProcessing;
import org.springframework.batch.core.launch.JobLauncher;
import org.springframework.boot.SpringApplication;
import org.springframework.boot.autoconfigure.SpringBootApplication;
import org.springframework.context.ConfigurableApplicationContext;
import org.springframework.context.annotation.ImportResource;

@SpringBootApplication
@EnableBatchProcessing
@ImportResource({ "classpath:batch-config.xml", "classpath:batch-beans-config.xml" })
public class BatchApplication {
  public static void main(String[] args) throws Exception {
    ConfigurableApplicationContext context =
        SpringApplication.run(BatchApplication.class, args);

    JobLauncher jobLauncher = (JobLauncher) context.getBean(JobLauncher.class);
    Job job = (Job) context.getBean("combinedJob");

    jobLauncher.run(job, createJobParameters(3));
    jobLauncher.run(job, createJobParameters(2));
    context.close();
  }
```

```java
    public static JobParameters createJobParameters(long recordCountToProcess) {
        return new JobParametersBuilder()
            .addLong("recordCountToProcess", recordCountToProcess)
            .toJobParameters();
    }
}
```

This main class uses the XML configuration we listed and executes combinedJob twice to highlight the resetting of counters and the JobScope and StepScope features. Both jobs are executed with a different value for the readCountToProcess parameter. When we run this main class, we see the output in Listing 9-65.

Listing 9-65. Output of XML Batch Scopes Example

```
2015-09-30 23:34:21.227  INFO 13386 --- [        main] o.s.b.c.l.support.
SimpleJobLauncher        : Job: [FlowJob: [name=combinedJob]] launched with the following
parameters: [{recordCountToProcess=3}]
2015-09-30 23:34:21.333  INFO 13386 --- [        main] o.s.batch.core.job.
SimpleStepHandler        : Executing step: [simpleRecordsStep]
2015-09-30 23:34:21.587  INFO 13386 --- [        main] n.l.b.e.chapter09.write.
WriteRepository  : Writing record: simple record 0 processed
2015-09-30 23:34:21.589  INFO 13386 --- [        main] n.l.b.e.chapter09.write.
WriteRepository  : Writing record: simple record 1 processed
2015-09-30 23:34:21.589  INFO 13386 --- [        main] n.l.b.e.chapter09.write.
WriteRepository  : Writing record: simple record 2 processed
2015-09-30 23:34:21.674  INFO 13386 --- [        main] o.s.batch.core.job.
SimpleStepHandler        : Executing step: [boilWaterStep]
2015-09-30 23:34:21.680  INFO 13386 --- [        main] n.l.b.e.c.step.
SimpleExecutablePoint       : After we processed 3 records, let's have a tea
2015-09-30 23:34:21.680  INFO 13386 --- [        main] n.l.b.e.c.step.
SimpleExecutablePoint       : Boil Water
2015-09-30 23:34:21.707  INFO 13386 --- [        main] o.s.batch.core.job.
SimpleStepHandler        : Executing step: [addTeaStep]
2015-09-30 23:34:21.734  INFO 13386 --- [        main] n.l.b.e.c.step.
SimpleExecutablePoint       : Add Tea
2015-09-30 23:34:21.821  INFO 13386 --- [        main] o.s.batch.core.job.
SimpleStepHandler        : Executing step: [addWaterStep]
2015-09-30 23:34:21.845  INFO 13386 --- [        main] n.l.b.e.c.step.
SimpleExecutablePoint       : Add Water
2015-09-30 23:34:21.901  INFO 13386 --- [        main] o.s.b.c.l.support.
SimpleJobLauncher        : Job: [FlowJob: [name=combinedJob]] completed with the following
parameters: [{recordCountToProcess=3}] and the following status: [COMPLETED]
2015-09-30 23:34:21.924  INFO 13386 --- [        main] o.s.b.c.l.support.
SimpleJobLauncher        : Job: [FlowJob: [name=combinedJob]] launched with the following
parameters: [{recordCountToProcess=2}]
2015-09-30 23:34:21.998  INFO 13386 --- [        main] o.s.batch.core.job.
SimpleStepHandler        : Executing step: [simpleRecordsStep]
2015-09-30 23:34:22.021  INFO 13386 --- [        main] n.l.b.e.chapter09.write.
WriteRepository  : Writing record: simple record 3 processed
2015-09-30 23:34:22.023  INFO 13386 --- [        main] n.l.b.e.chapter09.write.
WriteRepository  : Writing record: simple record 4 processed
2015-09-30 23:34:22.118  INFO 13386 --- [        main] o.s.batch.core.job.
SimpleStepHandler        : Executing step: [boilWaterStep]
```

```
2015-09-30 23:34:22.134  INFO 13386 --- [           main] n.l.b.e.c.step.
SimpleExecutablePoint    : After we processed 2 records, let's have a tea
2015-09-30 23:34:22.137  INFO 13386 --- [           main] n.l.b.e.c.step.
SimpleExecutablePoint    : Boil Water
2015-09-30 23:34:22.205  INFO 13386 --- [           main] o.s.batch.core.job.
SimpleStepHandler        : Executing step: [addTeaStep]
2015-09-30 23:34:22.216  INFO 13386 --- [           main] n.l.b.e.c.step.
SimpleExecutablePoint    : Add Tea
2015-09-30 23:34:22.293  INFO 13386 --- [           main] o.s.batch.core.job.
SimpleStepHandler        : Executing step: [addWaterStep]
2015-09-30 23:34:22.324  INFO 13386 --- [           main] n.l.b.e.c.step.
SimpleExecutablePoint    : Add Water
2015-09-30 23:34:22.378  INFO 13386 --- [           main] o.s.b.c.l.support.
SimpleJobLauncher        : Job: [FlowJob: [name=combinedJob]] completed with the following
parameters: [{recordCountToProcess=2}] and the following status: [COMPLETED]
```

The first job execution is limited to reading three records and processing them. This is recorded into the StepScope bean ReadCountRestricter. Notice that when the second Job is started, the counter stored in this bean is reset and a new value from JobParameter is retrieved to a fresh instance of this bean.

An example of a JobScope feature is shown in a transition of state between simpleRecordsStep and boilWaterStep. You can see that when we started preparing tea, we knew how many records were written in the previous step. At the same time, this state was reset between two Job runs.

Figure 9-6 shows the sequence diagram of state transitions during execution of combinedJob.

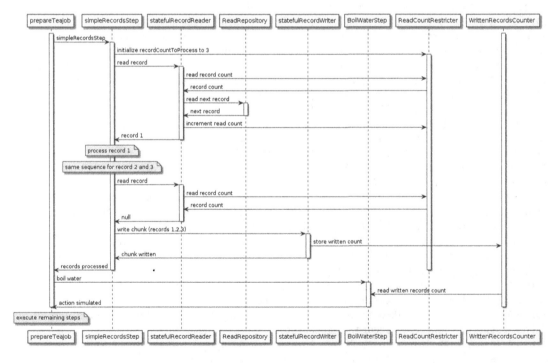

Figure 9-6. *Sequence diagram of XML batch scopes example*

To fit this diagram on the page, we skipped the stateless steps and SimpleRecordProcessor and added notes when they should be executed.

The ReadCountRestricter instance is used only during simpleRecordsStep to store the number of records we already read and decide whether we need to read another one. So it is used to transition the state between various statefulRecordReader.read() executions. This instance is also active only during this step execution. Each new execution of this step will create a new instance.

The WrittenRecordsCounter instance is used for the transition state (the written records count) between the steps simpleRecordsStep and boilWaterStep. This instance is abandoned after the prepareTeaJob execution is over. So a new execution of this Job will get a fresh instance from the Spring context.

Batch Scopes Java Example

Listing 9-66 shows an example of a bean configured with StepScope and a Java annotation.

Listing 9-66. StepScope Bean Configured with Java Annotation (0916-batch-scopes-javaconfig)

```java
package net.lkrnac.book.eiws.chapter09;
import lombok.Getter;
import lombok.Setter;
import org.springframework.batch.core.configuration.annotation.StepScope;
import org.springframework.beans.factory.annotation.Autowired;
import org.springframework.beans.factory.annotation.Value;
import org.springframework.stereotype.Component;

@Getter
@StepScope
@Component
public class ReadCountRestricter {
  private long countToProcess;

  @Setter
  private long readCount;

  @Autowired
  public ReadCountRestricter(
      @Value("#{jobParameters[recordCountToProcess]}") long countToProcess) {
    super();
    this.countToProcess = countToProcess;
  }
}
```

The @StepScope annotation defines the correct scope for this bean. Therefore, we can use late binding to JobParameter recordCountToProcess in the constructor injection. Listing 9-67 shows JobScope defined with a Java annotation.

Listing 9-67. JobScope Bean Configured with Java Annotation (0916-batch-scopes-javaconfig)

```java
package net.lkrnac.book.eiws.chapter09;
import lombok.Data;
import org.springframework.batch.core.configuration.annotation.JobScope;
import org.springframework.stereotype.Component;
```

```
@Data
@JobScope
@Component
public class ProcessedRecordsCounter {
  private int processedCount;
}
```

In this case, the @JobScope annotation does our trick. Listing 9-68 shows the Java batch configuration.

Listing 9-68. SB Flow for Batch Scopes Example with Java Configuration (0916-batch-scopes-javaconfig)

```
package net.lkrnac.book.eiws.chapter09;
import net.lkrnac.book.eiws.chapter09.process.SimpleRecordProcessor;
import net.lkrnac.book.eiws.chapter09.read.StatefulRecordReader;
import net.lkrnac.book.eiws.chapter09.step.tea.AddTea;
import net.lkrnac.book.eiws.chapter09.step.tea.AddWater;
import net.lkrnac.book.eiws.chapter09.step.tea.BoilWaterStateful;
import net.lkrnac.book.eiws.chapter09.write.StatefulRecordWriter;
import org.springframework.batch.core.Job;
import org.springframework.batch.core.Step;
import org.springframework.batch.core.configuration.annotation.EnableBatchProcessing;
import org.springframework.batch.core.configuration.annotation.JobBuilderFactory;
import org.springframework.batch.core.configuration.annotation.StepBuilderFactory;
import org.springframework.beans.factory.annotation.Qualifier;
import org.springframework.context.annotation.Bean;
import org.springframework.context.annotation.Configuration;

@Configuration
@EnableBatchProcessing
public class BatchConfiguration {
  @Bean
  public Step boilWaterStep(StepBuilderFactory stepFactory, BoilWaterStateful boilWater) {
    return stepFactory.get("boilWaterStep").tasklet(boilWater).build();
  }

  @Bean
  public Step addTeaStep(StepBuilderFactory stepFactory, AddTea addTea) {
    return stepFactory.get("addTeaStep").tasklet(addTea).build();
  }

  @Bean
  public Step addWaterStep(StepBuilderFactory stepFactory, AddWater addWater) {
    return stepFactory.get("addWaterStep").tasklet(addWater).build();
  }

  @Bean
  public Step simpleRecordsStep(StepBuilderFactory stepBuilderFactory,
      StatefulRecordReader statefulRecordReader,
      SimpleRecordProcessor simpleRecordProcessor,
      StatefulRecordWriter statefulRecordWriter) {
```

```
    return stepBuilderFactory.get("simpleRecordsStep")
        .<String, String> chunk(4)
        .reader(statefulRecordReader)
        .processor(simpleRecordProcessor)
        .writer(statefulRecordWriter)
        .listener(statefulRecordWriter)
        .build();
}

@Bean
public Job combinedJob(JobBuilderFactory jobBuilderFactory,
    @Qualifier("simpleRecordsStep") Step simpleRecordsStep,
    @Qualifier("boilWaterStep") Step boilWaterStep,
    @Qualifier("addTeaStep") Step addTeaStep,
    @Qualifier("addWaterStep") Step addWaterStep) {
    return jobBuilderFactory.get("combinedJob")
        .start(simpleRecordsStep)
        .next(boilWaterStep)
        .next(addTeaStep)
        .next(addWaterStep)
        .build();
}
}
```

This is a Java-configured exact mirror of the SB flow XML configuration from the previous example (Listing 9-63). The main class of this example is also similar; we excluded the annotations @EnableBatchProcessing (because this annotation is located in BatchConfiguration) and @ImportResource (because in this case we don't have any XML configuration files). The output of this example is again the same as in the previous example (Listing 9-65) and shows that batch scopes work as expected when transferring state.

Batch-Processing Listeners

Most of the Spring abstractions provide powerful mechanisms for their interceptions. SB is no exception, and we can intercept as follows:

- *Before* and *after* Job with the JobExecutionListener interface or @BeforeJob and @AfterJob annotations

- *Before* and *after* Step with the StepExecutionListener interface or @BeforeStep and @AfterStep annotations

- *Before, after,* and *after the chunk error* with the ChunkListener interface or @BeforeChunk and @AfterChunk annotations

- *Before, after,* and *on item read error* with the ItemReadListener<T> interface or @BeforeRead, @AfterRead, and @OnReadError annotations

- *Before, after,* and *on item process error* with the ItemProcessListener<T, S> interface or @BeforeProcess, @AfterProcess, and @OnProcessError annotations

- *Before, after,* and *on items write error* with the ItemWriteListener<S> interface or @BeforeWrite, @AfterWrite, and @OnWriteError annotations

- On *skip in read, process,* and *write* via SkipListener<T,S> or @OnSkipInRead, @OnSkipInProcess, and @OnSkipInWrite (Skip with listener is covered later in this chapter.)

- On *error, open, close in retry mode* via the Spring Core interface org.springframework. retry.RetryListener (Retry with listener is covered later in this chapter.)

If we don't need to use all the intercept methods of a particular listener, SB also provides empty convenience implementations of listeners with the suffix Support. This way, we can implement only the interception methods we are interested in. For example, if we want to intercept only after a chunkoperation, we can implement ChunkListenerSupport and override only the afterChunk() method.

XML Configuration of Job Interception Example

Listing 9-69 shows the job listener.

Listing 9-69. Annotated Job Listener (0917-job-listener-xml)

```
package net.lkrnac.book.eiws.chapter09;
import org.springframework.batch.core.annotation.AfterJob;
import org.springframework.batch.core.annotation.BeforeJob;
import org.springframework.beans.factory.annotation.Autowired;
import org.springframework.stereotype.Component;

import net.lkrnac.book.eiws.chapter09.step.SimpleExecutablePoint;

@Component
public class TeaJobListener {
  private SimpleExecutablePoint executablePoint;

  @Autowired
  public TeaJobListener(SimpleExecutablePoint executablePoint) {
    super();
    this.executablePoint = executablePoint;
  }

  @BeforeJob
  public void beforeTeaJob() {
    executablePoint.execute("It's tea time!");
  }

  @AfterJob
  public void afterTeaJob() {
    executablePoint.execute("Enjoy your tea!");
  }
}
```

We again use our simulation bean SimpleExecutablePoint to execute actions before and after the Job. In this case, we use the @BeforeJob and @AfterJob annotations to define the interception methods. Notice that we can pick names of interception methods, because annotations doesn't restrict them. Listing 9-70 shows the XML batch configuration.

Listing 9-70. XML Batch Configuration with Job Listener (File batch-config.xml in Folder src/main/ resource of Example Project 0917-job-listener-xml)

```xml
<?xml version="1.0" encoding="UTF-8"?>
<beans:beans xmlns:beans="http://www.springframework.org/schema/beans"
  xmlns:xsi="http://www.w3.org/2001/XMLSchema-instance"
  xmlns="http://www.springframework.org/schema/batch"
  xsi:schemaLocation="http://www.springframework.org/schema/batch
    http://www.springframework.org/schema/batch/spring-batch.xsd
    http://www.springframework.org/schema/beans
    http://www.springframework.org/schema/beans/spring-beans.xsd">

  <job id="prepareTeaJob">
    <step id="boilWaterStep" next="addTeaStep">
      <tasklet ref="boilWater"/>
    </step>
    <step id="addTeaStep" next="addWaterStep">
      <tasklet ref="addTea"/>
    </step>
    <step id="addWaterStep">
      <tasklet ref="addWater"/>
    </step>
    <listeners>
      <listener ref="teaJobListener"/>
    </listeners>
  </job>
</beans:beans>
```

This XML configuration is similar to prepareTeaJob we've already seen in the previous example. In this case, we register the teaJobListener bean as a listener for the job. We also reuse the BatchConfiguration class from Listing 9-7, which includes the batch-config.xml file and turns on batch processing via the @EnableBatchProcessing annotation. The main class of this example is the common Spring Boot main class in Listing 9-8. Notice that these classes are used a lot in batch listener examples. After running this main class, we can see the output in Listing 9-71.

Listing 9-71. Output of XML-Configured Job Listener Example

```
2015-10-01 20:09:14.852  INFO 22213 --- [          main] o.s.b.c.l.support.
SimpleJobLauncher    : Job: [FlowJob: [name=prepareTeaJob]] launched with the following
parameters: [{}]
2015-10-01 20:09:14.864  INFO 22213 --- [          main] n.l.b.e.c.step.
SimpleExecutablePoint    : It's tea time!
2015-10-01 20:09:14.886  INFO 22213 --- [          main] o.s.batch.core.job.
SimpleStepHandler    : Executing step: [boilWaterStep]
2015-10-01 20:09:14.904  INFO 22213 --- [          main] n.l.b.e.c.step.
SimpleExecutablePoint    : Boil Water
2015-10-01 20:09:14.931  INFO 22213 --- [          main] o.s.batch.core.job.
SimpleStepHandler    : Executing step: [addTeaStep]
2015-10-01 20:09:14.936  INFO 22213 --- [          main] n.l.b.e.c.step.
SimpleExecutablePoint    : Add Tea
2015-10-01 20:09:14.963  INFO 22213 --- [          main] o.s.batch.core.job.
SimpleStepHandler    : Executing step: [addWaterStep]
```

```
2015-10-01 20:09:14.968  INFO 22213 --- [            main] n.l.b.e.c.step.
SimpleExecutablePoint    : Add Water
2015-10-01 20:09:14.980  INFO 22213 --- [            main] n.l.b.e.c.step.
SimpleExecutablePoint    : Enjoy your tea!
2015-10-01 20:09:14.984  INFO 22213 --- [            main] o.s.b.c.l.support.
SimpleJobLauncher        : Job: [FlowJob: [name=prepareTeaJob]] completed with the following
parameters: [{}] and the following status: [COMPLETED]
```

Java Configuration of Job Interception Example

Listing 9-72 shows a different style of Job implementation.

Listing 9-72. JobListener Interface Implementation (0918-job-listener-javaconfig)

```java
package net.lkrnac.book.eiws.chapter09;
import net.lkrnac.book.eiws.chapter09.step.SimpleExecutablePoint;
import org.springframework.batch.core.JobExecution;
import org.springframework.batch.core.JobExecutionListener;
import org.springframework.beans.factory.annotation.Autowired;
import org.springframework.stereotype.Component;

@Component
public class TeaJobListener implements JobExecutionListener {
  private SimpleExecutablePoint executablePoint;

  @Autowired
  public TeaJobListener(SimpleExecutablePoint executablePoint) {
    super();
    this.executablePoint = executablePoint;
  }

  @Override
  public void beforeJob(JobExecution jobExecution) {
    executablePoint.execute("It's tea time!");
  }

  @Override
  public void afterJob(JobExecution jobExecution) {
    executablePoint.execute("Enjoy your tea!");
  }
}
```

This listener implements the JobExecutionListener interface, so the interception methods have to conform to its contract. We can't change the method names in this case. The jobExecution parameter is also enforced by the interface contract. This instance can be handy for accessing SB metadata. Listing 9-73 shows the Java configuration of the batch flow.

Listing 9-73. Java Configuration of JobExecutionListener (0918-job-listener-javaconfig)

```java
package net.lkrnac.book.eiws.chapter09;
import net.lkrnac.book.eiws.chapter09.step.tea.AddTea;
import net.lkrnac.book.eiws.chapter09.step.tea.AddWater;
import net.lkrnac.book.eiws.chapter09.step.tea.BoilWater;
import org.springframework.batch.core.Job;
import org.springframework.batch.core.Step;
import org.springframework.batch.core.configuration.annotation.EnableBatchProcessing;
import org.springframework.batch.core.configuration.annotation.JobBuilderFactory;
import org.springframework.batch.core.configuration.annotation.StepBuilderFactory;
import org.springframework.beans.factory.annotation.Qualifier;
import org.springframework.context.annotation.Bean;
import org.springframework.context.annotation.Configuration;

@Configuration
@EnableBatchProcessing
public class BatchConfiguration {
  @Bean
  public Step boilWaterStep(StepBuilderFactory stepFactory, BoilWater boilWater) {
    return stepFactory.get("boilWaterStep").tasklet(boilWater).build();
  }

  @Bean
  public Step addTeaStep(StepBuilderFactory stepFactory, AddTea addTea) {
    return stepFactory.get("addTeaStep").tasklet(addTea).build();
  }

  @Bean
  public Step addWaterStep(StepBuilderFactory stepFactory, AddWater addWater) {
    return stepFactory.get("addWaterStep").tasklet(addWater).build();
  }

  @Bean
  public Job prepareTeaJob(JobBuilderFactory jobBuilderFactory,
      @Qualifier("boilWaterStep") Step boilWaterStep,
      @Qualifier("addTeaStep") Step addTeaStep,
      @Qualifier("addWaterStep") Step addWaterStep,
      TeaJobListener teaJobListener) {
    return jobBuilderFactory.get("prepareTeaJob")
        .start(boilWaterStep)
        .next(addTeaStep)
        .next(addWaterStep)
        .listener(teaJobListener)
        .build();
  }
}
```

Again, this Java configuration is similar to that of prepareTeaJob in the previous examples. Notice how the listener is registered into the Job configuration while building its instance. The main class is again the common Spring Boot main class, and when we run it, we get the same output as for the previous example (Listing 9-71).

XML Configuration of Step Interception Example

Listing 9-74 shows the step listener implementation.

Listing 9-74. Annotated Step Listener (0919-step-listener-xml)

```
package net.lkrnac.book.eiws.chapter09;
import org.springframework.batch.core.ExitStatus;
import org.springframework.batch.core.StepExecution;
import org.springframework.batch.core.StepExecutionListener;
import org.springframework.beans.factory.annotation.Autowired;
import org.springframework.stereotype.Component;
import net.lkrnac.book.eiws.chapter09.step.SimpleExecutablePoint;


@Component
public class HotWaterStepListener implements StepExecutionListener {
  private SimpleExecutablePoint executablePoint;

  @Autowired
  public HotWaterStepListener(SimpleExecutablePoint executablePoint) {
    super();
    this.executablePoint = executablePoint;
  }

  @Override
  public void beforeStep(StepExecution stepExecution) {
    executablePoint.execute("Be careful with hot water!");
  }

  @Override
  public ExitStatus afterStep(StepExecution stepExecution) {
    executablePoint.execute("Step involving hot water manipulation is done");
    return ExitStatus.COMPLETED;
  }
}
```

As we implement StepExecutionListener, we can't change the names of the interception methods, because they need to match signatures from this interface. Signatures also include the parameter of StepExecution type. We don't use it in our example, but it can be used to access SB metadata in listeners. Listing 9-75 shows the XML configuration where this listener is used.

Listing 9-75. XML Batch Configuration with Step Listener (File batch-config.xml in Folder src/main/resource of Example Project 0919-step-listener-xml)

```xml
<?xml version="1.0" encoding="UTF-8"?>
<beans:beans xmlns:beans="http://www.springframework.org/schema/beans"
  xmlns:xsi="http://www.w3.org/2001/XMLSchema-instance"
  xmlns="http://www.springframework.org/schema/batch"
  xsi:schemaLocation="http://www.springframework.org/schema/batch
    http://www.springframework.org/schema/batch/spring-batch.xsd
    http://www.springframework.org/schema/beans
    http://www.springframework.org/schema/beans/spring-beans.xsd">
```

```
<job id="prepareTeaJob">
  <step id="boilWaterStep" next="addTeaStep">
    <tasklet ref="boilWater" />
    <listeners>
      <listener ref="hotWaterStepListener" />
    </listeners>
  </step>
  <step id="addTeaStep" next="addWaterStep">
    <tasklet ref="addTea" />
  </step>
  <step id="addWaterStep">
    <tasklet ref="addWater" />
    <listeners>
      <listener ref="hotWaterStepListener" />
    </listeners>
  </step>
</job>
</beans:beans>
```

Our listener is configured in the <step> tag and is reused for two steps. We did that to highlight fact that we can easily reuse listeners to intercept various SB steps. BatchConfiguration and the Spring Boot main class are again the same as for the previous XML examples. After running the main class, we get the output in Listing 9-76.

Listing 9-76. Output of XML-Configured Step Listener Example

```
2015-10-01 20:51:05.635  INFO 23623 --- [          main] o.s.b.c.l.support.SimpleJobLauncher
: Job: [FlowJob: [name=prepareTeaJob]] launched with the following parameters: [{}]
2015-10-01 20:51:05.668  INFO 23623 --- [          main] o.s.batch.core.job.
SimpleStepHandler    : Executing step: [boilWaterStep]
2015-10-01 20:51:05.673  INFO 23623 --- [          main] n.l.b.e.c.step.
SimpleExecutablePoint    : Be careful with hot water!
2015-10-01 20:51:05.687  INFO 23623 --- [          main] n.l.b.e.c.step.
SimpleExecutablePoint    : Boil Water
2015-10-01 20:51:05.692  INFO 23623 --- [          main] n.l.b.e.c.step.
SimpleExecutablePoint    : Step involving hot water manipulation is done
2015-10-01 20:51:05.715  INFO 23623 --- [          main] o.s.batch.core.job.
SimpleStepHandler    : Executing step: [addTeaStep]
2015-10-01 20:51:05.721  INFO 23623 --- [          main] n.l.b.e.c.step.
SimpleExecutablePoint    : Add Tea
2015-10-01 20:51:05.746  INFO 23623 --- [          main] o.s.batch.core.job.
SimpleStepHandler    : Executing step: [addWaterStep]
2015-10-01 20:51:05.748  INFO 23623 --- [          main] n.l.b.e.c.step.
SimpleExecutablePoint    : Be careful with hot water!
2015-10-01 20:51:05.751  INFO 23623 --- [          main] n.l.b.e.c.step.
SimpleExecutablePoint    : Add Water
2015-10-01 20:51:05.757  INFO 23623 --- [          main] n.l.b.e.c.step.
SimpleExecutablePoint    : Step involving hot water manipulation is done
2015-10-01 20:51:05.767  INFO 23623 --- [          main] o.s.b.c.l.support.SimpleJobLauncher
: Job: [FlowJob: [name=prepareTeaJob]] completed with the following parameters: [{}] and the
following status: [COMPLETED]
```

Both steps are intercepted as expected.

Java Configuration of Step Interception example

Listing 9-77 presents the StepExecutionListener implementation.

Listing 9-77. StepListener Implementation (0920-step-listener-javaconfig)

```
package net.lkrnac.book.eiws.chapter09;
import org.springframework.batch.core.ExitStatus;
import org.springframework.batch.core.annotation.AfterStep;
import org.springframework.batch.core.annotation.BeforeStep;
import org.springframework.beans.factory.annotation.Autowired;
import org.springframework.stereotype.Component;
import net.lkrnac.book.eiws.chapter09.step.SimpleExecutablePoint;

@Component
public class HotWaterStepListener {
  private SimpleExecutablePoint executablePoint;

  @Autowired
  public HotWaterStepListener(SimpleExecutablePoint executablePoint) {
    super();
    this.executablePoint = executablePoint;
  }

  @BeforeStep
  public void beforeHotWaterStep() {
    executablePoint.execute("Be careful with hot water!");
  }

  @AfterStep
  public ExitStatus afterHotWaterStep() {
    executablePoint.execute("Step involving hot water manipulation is done");
    return ExitStatus.COMPLETED;
  }
}
```

In this case, we use annotations to define the interception points. Notice that we don't need to use StepExecution parameters and we are allowed to pick the interception method names. But if we needed to, we could inject any SB metadata instance(s) as parameter(s) into these interception methods.

The option to change Step ExitStatus in the @AfterStep method if needed is also useful. This mechanism can be handy if we want to change ExitStatus of the StepExecution in the listener. Listing 9-78 shows the Java batch configuration.

Listing 9-78. Java Configuration of StepExecutionListener (0920-step-listener-javaconfig)

```
package net.lkrnac.book.eiws.chapter09;
import net.lkrnac.book.eiws.chapter09.step.tea.AddTea;
import net.lkrnac.book.eiws.chapter09.step.tea.AddWater;
import net.lkrnac.book.eiws.chapter09.step.tea.BoilWater;
import org.springframework.batch.core.Job;
import org.springframework.batch.core.Step;
import org.springframework.batch.core.configuration.annotation.EnableBatchProcessing;
```

```java
import org.springframework.batch.core.configuration.annotation.JobBuilderFactory;
import org.springframework.batch.core.configuration.annotation.StepBuilderFactory;
import org.springframework.beans.factory.annotation.Qualifier;
import org.springframework.context.annotation.Bean;
import org.springframework.context.annotation.Configuration;

@Configuration
@EnableBatchProcessing
public class BatchConfiguration {
  @Bean
  public Step boilWaterStep(StepBuilderFactory stepFactory,
      BoilWater boilWater,
      HotWaterStepListener hotWaterStepListener) {
    return stepFactory.get("boilWaterStep")
        .tasklet(boilWater)
        .listener(hotWaterStepListener)
        .build();
  }

  @Bean
  public Step addTeaStep(StepBuilderFactory stepFactory, AddTea addTea) {
    return stepFactory.get("addTeaStep").tasklet(addTea).build();
  }

  @Bean
  public Step addWaterStep(StepBuilderFactory stepFactory, AddWater addWater,
      HotWaterStepListener hotWaterStepListener) {
    return stepFactory.get("addWaterStep")
        .tasklet(addWater)
        .listener(hotWaterStepListener)
        .build();
  }

  @Bean
  public Job prepareTeaJob(JobBuilderFactory jobBuilderFactory,
      @Qualifier("boilWaterStep") Step boilWaterStep,
      @Qualifier("addTeaStep") Step addTeaStep,
      @Qualifier("addWaterStep") Step addWaterStep) {
    return jobBuilderFactory.get("prepareTeaJob")
        .start(boilWaterStep)
        .next(addTeaStep)
        .next(addWaterStep)
        .build();
  }
}
```

Notice that this is the exact Java configuration mirror of the XML configuration from the previous example in Listing 9-75. The main class is the same as the main Spring Boot class. After running it, we get the same output as in Listing 9-76.

XML Configuration of Chunk-Oriented Processing Listeners

Get ready for a listener-heavy example, as chunk-oriented processing can be intercepted quite extensively. Listing 9-79 shows the chunk listener.

Listing 9-79. Annotated Chunk Listener (0921-chunk-listener-xml)

```
package net.lkrnac.book.eiws.chapter09;
import org.springframework.batch.core.ChunkListener;
import org.springframework.batch.core.scope.context.ChunkContext;
import org.springframework.beans.factory.annotation.Autowired;
import org.springframework.stereotype.Component;
import net.lkrnac.book.eiws.chapter09.step.SimpleExecutablePoint;

@Component
public class SimpleChunkListener implements ChunkListener {
  private SimpleExecutablePoint executablePoint;

  @Autowired
  public SimpleChunkListener(SimpleExecutablePoint executablePoint) {
    super();
    this.executablePoint = executablePoint;
  }

  @Override
  public void beforeChunk(ChunkContext context) {
    executablePoint.execute("Starting chunk: " + context);
  }

  @Override
  public void afterChunk(ChunkContext context) {
    executablePoint.execute("After chunk: " + context);
  }

  @Override
  public void afterChunkError(ChunkContext context) {
    executablePoint.execute("Error occurred in chunk: " + context);
  }
}
```

The chunk can be intercepted before or after the chunk is read or after the chunk error occurs. Each time SB passes us an instance of ChunkContext. Because we are not using annotations, we need to name the interception methods according to the interface ChunkListener . Listing 9-80 shows the item reader listener.

Listing 9-80. Annotated Item Reader Listener (0921-chunk-listener-xml)

```
package net.lkrnac.book.eiws.chapter09;
import org.springframework.batch.core.ItemReadListener;
import org.springframework.beans.factory.annotation.Autowired;
import org.springframework.stereotype.Component;
import net.lkrnac.book.eiws.chapter09.step.SimpleExecutablePoint;
```

```java
@Component
public class SimpleItemReaderListener implements ItemReadListener<String> {
  private SimpleExecutablePoint executablePoint;

  @Autowired
  public SimpleItemReaderListener(SimpleExecutablePoint executablePoint) {
    super();
    this.executablePoint = executablePoint;
  }

  @Override
  public void beforeRead() {
    executablePoint.execute("Starting to read...");
  }

  @Override
  public void afterRead(String item) {
    executablePoint.execute("Read finished, item: " + item);
  }

  @Override
  public void onReadError(Exception ex) {
    executablePoint.execute("Error occurred while reading");
  }
}
```

We implement the ItemReadListener<String> interfa ce, which has three interception methods. Obviously, we don't know what item we're going to read out before we read. Therefore, the beforeRead() method doesn't have any parameters. After reading, SB injects an item instance. If an error occurs, SB injects that an exception instance occurred. Listing 9-81 shows item process listener.

Listing 9-81. Annotated Item Process Listener (0921-chunk-listener-xml)

```java
package net.lkrnac.book.eiws.chapter09;
import org.springframework.batch.core.ItemProcessListener;
import org.springframework.beans.factory.annotation.Autowired;
import org.springframework.stereotype.Component;
import net.lkrnac.book.eiws.chapter09.step.SimpleExecutablePoint;

@Component
public class SimpleItemProcessListener implements
    ItemProcessListener<String, String> {
  private SimpleExecutablePoint executablePoint;

  @Autowired
  public SimpleItemProcessListener(SimpleExecutablePoint executablePoint) {
    super();
    this.executablePoint = executablePoint;
  }
```

```java
  @Override
  public void beforeProcess(String item) {
    executablePoint.execute("Starting to process item: " + item);
  }

  @Override
  public void afterProcess(String item, String result) {
    executablePoint.execute("Processed item: " + result);
  }

  @Override
  public void onProcessError(String item, Exception e) {
    executablePoint.execute("Error occurred while processing item: " + item);
  }
}
```

In a before interception, we get an instance of the item before processing via the parameter. In an after process interception, SB injects an instance of the processed/converted item and the result of the processing operation. In an after process error interce ption method, we get the item and exception, which occurred during its processing. Obviously, we can't pick the names of methods, as we aren't using annotations. Listing 9-82 shows the interceptor for the item writer.

Listing 9-82. Annotated Item Write Listener (0921-chunk-listener-xml)

```java
package net.lkrnac.book.eiws.chapter09;
import java.util.List;
import org.springframework.batch.core.ItemWriteListener;
import org.springframework.beans.factory.annotation.Autowired;
import org.springframework.stereotype.Component;

import net.lkrnac.book.eiws.chapter09.step.SimpleExecutablePoint;

@Component
public class SimpleItemWriterListener implements ItemWriteListener<String> {
  private SimpleExecutablePoint executablePoint;

  @Autowired
  public SimpleItemWriterListener(SimpleExecutablePoint executablePoint) {
    super();
    this.executablePoint = executablePoint;
  }

  @Override
  public void beforeWrite(List<? extends String> items) {
    executablePoint.execute("Starting to write items...");
  }

  @Override
  public void afterWrite(List<? extends String> items) {
    executablePoint.execute("Items written successfully");
  }
```

```java
    @Override
    public void onWriteError(Exception exception, List<? extends String> items) {
        executablePoint.execute("Error occurred while writing items");
    }
}
```

The injections in the item writer are slightly different, as the writer is handling a List of items instead of items one by one. Otherwise, the injected values and interception points are similar to the reader and processor. Listing 9-83 shows the XML SB flow configuration.

Listing 9-83. XML Batch Configuration with Chunk Listener (File batch-config.xml in Folder src/main/resource of Example Project 0921-chunk-listener-xml)

```xml
<?xml version="1.0" encoding="UTF-8"?>
<beans:beans xmlns:beans="http://www.springframework.org/schema/beans"
  xmlns:xsi="http://www.w3.org/2001/XMLSchema-instance"
  xmlns="http://www.springframework.org/schema/batch"
  xsi:schemaLocation="http://www.springframework.org/schema/batch
    http://www.springframework.org/schema/batch/spring-batch.xsd
    http://www.springframework.org/schema/beans
    http://www.springframework.org/schema/beans/spring-beans.xsd">

  <job id="simpleRecordsJob">
    <step id="simpleRecordsStep">
      <tasklet>
        <chunk reader="simpleRecordReader" writer="simpleRecordWriter"
          processor="simpleRecordProcessor" commit-interval="4">
          <listeners>
            <listener ref="simpleChunkListener"/>
            <listener ref="simpleItemReaderListener"/>
            <listener ref="simpleItemProcessListener"/>
            <listener ref="simpleItemWriterListener"/>
          </listeners>
        </chunk>
      </tasklet>
    </step>
  </job>
</beans:beans>
```

All the listeners are registered as a subtag of <chunk>. The order of listeners is not relevant in this case, as they are used for different processing phases. If we registered various listeners for the same batch-processing phase, they would be executed in the order that they were registered.

We again use BatchConfiguration and the common main Spring Boot class in this example. Listing 9-84 shows the output if we run the main class.

Listing 9-84. Output of Chunk-Oriented Processing Listeners Example

```
2015-10-01 22:03:39.703  INFO 26035 --- [            main] o.s.b.c.l.support.SimpleJobLauncher
: Job: [FlowJob: [name=simpleRecordsJob]] launched with the following parameters: [{}]
2015-10-01 22:03:39.731  INFO 26035 --- [            main] o.s.batch.core.job.SimpleStepHandler
: Executing step: [simpleRecordsStep]
```

```
2015-10-01 22:03:39.746  INFO 26035 --- [            main] n.l.b.e.c.step.SimpleExecutablePoint
: Starting chunk: ChunkContext: attributes=[], complete=false, stepContext=Synchronized
AttributeAccessor: [], stepExecutionContext={batch.taskletType=org.springframework.batch.core.
step.item.ChunkOrientedTasklet, batch.stepType=org.springframework.batch.core.step.tasklet.
TaskletStep}, jobExecutionContext={}, jobParameters={}
2015-10-01 22:03:39.750  INFO 26035 --- [            main] n.l.b.e.c.step.SimpleExecutablePoint
: Starting to read...
2015-10-01 22:03:39.766  INFO 26035 --- [            main] n.l.b.e.c.step.SimpleExecutablePoint
: Read finished, item: simple record 0
2015-10-01 22:03:39.766  INFO 26035 --- [            main] n.l.b.e.c.step.SimpleExecutablePoint
: Starting to read...
2015-10-01 22:03:39.767  INFO 26035 --- [            main] n.l.b.e.c.step.SimpleExecutablePoint
: Read finished, item: simple record 1
2015-10-01 22:03:39.767  INFO 26035 --- [            main] n.l.b.e.c.step.SimpleExecutablePoint
: Starting to read...
2015-10-01 22:03:39.767  INFO 26035 --- [            main] n.l.b.e.c.step.SimpleExecutablePoint
: Read finished, item: simple record 2
2015-10-01 22:03:39.768  INFO 26035 --- [            main] n.l.b.e.c.step.SimpleExecutablePoint
: Starting to read...
2015-10-01 22:03:39.768  INFO 26035 --- [            main] n.l.b.e.c.step.SimpleExecutablePoint
: Read finished, item: simple record 3
2015-10-01 22:03:39.769  INFO 26035 --- [            main] n.l.b.e.c.step.SimpleExecutablePoint
: Starting to process item: simple record 0
2015-10-01 22:03:39.769  INFO 26035 --- [            main] n.l.b.e.c.step.SimpleExecutablePoint
: Processed item: simple record 0 processed
2015-10-01 22:03:39.770  INFO 26035 --- [            main] n.l.b.e.c.step.SimpleExecutablePoint
: Starting to process item: simple record 1
2015-10-01 22:03:39.770  INFO 26035 --- [            main] n.l.b.e.c.step.SimpleExecutablePoint
: Processed item: simple record 1 processed
2015-10-01 22:03:39.770  INFO 26035 --- [            main] n.l.b.e.c.step.SimpleExecutablePoint
: Starting to process item: simple record 2
2015-10-01 22:03:39.770  INFO 26035 --- [            main] n.l.b.e.c.step.SimpleExecutablePoint
: Processed item: simple record 2 processed
2015-10-01 22:03:39.770  INFO 26035 --- [            main] n.l.b.e.c.step.SimpleExecutablePoint
: Starting to process item: simple record 3
2015-10-01 22:03:39.770  INFO 26035 --- [            main] n.l.b.e.c.step.SimpleExecutablePoint
: Processed item: simple record 3 processed
2015-10-01 22:03:39.771  INFO 26035 --- [            main] n.l.b.e.c.step.SimpleExecutablePoint
: Starting to write items...
2015-10-01 22:03:39.784  INFO 26035 --- [            main] n.l.b.e.chapter09.write.
WriteRepository  : Writing record: simple record 0 processed
2015-10-01 22:03:39.785  INFO 26035 --- [            main] n.l.b.e.chapter09.write.
WriteRepository  : Writing record: simple record 1 processed
2015-10-01 22:03:39.785  INFO 26035 --- [            main] n.l.b.e.chapter09.write.
WriteRepository  : Writing record: simple record 2 processed
2015-10-01 22:03:39.785  INFO 26035 --- [            main] n.l.b.e.chapter09.write.
WriteRepository  : Writing record: simple record 3 processed
2015-10-01 22:03:39.786  INFO 26035 --- [            main] n.l.b.e.c.step.SimpleExecutablePoint
: Items written successfully
2015-10-01 22:03:39.794  INFO 26035 --- [            main] n.l.b.e.c.step.SimpleExecutablePoint
: After chunk: ChunkContext: attributes=[], complete=true, stepContext=SynchronizedAttribute
```

```
Accessor: [], stepExecutionContext={batch.taskletType=org.springframework.batch.core.step.item.
ChunkOrientedTasklet, batch.stepType=org.springframework.batch.core.step.tasklet.TaskletStep},
jobExecutionContext={}, jobParameters={}
2015-10-01 22:03:39.795  INFO 26035 --- [          main] n.l.b.e.c.step.SimpleExecutablePoint
: Starting chunk: ChunkContext: attributes=[], complete=false, stepContext=Synchronized
AttributeAccessor: [], stepExecutionContext={batch.taskletType=org.springframework.batch.core.
step.item.ChunkOrientedTasklet,  batch.stepType=org.springframework.batch.core.step.tasklet.
TaskletStep}, jobExecutionContext={}, jobParameters={}
2015-10-01 22:03:39.795  INFO 26035 --- [          main] n.l.b.e.c.step.SimpleExecutablePoint
: Starting to read...
2015-10-01 22:03:39.796  INFO 26035 --- [          main] n.l.b.e.c.step.SimpleExecutablePoint
: Read finished, item: simple record 4
2015-10-01 22:03:39.796  INFO 26035 --- [          main] n.l.b.e.c.step.SimpleExecutablePoint
: Starting to read...
2015-10-01 22:03:39.796  INFO 26035 --- [          main] n.l.b.e.c.step.SimpleExecutablePoint
: Read finished, item: simple record 5
2015-10-01 22:03:39.796  INFO 26035 --- [          main] n.l.b.e.c.step.SimpleExecutablePoint
: Starting to read...
2015-10-01 22:03:39.796  INFO 26035 --- [          main] n.l.b.e.c.step.SimpleExecutablePoint
: Read finished, item: simple record 6
2015-10-01 22:03:39.796  INFO 26035 --- [          main] n.l.b.e.c.step.SimpleExecutablePoint
: Starting to read...
2015-10-01 22:03:39.796  INFO 26035 --- [          main] n.l.b.e.c.step.SimpleExecutablePoint
: Read finished, item: simple record 7
2015-10-01 22:03:39.797  INFO 26035 --- [          main] n.l.b.e.c.step.SimpleExecutablePoint
: Starting to process item: simple record 4
2015-10-01 22:03:39.797  INFO 26035 --- [          main] n.l.b.e.c.step.SimpleExecutablePoint
: Processed item: simple record 4 processed
2015-10-01 22:03:39.797  INFO 26035 --- [          main] n.l.b.e.c.step.SimpleExecutablePoint
: Starting to process item: simple record 5
2015-10-01 22:03:39.797  INFO 26035 --- [          main] n.l.b.e.c.step.SimpleExecutablePoint
: Processed item: simple record 5 processed
2015-10-01 22:03:39.797  INFO 26035 --- [          main] n.l.b.e.c.step.SimpleExecutablePoint
: Starting to process item: simple record 6
2015-10-01 22:03:39.797  INFO 26035 --- [          main] n.l.b.e.c.step.SimpleExecutablePoint
: Processed item: simple record 6 processed
2015-10-01 22:03:39.797  INFO 26035 --- [          main] n.l.b.e.c.step.SimpleExecutablePoint
: Starting to process item: simple record 7
2015-10-01 22:03:39.797  INFO 26035 --- [          main] n.l.b.e.c.step.SimpleExecutablePoint
: Processed item: simple record 7 processed
2015-10-01 22:03:39.798  INFO 26035 --- [          main] n.l.b.e.c.step.SimpleExecutablePoint
: Starting to write items...
2015-10-01 22:03:39.798  INFO 26035 --- [          main] n.l.b.e.chapter09.write.
WriteRepository  : Writing record: simple record 4 processed
2015-10-01 22:03:39.798  INFO 26035 --- [          main] n.l.b.e.chapter09.write.
WriteRepository  : Writing record: simple record 5 processed
2015-10-01 22:03:39.798  INFO 26035 --- [          main] n.l.b.e.chapter09.write.
WriteRepository  : Writing record: simple record 6 processed
2015-10-01 22:03:39.798  INFO 26035 --- [          main] n.l.b.e.chapter09.write.
WriteRepository  : Writing record: simple record 7 processed
```

```
2015-10-01 22:03:39.798  INFO 26035 --- [              main] n.l.b.e.c.step.SimpleExecutablePoint
: Items written successfully
2015-10-01 22:03:39.803  INFO 26035 --- [              main] n.l.b.e.c.step.SimpleEx ecutablePoint
: After chunk: ChunkContext: attributes=[], complete=true, stepContext=SynchronizedAttribute
Accessor: [], stepExecutionContext={batch.taskletType=org.springframework.batch.core.step.item.
ChunkOrientedTasklet, batch.stepType=org.springframework.batch.core.step.tasklet.TaskletStep},
jobExecutionContext={}, jobParameters={}
2015-10-01 22:03:39.803  INFO 26035 --- [              main] n.l.b.e.c.step.SimpleExecutablePoint
: Starting chunk: ChunkContext: attributes=[], complete=false, stepContext=Synchronized
AttributeAccessor: [], stepExecutionContext={batch.taskletType=org.springframework.batch.core.
step.item.ChunkOrientedTasklet, batch.stepType=org.springframework.batch.core.step.tasklet.
TaskletStep}, jobExecutionContext={}, jobParameters={}
2015-10-01 22:03:39.804  INFO 26035 --- [              main] n.l.b.e.c.step.SimpleExecutablePoint
: Starting to read...
2015-10-01 22:03:39.804  INFO 26035 --- [              main] n.l.b.e.c.step.SimpleExecutablePoint
: Read finished, item: simple record 8
2015-10-01 22:03:39.804  INFO 26035 --- [              main] n.l.b.e.c.step.SimpleExecutablePoint
: Starting to read...
2015-10-01 22:03:39.804  INFO 26035 --- [              main] n.l.b.e.c.step.SimpleExecutablePoint
: Read finished, item: simple record 9
2015-10-01 22:03:39.804  INFO 26035 --- [              main] n.l.b.e.c.step.SimpleExecutablePoint
: Starting to read...
2015-10-01 22:03:39.804  INFO 26035 --- [              main] n.l.b.e.c.step.SimpleExecutablePoint
: Read finished, item: simple record 10
2015-10-01 22:03:39.804  INFO 26035 --- [              main] n.l.b.e.c.step.SimpleExecutablePoint
: Starting to read...
2015-10-01 22:03:39.805  INFO 26035 --- [              main] n.l.b.e.c.step.SimpleExecutablePoint
: Read finished, item: simple record 11
2015-10-01 22:03:39.805  INFO 26035 --- [              main] n.l.b.e.c.step.SimpleExecutablePoint
: Starting to process item: simple record 8
2015-10-01 22:03:39.805  INFO 26035 --- [              main] n.l.b.e.c.step.SimpleExecutablePoint
: Processed item: simple record 8 processed
2015-10-01 22:03:39.805  INFO 26035 --- [              main] n.l.b.e.c.step.SimpleExecutablePoint
: Starting to process item: simple record 9
2015-10-01 22:03:39.806  INFO 26035 --- [              main] n.l.b.e.c.step.SimpleExecutablePoint
: Processed item: simple record 9 processed
2015-10-01 22:03:39.806  INFO 26035 --- [              main] n.l.b.e.c.step.SimpleExecutablePoint
: Starting to process item: simple record 10
2015-10-01 22:03:39.806  INFO 26035 --- [              main] n.l.b.e.c.step.SimpleExecutablePoint
: Processed item: simple record 10 processed
2015-10-01 22:03:39.806  INFO 26035 --- [              main] n.l.b.e.c.step.SimpleExecutablePoint
: Starting to process item: simple record 11
2015-10-01 22:03:39.806  INFO 26035 --- [              main] n.l.b.e.c.step.SimpleExecutablePoint
: Processed item: simple record 11 processed
2015-10-01 22:03:39.806  INFO 26035 --- [              main] n.l.b.e.c.step.SimpleExecutablePoint
: Starting to write items...
2015-10-01 22:03:39.806  INFO 26035 --- [              main] n.l.b.e.chapter09.write.
WriteRepository  : Writing record: simple record 8 processed
2015-10-01 22:03:39.806  INFO 26035 --- [              main] n.l.b.e.chapter09.writ
e.WriteRepository  : Writing record: simple record 9 processed
```

```
2015-10-01 22:03:39.806  INFO 26035 --- [              main] n.l.b.e.chapter09.write.
WriteRepository  : Writing record: simple record 10 processed
2015-10-01 22:03:39.807  INFO 26035 --- [              main] n.l.b.e.chapter09.write.
WriteRepository  : Writing record: simple record 11 processed
2015-10-01 22:03:39.807  INFO 26035 --- [              main] n.l.b.e.c.step.SimpleExecutablePoint
: Items written successfully
2015-10-01 22:03:39.811  INFO 26035 --- [              main] n.l.b.e.c.step.SimpleExecutablePoint
: After chunk: ChunkContext: attributes=[], complete=true, stepContext=SynchronizedAttribute
Accessor: [], stepExecutionContext={batch.taskletType=org.springframework.batch.core.step.item.
ChunkOrientedTasklet, batch.stepType=org.springframework.batch.core.step.tasklet.TaskletStep},
jobExecutionContext={}, jobParameters={}
2015-10-01 22:03:39.812  INFO 26035 --- [              main] n.l.b.e.c.step.SimpleExecutablePoint
: Starting chunk: ChunkContext: attributes=[], complete=false, stepContext=Synchronized
AttributeAccessor: [], stepExecutionContext={batch.taskletType=org.springframework.batch.core.
step.item.ChunkOrientedTasklet, batch.stepType=org.springframework.batch.core.step.tasklet.
TaskletStep}, jobExecutionContext={}, jobParameters={}
2015-10-01 22:03:39.812  INFO 26035 --- [              main] n.l.b.e.c.step.SimpleExecutablePoint
: Starting to read...
2015-10-01 22:03:39.812  INFO 26035 --- [              main] n.l.b.e.c.step.SimpleExecutablePoint
: Read finished, item: simple record 12
2015-10-01 22:03:39.813  INFO 26035 --- [              main] n.l.b.e.c.step.SimpleExecutablePoint
: Starting to read...
2015-10-01 22:03:39.813  INFO 26035 --- [              main] n.l.b.e.c.step.SimpleExecutablePoint
: Read finished, item: simple record 13
2015-10-01 22:03:39.813  INFO 26035 --- [              main] n.l.b.e.c.step.SimpleExecutablePoint
: Starting to read...
2015-10-01 22:03:39.813  INFO 26035 --- [              main] n.l.b.e.c.step.SimpleExecutablePoint
: Read finished, item: simple record 14
2015-10-01 22:03:39.814  INFO 26035 --- [              main] n.l.b.e.c.step.SimpleExecutablePoint
: Starting to read...
2015-10-01 22:03:39.814  INFO 26035 --- [              main] n.l.b.e.c.step.SimpleExecutablePoint
: Starting to process item: simple record 12
2015-10-01 22:03:39.814  INFO 26035 --- [              main] n.l.b.e.c.step.SimpleExecutablePoint
: Processed item: simple record 12 processed
2015-10-01 22:03:39.814  INFO 26035 --- [              main] n.l.b.e.c.step.SimpleExecutablePoint
: Starting to process item: simple record 13
2015-10-01 22:03:39.814  INFO 26035 --- [              main] n.l.b.e.c.step.SimpleExecutablePoint
: Processed item: simple record 13 processed
2015-10-01 22:03:39.814  INFO 26035 --- [              main] n.l.b.e.c.step.SimpleExecutablePoint
: Starting to process item: simple record 14
2015-10-01 22:03:39.814  INFO 26035 --- [              main] n.l.b.e.c.step.SimpleExecutablePoint
: Processed item: simple record 14 processed
2015-10-01 22:03:39.814  INFO 26035 --- [              main] n.l.b.e.c.step.SimpleExecutablePoint
: Starting to write items...
2015-10-01 22:03:39.814  INFO 26035 --- [              main] n.l.b.e.chapter09.write.
WriteRepository  : Writing record: simple record 12 processed
2015-10-01 22:03:39.814  INFO 26035 --- [              main] n.l.b.e.chapter09.write.
WriteRepository  : Writing record: simple record 13 processed
2015-10-01 22:03:39.814  INFO 26035 --- [              main] n.l.b.e.chapter09.write.
WriteRepository  : Writing record: simple record 14 processed
```

```
2015-10-01 22:03:39.815  INFO 26035 --- [            main] n.l.b.e.c.step.SimpleExecutablePoint
: Items written successfully
2015-10-01 22:03:39.819  INFO 26035 --- [            main] n.l.b.e.c.step.SimpleExecutablePoint
: After chunk: ChunkContext: attributes=[], complete=true, stepContext=SynchronizedAttribute
Accessor: [], stepExecutionContext={batch.taskletType=org.springframework.batch.core.step.item.
ChunkOrientedTasklet, batch.stepType=org.springframework.batch.core.step.tasklet.TaskletStep},
jobExecutionContext={}, jobParameters={}
2015-10-01 22:03:39.832  INFO 26035 --- [            main] o.s.b.c.l.support.SimpleJobLauncher
: Job: [FlowJob: [name=simpleRecordsJob]] completed with the following parameters: [{}] and the
following status: [COMPLETED]
```

As you can see, this configuration-heavy example also is reflected in the output-heavy listing. But if you carefully step through it, you realize that the interceptions are happening as we expected.

Java Configuration of Chunk-Oriented Processing Listeners

Let's skip the verbose listener implementations for this example. The listeners for Chunk, ItemReader, ItemProcessor, and ItemWriter don't implement interfaces, but rather use annotations. The difference in this approach is that we are not forced to inject any parameters and are allowed to name interception methods differently. You can take a look at the 0922-chunk-listener-javaconfig example if you're interested in how these listeners are defined. Listing 9-85 shows the Java configuration.

Listing 9-85. Java Configuration of Chunk-Oriented Processing Listeners Example (0922-chunk-listener-javaconfig)

```
package net.lkrnac.book.eiws.chapter09;
import net.lkrnac.book.eiws.chapter09.process.SimpleRecordProcessor;
import net.lkrnac.book.eiws.chapter09.read.SimpleRecordReader;
import net.lkrnac.book.eiws.chapter09.write.SimpleRecordWriter;
import org.springframework.batch.core.Job;
import org.springframework.batch.core.Step;
import org.springframework.batch.core.configuration.annotation.EnableBatchProcessing;
import org.springframework.batch.core.configuration.annotation.JobBuilderFactory;
import org.springframework.batch.core.configuration.annotation.StepBuilderFactory;
import org.springframework.context.annotation.Bean;
import org.springframework.context.annotation.Configuration;

@Configuration
@EnableBatchProcessing
public class BatchConfiguration {
  @Bean
  public Step simpleRecordsStep(StepBuilderFactory stepBuilderFactory,
      SimpleRecordReader simpleRecordReader,
      SimpleRecordProcessor simpleRecordProcessor,
      SimpleRecordWriter simpleRecordWriter,
      SimpleItemReaderListener simpleItemReaderListener,
      SimpleItemProcessListener simpleItemProcessListener,
      SimpleItemWriterListener simpleItemWriterListener,
      SimpleChunkListener simpleChunkListener) {
```

```
    return stepBuilderFactory.get("simpleRecordsStep")
        .<String, String> chunk(4)
        .reader(simpleRecordReader)
        .listener(simpleItemReaderListener)
        .processor(simpleRecordProcessor)
        .listener(simpleItemProcessListener)
        .writer(simpleRecordWriter)
        .listener(simpleItemWriterListener)
        .listener(simpleChunkListener)
        .build();
}
@Bean
public Job simpleRecordsJob(JobBuilderFactory jobBuilderFactory,
    Step simpleRecordsStep) {
    return jobBuilderFactory.get("simpleRecordsJob")
        .start(simpleRecordsStep)
        .build();
}
}
```

The number of injected beans for the Step definition is far beyond the horizon of a wise parameter count. But as we wanted to highlight how to configure all listener types, please ignore that in this case. The order of registering doesn't matter, because listeners are for different phases of batch processing. If we registered various listeners for the same batch-processing phase, they would be executed in the order that they were registered.

The main class is again reused from previous examples, and when we run it, we get the same output as in the previous example (Listing 9-84).

ItemStream

Chunk-oriented processing often requires acquiring, updating, and releasing resources. Of course, Spring tries to handle these operations for us, for the most part. Examples can include opening and closing JMS or DB connections.

But for some technologies out there, Spring doesn't cover opening and closing their resources for us. These resources are often in the form of a stream, so SB came up with the name ItemStream. If we need to open, update, or close such resources in chunk-oriented processing, we can rely on this SB feature. We can think of it as a special interceptor executed at the right time to open or close the resource.

This support comes in three forms:

- ItemStream: Stand-alone interface defining open, update, and close actions as interception points. The advantage is that we can use this implementation separately from ItemReader and ItemWriter.

- ItemStreamReader<T>: A convenience subinterface for ItemReader<T> and ItemStream. The advantage is to define the ItemReader as a stream-aware SB component out of the box.

- ItemStreamWriter<S>: A convenience subinterface for ItemWriter<S> and ItemStream. The advantage is to define ItemWriter as a stream-aware SB component out of the box.

Notice that ItemStreamWriter<S> uses a different generic placeholder S than ItemStreamReader<T>. This is because we follow the notion of ItemProcessor<T, S>, where T is the type before the processing is passed into the processor, and S is the type after the processing is returned from the processor. Therefore, generic types after processing are marked with the placeholder S in this book.

XML Example of ItemStream Usage

Listing 9-86 shows a stand-alone implementation of the ItemStream interface.

Listing 9-86. Stand-alone Implementation of ItemStream interface (0923-item-stream-xml)

```java
package net.lkrnac.book.eiws.chapter09;
import net.lkrnac.book.eiws.chapter09.step.SimpleExecutablePoint;
import org.springframework.batch.item.ExecutionContext;
import org.springframework.batch.item.ItemStream;
import org.springframework.batch.item.ItemStreamException;
import org.springframework.beans.factory.annotation.Autowired;
import org.springframework.stereotype.Component;

@Component
public class RecordsReaderItemStream implements ItemStream {
  private SimpleExecutablePoint executablePoint;

  @Autowired
  public RecordsReaderItemStream(SimpleExecutablePoint executablePoint) {
    super();
    this.executablePoint = executablePoint;
  }

  @Override
  public void open(ExecutionContext executionContext)
      throws ItemStreamException {
    executablePoint.execute("Opening records reader");
  }

  @Override
  public void update(ExecutionContext executionContext)
      throws ItemStreamException {
    executablePoint.execute("Updating records reader");
  }

  @Override
  public void close() throws ItemStreamException {
    executablePoint.execute("Closing records reader");
  }
}
```

With this interface, we need to implement all three possible actions needed against the stream. For simplicity, we don't use a real resource, but rather simulate executions against our common execution point. In real life, we would open, update, or close the real resource. Listing 9-87 shows the ItemStreamWriter<T> implementation.

Listing 9-87. ItemStreamWriter<S> implementation (0923-item-stream-xml)

```java
package net.lkrnac.book.eiws.chapter09;
import java.util.List;
import net.lkrnac.book.eiws.chapter09.step.SimpleExecutablePoint;
import net.lkrnac.book.eiws.chapter09.write.WriteRepository;
import org.springframework.batch.item.ExecutionContext;
import org.springframework.batch.item.ItemStreamException;
import org.springframework.batch.item.ItemStreamWriter;
import org.springframework.beans.factory.annotation.Autowired;
import org.springframework.stereotype.Component;

@Component
public class StreamRecordWriter implements ItemStreamWriter<String> {
  private WriteRepository writeRepository;
  private SimpleExecutablePoint executablePoint;

  @Autowired
  public StreamRecordWriter(WriteRepository writeRepository,
      SimpleExecutablePoint executablePoint) {
    super();
    this.writeRepository = writeRepository;
    this.executablePoint = executablePoint;
  }

  @Override
  public void write(List<? extends String> items) throws Exception {
    writeRepository.writeRecords(items);
  }

  @Override
  public void open(ExecutionContext executionContext)
      throws ItemStreamException {
    executablePoint.execute("Opening records writer");
  }

  @Override
  public void update(ExecutionContext executionContext)
      throws ItemStreamException {
    executablePoint.execute("Updating records writer");
  }

  @Override
  public void close() throws ItemStreamException {
    executablePoint.execute("Closing records writer");
  }
}
```

As the ItemStreamWriter<String> implementation combines ItemWriter<String> with the ItemStream interface, we need to implement the write(), open(), update(), and close() methods. To simulate the ItemStream life-cycle actions, we need to inject the SimpleExecutablePoint instance. To write items in the write() method, we need the WriteRepository instance. Listing 9-88 shows the XML configuration of these stream handlers.

Listing 9-88. XML Configuration of ItemStream (File batch-config.xml in Folder src/main/resource of Example Project 0923-item-stream-xml)

```xml
<?xml version="1.0" encoding="UTF-8"?>
<beans:beans xmlns:beans="http://www.springframework.org/schema/beans"
  xmlns:xsi="http://www.w3.org/2001/XMLSchema-instance"
  xmlns="http://www.springframework.org/schema/batch"
  xsi:schemaLocation="http://www.springframework.org/schema/batch
  http://www.springframework.org/schema/batch/spring-batch.xsd
  http://www.springframework.org/schema/beans
  http://www.springframework.org/schema/beans/spring-beans.xsd">

  <job id="simpleRecordsJob">
    <step id="simpleRecordsStep">
      <tasklet>
        <chunk reader="simpleRecordReader" writer="streamRecordWriter"
          processor="simpleRecordProcessor" commit-interval="4" >
          <streams>
            <stream ref="recordsReaderItemStream"/>
          </streams>
        </chunk>
      </tasklet>
    </step>
  </job>
</beans:beans>
```

As a writer, we use the streamRecordWriter bean, which is aware of the resource and can handle its simulated life cycle. For other chunk handlers, we use the common simpleRecordReader and simpleRecordProcessor beans. The stand-alone recordsReaderItemStream needs to be registered via the <streams> XML tag. We again use the common BatchConfiguration class to import this XML configuration into the component scanning and @EnableBatchProcessing. When we run this example with the common Spring Boot main class, we get the output in Listing 9-89.

Listing 9-89. Output of XML ItemStream Example

```
2015-10-01 23:26:58.204  INFO 27880 --- [          main] o.s.b.c.l.support.
SimpleJobLauncher     : Job: [FlowJob: [name=simpleRecordsJob]] launched with the following
parameters: [{}]
2015-10-01 23:26:58.238  INFO 27880 --- [          main] o.s.batch.core.job.
SimpleStepHandler      : Executing step: [simpleRecordsStep]
2015-10-01 23:26:58.243  INFO 27880 --- [          main] n.l.b.e.c.step.
SimpleExecutablePoint    : Opening records reader
2015-10-01 23:26:58.243  INFO 27880 --- [          main] n.l.b.e.c.step.
SimpleExecutablePoint    : Opening records writer
2015-10-01 23:26:58.244  INFO 27880 --- [          main] n.l.b.e.c.step.
SimpleExecutablePoint    : Updating records reader
2015-10-01 23:26:58.244  INFO 27880 --- [          main] n.l.b.e.c.step.
SimpleExecutablePoint    : Updating records writer
2015-10-01 23:26:58.282  INFO 27880 --- [          main] n.l.b.e.chapter09.write.
WriteRepository  : Writing record: simple record 0 processed
2015-10-01 23:26:58.283  INFO 27880 --- [          main] n.l.b.e.chapter09.write.
WriteRepository  : Writing record: simple record 1 processed
```

```
2015-10-01 23:26:58.283  INFO 27880 --- [         main] n.l.b.e.chapter09.write.
WriteRepository  : Writing record: simple record 2 processed
2015-10-01 23:26:58.283  INFO 27880 --- [         main] n.l.b.e.chapter09.write.
WriteRepository  : Writing record: simple record 3 processed
2015-10-01 23:26:58.284  INFO 27880 --- [         main] n.l.b.e.c.step.
SimpleExecutablePoint      : Updating records reader
2015-10-01 23:26:58.284  INFO 27880 --- [         main] n.l.b.e.c.step.
SimpleExecutablePoint      : Updating records writer
2015-10-01 23:26:58.289  INFO 27880 --- [         main] n.l.b.e.chapter09.write.
WriteRepository  : Writing record: simple record 4 processed
2015-10-01 23:26:58.290  INFO 27880 --- [         main] n.l.b.e.chapter09.write.
WriteRepository  : Writing record: simple record 5 processed
2015-10-01 23:26:58.290  INFO 27880 --- [         main] n.l.b.e.chapter09.write.
WriteRepository  : Writing record: simple record 6 processed
2015-10-01 23:26:58.290  INFO 27880 --- [         main] n.l.b.e.chapter09.write.
WriteRepository  : Writing record: simple record 7 processed
2015-10-01 23:26:58.290  INFO 27880 --- [         main] n.l.b.e.c.step.
SimpleExecutablePoint      : Updating records reader
2015-10-01 23:26:58.290  INFO 27880 --- [         main] n.l.b.e.c.step.
SimpleExecutablePoint      : Updating records writer
2015-10-01 23:26:58.295  INFO 27880 --- [         main] n.l.b.e.chapter09.write.
WriteRepository  : Writing record: simple record 8 processed
2015-10-01 23:26:58.295  INFO 27880 --- [         main] n.l.b.e.chapter09.write.
WriteRepository  : Writing record: simple record 9 processed
2015-10-01 23:26:58.295  INFO 27880 --- [         main] n.l.b.e.chapter09.write.
WriteRepository  : Writing record: simple record 10 processed
2015-10-01 23:26:58.296  INFO 27880 --- [         main] n.l.b.e.chapter09.write.
WriteRepository  : Writing record: simple record 11 processed
2015-10-01 23:26:58.296  INFO 27880 --- [         main] n.l.b.e.c.step.
SimpleExecutablePoint      : Updating records reader
2015-10-01 23:26:58.296  INFO 27880 --- [         main] n.l.b.e.c.step.
SimpleExecutablePoint      : Updating records writer
2015-10-01 23:26:58.301  INFO 27880 --- [         main] n.l.b.e.chapter09.write.
WriteRepository  : Writing record: simple record 12 processed
2015-10-01 23:26:58.301  INFO 27880 --- [         main] n.l.b.e.chapter09.write.
WriteRepository  : Writing record: simple record 13 processed
2015-10-01 23:26:58.301  INFO 27880 --- [         main] n.l.b.e.chapter09.write.
WriteRepository  : Writing record: simple record 14 processed
2015-10-01 23:26:58.301  INFO 27880 --- [         main] n.l.b.e.c.step.
SimpleExecutablePoint      : Updating records reader
2015-10-01 23:26:58.301  INFO 27880 --- [         main] n.l.b.e.c.step.
SimpleExecutablePoint      : Updating records writer
2015-10-01 23:26:58.313  INFO 27880 --- [         main] n.l.b.e.c.step.
SimpleExecutablePoint      : Closing records reader
2015-10-01 23:26:58.313  INFO 27880 --- [         main] n.l.b.e.c.step.
SimpleExecutablePoint      : Closing records writer
2015-10-01 23:26:58.321  INFO 27880 --- [         main] o.s.b.c.l.support.
SimpleJobLauncher    : Job: [FlowJob: [name=simpleRecordsJob]] completed with the
following parameters: [{}] and the following status: [COMPLETED]
```

The simulated resource open(), update(), and close() actions were handled for
RecordsReaderItemStream and StreamRecordWriter as expected.

Java Configuration Example of ItemStream Usage

For a Java configuration example of ItemStream, we use all the same classes as for the previous example, except BatchConfiguration, as shown in Listing 9-90.

Listing 9-90. Java Configuration Example of ItemStream (0924-item-stream-javaconfig)

```java
package net.lkrnac.book.eiws.chapter09;
import net.lkrnac.book.eiws.chapter09.process.SimpleRecordProcessor;
import net.lkrnac.book.eiws.chapter09.read.SimpleRecordReader;
import org.springframework.batch.core.Job;
import org.springframework.batch.core.Step;
import org.springframework.batch.core.configuration.annotation.EnableBatchProcessing;
import org.springframework.batch.core.configuration.annotation.JobBuilderFactory;
import org.springframework.batch.core.configuration.annotation.StepBuilderFactory;
import org.springframework.context.annotation.Bean;
import org.springframework.context.annotation.Configuration;

@Configuration
@EnableBatchProcessing
public class BatchConfiguration {
  @Bean
  public Step simpleRecordsStep(StepBuilderFactory stepBuilderFactory,
      SimpleRecordReader simpleRecordReader,
      SimpleRecordProcessor simpleRecordProcessor,
      StreamRecordWriter StreamRecordWriter,
      RecordsReaderItemStream recordsReaderItemStream) {
    return stepBuilderFactory.get("simpleRecordsStep")
        .<String, String> chunk(4)
        .reader(simpleRecordReader)
        .processor(simpleRecordProcessor)
        .writer(StreamRecordWriter)
        .stream(recordsReaderItemStream)
        .build();
  }

  @Bean
  public Job simpleRecordsJob(JobBuilderFactory jobBuilderFactory, Step simpleRecordsStep) {
    return jobBuilderFactory.get("simpleRecordsJob").start(simpleRecordsStep).build();
  }
}
```

Notice that this is the mirror of the XML configuration from the previous example. Instead of the <stream> tag, we use the stream() method in step building. The output is the same as for the previous example (Listing 9-89).

Job and Step Inheritance

Sometimes we need to define a common configuration for Step or Job, which can be reused to define various Steps or Jobs. With a Java configuration, we use composition or inheritance for this purpose. But XML doesn't provide an easy composition out of the box. Therefore, the SB XML configuration support introduced the concept of Step or Job inheritance.

This example reuses TeaJobListener from Listing 9-69. Listing 9-91 shows the XML configuration.

Listing 9-91. XML Configuration of Job and Step Inheritance (File batch-config.xml in Folder src/main/ resource of Example Project 0925-job-inheritance)

```xml
<?xml version="1.0" encoding="UTF-8"?>
<beans:beans xmlns:beans="http://www.springframework.org/schema/beans"
  xmlns:xsi="http://www.w3.org/2001/XMLSchema-instance"
  xmlns="http://www.springframework.org/schema/batch"
  xsi:schemaLocation="http://www.springframework.org/schema/batch
  http://www.springframework.org/schema/batch/spring-batch.xsd
  http://www.springframework.org/schema/beans
  http://www.springframework.org/schema/beans/spring-beans.xsd">

  <step id="boilWaterStep" abstract="true">
    <tasklet ref="boilWater" />
  </step>
  <step id="addTeaStep" abstract="true">
    <tasklet ref="addTea" />
  </step>
  <step id="addWaterStep" abstract="true">
    <tasklet ref="addWater" />
  </step>

  <job id="prepareTeaJob" abstract="true">
    <listeners>
      <listener ref="teaJobListener"/>
    </listeners>
  </job>

  <job id="prepareMildTeaJob" parent="prepareTeaJob">
    <step id="boilWaterForMildTea" parent="boilWaterStep" next="addTeaForMildTea" />
    <step id="addTeaForMildTea" parent="addTeaStep" next="addWaterForMildTea"/>
    <step id="addWaterForMildTea" parent="addWaterStep"/>
  </job>

  <job id="prepareStrongTeaJob" parent="prepareTeaJob">
    <step id="boilWaterForStrongTea" parent="boilWaterStep" next="addTea1ForStrongTea" />
    <step id="addTea1ForStrongTea" parent="addTeaStep" next="addTea2ForStrongTea"/>
    <step id="addTea2ForStrongTea" parent="addTeaStep" next="addWaterForStrongTea"/>
    <step id="addWaterForStrongTea" parent="addWaterStep"/>
  </job>
</beans:beans>
```

We define two jobs here. One prepares mild tea, and the other prepares strong tea. We also want to register the same listener for both Jobs, so the listener definition is an abstract parent job, prepareTeaJob. Similarly, we specify the abstract parent Steps, where we use the common prepare tea Tasklets. This way, we can define the child Steps based on the parent Steps configuration. Notice that we also reuse one parent in two steps of the same job.

We again use the common BatchConfiguration and the Spring Boot main class. After running it, we can observe the output in Listing 9-92.

Listing 9-92. Output for Step and Job Inheritance Example

```
2015-10-03 17:40:44.303  INFO 23601 --- [           main] o.s.b.c.l.support.SimpleJobLauncher
: Job: [FlowJob: [name=prepareMildTeaJob]] launched with the following parameters: [{}]
2015-10-03 17:40:44.315  INFO 23601 --- [           main] n.l.b.e.c.step.
SimpleExecutablePoint      : It's tea time!
2015-10-03 17:40:44.336  INFO 23601 --- [           main] o.s.batch.core.job.
SimpleStepHandler      : Executing step: [boilWaterForMildTea]
2015-10-03 17:40:44.353  INFO 23601 --- [           main] n.l.b.e.c.step.
SimpleExecutablePoint      : Boil Water
2015-10-03 17:40:44.380  INFO 23601 --- [           main] o.s.batch.core.job.
SimpleStepHandler      : Executing step: [addTeaForMildTea]
2015-10-03 17:40:44.385  INFO 23601 --- [           main] n.l.b.e.c.step.
SimpleExecutablePoint      : Add Tea
2015-10-03 17:40:44.410  INFO 23601 --- [           main] o.s.batch.core.job.
SimpleStepHandler      : Executing step: [addWaterForMildTea]
2015-10-03 17:40:44.415  INFO 23601 --- [           main] n.l.b.e.c.step.
SimpleExecutablePoint      : Add Water
2015-10-03 17:40:44.427  INFO 23601 --- [           main] n.l.b.e.c.step.
SimpleExecutablePoint      : Enjoy your tea!
2015-10-03 17:40:44.430  INFO 23601 --- [           main] o.s.b.c.l.support.SimpleJobLauncher
: Job: [FlowJob: [name=prepareMildTeaJob]] completed with the following parameters: [{}] and
the following status: [COMPLETED]
2015-10-03 17:40:44.448  INFO 23601 --- [           main] o.s.b.c.l.support.SimpleJobLauncher
: Job: [FlowJob: [name=prepareStrongTeaJob]] launched with the following parameters: [{}]
2015-10-03 17:40:44.453  INFO 23601 --- [           main] n.l.b.e.c.step.
SimpleExecutablePoint      : It's tea time!
2015-10-03 17:40:44.466  INFO 23601 --- [           main] o.s.batch.core.job.
SimpleStepHandler      : Executing step: [boilWaterForStrongTea]
2015-10-03 17:40:44.471  INFO 23601 --- [           main] n.l.b.e.c.step.
SimpleExecutablePoint      : Boil Water
2015-10-03 17:40:44.492  INFO 23601 --- [           main] o.s.batch.core.job.
SimpleStepHandler      : Executing step: [addTea1ForStrongTea]
2015-10-03 17:40:44.497  INFO 23601 --- [           main] n.l.b.e.c.step.
SimpleExecutablePoint      : Add Tea
2015-10-03 17:40:44.537  INFO 23601 --- [           main] o.s.batch.core.job.
SimpleStepHandler      : Executing step: [addTea2ForStrongTea]
2015-10-03 17:40:44.541  INFO 23601 --- [           main] n.l.b.e.c.step.
SimpleExecutablePoint      : Add Tea
2015-10-03 17:40:44.564  INFO 23601 --- [           main] o.s.batch.core.job.
SimpleStepHandler      : Executing step: [addWaterForStrongTea]
2015-10-03 17:40:44.568  INFO 23601 --- [           main] n.l.b.e.c.step.
SimpleExecutablePoint      : Add Water
```

```
2015-10-03 17:40:44.577  INFO 23601 --- [           main] n.l.b.e.c.step.
SimpleExecutablePoint       : Enjoy your tea!
2015-10-03 17:40:44.580  INFO 23601 --- [           main] o.s.b.c.l.support.SimpleJobLauncher
: Job: [FlowJob: [name=prepareStrongTeaJob]] completed with the following parameters: [{}]
and the following status: [COMPLETED]
```

Configuring Restart

When SB executes the Step with or without the same JobParameters and it completes with RepeatStatus. FINISHED, SB doesn't allow it to start again. This is because the work represented by the Step is treated as done and shouldn't be performed again by default. This behavior, of course, can be changed by setting the XML attribute allow-start-if-complete of <tasklet> to true or via the allowStartIfComplete(true) call, when we build Step. These steps might be useful for validating or releasing resources after processing.

We can also define the number of times that Step can be executed. This can be configured via the start-limit XML attribute of <tasklet> or via the startLimit() method during the Java-configured Step construction. This can be handy—for example, when we need to pre-populate the database with initial metadata, we may want to ensure that it will run only once with the start limit configured to 1.

We also can configure the restarting behavior of the Job. By default, Job is restartable. If we want to disable the restarting of the job, we need to set up false for the restartable attribute of the XML tag <job> or use the preventRestart() method while building Job.

XML Configuration Example of Step Restart

Listing 9-93 shows the XML configuration.

Listing 9-93. XML Configuration of Step and Job Restart (File batch-config.xml in Folder src/main/resource of Example Project 0926-restart-xml)

```xml
<?xml version="1.0" encoding="UTF-8"?>
<beans:beans xmlns:beans="http://www.springframework.org/schema/beans"
  xmlns:xsi="http://www.w3.org/2001/XMLSchema-instance"
  xmlns="http://www.springframework.org/schema/batch"
  xsi:schemaLocation="http://www.springframework.org/schema/batch
  http://www.springframework.org/schema/batch/spring-batch.xsd
  http://www.springframework.org/schema/beans
  http://www.springframework.org/schema/beans/spring-beans.xsd">

  <step id="boilWaterStepParent">
    <tasklet ref="boilWater" allow-start-if-complete="true"/>
  </step>
  <step id="addTeaStepParent">
    <tasklet ref="addTea" allow-start-if-complete="true" start-limit="2"/>
  </step>
  <step id="addWaterStepParent">
    <tasklet ref="addWater"/>
  </step>

  <job id="prepareTeaJob">
    <step id="boilWaterStep" parent="boilWaterStepParent" next="addTeaStep"/>
```

```
    <step id="addTeaStep" parent="addTeaStepParent" next="addWaterStep"/>
    <step id="addWaterStep" parent="addWaterStepParent"/>
  </job>

  <job id="prepareTeaJobNotRestartable" restartable="false">
    <step id="boilWaterStepNR" parent="boilWaterStepParent" next="addTeaStepNR"/>
    <step id="addTeaStepNR" parent="addTeaStepParent" next="addWaterStepNR"/>
    <step id="addWaterStepNR" parent="addWaterStepParent"/>
  </job>
</beans:beans>
```

We have two Jobs configured here. The second one can't be restarted. If we try to run this job twice, this attempt will throw an exception.

Both Jobs use steps inherited from the parent Steps that are using our common Tasklets. The first Step definition, boilWaterStepParent, can be restarted anytime we need. The second Step definition, addTeaStepParent, can be restarted twice. If we try to run it a third time, it will throw an exception and fail the JobExecution.

The last Step definition, addWaterStepParent, uses the default restarting behavior, which does not execute the Step logic but allows the JobExecution to succeed.

This example again uses the common BatchConfiguration. The main Spring Boot class is shown in Listing 9-94.

Listing 9-94. Main Class of Job and Step Restart Example (0926-restart-xml)

```
package net.lkrnac.book.eiws.chapter09;

import org.springframework.batch.core.Job;
import org.springframework.batch.core.JobParameters;
import org.springframework.batch.core.launch.JobLauncher;
import org.springframework.boot.SpringApplication;
import org.springframework.boot.autoconfigure.SpringBootApplication;
import org.springframework.context.ConfigurableApplicationContext;

@SpringBootApplication
public class BatchApplication {
  public static void main(String[] args) throws Exception {
    ConfigurableApplicationContext context =
        SpringApplication.run(BatchApplication.class, args);
    JobLauncher jobLauncher = (JobLauncher) context.getBean(JobLauncher.class);

    Job job = (Job) context.getBean("prepareTeaJob");
    jobLauncher.run(job, new JobParameters());
    jobLauncher.run(job, new JobParameters());
    jobLauncher.run(job, new JobParameters());

    Job jobNotRestarteble =
        (Job) context.getBean("prepareTeaJobNotRestartable");
    jobLauncher.run(jobNotRestarteble, new JobParameters());
    jobLauncher.run(jobNotRestarteble, new JobParameters());
    context.close();
  }
}
```

We run prepareTeaJob three times and prepareTeaJobNotRestartable twice to highlight the restart features. After we run it, we get the output in Listing 9-95.

Listing 9-95. Output of Job and Step Restart Example

```
2015-10-03 19:26:16.013  INFO 26867 --- [              main] o.s.b.c.l.support.SimpleJobLauncher
: Job: [FlowJob: [name=prepareTeaJob]] launched with the following parameters: [{}]
2015-10-03 19:26:16.067  INFO 26867 --- [              main] o.s.batch.core.job.SimpleStepHandler
: Executing step: [boilWaterStep]
2015-10-03 19:26:16.086  INFO 26867 --- [              main] n.l.b.e.c.step.SimpleExecutablePoint
: Boil Water
2015-10-03 19:26:16.116  INFO 26867 --- [              main] o.s.batch.core.job.SimpleStepHandler
: Executing step: [addTeaStep]
2015-10-03 19:26:16.121  INFO 26867 --- [              main] n.l.b.e.c.step.SimpleExecutablePoint
: Add Tea
2015-10-03 19:26:16.172  INFO 26867 --- [              main] o.s.batch.core.job.SimpleStepHandler
: Executing step: [addWaterStep]
2015-10-03 19:26:16.179  INFO 26867 --- [              main] n.l.b.e.c.step.SimpleExecutablePoint
: Add Water
2015-10-03 19:26:16.205  INFO 26867 --- [              main] o.s.b.c.l.support.SimpleJobLauncher
: Job: [FlowJob: [name=prepareTeaJob]] completed with the following parameters: [{}] and the
following status: [COMPLETED]
2015-10-03 19:26:16.241  INFO 26867 --- [              main] o.s.b.c.l.support.SimpleJobLauncher
: Job: [FlowJob: [name=prepareTeaJob]] launched with the following parameters: [{}]
2015-10-03 19:26:16.263  INFO 26867 --- [              main] o.s.batch.core.job.SimpleStepHandler
: Executing step: [boilWaterStep]
2015-10-03 19:26:16.268  INFO 26867 --- [              main] n.l.b.e.c.step.SimpleExecutablePoint
: Boil Water
2015-10-03 19:26:16.296  INFO 26867 --- [              main] o.s.batch.core.job.SimpleStepHandler
: Executing step: [addTeaStep]
2015-10-03 19:26:16.300  INFO 26867 --- [              main] n.l.b.e.c.step.SimpleExecutablePoint
: Add Tea
2015-10-03 19:26:16.320  INFO 26867 --- [              main] o.s.batch.core.job.SimpleStepHandler
: Step already complete or not restartable, so no action to execute: StepExecution:
id=2, version=3, name=addWaterStep, status=COMPLETED, exitStatus=COMPLETED, readCount=0,
filterCount=0, writeCount=0 readSkipCount=0, writeSkipCount=0, processSkipCount=0,
commitCount=1, rollbackCount=0, exitDescription=
2015-10-03 19:26:16.323  INFO 26867 --- [              main] o.s.b.c.l.support.SimpleJobLauncher
: Job: [FlowJob: [name=prepareTeaJob]] completed with the following parameters: [{}] and the
following status: [COMPLETED]
2015-10-03 19:26:16.336  INFO 26867 --- [              main] o.s.b.c.l.support.SimpleJobLauncher
: Job: [FlowJob: [name=prepareTeaJob]] launched with the following parameters: [{}]
2015-10-03 19:26:16.358  INFO 26867 --- [              main] o.s.batch.core.job.SimpleStepHandler
: Executing step: [boilWaterStep]
2015-10-03 19:26:16.363  INFO 26867 --- [              main] n.l.b.e.c.step.SimpleExecutablePoint
: Boil Water
2015-10-03 19:26:16.400 ERROR 26867 --- [              main] o.s.batch.core.job.AbstractJob
: Encountered fatal error executing job
```

```
org.springframework.batch.core.JobExecutionException: Flow execution ended unexpectedly
        ...
Caused by: org.springframework.batch.core.StartLimitExceededException: Maximum start limit
exceeded for step: addTeaStepStartMax: 2
        ...
```

```
2015-10-03 19:26:16.407  INFO 26867 --- [          main] o.s.b.c.l.support.SimpleJobLauncher
: Job: [FlowJob: [name=prepareTeaJob]] completed with the following parameters: [{}] and the
following status: [FAILED]
2015-10-03 19:26:16.415  INFO 26867 --- [          main] o.s.b.c.l.support.SimpleJobLauncher
: Job: [FlowJob: [name=prepareTeaJobNotRestartable]] launched with the following parameters:
[{}]
2015-10-03 19:26:16.430  INFO 26867 --- [          main] o.s.batch.core.job.SimpleStepHandler
: Executing step: [boilWaterStepNR]
2015-10-03 19:26:16.434  INFO 26867 --- [          main] n.l.b.e.c.step.SimpleExecutablePoint
: Boil Water
2015-10-03 19:26:16.458  INFO 26867 --- [          main] o.s.batch.core.job.SimpleStepHandler
: Executing step: [addTeaStepNR]
2015-10-03 19:26:16.463  INFO 26867 --- [          main] n.l.b.e.c.step.SimpleExecutablePoint
: Add Tea
2015-10-03 19:26:16.492  INFO 26867 --- [          main] o.s.batch.core.job.SimpleStepHandler
: Executing step: [addWaterStepNR]
2015-10-03 19:26:16.501  INFO 26867 --- [          main] n.l.b.e.c.step.SimpleExecutablePoint
: Add Water
2015-10-03 19:26:16.511  INFO 26867 --- [          main] o.s.b.c.l.support.SimpleJobLauncher
: Job: [FlowJob: [name=prepareTeaJobNotRestartable]] completed with the following parameters:
[{}] and the following status: [COMPLETED]
Exception in thread "main" org.springframework.batch.core.repository.JobRestartException:
JobInstance already exists and is not restartable
        at org.springframework.batch.core.launch.support.SimpleJobLauncher.
run(SimpleJobLauncher.java:101)
        ...
```

The first execution prepares tea without any problems, as in the previous example. The second execution of prepareTeaJob finishes successfully, but the addWaterStep was already executed before, so SB doesn't execute it again. This means that the second tea is without water. Notice that this is the default behavior for Step with the same parameters.

The third execution of prepareTeaJob results in FAILED JobExecution, because we allow addTeaStepParent to run only twice. When we execute prepareTeaJobNotRestartable, it runs fine the first time, but the second time it throws an exception into the main thread, because we don't allow this job to run twice.

Java Configuration Example of Step Restart

Listing 9-96 shows the Java configuration of the same restarting behavior as in the previous example.

Listing 9-96. Java configuration to demonstrate restarting

```java
package net.lkrnac.book.eiws.chapter09;
import net.lkrnac.book.eiws.chapter09.step.tea.AddTea;
import net.lkrnac.book.eiws.chapter09.step.tea.AddWater;
import net.lkrnac.book.eiws.chapter09.step.tea.BoilWater;
```

```java
import org.springframework.batch.core.Job;
import org.springframework.batch.core.Step;
import org.springframework.batch.core.configuration.annotation.EnableBatchProcessing;
import org.springframework.batch.core.configuration.annotation.JobBuilderFactory;
import org.springframework.batch.core.configuration.annotation.StepBuilderFactory;
import org.springframework.beans.factory.annotation.Qualifier;
import org.springframework.context.annotation.Bean;
import org.springframework.context.annotation.Configuration;

@Configuration
@EnableBatchProcessing
public class BatchConfiguration {
  @Bean
  public Step boilWaterStep(StepBuilderFactory stepFactory, BoilWater boilWater) {
    return stepFactory.get("boilWaterStep")
        .tasklet(boilWater)
        .allowStartIfComplete(true)
        .build();
  }
  @Bean
  public Step addTeaStep(StepBuilderFactory stepFactory, AddTea addTea) {
    return stepFactory.get("addTeaStep")
        .tasklet(addTea)
        .allowStartIfComplete(true)
        .startLimit(2)
        .build();
  }

  @Bean
  public Step addWaterStep(StepBuilderFactory stepFactory, AddWater addWater) {
    return stepFactory.get("addWaterStep").tasklet(addWater).build();
  }

  @Bean
  public Job prepareTeaJob(JobBuilderFactory jobBuilderFactory,
      @Qualifier("boilWaterStep") Step boilWaterStep,
      @Qualifier("addTeaStep") Step addTeaStep,
      @Qualifier("addWaterStep") Step addWaterStep) {
    return jobBuilderFactory.get("prepareTeaJob")
        .start(boilWaterStep)
        .next(addTeaStep)
        .next(addWaterStep)
        .build();
  }

  @Bean
  public Job prepareTeaJobNotRestartable(JobBuilderFactory jobBuilderFactory,
      @Qualifier("boilWaterStep") Step boilWaterStep,
      @Qualifier("addTeaStep") Step addTeaStep,
      @Qualifier("addWaterStep") Step addWaterStep) {
    Job job = jobBuilderFactory.get("prepareTeaJobNotRestartable")
```

```
        .start(boilWaterStep)
        .next(addTeaStep)
        .next(addWaterStep)
        .preventRestart()
        .build();
    return job;
  }
}
```

Allowing the restart and defining the restart limit is done while building Steps. Disabling Job from restarting is done via calling preventRestart(). This example also uses the common Spring Boot main class, and the output looks the same as for the previous example (Listing 9-95).

Control Repeat of Step Execution

At times we need to decide programmatically whether Step needs to be repeated. We can control this aspect based on RepeatStatus returned from Tasklet. Listing 9-97 shows the bean that will be driving the Step repetition logic.

Listing 9-97. Job-Scoped Bean Deciding Whether Step Needs to Repeat (0928-repeat)

```
package net.lkrnac.book.eiws.chapter09.step.tea;
import org.springframework.batch.core.configuration.annotation.JobScope;
import org.springframework.beans.factory.annotation.Autowired;
import org.springframework.beans.factory.annotation.Value;
import org.springframework.stereotype.Component;

@JobScope
@Component
public class SugarCounter {
  private int currentSugarCount;
  private int desiredSugarAmount;

  @Autowired
  public SugarCounter(@Value("#{jobParameters[sugarAmount]}") int desiredSugarAmount) {
    super();
    this.desiredSugarAmount = desiredSugarAmount;
    this.currentSugarCount = 0;
  }

  public boolean addSugar() {
    boolean result = currentSugarCount < desiredSugarAmount;
    currentSugarCount++;
    return result;
  }
}
```

As a Spring component with the @JobScope annotation, its instance will live only for one JobExecution. JobScope also allows us to use late binding and retrieve the job parameter with the name sugarAmount. We store it and initialize currentSugarCount to 0. Listing 9-98 shows the implementation of AddSugar step.

Listing 9-98. Implementation of Repeatable Step (0928-repeat)

```java
package net.lkrnac.book.eiws.chapter09.step.tea;
import net.lkrnac.book.eiws.chapter09.step.SimpleExecutablePoint;
import org.springframework.batch.core.StepContribution;
import org.springframework.batch.core.scope.context.ChunkContext;
import org.springframework.batch.core.step.tasklet.Tasklet;
import org.springframework.batch.repeat.RepeatStatus;
import org.springframework.beans.factory.annotation.Autowired;
import org.springframework.stereotype.Component;

@Component
public class AddSugar implements Tasklet {
  private SimpleExecutablePoint simpleExecutableStep;
  private SugarCounter sugarCounter;

  @Autowired
  public AddSugar(SimpleExecutablePoint simpleExecutableStep,
      SugarCounter sugarCounter) {
    super();
    this.simpleExecutableStep = simpleExecutableStep;
    this.sugarCounter = sugarCounter;
  }

  @Override
  public RepeatStatus execute(StepContribution contribution,
      ChunkContext chunkContext) throws Exception {
    if (sugarCounter.addSugar()) {
      simpleExecutableStep.execute("Add one spoon of sugar");
      return RepeatStatus.CONTINUABLE;
    } else {
      return RepeatStatus.FINISHED;
    }
  }
}
```

We inject our common SimpleExecutionPoint to simulate the action. The second injection includes SugarCounter that we defined in the previous listing. This bean is used to decide whether we add a spoonful of sugar to our tea and also whether we should repeat the job. If we return ReturnStatus.CONTINUABLE, this step will be executed again. When the logic returns RepeatStatus.FINISHED, this step won't be executed again.

BatchConfiguration in this example is a simple flow of the tasklets BoilWater, AddTea, AddWater, and AddSugar. Because this configuration is straightforward and we've seen similar ones previously in this chapter, we'll skip it. Listing 9-99 shows the main class of this example.

Listing 9-99. Main Class of Repeat Example (0928-repeat)

```java
package net.lkrnac.book.eiws.chapter09;
import org.springframework.batch.core.Job;
import org.springframework.batch.core.JobParameters;
import org.springframework.batch.core.JobParametersBuilder;
import org.springframework.batch.core.launch.JobLauncher;
import org.springframework.boot.SpringApplication;
```

```
import org.springframework.boot.autoconfigure.SpringBootApplication;
import org.springframework.context.ConfigurableApplicationContext;

@SpringBootApplication
public class BatchApplication {
  public static void main(String[] args) throws Exception {
    ConfigurableApplicationContext context =
        SpringApplication.run(BatchApplication.class, args);

    JobLauncher jobLauncher = (JobLauncher) context.getBean(JobLauncher.class);
    Job job = (Job) context.getBean("prepareTeaJob");

    jobLauncher.run(job, createJobParameters(2));
    context.close();
  }

  public static JobParameters createJobParameters(long sugarAmount) {
    return new JobParametersBuilder()
        .addLong("sugarAmount", sugarAmount)
        .toJobParameters();
  }
}
```

We run the prepareTeaJob and specify that we want two spoonfuls of sugar. We can specify any amount of sugar desired. After running it, we get the output in Listing 9-100.

Listing 9-100. Output of Repeat Example

```
2015-10-03 21:03:27.469  INFO 30341 --- [           main] o.s.b.c.l.support.
SimpleJobLauncher      : Job: [SimpleJob: [name=prepareTeaJob]] launched with the following
parameters: [{sugarAmount=2}]
2015-10-03 21:03:27.496  INFO 30341 --- [           main] o.s.batch.core.job.
SimpleStepHandler       : Executing step: [boilWaterStep]
2015-10-03 21:03:27.514  INFO 30341 --- [           main] n.l.b.e.c.step.
SimpleExecutablePoint      : Boil Water
2015-10-03 21:03:27.538  INFO 30341 --- [           main] o.s.batch.core.job.
SimpleStepHandler       : Executing step: [addTeaStep]
2015-10-03 21:03:27.541  INFO 30341 --- [           main] n.l.b.e.c.step.
SimpleExecutablePoint      : Add Tea
2015-10-03 21:03:27.576  INFO 30341 --- [           main] o.s.batch.core.job.
SimpleStepHandler       : Executing step: [addWaterStep]
2015-10-03 21:03:27.587  INFO 30341 --- [           main] n.l.b.e.c.step.
SimpleExecutablePoint      : Add Water
2015-10-03 21:03:27.622  INFO 30341 --- [           main] o.s.batch.core.job.
SimpleStepHandler       : Executing step: [addSugarStep]
2015-10-03 21:03:27.723  INFO 30341 --- [           main] n.l.b.e.c.step.
SimpleExecutablePoint       : Add one spoon of sugar
2015-10-03 21:03:27.732  INFO 30341 --- [           main] n.l.b.e.c.step.
SimpleExecutablePoint       : Add one spoon of sugar
2015-10-03 21:03:27.752  INFO 30341 --- [           main] o.s.b.c.l.support.
SimpleJobLauncher       : Job: [SimpleJob: [name=prepareTeaJob]] completed with the following
parameters: [{sugarAmount=2}] and the following status: [COMPLETED]
```

Reacting to Failures

When batch processing contains steps, chunks, readers, processors, writers, and tasklets, often something goes wrong and the logic throws an exception. By default, SB fails the Step and the Job in such a situation. But some errors may be only temporary or not serious enough to fail all the processing. SB therefore provides various mechanisms to configure:

- *Skip* the item and configure the org.springframework.batch.core. SkipListener<T,S> listener.

- *Retry* the item and configure the org.springframework.retry.RetryListener listener. Notice that RetryListener is part of the common Spring module spring-retry.

SB also provides convenience abstract classes with the Support suffix for these interfaces (org.springframework.batch.core.SkipListenerSupport<T,S> and org.springframework.retry. RetryListenerSupport), where all methods have empty implementations. If we use abstract classes instead of interfaces, we don't need to implement all the interception methods. These mechanisms apply only to chunk-oriented processing.

XML Configuration of Skip and SkipListener

This example uses error simulation in the processor and writer. An error in the reader would have a similar effect as an error in the processor. For a reader, we reuse our common reader. Listing 9-101 shows the processor simulating an error.

Listing 9-101. Processor Simulating Error (0929-skip-xml)

```
package net.lkrnac.book.eiws.chapter09.process;
import org.springframework.batch.item.ItemProcessor;
import org.springframework.stereotype.Component;

@Component
public class SimpleRecordProcessor implements ItemProcessor<String, String> {
  private boolean errorSimulated = false;

  @Override
  public String process(String item) throws Exception {
    preProcessHook();
    return item + " processed";
  }

  public void preProcessHook() {
    if (!errorSimulated) {
      errorSimulated = true;
      throw new IllegalStateException("error occurred");
    }
  }
}
```

Before we process the first record, we simulate the error by throwing IllegalArgumentException. Subsequent processing attempts will succeed. Listing 9-102 shows the writer simulating an error.

Listing 9-102. Writer Simulating Error (0929-skip-xml)

```java
package net.lkrnac.book.eiws.chapter09.write;
import java.util.List;
import org.springframework.batch.item.ItemWriter;
import org.springframework.beans.factory.annotation.Autowired;
import org.springframework.stereotype.Component;

@Component
public class SimpleRecordWriter implements ItemWriter<String> {
  private WriteRepository writeRepository;
  private int errorSimulated = 0;

  @Autowired
  public SimpleRecordWriter(WriteRepository writeRepository) {
    super();
    this.writeRepository = writeRepository;
  }

  @Override
  @SuppressWarnings("unchecked")
  public void write(List<? extends String> items) throws Exception {
    preWriteHook();
    writeRepository.writeRecords((List<String>) items);
  }

  public void preWriteHook() {
    if (errorSimulated < 2) {
      errorSimulated++;
      throw new IllegalStateException("error occurred");
    }
  }
}
```

This writer simulates an error twice and then succeeds. Listing 9-103 shows the SkipListener implementation.

Listing 9-103. SkipListener Implementation (0929-skip-xml)

```java
package net.lkrnac.book.eiws.chapter09;
import net.lkrnac.book.eiws.chapter09.step.SimpleExecutablePoint;
import org.springframework.batch.core.SkipListener;
import org.springframework.beans.factory.annotation.Autowired;
import org.springframework.stereotype.Component;

@Component
public class SimpleSkipListener implements SkipListener<String, String> {
  private SimpleExecutablePoint executablePoint;
```

```
@Autowired
public SimpleSkipListener(SimpleExecutablePoint executablePoint) {
  super();
  this.executablePoint = executablePoint;
}

@Override
public void onSkipInRead(Throwable t) {
  executablePoint.execute("Skipping read because of error");
}

@Override
public void onSkipInWrite(String item, Throwable t) {
  executablePoint
      .execute("Skipping write of '" + item + "' because of error");
}

@Override
public void onSkipInProcess(String item, Throwable t) {
  executablePoint
      .execute("Skipping processing of '" + item + "' because of error");
}
}
```

When the read item is skipped, SB can inject its instance into the interception method. Therefore, it injects only an instance of Throwable as the root cause of the skip. But as we mentioned, there will be no error simulator in the reader for this example. We needed to implement this method because of the interface SkipListener<T, S>.

During the processor and writer interception, we also can use the instance of the item being skipped. SkipListener<T, S> uses two generic types, where T is the type before processing and S is the type after processing. In this case, both of these types are String, so the interface is used as SkipListener<String, String>. Listing 9-104 shows the XML configuration.

Listing 9-104. XML Configuration of Skip (File batch-config.xml in Folder src/main/resource of Example Project 0929-skip-xml)

```xml
<?xml version="1.0" encoding="UTF-8"?>
<beans:beans xmlns:beans="http://www.springframework.org/schema/beans"
  xmlns:xsi="http://www.w3.org/2001/XMLSchema-instance"
  xmlns="http://www.springframework.org/schema/batch"
  xsi:schemaLocation="http://www.springframework.org/schema/batch
    http://www.springframework.org/schema/batch/spring-batch.xsd
    http://www.springframework.org/schema/beans
    http://www.springframework.org/schema/beans/spring-beans.xsd">

<job id="simpleRecordsJob">
  <step id="simpleRecordsStep">
    <tasklet>
      <chunk reader="simpleRecordReader" writer="simpleRecordWriter"
        processor="simpleRecordProcessor" commit-interval="4" skip-limit="3">
        <skippable-exception-classes>
          <include class="java.lang.IllegalStateException"/>
```

```
      </skippable-exception-classes>
      <listeners>
        <listener ref="simpleSkipListener"/>
      </listeners>
    </chunk>
  </tasklet>
  </step>
  </job>
</beans:beans>
```

For a reader, we use our comm on `SimpleRecordReader` without error simulation. The processor and writer simulate errors as we've defined in Listings 9-101 and 9-102. The `skip-limit` attribute specifies the number of times we can skip each item before we fail the `JobExecution`. With the `<skippable-exception-classes>` tag, we define which exceptions are considered reasons to skip. `SkipListener` is registered in the standard `<listeners>` block, which is also used by all other listener types.

To define an exception list to skip, we can combine the `<include>` and `<exclude>` definitions of the exception types. This example did not fit into the scope of the book, and so is left for your experimentation.

`BatchConfiguration` and the main classes are again reused. Listing 9-105 shows the output.

Listing 9-105. Output of XML Skip Example (0929-skip-xml)

```
2015-10-03 21:53:59.714  INFO 32184 --- [          main] o.s.b.c.l.support.
SimpleJobLauncher       : Job: [FlowJob: [name=simpleRecordsJob]] launched with the following
parameters: [{}]
2015-10-03 21:53:59.736  INFO 32184 --- [          main] o.s.batch.core.job.
SimpleStepHandler       : Executing step: [simpleRecordsStep]
2015-10-03 21:53:59.782  INFO 32184 --- [          main] n.l.b.e.chapter09.write.
WriteRepository  : Writing record: simple record 2 processed
2015-10-03 21:53:59.782  INFO 32184 --- [          main] n.l.b.e.c.step.
SimpleExecutablePoint    : Skipping processing of 'simple record 0' because of error
2015-10-03 21:53:59.782  INFO 32184 --- [          main] n.l.b.e.c.step.
SimpleExecutablePoint    : Skipping write of 'simple record 1 processed' because of error
2015-10-03 21:53:59.787  INFO 32184 --- [          main] n.l.b.e.chapter09.write.
WriteRepository  : Writing record: simple record 3 processed
2015-10-03 21:53:59.792  INFO 32184 --- [          main]
    ...
n.l.b.e.chapter09.write.WriteRepository  : Writing record: simple record 13 processed
2015-10-03 21:53:59.803  INFO 32184 --- [          main] n.l.b.e.chapter09.write.
WriteRepository  : Writing record: simple record 14 processed
2015-10-03 21:53:59.816  INFO 32184 --- [          main] o.s.b.c.l.support.
SimpleJobLauncher       : Job: [FlowJob: [name=simpleRecordsJob]] completed with the
following parameters: [{}] and the following status: [COMPLETED]
```

As we can see, record 0 was skipped because of an error in the processor. But the writer behavior may be a surprise, because we simulated two errors in the writer. But when the write or whole chunk fails in chunk-oriented processing, SB tries to subsequently process each record one by one. This is because SB tries to write as many items as possible. This way, we are sure that one corrupted record won't cause write failure for other valid records belonging to the same chunk.

In this case, the first failure in the writer failed the whole chunk, so SB tried to write each record one by one afterward. The second error simulation failed record 1 processed. The rest of the records from the chunk, as well as all other chunks, were processed normally.

Java Configuration of Skip and SkipListener

This example uses the same classes as the previous one. The only difference is use of a Java configuration instead of XML. Listing 9-106 shows this configuration.

Listing 9-106. Java Configuration of Skip (0930-skip-javaconfig)

```java
package net.lkrnac.book.eiws.chapter09;

import net.lkrnac.book.eiws.chapter09.process.SimpleRecordProcessor;
import net.lkrnac.book.eiws.chapter09.read.SimpleRecordReader;
import net.lkrnac.book.eiws.chapter09.write.SimpleRecordWriter;

import org.springframework.batch.core.Job;
import org.springframework.batch.core.Step;
import org.springframework.batch.core.configuration.annotation.EnableBatchProcessing;
import org.springframework.batch.core.configuration.annotation.JobBuilderFactory;
import org.springframework.batch.core.configuration.annotation.StepBuilderFactory;
import org.springframework.context.annotation.Bean;
import org.springframework.context.annotation.Configuration;

@Configuration
@EnableBatchProcessing
public class BatchConfiguration {
  @Bean
  public Step simpleRecordsStep(StepBuilderFactory stepBuilderFactory,
      SimpleRecordReader simpleRecordReader,
      SimpleRecordProcessor simpleRecordProcessor,
      SimpleRecordWriter simpleRecordWriter,
      SimpleSkipListener simpleSkipListener) {
    return stepBuilderFactory.get("simpleRecordsStep")
        .<String, String> chunk(4)
        .reader(simpleRecordReader)
        .processor(simpleRecordProcessor)
        .writer(simpleRecordWriter)
        .faultTolerant()
        .skip(IllegalStateException.class)
        .skipLimit(3)
        .listener(simpleSkipListener)
        .build();
  }

  @Bean
  public Job simpleRecordsJob(JobBuilderFactory jobBuilderFactory, Step simpleRecordsStep) {
    return jobBuilderFactory.get("simpleRecordsJob").start(simpleRecordsStep).build();
  }
}
```

When we define the step, we again use the common reader and the error-simulating processor and writer. To configure the skip, we need to include the faultTolerant() call into the Step creation chain, so that we can configure skipLimit() and an exception to skip(). SkipListener is configured last, in the faultTolerant() section.

When we run this example, the behavior is exactly the same as for the previous example in Listing 9-105.

XML Configuration of Retry

This example uses common tasklets for the read and process items. The writer tasklet is reused from the previous example (Listing 9-102), simulating two errors for the first two write attempts. Listing 9-107 shows the retry listener.

Listing 9-107. Retry Listener Implementation (0931-retry-xml)

```java
package net.lkrnac.book.eiws.chapter09;
import net.lkrnac.book.eiws.chapter09.step.SimpleExecutablePoint;
import org.springframework.beans.factory.annotation.Autowired;
import org.springframework.retry.RetryCallback;
import org.springframework.retry.RetryContext;
import org.springframework.retry.listener.RetryListenerSupport;
import org.springframework.stereotype.Component;

@Component
public class SimpleRetryListener extends RetryListenerSupport {
  private SimpleExecutablePoint executablePoint;

  @Autowired
  public SimpleRetryListener(SimpleExecutablePoint executablePoint) {
    super();
    this.executablePoint = executablePoint;
  }

  @Override
  public <T, E extends Throwable> void onError(RetryContext context,
      RetryCallback<T, E> callback, Throwable throwable) {
    executablePoint.execute("Error occurred, retrying write of items");
  }
}
```

We are interested only in the onError interception, so we extended org.springframework.retry. RetryListenerSupport as a convenience empty implementation of org.springframework.retry. RetryListener. If we implemented org.springframework.retry.RetryListener, we would need to also implement the close() and open() interception methods. Listing 9-108 shows the XML configuration.

Listing 9-108. XML Configuration of Retry (File batch-config.xml in Folder src/main/resource of Example Project 0931-retry-xml)

```xml
<?xml version="1.0" encoding="UTF-8"?>
<beans:beans xmlns:beans="http://www.springframework.org/schema/beans"
  xmlns:xsi="http://www.w3.org/2001/XMLSchema-instance"
  xmlns="http://www.springframework.org/schema/batch"
  xsi:schemaLocation="http://www.springframework.org/schema/batch
    http://www.springframework.org/schema/batch/spring-batch.xsd
    http://www.springframework.org/schema/beans
    http://www.springframework.org/schema/beans/spring-beans.xsd">
```

```xml
<job id="simpleRecordsJob">
  <step id="simpleRecordsStep">
    <tasklet>
      <chunk reader="simpleRecordReader" writer="simpleRecordWriter"
        processor="simpleRecordProcessor" commit-interval="4" retry-limit="3">
        <retryable-exception-classes>
          <include class="java.lang.IllegalStateException"/>
        </retryable-exception-classes>
        <retry-listeners>
          <listener ref="simpleRetryListener"/>
        </retry-listeners>
      </chunk>
    </tasklet>
  </step>
</job>
</beans:beans>
```

We allow retrying each item three times, which is specified by the retry-limit attribute of <chunk>. If this retry limit is passed, an exception is thrown. StepExecution and JobExecution would fail in this case.

The <retryable-exception-classes> subelement defines a list of exceptions that we allow a retry for. The <retry-listeners> tag defines a list of retry listeners, which is in this case only our simpleRetryListener. Similar to the Skip feature, we can combine the <include> and <exclude> tags to fine-tune exceptions we are interested in. And as with the Skip example, we leave this feature for your experimentation.

BatchConfiguration and the main classes are our common implementations. After running this example, we can observe the output in Listing 9-109.

Listing 9-109. Output of XML Retry Example

```
2015-10-04 11:20:13.199  INFO 15982 --- [            main] o.s.b.c.l.support.
SimpleJobLauncher       : Job: [FlowJob: [name=simpleRecordsJob]] launched with the following
parameters: [{}]
2015-10-04 11:20:13.229  INFO 15982 --- [            main] o.s.batch.core.job.
SimpleStepHandler       : Executing step: [simpleRecordsStep]
2015-10-04 11:20:13.278  INFO 15982 --- [            main] n.l.b.e.c.step.
SimpleExecutablePoint       : Error occurred, retrying write of items
2015-10-04 11:20:13.281  INFO 15982 --- [            main] n.l.b.e.c.step.
SimpleExecutablePoint       : Error occurred, retrying write of items
2015-10-04 11:20:13.320  INFO 15982 --- [            main] n.l.b.e.chapter09.write.
WriteRepository. : Writing record: simple record 0 processed
2015-10-04 11:20:13.320  INFO 15982 --- [            main] n.l.b.e.chapter09.write.
WriteRepository  : Writing record: simple record 1 processed
2015-10-04 11:20:13.320  INFO 15982 --- [            main]
    ...
n.l.b.e.chapter09.write.WriteRepository  : Writing record: simple record 14 processed
2015-10-04 11:20:13.355  INFO 15982 --- [            main] o.s.b.c.l.support.
SimpleJobLauncher       : Job: [FlowJob: [name=simpleRecordsJob]] completed with the
following parameters: [{}] and the following status: [COMPLETED]
```

All the records were processed correctly, regardless of the two simulated errors, because we didn't reach the retry limit.

Java Configuration of Retry

We will use the same classes for the Java configuration example of Retry and replace only the XML configuration by BatchConfiguration in Listing 9-110.

Listing 9-110. Java Configuration of Retry (0932-retry-javaconfig)

```java
package net.lkrnac.book.eiws.chapter09;
import net.lkrnac.book.eiws.chapter09.process.SimpleRecordProcessor;
import net.lkrnac.book.eiws.chapter09.read.SimpleRecordReader;
import net.lkrnac.book.eiws.chapter09.write.SimpleRecordWriter;
import org.springframework.batch.core.Job;
import org.springframework.batch.core.Step;
import org.springframework.batch.core.configuration.annotation.EnableBatchProcessing;
import org.springframework.batch.core.configuration.annotation.JobBuilderFactory;
import org.springframework.batch.core.configuration.annotation.StepBuilderFactory;
import org.springframework.context.annotation.Bean;
import org.springframework.context.annotation.Configuration;


@Configuration
@EnableBatchProcessing
public class BatchConfiguration {
  @Bean
  public Step simpleRecordsStep(StepBuilderFactory stepBuilderFactory,
      SimpleRecordReader simpleRecordReader,
      SimpleRecordProcessor simpleRecordProcessor,
      SimpleRecordWriter simpleRecordWriter,
      SimpleRetryListener simpleRetryListener) {
    return stepBuilderFactory.get("simpleRecordsStep")
        .<String, String> chunk(4)
        .reader(simpleRecordReader)
        .processor(simpleRecordProcessor)
        .writer(simpleRecordWriter)
        .faultTolerant()
        .retry(IllegalStateException.class)
        .retryLimit(3)
        .listener(simpleRetryListener)
        .build();
  }

  @Bean
  public Job simpleRecordsJob(JobBuilderFactory jobBuilderFactory,
      Step simpleRecordsStep) {
    return jobBuilderFactory.get("simpleRecordsJob").start(simpleRecordsStep).build();
  }
}
```

The retry configuration needs to be initiated by the faultTolerant() method, similar to Skip. With retry(), we define the exception that can be retried, which in this case is IllegalArgumentException. The retry limit is configured to 3, and we also configure simpleRetryListener as the retry listener. Job uses only simpleRecordsStep. When we run this example, we get the same output as for the previous example (Listing 9-109).

Conditional Execution of Step

SB provides features to programmatically decide whether Step needs to be executed. This programmatic decision is done in the bean implementing JobExecutionDecider, which is then used in the <decision> XML element or by combination of the methods next(), on(), to(), and from() when we are building a Job with a Java configuration.

XML Configuration of Step Decision

Listing 9-111 shows the implementation of JobExecutionDecider.

Listing 9-111. JobExecutionDecider Implementation (0933-decision-xml)

```
package net.lkrnac.book.eiws.chapter09;
import org.springframework.batch.core.JobExecution;
import org.springframework.batch.core.StepExecution;
import org.springframework.batch.core.job.flow.FlowExecutionStatus;
import org.springframework.batch.core.job.flow.JobExecutionDecider;
import org.springframework.stereotype.Component;

@Component
public class TeaIngredientDecider implements JobExecutionDecider {
  @Override
  public FlowExecutionStatus decide(JobExecution jobExecution,
      StepExecution stepExecution) {
    String teaIngredient = jobExecution.getJobParameters().getString("teaIngredient");
    return ("milk".equals(teaIngredient))
        ? new FlowExecutionStatus(teaIngredient)
        : FlowExecutionStatus.COMPLETED;
  }
}
```

The component acting as JobExecutionDecider has to implement the decide() method, which has to return the FlowExecutionStatus type. We can use standard SB constants—for example, FlowExecutionStatus.COMPLETED or FlowExecutionStatus.FAILED. Notice that there are more out-of-the-box status constants in FlowExecutionStatus.

We can also wrap any string value into the FlowExecutionStatus type, which gives us an indefinite number of flow control opportunities in addition to the out-of-the-box status constants. In this case, we retrieve the teaIngredient job parameter from the injected jobExecution instance, and if milk is the desired ingredient, we indicate it in the return value; otherwise, the return status will be COMPLETED.

For this example we also introduce a new tasklet step called AddMilk. Because it is similar to all other tea tasklets, we skip its listing. It simulates the Add Milk action. Listing 9-112 shows the XML configuration.

Listing 9-112. XML Configuration of Conditional Step (File batch-config.xml in Folder src/main/resource of Example Project 0933-decision-xml)

```
<?xml version="1.0" encoding="UTF-8"?>
<beans:beans xmlns:beans="http://www.springframework.org/schema/beans"
  xmlns:xsi="http://www.w3.org/2001/XMLSchema-instance"
  xmlns="http://www.springframework.org/schema/batch"
  xsi:schemaLocation="http://www.springframework.org/schema/batch
```

```
    http://www.springframework.org/schema/batch/spring-batch.xsd
    http://www.springframework.org/schema/beans
    http://www.springframework.org/schema/beans/spring-beans.xsd">

  <job id="prepareTeaJob">
    <step id="boilWaterStep" next="addTeaStep">
      <tasklet ref="boilWater"/>
    </step>
    <step id="addTeaStep" next="addWaterStep">
      <tasklet ref="addTea"/>
    </step>
    <step id="addWaterStep" next="teaIngredientDecision">
      <tasklet ref="addWater"/>
    </step>
    <decision decider="teaIngredientDecider" id="teaIngredientDecision">
      <next on="milk" to="addMilkStep"/>
      <end on="COMPLETED"/>
    </decision>
    <step id="addMilkStep">
      <tasklet ref="addMilk"/>
    </step>
  </job>
</beans:beans>
```

The `AddWater` step defines `teaIngredientDecision` as the next Step. This decision block uses the `TeaIngredientDecider` bean as the decider logic. If the decider returns the `milk` value, we execute `addMilkStep`. If any other value is returned, we end the Job flow. Listing 9-113 shows the main class of this example.

Listing 9-113. Main Class of Decision Step Example (0933-decision-xml)

```
package net.lkrnac.book.eiws.chapter09;
import org.springframework.batch.core.Job;
import org.springframework.batch.core.JobParameters;
import org.springframework.batch.core.JobParametersBuilder;
import org.springframework.batch.core.launch.JobLauncher;
import org.springframework.boot.SpringApplication;
import org.springframework.boot.autoconfigure.SpringBootApplication;
import org.springframework.context.ConfigurableApplicationContext;

@SpringBootApplication
public class BatchApplication {
  public static void main(String[] args) throws Exception {
    ConfigurableApplicationContext context =
        SpringApplication.run(BatchApplication.class, args);

    JobLauncher jobLauncher = (JobLauncher) context.getBean(JobLauncher.class);
    Job job = (Job) context.getBean("prepareTeaJob");

    jobLauncher.run(job, createJobParameters("milk"));
    jobLauncher.run(job, createJobParameters(""));
    context.close();
  }
```

```
public static JobParameters createJobParameters(String teaIngredient) {
    return new JobParametersBuilder()
        .addString("teaIngredient", teaIngredient)
        .toJobParameters();
}
}
```

The job prepareTeaStep is executed first with the milk parameter teaIngredient and the second time without any tea ingredient. After running this example, we can observe the output in Listing 9-114.

Listing 9-114. Output of Decision Step Example

```
2015-10-04 13:14:01.678  INFO 19315 --- [            main] o.s.b.c.l.support.SimpleJobLauncher
: Job: [FlowJob: [name=prepareTeaJob]] launched with the following parameters:
[{teaIngredient=milk}]
2015-10-04 13:14:01.716  INFO 19315 --- [            main] o.s.batch.core.job.
SimpleStepHandler    : Executing step: [boilWaterStep]
2015-10-04 13:14:01.763  INFO 19315 --- [            main] n.l.b.e.c.step.
SimpleExecutablePoint      : Boil Water
2015-10-04 13:14:01.798  INFO 19315 --- [            main] o.s.batch.core.job.
SimpleStepHandler    : Executing step: [addTeaStep]
2015-10-04 13:14:01.803  INFO 19315 --- [            main] n.l.b.e.c.step.
SimpleExecutablePoint      : Add Tea
2015-10-04 13:14:01.833  INFO 19315 --- [            main] o.s.batch.core.job.
SimpleStepHandler    : Executing step: [addWaterStep]
2015-10-04 13:14:01.839  INFO 19315 --- [            main] n.l.b.e.c.step.
SimpleExecutablePoint      : Add Water
2015-10-04 13:14:01.869  INFO 19315 --- [            main] o.s.batch.core.job.
SimpleStepHandler    : Executing step: [addMilkStep]
2015-10-04 13:14:01.875  INFO 19315 --- [            main] n.l.b.e.c.step.
SimpleExecutablePoint      : Add Milk
2015-10-04 13:14:01.890  INFO 19315 --- [            main] o.s.b.c.l.support.SimpleJobLauncher
: Job: [FlowJob: [name=prepareTeaJob]] completed with the following parameters:
[{teaIngredient=milk}] and the following status: [COMPLETED]
2015-10-04 13:14:01.899  INFO 19315 --- [            main] o.s.b.c.l.support.SimpleJobLauncher
: Job: [FlowJob: [name=prepareTeaJob]] launched with the following parameters:
[{teaIngredient=}]
2015-10-04 13:14:01.915  INFO 19315 --- [            main] o.s.batch.core.job.
SimpleStepHandler    : Executing step: [boilWaterStep]
2015-10-04 13:14:01.921  INFO 19315 --- [            main] n.l.b.e.c.step.
SimpleExecutablePoint      : Boil Water
2015-10-04 13:14:01.945  INFO 19315 --- [            main] o.s.batch.core.job.
SimpleStepHandler    : Executing step: [addTeaStep]
2015-10-04 13:14:01.950  INFO 19315 --- [            main] n.l.b.e.c.step.
SimpleExecutablePoint      : Add Tea
2015-10-04 13:14:01.970  INFO 19315 --- [            main] o.s.batch.core.job.
SimpleStepHandler    : Executing step: [addWaterStep]
2015-10-04 13:14:01.975  INFO 19315 --- [            main] n.l.b.e.c.step.
SimpleExecutablePoint      : Add Water
2015-10-04 13:14:01.989  INFO 19315 --- [            main] o.s.b.c.l.support.SimpleJobLauncher
: Job: [FlowJob: [name=prepareTeaJob]] completed with the following parameters:
[{teaIngredient=}] and the following status: [COMPLETED]
```

The first execution occurs with addMilkStep, and the second without it, depending on whether we pass milk as the teaIngredient parameter. It also would be interesting to take a look at batch graph of this example, shown in Figure 9-7.

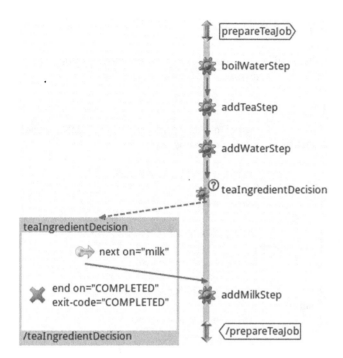

Figure 9-7. *Batch graph for decision step*

Java Configuration of Step Decision

Following our tradition, this Java example reuses all the classes from the previous XML-based example and replaces the XML configuration. Listing 9-115 shows the conditional Java-based configuration.

Listing 9-115. Java Configuration of Decision Step

```java
package net.lkrnac.book.eiws.chapter09;
import net.lkrnac.book.eiws.chapter09.step.tea.AddMilk;
import net.lkrnac.book.eiws.chapter09.step.tea.AddTea;
import net.lkrnac.book.eiws.chapter09.step.tea.AddWater;
import net.lkrnac.book.eiws.chapter09.step.tea.BoilWater;
import org.springframework.batch.core.Job;
import org.springframework.batch.core.Step;
import org.springframework.batch.core.configuration.annotation.EnableBatchProcessing;
import org.springframework.batch.core.configuration.annotation.JobBuilderFactory;
import org.springframework.batch.core.configuration.annotation.StepBuilderFactory;
import org.springframework.batch.core.job.flow.FlowExecutionStatus;
import org.springframework.beans.factory.annotation.Qualifier;
import org.springframework.context.annotation.Bean;
import org.springframework.context.annotation.Configuration;
```

```java
@Configuration
@EnableBatchProcessing
public class BatchConfiguration {
  @Bean
  public Step boilWaterStep(StepBuilderFactory stepFactory, BoilWater boilWater) {
    return stepFactory.get("boilWaterStep").tasklet(boilWater).build();
  }

  @Bean
  public Step addTeaStep(StepBuilderFactory stepFactory, AddTea addTea) {
    return stepFactory.get("addTeaStep").tasklet(addTea).build();
  }

  @Bean
  public Step addWaterStep(StepBuilderFactory stepFactory, AddWater addWater) {
    return stepFactory.get("addWaterStep").tasklet(addWater).build();
  }

  @Bean
  public Step addMilkStep(StepBuilderFactory stepFactory, AddMilk addMilk) {
    return stepFactory.get("addMilkStep").tasklet(addMilk).build();
  }

  @Bean
  public Job prepareTeaJob(JobBuilderFactory jobBuilderFactory,
      @Qualifier("boilWaterStep") Step boilWaterStep,
      @Qualifier("addTeaStep") Step addTeaStep,
      @Qualifier("addWaterStep") Step addWaterStep,
      @Qualifier("addMilkStep") Step addMilkStep,
      TeaIngredientDecider teaIngredientDecider) {
    return jobBuilderFactory.get("prepareTeaJob")
        .start(boilWaterStep)
        .next(addTeaStep)
        .next(addWaterStep)
        .next(teaIngredientDecider)
          .on("milk")
            .to(addMilkStep)
            .from(teaIngredientDecider)
          .on(FlowExecutionStatus.COMPLETED.getName())
            .end()
          .build()
        .build();
  }
}
```

The definition of steps is straightforward; we use our common tea tasklets with the AddMilk tasklet and inject it into the Job bean construction method. This is where the interesting constructs start. addWaterStep goes to teaIngredientDecider.

The following execution path depends on the decider's return value. If the decider returns the milk value, the branch with on("milk") is executed. It defines addMilkStep as the next step to execute. We also have to define the from() Step; otherwise, the Job will fail. If the decider returns FlowExecutionStatus.COMPLETED, the second branch of execution is applied. This value ends the execution of the batch flow.

Execution of the build() method is needed twice, because the first call builds the Job subflow initiated by the decider. The second build() call constructs the main Job instance. After we run this example, we can observe the same output as for the previous example (Listing 9-114).

Scaling and Parallel Processing

All the executions so far have been single-threaded. Sequential processing is often required by the nature of the data being processed, or simply isn't slow enough to represent a bottleneck in an enterprise system.

But often data doesn't have to be processed in sequence. In these cases, we can consider whether distributing the batch processing into separate threads or processes would boost overall performance. Fortunately, SB's creators considered such use cases and implemented support for the following:

- Multithreaded step (executed in a single process)

- Parallel steps (executed in a single process)

- Remote chunking of steps (executed in various processes)

- Partitioning a step (executed in various processes)

Multithreaded Step

The idea of using multiple threads for one Step is applicable only to Chunk-oriented processing. Each chunk is processed in a separate thread. The threads are handled by a thread pool configured for Step.

XML Configuration of Multithreaded Step

This example reuses the common chunk-oriented reader, processor, and writer as well as the common BatchConfiguration and Spring Boot main class. The only new part is the XML configuration introduced in Listing 9-116.

Listing 9-116. XML Configuration of Multithreaded Step (File batch-config.xml in Folder src/main/resource of Example Project 0935-multi-threaded-step-xml)

```xml
<?xml version="1.0" encoding="UTF-8"?>
<beans:beans xmlns:beans="http://www.springframework.org/schema/beans"
  xmlns:xsi="http://www.w3.org/2001/XMLSchema-instance"
  xmlns="http://www.springframework.org/schema/batch"
  xmlns:task="http://www.springframework.org/schema/task"
  xsi:schemaLocation="http://www.springframework.org/schema/batch
    http://www.springframework.org/schema/batch/spring-batch.xsd
    http://www.springframework.org/schema/task
    http://www.springframework.org/schema/task/spring-task.xsd
    http://www.springframework.org/schema/beans
    http://www.springframework.org/schema/beans/spring-beans.xsd">
```

```
<job id="simpleRecordsJob">
  <step id="simpleRecordsStep">
    <tasklet task-executor="taskExecutor">
      <chunk reader="simpleRecordReader" writer="simpleRecordWriter"
        processor="simpleRecordProcessor" commit-interval="4" />
    </tasklet>
  </step>
</job>

<task:executor id="taskExecutor" pool-size="10"/>
</beans:beans>
```

Multiple threads are handled by the TaskExecutor bean with a thread pool of size 10. When we define <tasklet> for our chunk-oriented step, we configure the taskExecutor bean via the task-executor attribute. Listing 9-117 shows the output when we execute this example.

Listing 9-117. Output of XML-Configured Multithreaded Step Example

```
2015-10-04 16:20:07.425  INFO 26949 --- [           main] o.s.b.c.l.support.SimpleJobLauncher
: Job: [FlowJob: [name=simpleRecordsJob]] launched with the following parameters: [{}]
2015-10-04 16:20:07.455  INFO 26949 --- [           main] o.s.batch.core.job.
SimpleStepHandler      : Executing step: [simpleRecordsStep]
2015-10-04 16:20:07.599  INFO 26949 --- [ taskExecutor-2] n.l.b.e.chapter09.write.
WriteRepository  : Writing record: simple record 4 processed
2015-10-04 16:20:07.599  INFO 26949 --- [ taskExecutor-3] n.l.b.e.chapter09.write.
WriteRepository  : Writing record: simple record 8 processed
2015-10-04 16:20:07.599  INFO 26949 --- [ taskExecutor-4] n.l.b.e.chapter09.write.
WriteRepository  : Writing record: simple record 0 processed
2015-10-04 16:20:07.599  INFO 26949 --- [ taskExecutor-1] n.l.b.e.chapter09.write.
WriteRepository  : Writing record: simple record 9 processed
2015-10-04 16:20:07.599  INFO 26949 --- [ taskExecutor-2] n.l.b.e.chapter09.write.
WriteRepository  : Writing record: simple record 5 processed
2015-10-04 16:20:07.600  INFO 26949 --- [ taskExecutor-3] n.l.b.e.chapter09.write.
WriteRepository  : Writing record: simple record 10 processed
2015-10-04 16:20:07.601  INFO 26949 --- [ taskExecutor-4] n.l.b.e.chapter09.write.
WriteRepository  : Writing record: simple record 1 processed
2015-10-04 16:20:07.601  INFO 26949 --- [ taskExecutor-1] n.l.b.e.chapter09.write.
WriteRepository  : Writing record: simple record 11 processed
2015-10-04 16:20:07.603  INFO 26949 --- [ taskExecutor-2] n.l.b.e.chapter09.write.
WriteRepository  : Writing record: simple record 6 processed
2015-10-04 16:20:07.604  INFO 26949 --- [ taskExecutor-3] n.l.b.e.chapter09.write.
WriteRepository  : Writing record: simple record 12 processed
2015-10-04 16:20:07.604  INFO 26949 --- [ taskExecutor-4] n.l.b.e.chapter09.write.
WriteRepository  : Writing record: simple record 2 processed
2015-10-04 16:20:07.604  INFO 26949 --- [ taskExecutor-1] n.l.b.e.chapter09.write.
WriteRepository  : Writing record: simple record 13 processed
2015-10-04 16:20:07.604  INFO 26949 --- [ taskExecutor-2] n.l.b.e.chapter09.write.
WriteRepository  : Writing record: simple record 7 processed
2015-10-04 16:20:07.604  INFO 26949 --- [ taskExecutor-3] n.l.b.e.chapter09.write.
WriteRepository  : Writing record: simple record 14 processed
2015-10-04 16:20:07.604  INFO 26949 --- [ taskExecutor-4] n.l.b.e.chapter09.write.
WriteRepository  : Writing record: simple record 3 processed
```

```
2015-10-04 16:20:07.663  INFO 26949 --- [              main] o.s.b.c.l.support.SimpleJobLauncher
: Job: [FlowJob: [name=simpleRecordsJob]] completed with the following parameters: [{}] and
the following status: [COMPLETED]
```

Two facts are worth noticing. First, the items are processed in random order. Second, one chunk is handled in a single thread. If you pair the item numbers with the names of the threads (for example, simple record 4 processed, simple record 5 processed, simple record 6 processed, and simple record 7 processed were handled by the thread named taskExecutor-2), you can see that each chunk is processed in a separate thread. This allows us to tune the processing throughput according to our requirements.

Java Configuration of Multithreaded Step

The Java configuration is shown in Listing 9-118.

Listing 9-118. Java Configuration of Multithreaded Step (0936-multi-threaded-step-javaconfig)

```java
package net.lkrnac.book.eiws.chapter09;
import net.lkrnac.book.eiws.chapter09.process.SimpleRecordProcessor;
import net.lkrnac.book.eiws.chapter09.read.SimpleRecordReader;
import net.lkrnac.book.eiws.chapter09.write.SimpleRecordWriter;
import org.springframework.batch.core.Job;
import org.springframework.batch.core.Step;
import org.springframework.batch.core.configuration.annotation.EnableBatchProcessing;
import org.springframework.batch.core.configuration.annotation.JobBuilderFactory;
import org.springframework.batch.core.configuration.annotation.StepBuilderFactory;
import org.springframework.context.annotation.Bean;
import org.springframework.context.annotation.Configuration;
import org.springframework.core.task.TaskExecutor;
import org.springframework.scheduling.concurrent.ThreadPoolTaskExecutor;

@Configuration
@EnableBatchProcessing
public class BatchConfiguration {
  @Bean
  public TaskExecutor customTaskExecutor() {
    ThreadPoolTaskExecutor threadPool = new ThreadPoolTaskExecutor();
    threadPool.setCorePoolSize(10);
    return threadPool;
  }

  @Bean
  public Step simpleRecordsStep(StepBuilderFactory stepBuilderFactory,
      SimpleRecordReader simpleRecordReader,
      SimpleRecordProcessor simpleRecordProcessor,
      SimpleRecordWriter simpleRecordWriter,
      TaskExecutor customTaskExecutor) {
    return stepBuilderFactory.get("simpleRecordsStep")
        .<String, String> chunk(4)
        .reader(simpleRecordReader)
        .processor(simpleRecordProcessor)
```

```
        .writer(simpleRecordWriter)
        .taskExecutor(customTaskExecutor)
        .build();
    }

    @Bean
    public Job simpleRecordsJob(JobBuilderFactory jobBuilderFactory,
        Step simpleRecordsStep) {
      return jobBuilderFactory.get("simpleRecordsJob").start(simpleRecordsStep).build();
    }
}
```

Configuring TaskExecutor for the chunk-oriented step is done by calling the taskExecutor() method while building the Step. The output for this example is similar to that of the previous example (Listing 9-117).

Parallel Steps

Not only chunks can be executed in parallel. Sometimes we might want to execute various steps in parallel.

XML Configuration of Parallel Steps

This example again reuses the common BatchConfiguration with the Spring Boot main class and all common chunk-oriented tasklets. We add one more, called AddSugar, which simulates the action named Add Sugar, similar to our common tasklets. Therefore, we show only the XML configuration in Listing 9-119.

Listing 9-119. XML Configuration of Parallel Steps (File batch-config.xml in Folder src/main/resource of Example Project 0937-parallel-steps-xml)

```xml
<?xml version="1.0" encoding="UTF-8"?>
<beans:beans xmlns:beans="http://www.springframework.org/schema/beans"
  xmlns:xsi="http://www.w3.org/2001/XMLSchema-instance"
  xmlns="http://www.springframework.org/schema/batch"
  xmlns:task="http://www.springframework.org/schema/task"
  xsi:schemaLocation="http://www.springframework.org/schema/batch
    http://www.springframework.org/schema/batch/spring-batch.xsd
    http://www.springframework.org/schema/task
    http://www.springframework.org/schema/task/spring-task.xsd
    http://www.springframework.org/schema/beans
    http://www.springframework.org/schema/beans/spring-beans.xsd">

  <job id="prepareTeaJob">
    <step id="boilWaterStep" next="addIngredientsSplit">
      <tasklet ref="boilWater" />
    </step>
    <split id="addIngredientsSplit" next="addWaterStep" task-executor="taskExecutor">
      <flow>
        <step id="addTeaStep">
          <tasklet ref="addTea" />
        </step>
      </flow>
```

```
      <flow>
        <step id="addSugarStep">
          <tasklet ref="addSugar" />
        </step>
      </flow>
    </split>
    <step id="addWaterStep">
      <tasklet ref="addWater" />
    </step>
  </job>

  <task:executor id="taskExecutor" pool-size="10"/>
</beans:beans>
```

The definition of parallel Steps starts with the <split> element named addIngredientsSplit. With task-executor, we define which thread pool will be used for parallel processing. Each <flow> subelement of <split> creates a boundary for execution in a single thread. In this case, each flow has only one step, so these two steps will be executed in parallel. Listing 9-120 shows the output of this example.

Listing 9-120. Output of XML Parallel Steps Example

```
2015-10-04 17:10:53.063  INFO 28783 --- [              main] o.s.b.c.l.support.SimpleJobLauncher
: Job: [FlowJob: [name=prepareTeaJob]] launched with the following parameters: [{}]
2015-10-04 17:10:53.099  INFO 28783 --- [              main] o.s.batch.core.job.SimpleStepHandler
: Executing step: [boilWaterStep]
2015-10-04 17:10:53.128  INFO 28783 --- [              main] n.l.b.e.c.step.SimpleExecutablePoint
: Boil Water
2015-10-04 17:10:53.190  INFO 28783 --- [ taskExecutor-1] o.s.batch.core.job.SimpleStepHandler
: Executing step: [addTeaStep]
2015-10-04 17:10:53.193  INFO 28783 --- [ taskExecutor-2] o.s.batch.core.job.SimpleStepHandler
: Executing step: [addSugarStep]
2015-10-04 17:10:53.206  INFO 28783 --- [ taskExecutor-2] n.l.b.e.c.step.SimpleExecutablePoint
: Add one spoon of sugar
2015-10-04 17:10:53.207  INFO 28783 --- [ taskExecutor-1] n.l.b.e.c.step.SimpleExecutablePoint
: Add Tea
2015-10-04 17:10:53.244  INFO 28783 --- [              main] o.s.batch.core.job.SimpleStepHandler
: Executing step: [addWaterStep]
2015-10-04 17:10:53.249  INFO 28783 --- [              main] n.l.b.e.c.step.SimpleExecutablePoint
: Add Water
2015-10-04 17:10:53.269  INFO 28783 --- [              main] o.s.b.c.l.support.SimpleJobLauncher
: Job: [FlowJob: [name=prepareTeaJob]] completed with the following parameters: [{}] and the
following status: [COMPLETED]
```

Notice that addTeaStep and addSugarStep are executed in separate threads in parallel. Figure 9-8 shows the batch graph.

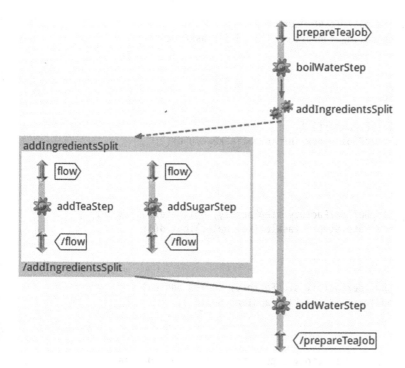

Figure 9-8. Bean graph of parallel steps example

Java Configuration of Parallel Steps

Again, we are building on the previous example. Listing 9-121 shows the Java configuration for the same behavior as in the previous example.

Listing 9-121. Java Configuration of Parallel Steps (0938-parallel-steps-javaconfig)

```
package net.lkrnac.book.eiws.chapter09;

import net.lkrnac.book.eiws.chapter09.step.tea.AddSugar;
import net.lkrnac.book.eiws.chapter09.step.tea.AddTea;
import net.lkrnac.book.eiws.chapter09.step.tea.AddWater;
import net.lkrnac.book.eiws.chapter09.step.tea.BoilWater;

import org.springframework.batch.core.Job;
import org.springframework.batch.core.Step;
import org.springframework.batch.core.configuration.annotation.EnableBatchProcessing;
import org.springframework.batch.core.configuration.annotation.JobBuilderFactory;
import org.springframework.batch.core.configuration.annotation.StepBuilderFactory;
import org.springframework.batch.core.job.builder.FlowBuilder;
import org.springframework.batch.core.job.flow.Flow;
import org.springframework.beans.factory.annotation.Qualifier;
import org.springframework.context.annotation.Bean;
import org.springframework.context.annotation.Configuration;
```

```java
import org.springframework.core.task.TaskExecutor;
import org.springframework.scheduling.concurrent.ThreadPoolTaskExecutor;

@Configuration
@EnableBatchProcessing
public class BatchConfiguration {
  @Bean
  public TaskExecutor customTaskExecutor() {
    ThreadPoolTaskExecutor threadPool = new ThreadPoolTaskExecutor();
    threadPool.setCorePoolSize(10);
    return threadPool;
  }
  @Bean
  public Step boilWaterStep(StepBuilderFactory stepFactory, BoilWater boilWater) {
    return stepFactory.get("boilWaterStep").tasklet(boilWater).build();
  }

  @Bean
  public Step addTeaStep(StepBuilderFactory stepFactory, AddTea addTea) {
    return stepFactory.get("addTeaStep").tasklet(addTea).build();
  }

  @Bean
  public Step addSugarStep(StepBuilderFactory stepFactory, AddSugar addSugar) {
    return stepFactory.get("addSugarStep").tasklet(addSugar).build();
  }

  @Bean
  public Step addWaterStep(StepBuilderFactory stepFactory, AddWater addWater) {
    return stepFactory.get("addWaterStep").tasklet(addWater).build();
  }

  @Bean
  public Job prepareTeaJob(JobBuilderFactory jobBuilderFactory,
      @Qualifier("boilWaterStep") Step boilWaterStep,
      @Qualifier("addTeaStep") Step addTeaStep,
      @Qualifier("addSugarStep") Step addSugarStep,
      @Qualifier("addWaterStep") Step addWaterStep,
      TaskExecutor customTaskExecutor) {
    return jobBuilderFactory.get("prepareTeaJob")
        .start(boilWaterStep)
        .split(customTaskExecutor)
        .add(new FlowBuilder<Flow>("addIngredientsSplit")
            .from(boilWaterStep).next(addTeaStep)
            .from(boilWaterStep).next(addSugarStep)
            .end())
        .next(addWaterStep)
        .end()
        .build();
  }
}
```

The definition of the thread pool bean and the creation of Step beans isn't new for us. When we create the Job definition, the split() method allows us to specify the thread pool instance to use for parallel definition. In the add() method, we define parallel branches of execution. As use of split() and add() converts SimpleJob to FlowJob, we need to use the end() method to close the parallel subflow and the main job. The output after execution of this example is similar to Listing 9-120 shown previously.

Remote Chunking of Step

Remote chunking is a concept that can help when we are dealing with chunk-oriented processing and the processing or writing of items is resource intensive. The idea is to delegate the processing and writing part of the chunk to one remote JVM process or various processes. These processes can, of course, be hosted on remote machines.

Reading of chunks is done in the master process. The master communicates with the remote slave(s) via a message queue. So communication between master and slaves is asynchronous. The SB framework takes advantages of the Spring Integration framework to configure this communication. Two separate message queues are needed for the following:

- Sending command from master to slave(s)

- Sending responses from slave(s) back to master

As communication is done via the messaging interface, work is divided dynamically to remote slaves, and load balancing in case of various slaves is automatic. Let's explain this natural load balancing. The master sends a command to the message queue, where various slaves are listening. As the message queue is configured for point-to-point messaging, only one slave can read this command. The first slave that picks up the message does the processing and writing. Naturally, the least busy slave will be the first to read this command message from the master.

SB uses the standard ItemReader, ItemProcessor, and ItemWriter interfaces for performing the work. ChunkProcessor<I> is the interface helping with work delegation to the slave process(es). SimpleChunkProcessor is the out-of-the-box implementation that the SB framework provides.

Notice that our example for this feature is covered only with an XML configuration. The example combines Spring Integration flow with SB flow, and XML configurations seem to be more concise in this case, so the Java configuration was skipped.

JMS Configuration Used for Master-Slave Communication

We will use a HornetQ server as the messaging middleware for this communication. Chapter 5 showed how to download and easily start a HornetQ server instance. Now we need to configure message queues for master-slave communication. Listing 9-122 shows the HornetQ definition of these queues.

Listing 9-122. HornetQ Configuration for Master-Slave Communication (File config/stand-alone/non-clustered/hornet-jms.xml of HornetQ Installation)

```
<queue name="MasterCommands">
    <entry name="/queue/MasterCommands"/>
</queue>
<queue name="SlaveResponses">
    <entry name="/queue/SlaveResponses"/>
</queue>
```

We need to add these two top-level elements to the HornetQ configuration. After we start the server, the queues will be available. The queue named `MasterCommands` will be used for sending messages from the master to the slave. The `SlaveResponses` queue will be used for replies from the slave. Listing 9-123 shows the JMS communication, which will be present in the master and the slave projects.

Listing 9-123. XML Configuration for JMS Access (File jms-config.xml in Folder src/main/resource of Example Project 0939-remote-chunking-slave and 0939-remote-chunking-master)

```xml
<?xml version="1.0" encoding="UTF-8"?>
<beans xmlns="http://www.springframework.org/schema/beans"
  xmlns:xsi="http://www.w3.org/2001/XMLSchema-instance"
  xmlns:util="http://www.springframework.org/schema/util"
  xmlns:jee="http://www.springframework.org/schema/jee"
  xsi:schemaLocation="http://www.springframework.org/schema/jee
    http://www.springframework.org/schema/jee/spring-jee.xsd
    http://www.springframework.org/schema/beans
    http://www.springframework.org/schema/beans/spring-beans.xsd
    http://www.springframework.org/schema/util
    http://www.springframework.org/schema/util/spring-util.xsd">

  <util:map id="jndiProperties" map-class="java.util.Properties">
    <entry key="java.naming.factory.initial"
      value="org.jnp.interfaces.NamingContextFactory" />
    <entry key="java.naming.factory.url.pkgs"
      value="org.jboss.naming:org.jnp.interfaces" />
    <entry key="java.naming.provider.url" value="jnp://localhost:1099" />
  </util:map>

  <jee:jndi-lookup id="connectionFactory" jndi-name="/ConnectionFactory"
    environment-ref="jndiProperties" />
  <jee:jndi-lookup id="masterCommands" jndi-name="/queue/MasterCommands"
    environment-ref="jndiProperties" />
  <jee:jndi-lookup id="slaveResponses" jndi-name="/queue/SlaveResponses"
    environment-ref="jndiProperties" />
</beans>
```

The JMS connection via JNDI is the same as we used in the JMS examples as well as the JNDI lookup for connectionFactory bean. JNDI lookups for master-slave communication queues follow, which registers them as JMS destinations in the Spring context. Again, the same configuration is used in the master and slave project for JMS access.

Configuration of Slave for Remote Chunking

This example reuses our common writer and processor to work on the slave piece of remote chunking. Listing 9-124 shows the XML slave configuration.

Listing 9-124. XML Configuration of Remote-Chunking Slave (File batch-slave-config.xml in Folder src/main/resource of Example Project 0939-remote-chunking-slave)

```xml
<?xml version="1.0" encoding="UTF-8"?>
<beans xmlns="http://www.springframework.org/schema/beans"
  xmlns:xsi="http://www.w3.org/2001/XMLSchema-instance"
  xmlns:batch="http://www.springframework.org/schema/batch"
```

```
xmlns:int="http://www.springframework.org/schema/integration"
xmlns:int-jms="http://www.springframework.org/schema/integration/jms"
xsi:schemaLocation="http://www.springframework.org/schema/batch
  http://www.springframework.org/schema/batch/spring-batch.xsd
  http://www.springframework.org/schema/beans
  http://www.springframework.org/schema/beans/spring-beans.xsd
  http://www.springframework.org/schema/integration/jms
  http://www.springframework.org/schema/integration/jms/spring-integration-jms.xsd
  http://www.springframework.org/schema/integration
  http://www.springframework.org/schema/integration/spring-integration.xsd">

<import resource="classpath:jms-config.xml"/>

<int-jms:message-driven-channel-adapter id="inSlaveAdapter"
  destination="masterCommands" channel="inSlaveChannel" />
<int:channel id="inSlaveChannel" />

<int:service-activator id="slaveServiceActivator" method="handleChunk"
  input-channel="inSlaveChannel" output-channel="outSlaveChannel" ref="slaveChunkHandler"/>

<bean id="slaveChunkHandler"
  class="org.springframework.batch.integration.chunk.ChunkProcessorChunkHandler">
  <property name="chunkProcessor" ref="slaveChunkProcessor" />
</bean>

<bean id="slaveChunkProcessor"
  class="org.springframework.batch.core.step.item.SimpleChunkProcessor">
  <property name="itemProcessor">
    <bean
      class="net.lkrnac.book.eiws.chapter09.process.SimpleRecordProcessor" />
  </property>
  <property name="itemWriter">
    <bean class="net.lkrnac.book.eiws.chapter09.write.SimpleRecordWriter" />
  </property>
</bean>

<int:channel id="outSlaveChannel" />
<int-jms:outbound-channel-adapter id="outSlaveAdapter"
  destination="slaveResponses" channel="outSlaveChannel"/>
</beans>
```

First, we import the JMS configuration. Next we use a Spring Integration construct to define the inbound channel adapter, which will be receiving messages from the master. The items to process will arrive via the JMS queue masterCommands, and this inbound channel adapter will pace them onto the local Spring Integration channel inSlaveChannel, where they will be picked up by the service activator named slaveServiceActivator.

This service activator delegates items to process to ChunkProcessorChunkHandler, which is a wrapper for SimpleChunkProcessor. SimpleChunkProcessor is the bean where we define ItemProcessor and ItemReader—in this case, our common SimpleRecordProcessor and SimpleRecordWriter.

Responses from the simpleChunkHandler bean will be sent to the Spring Integration channel outSlaveChannel as a reply message from slaveServiceActivator. Last, outSlaveChannel is connected to outSlaveAdapter, which will send responses to the JMS queue slaveResponses.

Figure 9-9 shows the Spring Integration graph of processing messages from the master.

Figure 9-9. Spring Integration graph of slave message flow

Configuration of Master for Remote Chunking

Listing 9-125 shows the remote chunking of the master configuration.

Listing 9-125. XML Configuration of Remote-Chunking Master (File batch-config.xml in Folder src/main/ resource of Example Project 0939-remote-chunking-master)

```xml
<?xml version="1.0" encoding="UTF-8"?>
<beans xmlns="http://www.springframework.org/schema/beans"
  xmlns:xsi="http://www.w3.org/2001/XMLSchema-instance"
  xmlns:batch="http://www.springframework.org/schema/batch"
  xmlns:int="http://www.springframework.org/schema/integration"
  xmlns:int-jms="http://www.springframework.org/schema/integration/jms"
  xsi:schemaLocation="http://www.springframework.org/schema/batch
    http://www.springframework.org/schema/batch/spring-batch.xsd
    http://www.springframework.org/schema/beans
    http://www.springframework.org/schema/beans/spring-beans.xsd
    http://www.springframework.org/schema/integration/jms
    http://www.springframework.org/schema/integration/jms/spring-integration-jms.xsd
    http://www.springframework.org/schema/integration
    http://www.springframework.org/schema/integration/spring-integration.xsd">

  <import resource="classpath:jms-config.xml"/>

  <bean class="org.springframework.batch.core.scope.StepScope">
    <property name="proxyTargetClass" value="true"/>
  </bean>

  <bean id="messagingTemplate" class="org.springframework.integration.core.
  MessagingTemplate">
    <property name="defaultChannel" ref="outMasterAdapter" />
    <property name="receiveTimeout" value="2000" />
  </bean>

  <int-jms:outbound-channel-adapter id="outMasterAdapter"  destination="masterCommands"/>
```

```
<int:channel id="inMasterChannel">
  <int:queue />
</int:channel>

<int-jms:message-driven-channel-adapter
  id="inMasterAdapter" destination="slaveResponses" channel="inMasterChannel" />

<batch:job id="simpleRecordsJob">
  <batch:step id="simpleRecordsStep">
    <batch:tasklet>
      <batch:chunk reader="simpleRecordReader" writer="remoteRecordWriter"
        commit-interval="4" />
    </batch:tasklet>
  </batch:step>
</batch:job>

<bean id="remoteRecordWriter" scope="step"
  class="org.springframework.batch.integration.chunk.ChunkMessageChannelItemWriter">
  <property name="messagingOperations" ref="messagingTemplate" />
  <property name="replyChannel" ref="inMasterChannel" />
</bean>
</beans>
```

The JMS configuration is imported. Next we define the StepScope bean. When we use XML configuration, we need to enable batch scopes by configuring them as beans with proxyTargetClass enabled. If we didn't configure these beans, Spring wouldn't know about SB scopes at all.

The MessagingTemplate bean is used for communication with the slave application. Its defaultChannel is connected to outMasterAdapter, which is the JMS outbound channel adapter connected to the JMS queue masterCommands. This route is used for sending items for remote processing and writing.

Responses from the slave are received via the JMS inbound channel adapter inMasterAdapter and gathered in inMasterChannel, which is of type QueueChannel. So it stores responses in memory for master job processing.

The chunk-oriented processing Job is defined with the local reader bean simpleRecordWriter, but for a writer we use the special bean named remoteRecordWriter.

This is defined with the step scope and is of type ChunkMessageChannelItemWriter, which delegates writing of messages to messagineTemplate. The replyChannel attribute is configured to inMasterChannel. So this SB component polls inMasterChannel and waits for responses from the slave.

Running the Remote Chunking Example

To execute this example, we need to start three processes. First, the HornetQ server needs to be running; otherwise, the master and slave couldn't communicate at all. We can start the HornetQ server via the command bin/run.sh or bin/run.bat.

The second process is started by the main class shown in Listing 9-126.

Listing 9-126. Main Class of Remote Chunking Slave Project (0939-remote-chunking-slave)

```
package net.lkrnac.book.eiws.chapter09;
import org.springframework.batch.core.configuration.annotation.EnableBatchProcessing;
import org.springframework.boot.SpringApplication;
import org.springframework.boot.autoconfigure.SpringBootApplication;
import org.springframework.context.annotation.ImportResource;
```

```java
@SpringBootApplication
@EnableBatchProcessing
@ImportResource("classpath:batch-slave-config.xml")
public class BatchSlaveApplication {
  public static void main(String[] args) throws InterruptedException {
    SpringApplication.run(BatchSlaveApplication.class, args);
  }
}
```

This imports the slave XML configuration, enables batch processing, and executes this configuration as a Spring Boot application. We need to execute the slave process first, because it will be listening for items to process from the master.

Finally, we execute the master process via the main class in Listing 9-127.

Listing 9-127. Main Class of Remote Chunking Master Project (0939-remote-chunking-master)

```java
package net.lkrnac.book.eiws.chapter09;

import org.springframework.batch.core.configuration.annotation.EnableBatchProcessing;
import org.springframework.boot.SpringApplication;
import org.springframework.boot.autoconfigure.SpringBootApplication;
import org.springframework.context.annotation.ImportResource;

@SpringBootApplication
@EnableBatchProcessing
@ImportResource("classpath:batch-config.xml")
public class BatchApplication {
  public static void main(String[] args) throws InterruptedException {
    SpringApplication.run(BatchApplication.class, args);
  }
}
```

This configuration class imports the master XML configuration, enables batch processing, and runs this configuration as the Spring Boot main class. When we execute this third process, we see the output in Listing 9-128.

Listing 9-128. Output of Master Process for Remote Chunking Example

```
2015-10-04 21:58:02.229  INFO 4487 --- [          main] o.s.b.c.l.support.SimpleJobLauncher
: Job: [FlowJob: [name=simpleRecordsJob]] launched with the following parameters: [{}]
2015-10-04 21:58:02.253  INFO 4487 --- [          main] o.s.batch.core.job.
SimpleStepHandler      : Executing step: [simpleRecordsStep]
2015-10-04 21:58:02.657  INFO 4487 --- [          main] o.s.b.i.c.ChunkMessageChannelItem
Writer  : Waiting for 4 results
2015-10-04 21:58:02.688  INFO 4487 --- [          main] o.s.b.c.l.support.SimpleJobLauncher
: Job: [FlowJob: [name=simpleRecordsJob]] completed with the following parameters: [{}] and
the following status: [COMPLETED]
```

We can see that Job in the master process was executed and also finished successfully. But where are our write log entries? Notice that the remote chunking delegated the process and write work to the slave process. So when we switch to slave log entries, we can see the output in Listing 9-129.

Listing 9-129. Output of Slave Process for Remote Chunking Example

```
2015-10-04 21:57:36.627  INFO 4384 --- [           main] n.l.b.e.chapter09.
BatchSlaveApplication  : Started BatchSlaveApplication in 4.818 seconds (JVM running for 5.26)
2015-10-04 21:58:02.485  INFO 4384 --- [erContainer#0-1] n.l.b.e.chapter09.write.
WriteRepository  : Writing record: simple record 0 processed
        ...
2015-10-04 21:58:02.661  INFO 4384 --- [erContainer#0-1] n.l.b.e.chapter09.write.
WriteRepository  : Writing record: simple record 14 processed
```

Notice that if we wanted to use various slave processes/machines, we would run all the slaves first. The master should be executed last in this example.

Partitioning a Step

Step partitioning is an SB feature that delegates the batch processing load to remote processes completely. It also applies only to chunk-oriented processing, where processing is fully done in slave processes. This mechanism is handy when we are dealing with I/O bound requirements.

We also have to emphasize that an inner process mode of partitioning is possible; work is delegated to local threads instead of remote processes. But this execution is handled in a single process and can be easily covered by the parallel steps feature. Parallel processing is easier to configure. Therefore, we will focus purely on partitioning remote processes.

The idea is to divide the reading data set into partitions so that each partition can be executed in a separate remote process. We again have master and slave processes, and the master defines partitions. Partition boundaries are usually defined by one dimension of the data set. For example, if we have a data set of user interactions, we can divide this data set based on the interaction date and time into various time buckets. Data belonging to each bucket can represent the data set for one partition.

For each partition, the master creates a separate ExecutionContext instance in which the partition's boundary information is stored. This is done in the component defined by the Partitioner interface. Most of the time, this component is implemented by application developers.

After the partitions are defined and wrapped into ExecutionContext, the master sends commands via the messaging interface to the slave processes. The slave process will retrieve information about partition boundaries from the ExecutionContext instance it receives. The slave then performs chunk-oriented processing on the defined partition data set, and after the work is done, sends the results to the master.

For handling partitions, SB provides three implementations of PartitionHandler:

- TaskExecutorPartitionHandler: Uses TaskExecutor for delegating work to the slave's local threads.

- JsrPartitionHandler: Uses ThreadPoolTaskExecutor for delegating work to the slave's local threads. Conforms to the JSR-352 partitioning standard.

- MessageChannelPartitionHandler: This is the most interesting implementation in terms of true distributed scaling, where MessagingTemplate is used to delegate work to the slave's remote processes. This scaling is again dependent on the least busy slave reading the message from the master first.

If we are using MessageChannelPartitionHandler for remote partitioning, the master and slaves need to share a database for storing SB metadata. Thi s DB instance should be used by the master and all slave processes directly via JDBC.

Partitioning Step Example

The example for this chapter uses only an XML configuration, for the same reasons as the remote chunking examples. To cover this feature, we will use three projects and will run several processes:

- HornetQ server for handling messaging between master and slaves

- Shared database server

- Master project

- Slave project, where we will run various processes

Shared Database Project

For a shared database, we will use the Spring Boot application running an instance of an H2 database stored in the file. Listing 9-130 shows the script used when we start this project.

Listing 9-130. Initialization SQL Script for Partitioning Example (File h2-purge.sql in Folder src/main/ resource of Example Project 0940-remote-partitioning-sql-server)

DROP ALL OBJECTS

Because we are not using H2 mode where it persists into the file, this script wipes out all the objects in the database so that we always start our example with a clean sheet. In the real world, we wouldn't want to do this, but for example purposes, it is good to start with an empty DB. Listing 9-131 shows the XML configuration for this example project.

Listing 9-131. XML Configuration of Shared SB Project (File sql-server-config.xml in Folder src/main/ resource of Example Project 0940-remote-partitioning-sql-server)

```xml
<?xml version="1.0" encoding="UTF-8"?>
<beans xmlns="http://www.springframework.org/schema/beans"
  xmlns:xsi="http://www.w3.org/2001/XMLSchema-instance"
  xmlns:jdbc="http://www.springframework.org/schema/jdbc"
  xsi:schemaLocation="http://www.springframework.org/schema/jdbc
    http://www.springframework.org/schema/jdbc/spring-jdbc.xsd
    http://www.springframework.org/schema/beans
    http://www.springframework.org/schema/beans/spring-beans.xsd">

  <bean id="org.h2.tools.Server" class="org.h2.tools.Server" lazy-init="false"
    factory-method="createTcpServer" init-method="start" destroy-method="stop">
    <constructor-arg>
      <array>
        <value>-tcp</value>
        <value>-tcpAllowOthers</value>
        <value>-tcpPort</value>
        <value>8043</value>
        <value>-properties</value>
        <value>"~/partition-test"</value>
      </array>
    </constructor-arg>
  </bean>
```

```
<jdbc:initialize-database data-source="dataSource">
  <jdbc:script location="classpath:h2-purge.sql"/>
</jdbc:initialize-database>

<bean id="dataSource" class="org.springframework.jdbc.datasource.DriverManagerDataSource">
    <property name="driverClassName" value="org.h2.Driver"/>
    <property name="url" value="jdbc:h2:tcp://localhost:8043/~/partition-test"/>
    <property name="username" value="sa"/>
    <property name="password" value=""/>
  </bean>
</beans>
```

The first bean creates an H2 database instance, which is exposed via TCP and allows other processes to connect to it. The TCP port used for the DB connection is configured to 8043. The last configuration flag specifies the location of the file the H2 DB instance is using to store the data.

The XML tag `<jdbc:initialize-database>` will run the h2-purge.sql script from Listing 9-130, which ensures a clean sheet in the database after we start this project. The dataSource bean is needed to execute this script. The URL uses an H2 convention to access the TCP-hosted database located in the file ~/partition-test. The tilde character (~) indicates the user's home directory.

Listing 9-132 shows the main class of this project.

Listing 9-132. Main Class of SQL Server for Remote Partitioning Example (0940-remote-partitioning-sql-server)

```
package net.lkrnac.book.eiws.chapter09;

import org.springframework.boot.SpringApplication;
import org.springframework.boot.autoconfigure.SpringBootApplication;
import org.springframework.boot.autoconfigure.jdbc.DataSourceAutoConfiguration;
import org.springframework.context.annotation.ImportResource;

@SpringBootApplication(exclude = { DataSourceAutoConfiguration.class })
@ImportResource("classpath:sql-server-config.xml")
public class SqlServerApplication {
  public static void main(String[] args) throws InterruptedException {
    SpringApplication.run(SqlServerApplication.class, args);
  }
}
```

This imports the XML configuration we described previously in Listing 9-131. When Spring Boot, executed with autoconfiguration, finds the H2 database dependency on the classpath, by default it configures an in-memory database. But we want to avoid this feature, because we have our special TCP configuration that we want to expose to other processes also. So we exclude the Spring Boot DataSourceAutoConfiguration from autoconfiguration so it doesn't conflict with our configuration.

Slave Partitioning Project

Listing 9-133 shows the repository we will use in our example.

Listing 9-133. Read Repository Used for Partitioning Example (0940-remote-partitioning-slave)

```
package net.lkrnac.book.eiws.chapter09.read;
import java.util.List;
import java.util.stream.Collectors;
import java.util.stream.IntStream;
import org.springframework.stereotype.Repository;

@Repository
public class IndexedReadRepository {
  private static final List<String> RECORDS_LIST = generateRecords(16);

  public synchronized String getRecord(int index) {
    return RECORDS_LIST.get(index);
  }

  private static List<String> generateRecords(int count) {
    return IntStream.range(0, count)
        .mapToObj(idx -> "simple record " + idx)
        .collect(Collectors.toList());
  }
}
```

This class represents a data set to process. As we will need to separate the data set into partitions, we allow reading the example records via indexes, so that each slave can index the record belonging to the partition it should process. Each record will be exposed via the getRecord() method. Listing 9-134 shows ItemReader for this slave project.

Listing 9-134. ItemReader Implementation for Partitioned Example (0940-remote-partitioning-slave)

```
package net.lkrnac.book.eiws.chapter09.read;
import org.springframework.batch.core.StepExecution;
import org.springframework.batch.core.annotation.BeforeStep;
import org.springframework.batch.item.ExecutionContext;
import org.springframework.batch.item.ItemReader;
import org.springframework.beans.factory.annotation.Autowired;
import org.springframework.stereotype.Component;

@Component
public class PartitionedRecordReader implements ItemReader<String> {
  private IndexedReadRepository readRepository;
  private ExecutionContext executionContext;
  private int partitionEnd;

  @Autowired
  public PartitionedRecordReader(IndexedReadRepository readRepository) {
    super();
    this.readRepository = readRepository;
  }
```

```java
@BeforeStep
public void storeExecutionContext(StepExecution stepExecution) {
  this.executionContext = stepExecution.getExecutionContext();
  this.partitionEnd = executionContext.getInt("partitionEnd");
}

@Override
public String read() {
  int currentIndex = executionContext.getInt("currentIndex");
  String item = (currentIndex <= partitionEnd)
      ? readRepository.getRecord(currentIndex)
      : null;
  executionContext.putInt("currentIndex", currentIndex + 1);
  return item;
}
}
```

This item reader injects IndexedReadRepository to read from. It also injects the ExecutionContext instance via the @BeforeStep annotation. Notice that this ExecutionContext instance will be sent to this slave process from the master and defines the partition boundaries that this slave should process.

In this case, the partition boundaries are stored in the currentIndex, and partitionEnd properties are stored in ExecutionContext. On each read() execution, this reader will check whether we reached the end of the partition. If not, it will read the record and increase currentIndex in the execution context. If the reader returns null, it means the end of work for this slave.

This example uses the same JMS configuration from Listing 9-123 of the previous example, where we define access to the JMS destinations MasterCommand and SlaveResponses. These will be used for communication with the master. The slave Spring configuration is presented in Listing 9-135.

Listing 9-135. Slave XML Configuration for Remote Partitioning Example (File batch-slave-configuration. xml in Folder src/main/resource of Example Project 0940-remote-partitioning-slave)

```xml
<?xml version="1.0" encoding="UTF-8"?>
<beans xmlns="http://www.springframework.org/schema/beans"
  xmlns:xsi="http://www.w3.org/2001/XMLSchema-instance"
  xmlns:batch="http://www.springframework.org/schema/batch"
  xmlns:int="http://www.springframework.org/schema/integration"
  xmlns:int-jms="http://www.springframework.org/schema/integration/jms"
  xsi:schemaLocation="http://www.springframework.org/schema/batch
    http://www.springframework.org/schema/batch/spring-batch.xsd
    http://www.springframework.org/schema/beans
    http://www.springframework.org/schema/beans/spring-beans.xsd
    http://www.springframework.org/schema/integration/jms
    http://www.springframework.org/schema/integration/jms/spring-integration-jms.xsd
    http://www.springframework.org/schema/integration
    http://www.springframework.org/schema/integration/spring-integration.xsd">

  <import resource="classpath:jms-config.xml" />
```

```xml
<bean id="dataSource" class="org.springframework.jdbc.datasource.DriverManagerDataSource">
    <property name="driverClassName" value="org.h2.Driver"/>
    <property name="url" value="jdbc:h2:tcp://localhost:8043/~/partition-test"/>
    <property name="username" value="sa"/>
    <property name="password" value=""/>
</bean>

<bean id="stepExecutionRequestHandler"
  class="org.springframework.batch.integration.partition.StepExecutionRequestHandler">
    <property name="jobExplorer" ref="jobExplorer" />
    <property name="stepLocator" ref="stepLocator" />
</bean>

<bean id="stepLocator"
  class="org.springframework.batch.integration.partition.BeanFactoryStepLocator" />

<batch:step id="simpleRecordsStep">
  <batch:tasklet allow-start-if-complete="true">
    <batch:chunk reader="partitionedRecordReader" writer="simpleRecordWriter"
      processor="simpleRecordProcessor" commit-interval="4"/>
  </batch:tasklet>
</batch:step>

<int:channel id="inSlaveChannel" />
<int-jms:message-driven-channel-adapter
  id="inSlaveAdapter" destination="masterCommands" channel="inSlaveChannel" />

<int:service-activator ref="stepExecutionRequestHandler"
  input-channel="inSlaveChannel" output-channel="outSlaveChannel" />

<int:channel id="outSlaveChannel" />
<int-jms:outbound-channel-adapter id="outSlaveAdapter"
  destination="slaveResponses" channel="outSlaveChannel" />
</beans>
```

First, we import the JMS configuration, so that the slave process can access the JMS messaging server in order to receive commands from the master. The dataSource bean is used to access the shared database hosted by the example project 0940-remote-partitioning-sql-server.

Next, the StepExecutionRequestHandler bean is the MessagingEndpoint used to handle commands from the master process. These commands will arrive as a StepExecutionRequest instance, and this handler should respond to the master with a StepExecution instance. The jobExplorer property of this bean is created by Spring Boot autoconfiguration and is used to access the SB metadata stored in the shared database. The stepLocator property is a bean created by the next bean definition and is of type BeanFactoryStepLocator. It is used for scanning the Spring context for SB Step instances. Step located in this Spring context will be used to perform SB work.

This Step instance is defined by the <batch:step> XML tag and configured to use chunk-oriented processing for this slave. For the ItemReader, we use PartitionedRecordReader shown in the previous listing. The processor and writer instances are our common beans used across the chapter.

The following beans define JMS communication with the master. The commands are received from the JMS queue masterCommands and forwarded to the local Spring Integration channel inSlaveChannel. This channel is connected to stepExecutionRequestHandler, which performs batch processing. Its reply is forwarded to Spring Integration's outSlaveChannel and passed to the JMS queue slaveResponses, respectively.

Figure 9-10 shows the Spring Integration graph for this slave configuration.

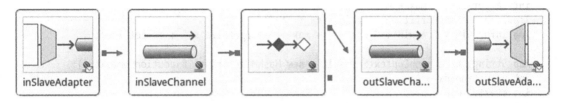

Figure 9-10. *Spring Integration graph for slave configuration of remote partitioning example (file batch-slave-configuration.xml in folder src/main/resource of example project 0940-remote-partitioning-slave)*

Listing 9-136 shows the main class of the slave project.

Listing 9-136. Main Class of Remote Partitioning Slave (0940-remote-partitioning-slave)

```
package net.lkrnac.book.eiws.chapter09;
import org.springframework.batch.core.configuration.annotation.EnableBatchProcessing;
import org.springframework.boot.SpringApplication;
import org.springframework.boot.autoconfigure.SpringBootApplication;
import org.springframework.context.annotation.ImportResource;

@SpringBootApplication
@EnableBatchProcessing
@ImportResource("classpath:batch-slave-config.xml")
public class BatchSlaveApplication {
  public static void main(String[] args) throws InterruptedException {
    SpringApplication.run(BatchSlaveApplication.class, args);
  }
}
```

We include the slave XML configuration and run the Spring Boot application with batch processing enabled.

Master Partitioning Project

Listing 9-137 shows the Partitioner implementation.

Listing 9-137. Partitioner Implementation (0940-remote-partitioning-master)

```
package net.lkrnac.book.eiws.chapter09;
import java.util.HashMap;
import java.util.Map;
import lombok.extern.slf4j.Slf4j;
import org.springframework.batch.core.partition.support.Partitioner;
import org.springframework.batch.item.ExecutionContext;
import org.springframework.stereotype.Component;
```

```java
@Slf4j
@Component
public class RecordsPartitioner implements Partitioner {
  @Override
  public Map<String, ExecutionContext> partition(int gridSize) {
    int min = 0;
    int max = 16;
    int targetSize = (max - min) / gridSize;
    log.info("***** Partition distribution *****");
    log.info("min = " + min + " max = " + max + " targetSize = " + targetSize);

    Map<String, ExecutionContext> result = new HashMap<String, ExecutionContext>();
    int partitionIdx = 0;
    int start = min;
    int end = start + targetSize - 1;

    while (start < max) {
      ExecutionContext value = new ExecutionContext();
      result.put("partition" + partitionIdx, value);

      if (end > max) {
        end = max - 1;
      }
      log.info("partitionStart" + partitionIdx + " = " + start);
      log.info("partitionEnd" + partitionIdx + " = " + end);

      value.putInt("currentIndex", start);
      value.putInt("partitionEnd", end);
      start += targetSize;
      end += targetSize;
      partitionIdx++;
    }

    log.info("partitions = " + result.size());
    log.info("*******************************");
    return result;
  }
}
```

This SB component divides partitions into separate ExecutionContext instances, based on the given gridSize (number of partitions). Each ExecutionContext instance contains a start and end index of the partition it belongs to. The size of the data set (records to process) is hard-coded to 16, because IndexedReadRepository for this example has only 16 records to process.We hope you excuse this fact, which is created to make this example simple. So, for example, with a gridSize of 2 partitions, we would create two ExecutionContexts with the partition boundaries 0..7 and 8..15.

■ **Note** This algorithm as well as other constructs in this partitioning example are highly influenced by Michael Minella's remote partitioning example at https://github.com/mminella/Spring-Batch-Talk-2.0.

Listing 9-138 shows the XML configuration of the master.

Listing 9-138. Master Configuration for Remote Partitioning Example (File batch-configuration.xml in Folder src/main/resource of Example Project 0940-remote-partitioning-master)

```xml
<?xml version="1.0" encoding="UTF-8"?>
<beans xmlns="http://www.springframework.org/schema/beans"
  xmlns:xsi="http://www.w3.org/2001/XMLSchema-instance" xmlns:batch="http://www.
  springframework.org/schema/batch"
  xmlns:int="http://www.springframework.org/schema/integration"
  xmlns:int-jms="http://www.springframework.org/schema/integration/jms"
  xsi:schemaLocation="http://www.springframework.org/schema/batch
    http://www.springframework.org/schema/batch/spring-batch.xsd
    http://www.springframework.org/schema/beans
    http://www.springframework.org/schema/beans/spring-beans.xsd
    http://www.springframework.org/schema/integration/jms
    http://www.springframework.org/schema/integration/jms/spring-integration-jms.xsd
    http://www.springframework.org/schema/integration
    http://www.springframework.org/schema/integration/spring-integration.xsd">

  <import resource="classpath:jms-config.xml" />

  <bean id="dataSource" class="org.springframework.jdbc.datasource.DriverManagerDataSource">
      <property name="driverClassName" value="org.h2.Driver"/>
      <property name="url" value="jdbc:h2:tcp://localhost:8043/~/partition-test"/>
      <property name="username" value="sa"/>
      <property name="password" value=""/>
  </bean>

  <batch:job id="masterJob">
    <batch:step id="masterStep">
        <batch:partition partitioner="partitioner" handler="partitionHandler" />
    </batch:step>
  </batch:job>

  <bean id="partitioner" class="net.lkrnac.book.eiws.chapter09.RecordsPartitioner"/>

  <bean id="partitionHandler"
    class="org.springframework.batch.integration.partition.MessageChannelPartitionHandler">
    <property name="stepName" value="simpleRecordsStep" />
    <property name="replyChannel" ref="inMasterAggregatedChannel"/>
    <property name="gridSize" value="2" />
    <property name="messagingOperations" ref="messagingTemplate">
    </property>
  </bean>

  <bean id="messagingTemplate" class="org.springframework.integration.core.
  MessagingTemplate">
    <property name="defaultChannel" ref="outMasterAdapter" />
    <property name="receiveTimeout" value="5000" />
  </bean>
```

```
<int-jms:outbound-channel-adapter id="outMasterAdapter"
  destination="masterCommands" />

<int:channel id="inMasterChannel" />
<int-jms:message-driven-channel-adapter
  id="inMasterAdapter" destination="slaveResponses" channel="inMasterChannel" />

<int:channel id="inMasterAggregatedChannel">
  <int:queue />
</int:channel>
<int:aggregator ref="partitionHandler" input-channel="inMasterChannel"
  output-channel="inMasterAggregatedChannel" />
</beans>
```

The master configuration also imports the JMS configuration to be able to send commands and receive responses from slaves. The dataSource bean accesses a shared database hosted in the 0940-remote-partitioning-sql-server example project.

The SB job definition follows. For Step, we use the <batch:partition> construct to define the remote execution for this processing. We need to define two properties here. A reference to the partitioner is covered by our work distribution algorithm in RecordsPartitioner from the previous listing.

The second bean used in the job is partitionHandler. This is the main bean of the master processing of type MessageChannelPartitionHandler, because it coordinates the slave processing via messaging middleware. We define gridSize (the number of partitions to process), stepName (the name of the step to execute in the slave processes), and replyChannel (the Spring Integration channel where the master expects replies from the slave processes). The last parameter of partitionHandler specifies the MessagingTemplate instance that will be used for communication with slaves.

This communication uses Spring Integration's JMS outbound channel adapter outMasterAdapter connected to the JMS queue master commands. Responses from slaves are received from the JMS queue slaveResponses, temporarily stored in the Spring Integration QueueChannel named inMasterAggregatedChannel. So this channel is asynchronous. The last component is a Spring Integration aggregator using, again, partitionHandler to aggregate slave responses.

Listing 9-139 shows the main class of the master application.

Listing 9-139. Main Class of Master Project for Remote Partitioning Example (0940-remote-partitioning-master)

```
package net.lkrnac.book.eiws.chapter09;
import org.springframework.batch.core.configuration.annotation.EnableBatchProcessing;
import org.springframework.boot.SpringApplication;
import org.springframework.boot.autoconfigure.SpringBootApplication;
import org.springframework.context.annotation.ImportResource;
import org.springframework.scheduling.annotation.EnableScheduling;

@SpringBootApplication
@EnableBatchProcessing
@EnableScheduling
@ImportResource("classpath:batch-config.xml")
public class BatchApplication {
  public static void main(String[] args) throws InterruptedException {
    SpringApplication.run(BatchApplication.class, args);
  }
}
```

Alongside importing the master Spring configuration, this Spring Boot main class needs to enable batch processing and enable scheduling for asynchronous polling of inMasterAggregatedChannel by the partitionHandler bean.

Executing Remote Partitioning Example

It is obvious that this last example is the most complicated in the entire book. When we execute it, the load balancing between slaves is natural; the least busy slave will read the messages from the masterCommands JMS queue first. So this least busy slave will perform the processing. In real life, this load balancing is fine.

But my machine has four cores, and when I use two slave processes with two partitions, they are mostly processed by the same process, and the second slave lays there unused. Therefore, we will run three slave processes to increase the possibility of dividing the load into separate slave processes.

To execute this example we need to do the following:

- Start a HornetQ server with the same configuration as in the previous example (Listing 9-122).

- Start a SQL server via the SqlServerApplication class from the example project 0940-remote-partitioning-sql-server.

- Start three slave processes via BatchSlaveApplication from example project 0940-remote-partitioning-slave. Just run the same project three times.

- Start the master process via BatchConfiguration from example project 0940-remote-partitioning-master.

After running this sequence, we can observe master process output similar to Listing 9-140.

Listing 9-140. Master Output of Remote Partitioning Example

```
2015-10-06 22:36:52.616  INFO 32581 --- [          main] o.s.b.c.l.support.SimpleJobLauncher
: Job: [FlowJob: [name=masterJob]] launched with the following parameters: [{}]
2015-10-06 22:36:53.000  INFO 32581 --- [          main] o.s.batch.core.job.
SimpleStepHandler      : Executing step: [masterStep]
2015-10-06 22:36:53.111  INFO 32581 --- [          main] n.l.b.eiws.chapter09.
RecordsPartitioner  : ***** Partition distribution *****
2015-10-06 22:36:53.112  INFO 32581 --- [          main] n.l.b.eiws.chapter09.
RecordsPartitioner  : min = 0 max = 16 targetSize = 8
2015-10-06 22:36:53.112  INFO 32581 --- [          main] n.l.b.eiws.chapter09.
RecordsPartitioner  : partitionStart0 = 0
2015-10-06 22:36:53.112  INFO 32581 --- [          main] n.l.b.eiws.chapter09.
RecordsPartitioner  : partitionEnd0 = 7
2015-10-06 22:36:53.116  INFO 32581 --- [          main] n.l.b.eiws.chapter09.
RecordsPartitioner  : partitionStart1 = 8
2015-10-06 22:36:53.116  INFO 32581 --- [          main] n.l.b.eiws.chapter09.
RecordsPartitioner  : partitionEnd1 = 15
2015-10-06 22:36:53.116  INFO 32581 --- [          main] n.l.b.eiws.chapter09.
RecordsPartitioner  : partitions = 2
2015-10-06 22:36:53.116  INFO 32581 --- [          main] n.l.b.eiws.chapter09.
RecordsPartitioner  : ******************************
2015-10-06 22:36:55.651  INFO 32581 --- [          main] o.s.b.c.l.support.SimpleJobLauncher
: Job: [FlowJob: [name=masterJob]] completed with the following parameters: [{}] and the
following status: [COMPLETED]
```

The job completed successfully, with partitions split as we expected. Listing 9-141 shows the output of the first slave.

Listing 9-141. Output of First Slave for Remote Partitioning Example

```
2015-10-06 22:36:55.141  INFO 32483 --- [erContainer#0-1] n.l.b.e.chapter09.write.
WriteRepository  : Writing record: simple record 8 processed
2015-10-06 22:36:55.142  INFO 32483 --- [erContainer#0-1] n.l.b.e.chapter09.write.
WriteRepository  : Writing record: simple record 9 processed
2015-10-06 22:36:55.143  INFO 32483 --- [erContainer#0-1] n.l.b.e.chapter09.write.
WriteRepository  : Writing record: simple record 10 processed
2015-10-06 22:36:55.144  INFO 32483 --- [erContainer#0-1] n.l.b.e.chapter09.write.
WriteRepository  : Writing record: simple record 11 processed
2015-10-06 22:36:55.210  INFO 32483 --- [erContainer#0-1] n.l.b.e.chapter09.write.
WriteRepository  : Writing record: simple record 12 processed
2015-10-06 22:36:55.210  INFO 32483 --- [erContainer#0-1] n.l.b.e.chapter09.write.
WriteRepository  : Writing record: simple record 13 processed
2015-10-06 22:36:55.210  INFO 32483 --- [erContainer#0-1] n.l.b.e.chapter09.write.
WriteRepository  : Writing record: simple record 14 processed
2015-10-06 22:36:55.211  INFO 32483 --- [erContainer#0-1] n.l.b.e.chapter09.write.
WriteRepository  : Writing record: simple record 15 processed
```

Listing 9-142 shows the output of the second slave.

Listing 9-142. Output of Second Slave for Remote Partitioning Example

```
2015-10-06 22:36:54.670  INFO 32427 --- [erContainer#0-1] n.l.b.e.chapter09.write.
WriteRepository  : Writing record: simple record 0 processed
2015-10-06 22:36:54.671  INFO 32427 --- [erContainer#0-1] n.l.b.e.chapter09.write.
WriteRepository  : Writing record: simple record 1 processed
2015-10-06 22:36:54.671  INFO 32427 --- [erContainer#0-1] n.l.b.e.chapter09.write.
WriteRepository  : Writing record: simple record 2 processed
2015-10-06 22:36:54.671  INFO 32427 --- [erContainer#0-1] n.l.b.e.chapter09.write.
WriteRepository  : Writing record: simple record 3 processed
2015-10-06 22:36:54.733  INFO 32427 --- [erContainer#0-1] n.l.b.e.chapter09.write.
WriteRepository  : Writing record: simple record 4 processed
2015-10-06 22:36:54.733  INFO 32427 --- [erContainer#0-1] n.l.b.e.chapter09.write.
WriteRepository  : Writing record: simple record 5 processed
2015-10-06 22:36:54.733  INFO 32427 --- [erContainer#0-1] n.l.b.e.chapter09.write.
WriteRepository  : Writing record: simple record 6 processed
2015-10-06 22:36:54.733  INFO 32427 --- [erContainer#0-1] n.l.b.e.chapter09.write.
WriteRepository  : Writing record: simple record 7 processed
```

As we can see, processing was successfully distributed across the various slave processes.

Spring Batch Admin

Often we need to monitor and manually control batch processing. For example, we might need to restart a certain JobExecution, because previously corrupted data was manually fixed. SB provides for this purpose a project called Spring Batch Admin (http://docs.spring.io/spring-batch-admin).

This is a web application that can be embedded into our batch processing application to control and monitor batch processing. Because it is a web component, it needs to be hosted in the servlets container. We can use `spring-batch-admin-manager` and `spring-batch-admin-resources` and place our Jobs XML configuration into the directory `META-INF/spring/batch/jobs`.

To cover the features of Spring Batch Admin, we will use an example application that can be downloaded from the Spring Batch Admin site (`http://docs.spring.io/downloads/nightly/release-download.php?project=BATCHADM`). We used version 1.3.1.RELEASE in this example. When we run this application on a local servlet container with port 8080 (for example, using the default Pivotal tc Server in STS), we can enter the `http://localhost:8080/spring-batch-admin-sample` address into the browser to control batch processing.

■ **Note**   All of the following figures were downloaded from the spring.io site at `http://docs.spring.io/spring-batch-admin/screenshots.html`.

Figure 9-11 shows how we can browse jobs that are available in the batch application, along with their main attributes and statistics. Figure 9-12 shows a screen for a single job.

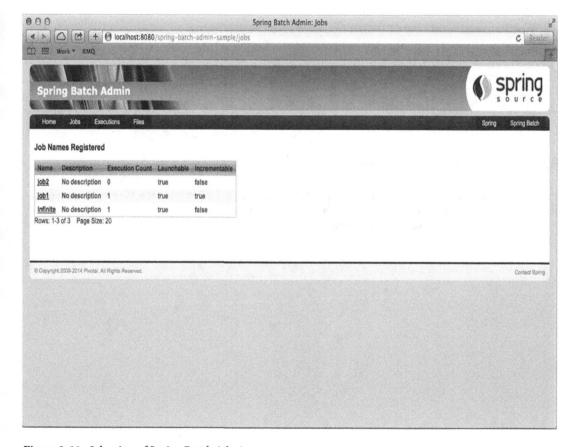

Figure 9-11. Jobs view of Spring Batch Admin

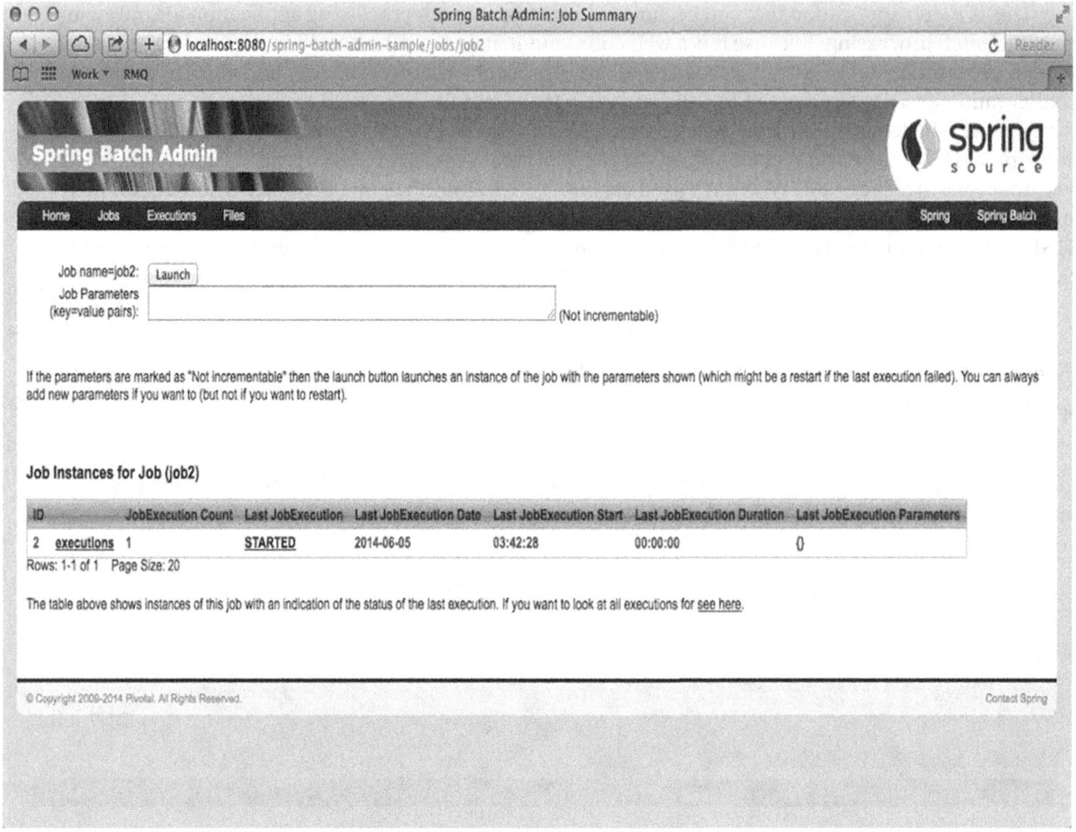

Figure 9-12. *Single job view of Spring Batch Admin*

From this screen, we can run the job and specify the parameters for JobInstance. We can also see past or running job instances, including their status and main statistics.

Figure 9-13 shows the Job Executions screen.

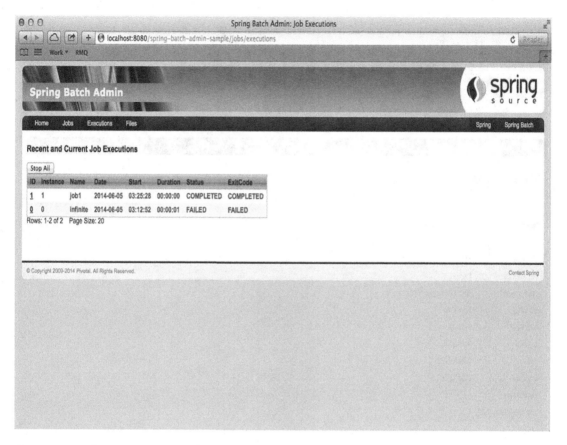

Figure 9-13. *Job Executions screen of Spring Batch Admin*

From this screen, we can observe the past and current JobExecution instances and their statuses and statistics. We can also terminate all executions by clicking the Stop All button.

Figure 9-14 shows the screen for a single JobExecution.

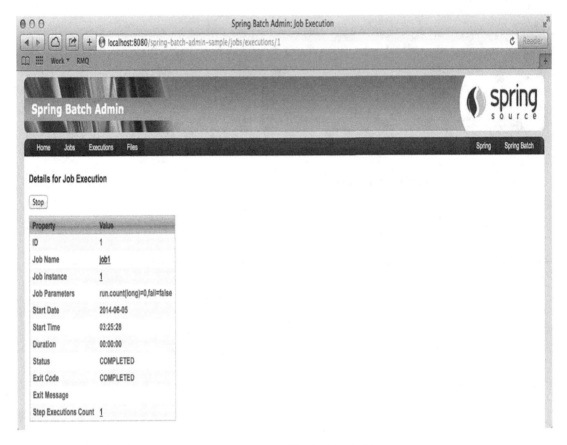

Figure 9-14. *Single JobExecution without error screen of Spring Batch Admin*

On this screen, we can see statistics for a concrete JobExecution instance. We also can terminate the instance by clicking the Stop button.

Figure 9-15 shows the screen of a single JobExecution with an error.

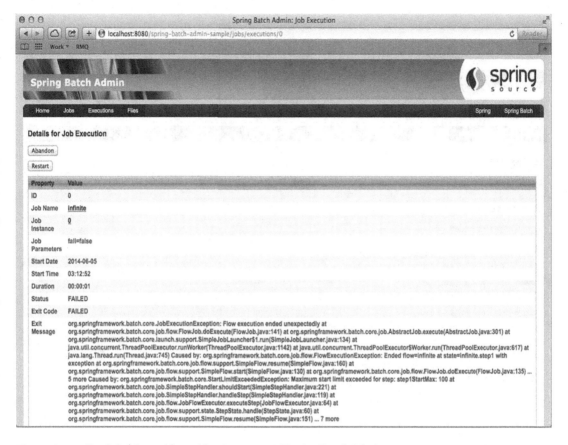

Figure 9-15. *Single JobExecution with error screen of Spring Batch Admin*

Here Spring Batch Admin can provide us a stack trace of the error that occurred in JobExecution.
Figure 9-16 shows a screen of the chunk-oriented StepExecution. Here we can see all the stats for
StepExecution of the chunk-oriented processing Step.

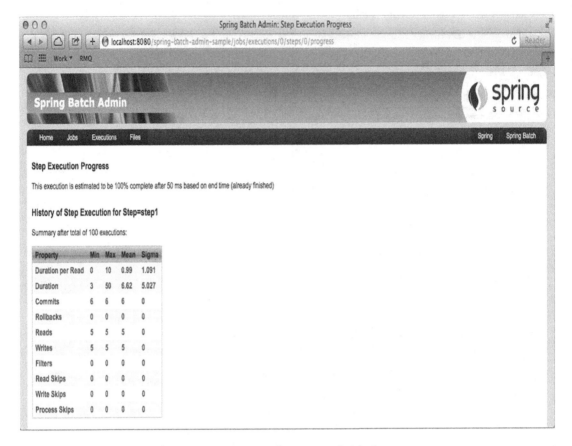

Figure 9-16. *Chunk-oriented StepExecution screen of Spring Batch Admin*

Summary

This chapter focused on background processing in the enterprise, where the Spring Batch framework has a unique position as one of the first abstractions in the Java world and a reference implementation for the JEE 7 standard for batch processing.

We covered the Spring Batch domain, which consists of Job and Step as its main pillars. Chunk-oriented processing is the most common mechanism for handling batch requirements, but we also have the option to use Tasklet, a one-time task to perform batching work.

Various options for running the job programmatically and from the command line were shown, alongside possibilities for executing Job with parameters. To allow for state sharing, we showed how to pass ExecutionContext between Spring Batch constructs. We also covered special Spring Batch scopes as an alternative to the ExecutionContext approach.

Next we explored the rich possibilities for intercepting processing of the Spring Batch framework and how to open/close/update third-party resources. Job and Step inheritance allows us to consolidate XML configuration for Spring Batch. The following sections dived into the mechanisms for controlling Spring Batch flow to repeat certain tasks, perform conditional Steps, and react to errors.

The remaining parts focused on scaling and parallel processing, so that we can boost our application's performance.

Index

Get the eBook for only $5!

Why limit yourself?

Now you can take the weightless companion with you wherever you go and access your content on your PC, phone, tablet, or reader.

Since you've purchased this print book, we're happy to offer you the eBook in all 3 formats for just $5.

Convenient and fully searchable, the PDF version enables you to easily find and copy code—or perform examples by quickly toggling between instructions and applications. The MOBI format is ideal for your Kindle, while the ePUB can be utilized on a variety of mobile devices.

To learn more, go to www.apress.com/companion or contact support@apress.com.

Printed in the United States
By Bookmasters